HEIDEGGER AND THE WILL

Northwestern University
Studies in Phenomenology
and
Existential Philosophy

Founding Editor †James M. Edie

General Editor Anthony J. Steinbock

Associate Editor John McCumber

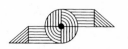

HEIDEGGER AND THE WILL

On the Way to *Gelassenheit*

Bret W. Davis

Northwestern University Press
Evanston, Illinois

Northwestern University Press
www.nupress.northwestern.edu

Printed in the United States of America

10 9 8 7 6 5 4 3 2 1

ISBN-13: 978-0-8101-2034-1 (cloth)
ISBN-10: 0-8101-2034-8 (cloth)
ISBN-13: 978-0-8101-2035-8 (paper)
ISBN-10: 0-8101-2035-6 (paper)

Library of Congress Cataloging-in-Publication data are available from the
Library of Congress.

⊗ The paper used in this publication meets the minimum requirements of the
American National Standard for Information Sciences—Permanence of Paper
for Printed Library Materials, ANSI Z39.48-1992.

For three generations of women who have taught me more than they think about attentive letting-be: in appreciation of the ever-caring companionship of my wife, Naomi Davis; in gratitude for the steadfast and loving support of my mother, Barbara Davis; and in memory of the gentle sternness and stern gentleness of my grandmother, Alberta Stephen (1909–1994)

Contents

Preface

This book was written with the aim of filling what appeared to me to be nothing less than an astonishing lacuna in Heidegger scholarship. Despite the numerous books on Heidegger that appear each year, for decades now no study has thoroughly treated the multifaceted problem of the will in his thought-path from *Being and Time* (1926) through "Time and Being" (1962). Such a lacuna is striking given that, according to my interpretation at least, this problematic lies at the very heart of Heidegger's *Denkweg*. While I have throughout attempted to make explicit my debt to previous research which either supports, supplements, or provides contrast to my interpretations, since no major study is available that specifically treats this crucial issue in all its manifold complexity, I found it necessary to proceed by way of my own detailed analysis of Heidegger's texts. The more I dug in my reading of Heidegger, the more I found a labyrinth of interconnecting *Holzwege* concerning the problem of the will. My project was to shed some light on these paths, to open a clearing in which their intersections begin to make sense, and to attempt to give some indications for thinking the problem of the will "after Heidegger."

Back in 1996 I quickly abandoned, or rather reduced in scope, my original research project, which was even more ambitious. I initially thought of bringing my two major areas of interest together, and writing a comparative (or rather "dialogical") work on the problem of the will in Heidegger and in the Zen Buddhist philosophy of Nishitani Keiji. As it turns out, most of the writing of this book was done while residing in Japan. I was studying and teaching in Kyoto for a number of years, simultaneously pursuing in part the "other side" of the original project in a second doctoral and postdoctoral career at Otani University and Kyoto University, with the generous support of research fellowships from the Japanese Ministry of Education and the Japan Society for the Promotion of Science. (For some of the directly related results of this parallel research, I refer the English reader in particular to my lengthy article, "Zen after Zarathustra: The Problem of the Will in the Confrontation between Nietzsche and Buddhism.")

I believe that a thoroughgoing study of Heidegger's thought-path ultimately leads one in two directions: back to the Greeks and over to the East. Both of these orientations remain necessary: in order to read Heidegger one cannot circumvent an engagement with the tradition of Western philosophy; yet in reading Heidegger one is also invited to disengage from the metaphysical moorings of this tradition and open oneself to an encounter with the "few other great beginnings" of thought, and in particular that of East Asia. The "dialogue with the Greek thinkers" is, for Heidegger's path of thinking, the "precondition for the inevitable dialogue with the East Asian world." For my part, while attempting to remain in conversation with the many dedicated Heidegger scholars who critically follow his indications for rereading the Greeks, I have set out on a woodpath, or a silk road, that is comparatively less traveled. Be that as it may, in either case one must first and foremost travel through a rigorous engagement with Heidegger's texts themselves. Hence, while written in Kyoto, and while no doubt essentially supplemented in more ways than one by my life and studies in Japan, the present work for the most part postpones entering into the dialogue between Heidegger's thought and the East. The focus in this book is, from beginning to end, Heidegger's thought-path itself. It proceeds by way of a close and critical reading of his texts, and these texts are considered here predominantly, if not exclusively, in the context in which they were written, that of the Western philosophical tradition.

Before embarking on this journey through Heidegger's texts, I would like to take this opportunity to thank those who helped me along the way. The most obvious regard in which "thinking" is intimately related to "thanking" lies in the fact that it is only thanks to a number of individuals and institutions that one is given the guidance and companionship, as well as the emotional and material support, needed to think.

Let me begin by expressing my gratitude to my teachers in the United States, whose "authentic care" provided just the right balance between guided instruction and timely releasement to my own wanderings. Professors Lawrence Kimmel and Charles Salman at Trinity University first introduced me to the wonder and rigor of Greek and Continental philosophy. During my years of graduate study at Vanderbilt University, I had the great fortune to work closely with Professors Charles Scott, John Sallis, and David Wood, and also learned much from doing coursework with others in the department, including Professors John Compton and Idit Dobbs-Weinstein. The present book grew out of my doctoral dissertation for Vanderbilt, which was written and rewritten between 1995 and 2001. I would like to thank David Wood, my dissertation advisor, for encouraging me early on to pursue the project thoroughly and with the aim of eventually preparing it for publication. I also received helpful instruction and feedback from the other members of my dissertation committee, Professors Gregg Horowitz, Michael Hodges, John Lachs, and William Franke.

I profited greatly over the years from my participation in the Collegium Phaenomenologicum held in Città di Castello, Italy, where I was able to attend courses and lectures on Heidegger's thought by Günter Figal, François Dastur, Hans Ruin, Miguel de Beistegui, Robert Bernasconi, and Daniel Dahlstrom, as well as several of the other distinguished Heidegger scholars named here. At the Collegium I was able to keep in touch with or get to know John Sallis, Charles Scott, Susan Schoenbaum, David Wood, Dennis Schmitt, James Risser, Larry Hatab, Peg Birmingham, François Raffoul, and Rodolphe Gasché, most of whom offered me advice or an encouraging word with regard to this project. I thank Professor Sallis for permission to quote (in chapter 2) from personal correspondence, in which he relayed Heidegger's comments to him during a conversation held in 1975. Let me express my gratitude here to Alejandro Vallega and Daniela Vallega-Neu, two more noteworthy Heidegger scholars, for inviting me to lead a seminar on "Time and Being" at the 2004 Collegium, and also convey my thanks to the excellent group of seminar participants I had the pleasure to work with at that time.

I would like to express my appreciation to David Michael Levin, who, although I had not yet met him at the time, read carefully through an earlier version of my entire manuscript and generously offered his extensive, encouraging, and critical commentary. To my embarrassment, I only subsequently discovered the extent to which his own works insightfully address the issue of *Gelassenheit*. (I have since attempted to make amends for this oversight in my notes and bibliography.) Levin's works are particularly noteworthy for his attention to the question of the embodiment of *Gelassenheit*, as well as for his courage to look beyond the boundaries of the Western tradition. I also benefited significantly from the insightful reading and discerning comments given by my two anonymous reviewers at the Northwestern University Press. They helped me improve the manuscript in several respects. Thanks to the patience and flexibility of the editors at Northwestern, I have had the opportunity to both cut and add several whole chapters and sections, in addition to rewriting and refining the entire text. Although I have tried to take all the advice I have received into account during this process of revision, it goes without saying that I am alone responsible for the remaining errors and insufficiencies, as well as for whatever controversial views are expressed in this somewhat ambitious project.

(One editorial decision in particular deserves comment, namely the use of "man" as a translation for Heidegger's *der Mensch*. In general I am in agreement with many in today's academy that the male bias implied in the use of "man" as a generic term for *anthropos* or *der Mensch* is problem-

atic and probably ineradicable, and therefore that wherever possible the
term should be replaced with a more gender inclusive expression like
"human being." In fact, in the first draft of the manuscript of this book I
had rendered *der Mensch* as "human being." However, one of the anonymous reviewers with Northwestern University Press objected that this
translation led to too many ambiguities, especially given the fact that Heidegger also uses such terms as *Menschsein* and *Menschenwesen;* and with
Heidegger, of course, it is best to avoid ambiguous uses of the term "being." In response I attempted something novel but ultimately unsatisfac-
tory. I used the traditional term "man," but with the feminine pronouns
"she" and "her." However, as my copy editor let me know in no uncertain
terms, such "bizarre attempts at gender equity simply do not work," and
in this case it is better to bite the bullet and stay with conservative yet clear
language. In the eleventh hour I accepted the editor's change of these
pronouns to the masculine. Hence, with some trepidation I have allowed
my concern for terminological clarity and precision in this case to over-
rule my support for the revision of our language in the name of more unambiguous gender inclusiveness.)

My lengthy residence in Japan has indeed turned out to be fortu-
itous, and not only for the "hermeneutical distance" gained by stepping
outside the Western tradition. As is well known, there is a long and rich
tradition of Heidegger scholarship in Japan, which dates back to the first
article ever to appear in any language on Heidegger, written by Tanabe
Hajime upon his return from Freiburg in 1924! Japanese interpretations
of Heidegger, while always grounded in solid and painstaking scholarship, are often able to shed new light on issues by way of drawing on their
East Asian and Buddhist background. The problem of the will is a case in
point. In fact, one of the only significant studies in any language that explicitly addresses the problem of the will in Heidegger is a book originally
written in German (and later expanded in a Japanese version) in 1975 by
the Japanese philosopher Ōhashi Ryōsuke, *Ekstase und Gelassenheit: Zu
Schelling und Heidegger.* At that time Ōhashi remarked on the lack of attention given (even by scholars such as Otto Pöggeler) to the topic of *Gelassenheit* in Heidegger studies, despite its centrality to his later thought. Ōhashi
was encouraged in his treatment of the theme by his teacher Tsujimura
Kōichi, who, together with Ueda Shizuteru (the central contemporary figure in what has come to be known as the Kyoto School), was a student of
Nishitani Keiji, who in turn studied with Heidegger during the time the
latter was beginning to lecture on Nietzsche's will to power (1937–39).
Nishitani not only submitted to Heidegger at this time an impressive essay on Nietzsche and Meister Eckhart, but was also frequently asked to
Heidegger's home to teach him about Zen. Above and beyond questions

of influence and counterinfluence, however, it is clear that, as I briefly indicate in the closing section of chapter 2, the East Asian Buddhist background these thinkers bring to the study of Heidegger allows them a uniquely significant hermeneutical entry point into the problem of the will in his thought.

Even before I had read much of the relevant Japanese literature, I was pleasantly surprised at the ease with which I could discuss the topic of this project with philosophers in Japan. While my presentations and publications in Japanese have generally focused more on Japanese philosophy and less directly on Heidegger, I have nevertheless learned much from conversations on Heidegger and related topics with teachers and colleagues in Japan over the years. Let me take this opportunity to thank some of those under or with whom I have had the good fortune to study (names written in Japanese order, with family name first): Professors Ueda Shizuteru, Fujita Masakatsu, Horio Tsutomu, Mori Tetsurō, Ōhashi Ryōsuke, Okada Katsuaki, and Hase Shōtō. I have also benefited from my contact with Professors Tsujimura Kōichi, Matsumaru Hisao, Mine Hideki, Ōkōchi Ryōgi, Keta Masako, and Ogawa Tadashi, and well as with colleagues such as Kajitani Shinji and Wu Guanghui. Let me also mention here Professors Graham Parkes and John Maraldo, both of whom I got to know during their visits to Japan, and who have been constant sources of inspiration and encouragement for my research orientations. I would like to express my gratitude to Matsumoto Naoki, Minobe Hitoshi, Akitomi Katsuya, Mizuno Tomoharu, Sugimoto Kōichi, and Yoshie Takami for their company not only in philosophical discussions, but also in the study and practice of Zen. I am profoundly indebted to Tanaka Hōjū Rōshi and the monks of Shōkokuji Rinzai Zen monastery in Kyoto for their guidance in the holistic rigors of an embodied and inspirited practice of *Gelassenheit*.

I would also like to gratefully acknowledge here a number of other colleagues and companions who have shared with me their time, thoughts, dinner tables, and above all laughter. These include John Lysaker, Andy Fiala, and Rob Metcalf among the many fellow graduate students and lasting friends from Vanderbilt; Brian Schroeder, Silvia Benso, Jason Wirth, Hans Ruin, and Rick Lee, to name a few of those whom I first met at the Collegium Phaenomenologicum; and Rolf Elberfeld, Ralf Müller, and Steffen Döll, each of whom I got to know in Japan and then in Germany. A special word of thanks is due to Rolf for his hospitality on more than one occasion in Wuppertal, to Ralf for hosting my stay in Berlin, and to Steffen for countless hours of lively multilingual conversation (at our "Stammtisch" in Honyaradō and in his tiny yet *gemütliche* apartment in Munich), and for frequently sending me valuable research materials from Germany. I am also very grateful to Jeff and Dominique Wisdom for generously opening their home to us during our several summer sojourns in Munich.

Over the years such friends have helped me bear in mind that, while for many of us it may indeed be the case that "the unexamined life is not worth living," it would be truer still to say that "the unlived life is not worth examining."

Most recently I would like to thank my new colleagues in the philosophy department of Loyola College in Maryland for easing our transition back to the United States and for welcoming me into this truly exceptional environment for teaching and research. It has been a pleasure to be among their company during the final stages of working on this book. Let me also thank once again the editors at Northwestern University Press, this time for their meticulous and insightful copyediting and in general for the friendly and professional manner in which they have carried out the production of this book.

Last but certainly not least, I would like to express my deepest gratitude to my family, whose attentive patience has helped me commit the years of unhurried concentration needed to complete this book. My wife, Naomi, has seen me through each day of the decade of research and writing, and has nursed my "swollen brain" innumerable times with a walk along Kamogawa and a dose of Kansai cuisine. Her bilingual typing and editing skills have also contributed to this and other projects. Our son, Toshi Field Davis, decided to come into the world and hop on board for the last years of the rewriting ride. His smile and his giggle remind me every morning how wonderfully amusing the little things in life really are, like a toothbrush or an earlobe. With this book on its way, I hope now to pay better attention during his lessons on the little things! Our daughter, Koto Fair Davis, came along to bless us with her adorable presence just as this book was going to press. I sincerely thank my mother, Barbara Davis, for all the encouragement and unconditional support she gave to my educational career over the years; looking back, I am particularly grateful for her unwavering perseverance during earlier, more difficult times. The fraternal ties of friendship with my brothers, Peter, Chris, and Sean, have always remained immeasurably closer to me than anything one can calculate in the miles and oceans that limit our occasions to gather. To the memory of Charles Anderson I feel special gratitude for a true gift, one that expects neither to witness a return nor to know the destination. And finally, I would like to thank my grandmother, Alberta Stephen, for the many true gifts she left behind, gifts which live on in those of us who shall always remember the down-to-earth wisdom of her words and the composed releasement of her smiling silence.

Abbreviations

The following abbreviations are used in the text and notes when citing from Heidegger's works. Citations include cross-references to page numbers in existing English translations, except in cases where the translation includes the German pagination. The German page(s) shall be given first, followed by a slash and the English page(s). For the sake of literal precision and consistency, I have frequently revised the translations listed here. For works in the *Gesamtausgabe* (Frankfurt am Main: Vittorio Klostermann, 1975–), which are listed here first, I use the conventional abbreviation *GA* followed by volume number.

Gesamtausgabe (Collected Edition)

GA 1   *Frühe Schriften.* (Written 1912–16.)

GA 5   *Holzwege.* (Written 1935–46.)
Pp. 1–74: "The Origin of the Work of Art." In *Basic Writings*, rev. and exp. ed. Edited by David Farrell Krell. New York: Harper and Row, 1977.
Pp. 75–113: "The Age of the World Picture." In *The Question Concerning Technology.* Translated by William Lovitt. New York: Harper and Row, 1977.
Pp. 115–208: *Hegel's Concept of Experience.* New York: Harper and Row, 1970.
Pp. 209–67: "The Word of Nietzsche: 'God Is Dead.'" In *The Question Concerning Technology.*
Pp. 269–320: "What Are Poets For?" In *Poetry, Language, Thought.* Translated by Albert Hofstadter. New York: Harper and Row, 1971.
Pp. 321–73: "The Anaximander Fragment." In *Early Greek Thinking.* Translated by David Farrell Krell and Frank Capuzzi. New York: Harper and Row, 1975.

GA 9   *Wegmarken.* 2nd ed. (Written 1919–61.)
Pathmarks. Edited by William McNeill. Cambridge: Cambridge University Press, 1998.

GA 12   *Unterwegs zur Sprache.* (Written 1950–59.)

Pp. 7–30: "Language." In *Poetry, Language, Thought.*
Pp. 31–end: *On the Way to Language.* Translated by Peter D. Hertz.
New York: Harper and Row, 1971.

GA 13   *Aus der Erfahrung des Denkens: 1910–1976.*
Pp. 75–86: "The Thinker as Poet." In *Poetry, Language, Thought.*

GA 15   *Seminare.* (Written 1951–73.)
Pp. 271–407: *Four Seminars.* Translated by Andrew Mitchell and
François Raffoul. Bloomington: Indiana University Press, 2003.

GA 16   *Reden und andere Zeugnisse eines Lebensweges: 1910–1976.*
Included in this volume are the texts published as "Political Texts,
1933–1934." Translated by William S. Lewis. In *The Heidegger Controversy.* Edited by Richard Wolin. Cambridge, Mass.: MIT Press,
1993.

GA 24   *Die Grundprobleme der Phänomenologie.* 2nd ed. (Written 1927.)
The Basic Problems of Phenomenology. Translated by Albert Hofstadter.
Bloomington: Indiana University Press, 1982.

GA 26   *Metaphysische Anfangsgründe der Logik im Ausgang von Leibniz.* (Written 1928.)
The Metaphysical Foundations of Logic. Translated by Michael Heim.
Bloomington: Indiana University Press, 1984.

GA 29/30 *Die Grundbegriffe der Metaphysik: Welt–Endlichkeit–Einsamkeit.* (Written
1929–30.)
The Fundamental Concepts of Metaphysics: World, Finitude, Solitude.
Translated by William McNeill and Nicholas Walker. Bloomington: Indiana University Press, 1995.

GA 31   *Vom Wesen der menschlichen Freiheit: Einleitung in die Philosophie.*
(Written 1930.)
The Essence of Human Freedom: An Introduction to Philosophy. Translated by Ted Sadler. London/New York: Continuum, 2002.

GA 36/37 *Sein und Wahrheit.* (Written 1933–34.)

GA 38   *Über Logik als Frage nach der Sprache.* (Written 1934.)

GA 39   *Hölderlins Hymnen "Germanien" und "Der Rhein."* (Written 1934–35.)

GA 45   *Grundfragen der Philosophie: Ausgewählte "Probleme" der "Logik."*
(Written 1937–38.)
Basic Questions of Philosophy: Selected "Problems" of "Logic." Translated
by Richard Rojcewicz and André Schuwer. Bloomington: Indiana
University Press, 1984.

GA 49   *Die Metaphysik des deutschen Idealismus: Zu erneuten Auslegung von
Schelling: Philosophische Untersuchungen über das Wesen der*

menschlichen Freiheit und die damit zusammenhängenden Gegenstände (1809). (Written 1941–43.)

GA 53   *Hölderlins Hymne "Der Ister."* (Written 1942.)
Hölderlin's Hymn "The Ister." Translated by William McNeill and Julia Davis. Bloomington: Indiana University Press, 1996.

GA 54   *Parmenides.* (Written 1942.)
Parmenides. Translated by André Schuwer and Richard Rojcewicz. Bloomington: Indiana University Press, 1992.

GA 55   *Heraklit.* (Written 1943–44.)

GA 56/57 *Zur Bestimmung der Philosophie.* (Written 1919.)

GA 60   *Phänomenologie des religiösen Lebens.* (Written 1920–21.)
The Phenomenology of Religious Life. Translated by Matthias Fritsch and Jennifer Anna Gosetti-Ferencei. Bloomington: Indiana University Press, 2004.

GA 65   *Beiträge zur Philosophie (Vom Ereignis).* (Written 1936–38.)
Contributions to Philosophy (From Enowning). Translated by Parvis Emad and Kenneth Maly. Bloomington: Indiana University Press, 1999.

GA 66   *Besinnung.* (Written 1938–39.)

GA 67   *Metaphysik und Nihilismus.* (Written 1938–39 and 1946–48.)

GA 69   *Die Geschichte des Seyns.* (Written 1938–40.)

GA 77   *Feldweg-Gespräche (1944/45).*

GA 79   *Bremer und Freiburger Vorträge.* (Written 1949 and 1957.)
Pp. 68–77: "The Turning." In *The Question Concerning Technology.*

Other Editions

D   *Denkerfahrungen: 1910–1976.* Frankfurt am Main: Vittorio Klostermann, 1983.

"EdP"   "Europa und die deutsche Philosophie." In *Europa und die Philosophie,* ed. Hans-Helmut Gander. Frankfurt am Main: Vittorio Klostermann, 1993. (Written 1936.)

EHD   *Erläuterungen zu Hölderlins Dichtung.* 6th ed. Frankfurt am Main: Vittorio Klostermann, 1996. (Written 1936–69.)
Elucidations of Hölderlin's Poetry. Translated by Keith Hoeller. New York: Humanity Books, 2000.

EM   *Einführung in die Metaphysik.* 5th ed. Tübingen: Max Niemeyer, 1987. (Written 1935.)

Introduction to Metaphysics. Translated by Gregory Fried and Richard Polt. New Haven: Yale University Press, 2000.

G   *Gelassenheit.* 10th ed. Pfullingen: Neske, 1992. (Written 1944–55.) *Discourse on Thinking.* Translated by John M. Anderson and E. Hans Freund. New York: Harper and Row, 1966.

ID   *Identität und Differenz.* Published in a bilingual edition as *Identity and Difference.* Translated by Joan Stambaugh. New York: Harper and Row, 1969. (Written 1956–57.)

N1   *Nietzsche. Erster Band.* 5th ed. Pfullingen: Neske, 1989. (Written 1936–39.)
Pp. 11–254: *Nietzsche,* Vol. 1, *The Will to Power as Art.* Translated by David Farrell Krell. New York: Harper and Row, 1979.
Pp. 254–472: *Nietzsche,* Vol. 2, *The Eternal Recurrence of the Same.* Translated by David Farrell Krell. New York: Harper and Row, 1984.
Pp. 473–658: *Nietzsche,* Vol. 3, *The Will to Power as Knowledge and as Metaphysics,* "The Will to Power as Knowledge." Translated by Joan Stambaugh, David Farrell Krell, and Frank A. Capuzzi. New York: Harper and Row, 1987.

N2   *Nietzsche. Zweiter Band.* 5th ed. Pfullingen: Neske, 1989. (Written 1939–46.)
Pp. 7–29: *Nietzsche,* Vol. 3, *The Will to Power as Knowledge and as Metaphysics,* "The Eternal Recurrence of the Same and the Will to Power."
Pp. 31–256: *Nietzsche,* Vol. 4, *Nihilism,* "European Nihilism." Translated by Frank A. Capuzzi. Edited by David Farrell Krell. New York: Harper and Row, 1982.
Pp. 257–333: *Nietzsche,* Vol. 3, *The Will to Power as Knowledge and as Metaphysics,* "Nietzsche's Metaphysics."
Pp. 335–98: *Nietzsche,* Vol. 4, *Nihilism,* "Nihilism as Determined by the History of Being."
Pp. 399–457: *The End of Philosophy,* "Metaphysics as History of Being." Translated by Joan Stambaugh. New York: Harper and Row, 1973.
Pp. 458–80: *The End of Philosophy,* "Sketches for a History of Being as Metaphysics."
Pp. 481–90: *The End of Philosophy,* "Recollection in Metaphysics."

"PMH"   "Preface by Martin Heidegger." In William J. Richardson. *Heidegger: Through Phenomenology to Thought.* 3rd ed. The Hague: Nijhoff, 1974. The German original appears on facing pages. (Written 1962.)

R   *Die Selbstbehauptung der deutschen Universität: Das Rektorat 1933/34.*
           Frankfurt am Main: Vittorio Klostermann, 1983. (Written 1933
           and 1945.)
           Pp. 9–19: "The Self-Assertion of the German University." Translated
           by William S. Lewis. In *The Heidegger Controversy.*
           Pp. 21–43: "The Rectorate 1933/34: Facts and Thoughts." In *Martin Heidegger and National Socialism.*

SA   *Schellings Abhandlung Über das Wesen der menschlichen Freiheit (1809).*
           2nd ed. Tübingen: Max Niemeyer, 1995. (Written 1936 and
           1941–43.)
           Schelling's Treatise on the Essence of Human Freedom. Translated by
           Joan Stambaugh. Athens: Ohio University Press, 1985.

SG   *Der Satz vom Grund.* 7th ed. Pfullingen: Neske, 1992. (Written
           1955–56.)
           The Principle of Reason. Translated by Reginald Lilly. Bloomington:
           Indiana University Press, 1991.

SP   "Nur noch ein Gott kann uns retten." Interview which took place
           in 1966, and published posthumously in *Der Spiegel* in 1976.
           Reprinted in *Antwort: Martin Heidegger im Gespräch.* Edited by
           Günther Neske and Emil Kettering. Pfullingen: Neske, 1988.
           "'Only a God Can Save Us': *Der Spiegel*'s Interview with Martin Heidegger." Translated by Maria P. Alter and John D. Caputo. In *The
           Heidegger Controversy.*

SZ   *Sein und Zeit.* 17th ed. Tübingen: Max Niemeyer, 1993. (Written
           1926.)
           Being and Time. Translated by John Macquarrie and Edward Robinson. New York: Harper and Row, 1962.
           Being and Time. Translated by Joan Stambaugh. Albany: SUNY
           Press, 1996.

VA   *Vorträge und Aufsätze.* 7th ed. Pfullingen: Neske, 1994. (Written
           1936–54.)
           Pp. 9–40: "The Question Concerning Technology." In *Basic Writings.*
           Pp. 41–66: "Science and Reflection." In *The Question Concerning
           Technology.*
           Pp. 67–95: "Overcoming Metaphysics." In *The Heidegger Controversy.*
           Pp. 97–122: "Who Is Nietzsche's Zarathustra?" In *Nietzsche,* Vol. 2,
           The Eternal Recurrence of the Same.
           Pp. 139–56: "Building Dwelling Thinking." In *Poetry, Language,
           Thought.*
           Pp. 157–79: "The Thing." In *Poetry, Language, Thought.*
           Pp. 181–98: ". . . Poetically Man Dwells . . ." In *Poetry, Language,
           Thought.*

Pp. 199–221: "Logos (Heraclitus, Fragment B 50)." In *Early Greek Thinking.*

Pp. 223–48: "Moira (Parmenides VIII, 34–41)." In *Early Greek Thinking.*

Pp. 249–74: "Aletheia (Heraclitus, Fragment B 16)." In *Early Greek Thinking.*

WhD   *Was heisst Denken?* 4th ed. Tübingen: Max Niemeyer, 1984. (Written 1951–52.)
What Is Called Thinking? Translated by J. Glenn Gray. New York: Harper and Row, 1968.

WP   "Was ist das—die Philosophie?" Published in a bilingual edition as *What Is Philosophy?* Translated by William Kluback and Jean T. Wilde. New Haven: College and University Press, 1958. (Written 1955.)

Z   *Zollikoner Seminare: Protokolle–Zwiegespräche–Briefe.* Edited by Menard Boss. Frankfurt am Main: Vittorio Klostermann, 1987. (Written 1959–71.)
Zollikon Seminars: Protocols–Conversations–Letters. Edited by Menard Boss. Translated by Franz Mayr and Richard Askay. Evanston, Ill.: Northwestern University Press, 2001.

ZSD   *Zur Sache des Denkens.* 3rd ed. Tübingen: Max Niemeyer, 1988. (Written 1962–64.)
On Time and Being. Translated by Joan Stambaugh. New York: Harper and Row, 1972.

Introduction: On *Gelassenheit* and Heidegger's Path of Thought

Sich auf den Sinn einlassen, ist das Wesen der Besinnung. . . .
Sie ist die Gelassenheit zum Fragwürdigen. (*VA* 64)[1]

Der Übergang aus dem Wollen in die Gelassenheit scheint mir
das Schwierige zu sein. . . . Vollends dann, wenn uns das Wesen
der Gelassenheit noch verborgen ist. (*G* 33)

The topic of this study is the problem of the will and the possibility of non-willing in the thought of Martin Heidegger. I attempt to show that this problematic lies at the very heart of his path of thought, and that following its development through a close examination of his texts involves nothing less than explicating the very movement (*Bewegung*) of his *Denkweg*. The topic is not just limited, then, to the later Heidegger's explicit critique of the culmination of the history of metaphysics in the technological "will to will" (*der Wille zum Willen*), or to his explicit anticipations of a "releasement" from the will to a radically other way of being. Over the course of this study I shall show how the question of the will—at first remaining problematically unthematized ("unthought"), then explicitly thematized yet fatefully unproblematized, before finally becoming radically criticized—is crucially at issue in the various twists and turns of Heidegger's path of thought from beginning to end.

The problem of the will is thus a problem "in Heidegger's thought" in the dual sense of, on the one hand, a problem which his thought explicitly and painstakingly takes up as a theme for thoughtful questioning, and, on the other hand, a problem to which his thinking itself at times succumbs. The task of this study is to learn from both of these aspects, by explicating and interpreting the former, while critically exposing the latter. Only by way of a careful and critical reading of both aspects of the problem of the will in his thought can we work towards disclosing a way of thinking the possibility of non-willing in and after Heidegger.

I attempt in this study to think "*after* Heidegger" (*nach* Heidegger), to be sure in the sense of following in the wake of and carrying forward the way of his thought; but also in the sense of reflecting back from a certain critical distance—a distance that is itself gained largely, if not exclusively, by way of following the sense and direction (*Sinn*) of a path opened up in the movement of his thinking. This approach in no way then precludes a critical reading; it does, however, involve first and foremost a patient attempt to understand the movement and tensions at play in the texts themselves. A careful reading shall thus allow for an "immanent critique" of the problem of the will in Heidegger's thought, above all a critique of the "embrace of the will" in his political misadventure during the early years of the Nazi regime. We shall find, however, that neither the problem nor the problematization of the will in Heidegger's thought either began in 1933 or ended in 1934. His philosophical embrace of the will began a few years prior and lingered on for several years after his political voluntarism. Moreover, if anticipations of his later thought of *Gelassenheit* can already be found in his earliest phenomenological writings, and if a radical interruption of willing is one thread in the ambiguous text of *Being and Time*, it is also the case that certain residues of the will remain in his thought to the end. Nevertheless, at the midpoint of his career, around 1940, we do find a decisive "turn" in Heidegger's thought toward an explicit and relentless problematization of the will in its various guises and disguises.

Following the path of Heidegger's thought, then, reveals both moments of a profound failure with regard to, and a profound search for a way of recovery from, the problem of the will. According to the later Heidegger's thought of "the history of being," however, the search for a path of recovery is not simply Heidegger's personal endeavor; it involves nothing less than the historical destiny of the West and indeed of the entire Westernizing world. Heidegger reads the history of metaphysics as a series of epochs linked together by a narrative of the rise of willful subjectivity, a story that culminates in the technological "will to will." It is thought to be this will to will that drives today's globalizing "world civilization," displacing the various peoples of the earth from their traditional contexts of dwelling and replacing them in a Euro-Americanocentric system of economic and technological manipulation.[2]

Yet Heidegger does not simply call for a retreat from the world of technology. What he says is that we need to learn to "let technical devices enter our daily life, and at the same time leave them outside." This "letting," which says "no" and "yes" at the same time, Heidegger calls, drawing on "an old word," "releasement toward things [*Gelassenheit zu den Dingen*]" (*G* 23/54). This comportment of *Gelassenheit,* which would lie beyond both the activity and the passivity of the subject of will, is one of the key words Heidegger uses to speak of what I shall translate as "non-willing" (*Nicht-Wollen*). *Gelassenheit* is one among a number of expressions through which Heidegger attempts to think non-willing(ly), though it in particular has become recognized as a key term of his later thought. Some introductory discussion is called for here on how Heidegger adopts and adapts this "old word," while also distancing himself from its past and present connotations.

While the word *Gelassenheit* has become familiar to many English-speaking philosophers through Heidegger's thought itself, the connotations it carries—for better or for worse—in German should be acknowledged. As the nominalized form of the perfect participle of *lassen* (to let, allow, leave), *Gelassenheit* can be translated as "releasement." But this English word does not speak to us with the nuances of the German, and *Gelassenheit* is thus sometimes translated as "composed releasement" or even as "letting-be." A current popular collection of sayings and texts by various authors from antiquity to modern times, *Von der Gelassenheit: Texte zum Nachdenken,* refers to "*apatheia, ataraxia, indifferentia, délaissement* and calmness" as names for *Gelassenheit* that can be found in other tongues.[3] Andreas Nießeler informs us that the German youth of today have added to this list of synonyms the English expression "cool." Nießeler points out the irony here, insofar as "cool" is meant to imply "a youth who has a total grip on himself and only does what he wants [*was er will*]."[4] The cool *Gelassene* would apparently not be released from, but rather delivered over to, the arbitrariness (*Willkür*) of his whim. The rhetoric of *Gelassenheit* thus even gets ironically co-opted for the egoism of *das Man* (or *das Jugendliche,* as the case may be). Given such contemporary connotations, and given the fact that Heidegger was wary of linking his thought of *Gelassenheit* too closely to the Stoic, Christian, or modern secular uses of the term, it is perhaps not surprising that the editor of *Von der Gelassenheit* was not allowed to reprint a passage from Heidegger's text entitled *Gelassenheit* (translated into English as *Discourse on Thinking*).

It is nevertheless important to bear in mind not only the current connotations but also the semantic history of the term *Gelassenheit,* a history that Heidegger takes over in his own critically innovative manner. As the article on "Gelassenheit" in the *Historisches Wörterbuch der Philosophie* informs us, the term was used by the medieval German mystics to refer to an emptying of the "creaturely" in order to be filled with the grace of God—or as Johannes Tauler puts it, true *Gelassenheit* is a matter of a "will-lessness" (*Willenslosigkeit*) that prepares one to sink back into the ground of the divine Will.[5] Luther and the theologians of the Reformation took over this notion of abandoning self-will (*Eigenwille*) in order to entrust oneself to the Will of God. While the theosophists of the baroque era and the theologians of Pietism continued to develop the religious notion of *Gelassenheit* as involved in a turn to God, in the late eighteenth century the term became popular in secular literature as synonymous with "gentleness" (*Sanftmut*), "calm" (*Ruhe*), "contentment" (*Zufriedenheit*), and "equanimity" (*Gleichmut*), if not perhaps "indifference" (*Gleichgültigkeit*). It was against the apparent passivity and disengagement of this literary ideal of calmness and *Gelassenheit* that the pathos-filled authors of the Sturm und Drang movement rebelled. Only after nineteenth-century thinkers such as Schopenhauer and, in his own manner, Nietzsche managed to rehabilitate the positive implications of *Gelassenheit*, were "existentialists," such as Jaspers, able to bring the term into twentieth-century philosophical use.

The *Brockhaus* encyclopedia currently defines *Gelassenheit* as "the comportment, attained by way of letting go of one's own wishes and cares, the comportment of a calm mental preparedness to willingly accept fateful dispensations of every kind." As historical predecessors, we are referred to Meister Eckhart's notion of "detachment" (*abgescheidenheit*) and the Stoic and Epicurean ideals of *apatheia* and *ataraxia*.[6] It is Eckhart, in fact, who introduced the nominalized form of *Gelassenheit* (*gelāzenheit*), and, as we have seen, since then the idea has had a long and varied history, both religious and secular.[7] The term has at times been praised as a releasement from worldly concerns into a devotion to God (and his Will), or as a detachment which allows for theoretical objectivity. On the other hand, it has at times been derided as a heretical "indifference" to ethical duties (and even to the performance of God's Will), as a quietism that withdraws from the world, or as a calm equanimity unacceptable to the passionate rebelliousness of the proponents of Sturm und Drang. As we shall see, however, Heidegger attempts to think a sense of *Gelassenheit* beyond the very domain of this conflict between passive aloofness and willful rebellion.

Is *Gelassenheit* compatible with the *vita activa*? A strict distinction (a "binary opposition") between activity and passivity—and the ensuing reductive restriction of *Gelassenheit* to the latter category, i.e., as a mere absence of action if not a negation of life itself—is, to be sure, a deep-rooted prejudice of the tradition we inherit. That we find it difficult to understand a "positive" sense of "letting-be," of attentively releasing something or someone into their own, testifies to the dominance of what Heidegger calls "the domain of the will" in our language, thought, and behavior.

One should note, moreover, that the English word "to let" (not to mention the prevalence of the liberal concept of "negative freedom") may exacerbate this prejudice. The German *Lassen* is used as a modal auxiliary not only in the sense of passively *letting* something happen or *allowing* someone to do something, but also in the sense of *having* something done.[8] Moreover, *Sicheinlassen auf etwas* means "to engage oneself in something." Hence, while *Seinlassen* (letting-be) may be used in common speech to mean "to leave alone or stop doing," Heidegger's *Sein-lassen* involves rather a *Sicheinlassen auf* in the sense of "getting into, engaging with, getting involved with things"; in other words, "actively letting" beings be themselves.[9] Thus, for Heidegger it would in fact hardly be oxymoronic to speak of an "engaged releasement" (*engagierte Gelassenheit*).[10]

In an important passage in this regard, which attempts to articulate an originary sense of freedom prior to the opposition of its "positive" and "negative" senses, Heidegger writes:

> Freedom for what is opened up in an open region lets beings be the beings they are. Freedom now reveals itself as letting beings be. . . . Ordinarily we speak of letting be . . . in the negative sense of leaving something alone, of renouncing it, of indifference and even neglect. . . . However, the phrase required now—to let beings be—does not refer to neglect and indifference but rather the opposite. To let be is to engage oneself with beings [*Sein-lassen ist das Sicheinlassen auf das Seiende*]. On the other hand, to be sure, this is not to be understood only as the mere management, preservation, tending, and planning of the beings in each case encountered or sought out. To let be—that is, to let beings be as the beings that they are—means to engage oneself with the Open and its openness into which every being comes to stand, bringing that openness, as it were, along with itself. (*GA* 9:188/144)

Some traditional connotations of *Gelassenheit*—for example, as a releasement from willfulness, and as a rest (*Ruhe*) within movement or an "inner calm" in the very midst of activity—are indeed positively taken over into Heidegger's thought. But, perhaps in an attempt to free its sense from the categories of metaphysical thinking, Heidegger limits his references back to the semantic history of the term.[11] One significant exception in this regard is his reference to Meister Eckhart. Heidegger refers to Eckhart's notion of *Gelassenheit* both in order to link his own idea with, and to distance it from, the Christian mystical tradition of releasement.

For Eckhart *Gelassenheit* has, to begin with, a double meaning, corresponding to the two senses of the Middle High German word *lāzen*: *verlassen* (to abandon or leave behind) and *überlassen* (to defer or "give over to"). One must leave (*relinquere*) the world of creatures and give oneself up to (*committere*) God.[12] Only by way of abandoning (*Ablassen*) all self-will can one open oneself up to receive the grace of God, i.e., "the birth of the Son in the soul." And only by way of this birth can one be united with God's Will and perform his works in the midst of worldly activity. For Eckhart, this releasement *from* self-will and *to* God's Will in the end releases one *back into* the world of the *vita activa*. Heidegger's *Gelassenheit* shares an analogous tripartite structure: a releasement from willful subjectivity, to a cor-respondence with the address of being (and to an openness for its mystery of self-concealment), and back into an engagement with letting things be.

However, Heidegger explicitly distances his notion of *Gelassenheit* from that of Eckhart, inasmuch as the latter, he claims, remains within "the domain of the will" (*G* 33–34/62). As Friedrich-Wilhelm von Herrmann points out, what must be abandoned (*abgelassen*) for Heidegger is not sinful selfishness, but rather "the essential restriction of modern thought in its being stamped with character of will." A recovery from this willful mode can then release us into (*einlassen*) an other way of thinking, by attuning us to that which admits (*einlässt*) or allows (*zulässt*) us into our being-in-the-world.[13] Emil Kettering emphasizes what he sees as the fundamental difference between the conceptions of *Gelassenheit* in the mystics and in Heidegger in the following manner:

> The greatest parallel between the mystical and Heideggerian conceptions appears to be the idea of will-lessness [*Willenslosigkeit*]. But appearances are deceptive here. While the mystics are concerned only with the overcoming of self-will in favor of divine Will, and so continue to hold fast to thinking in terms of will [*das Willensdenken*], Heidegger attempts to recover from every form of thinking as willing, including not-willing [*Nichtwollen*], which as negation itself remains bound to the circle of representation of willing.[14]

While Kettering may be unfair in his critical interpretation of the mystics—he does not attend, for example, to the radical (re)affirmation of the *vita activa* in Eckhart, nor to the ways in which the strictures of not just human but also divine "will" are challenged and indeed "broken through" in the most radical moments of Eckhart's mystical thought—he rightly points out Heidegger's attempt to get beyond the very domain of the will. The releasement from the will would lead neither to a passive quietism nor to a deference to a higher Will.

Heidegger's being (*Sein*) is not a higher being (*Seiendes*) or a meta-Subject possessed of Will. Perhaps not altogether incomparable to Eckhart's radical notion of "detachment," which is said to be not only the highest human virtue but also of the very essence of God (or, more precisely speaking, of the *Gottheit* before and beyond the Will of God the Father), Heidegger thinks "that the most profound meaning of being is *Lassen.* Letting beings be" (*GA* 15:363/59).[15] In the latter chapters of this study we shall consider Heidegger's specific notions of *Sein-lassen* and *Gelassenheit* in more detail, in the context of a more general concern with the problem of the will and the possibility of non-willing in his later thought.

Let us remark here on how he distances his own thought from earlier notions of *Gelassenheit* in the context of his conception of the history of philosophy. For Heidegger, "philosophy" has been determined as metaphysics, as "onto-theology," and the task of transforming thinking at "the end of philosophy" requires that the very language of this history be transformed by way of a radically deconstructive repetition. Heidegger cannot, then, simply appeal to a prior definition of *Gelassenheit,* insofar as any prior notion would be bound to an earlier epoch in the history of metaphysics. Hence, Heidegger says that Eckhart *still* thinks within the domain of the will (*G* 33/61). (Whether and to what extent this is the case shall be the topic of chapter 5.)

Yet are we even today prepared to think *Gelassenheit* postmetaphysically, beyond the strictures of an onto-theological or subjective voluntarism? Are we not, according to Heidegger, bogged down still deeper in this horizonal domain of the will, as in a well that limits our view the farther down we fall? Or is the dark abyss of this "well of will," as Heidegger suggests, a danger in the midst of which a flash of insight first becomes possible? Does our distressful condition harbor the possibility of a thoughtful intimation of what lies beyond the shrinking horizon of the cybernetic will to will; does a critical reflection prepare us to follow hints of a region of non-willing, a region that is always already there but to which we have not yet properly corresponded?

For Heidegger, we are still, at best, on the way to *Gelassenheit.* Our Dasein is not yet "there" in the region of non-willing; we have not yet properly made the leap (back) into the *Da* of *Sein.* Being on the way involves a manifold and relentless problematization of the will. Prior still, for Heidegger on the wandering path of his *Denkweg,* it required first *discovering* the problem of the will; that is to say, he first had to find the path of problematizing the will. Having stumbled over and then explicitly returned to clear this path, Heidegger's mature critique of the will compels us to consider this problem as one of the most decisive issues for thinking today. At the very least, this study shall demonstrate how the problem of the will can—with scarcely more than a touch of interpretive emphasis—be read as the problem of problems on Heidegger's path of thought.

This reading does not mean to displace the question of being; on the contrary, it reveals that the *Seinsfrage* involves, at its core, the question of the will. The question of the will is just as intertwined with the question of being as is the latter with the question of the essence of man. Heidegger repeatedly stated that the relation between being and man is "in fact the one single question which all previous thinking must first be brought to face" (*WhD* 74/79). Yet how is the relation between being and man to be thought in its *Grundstimmung;* how are we to be a-tuned to being? It is here that we find a radical turn in Heidegger's thought-path, one that, following a profound ambivalence toward the will in *Being and Time,* traverses a zealous embrace of the will in the first half of the 1930s, before leading to his mature attempts to patiently prepare for thinking non-willing(ly).

Undoubtedly, the ground zero of Heidegger's failure to problematize the will is found in his political speeches from 1933–34, where, for example, he enthusiastically calls for a "threefold 'Sieg Heil!'" to "the towering will of our Führer" (*GA* 16:236/60). Here as elsewhere Heidegger's "political blunder" is not simply a tangential diversion unrelated to his properly philosophical endeavor. The will first secures its place at the very core of Heidegger's thought by 1930, specifically in his affirmation of "pure willing" as the answer to the question of the essence of human freedom, a question that is said to underlie even the question of being (*GA* 31:303). This idea of a concrete will that "actually wills willing and nothing else besides" (285) ironically prefigures in some respects the "will to will" that later becomes the very focus of Heidegger's critique of the modern epoch. After Heidegger turns to this radical critique of the will, freedom is then rethought as a "letting-be" that is "*originally* not connected with the will" (*VA* 28/330).

Both the early quasi-transcendental claim that finite resolute Dasein chooses its possibilities for being, and the subsequent claim that the human will-to-know (*Wissen-wollen*) must violently bring to a stand the overpowering onslaught of being, themselves become questionable in Heidegger's mature being-historical thought, according to which being is revealed-in-(extreme)-concealment as will in the epoch of modernity. "To modern metaphysics," Heidegger writes, "the being of beings appears as will," and this means that "human-being [*Menschsein*] must appear in an emphatic manner as a willing" (*WhD* 36/91–92). Modern man has fallen into a purportedly self-grounding subjectivity, and things can appear only as representations (*Vorstellungen*) within the horizon of its will to power. To such willful subjectivity, the "earth itself can show itself only as the object of assault, an assault that, in human willing, establishes itself as unconditional objectification" (*GA* 5:256/100). Ultimately, in the age of nihilism as the most extreme "epoch" of the history of being (the *epoche* in which being is forgotten and withdraws to the extreme point of abandonment), beings are produced (*hergestellt*), ordered about (*bestellt*), and distorted (*verstellt*) within an enframing (*Ge-stell*) set up and driven by the technological "will to will." Human beings too, themselves threatened with reduction to "human resources," are "willed by the will to will without experiencing the essence of this will" (*VA* 85/82).

How, then, might we step back into a proper, non-willing relation of cor-respondence to being, as "place-holders" and "guardians" of its clearing, and thereby into a proper comportment to beings, one that cultivates and preserves them in a manner that genuinely lets them be? Heidegger writes: "Being itself could not be experienced without a more original experience of the essence of man and vice versa" (*GA* 55:293). He also tells us that "salvation [from the technological will to will] must come from where there is a turning with mortals in their essence" (*GA* 5:296/118). Yet how are we—in the midst of finding our historical essence thoroughly determined by the will to will—to turn and find our way to *Gelassenheit*? This problem of the will and the possibility of non-willing is undoubtedly one of the most question-worthy issues on Heidegger's path of thought.

HEIDEGGER AND THE WILL

The Will, Non-Willing, and the Domain of the Will: Preliminary Determinations

Every exposition must of course not only draw upon the matter of the text; it must also, without presuming, imperceptibly give to the text something out of its own problematic [*Eigenes aus ihrer Sache*]. (*GA* 5:213–14/58)

Philosophy will never seek [*wollen*] to deny its "presuppositions," but neither may it simply admit them. It conceives them, and it unfolds with more and more penetration both the presuppositions themselves and that for which they are presuppositions. The methodological considerations now demanded of us will have this very function. (*SZ* 310)

Reentering the Hermeneutical Circle

One cannot (therefore) have begun. . . . For one will always only have begun again, redoubling what will always already have commenced.
　　—John Sallis[1]

Thus we constantly find ourselves moving in a circle. And this is an indication that we are moving within the realm of philosophy. Everywhere a kind of circling. (*GA* 29/30:266/180)

Philosophy perhaps always involves the frustrated attempt to get back to where we have already begun, to get this foundation in full view, if not indeed to lay it ourselves. We then repeat this backward step with an introduction to what we have disclosed, trying to determine the very reading of the reading we have given. This backward stepping is both the virtue and the folly of philosophy; it is also not unrelated to the problem of the will. Lest I simply repeat a will to ground and control at the very moment when I embark on an essay that problematizes the will, let me reflect at the outset on the sense in which I shall, in this chapter, give a preliminary account of the terms of this inquiry. I offer these opening reflections, not in an attempt to definitively determine all that follows, but in order to break once more the hermeneutical ice, to sketch, as Plato would write, "where we have come from and where we are going."[2]

Recalling Heidegger's analysis of "the fore-structure of interpretation" (*SZ* section 32), we are called on to approach his texts with a certain amount of hermeneutical distance, or rather to reflect on the distance we have always already taken. Moreover, inasmuch as Heidegger asked for his texts to be read as "ways—not works [*Wege—nicht Werke*]" (*GA* 1:437), we are invited to pursue the paths of thought his texts open up, rather than forever attempting merely to faithfully reconstruct his "system." In order to genuinely read a great thinker, both critically and "faithfully," one must go beyond merely reproducing his or her thought "in their own terms." Reading is interpreting; thinking is being on the way of a thought, and happily so. The task is to attune oneself to what is question-worthy in a thinker's thoughts, to take up his way and not simply to imitate his works.

> The wish to understand a thinker in his own terms is something else entirely than the attempt to inquire into a thinker's question in the question-worthiness of what he has thought [*das Fragen eines Denkers in die Fragwürdigkeit seines Gedachten hineinzufragen*]. The first is and remains impossible. The second is rare, and of all things the most difficult. We shall not be allowed to forget this difficulty for a single moment while on our way. (*WhD* 113/185)

Heidegger went so far as to write the following to Otto Pöggeler near the end of his career: "I think now would be the time to stop writing *about* Heidegger. A substantive discussion would be more important."[3] The present study is ultimately an attempt to engage in such a substantive discussion regarding the problem of the will and the possibility of non-willing. Attending to the matter itself, that is to say, to "the question-worthiness of what [Heidegger] has thought," my interpretation of and engagement in this discussion shall not only rely on Heidegger's explicit nomenclature, but shall also develop a few guiding terms of its own.

Nevertheless, it is also the case that we still have much to learn from a close reading of Heidegger's texts, and it would be shortsighted to simply import our own presuppositions, and to hastily rush ahead with our own assumptions of the direction his path of thinking should take, or should have taken. I agree with Pöggeler's response to Heidegger's comment, namely, that "both are still necessary: to bring into view appropriately the impetus which can emanate from Heidegger's thinking and to wean oneself from these initiatives in order to travel one's own ways."[4] The former task alone is a considerable one, and in fact the greater part of this book shall be devoted to it. Only at certain points, already here in the initial defining of terms and more clearly in later chapters, shall I attempt a few small steps toward finding a way of thinking the problem of the will and the possibility of non-willing "after Heidegger."

In this chapter I give some preliminary determinations of the terms of this inquiry. These terms include "will," "not-willing," "deferred-willing," "covert-willing," "the domain of the will," and "non-willing." I shall attempt to lay out the perspective from which I shall read Heidegger, a perspective which has itself, however, been gained for the most part through reading his texts. I acknowledge the circle, and merely pause here at the outset of writing in order to invite the reader into this dynamic of my reading/interpreting Heidegger's thought.

The Will as a Fundamental (Dis)Attunement

Let us begin with the term "will." What is the will? As heirs of the modern Western philosophical tradition, we tend to understand the will as a "faculty of the subject," to be distinguished from "thinking" or "feeling." To be sure, a standard historical introduction to the notion of will in the West would involve an examination beginning at least with the ancient Greeks, perhaps asking why they had not yet "discovered" the unity of this faculty.[5] One might then move on to the gradual piecing together of the faculty of the will in the Stoics, and then to its first unified appearance in Augustine's *voluntas*.[6] Next, one might consider the debates in Scholastic theology over whether the faculty of will or that of intellect is the "higher faculty." After working through Kant's critical delimitations of the spheres proper to each faculty, one could argue, against both irrational voluntarism and disengaged intellectualism, for a balance of powers. Since on this account the faculty of the will could be shown to be the backbone of action, any predilection for "non-willing," such as Heidegger's thought of *Gelassenheit*, might then be criticized as yet another reoccurrence of the old philosopher's prejudice for "thinking" over "acting," a prejudice harmless enough in the ivory tower but dangerous to the political sphere which requires not only thought but also action and thus will.[7] This is, in fact, roughly the manner in which Hannah Arendt analyzes the will.

Yet despite Arendt's illuminating account of the relation between the faculties of thought and will (unfortunately she died before finishing the third part of her study, which would have treated the faculty of judgment) through the history of philosophy, if we are to pursue Heidegger's path of rethinking the will, we must more radically call into question the traditional assumption that the will is simply a "faculty of the subject." To begin with, what if it were the case that something akin to the opposite were true—that subjectivity is rather, as it were, a "faculty of the will"? What if the will underlies the subject, and not vice versa? In other words, what if it were the case that thinking in terms of a subject who possesses faculties, a "subject who wills," already involves a particular willful mode of being-in-the-world? That is, what if the very ontology which sets up a subject who stands over against a world of objects, to which it then reaches out by means of faculties, powers of representational thought and volitional action, is itself determined by a willful manner of being and thinking?

This, indeed, is the direction of questioning which Heidegger's thought engenders. He writes:

> By the word "will" I mean, in fact, not a faculty of the soul, but rather—
> in accordance with the unanimous, though hardly yet thought-through
> doctrine of Western thinkers—that wherein the essence of the soul,
> spirit, reason, love, and life are grounded. (*GA* 77:78)

Rather than seeing willing and thinking as separate and competing faculties, Heidegger attempts to show that traditional (especially modern) thinking, as representing, is a kind of willing: "Thinking is willing, and willing is thinking" (*G* 30/59). His own task, as we shall see, is to attempt a thinking which "is something other than willing" (ibid.), not because it chooses the one faculty over the other, and not because it is a mere passivity—indeed Heidegger sometimes suggests that genuine thinking involves "a higher activity [*ein höheres Tun*]" (*G* 33/61)—but because such thinking, together with "dwelling" and "building," would be *other than* willing. Before broaching this question of "non-willing," however, we need to get clear on what is meant by the term "will."

What then is the will if not first of all a faculty of the subject? Let me introduce a certain interpretive extrapolation at this point. I suggest that we can understand the notion of will by way of what Heidegger calls a "fundamental attunement" (*Grundstimmung*). Let us develop the sense in which this interpretive connection of terms is intended here. Heidegger writes:

An attunement is a way [*eine Weise*] . . . in the sense of a melody that does not merely hover over the so-called proper being at hand of humans, but that sets the tone for such a being, i.e., attunes and determines the manner and way [*Art und Wie*] of their being. . . . [Attunement] is . . . the *fundamental manner in which Dasein is as Dasein* [*die* Grundweise, wie das Dasein als Dasein ist]. . . . [It] is not—is never—simply a consequence or side-effect of our thinking, doing, and letting. It is—to put it crudely—the presupposition for such things, the "medium" within which they first happen. (*GA* 29/30:101; see also *GA* 9:110/87)

In another text Heidegger writes:

A deep-rooted and very old habit of experience and speech stipulates that we interpret feelings and attunements [*Gefühle und Stimmungen*]—as well as willing and thinking—in a psychological-anthropological sense as occurrences and processes within an organism. . . . This also means that we are "subjects," present at hand, who are displaced *into* this or that attunement [*Stimmung*] by "getting" them. In truth, however, it is the attunement that displaces us, namely into this or that understanding or disclosure of the world, into such and such a resolve or occlusion of one's *self*, a self which is *essentially* a being-in-the-world. (*GA* 45:161)

Although Heidegger does not usually explicitly connect the notion of *Grundstimmung* with that of the will, at one point in his analysis of Nietzsche's conception of will—the conception which most directly influenced his own—he writes the following:

Will is command. . . . In commanding, "the innermost conviction of superiority" is what is decisive. Accordingly, Nietzsche understands commanding as the fundamental attunement of one's being superior [*die Grundstimmung des Überlegenseins*]. . . . (*N1* 651/152)

Although in at least this passage Heidegger does explicitly refer to the will as a fundamental attunement, I shall not pursue further here the textual question of the relation between the two terms in Heidegger's corpus.[8] My point is that an entry into what Heidegger understands by the notion of will, the sense in which he does not mean by it one "faculty of the subject" among others, can be gained by way of thinking the will as a fundamental attunement.

A fundamental attunement is a comportment "prior to" the determination of any subject, object, or intentional relation between them. We cannot, therefore, begin by defining the will as a faculty of the subject, because our thinking in terms of a "subject equipped with faculties for confronting the world" is dependent on a certain already "willful" mode of being-in-the-world. Part of what is at stake in Heidegger's critique of the will is to see that the very understanding of the being of beings in terms of "subjects" and "objects" is implicated in a particular willful *Grundstimmung*. Only *within* this particular fundamental attunement does it make sense to speak of the subjective act of willing or of "the faculty of the will."

A fundamental attunement would be "fundamental" in the sense that it first opens (one) up (to) a world, prior to the determination of "who" is opened up to "what." We reflectively find ourselves always already involved in such an attunement, just as we perceptively find the world always already disclosed through such an attunement. A willful fundamental attunement first determines the ontology wherein a subject is open to a world of objects in such a manner that the "open to" of this relation is distorted (constricted) into the representation of objects present-at-hand, if not indeed into the securing of a totality of materials ready for willful manipulation.

Heidegger, in fact, goes even "further" than this in his determination of the term "will." The will, for the later Heidegger, is not only a matter of the fundamental attunement of the subject who seeks to dominate the world; it is, prior still, the name for the being of beings in the epoch of modernity. Thus he writes:

> The will in this willing does not mean here a faculty [*Vermögen*] of the human soul . . . ; the word "willing" here designates the being of beings as a whole. Every single being and all beings as a whole have their essential powers [*das Vermögen seines Wesens*] in and through the will. (*WhD* 35/91)

For Heidegger, the fundamental attunement (*Grundstimmung*) of man's historical essence is in turn determined (*bestimmt*) by a "sending of being." This sending (*Seinsgeschick*) is always a granting-in-withdrawal, and thus always involves an interplay of revealing/concealing; yet in the modern epoch of will this occurs as an *extreme* self-withholding of being, a denial which abandons man to the fundamental (dis)attunement of will.

A turn to the "proper fundamental attunement" of non-willing could, then, only take place by way of a turning in the sending of being. The crucial question of how man is to "participate" in this sending—and specifically of how he is to "wait for," "prepare for," or "cor-respond to" the turning—shall be a central concern of this study. It may turn out that we need to think in terms of a "double genitive" in the turning to non-willing as a "fundamental a-tunement *of* man"; or rather, as with the case of the "thinking *of* being" (see *GA* 9:313ff./239ff.), it may be necessary to liberate ourselves from the very framework of the subject/predicate grammar that compels us to think in terms of a dichotomy between an active agent and a passive recipient.

The Will as Ecstatic-Incorporation, as the Will to Will, and as Power-Preservation/Power-Enhancement

Let us return to the task at hand, that of giving a preliminary account of the notion of "will." What characterizes the fundamental (dis)attunement of willing? Heidegger develops his mature conception of the will chiefly through his encounter with Nietzsche. In Heidegger's first lecture course on Nietzsche in 1936, he draws on Nietzsche's thought to give a kind of phenomenological account of the will, laying out the following points.[9]

Willing must first be distinguished from a "mere striving" (*blosse Streben*) which, as it were, merely pushes one from behind. While "it is not possible for us to strive beyond ourselves, . . . will . . . is always a willing out beyond oneself [*über sich hinaus wollen*]" (*N1* 51/41). The will is thus not a matter of a simple "encapsulation of the ego from its surroundings" (59/48), but is a mode in which Dasein ecstatically exists out into the world. Nevertheless, "he who wills stations himself abroad among beings *in order to* keep them firmly within his field of action" (ibid., emphasis added). In other words, if the subject who wills always wills out beyond himself, opening himself up to the world, this involves at the same time a movement of bringing the world back into the realm of his power, the domain of his will.

There is thus a double movement essential to willing. "Willing always brings the self to itself; it *thereby* finds itself out beyond itself" (63/52, emphasis added); or as Heidegger writes in his Schelling interpretation, it is a matter of "what always strives back to itself, and yet expands itself" (*SA* 155/128). In willing, we exceed ourselves only to bring this excess back into the self; "in willing we [seek to] know ourselves as out beyond ourselves; we have the sense of having somehow achieved a state of being-master [*Herrsein*] over [something]" (*N1* 64/52). The *ekstasis* of willing is thus always incorporated back into the domain of the subject; the will's movement of self-overcoming is always in the name of an expansion of the subject, an increase in his territory, his power. Willing is, in short, "being-master-out-beyond-oneself [*Über-sich-hinaus-Herrsein*]" (76/63). I shall call this double-sided or "duplicitous" character of will: *ecstatic-incorporation*.[10]

Let me briefly refer here to two other thinkers who have insightfully indicated this ambivalently "duplicitous" character of the will as what I am calling "ecstatic-incorporation": Levinas and Nishitani. Given the diversity of their Judaic and Buddhist backgrounds, not to mention the complexity of their relations to Heidegger, it might be provocative as well as illuminating to point out a congruence between them with regard to the problem of the will.

The fundamental (dis)attunement of willing is characterized, as we have seen, by a circular movement where the subject steps out and forcefully brings the other-than-itself back into the domain of his power. Levinas speaks of this as the "reduction of the Other to the Same." The will is a movement of reducing otherness to sameness, difference to identity, even when paradoxically this has the alienating effect of solidifying dichotomies. The subject of will alienates himself from others, even when—or precisely because—he attempts to forcefully bring them back into his own domain. On the one hand, the will to the Same is a denial and refusal of alterity. On the other hand, however, the subject of will, in the *ekstasis* of his ecstatic-incorporation, cannot help but run the risk of exposing himself to the threat of otherness. In order to embark on a mission of conquest, the fortress gates must be opened to that which lies beyond the walls and is not yet conquered. Moreover, in the very will to conquer and incorporate others, the will to lay claim to their exterior bodies as one's own territory, one inevitably exposes oneself to a recognition of the trace of radical alterity in their faces, the trace of that interiority which forever withdraws from and resists conquest and assimilation. Hence, as Levinas puts it, there is "this ambiguity of voluntary power, exposing itself to the others in its centripetal movement of egoism."[11] The will wants the impossible: to possess others *as other;* but the moment it succeeds in possessing them, they are stripped of their otherness. The will therefore fails even when it succeeds, and its movement of restless self-expansion must continue without end.

Nishitani critically reworks Heidegger's early phenomenological analysis of being-in-the-world by way of linking the Buddhist notion of "karma" with Heidegger's own later critique of the nihilistic "will to will."[12] He describes how our everyday karmic Dasein remains tethered to itself, "tying itself up with its own rope," even as it steps out into the world. Our everyday Dasein "endlessly stands outside itself," and yet at the same time, in this everyday mode of *ekstasis*, "remains shut up perpetually within itself, never radically departing from its own abode."[13] Nishitani interprets "the darkness of ignorance" (*mumyō, avidyā*)—which is generally understood alongside "craving" (*tanhā*) to be the root cause of suffering in Buddhism—as this "radical self-enclosure, the self-centeredness that is the wellspring of endless karmic activity."[14] Buddhist enlightenment would break through the darkness of this self-enclosure, and implies at once an extinguishing (*nirvana*) of the will of craving and a compassionate engagement (*karuna*) in the world beyond the walls of the ego.[15]

Heidegger's own pointed critique of this dual character of the will is clearly articulated in his later lectures and writings on Nietzsche. But before looking there, let us first note another important element of Heidegger's understanding of the will that is already apparent in his early lectures on Nietzsche: the will is ultimately "the will to will." The will is essentially a matter of "commanding" or "mastery," of reaching out beyond oneself— to what? To power. What then is power? Power is "nothing else than the essence of will. Hence will to power is will to will, which is to say, willing is a self-willing" (*N1* 46/37). "Willing itself is mastery over [something], which reaches out beyond itself; will is intrinsically power. And power is willing that is constant in itself. Will is power; power is will" (52/41).

There is a certain doubling-back character of the will to power; it is finally a self-willing even as it always wills out beyond itself. But there is also a constant movement to willing, an insatiability. "Every willing is a willing-to-be-more [*ein Mehr-sein-wollen*]. Power itself only *is* inasmuch as, and as long as, it remains a willing-to-be-more-power" (72/60). Thus, even though will is power, the phrase "will to power" is not simply redundant. The will to power is the will *to* power. "In the will, as a willing-to-be-more, in the will as the will to power, enhancement and heightening [*die Steigerung, die Erhöhung*] are essentially implied" (ibid.). The will is the insatiable, ever expanding, yet always essentially to more of the same, "will to will."

Heidegger later develops these thoughts in an increasingly critical fashion. In 1943 he writes the following concerning the essential character of the will.

> To will is to will-to-be-master [*Wollen ist Herr-sein-wollen*]. . . . The will is not a desiring, and not a mere striving after something, but rather, willing is in itself a commanding. . . . What the will wills it does not merely strive after as something it does not yet have. What the will wills it has already. For the will wills its will. Its will is what it has willed. The will wills itself. It mounts beyond [*übersteigt*] itself. Accordingly, the will as will wills out beyond itself and must at the same time in that way bring itself behind and beneath itself. Therefore Nietzsche can say: "To will at all is the same thing as to will to become *stronger*, to will to grow. . . ." (*The Will to Power*, section 675, 1887–88). (*GA* 5:234/77–78)

The will to power must not rest for a moment in its quest for more power, for even "a mere pause in power-enhancement . . . is already the beginning of the decline of power" (234–35/78). And yet, on the other hand, the movement of power-enhancement needs the moment of "power-preservation" as well. "The making secure of a particular level of power is the necessary condition for the heightening of power" (236–37/80). The will to power involves both moments of increasing and securing, securing and increasing, which mutually enable one other.

> The will to power must, above all, posit conditions for power-preservation [*Machterhaltung*] and power-enhancement [*Macht-steigerung*]. To the will belongs the positing of these conditions that belong intrinsically together. (237/80)

We return then once again to the double-sided character of the will, the will as ecstatic-incorporation, but now with an even greater critical edge, for even the ecstatic moment is revealed to be a matter of sheer extension of power for the sake of power. The will is after all, we now see, a kind of *dynamic* "encapsulating of the ego," not, to be sure, in the timid sense of shutting out the world, but in the aggressive sense of expanding the territory of the subject to include the world within his domain of power. Ultimately: "Willing wills the one who wills, as such a one; and willing posits the willed as such" (*NI* 51/40). "In this way [the will] continually comes as the selfsame [*der gleiche*] back upon itself as the same [*den Gleichen*]" (*GA* 5:237/81). The will, in willing itself, reaches out to the world as something it posits and represents as a means for its movement of power-enhancement and hence power-preservation, of power-preservation and hence power-enhancement.

The "egoism" of the will, of course, need not be that of an individual ego. Heidegger in fact persistently warns against this "moral" simplification of the problem of the will (see *GA* 54:203–4). To restrict the problem of the will to that of individual egoism would be to fail to see that nationalism and even humanism (anthropocentrism) or religion (missionary zeal) can repeat the problem of the will even as they call for the self-sacrifice of individual egos. The collective will to the protection and development of "national interests," or to the technological progress of humanity in the conquest of nature, or to the missionary assimilation of all remaining heathens under the reign or reins of our God's Will: all these can remain but altered formations of self-overcoming for the sake of self-expansion. We shall return to the issue of overt and covert sublations and sublimations of the will when we discuss the manifold "domain of the will."

Two more elements of the will should be mentioned here at the outset, namely, its connections with "representation" (*Vorstellung*) and with "metaphysics." For Heidegger, as we have noted, thinking "understood in the traditional way, as representing is a kind of willing" (*G* 29/58). "Representation inspects everything encountering it from *out* of itself and in reference *to* itself" (*N2* 295/219). In representing the world, one brings it into one's sphere of knowing and acting, and thus the world is reduced to an environment (*Umwelt*) pivoting on (*sich drehen um*) one's will. Ultimately, Heidegger attempts to show, representation reduces the things of the world to objects and finally to "standing-reserve" (*Bestand*) for willful technological manipulation.

Not unrelated to knowing as representing is the attempt of "metaphysics" to "ground" beings, to lay out with certainty the essence of all existence, or even ultimately to establish man himself, in the form of the subject (as *hypokeimenon, subiectum,* or the "transcendental ego"), as the ground of beings. The history of metaphysics not only completes itself in the modern metaphysics of the will; from the beginning the project of metaphysics itself was in this sense a project of the will. The dilemma endemic to metaphysics as such lies in the fact that its "will to ground and found" (see *GA* 77:164ff.), its will to submit beings to the shadowless light of the principle of calculative reason, or the will to posit the human subject himself as the ground, hinders an originary experience of the granting-in-withdrawal of being which lets beings be in their presencing and absencing.[16]

Following Heidegger, I have developed here in a broad sense the meaning of the term "will," and have in the process suggested the sense in which this will is a problem. It has also been suggested that the problem of the will cannot simply be overcome by means of sacrifice to a greater cause, a larger Will. What then would it mean to move beyond the will? Insofar as the will is a *fundamental* attunement, such a move must involve a shift at this basic level. But if an attunement is truly "fundamental," on what ground could a shift take place? Here we must further problematize the phrase "fundamental attunement." Indeed, from the beginning does the phrase perhaps involve a paradoxical coupling: does not being "a-tuned" imply an original *ekstasis* which prohibits the attunement itself from being its own source of origin or ground—that is, from being in this sense "fundamental"?

The will, as we have seen, apparently involves precisely *not* being a-tuned to an other; it is rather an attempt to impose one's "tune" on others, to assimilate their voices into one's own monologue or communally into one's own chorus. But if it were the case that man is fundamentally attuned to that which is other than his own possession, then the fundamental attunement of willing would involve a tension or even contradiction within itself. The will, of necessity, draws its being from a relation with an otherness or exteriority which exceeds its domain, while at the same time denying or disguising this originary dispossession of itself. In this sense, the fundamental attunement of the will would be an *inauthentic* fundamental (dis)attunement.

A critique of this inauthenticity, it could be said, is one prevalent orientation of Heidegger's thought from early on, from *Being and Time*'s description of Dasein as ecstatic being-in-the-world to his later thought of man as essentially in a relation of cor-respondence to the address of being. Heidegger attempts to intimate an a-tunement more fundamental (originary) than that of the inauthentic (dis)attunement of the will as ecstatic-incorporation. This authentic fundamental attunement would involve a way of being that is fundamentally a-tuned to the otherness of being and to the being of others, and not an attunement that is "fundamental" in the sense of willfully positing its own ground and imposing the tune of this ground on others.

Suffice it to note at this point that the will is a comportment of the subject that attempts to close off, to forget, his originary ecstatic openness to what lies beyond his grasp. The subject of will can only see self and other through the either/or lens of an inside to be firmly grasped and asserted or an outside to be conquered and assimilated—rather than as that to which one essentially cor-responds by way of an engaged listening-belonging (*Gehören*).[17] It is this more originary comportment, this authentic fundamental a-tunement, which is indicated by the term "non-willing."

Non-Willing

> Where there is attunement, there is the possibility of a change
> in attunement, and thus also of *awakening attunement*. (*GA* 29/
> 30:268/181)

With the term "non-willing," it is above all important not to overdetermine our preconception from the outset. I shall therefore restrict my remarks here to an indication of the basic sense or direction in which this term is intended. "Non-willing" translates Heidegger's term *Nicht-Wollen*. Yet Heidegger says that the latter term can mean various things (see *GA* 77:76). He himself employs the term in two particular senses: (1) "willingly to renounce willing" and (2) "what remains strictly outside any kind of will" (*G* 30/59). The latter is the ultimate sense intended in the term "non-willing." Non-willing would be radically *other than willing*. The former sense of *Nicht-Wollen* speaks of non-willing in the context of the transitional "will to not will" or the "will to non-willing" (*Wollen das Nicht-Wollen*), which shall also be an important focus of attention (see in particular chapter 7).

A third possible sense of *Nicht-Wollen*, one which Heidegger critically comments on but does not himself employ, is the simple negation or absence of willing. Taking advantage of the fact that English offers two ways to translate the *Nicht* of *Nicht-Wollen*, as "not" and as "non," I shall refer to the simple negation or absence of willing as "*not*-willing," and to the radically other than willing as "*non*-willing." Maintaining this distinction shall be crucial, since it is precisely the conflation of these two senses of *Nicht-Wollen* that lies behind any number of misinterpretations of Heidegger's attempt to think a *non*-willing sense of *Gelassenheit*.

Because the comportment of willing lends itself to hypostatization as "a faculty" or indeed as "the ground of beings," it is appropriate to speak in the nominative of "the will." Heidegger is not always clear on (or concerned with) the distinction between "willing" and "the will," and indeed he claims at one point that the word for this relation is lacking. Nevertheless, he does suggest there that while "the word 'will' ['*Wille*']" indicates that which grounds the essence of the soul according to the metaphysical tradition, the word "willing" (*Wollen*) would indicate "the carrying out of this will" (*GA* 77:78). The deeper matter at stake is thus the will; for "we are always in the scope of the will, even when we are unwilling" (*N1* 57/57). Genuine non-willing would involve a *radical* negation, not just of "willing," but of the hypostatized "will" itself; "*Nicht-Wollen* [ultimately] bespeaks then," Heidegger writes, "*Nicht-Wille*" (*GA* 77:79).

And yet I prefer to use the quasi-verbal term "non-willing," rather than "non-will"; for the comportment of non-willing would neither be a faculty of the subject nor a substantial metaphysical ground, but rather a way of fundamentally comport*ing* oneself, of *being* (verbal) fundamentally a-tuned, of be*ing*-in-the-world in a manner other than willing. Refusing to reify "non-willing" into a noun, we acknowledge the fact that to think the possibility of non-willing we must call into question the very grammar in which we think. Thus, for Heidegger the question of how to think in the manner of a "thinking [which] would be something other than willing" (*G* 30/59) is inseparable from the question of how to think the fundamental attunement of non-willing. Ultimately, to think non-willing would require thinking non-willingly (see *GA* 77:67).

One grammatical form which Heidegger's thought often recalls at decisive points is that of "the middle voice," which expresses a way of speaking in neither the active nor the passive voice, and which intimates an "activity" prior to or other than that which can be articulated in a subject/

predicate grammar and a subject/object ontology. Already in his early phenomenological writings Heidegger attempted to "formally indicate" the "it worlds" (*es weltet*) prior to the epistemological split between the representing categorizing subject and the represented categorized object.[18] In *Being and Time* Heidegger points to the middle voice as proper to the original sense of "phenomenon," as "that which shows itself from itself" (*SZ* 28), and he subsequently often, and in key moments of his texts, employ certain quasi-middle-voiced expressions such as "temporality temporalizes," "the world worlds," "the thing things," and "the region regions." Perhaps non-willing could only be expressed in the middle voice, as what John Llewelyn calls that "place between activity and passivity, rarely indicated on maps of so-called Western thought."[19] We shall need to attune our ears to this voice as we attempt to follow Heidegger in his most radical moments of thinking non-willing(ly).

If it is a question of thinking what is radically other than willing, why, one may wonder at this point, should one still name the possibility of "non-willing" by way of quasi-opposition or even radical negation, that is, still in terms of a certain relation of contrast with the will? Would it not be best to free the expression from any reference whatsoever to that which it would be radically other than? Just as Heidegger finally claims that we should "cease all overcoming, and leave metaphysics to itself" (*ZSD* 25/24), should we not cease all attempts to relate what is other than the will back to the will, and simply—speak differently? Were this to be possible for us here and now, perhaps the answer would be yes. And yet, I wish to maintain the *question* of the "possibility" of non-willing; I wish to hesitate at a critical distance from any claim to have conclusively thought non-willing(ly). To begin with, it is for this reason that I leave a trace of a relation to the will in the expression "non-willing," even as this expression gestures towards that which would in itself presumably be wholly unrelated to the will.

Does Heidegger claim to have thought non-willing(ly)? He does suggest that in the midst of the radical negation in the expression *Nicht-Wollen,* as in our darkening epoch in general, something "withdraws and yet brings forth." "When we say 'non-willing,' something is nevertheless given to us" (*GA* 77:68). Moreover, Heidegger does indeed in a variety of manners attempt to think a way of being, and to think in a manner, other than willing. Perhaps the most remarkable and suggestive expression for non-willing is his term *Gelassenheit.* Yet it should be pointed out that this term also speaks in part of a negation: it speaks of releasement *from* as well as a releasement *into,* of a letting go as well as a letting be. Do *Gelassenheit* and "non-willing" remain transitional terms, insofar as they still drag along with them a problematical relation to the will? Would these names eventually disappear into the region towards which they point from a certain distance?[20]

In any case, I shall retain the "quasi-negative" or "radically negative" expression "non-willing" first of all in order to emphasize the difficulty of attempting to name an other than the will without simply covering up and repeating in another form the problem of the will. Heidegger is careful to note, for example, that while "something like power of action and resoluteness [*Entschlossenheit*]" do indeed "also reign in *Gelassenheit*," "all such names at once misinterpret *Gelassenheit* as pertaining to the will" (*G* 58/80). This warning urges us to proceed cautiously when attempting to stake out a region beyond the domain of the will. Even given the possibility of non-willing, a premature claim to have succeeded in thinking non-willing(ly) would only distort and complicate matters—just as self-sacrifice only multiplies and shifts the site of the problem when it is done in the name of another('s) will.

Moreover, Heidegger in fact must hesitate to claim to have thought non-willing(ly) insofar as his thought remains preparatory, *unterwegs,* that is to say, insofar as it seeks to help prepare for a turning in the history of being itself, a turning to an "other beginning" that would clear the way for being in a region otherwise than willing. Insofar as our epoch remains that of the technological will to will, however Janus-faced these dangerous times may be, we must not forget our epochal tethers to the domain of the will. The best we can do is to prepare for non-willing by means of patient and rigorous reflection on the tenacious problem of the will as a "twisting free" of its multifaceted domain.[21]

I add to this an additional hesitancy to "positively" name non-willing. I wish to preserve a space for the critical question of whether there could *ever* be, in any epoch or even in a time beyond the epochs of metaphysics, a final releasement from willing. In other words, I wish to hold open the critical question of whether non-willing could ever be entered into such that it would no longer need to be named in any relation (even in the radical negation of a "*non*-willing") to the will. Could we ever be over and done with the problem of the will? Or would any attempt to stake out a region free once and for all from the problem of the will inevitably serve to conceal and repeat the will in one form or another? This question shall return most clearly in the later chapters of this study. Here, in this preliminary determination of terms, let us look more closely at the various deceptive partial negations, sublations, and sublimations of willing in "the domain of the will."

The Domain of the Will: Willing, Not-Willing, Deferred-Willing, and Covert-Willing

The "domain of the will" includes, to begin with, the polar extremes of a straightforward assertive willing on the one hand, and the simple negation or lack of willing on the other. The domain of the will thus encompasses not only voluntarism, but also its simple negation, the deficient states of willing that often go by such names as quietism, resignationism, passivism, and fatalism, and that I shall refer to in general as "*not-willing*." Not-willing is understood to be the simple opposite of assertion of will, passivity as opposed to activity, and is to be rigorously distinguished from what is being called non-willing. Perhaps the initial and one of the most persistent difficulties in the attempt to think *non*-willing is distinguishing it from this mere passivity of not-willing. Yet, as Heidegger says of *Gelassenheit*, non-willing would lie "beyond the distinction between activity and passivity . . . because [it] does *not* belong to the domain of the will [*Bereich des Willens*]" (*G* 33/61). It is crucial to the present study that the parameters of this "domain of the will" be outlined; for only by clarifying the various modes *within* this domain can we begin to think what a radical negation of the domain itself would imply.

The *radical* negation implied in *non*-willing must be thought otherwise than as an oppositional negation that remains determined within the domain of that against which it speaks. "Everything 'anti,'" Heidegger writes, "remains in the spirit of that against which it is 'anti'" (*GA* 54:77); mere opposition remains a slave to that which it opposes (see *GA* 77:51). Elsewhere he condemns in even harsher terms any "crude reversing" (*grobe Umkehrung*), in which it is said "the most ruthless and captious enslaving prevails; reversing overcomes nothing but merely empowers the reversed" (*GA* 65:436). Simply to rebel against or to refrain from the activity of willing would not free one from the domain of the will. Just as simply not acting remains within the domain of action, namely as the neglect or refusal to act, so does not-willing remain a mere lack of or refusal to will, and does not call into question the domain of the will as such.

Nor would deferring one's will to another, by passively following or actively becoming the "vessel" for their will, free one from the domain of the will. Such "*deferred-willing*" too is strictly bound to the domain of the will. Regardless of whether one sacrifices one's will to the will of a political leader or to that of a religious guru, or for that matter to the Will of a transcendent Being, the axis of the will is merely shifted while the domain of the will itself remains in place.

Such deferred-willing could be genuine, as in the case where one would actually sacrifice one's will to that of another (whether and to what extent this is possible is another question), or it could be feigned, as in the case where one asserts one's own will indirectly by projecting a larger will (e.g., the Will of the *Volk* or the Will of God) for which one would, as it were, merely be acting as the servant and perhaps mouthpiece. This latter species of will, where one feigns deferred-willing for the sake of increasing one's power, I shall refer to as "*covert-willing.*"

Covert-willing could assume the guise of not-willing as well as that of deferred-willing. In the former case, one would pretend to have renounced all willing, or indeed to have abnegated the very will-to-live as such. In the latter case, one would claim to have sacrificed one's individual will for the sake of becoming the vehicle for the expression of a "higher Will." Moreover, covert-willing could be either conscious or unconscious; in the latter situation one would conceal even from oneself the dynamics of this sublimation, genuinely believing that one has sacrificed one's will to another, or negated the will as such. In short, covert-willing would be the feigning of a transfer of one's will to another (i.e., a feigned deferred-willing) or of a negation of the will as such (i.e., a feigned not-willing) in the concealed attempt (conscious or unconscious) to preserve and enhance one's own domain of power.

In his demand for an honest recognition of the ubiquity of the will to power, Nietzsche was himself the sharpest critic of covert-willing. He sought to expose, for example, the covert-willing of *ressentiment,* and the hidden thirst for revenge, at work in such ideas as the "kingdom of God" wherein "the meek shall inherit the earth."[22] What Nietzsche calls the "ascetic priest" only appears to negate his will, while in fact it is sublated into the convoluted and hypocritical form of a self-serving mouthpiece for the projected higher Will of God. Nietzsche ascribes this fabrication of the "Will of God" to "the conditions for the preservation of priestly power."[23] According to Nietzsche, any apparent twisting free of the will actually results only in a twisted form of will to power.

As for the renunciation of will, Nietzsche writes: "I regard a philosophy which teaches denial of the will as a teaching of defamation and slander."[24] He no doubt had in mind here the philosophy of his early "educator" and then foil, Schopenhauer. In a sense, Nietzsche begins by attempting to affirm what Schopenhauer denies,[25] that is, by attempting to give the opposite response to what Schopenhauer calls "the great question" of "the willing or not-willing [*Nichtwollen*] of life."[26] Whereas Nietzsche attempts to unconditionally affirm the fact of the world and oneself as "the will to power—and nothing besides,"[27] Schopenhauer teaches a philosophy of "giving up . . . of the whole of the will-to-live itself," which leads to a "state of voluntary renunciation [*freiwilligen Entsagen*], resignation, true composure [*wahren Gelassenheit*], and complete will-lessness [*gänzlichen Willenslosigkeit*]."[28] For Schopenhauer, *Gelassenheit* would be a matter of a complete and utter denial of the will-to-live, more of an extreme not-willing, a pessimistic rejection of the world, than a gateway to an other way of affirmatively being-in-the-world. In general Schopenhauer's pessimism takes the critique of the will only in the direction of an oppositional negation (*Verneinung*) or renunciation (*Entsagen*) of the will, which leads to a mere state of resignation (*Resignation*).[29]

Whether such pessimistic renunciation of the will-to-live is possible, or whether the ascetic denial of life is, as Nietzsche suspects, "only apparent" and leads to a hypocritical "artifice for the *preservation* of life,"[30] in either case both a genuine philosophy of not-willing and a (self-) deceptive one of covert-willing would remain wholly within the domain of the will as such, just as would a philosophy that explicitly affirms the will, either in one's own person or by way of deference to the will of another, be that other an otherworldly overseer or a futuristic overman. In short, this battle of the giants, between Schopenhauer's negation and Nietzsche's affirmation of willing, takes place predominantly (if not exclusively) within the ring of the domain of the will.

The later Heidegger is well aware of the various simple or partial negations of willing that only shift positions within the domain of the will without calling into question this domain as such. Thus, when Heidegger thinks *Gelassenheit* as *Nicht-Wollen*, he is quick to add that this does not mean a simple "denial of willing" (*GA* 77:77), nor does it mean "letting self-will go in favor of the divine Will" (*G* 34/62). The latter would reduce *Gelassenheit* to a matter of deferred-willing, or perhaps, after the death of God, to a covert-willing. Heidegger's *Gelassenheit*, as *non*-willing, would not be a shift within the domain of the will, but would indicate an *other than* willing. Moreover, as we shall see, recoiling from his own disastrous blunder of calling for a deference to the will of the Führer in 1933–34, Heidegger learns to be wary of any sublated or sublimated expression of the will, to be suspicious of any partial negation of one's will for the sake of the will of the *Volk* or its leader. Through "the insertion of the I into the we," Heidegger writes, subjective egoism "only gains in power" (*GA* 5:111/152). The decisive question is whether the later Heidegger succeeds in clearing a path that leads beyond these pitfalls to intimate a region of genuine *non*-willing.

A difficult question arises here at the end of this preliminary determination of terms: Are not the fascist will of Hitler and the loving Will of the Judeo-Christian God utterly and essentially different in kind? Does not the Will of God (at least, some might want to argue, as he is revealed in the New Testament) ultimately involve the letting-be of forgiveness and grace, and perhaps even the pure giving of a self-emptying kenosis, rather than the power-preservation/power-enhancement of ecstatic-incorporation? And what of the human "good will"? Is not the good will, whether in the Kantian rational version or in the common emotive sense, itself essentially opposed to the will to power? Does not, for example, the Kantian notion of the good will involve the rational suspension of all egoistic inclinations, all willful arbitrariness, and the consideration of the good of the other as an end in itself—and thus precisely *not* the preservation and enhancement of one's own will to power?

Is the extreme claim being made here that, in William Blake's words: "There can be no Good Will. Will is always Evil; it is perniciousness to others or suffering"?[31] Heidegger does at one point suggest that it is perhaps "in general the will itself that is evil" (*GA* 77:208). Does every use of the term "will" then necessarily draw on its essential determination as ecstatic-incorporation? This would be a rash claim, and to blindly assert this would probably conceal more than it would reveal. While Heidegger's epochal history of metaphysics does seem to suggest an essential continuity to at least all determinations of "will" in the modern Western tradition, one might remain suspicious of a certain paradoxical "will to unity" at work in this very comprehensive framing of the problem of the will (see chapter 9). In any case, I do not wish to presume from the outset that the four-letter word "will" has been and could only ever be used in the precise sense of ecstatic-incorporation. And yet, on the other hand, after Heidegger's radical critique of the will we are also called on to be suspicious of any use of this term which would purport to be *wholly and simply* unrelated to this sense; that is to say, we must remain vigilantly on guard against any unproblematized use of the term "will."

To unequivocally collapse the "will" of the monotheistic God and the "will" of a fascist dictator into a single sense would no doubt be an impermissible act of interpretive violence. And yet, to unquestioningly assume from the start that they are utterly and essentially different, that there could be absolutely no overlapping relation or "family resemblance" between the two, would be to arbitrarily cut short the depth and range of Heidegger's critique of the will. Was the deferred-willing of those involved in the Crusades or in the Inquisition, for example, wholly and essentially unrelated to the deferred-willing of Nazi middlemen like Adolf Eichmann, who claimed to have sacrificed his own compassionate sensibilities to the authority of his Führer's will? Is the missionary zeal to colonize the world in the name of expanding Christendom purely distinguishable from the will that drives corporate globalization as economic ecstatic-incorporation? And does not even the moral dictum, "Do unto others as you would have them do unto you," still harbor the danger of imposing on others one's own idea of the good life? Does not even the Kantian good will harbor the danger of incorporating others into one's own conception of justice and goodness?[32]

While on the one hand each particular use of the term "will" would have to be considered in its own context, on the other hand we should not confine Heidegger's critique of the will to merely one particular sense of the term, believing that other senses remain innocent, and can therefore continue to be used innocently. Just as each use of the term "will" needs to be questioned *in turn*, each *needs to be questioned* in turn. While this enormous and multifarious task obviously exceeds the limits of the present study, we shall no doubt be better prepared for it after having worked through the problem of the will in Heidegger's path of thought.[33]

Summary of Terms

In closing, let me summarize the terms developed in this introductory chapter. While the following preliminary determinations may be expanded or modified in some respects as we proceed, with other terms being added on occasion, these may serve as a stepping-stone for our hermeneutical (re)entry into the circle of interpreting the problem of the will in the context of Heidegger's thought.

The Will: The "fundamental (dis)attunement" of "ecstatic-incorporation"; that is, the basic comportment of "being master out beyond oneself," of representing and treating that which is other to oneself as a means for the preservation and enhancement of one's own power.

Not-Willing: The simple negation or deficient state of willing; passive resignation as opposed to active assertion of willing. A philosophy of not-willing would be quietism as opposed to voluntarism.

Deferred-Willing: Letting one's own will go in favor of the will of another, whether passively acquiescing to, or actively becoming a vessel for, this other will, whether this other be the leader of a state, a god, and so on.

Covert-Willing: The form of willing which conceals itself (perhaps even from itself) under the guise of not-willing or deferred-willing; in other words, the feigning of the negation or deferral of one's will for the sake of preserving and increasing its power.

The Domain of the Will: The entire range of possible modes of willing, including not only the straightforward assertion of will, but also not-willing, deferred-willing, and covert-willing. Note that "the problem of the will" needs to be fully understood as the problem of this entire domain of the will.

Non-Willing: The "(proper) fundamental attunement" of *Gelassenheit,* which could not be determined as either willing, not-willing, deferred-willing, or covert-willing. The prefix "non-," as distinct from the simple negation of a "not-" or the polar opposition of an "anti-," expresses a *radical negation;* and thus "non-willing" would indicate a region of *Gelassenheit* outside and other than the entire domain of the will.

2

The Ambiguous Role of the Will in *Being and Time*

> *Being and Time* is a *way* and not a lodging. Whoever cannot walk should not set himself down to rest in it. (*SA* 78/64)[1]

The "Unsaid" Problem of the Will

> For all genuine thoughts belonging to an essential thinking remain—and indeed for essential reasons—ambiguous [*mehrdeutig*]. . . . Therefore we must seek out thinking and its thoughts always in the element of its ambiguity [*Mehrdeutigkeit*], or else everything will remain closed to us. (*WhD* 68/71)

In this chapter I shall demonstrate that this claim of the later Heidegger is particularly true of that central concept—*Entschlossenheit* (resoluteness or resolute openness)—of his own first major publication. My thesis in this chapter is that there is a fundamental ambiguity to the role of the will in *Being and Time,* and that in this ambiguity are foreshadowed *both* Heidegger's embrace of the will in the first half of the 1930s *and* his later critique of the will beginning in the later part of that decade. *Being and Time* oscillates between embracing a resolute willing as the existentially decisive moment, and proposing that a shattering of the will is what is most proper to Dasein.

The claim that there is an essential ambiguity at the heart of this text may not surprise readers who are accustomed to the ambivalences *explicitly* cultivated by Heidegger's Dasein analysis: Dasein is both thrown into and projects its world. It discloses its past from out of its future. Its concrete possibilities for authentic living are appropriated by running forward in anticipation of its own death, as its ownmost possibility of no possibility at all. Intricately weaving such tensions together is undoubtedly a significant aspect of the book's rigor and its genius. However, I shall argue that a certain crucial and largely *implicit* ambiguity with regard to the will marks an unintended inconsistency of *Being and Time,* and ultimately a failure to disclose the problem of the will. It is this implicit ambiguity that left open both the door to an explicit embrace of the will—an embrace that led seven years later to Heidegger's political speeches on behalf of Hitler's "one great will of the state"—as well as the door to his radical critique of the will developed after the misadventure of his political involvement. In the reading given here, the possibility of *both* interpretative directions is traced back to a fundamental ambiguity in the text itself.

As a negative symptom of this ambiguity, one can note that the text itself is silent to the point of avoidance on the question of the role of "the will." When it does briefly consider "willing," it is only to assure us that it is not a phenomenon of ontological significance. I shall argue that willing cannot be confined to the unessential ontical role it is given in the text, and that in fact it turns out to be a problem of critical ontological consequence.

In his interpretations of previous philosophers, Heidegger often suggests that it is the "unsaid" (*das Ungesagte*)—i.e., the implicit problematic which determines a text without being explicitly articulated—that is most decisive.[2] In a certain sense I shall read the problematic of the will as the "unsaid" in *Being and Time.* In order to bring this unsaid to the surface, I shall point out the inadequacy of restricting willing to the limited role it officially plays in the analytic of Dasein, and then demonstrate how a discourse on the will (re)appears in more or less implicit forms in decisive moments of the text. Having uncovered this unsaid problematic of the will, we shall discover *both* elements of a voluntarism *and* elements of a radical critique of the will.

The direction Heidegger's thought, and his politics, did in fact take in the years following the publication of *Being and Time* might encourage one to stress the voluntaristic aspects of the text. Or one might attempt to show that the flip-flopping between voluntarism (willing) and fatalism (not-willing), or deference to a higher sort of communal will (an active deference to the higher will of the spiritual *Volk* as opposed to a passive deference to the fallen *das Man*), had already begun in the later sections of the book. This is indeed a possible—and critically significant—interpretation (one to which I shall return in the following chapter); and yet it reveals only part of the ambiguous story. *Being and Time* also prepares in a number of important ways for Heidegger's mature thought and its rigorous critique of the will. Moreover, this early text itself offers several indications for thinking non-willing(ly). Later we shall consider not only the notion of being-towards-death as involving a shattering of the will, but also one possible interpretation of the key notion of *Ent-schlossenheit* (particularly as hyphenated and [re]interpreted by the later Heidegger himself) as a kind of non-willing openness to being. To begin with, let us look at how the method of "phenomenology" itself, as Heidegger adopts and develops it, can be understood as under way to a thinking of non-willing.

Phenomenology on the Way to Non-Willing

The movement of phenomenology, as the attempt to return "back to the things themselves" (*zurück zu den Sachen selbst*), has perhaps always been in its best moments an attempt to think without either actively or passively imposing one's own biases of interpretation, that is, an attempt to think non-willingly in order to let things show themselves. As is evident in the following passage from *The Basic Problems of Phenomenology*, what is required is first of all a rigorous will to non-willing.

> [The] success or failure [of phenomenological endeavors] depends primarily on . . . how far, in correspondence with its own principle, it is unbiased in the face of what the things themselves demand. . . . [What] is most essential is . . . for one thing, to learn to wonder scientifically about the mystery of things and, for another, to banish all illusions, which settle down and nest with particular stubbornness precisely in philosophy. (*GA* 24:467)

In *The Fundamental Concepts of Metaphysics* we even find an early use of the term *Gelassenheit* to depict the deconstructive "releasement of our free, everyday perspective" from the "traditional perspectives that have ossified" (*GA* 29/30:137).

In his earliest phenomenological efforts (beginning in 1919), Heidegger attempted to develop a "pre-theoretical science" (*GA* 56/57:63) of "hermeneutical intuition" (117) that would give access to a pre-ontological dimension—or what Heidegger then calls "the pre-theoretical something" (*das vortheoretische Etwas*) that gets covered up by the hardened traditional categories of theory. By holding itself back to the level of "formal indication," rather than attempting a reduction of phenomena to the grasp of concepts, phenomenology would let the "immediacy of everyday Dasein" show itself through the cracks of hardened traditional concepts, concepts which are imposed not only at the level of theory but which already pervade what Heidegger will come to call the inauthentic everydayness of *das*

Man. In an effort to get back to the things themselves in a way that discloses with minimal imposition of concepts, Heidegger adopted (through Emil Lask) an idea from the mystics: *Hingabe,* or "dedicative submission" (61).

Hingabe would indicate the radical act of giving oneself over to the things themselves; but it is an "act" which would paradoxically require the restraint of all (willful) acting on the subject's part in order to let things show themselves. As John van Buren points out, "the mystical overtones of Meister Eckhart's *Gelassenheit,* abandonment, releasement, letting-be" can be heard resonating in this phenomenological *Hingabe.*[3] As in the case of *Gelassenheit,* the (non)act of *Hingabe* requires both a negative restraining moment, a releasement-from, and a positive moment, a releasement-to, in order to let beings be. One perhaps cannot help but wonder here to what extent Heidegger's later turn to *Gelassenheit* might be interpreted as a return to this fundamental attunement of dedicative submission.

And yet Heidegger himself, it appears, increasingly came to find this attitude too passive; an openness to beings must be grounded with the resoluteness of authentic decision. The young Heidegger's "Protestant turn" to a Paulian-inspired *kairos,* the existential *Augenblick* of decision, necessitated a turn away from the *Stimmung* of *Gelassenheit* understood as *Hingabe.* In fact, already in 1919 Heidegger was concerned with a certain tension in his phenomenology between "dedicative submission" (*Hingabe*) and "the scientific will to know"; that is to say, he was already struggling with "the constant tension between the higher receptivity of acknowledgement and the critical productivity of research."[4] The methodological question that Heidegger takes into *Being and Time* was, in Theodore Kisiel's words:

> Do we really apprehend, grasp, take . . . the immediacy of experience in its sense? [Or rather] instead of *Hinsehen,* a *Hingabe,* a receptive submission: heeding, and not looking, more of a suffering than an action? Or somewhere in the middle, that Greek voice which will continue to recur as Heidegger moves from Paul's verbs *of* God to Aristotle's search for a middle between passion and action?[5]

It is precisely the grammar of the middle voice on which Heidegger draws in *Being and Time* to depict the fundamental manner in which things show themselves; the task of the phenomenologist is to find the proper attunement and method with which to assist in letting these things show themselves from themselves.

In the introduction to *Being and Time,* Heidegger breaks down the word "phenomenology" into its two component parts: "phenomenon" (from the Greek *phainomenon*) and "logy" (from the Greek *logos*). As Charles

Scott notes, "Heidegger's discussion of 'phenomenon' is based on the Greek *phainesthai,* the middle voice of *phaino* . . . an occurrence that was neither active nor passive nor even necessarily reflexive."[6] As the verb *phaino* means "to bring to the light of day, to put to light," Heidegger understands "phenomena" to be the middle-voiced self-showing of beings.

Now, although a being can show itself in many ways, including that of showing itself "as something which it is *not,*" it is crucial that we not equate, as the tradition tends to do, "phenomenon" in the primordial sense with such second-order notions as that of "mere appearance" or "semblance." Even when one speaks of "phenomenon" as a "semblance," "the primordial signification (the phenomenon as the manifest) is already included as that upon which the second signification is founded" (*SZ* 29). "Phenomena," in Heidegger's "primordial signification," "are *never* appearances, though on the other hand every appearance is dependent on phenomena" (30). Phenomena are not appearances behind which would lie something (e.g., a Kantian thing-in-itself); on the contrary, they could even—as the Greeks "sometimes" did—be "identified simply with *ta onta* (beings)" (28; see also *EM* 77). Thus "phenomenology is the science of the being of beings—ontology" (*SZ* 37).

Heidegger also says this the other way around: "*Ontology is only possible as phenomenology*" (35). What then is phenomeno*logy*, and why is it necessary at all if the things themselves occur primordially as showing-themselves? Moreover, why does Heidegger claim that "the meaning of phenomenological description as a method is *interpretation*" (37); why would self-showing beings need to be revealed by a logos with the character of a *hermeneuein*? Why is simple perception not enough to let beings show themselves as they are in themselves? The answer lies in what he calls "covered-up-ness" (*Verdecktheit*) as "the counter-concept to 'phenomenon'" (36). Although, on the one hand, it is true that there is essentially nothing "behind" the phenomena to be investigated, "on the other hand, what is to become a phenomenon can be concealed. And precisely because the phenomena are proximally and for the most part *not* given, there is need for phenomenology" (36).

This concealment or covered-up-ness can occur in various ways. A phenomenon can be simply not yet discovered; or its prior self-showing can subsequently become "buried over," either completely or partially, leaving a mere semblance. But it is the case of "distortion" or "disguise," Heidegger tells us, that is "the most frequent and the most dangerous," for here phenomena are revealed with apparent clarity—for example within the "systems" of philosophy and their hardened concepts. In such systems, an expression of a phenomenon originally won from the primordial experience of a culture or a thinker loses its "groundedness" (*Bodenständig-keit*) and "becomes a free-floating thesis" (36). Heidegger's hermeneut-ical phenomenology, particularly in the *Destruktion* of the tradition of ontology in the planned part 2 of *Being and Time,* would attempt to dig down beneath such "free-floating theses" to the original experiences of phenomena on which they were based.

Hence, a certain type of logos is necessary to uncover the primordial phenomena. Or, to put it the other way around, a "phenomenon," in the original sense of "the showing-itself-in-itself," is not just any given thing which appears, but rather "signifies a distinctive way in which something can be encountered" (31). Or again: "These beings must show themselves with the kind of access which genuinely belongs to them" (37). What is this distinctive way of encountering or accessing beings; how are humans to go to the encounter with beings in such a way that the latter can show themselves from themselves as they are in themselves?

To begin with, this cannot be a mere passive looking. Indeed, *Being and Time* is above all critical of the traditional notion of knowledge based on the passivity of "pure intuition." He even claims that primordial knowl-edge of phenomena must be "wrested" (*abgewonnen*) from objects, and that this "grasping [*Erfassung*] and explicating phenomena in a way that is 'original' and 'intuitive' is directly opposed to the naiveté of a haphaz-ard, 'immediate,' and unreflective 'beholding' ['*Schauen*']" (37). The later Heidegger, however, while continuing to reject the idea of a knowl-edge based on mere passive intuition, also grows increasingly suspicious of the willful overtones of conceiving knowledge as a "grasping" (*Greifen*) of concepts (*Begriffe*) (see *WhD* 128/211). The task is then to think a know-ing through *Gelassenheit* or "letting-be," a knowing which is neither a blank staring nor a willful manipulating. This knowing as letting-be would take place by way of attuning oneself in a proper responsiveness to the middle-voiced self-showing of beings.

And yet already in *Being and Time* it is claimed that the logos of phe-nomenology involves a kind of non-passive letting. Indeed, logos is under-stood here as responsively taking part in the middle-voiced self-showing of phenomena. As Scott puts it, to the question "How are we to 'address' phenomena in light of their accessibility in the middle voice?" Heidegger answers: "Speaking may let something come to light. *Logos,* taken in its meaning of speech (*apophansis*), is self-showing (*apophainesthai*) as it is spoken about. Words let something be seen in self-showing occurrences."[7] Prior to being "translated" (which means, for Heidegger, interpreted) as "reason," "judgment," etc., the basic meaning of "logos" is "speech" (*Rede*); but this notion too must be understood in the right way. "Speech," understood primordially, "'lets something be seen' *apo* [from] . . . : that is, it lets us see something from the very thing which the speech is about" (*SZ* 32). Logos is thus a "letting something be seen" (ibid.).

The method of phenomenology that Heidegger develops in *Being and Time* appears, then, to be at least a foreshadowing of his later efforts to think non-willing(ly). Consider now the definition he gives of this method in the introduction to *Being and Time:*

> Thus "phenomenology" means: *apophainesthai ta phainomena*—to let that which shows itself be seen from itself in the very way in which it shows itself from itself. (34)

Phenomenology involves an effacing of one's prejudices, "standpoints," or "any special direction" (27) one might be inclined toward, in order to let the things themselves present themselves as they are in themselves. In other words, phenomenology involves not imposing one's will on the phenomena to be thought; it involves, to begin with, a refraining from willing.

And yet, furthermore, to let a phenomenon show itself can never be accomplished by simply blankly staring at what lies in front of one; for this would be merely to see things as one is accustomed to seeing them, namely, through one's accustomed prejudices.[8] As *Being and Time* makes explicit in its analyses, phenomenology, far from being a passive description, must involve the most radical kind of "interpretation." And interpretation, Heidegger makes clear, must first disclose unacknowledged prejudices.

> Interpretation is never a presuppositionless apprehending of something presented to us. If, when one is engaged in a particular concrete kind of interpretation, . . . one likes to appeal to what "stands there," then one finds that what "stands there" in the first instance is nothing other than the obvious undiscussed assumption of the person who does the interpreting. (150)

Interpretation cannot begin from any "view from nowhere," for such is always only a matter of ignorance as to its own whereabouts. Interpretation necessarily moves in a "hermeneutical circle," looking from a particular standpoint, and in turn letting what is disclosed illuminate the context within and the place from which one begins to look. But this means that interpretation must take its stand from a particular starting place; and thus even phenomenology always involves a certain kind of interpretive "violence" (*Gewaltsamkeit*) of projection.

In *Being and Time* Heidegger acknowledges that his own investigation can move forward only by violently throwing off the prejudices of the tradition; but as for the danger of doing violence to the things themselves, he remains optimistically sure of the uniqueness of the perspective and methods employed in his own hermeneutical phenomenology. In section 65 of *Being and Time* Heidegger explicitly refers to the necessary violence of interpretation, including that of his own existential analysis: "because the understanding which develops in interpretation has the structure of projection." And yet Heidegger assures us (and himself?) of the propriety of the violence of his method. "Ontological interpretation," properly done, "projects the entity presented to it upon the being *which is that entity's own*" (312, emphasis added), and thus would merely violently return it to its own proper self-showing by means of wresting it away from its traditional or everyday covered-up-ness.

The hermeneutical circle of interpretation cannot be avoided. But this circle, Heidegger tells us, is not necessarily a vicious circle. "What is decisive is not to get out of the circle but to come into it in the right way. . . . In the circle is hidden a positive possibility of the most primordial kind of knowing" (153). Everything rests on finding the right point of entry. For the author of *Being and Time,* the right point of entry is the "existential analytic of Dasein," as the self-interpretation of that being for whom being is at issue.

Dasein is first shown to be the structured whole of being-in-the-world. Then, in the analysis of anxiety, which is ultimately shown to involve opening oneself to the possibility of one's own death, a fundamental mood is found which discloses being-in-the-world as such and as a whole. Hence, willing-to-have-a-conscience (*Gewissenhabenwollen*) as a readiness for anxiety (see 296) is the key to the proper way of letting the phenomenon of being-in-the-world show itself from itself. In its most radical form, I shall suggest, this *Gewissenhabenwollen* is *Being and Time*'s version of a will to interrupt willing. In the fundamental experience of anxiety, resolutely repeated in "running ahead to one's own death," Dasein's "will" would be shattered along with the tradition of hardened concepts, thus allowing beings to shine forth from themselves anew. Here, one could read *Being and Time* as radically problematizing the will and clearing the way for Heidegger's later thinking of non-willing.

I shall return to this possibility of interpretation in the final part of this chapter; we must first, however, make our way toward that other face of *Being and Time,* the side which, far from problematizing the will, threatens to glorify it. *Being and Time* serves to displace a number of traditional prejudices; others linger on. To what extent was the great modern prejudice of willful subjectivity deconstructed? The modern metaphysical positing of the human subject as a consciousness that represents things as objects is no doubt severely criticized in *Being and Time*. And yet, it is not until the late 1930s that Heidegger explicitly and unambiguously makes the essential connection between the subject of representation and the subject of will.[9] The question at hand is this: To what extent is a critique of the will already implicit in *Being and Time*, and to what extent does *Being and Time* unwittingly repeat this voluntaristic prejudice of the modern tradition?

The Official Doctrine and the Unofficial Resonances of Willing

For the Sake of . . . a Will?

The official doctrine of "willing" in *Being and Time* is, as we shall see, less than satisfying. "Willing" is considered only briefly, and only in order to assure us that it is not a phenomenon of consequence. More fundamental, it is claimed, is "care" (*Sorge*), which characterizes the entirety of the structural whole of being-in-the-world. The ontic phenomenon of willing can be understood only on the basis of the fundamental ontology of care. What is this "care" that would apparently be misconstrued if thought of in terms of "will"? Would care perhaps name, as it were, an underlying fundamental attunement of non-willing, and would authentic existence then be a matter of properly recovering this attunement? To begin with, however, does the distinction between care and will hold up?

On the contrary, at least in the first analyses of "world," it seems as if the totality of being-in-the-world is thoroughly structured by something like Dasein's "will." Things are to be properly understood as first of all ready-to-hand, as pieces within a referential totality of significations. The "world," we are told, is first of all to be thought of in terms of this totality of significations. Things in themselves are to be understood in their "towards-which" (*Wozu*) character. The hammer is for the task of nailing, which in turn is for the sake of building a house, and so on. Finally we come up against a "for-the-sake-of-which," a grand project of Dasein that provides the referential totality with a telos. "The primary 'towards-which' is a 'for-the-sake-of-which'" (*SZ* 84).

Heidegger's investigation into worldhood in general orients itself from an analysis of that "world of everyday Dasein which is closest to it," namely, what he calls "the *environment* [Umwelt]" (66). (The *Um-* of Heidegger's *Umwelt*, as we shall see, refers not only to the "surrounding" character of Dasein's world, but also to its *um zu*—i.e., its "for the sake of" or "in order to"—character.) The *Umwelt* is structured by Dasein's projects. In this "instrumental world" things reveal themselves "first of all" as ready-to-hand within the parameters of a task projected by Dasein. Is this not an essentially egocentric "willful" world view, which understands things as "first of all" or even "in themselves" to be tools in an environment of human projection? Is *this* the result of Heidegger's phenomenological attempt to break out of the theoretical constituting ego and return to the original sphere of the self-showing of the things themselves? Is the *theoretical* constituting ego not simply replaced here by an unabashed ego of *practical* projection?

Heidegger writes in italics: "*Readiness-to-hand is the way in which beings as they are 'in themselves' are defined ontologico-categorially*" (71). Later he again stresses: "*beings . . . are encountered in a world with involvement (readiness-to-hand) as their kind of being, and which can thus make themselves known as they are in themselves* [in seinem An-sich]" (87).

What an astonishing claim: that things are most originally revealed—not merely in our access to them, but "in themselves"—as ready-to-hand "equipment" in a world structured by Dasein's projects! Is this anything more than an unabashed anthropocentric egoism? Is this primacy given to human projects, to a world disclosed most primordially as a "workshop" for our tasks of "production," not precisely what the later Heidegger criticizes as the decline of the modern West into the epoch of technological manipulation?[10]

In *Being and Time,* readiness-to-hand is considered the most original mode in which things are revealed. Aside from a few cryptic references to "the primitive world" (82) and to "nature as that which 'stirs and strives'" (90), the only other option to the world disclosed as the totality of equipment ready-to-hand that the text considers in detail is the derivative mode of "present-at-hand."[11] Things reveal themselves as present-at-hand when Dasein "just stares" at things without the "concernful absorption" attitude that reveals the ready-to-hand. "In this kind of '*dwelling*' as a holding-oneself-back [*Sichenthalten*] from any manipulation or utilization, the *perception* of the present-at-hand is consummated" (61). But this "objective" attitude of "holding-oneself-back from any production [*Herstellen*], manipulation [*Hantieren*], and the like" is argued to be, in fact, a parasitic or derivative mode of revealing.

Heidegger gives the example of a broken tool: "The helpless way in which we stand before it is a deficient mode of concern [*Besorge*], and as such it uncovers the being-just-present-at-hand-and-no-more of something ready-to-hand" (73). The passive attitude which just stares at an object does not let the object reveal itself as it is in itself, but merely reveals a deficient mode of that more original encounter with the thing which would let it show itself as it is. What is this more original comportment? We might suppose that if the passivity or not-willing of holding-oneself-back which reveals the present-at-hand is a deficient mode of that comportment which reveals the ready-to-hand, the latter would be an active mode of willing. The world of things as "equipment" oriented to Dasein's projects is said to be a world unified by "care" (*Sorge*). As the above passage has it, the passivity of standing before the present-at-hand is a deficient mode of "concern" (*Besorge*). We return, then, to the question of the relation of "care" to the will. The ambiguity of this relation is reflected in the following passage where Heidegger discusses the way in which the thing is revealed as ready-to-hand in terms of "letting something be involved":

> Previously letting something "be" does not mean that we must first bring it into its being and produce it; it means rather that something which is already "a being" must be discovered in its readiness-to-hand, and that we must thus let the being which has this being be encountered. This "*a priori*" letting-something-be-involved is the condition for the possibility of encountering anything ready-to-hand. (85)

Already in *Being and Time* Heidegger thus speaks of the proper manner in which things are revealed as one of "letting-be." This is an interesting passage to note in relation to Heidegger's 1953 comment (to be considered below) that "all willing should be grounded in letting-be." The point here would be that all "willful" manipulation of things ready-to-hand must first be grounded in a letting-be which reveals these things as they are in themselves. A non-willful letting would precede and underlie any act of willing.

And yet, let us not forget that the things that are revealed "in themselves" are revealed as "equipment" in a world structured by Dasein's projected "for-the-sake-of-which." "Letting an entity be involved," we are told, is a matter of "freeing it for its readiness-to-hand within the environment" (ibid.); in other words, letting a thing be is here a matter of letting it serve a purpose in Dasein's totality of equipment. A letting is required to reveal things, but these things are revealed—one is tempted to say—as ready-for-willing.[12]

The ambiguous role of the will in *Being and Time* is reflected here already in the question of how things are said to be revealed in themselves; but we have only begun to reveal the ambiguity of the role of the will in this text. Why is it that things are "first of all" ready-to-hand? "Relevance" or "involvement" (*Bewandtnis*) is "the being of innerworldly beings, for which they are always initially freed," or "let-be-involved [*Bewendenlassen*]" (84). This relatedness of beings has a certain direction, a "what-for" or "where-to" (*Wozu*). Ultimately, this "structure of relevance" leads to none other than "the being of Dasein itself as the proper and unique for-the-sake-of-which" (ibid.). The being of things leads back to Dasein because the world in which these things are found is structured first of all by Dasein's projected for-the-sake-of-which.

The question of the role of the will thus hinges on the question of the nature of this "for-the-sake-of-which" which opens up and structures Dasein's world. While the English translation may leave ambiguous the character of the formation of the involvements leading up to this master project, the German is revealing: "For-the-sake-of" translates *Umwillen;* and hence "The primary 'what-for' or 'where-to' is a for-the-sake-of-which" translates: *"Das primäre 'Wozu' ist ein Worum-willen"* (ibid.). "For what sake" is a question of "for what will." Does not everything then come down in the end to Dasein's will? Are not beings given their proper being, allowed to be involved in Dasein's world, merely as tools functioning "in order to" (*umwillen*) carry out the projects of Dasein's will (*Wille*)?

A Mere Ontic Phenomenon or a Transcendental Will?

And yet, far from being explicitly elevated to such a prominent ontological status, the official role of "willing" in *Being and Time* is in fact quite restrictive and mundane. It is treated as a second-order phenomenon, more of an ontic than an ontological concern. "Willing," we are told, is always directed toward an object in the world, and as such always presupposes a world disclosed beforehand. Willing might characterize relations within a world, but would not be involved in the prior disclosing of that world.

> *Hence,* to any willing there belongs something willed, which has already been determined in terms of a for-the-sake-of-which [Deshalb *gehört zum Wollen je ein Gewolltes, das sich schon bestimmt hat aus einem Worum-willen*]. If willing is to be possible ontologically, the following factors are constitutive for it: [1] the prior disclosedness of the for-the-sake-of-which in general (being-ahead-of-itself); [2] the disclosedness of something with which one can concern oneself (the world as the "wherein" of being-already); [3] the understanding self-projection of Dasein upon a potentiality-for-being towards a possibility of the entity "willed." In the phenomenon of willing, the underlying totality of care shows through. (194)

Although the being of Dasein itself is "the proper and unique *Worum-willen*" (84), "care," which names the being of Dasein, is ontologically prior to any "willing." Thus, even while the internal relations of the world might be understood to be saturated with willing, the *Worum-willen* which orients relations in the world would not be determined on the basis of a "willing." Willing, restricted to an inner-worldly intentional comportment to something willed, could not characterize the projection (*Entwurf*) upon a potentiality-for-being (*Seinkönnen*) which is responsible for opening a world in the first place. The ontologically more fundamental term "care," on the other hand, would extend beyond the ontic realm of willing to involve this ontological projection as well.[13]

But does such restriction of *the term* "willing" solve, or even address, the real problem of the will? Could it not be argued rather that care bespeaks a deeper and more inclusive form of will, one which has as its "objects" not just beings within an already disclosed world, but first of all the ontologically prior potentiality-for-being? Far from disrupting the centrality of willful subjectivity, this idea of care would appear to confirm and sublate it.

Indeed, I do not simply introduce this interpretive linking of care to a not merely ontic "will" from outside Heidegger's texts. In a lecture course from 1928 Heidegger writes: "World . . . is primarily defined by the for-the-sake-of-which. . . . But a for-the-sake-of-which, a purposiveness [*Umwillen*], is only possible where there is a will [*Willen*]" (*GA* 26:238). The 1929 essay "The Essence of Ground" confirms this idea of a higher type of "will" which, rather than being restricted to operations within the world structured by the *Umwillen*, would be responsible for "forming" (*bilden*) the *Umwillen* as such. We read:

> This surpassing that occurs "for the sake of" [*Der umwillentliche Überstieg*] does so only in a "will" [*Willen*] that as such projects itself upon possibilities of itself. . . . This will cannot be a particular willing, an "act of will" as distinct from other kinds of comportment. . . . Every kind of comportment is rooted in transcendence. The "will" in question, however, must first "form" the for-the-sake-of as and in a surpassing [*Jener "Wille" aber soll als und im Überstieg das Umwillen selbst "bilden"*]. (*GA* 9:163/126)

That surpassing ontological act of transcendence by which the world is structured, given meaning, is here explicitly characterized as a kind of "will." A transcendental voluntarism par excellence, it would seem. In this text, written but a few years after *Being and Time*, no longer does Heidegger shy from using the language of "will," even if still only with the hesitation of quotation marks.

(As I shall show in the next chapter, the "will" soon thereafter gets unleashed from these hesitation marks, first by way of a particularly violent interpretation of Kant's practical philosophy in 1930, and then in an unabashed self-assertion of will in Heidegger's political misadventure of

1933–34. But let us not rush to assimilate the subtleties and ambiguities of his earlier texts too quickly forward into his subsequent embrace of the will.)

Heidegger warns us in "The Essence of Ground" not to understand him as proposing an outright metaphysical idealism: "Ontological interpretation of being in and out of the transcendence of Dasein is by no means equivalent to the ontical derivation of the entirety of non-Dasein-like beings from this being qua Dasein" (*GA* 9:162/371). Nor, he cautions, should we mistake it as entailing an immoral "egoism": "The statement: *Dasein exists for the sake of itself,* does not contain the positing of an egoistic or ontic end from some blind narcissism on the part of each factical human" (*GA* 9:157/122). But even if not peddling a philosophy of individual egoism, does not Heidegger take over here, in his own manner, the German idealist tradition of positing a supra-empirical will, and would this not imply, in some sense, the repetition of "transcendental egoism"? Might not this "will" that "forms the *Umwillen*" even be referred to as a curious sort of "transcendental will"?[14] To be sure, what would distinguish Heidegger's "transcendental will" of Dasein (and what makes it curious) is the finitude of its thrownness and its *Jemeinigkeit.* Dasein's willing of a project which gives a meaningful structure to its world is always interrupted by its nonsublatable facticity; and thus the willing-projection must ever again be repeated in response to its current factical situation. But in what way does all this alter its character as will?

As we shall see, the "transcendental will" of idealism becomes one of the explicit targets of Heidegger's later critique of the history of metaphysics. The later Heidegger would no doubt, in retrospect, object to a reading which links his early notion of Dasein with idealism's transcendental ego; I am merely trying to point out here the difficulty of making this objection, without going so far as to deny certain significant differences. Once again, my argument is that the early Heidegger's relation to the will is inherently ambivalent and thus open to several directions of interpretation.

One of these directions leads to his post-(circa)1940 critique of the transcendental will of idealism as preparing the metaphysical ground for the will to power and the technological will to will; another leads to Heidegger's 1933–35 embrace of the language of spirit and will. In 1935 Heidegger writes:

> World is always *spiritual* [geistige] world. The darkening of the world contains within itself a *disempowering of spirit* [*eine* Entmachtung des Geistes] . . . [and the so-called] "collapse of German idealism" . . . is a kind of shield behind which the already dawning spiritlessness, the dissolution of spiritual powers [*geistigen Mächte*], the deflection of all origi-

nal questioning about grounds and the bonding to such grounds, are hidden and obscured. For it was not German idealism that collapsed; rather, the age was no longer strong enough to stand up to the greatness, breadth, and originality of that spiritual world. (*EM* 34–35)

And in the following year, in the first of his lecture courses on Nietzsche, Heidegger will deride the (Schopenhauerian) fall from the heights of "the might of thoughtful will in German idealism" which "thought being as will" (*N1* 73–75/61–63).

An Existential Voluntarism?

We have gotten ahead of ourselves and the text at hand. *Being and Time* does not yet speak of will and spirit, at least not as ontologically decisive matters or not without hesitation marks. Yet to the extent that it is possible to read the term "care" not as an alternative to or deeper dimension *than* will but as a deeper dimension *of* will,[15] and thus Dasein not as an utter disruption of the subject but as a curious sort of finite-transcendental "subject,"[16] then, far from disrupting the centrality of willful subjectivity, the text would appear to remodel it into a peculiar synthesis of the transcendental will of idealism and an existential voluntarism.

Not only the resonances of idealism, but also the existentialist thrust of the text, as shown in passages such as the following, seem to confirm the suspicion that *Being and Time* proffers a philosophy of will, in this case a kind of individualistic voluntarism:

> Dasein always understands itself in terms of its existence—in terms of a possibility of itself: to be itself or not itself. Dasein has either *chosen these possibilities itself,* or stumbled upon them, or grown up in them already. Only the particular Dasein *decides* its existence, whether it does so by *seizing upon* [Ergreifens] or by neglecting. (*SZ* 12, emphases added)

Heidegger later makes clear that the first of these possibilities—where Dasein *chooses, decides,* and *seizes upon* itself—is the authentic, proper (*eigentliche*) mode of Dasein's being. On the other hand, merely stumbling upon, passively inheriting, or neglecting to decide for itself its possibilities, characterizes Dasein's inauthentic, improper mode of existence, its deference to "the they" (*das Man*).

To be sure, Heidegger stresses that we are always already thrown into circumstances and falling into a passive adoption of possibilities offered up by the anonymous "they." And yet, even when always essentially qualified by falling and facticity, the absolute choosing of oneself remains an operative ideal in the text. In choosing itself, it would seem, Dasein wills itself, wills its projections and even its factical limitations. While fully facing up to its always already having been thrown into a world of facticities and limited possibilities, in a supreme and ingenious act of ecstatic-incorporation, Dasein would take over these limits as its own: in its ideal moments of authentic choosing, Dasein then perhaps becomes like Nietzsche's Zarathustra, who finally succeeds in "willing backwards" by changing every "it was" into a "thus I willed it!"[17] And to the extent that *Being and Time* repeats this Nietzschean motif, it too would be a philosophy of radical affirmation of will, a philosophy which teaches that "will" is "the name of the liberator and joy-bringer."

Heidegger does not in fact directly state that authenticity is a matter of will. In places, however, he does go so far as to explicitly link inauthentic existence with a lack of will, and thus by implication, at least, authentic existence with an abundance of will. We are told that "Dasein *can* comport itself also *unwillingly* to its possibilities; it can be inauthentic" (*SZ* 193); and he writes that such inauthenticity would be a kind of "tranquilized 'willing' under the guidance of the 'they'" (239). Heidegger is sharply critical of deference to "the they" (*das Man*), or what he calls "*subjection* to 'the others'" and "the dominion of public interpretedness." "What is decisive is just the inconspicuous mastery by others. . . . One belongs to the others oneself and solidifies their power [*Macht*]," and it is precisely in the anonymity of "the they," which is everyone and no one in particular, that "the real dictatorship of the they unfolds itself" (*SZ* 126).[18]

Of course, these passages could be read as a critique of the not-willing or deferred-willing of inauthenticity without *necessarily* asserting that authenticity is a matter of assertion of will. In breaking free of subjugation to the dictatorship of *das Man*, would one will one's own choices, or would one twist free to a third option beyond the dichotomy of willing and deferred-willing? But without (the search for) a "third option" (i.e., non-willing) being clearly articulated, it is all too easy to read such passages as implying that authenticity is a matter of voluntaristic assertion.

According to our analysis in this section, the cards may seem stacked against any reading of *Being and Time* as a disruption of willful subjectivity, despite Heidegger's avoidance of the term "will." Yet the issue is not nearly so simple. It perhaps remains necessary to proceed in this at first sharply critical manner in order to counteract Heidegger's own later self-(re)interpretations of *Being and Time*, according to which the fundamental thought of the book "has nothing to do with the will." We shall come to this "rebuttal" shortly. We also have yet to consider the important "interruption" of Dasein's ("willful") projects in the crucial moment of "running ahead to one's own death," and in the "call of consciousness" which brings one back from (the deferred-willing of) a fallenness into the they.

Entschlossenheit and the Will: Four Interpretations

The complexity of the question—and the ambiguity of the answer—regarding the role of the will in *Being and Time* fully emerges when we look at what is said to characterize Dasein's most proper way of being: *Entschlossenheit* (usually rendered as "resoluteness," but it shall soon become apparent why I leave this term untranslated). "In *Entschlossenheit* we have now arrived at that truth of Dasein which is most primordial because it is *authentic*" (*SZ* 297). But what is *Entschlossenheit*? It is first defined as the existential name for that "existentiell choosing to choose a kind of being-one's-self" (270); however, as we shall see, this voluntaristic-sounding "choosing to choose" must in the end be thought together with the other central notions of anxiety, running ahead to one's own death, and willing-to-have-a-conscience.

Initially at least, the term "resoluteness," like "projection" and "choosing," conveys what appear to be undeniable and ineradicable overtones of willfulness. And yet on closer examination of the term, this initial impression becomes questionable. For Heidegger *Entschlossenheit* is intimately related (see 297) to the notion of *Erschlossenheit* (disclosedness). This notion of dis-closing in turn is related to Heidegger's conception of truth as *a-letheia*, "unconcealment" or "unhiddenness" (*Entborgenheit, Unverborgenheit*). Thinking of unconcealment in terms of a "clearing" (*Lichtung*) ultimately leads him to think truth "topologically" as the "location" (*Ortschaft*) or "locality" (*Örtlichkeit*) of being (*GA* 15:335/41). It is this "topology of beyng" that we find in his later thinking of the region (or the open-region, *die Gegnet*) and the Open (*das Offene*) as that place of the revealing/concealing of beings wherein mortal humans most properly dwell. Hence, the later Heidegger defines or redefines (that is the question!) *Entschlossenheit* in this context as "the *specifically* [eigens] undertaken self-opening of Dasein *for* the Open" (*G* 59/81).

Etymologically, *Entschlossenheit* derives from the word *schließen* (to close, shut, fasten) and the prefix *ent-*, indicating opposition or separation; hence *entschließen* is said to have originally meant "to open, unlock."[19] The term *Entschlossenheit* would therefore "literally" mean "to be un-closed or opened-up" (*aufgeschlossen*). That Heidegger reads the term in this manner in his later writings is clear from such passages as the following, where *Entschlossenheit* finds its place (gets reinterpreted?) in a philosophy of *Gelassenheit:* "As letting beings be, freedom is intrinsically the resolutely open bearing that does not close up in itself [*das entschlossene, d.h. das sich nicht verschließende Verhältnis*]" (*GA* 9:194/149). The later Heidegger often hyphenates the word as *Ent-schlossenheit,* stressing this etymologically original ecstatic meaning.

But is this "being opened-up" *unequivocally* the sense of *Entschlossenheit* already intended in *Being and Time?* Let us consider for a moment the other, modern, everyday, if etymologically non-original, sense of the term. While originally meaning to open or unlock, from around the sixteenth century, *entschließen* came to be used (with the reflexive *sich*) in the sense of "to decide, reach a decision." The perfect participle *entschlossen* then came to mean "resolute," and the noun *Entschluss* to mean "decision or resolution," a matter of a "decision of will" (*Willensentscheidung*) to carry out a certain intention.[20] What would be unlocked, in a usual modern understanding, would not be the doorway to a region of non-willing, but rather one's own barrier of indecisiveness concerning what one willed to do. There is in fact another sense of the prefix "ent-" that supports this modern understanding, namely as "indicating the establishment of the condition designated by the word to which it is affixed."[21] If read in this usual modern sense, *Entschlossenheit* would mean "the establishing of a closing off," that is, a rejection of other possibilities in a firm grasping of a particular one. In the context of *Being and Time,* Dasein would, in freeing itself from its everyday deference to the they, resolutely choose its own possibility of being. This would clearly seem to imply a comportment of willing.

And yet, in a conversation with John Sallis in 1975, Heidegger reportedly strongly protested against relating *Entschlossenheit* to the will. Stating unequivocally, "It has nothing to do with the will," he suggested instead that *Entschlossenheit* be understood in the sense of *Geöffnetsein.*[22] Which reading is correct? Is *Entschlossenheit* a resolute willing of one's own potentiality-for-being, or is it an un-locked open(ed)ness to being?

In fact, I shall demonstrate, in the context of *Being and Time* there are not only two, but four possible ways of reading the term:

1. The notion of *Entschlossenheit* in *Being and Time* is—despite later developments in Heidegger's thinking and despite his later self-reinterpretations—a matter of willful resolve.
2. Despite certain misleading expressions in *Being and Time,* which can be attributed to "the metaphysical residues" inappropriate to the "original experience" behind the text, the term *Entschlossenheit* already ex-

clusively refers to the later Heidegger's "non-willing" explanations of
Ent-schlossenheit.

3. The inconstancies between the various connotations of *Entschlossenheit*
   in *Being and Time* are irresolvable. It contains undeniable elements
   of will, while in other respects foreshadowing his later thought of
   Gelassenheit.

4. The ambiguity of *Entschlossenheit* is rather that of a dynamic ambivalence, where authentic Dasein not only wills to resolutely choose its
   possibility of being, but also resolves to repeat an interruption of this
   willing.

Let us consider each of these interpretations in turn.

Entschlossenheit as Willful Resolve

It is not difficult to hear certain willful overtones—if not indeed the
marching tune of an existential voluntarism plain and simple—in the notion of "resoluteness" in such passages as the following:

> In the light of the for-the-sake-of-which of one's self-chosen potentiality-
> for-being, resolute Dasein frees itself for its world. . . . According to its
> ontological essence, resoluteness is always the resoluteness of some facti-
> cal Dasein at a particular time. The essence of this entity is its existence.
> Resoluteness "exists" only as a resolution [*Entschluss*] that projects itself
> understandingly. But to what does Dasein resolve itself in resoluteness?
> On what is it to resolve? *Only* the resolution itself can give the answer.
> (*SZ* 298)

In anxiety, one could infer, individual Dasein comes face-to-face with its
lack of ground (*Abgrund*), with an abysmal Nothing, and in the face of
this Nothing resolutely wills a project that gives structure and meaning to
its world. Read in this manner, the Heidegger of *Being and Time,* in the
wake of Nietzsche and his proclamation of the death of God, calls on each
of us to resolutely will to take on the burden of imposing meaning on an
otherwise meaningless world. *Being and Time* would be, despite Heidegger's belated objections, a voluntaristic existentialism.

Sartre would not then, after all, have completely mistaken the implications of *Being and Time* when he aligned it with his own atheistic and
humanistic existentialism. Referring to Heidegger, Sartre writes:

> What is meant here by saying that existence precedes essence? It means
> that, first of all, man exists, turns up, appears on the scene, and, only
> afterwards, defines himself. . . . Not only is man what he conceives him-

self to be, but he is also only what he wills himself to be after this thrust toward existence. . . . [Man] will be what he will have planned to be. Not what he will want to be. Because by the word "will" we generally mean a conscious decision, which is subsequent to what we have already made of ourselves . . . ; but all that is only a manifestation of an earlier, more spontaneous choice that is called "will."[23]

Man's essence is not created by the will of God; in existing he creates his own essence by means of his own will. In his response to Sartre's "misappropriation" of *Being and Time*'s statement "The 'essence' of Dasein lies in its existence" (*SZ* 42), Heidegger later points out, in the 1947 "Letter on Humanism," that "the reversal of a metaphysical statement remains a metaphysical statement" (*GA* 9:328/250). We could take this to imply that a mere shift in agency (i.e., from God to man) within the domain of the will does not break free of the metaphysics of will as such.

Yet despite Heidegger's explicit disavowals of Sartre's existentialist appropriation of his thought (see *GA* 9:325ff./247ff.), *Being and Time*'s notion of *Entschlossenheit* continues often enough to be accused of voluntarism. Frequently this charge is made by readers who are no more subtle in their criticism than Sartre was in his appropriation; but we also find a powerful critique in this regard by an astute interpreter like Michel Haar:

> At the end of the day, then, what are being-towards-death and running ahead if not the *forms* of *Dasein*'s self-appropriation, forms eternally devoid of content? . . . Running ahead could just as well be called *resoluteness*. . . . It seems that the two allow *Dasein* radically to take hold of its initial disclosedness, to capture its own light, to enter absolutely into possession of itself, of its "freedom," to learn to "choose its choice" [*SZ* 268]. An extreme voluntarism.[24]

In the moment of *Entschlossenheit*, Dasein would appropriate, hold within its circle of power and knowledge, its own potentiality-for-being, which in turn structures its world. A philosophy of will indeed, one is tempted to conclude without further ado.

Nor do we have to rely on an interpretation to explicitly make the connection between *Entschlossenheit* and will in Heidegger's thought. As late as 1936, in the first stages of Heidegger's confrontation with Nietzsche (when, as Arendt puts it, Heidegger still largely "goes along with" Nietzsche), he himself writes:

> Will is, in our terms, *Ent-schlossenheit*, in which he who wills stations himself abroad among beings in order to keep them firmly within his field of action. (*NI* 59/48)

Even when hyphenating the word, then, *Ent-schlossenheit* is explicitly equated with the will, and indeed in connection with Nietzsche's will to power. And although *Ent-schlossenheit* or the will is not understood here as an isolating act or an "encapsulation of the ego from its surroundings," it does stand out in these surroundings in order to "keep them firmly within his field of action." *Ent-schlossenheit* would be a matter of will as ecstatic-incorporation.

This comment from the early *Nietzsche* lectures was written during the years when Heidegger was struggling to think a "most proper" form of will, a troubled and transitional time that shall be the focus of the latter part of the following chapter. Here let us note one further place where Heidegger explicitly makes the connection between *Entschlossenheit* and will. In *Introduction to Metaphysics* (1935), Heidegger speaks of a positive notion of will in connection with the proper manner of knowing: the question of being must proceed, he says, by way of *Wissen-wollen*. In this connection he also mentions *Entschlossenheit*.

> Questioning is willing-to-know [*Wissen-wollen*]. Whoever wills, whoever lays his whole Dasein into a will, *is* resolute [*entschlossen*]. Resoluteness delays nothing, does not shirk, but acts from the moment and without fail. *Ent-schlossenheit* is no mere resolution to act, but the decisive [*entscheidende*] inception of action that reaches ahead and through all action. To will is to be resolute. (*EM* 16)

Is there any room left to contest the idea that Heidegger's early philosophy of *Entschlossenheit* is a philosophy of will, pure and simple?

Ent-Schlossenheit as Non-Willing Openness to Being: The Question of Heidegger's Self-(Re)Interpretations

There is indeed, according to the later Heidegger himself, who steps in at this point with a comment appended to the above passage in the 1953 publication of *Introduction to Metaphysics*. This comment reads:

> The essence of willing is traced back here to *Ent-schlossenheit*. But the essence of *Ent-schlossenheit* lies in the de-concealment [*Ent-borgenheit*] of human Dasein *for* the clearing of being, and by no means in an accumulation of force [*Kraftspeicherung*] for "activity." . . . The relation to being is rather one of letting. That all willing should be grounded in letting strikes the understanding as strange. (*EM* 16)

To will is to be resolved (*entschlossen*), but to be resolved is to be un-closed (*ent-schlossen*), standing-out in a relation of letting-be in the clearing of being. Willing is thus grounded in letting, an idea that would seem paradoxical only to those who do not see through to the proper, more "original" sense of the middle term *Ent-schlossenheit.*

In a "slightly revised" version of a text originally composed in 1936, "The Origin of the Work of Art," and again in defense of an affirmative use of the notion of willing-to-know, Heidegger writes:

> The willing here referred to, which neither merely applies knowledge nor decides beforehand, is thought of in terms of the fundamental experience [*Grunderfahrung*] of thinking in *Being and Time.* Knowing that remains a willing, and willing that remains a knowing, is the existing human's ecstatic engagement [*ekstatische Sicheinlassen*] in the unconcealedness of being. The *Ent-schlossenheit* thought in *Being and Time* is not the deliberate action of a subject, but the opening up of man, out of his captivity in beings, to the openness of being. (*GA* 5:55/192)

The willing *here* referred to (unlike, it is implied, the willing that is the target of Heidegger's critique of modernity and technology after the late 1930s) is not only not opposed to knowledge, but is properly a matter of man's *Sicheinlassen* in the unconcealedness of being. Willing is thus, properly understood, not a matter of "self-assertion," but a matter of opening up to the (non-willing) event of being. This is the sense, Heidegger claims, of the *Entschlossenheit* of *Being and Time,* given that we understand that work—not only, it is implied, in the letter of its text, but first of all—in the *Grunderfahrung* of its thinking.

In the 1942 course, "Parmenides," Heidegger attempts to sharply distinguish between, on the one hand, "the Greek" and his own notion of *Ent-schlossenheit,* which he explains as "the self-disclosing opening up [*Aufschließerung*] toward being," and, on the other hand, the modern understanding of *Entschlossenheit,* which he characterizes as "the act of will of man positing himself willfully on himself and only on himself," that is, as precisely the "will to will" (*GA* 54:111–12).

These later texts involve a twofold self-reinterpretation by the later Heidegger.[25] On the one hand, there is the self-critical (and wholly legitimate) attempt to rethink certain key terms of his own earlier thought. But, on the other hand, there is also an attempt to read these later developments back into the earlier texts, as if he were *simply* clarifying what had been originally intended there. Separating these two aspects of his self-(re)interpretations is as difficult as it is important, as the earlier thought does indeed often contain saplings which, when cultivated (i.e., both watered and pruned), grew into the later thought. Therefore, while the later Heidegger's self-(re)interpretations should carefully be attended to, they should certainly not be considered as exclusively authoritative; we must rather, as Heidegger puts it, "seek out thinking and its thoughts always in the element of its ambiguity" (*WhD* 68/71)—in this case, in the ambiguity and ambivalence of his early thought with regard to the will.

In the passages quoted above, Heidegger is reinterpreting two phases of his earlier thought. On the one hand he gives a (re)reading of *Being and Time*'s notion of *Entschlossenheit,* and on the other he attempts to reconcile (or at least smooth over the discontinuities in the transition between) his attempt in the 1930s to think a proper mode of willing (e.g., in the notion of *Wissen-wollen*) and his later attempt to move beyond the (epoch of) will altogether. It is the former attempt which concerns us at the moment: the (re)interpretation of the resoluteness of *Entschlossenheit* as a non-willing *Ent-schlossenheit,* a being-open(ed) to the clearing event of being. Far from being a decisive act of willful subjectivity, closing itself off from the world, or rather seeking to incorporate the world into its closed realm of control, *Ent-schlossenheit* is here thought as the "un-closedness" or openness to the event of being, as a released engagement (*Sicheinlassen*) in the worlding of the world.

But since it cannot be denied that in *Being and Time* resoluteness is connected with Dasein's "projection" of its potentiality-for-being, Heidegger needs to give a new interpretation of "projection" as well. This he does in the 1936–38 *Contributions to Philosophy* (see *GA* 65:304) and then again as follows in the 1947 "Letter on Humanism."

> If we understand what *Being and Time* calls "projection" as a representational positing, we take it to be an achievement of subjectivity and do not think it in the only way the "understanding of being" in the context of the "existential analysis" of "being-in-the-world" can be thought— namely as the ecstatic relation to the clearing of being. (*GA* 9:327/249)[26]

Moreover, the "Letter" seeks to decisively remove *Being and Time*'s central notion of "care" from any possibility of being "misunderstood" as related to a willfulness. In the language of his mature thought, Heidegger writes:

> Man does not decide whether and how beings appear. . . . The advent of beings lies in the destiny [*Geschick*] of being. But for humans it is ever a question of finding what is fitting in their essence which corresponds to such destiny; for in accord with this destiny man as ek-sisting has to guard [*hüten*] the truth of being. Man is the shepherd [*der Hirt*] of being. It is in this direction alone that *Being and Time* is thinking when ecstatic existence is experienced as "care." (*GA* 9:330–31/252; compare *GA* 65:16)

It is with this language of "guarding," "shepherding," and "corresponding" that the later Heidegger attempts to think non-willing(ly). In the present context we are concerned with the way in which the key terms of *Being and Time* are being (re)interpreted from the vantage point of this later perspective.

Did the notion of "care" in his early work already bespeak a shepherding the truth of being or a corresponding to the *Seinsgeschick?* Was not *Sorge* rather first of all a matter of Dasein's concern for its own potentiality-for-being, for its projection of possibilities which structure the world and thus "let beings be" as referential points within this totality of signification? And *Entschlossenheit?* Haar argues that Heidegger's

> self-interpretation [in the passage from "The Origin of the Work of Art" cited above] hardens nuances with the aid of half-truths: certainly resoluteness was never "the decided action of a subject," since it was the possibility of being-in-the-world (which is not closed in on itself like a subject) choosing its own ipseity, yet the self-appropriation of Dasein was not yet the "ekstatic abandonment of existing man to the unconcealment of being." . . . In *Being and Time* there was no way in which resoluteness could mean being open to the openness of being. . . . Resoluteness was the very search for the pure form of the self in one's ownmost temporality. . . .[27]

In fact, that search was perhaps already condemned to failure within *Being and Time* itself, namely in its anticipations of a turn from Dasein's *Zeitlichkeit* to the *Temporalität* of being itself in the never-completed division 3 of part 1, where, according to Heidegger, "everything is turned around" (*GA* 9:328/250). Haar writes in this regard:

> That temporality that cannot be appropriated draws the widest circle, encompassing all the structures, and secretly holds whoever believes he holds it. This aspect of *Being and Time*, the reverse of its voluntarism, is not so explicit, yet it produces a gap that is quite fundamental and that undermines the quest for one's own self, condemns it to fail at its very end.[28]

Despite these intimations of a turn, however, Haar rightly insists that we cannot ignore the willful aspect of *Entschlossenheit* in *Being and Time*. There is at least an ambiguity in this early text, an ambiguity that Heidegger's later self-(re)interpretations often tend to conceal in an attempt to exclusively reveal the connections with his later thought.

Entschlossenheit as Irredeemably Ambiguous

According to *Being and Time*, authentic Dasein is resolute in the face of its own death. What is this being-towards-death? In running ahead towards its own death, Dasein resolutely takes over its own finite potentiality-for-being; it comes back to itself from an anticipation of its ownmost "possibility of no-longer-being-able-to-be-there [*Nicht-mehr-dasein-können*]" (*SZ* 250) to resolutely take up a particular possibility of being. Is this being-towards-death the ultimate experience and recognition of finitude? Or is it the attempt to gain control over, to assert one's will even in the face of the limits of one's control, one's power?

It is once again Haar who most sharply poses the critical question: "[Is] not being-towards-death a name for the will to self-possession, to the self-appropriation of Dasein?"[29] Later on he concludes:

> We can thus comprehend the ultimate significance of running ahead. It is Dasein's turning back on itself in attaining the "absolute" point at which it can give itself what is possible for it. "Dasein can only *authentically* be *itself* if it makes this possible for itself of its own accord" [*SZ* 263]. Do we not have a full-blown idealism? Dasein wants itself, posits itself in its most extreme possibility, like the absolute Hegelian Subject and like the Will to Power. Dasein takes every possibility back to itself and into itself by force, by an act of will.[30]

Interpreted from this critical angle, in running ahead to its ownmost possibility of death, Dasein would will to master even that inescapable possibility of the demise of all its power of mastery. No longer fleeing in the face of its own mortality, authentic Dasein would turn the tables, perhaps reciting Zarathustra's monologue: "Now that which has hitherto been your ultimate danger has become your ultimate refuge."[31] Perhaps in this thought of willfully taking charge of one's life from the limit experience of deathliness, Heidegger silently already interpretively appropriates Hölderlin's line: "But where danger is, grows / Also that-which-saves," a line which later gets explicitly employed by Heidegger to depict the down-going (*Untergehen*) through an extreme epochal abandonment to the technological will to will towards intimations of a way of being other than willing. In this early context, however, it would be a matter of facing up to and usurping the power of that mortal enemy—mortal finitude itself—that threatens Dasein's wholeness and certainty at every projecting moment. In "anticipatory resoluteness" (*vorlaufende Entschlossenheit*), in running ahead in a constant certainty of that inescapable possibility of death, Dasein would at last and paradoxically attain a "self-constancy" (*SZ* 322), that is, "a certainty which is authentic and whole" (308).

On the other hand, a reading that would lead (only) to these conclusions must be qualified by another that attends to the radically *interruptive* moment of running ahead to one's own death, the moment of letting itself be *"thrown back upon its factical 'there' by shattering itself against death"* (385). Haar, for his part, qualifies his critique (or adds an element of ambiguity) by writing a few pages down from the passage quoted above: "Does not the call of conscience, therefore, instead of giving Dasein absolute mastery over itself, in truth lead it towards an initial dispossession?"[32] Dasein, it turns out, does not "master" its death any more than its thrownness (see *GA* 9:117/93). Indeed, Heidegger explicitly rejects the idea that Dasein can "overcome" death: "Anticipatory resoluteness is not a way of escape, fabricated for the 'overcoming' of death; it is rather that understanding which follows the call of conscience and which frees for death the possibility of *gaining power over* Dasein's *existence* [*der* Existenz *des Daseins* mächtig *zu werden*]" (*SZ* 310).

And yet again, we are later told that by running ahead Dasein not only "lets death become powerful in itself," but that Dasein, as now "free for death," "understands itself in its own *higher power* [Übermacht] of its finite freedom," a higher power in which Dasein can take over its "powerlessness" of being abandoned to that freedom which "is" only in authentically "choosing to choose" its possibilities (384). A complex thought, and, with regard to the question of the will, an ambiguous one at that. What is the relation between the power of death and the higher power of Dasein; and why is this relation thought in terms of "power" to begin with?

But let us not fail to notice the crucial point that it is a *finite* freedom, a *finite* power, that Dasein has, and it chooses to choose knowing that its choice is a finite one, and will have to be repeated with every new "situation" into which it is thrown. Moreover, "resoluteness" must ultimately be understood in its intimate connection with the "call of conscience," wherein Dasein is called back from its lostness in any single possibility, regardless of whether this was a possibility that it previously chose ("willed") or one that it passively received from the "anonymous will" of the they. And thus if willing-to-have-a-conscience (*Gewissenhabenwollen*) is indeed a form of "will," it is one which, as we shall see below in a fourth interpretation of *Entschlossenheit*, "resolves to repeat" an interruption of willing.

How then are we to understand this ambiguity of *Entschlossenheit*, that it on the one hand leans toward a supreme will to mastery, a mastery over even Dasein's own death, and on the other hand that it is a resolve to repeat the interruption of every project of Dasein that tends to forget its own finitude?

It is of course possible to criticize the role of will in *Being and Time* as irredeemably ambiguous, and leave it at that. This is the third possibility of interpretation I am noting, and is the approach followed for the most part by Haar. If we try to directly reconcile Heidegger's later (re)interpretations of *Entschlossenheit* with the undeniable element of voluntarism in *Being and Time* itself, perhaps this frustrated conclusion is inevitable. In fact, Heidegger himself claims that the project of *Being and Time* ended abruptly because "thinking failed in the adequate saying of [the] turning and did not succeed with the help of the language of metaphysics" (*GA* 9:328/231). Moreover, he tells us elsewhere: "The reason for the disruption is that the attempt and the path it chose confront the danger of unwillingly becoming merely another entrenchment of subjectivity" (*N2* 194/141). The implication of such self-criticism is that the original experience of *Ent-schlossenheit* (released openness to being) is distorted by the attempt to explicate it with a language of analysis that is still entangled with the metaphysics of willful subjectivity.

Thought in this manner, the task of reading the *Entschlossenheit* of *Being and Time* would be the double one of, on the one hand, criticizing the residual tendencies of Dasein-analysis toward "becoming another entrenchment" in that from which the text is attempting to free itself: the self-understanding of man as willful subjectivity; and, on the other hand, catching glimpses of what is to come: the "mortal" who dwells beyond the epoch of will in a region of *Gelassenheit* or non-willing.

This is the manner in which, for example, Ryosuke Ohashi (Ōhashi Ryōsuke) interprets the ambiguity of this early notion of *Entschlossenheit*. Arguing that "a willful character of thinking [*Willenscharakter des Denkens*] pervades the entire way of the early Heidegger," Ohashi understands the idea of "resolutely choosing oneself" as "the supreme form of willing for finite Dasein." However, he adds, "this thinking as willing already shows signs of a rupture in *Being and Time*."[33] This disruption is namely Dasein's confrontation with the nothingness exposed in anxiety; and it is the same resolute running ahead which opens Dasein to this nothingness. Thus, while on the one hand "resolute running ahead . . . is the highest willing of Dasein," on the other hand it is "a prefiguring [*Vorform*] of *Gelassenheit*."[34] Ohashi thus concludes that, although only by investigating the early Heidegger can we fully see the necessity of the mature position of *Gelassenheit*, it is only with the latter thought that Heidegger succeeds in overcoming a thinking that is a willing.[35]

Although I concur with the idea that the will is clearly problematized, and the possibility of a way of thinking other than willing explicitly elaborated, only in the later Heidegger, I wish to pause before leaving *Being and Time* to ask: is there not perhaps a more positive sense to the ambiguity of *Entschlossenheit* that can be found within the text itself? This is the fourth possibility which I shall, perhaps somewhat more interpretively, explore below: the possibility of reading this ambiguity as an essential ambivalence, namely as the dynamic tension of a "will to repeat the interruption of willing."

Entschlossenheit as the Will to Repeat the Interruption of Willing

In order to develop this most radical interpretation of *Entschlossenheit* in *Being and Time*, we need to consider in more detail the intimately related notions of being-towards-death, anxiety, and the call of conscience. First let us return to the idea of being-towards-death. We have seen how this notion may be critically interpreted as repeating the "idealistic" attempt of the subject to fully master himself (and his world) by experiencing even death—what Hegel calls that most "tremendous power of the negative" (*die ungeheure Macht des Negativen*)—as a "determinate negation" on the way to a higher synthetic recovery of the subject. According to Hegel, Spirit is precisely this "magical power" of "tarrying with the negative" which "converts it into being." Even the disruptive force of death would be incorporated into the will to expand the subject's realm and reign. Would Heidegger's finite Dasein, like Hegel's absolute Spirit, "win its truth only when, in utter dismemberment [*absoluten Zerrissenheit*], it finds itself"?[36] In authentically being-towards-death, Dasein, like Spirit, would then be a power of "life that endures death and maintains itself in death."[37]

Perhaps *Being and Time*'s being-towards-death does in fact, even if only in part, repeat this Hegelian motif. But there is another aspect, another thrust to the centrality of finite mortality in the text, namely an attempt not to overcome death but to let it be the disruptive force that it is. There is thus another way to read being-towards-death, a way that is perhaps more straightforward, yet is far more difficult to understand in the radicality of its consequences for any systematic "book" of philosophy, including *Being and Time*.[38] Charles Scott interprets the radical consequences of being-towards-death as follows:

> When dasein's *eigenste Möglichkeit* (most proper possibility) is named death . . . , the meaning of *most proper* or *ownmost* or *most essential* is thus interrupted. . . . It rather discloses human being as non-selflike possibility without identity of subjectivity. . . . When Heidegger says that an individual is forced by the forward run [*Vorlaufen*] of existence to take over its most proper and true being in possibility, he is saying that the individual's world and life are decentered and ruptured by the individual's resolve. In this resolve the thought of selfhood, subjectivity, and self-

constitution are set aside. In resolve one opens out in the world in the "understanding design" of dasein's mortal openness.[39]

Scott goes on to argue that resoluteness should not be understood as "self-constitution," but rather that Heidegger's notion of authenticity must be read in terms of a "middle-voiced" movement which is "beyond will."[40] Although Scott passes over the sense in which *Being and Time*'s resolute taking up of "the possibility of no possibility at all" does indeed bear elements of an attempt at (willful) self-constitution at the limit of death, he offers here a significant counter-interpretation to that which would see the role of death in the text *only* as one of ultimate self-mastery. In running ahead to death, Dasein's worldly willful projects of self- and world-constitution are interrupted, revealed in their finitude, and thus in their ultimate groundlessness. The centrality of death in *Being and Time* marks the place of an essential interruption of will, even if it also at times threatens to be appropriated and inserted as a precariously unstable keystone for the circle of ecstatic-incorporation.

Although after *Being and Time* Heidegger no longer accords the same central place in his texts to the thought of death, at one key point in *Introduction to Metaphysics* (1935) a consideration of the interruptive character of death brings pause to an otherwise rather "willful" analysis of Dasein. In this text, as we shall see in the following chapter, Dasein is thought of as essentially "violent," as willfully wresting truth from the "overpowering" onthrusts of being. And yet, we are told:

> There is only *one* thing against which all violence-doing directly shatters. That is death. It is an end beyond all completion [*Er über-endet alle Vollendung*], a limit beyond all limits [*über-grenzt alle Grenzen*]. Here there is no . . . capturing and subjugating. But this un-canny thing [*Un-heimliche*], which dislodges us simply and suddenly from everything in which we are at home, is no particular event that must be named among others because it, too, ultimately occurs. Man has no way out in the face of death, not only when it is time to die, but constantly and essentially. (*EM* 121; compare *SZ* 385)

The willful language of the text is suddenly brought to a halt when Dasein's mortal finitude becomes the issue. It should be pointed out, however, that even here there follows a problematical attempt to reincorporate this ultimate limit by way of "naming" it: "With the naming of *this* strange and powerful thing [i.e., "death"], the poetic project of being and human essence *sets its own limit on itself*" (*EM* 121, second italics added). Nevertheless, what is named is a constant and essentially interruptive event; all violence, all willing, shatters against death.

In *Being and Time,* death is the ownmost possibility of Dasein, but in the disruptive sense of being "the possibility of the absolute impossibility of Dasein" (*SZ* 250). The experience of anxiety—which, unlike fear, is anxious in the face of no particular entity, but rather in the face of the nothingness of the world as such—is ultimately the experience of death-liness (251). Death is, as Heidegger later puts it, the "place-holder of the Nothing" (*GA* 9:118/93). The experience of running ahead to one's own death is the experience of the finitude of every possible project; it is the ever-repeatable interruption of every attempt of Dasein to give final meaning to its world. Anxiety or running ahead to death ever again shatters the *Umwillen* that would orient the world around Dasein.

Entschlossenheit would, therefore, not only be the willful resolve of Dasein to a particular project, but would also be the resolve to repeat (or to be open to the repetition of) the interruption of willing in the experience of deathliness. *Entschlossenheit* must then be understood as "anticipatory resoluteness" (*vorlaufende Entschlossenheit*) which "resolves to repeat" the self-denuding experience of running ahead to one's own death. In authentic resoluteness, Dasein "cannot become rigid" in its resolve, but must "be *held open*" to the changing factical situation and the disruption it brings to the project of any given choice.

> The certainty of the resolution means that *one holds oneself free for* the possibility of *taking it back,* a possibility which is always factically necessary. . . . [This] holding-for-true, as resolute holding-oneself-free for taking it back, is *authentic resoluteness which resolves to keep repeating itself* [Entschlossenheit zur Wiederholung ihrer selbst]. (*SZ* 307–8)

And—let us emphasize here in this final reading of *Entschlossenheit*—what gets repeated is not simply the constructive moment of (willful) resolute projection, but is first of all the deconstructive moment of anxiety in being-towards-death. In another place in the text we read: "*This reticent self-projection upon one's ownmost being-guilty, in which one is ready for anxiety—*we call '*resoluteness*'" (296–97). Thus Dasein, in its most proper comportment, is not simply willfully resolved to take up a particular project; it is resolved first to expose itself to abyssal deathliness, second to choose a particular possibility within the limits of its thrown facticity, and finally to repeat this movement of destruction/construction or interruption/projection without end. There would always be a moment of interruption in counterbalance to any affirmation, a will to the interruption of any willing to will (choosing to choose).

Hence, *Entschlossenheit* would not only be resolve (decisive) *in the face of death,* it would also be resolved (opened up) *to face death,* and to do so repeatedly. This is the ambivalence we finally come down to in this central thought of *Being and Time. Entschlossenheit,* which first strikes one as un-equivocally a matter of decisive willfulness, shows itself to also entail the sense of an open willingness to repeatedly interrupt willing.

We can also approach this fundamental ambivalence from the other side, as it were, through the notion of "conscience" (*Gewissen*), which is presented both as "the call of conscience" (*der Ruf des Gewissens*) and as a "willing-to-have-a-conscience" (*Gewissenhabenwollen*).

"Conscience" is that peculiar "voice" that is both one's own and not one's own. It speaks to one, reprimands one, calls one back from one's will-ful doings, and yet it is not simply external to one. As Heidegger says, its "call comes *from* me and yet *from beyond me*" (*SZ* 275). While on the one hand it is not a call to passively heed the will of an other; on the other hand, neither can the call of conscience be understood as the internal monologue of one's own autonomous will with itself. Indeed,

> the call is precisely something which *we ourselves* have neither planned nor prepared for nor voluntarily performed, nor have we ever done so. "It" calls, against our expectations and even against our will. (Ibid.)

As Heidegger puts this point in a slightly later text: "We are so finite that we cannot even bring ourselves originally before the Nothing through our own decision and will" (*GA* 9:118/93).

Nevertheless, our "understanding of the appeal reveals itself as our *willing-to-have-a-conscience*" (*SZ* 269–70). In this sole explicit and repeated employment of a term involving "*Wollen*" in *Being and Time* (aside from de-rivative terms like *Umwillen*), Heidegger speaks of the "active" part Dasein plays in being ready for the call of conscience as a matter of "willing-to-have." This willing-to-have-a-conscience is sometimes referred to by commentators as representative of "the voluntaristic or willful strain" in *Being and Time.*[41] And yet this tells but half the story; for what is being "willed" is initially nothing other than *the interruption of willing.* One wills to let the call of conscience bring one back from one's (willful) projects to the abyssal experience of anxiety. Like resoluteness, "willing-to-have-a-conscience becomes a readiness for anxiety" (296). The "will" of willing-to-have-a-conscience wills to let the call of conscience bring one back to the experience of anxiety as the interruption of willing. It is a will to inter-rupt willing, or rather to *let* this interruption occur.

Moreover, the call of conscience does not give any content of its own, but speaks only in a "keeping silent" (ibid.). "The Heideggerian *Gewissen,*" Haar points out, "like Socrates' daimon, interrupts the impulse to act, rather than provoking it."[42] The call of conscience interrupts our (willful) action or our passive fallenness into the they, without prescribing a particular course of conduct in their place. The "primordial being-guilty," to which the call of conscience calls Dasein back, cannot then "be defined by morality, since morality already presupposes it for itself" (*SZ* 286). It interrupts not only one's own will, but any morality as the "common will" of the community to which one could defer. As Scott writes: "Dasein's deathly openness ek-sists its selfhood as well as its ethos. . . . [It] interrupts one's historical and community identity."[43] Of itself the call of conscience gives no positive content; it gives no explicit instruction in its reprimand; it simply interjects an abrupt pause in the restless willful (or deferential) flow of life.

However, just as resoluteness has its other side, the call of conscience in *Being and Time* is not *only* a matter of interruption of will; for it is also a call to once again will resolutely. What gets repeated is not only the interruption of will, but also the call to fill this void yet once again with a (willful) projection, a resolute choosing of a possibility. Heidegger tells us that the call is "not merely critical" (288), it does not function "only negatively" (294). The call of conscience does not only "call Dasein *back*" from willing and losing itself in its willful projects; the call also "calls Dasein *forth*" to the willing of a new factical resolution.

> The summons calls back by calling forth: it calls Dasein *forth* to the possibility of taking over, in existing, that thrown entity which it is; it calls Dasein *back* to its thrownness so as to understand this thrownness as the null ground which it has to take up into existence. (287)

The call thus calls one back to one's thrownness in order to take this null basis up into one's existential projection. The call reminds Dasein of "the null ground of its null project" (ibid.), but does not renounce this world-forming projecting altogether; on the contrary, it calls one forth to project all the more "resolutely," to take over and be this null ground itself. On the one hand, if one expects unequivocal maxims for calculating one's actions, "the conscience would deny to existence nothing less than the very *possibility of acting*" (294); on the other hand, "when the call is rightly understood . . . as a *calling back* which *calls forth* into its factical potentiality-for-being-its-self *at the same time*" (ibid., emphases added), then: "To hear the call authentically signifies bringing oneself into a factical acting" (ibid.).

The call of conscience is thus ambiguous, or, more precisely speaking, ambivalently two-sided. On the one hand, like the Socratic daimon, it calls one back from, interrupts, any particular (willful) project. On the other hand, it calls one forth to the resolute taking up of a new project, albeit in resolute awareness of one's thrown facticity and of the fact that this new project too will subsequently need to be interrupted and recast, and so on without end—or rather until the actual event (not the possibility, which, to be sure, is considered by Heidegger to be ontologically more significant than the ontic event) of death.

From Being-Towards-Death to the Great Death: An Exhortation from Zen

> First of all, the Great Death; after cutting off completely, once again coming back to life.
> —Zen saying[44]

> Leben ist Tod, und Tod ist auch ein Leben.
> —Hölderlin[45]

> Insofar as death comes, it vanishes. The mortals die the death in life. (*EHD* 165/190)

Could the ambivalence of *Being and Time*'s *Entschlossenheit*—as an open resolve to repeat (the interruption of) willing—ever twist free of the "willful" character of being-in-the-world as such? Might not a thorough opening of the abyssal ground of existence essentially or "existentially" alter one's very way of being, not only *interrupting* each particular projection, but *disrupting* the willful character of "projecting" as such? Could there occur an existential shift so radical that Dasein would no longer structure the world according to its own *Worum-willen,* but would become fundamentally (more) open to the worlding of the world in a different manner?

Let me bring this chapter to a close by briefly introducing a parallel to *Being and Time*'s being-towards-death—as well as an exhortation to proceed "one step further" on this way back to authentic dwelling-in-the-world as a mortal—from Zen Buddhism. This parallel and exhortation have been insightfully articulated by several philosophers of the Kyoto School,[46] who not only had firsthand experience with the thought and practice of Zen, but were also on familiar terms with Heidegger and his path of thought.

Alluding to the early Heidegger's expression "being held out into the Nothing [*Hineingehaltenheit in das Nichts*]" from the 1929 lecture "What Is Metaphysics?" (*GA* 9:115/91), Nishitani Keiji suggests that, despite the fact that Heidegger introduced the idea of "the Nothing" precisely in order to mark the ontological difference (i.e., the notion that being is no-thing), insofar as the early Heidegger thought of the Nothing as an abyss into which Dasein is suspended in a state of anxiety (*Angst*), "traces of the representation of the Nothing as some 'thing' [which threatens Dasein from without] still remain."[47] In the wake of Nishitani's critique, Ueda Shizuteru traces a deepening movement within Heidegger's thought itself with regard to the Nothing. When the Nothing of the world first presents itself, and "beings as a whole slip away" as we are turned away from our everyday "running around amidst beings [*Umtrieben an das Seiende*]" (*GA* 9:116/92), anxiety besets us. And yet, writes Ueda, "the Nothing that is revealed in the manner of anxiety is not in fact the originary aspect of the Nothing." It does, however, serve to "call us toward a fundamental conversion in our relation towards the Nothing."[48] Ueda finds this conversion under way in Heidegger's path of thought.

> When the Nothing is revealed, the "Da" of Dasein too gets under way. Near the very end of "What Is Metaphysics?" Heidegger speaks of "releasing oneself into the Nothing [*das Sichloslassen in das Nichts*]" [*GA* 9:122/96]. In fact, it is perhaps by letting oneself go, casting oneself into the Nothing revealed in anxiety, that the mood of anxiety is broken through and an originary manifestation of the Nothing becomes, as it most properly should be, the "Da" of Dasein. To begin with this is realized as the "resolute anticipation of death" and the "being-towards-death" of Dasein; yet this remains, it must be said, but a station on the way to the [genuine] manifestation of the Nothing. As a matter of fact, the notion of "releasing oneself into the Nothing" is radicalized in the later Heidegger's thought into the notion of *Gelassenheit,* and "being-towards-death" into the notion of "the mortal" as one who is able to die.[49]

Ueda goes on to write that "through this deepening conversion from anxiety threatened by the Nothing to *Gelassenheit* as releasing oneself into the Nothing, by going from the Nothing of *Angst* to the Nothing of *Gelassenheit,*" and through this releasement becoming "able to die," one is first truly "able to be" and able to let beings be.[50]

Might it be possible, then, not merely to "anxiously anticipate" death in an experience of "being held out into the Nothing," but rather to be released through and from this anxiety into an experience of the Nothing as none other than the open place wherein one recovers one's "original face" of freedom and response-ability? Perhaps one could willingly undergo, on the way to this *Gelassenheit,* a kind of "existential death"—a death without sublation of the subject, where what gets reborn or uncovered is rather a non-ego (*muga*) or a "self that is not a self" (*jiko narazaru jiko*). Such a Great Death (*daishi*) would not simply periodically interrupt, but would also break through and reorient the willful ground of the self as such. A well-known Zen saying describes this path as follows: "Become a dead man, remaining alive; become thoroughly dead; then do as your mind pleases, all your works are then good."[51] This could be paraphrased as "Die once, and do what you will," with the qualification that having undergone this Great Death of the ego-subject, "what you will" would in fact no longer be a matter of "will" at all, but would be grounded (or groundlessly) in a way of being other than willing.

Tsujimura Kōichi (another Zen adept who studied under both Nishitani and Heidegger) suggests that the "transcendental will" which he finds underlying Heidegger's early thought[52] could be understood, in the context of Buddhism, to be the basis of the formation of the world of samsara (in Japanese, shōji, [the cycle of] birth and death [of the ego]). Having broken through this ground, that is, having gone all the way to the bottom of the abyss (Abgrund) exposed in the fundamental mood of anxiety, this mood itself should, Tsujimura writes, give way to a fundamentally other kind of attunement.[53] For Nishitani, this is a matter of returning to the "standpoint of emptiness (śūnyatā)," a standpoint which is "first established at a bottomless place that exceeds by way of absolute negation all standpoints of any kind related to will."[54]

In radically stepping back through the nihilism of "relative nothingness" (the Nothing of anxiety) to "the place of Absolute Nothingness" (zettaimu no basho) or "the field of emptiness" (kū no ba), one would learn to dwell without metaphysical ground or reason (ohne Grund). Perhaps there, as an awakened place-holder of this originary freedom and response-ability of emptiness, one's "non-artificial doing" or "non-acting activity" (wei-wuwei, mui-no-i) would recover the spontaneous naturalness (jinen) of an originary attunement of non-willing. The practice of this recovery, to be sure, would be without end; "Shakyamuni and Amitabha Buddha too are still engaged in practice." Indeed, as Dōgen stresses, practice is not a means to the end of releasement; awakening to one's original "Buddha-nature" would not be the end of the Way, but the beginning of the realization of the "non-duality of practice and enlightenment" (shushō-ittō).[55] "Those who are able to see the Way, practice the Way." And yet, even for Dōgen, there is a radical shift—a "suddenness" of enlightenment (tongo)— that takes place when the "body and mind" of the ego "drop off" (shinjin-datsuraku) and one awakens to the practice of being on the way to/of releasement.[56]

While I cannot pursue further here the critique of the will and the intimations of non-willing which lie at the heart of the path of Zen Buddhism,[57] it has often been pointed out, both by the Kyoto School[58] and by Western scholars,[59] that many aspects of Heidegger's thought invite dialogue with East Asian traditions. In particular, his later thought of being on the way to *Gelassenheit* resonates well with Zen's path of awakening to a non-egoistic and non-dual manner of being-in-the-world by way of an existential death of the ego-subject of will. The later Heidegger no longer thinks mortality as an abysmal anxiety in the face of which Dasein must resolutely project the meaning of being. Rather, for the mortal dwelling in the fourfold (of earth, sky, mortals, and divinites), death is "the shrine of the Nothing" as "the mystery of being itself" (*VA* 171/178). The mortal, who alone is capable of death as death, dies "continually, as long as he stays on this earth, so long as he dwells" (190/222). Thoroughly dying to the will to posit himself as the ground and center of beings, the mortal shelters the no-thing of being, and, cor-responding to the appropriating event of the fourfold, plays his part in letting beings be.

However, the early Heidegger's thought of resolutely running ahead to death is, as we have seen, highly ambiguous in regard to the problem of the will. *Being and Time* leaves us, at best, with an ambivalent circling between resolute willing and an open resolve to interrupt willing; no third possibility is clearly indicated, even if we may take the dynamic of this to-and-fro to be obliquely negotiating a circuitous path toward non-willing. Yet regardless of the extent to which *Being and Time* can be read in hindsight as already on the way to *Gelassenheit,* its failure to *explicitly* take up the will as a problem for thought is a profound one. The neglect to overtly problematize the will, and the consequent unsaid ambiguity of the role of the will in this text are disturbing, not merely because a radical critique of the will assumes such a central place in the later Heidegger's own thought, but most of all because this neglect facilitated, or at least failed to prevent, his dubious philosophical and disastrous political embrace of the will in the early 1930s.

3

The Turn Through an Embrace of the Will

> [A] genuine and substantively necessary overturning is always a
> sign of inner continuity and thus can be grasped only from the
> whole problematic. (*GA* 31:267)

> In the woods are paths that mostly wind along until they end
> quite suddenly in an impassable thicket. . . . Each goes its
> peculiar way, but in the same forest. Often it seems as though
> one were identical to another. It only seems so. (*GA* 5:iv)

In this chapter I consider the twistings and turnings of Heidegger's
thought-path during the transitional decade of the 1930s. In this decade
Heidegger's thought undergoes its much-remarked yet controversial
"turn," and our first task shall be to understand this turn in relation to the
problem of the will. We shall find that it is necessary to speak of at least
two interconnected yet distinguishable turns (or stages of the turn) in
Heidegger's thought, the second involving an explicit and radical critique
of the will.

Heidegger's turn to non-willing, or more precisely stated, his turn
to the task of thinking the problem of the will and the possibility of non-
willing, takes place only after wandering down the dead-end path of a disastrous embrace of the will. Yet this wandering cannot be simply written
off as a disconnected aberration of Heidegger's *Denkweg;* for, as we have
seen, an ambivalence with regard to the will lay at the heart of his pre-turn
thought. It is only by way of carefully working through the inflections of
the will embedded in Heidegger's thought at the time that we can understand both the continuity and the discontinuity—the immanent overturning and radical twisting free—at work in Heidegger's turn through
and from the will.

After an explication of the "turn(s)" in Heidegger's thought in the first section of this chapter, in the second section I examine Heidegger's voluntaristic interpretive appropriation of Kant's practical philosophy, and then his infamous political "blunder" as a certain ground zero of the problem of the will in Heidegger's thought-path. In the Rectoral Address and in political speeches during this brief but spirited involvement with the Nazi politics of assertion and sacrifice of will, the Heidegger of 1933–34 himself provides us with a foil for his later critique of the domain of the will. In the third section I consider Heidegger's attempts to think a "proper will" in his works in the middle and latter years of this decade, in particular *Introduction to Metaphysics* and *Contributions to Philosophy (From Enowning)*. In these works we see Heidegger's first attempts to come to grips with his blunder of 1933–34, to resituate or rethink the philosophy of "will" he committed himself to embracing. Increasingly, however, particularly in the solitary meditations of *Contributions,* this "proper will" comes to signify a radical critique of the subjective will of self-assertion, a critique which eventually leads to his break with the language and thought of "will" altogether. With this break is inaugurated the "later Heidegger" as concerns this study, the Heidegger after his turn to a radical critique of the will, the Heidegger on the way of twisting free towards an other-than-willing.

The Problem of the Will in Heidegger's Turn(s)

The content and dating of Heidegger's "turn" continues to be the subject of much debate. I shall argue that it is necessary to distinguish several distinct, though complexly interrelated, senses of the turn.[1] Heidegger himself at times prefers to speak of the *Kehre* as belonging to the matter (*Sachverhalt*) itself, in distinction from what he called "a change or turn in my thinking" (*eine Wendung in meinem Denken*) which would reflect his attempt to correspond to the turning of beyng or *Ereignis*.[2] In his first published mention of the *Kehre* in the "Letter on Humanism," Heidegger tells us that the third section of *Being and Time,* "Time and Being," where "everything would be turned around [*Hier kehrt sich das Ganze um*]," was held back because "thinking failed in the adequate saying of this *Kehre*" (*GA* 9:328/ 250). Unable to free itself from "the language of metaphysics," *Being and Time* ultimately failed in the "adequate understanding and cooperative carrying out [*Nach- und Mit-vollzug*] of this other thinking that abandons subjectivity" (327/249). The *Wendung im Denken* is thus to cor-respond to the *Kehre* in the matter itself. As Heidegger tells us in his letter to William Richardson:

> [The] "being" into which *Being and Time* inquired cannot remain something that the human subject posits. It is rather being, stamped as presencing (*An-wesen*) by its time character, that goes forth to Da-sein. As a result, even in the initial steps of the question of being in *Being and Time* thought is called upon to undergo a change [*Wendung*] whose movement corresponds to the *Kehre*. ("PMH" xviii/xix)

What then is the *Kehre* in the matter itself for Heidegger? Here too, I submit, we find two distinct but related meanings. With the publication of *Contributions* it has become particularly evident that Heidegger developed a specific sense of the term *Kehre* in connection with, or even as a way of depicting, the event of appropriation (*Ereignis*) itself. The *Kehre* is one way of speaking about the counter-swing or counter-resonance (*Gegenschwung*) between beyng's needful-usage (*Brauchen*) of man and man's belonging (*Zugehören*) to beyng (*GA* 65:251). There is "a turning, or rather *the* turning [die *Kehre*], that indicates just this essence of being itself as the immanent counter-resonating event of appropriation [*das in sich gegenschwingende Ereignis*]" (261).

The fourth Bremen lecture of 1949, entitled "Die Kehre," provides us with the second meaning of the *Kehre* in the matter itself.[3] There he writes: "In the essence of the danger is concealed the possibility of a turning [*Kehre*], in which the oblivion of the essence of being so turns [*wendet*] itself that, with this turning [*Kehre*] the truth of the essence of beyng itself returns [*einkehrt*] to beings" (*GA* 79:71/41). The *Kehre* here is not just a structural dynamic within *Ereignis,* but anticipates "the advent of this turning [*die Ankunft dieser Kehre*]" from "the oblivion of being to the safekeeping of the essence of beyng" (ibid.). In this context it is possible to speak of a being-historical turning (*eine seinsgeschichtliche Kehre*) from the abandonment of being in the extreme epoch of the technological will to will to a time of a more originary cor-respondence with being: a turning to non-willing.

Connecting Heidegger's two senses of the *Kehre* in the matter itself is possible insofar as the being-historical turn to an other beginning enables a more originary cor-respondence within the counter-swing of *Ereignis.* Moreover, the *Wendung* in Heidegger's *Denkweg* is certainly not unrelated here, since it would occur as an attempt to thoughtfully enter into participation with the *Kehre* in the matter itself.

Influenced by Heidegger's own enigmatic remarks and qualified acknowledgment of Richardson's distinction between "Heidegger 1" and "Heidegger 2," interpreters have often used and sometimes misused the term *Kehre* to refer to a major shift, and perhaps even a kind of "reversal," along the way of Heidegger's thought-path. Reacting to past ambiguities and excesses in this regard, some scholars have recently argued that we should keep the terminology distinct, and only refer to "Heidegger's turn" as a *Wendung im Denken*.[4] I shall generally refer to this *Wendung* as a "turn" and to the *Kehre* of or in the matter itself as a "turning." It is necessary, I maintain, to speak of two turns, or at the very least of two relatively distinct moments of the turn, in Heidegger's path of thought.

Heidegger's turn is often understood to involve a shift from an emphasis on Dasein's thrown-*projection* of its own possibilities for being to a thought which gives primacy to the sendings that appropriate humans into their being-historical time-space.[5] As *Contributions* puts it: "The thrower itself, Da-sein, is thrown, a-propriated [*er-eignet*] by beyng" (*GA* 65:304). Yet a turn of primary orientation from Dasein to being would not on its own be decisive with regard to the problem of the will. "Reversing" the emphasis of direction in the relation, from that of "Dasein's projection" to that of "being's sendings," does not *necessarily* overcome thinking within "the domain of the will." If the relation can still be considered in binary terms of activity/passivity, then the turn would only be an inversion *within* the domain of the will and not a turn beyond, a twisting free of the domain of the will as such. The turn of focus from Dasein to being would not yet decisively instigate the turn from the will toward *Gelassenheit*.

No amount, for example, of tempering the power of Dasein's will by emphasizing its exposure to the "overpowering" force of being would fundamentally alter the very terms of will and power in which this relation is thought. Thus in 1935 Dasein's role would still be thought as one of "the use of power/violence [*Gewalt-brauchen*] against the overpowering/overwhelming [*Überwältigende*]" (*EM* 122). We shall see that a willful attitude of Dasein is called forth by the (willful) "overpowering" character attributed to being (*physis*) in this period. Moreover, even after, or precisely when, Heidegger begins to recoil from Dasein's assertion of will, the flip side of the problem of the (domain of the) will, the problem of passive not-willing or deferred-willing, is prone to rear its head. Indeed, many critics have stopped here and written off Heidegger's later thought as a mere "turnaround" from a willful assertion to a sacrifice of will, from voluntarism to fatalism, or from willful decisionism to will-less quietism.[6] It is one of the purposes of this study to show the limits of this simplistic understanding of Heidegger's turn as a "turnabout." We have already explored the highly ambiguous role of the will in *Being and Time,* and in later chapters we shall look in detail at Heidegger's attempts to twist free of the very domain of the will. The ultimate turn in Heidegger's thought involves not only a turn of focus from Dasein to being, but crucially *a turn from thinking this relation in terms of the (domain of the) will.*

In short, there are at least two "turns" (or at least two significant moments of "the turn") in Heidegger's path, which occur almost a decade apart. Roughly put: the "initial turn" (under way by 1930), from a focus on an analysis of Dasein toward a thinking of being, does not yet radically problematize the will; the decisive turn toward a radical critique of the will, and toward an attempt to think the relation between man and being otherwise than willing, is first carried out in the late 1930s and early 1940s. Though prepared for in the preceding (and partially overlapping) attempt to think a non-subjective "proper will" in *Contributions,* the second turn is most clearly witnessed in the course of Heidegger's prolonged *Auseinandersetzung* with Nietzsche (1936–46). With regard to the problem of the will, it can be said that by around 1940 the post-turn thought of the "later Heidegger" is under way.

Several commentators have emphasized this turn from the will to an "altered *Stimmung,*"[7] and Hannah Arendt even tempts us to "date the reversal as a concrete autobiographical event precisely between volume 1 and volume 2" of Heidegger's *Nietzsche,* that is, sometime in 1939.[8] Yet while Heidegger's interpretation of Nietzsche's will to power does become increasingly critical at this time, the change cannot simply be reductively ascribed to a sudden autobiographical event, for the "twisting and turning" in his thought had begun long before, and in the context of his rigorous engagements with the tradition of philosophy. Moreover, as I shall show, Heidegger did not *abruptly* turn away from the will, but first spent several years attempting to think a "proper will" (e.g., a will of "reservedness") in distinction from subjective assertion of will, the latter becoming fairly early on an explicit target of his critique. Although Heidegger eventually breaks with any positive use of the term "will" altogether, the thought experiments in this troubled decade are instructive in their failings as well as in their foreshadowing of Heidegger's mature thought.

Heidegger's turn toward a critique of the will beginning in the latter years of the 1930s, however, gets under way only after a disastrous lapse in 1933–34, during which time Heidegger embraces the will resolutely, and in the name of the most infamous fascist state of the twentieth century. The tentative (and still largely implicit) problematization of the will achieved in *Being and Time* is here forgotten, and for a time the will is embraced as the essence of human freedom, the essence of the state, and the essence of their relation to each other and to history. We must first reflect on this decisive lapse, this ground zero in Heidegger's problematization of the will, before considering the steps taken in the remaining years of the 1930s on the long road of recovery and transformation.

The Embrace of the Will: In Thought and in Politics

> The evil and thus keenest danger is thinking itself. It must think against itself, which it can only seldom do. (*GA* 13:80/8)

In tracing the course of the avoidance, questioning, and then suddenly uninhibited use of the term "spirit" (*Geist*) in Heidegger's writings, Derrida reveals the dramatic yet unannounced "lifting of the quotation marks" from this term in Heidegger's Rectoral Address of 1933, "The Self-Assertion of the German University." While this metaphysically charged term had always been "avoided" or placed in quotation marks by Heidegger before this time, all critical hesitancy lapses in his spiritual resolve to support Hitler's regime. The Rectoral Address is thus shown to be as dubious philosophically as it is politically.[9]

In a by no means less troubling manner, in the Address the term *Wille* too has been unleashed from all "hesitation marks." In the wake of German idealism, the synchronized reappearance of these terms, "spirit" and "will," would not be mere coincidence; in Heidegger's later words: "The completion of metaphysics begins with Hegel's metaphysics of absolute knowledge as that of the Will of Spirit" (*VA* 72/89; see also *GA* 5:115ff.). We have seen in the previous chapter how the term "will" was "avoided" in *Being and Time* as a phenomenon of purportedly no ontological significance, and how it was then introduced, if still only in quotation marks, at the very center of Heidegger's ontology in the 1929 "The Essence of Ground" (see *GA* 9:163/126). There we do indeed already have a clear foreshadowing of the "unleashing" that occurs by the time of the Rectoral Address of 1933. In his political debut, we shall see, the language of will is explicitly and without reservation employed at the center of Heidegger's thought.

Being Rooted in Pure (Yet) Finite Willing: A Unilateral Appropriation of Kantian Autonomy

In between "The Essence of Ground" and the Rectoral Address we find an important lecture course wherein the process of removing the hesitation marks from the "will" can most clearly be witnessed—namely, in the summer course of 1930 where Heidegger interpretively appropriates the "pure will" of Kant's practical philosophy.[10] In the final part of this course, Heidegger's "violent" reinterpretation of the categorical imperative as "*the fundamental law of a finite pure willing*" (*GA* 31:280) sets down an important stepping-stone, indeed a springboard for his subsequent political voluntarism.

The course is entitled "The Essence of Human Freedom." As the subtitle "An Introduction to Philosophy" indicates, the question of freedom is said to lie at the very heart of philosophy. Indeed, in claiming that "'going-after-the-whole' must be grasped as 'going-to-the-roots'" (19)—which he will later clarify as "going-to-our-roots [*Uns-an-die-Wurzel-Gehen*]" (131)—Heidegger here subordinates the "leading question" of metaphysics, that of "being and time," to the "fundamental question" (*die Grundfrage*) of the "essence of human freedom." He now claims: "*The essence of freedom only comes properly into view if we seek it as the ground of the possibility of Dasein, as something that lies prior even to being and time*" (134). "Thus *the question concerning the essence of human freedom is the fundamental question of philosophy, in which is rooted even the question of being*" (300).

Freedom is "the root of being and time." The categories through which beings show themselves, such as "causality" and "movement," are contingent upon an understanding of being that is in turn grounded in the essence of human freedom as "*the condition of the possibility of the manifestness of the being of beings*" (303). Heidegger is careful here to subordinate man to this metaphysical freedom and not the other way around. "Human freedom now no longer means: freedom as a property of man; but rather the reverse: *man as a possibility of freedom*" (135). But insofar as this freedom "breaks through in man and takes him up unto itself," then "man, as *grounded* in his existence upon and *in* this freedom, becomes the site and opportunity at which and with which beings in the whole become manifest. . . . [Man] exists as the entity in whom the being of beings, thus beings as a whole, are revealed" (ibid.).

Kant's mistake, according to Heidegger, was to unduly subordinate the question of freedom to that of causality, whereas in fact causality, as *one* way in which beings can show themselves in their interconnectedness, is possible only on the basis of freedom. But nevertheless "Kant was the first to see the problem of freedom in its most radical philosophical consequences" (137). Kant's most radical thinking of freedom can be found, it turns out, not in his "first way," that is, by way of the theoretical question of "a possible kind of causality in the world," but rather in the "second way" found in his philosophy of practical reason. In the latter Kant seeks to demonstrate not just the theoretical possibility but an "actually existing freedom [*die wirkliche Freiheit*] as the freedom of the ethically acting human being" (265). Unique among the "ideas of reason," we can experience freedom as a fact in practical will-governed action, or *willentlichen Handeln* (269–71).

For Kant, as we know, it is the *purely rational and therefore autonomous* will that provides the basis for a praxis of freedom by revealing *universal laws*. But Heidegger is more interested in the autonomy and the purity of the will—as demonstrated, not in a transcendental freedom of abstraction from factical life but in the "*facticity of freedom*" (273)—than he is with its disclosure of universal rational laws.[11] "What," Heidegger needs to ask well into his discussion of Kant's practical philosophy, "does the pure will have anything to do with laws . . . ?" (278). Yet for Kant, from the beginning the "purity" of the will indicates not just its freedom *from* the impurity of desire, but also its freedom *for* the wholly rational law of the categorical imperative. Only because the pure will is wholly rational and unaffected by the factical desires of the empirical self can it give itself the universal law that is valid for everyone at all times.

For Heidegger, on the other hand: "What is genuinely law-giving for willing is the actual pure willing itself [*das wirkliche reine Wollen selbst*] and nothing else" (279). No particular transcendental rational form can be allowed to dictate the factical actuality of pure willing; for Heidegger the will must be purified of all formulas. "In actual willing we bring ourselves into the situation where we must decide on the determining grounds of our action" (290). Is this anything other than an existential voluntarism, where our only duty is to decisively institute a law, to auto-nomously will a determination of our indeterminate essence?

As an interpretation of Kant, in any case, Heidegger's philosophy of "actual pure willing" is more violent than compelling. In the end it may serve best, indirectly and by way of hyperbole, to indicate certain problems with Kant's peculiar philosophy of a purely autonomous rational will, rather than to offer an appealing development of his practical philosophy. In order to fully respond to Heidegger's interpretive appropriation (which, as we shall see, ironically lays the groundwork for his later *criticism* of Kant's "philosophy of the will"), it would be necessary to clarify the tensions and difficulties within Kant's own position, a position that itself undergoes significant development. We would need to examine the tensions in Kant's thought between the universal rational will (*Wille*) and the finite factical "will" (*Willkür*) that chooses either to submit itself to this universal will of reason or to follow the natural inclinations of desire of the finite self.[12] As this would take us beyond the limits of this study, I shall limit myself here to marking several points where Kant's "categorical imperative" decisively resists incorporation into Heidegger's interpretive appropriation of it as "*the fundamental law of a finite pure willing* [das Grund-gesetz eines endlichen reinen Willens]" (281).

According to Heidegger, it is the "pure will" that *unilaterally* determines the law of practical reason, and not the other way around. The pure will is only experienced as a command or an imperative when "the pure will does not unreservedly follow its essence" (280). The essence of the will is not, however, to conform itself wholly to reason; for to "the holy will . . . the law is simply the willing of the will" (ibid.). It is crucial for Heidegger to repeatedly insist on this order: the pure will is not a mental perceptual event of the value of "an independently existing law [*eines an sich seienden Gesetzes*]"; on the contrary, "only because, and insofar as, the pure will wills, does the law exist [*ist das Gesetz*]" (295).

But for Kant, the autonomy of self-legislation was only half the story of the will; it is also a respectful response to the imperative of a wholly rational law. For Kant, the pure will and the law of practical reason cannot be separated; yet for heuristic purposes it would be more appropriate to say that the will is pure only to the extent that it conforms to the rational law, rather than to the extent that it forces the law to conform to it. In that the will is pure only insofar as it is rational, it would be misleading to say that Kant's law of practical reason is derived from the factical enactment of pure will. Heidegger himself clearly marks this distance between Kant and his own "fundamentally different problematic" when he writes:

> It is not a formula and rule that we come to understand, but the character of the specific actuality of that which is and becomes actual in and as action. *However,* Kant remains a long way from explicitly making this factuality as such into a central metaphysical problem, and from in this way bringing its conceptual articulation over into the essence of man and thereby reaching the threshold of *a fundamentally different problematic*. (294, emphases added)

Kant says that "we become conscious of the moral law 'as soon as we construct maxims for the will'" (285–86); but this "becoming conscious" is a factical enactment, not a factical creation. For Kant, the form of the law is thus not willed into existence in any arbitrary sense; it is revealed as universal. It is our capacity for rationally abstracting ourselves from our sensible inclinations—and in this sense, our ability to transcend our factical embeddedness—according to Kant, that gives us our autonomy, not our capacity to freely choose a maxim by which to live, and through which to disclose the world. In fact, as becomes more evident in the increasingly exact terminological development of Kant's thought, it is the *Willkür* that is our power of free choice, i.e., what we normally think of as the faculty of the will. Kant's peculiar notion of *Wille*, as the "purely rational law of freedom," can be chosen, submitted to or not; but its content is not subject to arbitrary factical decision.

A holy will, were it to exist, would indeed be wholly rational and therefore identical with the law. But since we are in fact beings internally torn between sensible desires (or more damningly still what Kant comes to see as "radical evil," an ineradicable wicked inclination to self-love in our natures) and a rational *Wille*, the law appears for us first and foremost as a *duty* and an *imperative* to which we, however reluctantly, must submit. Thus Kant can write, not just a treatise on autonomy, but also a "hymn to duty."

> Duty, though sublime and mighty name, that dost embrace nothing charming but requirest submission and yet seekest not to move the will by threatening . . . but only holdest forth a law which of itself finds entrance into the mind and gains reluctant reverence. . . .[13]

For Kant, then, factical human will is only free, pure, to the extent that it heeds this call of the rational moral law. Laying the "groundwork" for morals is a matter of making explicit the unequivocal form of the universal law, not a matter of willfully giving form to the formless. Hence, to call into question Kant's formulations of the categorical imperative is to call into question the very foundations of his practical philosophy.

According to Heidegger's interpretive appropriation, however, the "*fundamental law of the pure will, of pure practical reason*, is nothing other than the *form of law-giving* [Gesetzgebung]" (279). The only form of law that the pure will must obey is that which dictates that it must itself give the law form. The particular forms of the law that Kant gave are even said to be arbitrary! Heidegger, understandably, favors that form which says: "So act that the maxim of your will could always hold at the same time as the principle of a universal legislation."[14] But, Heidegger claims, it is not necessary to understand "the fundamental law of pure practical reason" in terms of "the formula of the Kantian categorical imperative." It is not the formula that is important, he tells us, for it is "only one among many philosophical interpretations" (291); Kant himself, it is pointed out, gave several different versions.

What is most revealing is the way Heidegger interprets the second Kantian formulation of the law: "Act so that you treat humanity, whether in your own person or in that of another, always as an end and never as a means only."[15] One would think that Kant is stressing here an imperative openness to the otherness of the other person which cannot, must not, be reduced to the circle of significations centered on the projection of a self-understanding. For Heidegger, however, the message here is first and foremost, not that of respect for the other as an end in him- or herself, but rather that of "self-responsibility: to bind oneself to oneself." To be sure, Heidegger claims that this is not to be done "egoistically and in relation to the accidental 'I,'" but rather in relation to the "the essence of one's self" (293). But how are we to distinguish the accidental self from the essential self without preserving some way (some form) of marking the distinction between the transcendental law and the law willed into existence by the factically existing Dasein? Can Heidegger's practical philosophy here, which resolutely subordinates the law to "concrete willing," maintain the crucial distinction between the "accidental ego" and the "essence of the self"? Whose concrete willing would lay the basis for the concrete laws of communal existence? We are left with Heidegger's assurances, in a passing cryptic remark, that the "actual willing, i.e., essential willing," will indeed bring about "understanding with the other, whose community is only the force of mystery, of the hidden actual willing of the individual" (294). Respect for the other person will follow; first learn to respect the pure willing of your own individual Dasein. This voluntarism of "finite [yet] pure willing" is the precarious groundwork for community that Heidegger's interpretation of Kant left one with in the summer of 1930.

In the following key passage of Heidegger's interpretive appropriation, Kant's practical philosophy, according to which autonomy is found only in respect for the law of reason, is hardly any longer recognizable.

> The purity of willing grounds the possibility of the universal validity of the law of the will. The reverse does not apply, i.e., the purity of willing is not a consequence of the universal validity of the law which is followed. If this willing of the pure will transcends the contingency of empirical action, this does not amount to becoming lost in the empty abstraction of a form of lawfulness valid in itself, such that what one is to do would remain entirely indeterminate. Rather, this transcending to pure willing is the coming into operation of one's own concrete willing, concrete because it actually wills willing and nothing else besides. (284–85)

In this affirmative teaching of *das Wollen wirklich wollen* we ironically find an early version of a *Wille zum Willen* in Heidegger's thought—not as a critical expression for the essence of technological nihilism, as it becomes for him later, but as the very essence of freedom.

One cannot, to be sure, simply equate this earlier affirmative notion with that later critical notion of the will to will, and it may in fact be more or less possible (in a more generous reading than I have seen fit to give here in this context) to interpretively retrieve and develop a sense of "obligation to ek-sistence" maintained in Heidegger's interpretive appropriation of Kant's practical philosophy, and to set this aspect in opposition to the self-positing will of subjectivity and to the utmost closure of ek-sistence in the immanent repetitions of the technological will to will.[16] Yet in light of the manner in which Heidegger himself politically applied this practical philosophy after 1930, and in reflecting back by way of imma-nent critique from the vantage point of Heidegger's own later radical cri-tique of all forms of voluntarism, it is also plainly necessary to indicate the profound dangers involved in attempting to think the freedom of Dasein in terms of a pure and yet concrete will that wills nothing but its own will-ing. And while it is certainly a possible and fruitful endeavor "to read the philosophy of Heidegger as a whole as a philosophy of freedom,"[17] one must nevertheless clearly mark not just the aspects of continuity, but also the decisive turn between this 1930 understanding of freedom as a "will-ing of will" and Heidegger's later understanding of freedom as a "letting beings be" (*GA* 9:188/144) that is "*originally* not connected with the will" (*VA* 28/330).

Between Voluntarism and Deference of Will: A Politics of Self-Assertion and Sacrifice

In the opening paragraphs of the Rectoral Address (given on May 27, 1933), we are told that the spiritual mission of the university, its role in the fate of the German *Volk* as a whole, must be *willed* (Heidegger's emphasis) if it is to have "the power to shape our existence" (*R* 9/29). He then goes on to explain these key terms of the Address—spiritual mission, German *Volk*, self-assertion, will to essence—as follows:

> The self-assertion of the German university is the original, common will to its essence. . . . The will to the essence of the German university is the will to science as the will to the historical spiritual mission of the German *Volk* as a *Volk* that knows itself in its state. Science and German destiny must, in this will to essence, achieve power *at the same time*. (10/30)

"The will to essence" alone can guarantee the success of the "struggle" of the university to assist in the struggle of the *Volk* to "fulfill its historical destiny." The university, in "asserting itself," contributes to the willing of the destiny of the state. Near the close of the speech Heidegger writes: "Whether such a thing [as the collapse of the "moribund pseudo-civilization" of the West] occurs or does not occur, this depends solely on whether we as a historico-spiritual *Volk* will ourselves. . . . But it is our will that our *Volk* fulfill its historical mission. . . . We will ourselves" (19/38).

The Rectoral Address fully unleashes what Derrida calls a "massive voluntarism" in thought and in politics. It is followed by a number of political speeches in which Heidegger draws freely on the rhetoric of the will, calling for self-assertion of the will of the German *Volk* as well as arguing for the need to sacrifice or defer one's will to the will of the state and specifically to the will of its Führer. In short, during his time as rector Heidegger traversed freely between extremes, while remaining firmly within the domain of the will. In an almost frenzied employment of the rhetoric of both self-assertion (willing) and sacrifice (deferred-willing), Heidegger not only entangles himself in the web of politics/metaphysics within the domain of the will, but does so in such a way as to reveal its dark side as few—if any—thinkers of his stature ever have.

One strategy I will take in this section is to let Heidegger speak against himself; that is, to show how he later rebukes precisely the elements of will that he embraces during his time as rector. My purpose in taking this approach of immanent critique is not merely to suggest that Heidegger learned his lesson and mended his ways, but rather (1) to show that many of his later criticisms of the will can be read as self-criticisms, and (2) to give concrete, if ironic, examples for what his later thought helps us to think against.

In this regard let us look for a moment at another passage from the Rectoral Address. It is claimed that "the will to the essence of the German university" arises out of "the resolve of the German students to stand firm in the face of the extreme distress of German fate" (*R* 15/34). In this context, Heidegger calls for "a true will" (*ein wahrer Wille*) as a kind of quasi-Kantian freedom of giving the law to oneself:

> This will is a true will, provided that the German students, through the new Student Law, place themselves under the law of their essence and thereby delimit this essence for the first time. To give law to oneself is the highest freedom. (15/34)

In striking contrast, approximately a decade later Heidegger argues that the autonomous self-will of idealism cuts the cloth in preparation for the will to power and ultimately the technological will to will. In "Overcoming Metaphysics" (1936–46) he writes:

> The aimlessness, indeed the essential aimlessness of the unconditional will to will, is the completion of the essence of will which was incipient in Kant's concept of practical reason as pure will. Pure will wills itself, and as the will is being. (*VA* 85/81)

In reading these two passages together, we can clearly see Heidegger's recoil from his philosophical embrace of the will and its unbounded employment in his political speeches of 1933–34. The quasi-Kantian exaltation of self-willing to the status of the highest freedom in the former is matched by its vilification as a step on the way to the aimless technological will to will in the latter.

The term "self-assertion," used in the title of the Rectoral Address, "The Self-Assertion of the German University," is also charged with resonances of willfulness; and this term too is later criticized by Heidegger himself as an element of voluntaristic "value thought" (see *N2* 67/33).[18] The Rectoral Address, however, teems with Heidegger's 1933 resolve to philosophically legitimize willful assertion, and it is hardly a coincidence that it simultaneously marks his debut in an involvement with the politics of fascism.

And yet, to be fair to the text, the Address still speaks in the name of a certain independence of the university; it calls for a self-assertion of the university, for its "self-governance"—this, he claims, "shall be preserved" (*R* 9/29). As is made clear in a lecture course given shortly after the Address, Heidegger's intention was to root the political destiny of the nation in its "spiritual-communal mission" (*geistig-volkliche Auftrag*), in other words, to root politics in a philosophy of the *Volk* and not the other way around (*GA* 36/37:3).[19] Moreover, the Address calls for a balance of power between leading and following; indeed, it is claimed, this "essential opposition . . . must neither be covered over nor . . . obliterated altogether" (18/38). The Rectoral Address is not yet a simple call for deference of the individual's will to the will of the state, even if in Heidegger's subsequent political speeches we do, on more than one occasion, find shockingly unqualified calls for asserting one's will only by way of sacrificing it in deference to the "towering willing of the *Führer.*"

While we must take care not to simply conflate the contexts of (and thus perhaps the degrees of "compromise" involved in) various types of text, Heidegger's subsequent speeches, articles, and memos presented during his brief tenure as rector are deplorable examples of a "thought" embedded in the most hideous corners of the domain of the will. Here we find, in two passages from political speeches during his time as rector, what can only be called the absolute zero point in Heidegger's (lack of) thought with regard to the problem of the will:

> There is only the one will to the full Dasein of the state [*Es gibt nur den einen Willen zum vollen Dasein des Staates*]. . . . The *Führer* has awakened this will in the entire *Volk* and has welded it into a single resolve [*Entschluss*]. (*GA* 16:189/49)

> For in what this will wills, we are only following the towering willing of our *Führer.* . . . To the man of this unprecedented will, to our *Führer* Adolf *Hitler*—a threefold "Sieg Heil!" (236/60)

In such passages Heidegger calls on students and others to wholly submit to the will of Hitler, who is said to embody the will of the *Volk* and the state. His call demands a deferral of one's will, an offering it up in service of a greater will. Dasein is here expanded to the Dasein of the state. The individual Dasein of the student is called upon to authentically will by sacrificing his or her will to "the one great will of the state" (235/59), a will that is unified in and by the will of its fascist leader, Adolf Hitler.

In these statements from Heidegger's political speeches we find the full range of the domain of the will in play. We are presented with a rhetoric of willful self-assertion coupled with a call to a deferential self-sacrifice, in other words, a call not simply to abandon one's will but to actively defer it to "the towering willing of the *Führer*." And who makes this call and in the name of what? The Führer himself, or rather, in this case his spokesman: the leader of the leader (*der Führer des Führers*), the would-be philosopher of the king. Neither leader, to be sure, simply and straightforwardly commands obedience to his individual arbitrary will. Rather, they each present their own personal will as the embodied (Hitler) or en-spirited (Heidegger) will of the German *Volk* and its historical mission. Voluntarism is thus thoroughly entwined with a quasi-fatalistic notion of destiny.

Heidegger's political speeches of 1933–34 are thus classic examples of the intertwining of (apparent) opposites within the domain of the will. A pivotal moment, which facilitates this flip-flopping among positions within the domain of the will, is the transference of the locus of authenticity from the individual to the group, from the Dasein that is in each case mine to the communal Dasein of the *Volk*. The radically individualized Dasein facing its own unique and non-transferable death gets reinscribed as the collective Dasein who inherits the destiny of the German nation. In retrospect, this transition can be interpreted as already (at least potentially) under way in the later sections of *Being and Time* (see SZ 384), where a Dasein and its "fate" (*Schicksal*) are placed within the "destiny" (*Geschick*) of a people.

The question of this transformation, from a *Je-meinigkeit* to a kind of *Je-unsrigkeit*, or from a *je einiges Dasein* to a *deutsches Dasein*,[20] is at issue in the "Logic" lectures from the summer of 1934. Although Heidegger's original manuscript inexplicably disappeared sometime after 1954 (see *GA* 38:173), these lectures have now been published from several sources of student notes as volume 38 of the *Gesamtausgabe*. Based on an earlier, overtly polemical publication of one set of notes, Rüdiger Safranski interprets the transformation that reportedly took place in these lectures as follows:

> "The self," [Heidegger] argued, "is not a distinguishing determination
> of the 'I.'" What is important is the "we-ourselves." In his endeavors for

the "I-myself," the individual loses the ground under his feet; he "stands in the lostness to the Self" because he seeks the Self in the wrong place, in the detached "I." It can be found only in the "We." . . . The inauthentic We is the They, the authentic We is the nation that asserts itself as one man. "A national whole, therefore, is a man on the large scale."[21]

Based on the more complete and scholarly edition of these lectures now available, let us give here a bit more nuanced account. Heidegger does clearly state: "The self [*Selbst*] is not a distinguishing determination of the I. This is the fundamental error of modern thinking" (*GA* 38:38), and in particular of "liberalism" (see 149). But he also claims that the "we" does not necessarily have priority over the "I," at least "as long as in this case the task is not grasped and presented for the wise" (51). The question of the "we," just as the question of the "I," must be based on the question of the "self," and not vice versa. Properly grasped in this manner, the question of the "we-self" does end up taking precedence. "We nevertheless asked: 'Who are *we* ourselves [*Wer sind* wir *selbst*]?' In this way we avoid equating the I and the self. This also affords us an advantage, namely that the question, who *we* ourselves are, is appropriate to the times [*zeitgemäß*], in distinction from the time of liberalism, the I-time. Now would be the we-time" (50–51). Asking the question in terms of the "we," however, is said to in no way guarantee that the question of the self is properly raised. "With the outcry 'we!' we can mistake our self just as much as in the glorification of the I" (51). Indeed, Heidegger recognizes that the cry "We!" carries with it the dangerous potential to "even drive self-being into criminality" (ibid.). Nevertheless, while he consistently resists defining the "we" or the *Volk* merely in terms of geography or biology (see 56), Heidegger continues to pursue the question of the self in terms of the we, and specifically in terms of the *Volk* and the state as the "historical being of the *Volk*" (165). The we, he says, is founded in a type of decision (*Entscheidung*), namely, in historical resoluteness (*geschichtliche Entschlossenheit*).

Heidegger does not want to "describe," but rather to enact this resolute decision that carries out the determination of the we. He thus addresses his students directly:

> In that we are involved in these demands of the university, we will the will of a state, which itself wills to be nothing other than the master will and master form of a *Volk* over itself. As Dasein we insert ourselves in our own way into the belongingness to a *Volk*; we stand in the being of the *Volk*; we are this *Volk* itself. . . . What happened? We submitted ourselves to the *Augenblick*. With the turn of expression, "We are here [*Wir sind da*]," engaged in an educational happening, something is carried

> out. . . . We can test this by examining whether we, in our speaking
> together, can say what has just been expressed: "Yes, this is what I will. I
> will to place myself under these demands, to submit myself to the power
> of a will, to stand together with will [*mich fügen in die Macht eines Willens,
> mit Willen mitstehen*]. (57)

Heidegger explicitly denies that this willful decision to the we-self
can be thought in terms of egoism (64), or that the Dasein of this we-self
that wills itself can be understood in terms of modern "subjectivity"
(156ff.). "Through this decision we are rather sent out beyond ourselves
into the belongingness to the *Volk*" (64). "Resoluteness," for its part, "is
not a matter of a blind amassing of a large amount of so-called willpower";
it involves rather an "un-locking for the mystery" and an "acting drawn
away into being," which essentially entails "the possibility of going-under
[*Untergangs*], i.e., sacrifice" (160). In any case, a resolute deference of the
I to the we is affirmed here as a willing and willful sacrifice of will to a
greater will, namely to that of the *Volk* and its own historical mission of
sacrifice and mastery. Regardless of whatever essential differences remained between the reality of racist Nazism and Heidegger's spiritual vision of its potential "inner truth and greatness," the *Volk* philosophy that
Heidegger affirmatively taught in 1934 appears disturbingly similar to
what we shall in a moment see him later critically denouncing (or renouncing), namely, the deceptive transference of the locus of will—and
he eventually comes to see the will as inseparable from subjectivity—by
way of an "insertion of the I into the we."

But before we move to this (self-)critique, let us elaborate on what
we might call a "logic of deferred-willing." When the locus of subjectivity
is transferred from the individual to the collective whole, or to a leader
who stands for that whole, and when subjectivity is essentially willful subjectivity, then individuals, in the name of their own higher authenticity,
are called on to sacrifice, to actively defer, their wills to this whole. In such
a case, as Richard Wolin has correctly noted, "voluntarism and fatalism go
hand in hand"; thus "National Socialist ideology emphasized—at times in
the same breath—both the importance of German historical 'destiny' as
well as the unshakable character of the 'will' of the German *Volk*."[22] Wolin
cites in this regard a passage from J. P. Stern's book, *Hitler: The Führer and
the People*, that is worth reproducing here; for it offers an illuminating account of the peculiar pendulum swings in fascist regimes between one extreme and the other within the domain of the will.

> It is obvious that the more "absolute" the Will becomes, and therefore
> the further removed from all concrete means, the more ineffectual it will

be, and the more its assertions will resemble childish tantrums. . . . [At] the point where the self is so imperiously asserted a curious reversal, from complete subjectivity and arbitrariness to what looks like its opposite is said to take place. In declaring "the Will" absolute, the ideologist makes a show of replacing the subjective self by an objective principle; "the will" is now to be seen as a cosmic "law" *and* as an element of a religious faith.[23]

The individual's will, frustrated in its overt attempts at dominance, looks to a higher Will to which the individual can defer and receive in return a partitioning of its power and protection, perhaps even a title to its representation; or else the individual cunningly projects this higher Will himself in a deceptive act of covert-willing.

Did Heidegger's path of thought lead him down such a deceptive and destructive dead-end road? Was his deference to the destining of being through the medium of the German *Volk* an enormous exercise in deferred-willing? Was his political attempt—or more precisely his attempt to ground politics in something more fundamental—to "lead the leader" merely a power politics strategy of covert-willing? Was the thinker's access to the "sending of being," which determines the entire history of the West, a trump card that Heidegger played in this poker game of covert-willing only after being excluded from Hitler's charade of embodying the will of the German *Volk*?

As we shall see, even after Heidegger's withdrawal from the political arena, the language and what might be called the "ur-politics" of will and power do not simply fade away. Stepping down from the rectorship, Heidegger did not immediately attain insight into the full reach of the problem of the domain of the will. Indeed, his retreat back into that "more essential" dimension of thought did at times seem more like a search for a trump card in the game of power politics than a problematization of this game as such. In a revealing passage from his 1935 *Introduction to Metaphysics,* for instance, in speaking of the destinal role of Germany, that "most metaphysical of *Volk*" in the center of Europe, Heidegger claims that "this *Volk* . . . must transpose itself and thereby the history of the West . . . into the originary realm of the powers [*Mächte*] of being. . . . [The] great decision regarding Europe . . . can come about only through the development of new, historically spiritual forces [*geistiger Kräfte*] from the center" (*EM* 29). One cannot help but suspect that the problem of the will is here, far from being overcome, repeated on a deeper level. If Nazi "political science" is rejected as "fishing in the troubled waters of 'values' and 'totalities'" (*EM* 152), then on behalf of his *Volk* Heidegger would descend into the covert depths to reveal its destiny sent by the greater powers that be.

It may be tempting to write off the history of being (and even Heidegger's later thought altogether) by reference to these moments or aspects of covert-willing; and in fact hasty critics looking for an excuse not to have to follow the more radically challenging implications of Heidegger's path of thought are often quick to highlight and exaggerate this aspect. Such critics, situating Heidegger's thought wholly within the domain of the will (and hence reading the "turn" as merely a further flip-flopping between voluntarism and fatalism), are quick to close the book on the Heidegger case: *Entschlossenheit* equals voluntaristic resoluteness; the *Volk*, the destiny of the West, being equal objects of a fatalistic deferred-willing, if not projections of a cunning covert-willing; case closed. But what this reductionist reading misses, among other things, is the *movement* of Heidegger's thought, a movement of self-critique as well as a twisting free toward something other than the domain within which such impatient critics insist on situating their reading, a movement which, despite its points of slippage and regression (points which must indeed not only be admitted but vigilantly exposed *and thought*), cannot be reduced to a pendulum swing within this domain. Whether or not there is anything worth salvaging from that great "blunder of thought" that occurred in Heidegger's politics of 1933–34, his subsequent path of thought cannot be summed up in, or reduced to, the language of voluntarism/fatalism; it is indeed Heidegger's later thought which helps us critically expose the metaphysical roots of this very domain of the will.

To be sure, after thoroughly entangling himself and his thought in the domain of the will during the period of his political errancy, a recovery did not come easy; yet here too we have much to learn by retracing Heidegger's firsthand struggle towards (seeing the task of thought as one of) twisting free of the domain of the will.

Heidegger's Later (Self-)Critique of Deferred-Willing

Let us look here at several points on his thought-path where Heidegger doubles back in (self-)critique of the voluntarism/fatalism of (his support of) Nazism. In the years following his own embrace of such notions, Heidegger recoils from the idea of a "common will," and specifically from the idea that the willfulness of individualism should be overcome by calling on individuals to sacrifice their wills to the higher will of the state or its leader.

In the 1936–38 *Contributions to Philosophy,* Heidegger continues to see the *Volk* as an important philosophical category ("Who would deny," he asks, "that philosophy is philosophy 'of a *Volk*'?" [*GA* 65:42]). And yet, he not only chastises those who think they know what a *Volk* is (especially those who think it is based on race!), but is also sharply critical of the idea of the *Volk* as an end in itself; "for, preservation of a *Volk* is never a possible goal but only the condition for setting goals" (*GA* 65:99; see also 139). For his own part, Heidegger strictly subordinates the *Volk* to Da-sein, the latter in turn grounding and grounded by being. He also begins to critically connect the notion of *Volk*-centered thought with the "liberal" notion of the "ego" (i.e., egoism), and writes of the danger involved in raising the question of "who we are." A few years after having given speeches identifying the "true will" as that which wills itself in willing its allegiance to Hitler's National Socialism, Heidegger writes the following in *Contributions:*

> For us the danger involved in this question [of who we are] is in itself
> essential; the danger that it looses the appearance of being in opposition
> to the new German will. . . . But [above all] the question "who we are?"
> must remain purely and fully enjoined with the grounding question:
> how does beyng essence [*wie west das Seyn*]? (54)

In these lines Heidegger gives us a key for understanding his involvement with and move away from National Socialism. The danger, to which Heidegger himself presumably succumbed in 1933, would be that of collapsing the notion of the self-willing of a community with that of the proper will which "wills the truth of beyng" (48). The latter must be distinguished, Heidegger writes, from any self-willing insofar as "the will to self-*being* invalidates the question" (49). The question of who we are is not answered by willing ourselves, but only by way of standing outside ourselves in resolutely asking the question: *Wie west das Seyn?* A "turn" in the primary orientation of Heidegger's thinking, from the being of the individual Dasein to the Da-sein of being, is thus decisively made by this point; but on the path of this turn Heidegger stumbled in 1933 towards the pitfall of an inflated form of willful subjectivity: the German *Volk* as a political entity. In the sequel volume of notes from 1938–39, *Besinnung* (*Mindfulness*), Heidegger goes so far as to ridicule "the poor fool" who would make the "comical claim that the individual subject (in *Being and Time*) would now have to be replaced by the *Volk*-subject" (*GA* 66:144). Yet had he himself not fallen into the proximity of such foolery?

By 1947, in any case, Heidegger had worked out his own severe critique of nationalism, Nazi or otherwise: "Every nationalism is metaphysically an anthropologism, and as such subjectivism" (*GA* 9:341/260). In passages such as this and the following, Heidegger comes as close as he ever does to a penetrating (self-)critique of the Nazi state, or of any attempt to solve the problem of the will by way of immersion in a larger communal Will.

> Man has become *subiectum*. He can determine and realize the essence of
> subjectivity, always in keeping with the way in which he conceives him-
> self and wills himself. Man as a rational being in the age of the Enlight-

enment is no less subject than is man who grasps himself as a nation, wills himself as a *Volk,* fosters himself as a race, and, finally, empowers himself as lord of the earth. Still in all these fundamental positions of subjectivity, a different kind of I-ness and egoism is also possible; . . . Subjective egoism . . . can be canceled out through the insertion of the I into the we. Through this, subjectivity only gains in power. (*GA* 5:110–11/152; see also *GA* 54:204–5)

Heidegger acutely points out here that the problem of egoism cannot be resolved by the insertion of the willful I into a willful We, that is, into an "egoism of a *Volk.*"

It is nevertheless also necessary here to critically analyze the implications of Heidegger's criticism. With respect to the logic operating in such passages, which tend to reduce the problem of Nazi fascism to the "more basic" or "more encompassing" problem of subjectivism seen on the "deeper level" or "larger scale" of the history of being, there arises the question of whether in the fascist state the subjectivism underlying the entire modern epoch is revealed in the horrible form it can and did take, or whether Heidegger thereby belittles the evils of Nazism (and hence his involvement in it) by reducing it to one more example of the general problem of subjectivity, technology, and will.

Soon after stepping down from the rectorship, in his lectures Heidegger began to criticize the reality (if not "the inner truth and greatness" [*EM* 152], that is, his own "private National Socialism" [*R* 30/23]) of Nazism as among the manifestations of the frenzy of technology and its forgetfulness of the essential. Already in 1935 he writes in scorn of the "mass meetings attended by millions" (read: the Nuremberg rallies) as a technological "transformation of humans into masses" (*EM* 29); and such criticisms abound in his lectures until the end of the war, at least for "anyone with ears to hear" (*SP* 93/101). By the time of his 1945 "apology" ("The Rectorate 1933/34: Facts and Thoughts"), Heidegger criticizes Nazi fascism (along with the other modern political forms of "world democracy" and "communism") as being part of the nihilistic reality of "the universal rule of the will to power within planetary history" (*R* 25/18).

Heidegger's penetrating insight into the pervasiveness of the various facets of technology and will, facets which infect or even underlie some of our most cherished ideals, is both the merit of his thought and its danger; for while "essentially connecting" fascism and democracy (or, as Lacoue-Labarthe's controversial statement has it, Nazism and humanism)[24] may open up an important possibility of critically viewing that prevailing ideology of our own age, certainly it also covers over some quite essential differences. Vital differences are also infamously covered over when on one occasion Heidegger "essentially" equates the "motorized food industry" with "the gas chambers and the extermination camps" (*GA* 79:27).[25] Perhaps, as Derrida suggests, the most generous reading of Heidegger's silence regarding the unique horror of the Holocaust is one which sees it as a confession of an inability to say anything, a failure of his thought to provide the terms with which to think that atrocity in its singularity, in its ghastly difference from other mundane forms of technological manipulation.[26]

In chapter 9 we shall return to a number of questions regarding the residues of will in Heidegger's later thought. In the present context, however, it has been important to also note the extent to which Heidegger does indeed criticize the problem of the (domain of the) will in Nazism, and, at least implicitly, in the blunder of his own involvement therewith. We have seen that the later Heidegger explicitly repudiates the idea that the will can be overcome by its insertion into a "larger will," and specifically the notion that a "nationalism," by purportedly overcoming individual willfulness in the forging of the common will of a *Volk,* thereby overcomes the problem of the will as such. In such deferential sublations, the will of subjectivity "only gains in power."

Thinking the Affair: On Relating Heidegger's Nazism to His Philosophy

The "Heidegger Affair" or "Heidegger Controversy" has become something of a boom—if not in every case living up to its potential as a boon—for thought over the years.[27] It is perhaps one of the most decisive, and certainly one of the most divisive, philosophical issues of our time. If the "Heidegger Controversy" is to contribute to a genuine questioning, of Heidegger *and of ourselves,* it must not be just another occasion to rewind and repeat certain self-assured liberal democratic/free-market capitalist platitudes, but must become an occasion to critically question and be questioned, to think.

Nevertheless, despite Heidegger's persistent skepticism (see *SP* 96/ 104), I do believe that we must at least agree with Lacoue-Labarthe when he writes that democracy is for us today "the only more or less livable political reality."[28] Heidegger's (mis)understanding and distrust of democracy, while thought-provoking, is one of the most problematical aspects of his thought. He failed to see that a central thrust behind the movement of democracy (and democracy is at its best always on the move) is the attempt to let individuals and groups be heard, to let them be in their differences within and from the political whole; democracy is not just a matter of reducing the political to a regulated space of a battle between egoistic wills, though it is too often this too. In any case, an acceptance and even active support of liberal democracy as the best, or at least the "most livable" of today's political options should not prevent one from rigorously continuing to question its current forms, and their (essential?) compromises with technological and capitalistic willfulness.

In this regard we may still have much to learn from Heidegger's thought, despite his errant haste in 1933–34, and despite the residues of cultural chauvinism that remain in his thought to the end. Only if we overcome the all too easy black-and-white confidence of victor's justice, that is, the tendency to completely whitewash ourselves (the realities as well as the ideals of liberal democracy and free-market capitalism) in contrast to the clearly abhorrent evils of the Third Reich, only if we learn to question ourselves without blurring what we must stand against, can we break out of the logic which simply equates the lesser of two evils, or even what is clearly a relative good, with an absolute and *unquestionable* good.

Moreover, Heidegger's thought can, if we interpretively engage in letting it, participate in our questioning and thinking the errant revolution of Nazism. Thinking with Heidegger, we learn, among other things, to question Heidegger in certain illuminating ways. Despite, then, Heidegger's infamous "silence" after the war regarding the Nazi Holocaust, we should take seriously his own later (too often implicit) criticisms of his blunder—not only his political blunder but (if the two can be separated) his blunder in thought, his reduction of thought to a matter of will. Heidegger is at times and in places his own best critic, and his own best foil. We must at least begin here with the attempt at an "immanent critique." Only by having learned to "think *with* Heidegger *against* Heidegger," can we begin to think *after* Heidegger.[29] This is not meant as a general imperative for thought. I do not presume to claim that "because Heidegger is the greatest thinker of our time," in order to "think" at all one must pass through Heidegger. But I do want to claim that *if* one is to critically think *about Heidegger,* then one should at least in part begin by attempting to think *with him,* according to his way of thought, including the manner in which, as we have seen, this way doubles back in implicit critique of his own embrace of the will.

On the other hand, there is the question of the connection between Heidegger's early philosophy and his political involvement. While Heidegger's resolute decision to support Hitler's political will in 1933 cannot be simply deduced from his 1930 philosophical affirmation of "pure factical willing," his philosophical embrace of the will certainly did help free up the way for his political commitment. When we look back to *Being and Time,* it is yet more difficult to ascertain the extent to which Heidegger's philosophy led him toward his political disaster and the extent to which Heidegger failed to live up to the critical possibilities of his philosophy when he lapsed into participation with the politics of willful resolve.[30] Critics such as Karl Löwith have argued unequivocally for the former: "Heidegger did not 'misunderstand himself' when he supported Hitler; on the contrary, anyone who did not comprehend how he could do this, did not understand him."[31]

And yet, we have seen that *Being and Time* in part problematizes the will, by showing how the call of conscience calls for its repeated interruption, and by showing the inauthenticity of deferring decisions to "the they." Decisions must be made by the individual Dasein in the face of its deathliness, and in the resolve to "take it back" as the factical situation demands. Willful resolve is tempered by a resolute openness to the need to repeatedly let one's projects be interrupted and to recast them in light of changing circumstances. The call of conscience would presumably never call on one to sacrifice one's will to the will of another, for such a deferential act would amount to forsaking one's responsibility in the face of one's own existential mortality, and falling into a passive submission to "the they."

However, it is also the case that the radically individualized existentialism which pervades most of *Being and Time* gives way in its later sections to discussions of "co-historizing" (see *SZ* 384); and certain passages there can in fact, in retrospect in any case, be read as foreshadowing a deference to a communal will. And despite the fact that the call of conscience is connected with the radically individuating moment of running ahead to one's own death, in one cryptic passage, for instance, Heidegger writes that when "Dasein is resolute, it can become the 'conscience' of others" (*SZ* 298). Would this imply that some would defer their own proper willing-to-have-a-conscience to that of another? Heidegger claims that in being resolute we can authentically be with one another communally, as opposed to the inauthentic herding together of the they. In one of the most suggestive (if unfortunately underdeveloped) passages on "being-with" (*Mitsein*) in *Being and Time*, Heidegger makes a distinction between "leaping-in" for another and "leaping-ahead" for him. The former would entail taking over the other's task for him, wherein "the other can become one who is dominated and dependent, even if this domination is a tacit one and remains hidden from him" (*SZ* 122)—a classic covert tactic in power politics within the domain of the will. In contrast to this usurpation of the other's care, however, the second possibility of "authentic care" "helps the other to become transparent to himself *in* his care and to become free for it" (ibid.). Here is perhaps intimated a non-willing manner of being-with, perhaps even the seeds of a non-willing "community of those with nothing in common," based neither on the formation of a communal will nor on a piecemeal social contract of fundamentally antagonistic wills, but on a shared exposure to mortal finitude.

And yet, Heidegger's own political speeches of 1933–34 are hardly a lesson in authentic being-with, and the call there to sacrifice one's will to the will of the Führer makes highly suspicious in retrospect *Being and Time*'s talk of the possibility of Dasein to "choose its hero" (*SZ* 385). Would the ultimate choice then be a matter of choosing to whom the burden of choice would henceforth be deferred, choosing that greater Will to which one's own will would be sacrificed and offered up?

The relation of Heidegger's 1933–34 politics to his previous philosophy is thus an extremely ambiguous one, reflecting the ambiguity of the role of the will in the text of *Being and Time* itself. In the next section of this chapter I move on to examine some of Heidegger's writings in the years following his political failure. One might expect to find an about-face, a sudden awaking from his political folly and an immediate repudiation of thinking within the domain of the will. We might expect that the "autobiographical event" of his failure in politics would lead him to cast off the philosophy of will and leap into his mature thought which sees the will, not favorably as the essence of human freedom, but critically as the historical curse of modernity. But the case is far from this simple; his turn from the will does not take place as an overnight conversion. The will remains an essential element of Heidegger's thought throughout most of the 1930s, and in these years undergoes alteration, bifurcation, and qualification before finally being claimed unsalvageable and abandoned, or rather repositioned as the nemesis in Heidegger's critique of modern metaphysics and the technological worldview.

Heidegger's later thought itself (as we shall see in chapter 9) is not wholly innocent of the problem of the will, and his continued Greco-German ethnocentrism, for example, carries forward certain themes of his *Volk*-politics from the 1930s.[32] His later thought does, however, increasingly develop a radical critique of the will. The later Heidegger learns, and can teach us, to critically think not only passive fallenness and willful projection, but also the self-assertion of and/or deference to a "higher Will." But learning to see the task of thought as one of twisting free of the very domain of the will, we shall now see, takes a number of years and several major texts following his withdrawal from politics in 1934.

The Search for a Proper Will After 1934

The Indirect Path of Hölderlin's Poetry

It is noteworthy that one year after his political failure Heidegger gave his first lecture course on poetry. This step back from the apparently all too

ontic arena of politics to the more fundamental realm of thinking in cor-
respondence to the *Dichtung* of that "poet of poets," Hölderlin, signals a
significant shift in Heidegger's thought. This shift is manifold. On the one
hand, it prolongs his political aspirations by rooting them in this purportedly more decisive and uncompromised ur-political realm of discourse. Hölderlin is also, for Heidegger, the "poet of the Germans," the
poet who sings their destiny at the center of Europe. In his 1934–35 course
on Hölderlin, Heidegger claims: "The historical Dasein of a *Volk* . . . originates in poetry. From the latter [arises] authentic knowing, in the sense
of philosophy. From these two, the actualization of the Dasein of a *Volk* as
a *Volk* through the state—politics originates" (*GA* 39:51).[33] In this respect,
the turn to Hölderlin continues rather than disrupts Heidegger's ethno-
centric ur-politics, his spiritual version of Nazism.[34]

Moreover, the elements of voluntarism/fatalism in Heidegger's
thought did not simply evaporate even when interpreting Hölderlin's
poetry. The poet's task, he claims in the 1934 lectures, is to suffer and endure the fate of being; but this suffering, he tells us,

> does not mean the merely passive being struck by another, but rather
> suffering [*Er-leiden*] as *struggling against and creating beyng only in enduring*
> [Leiden]. Beyng as fate [*Schicksal*] has its origin not in the pushing of
> something decreed, or assigned, as purely unalterable "lot," . . . but
> rather surmounting the breach and willing-back [*Zurückwollen*] from
> there into the origin characterize beyng as fate. (*GA* 39:235)

This interplay between polarities within the domain of the will, between
suffering and struggle or fate and will, characterizes Heidegger's thought
of the mid-1930s, as we shall see when we examine the central text from
that period, *Introduction to Metaphysics*.

On the other hand, however, the turn to Hölderlin is not merely a
change of turf, but marks the beginning of a genuine turn from (the Nazi
politics of) the will. The "fundamental attunement" which Heidegger
gleans from his reading of Hölderlin—for whom, as D. F. Krell points out,
"poetizing was anything but willful assertion"—is that of "sacred mourning" for the gods that have flown. In contrast to a self-assertion in the face
of "the death of God" (see *R* 13/33), the attitude is now that of a "resolute
preparedness for the awaiting of the divine" (*GA* 39:95). As Miguel de
Beistegui points out, "this readiness is now progressively stripped from the
activistic and voluntaristic overtones in which it was draped in 1933," and
yet neither does it represent a turnabout to a mere passivity.[35]

Looking ahead to a text on Hölderlin from 1943, for example, after
Heidegger has himself ceased to use the term "will" in a positive sense, he

takes great pains to defuse any possible "misunderstanding" of the appearance of this word in a line from Hölderlin which reads: "But that which comes is what I will." Heidegger interprets:

> What is meant by "will" here is in no way the egoistically driven compulsion of a selfishly calculated desire. Will is the knowing readiness for belonging to destiny. This will wills only what is coming, for what is coming has already addressed this will, "calling" [*heißt*] on it to know and stand in the wind of its promise [*Verheißung*]. (*EHD* 87/111)

Amidst the storm of willful assertion and sacrifice, even Heidegger's earliest interpretations of Hölderlin foreshadow his increasingly self-conscious attempt to intimate a gentler current of thoughtful correspondence to the address of being.

By 1942 Heidegger becomes convinced through his reading of Hölderlin that if a "measure" is to be found on this earth, this can happen neither by way of actively willing nor by way of passively not-willing.

> If we merely attempt to set or seize upon the measure with our own power, then it becomes measureless and disintegrates into nothingness. If we merely remain thoughtless and without the alertness of a searching anticipation [*prüfenden Ahnens*], then again no measure is revealed. (*GA* 53:205)

In 1963 Heidegger makes clear that this *Prüfung* has nothing to do with a willful "testing" or "scrutinizing," but is of a kind where all "willfulness must bow down and fall away" (*EHD* 196/225).

The influence of Hölderlin on Heidegger's "second turn" should not be underestimated, and much of his later attempt to think non-willing(ly) is developed in dialogue with Hölderlin's poetry. And yet, Heidegger tells us in his preface to the *Nietzsche* volumes that "the *Elucidations of Hölderlin's Poetry* . . . sheds only indirect light" on "the path of thought I followed from 1930 to the 'Letter on Humanism' (1947)" (*NI* 10/xl). It is the *Nietzsche* volumes themselves, he tells us, that provide the direct view of this path. It is indeed in his *Auseinandersetzung* with Nietzsche's philosophy of the will to power that we find the most decisive site of his turn away from the will.

The dialogue with the poets, while essential, is of a different nature than is his dialogue with other philosophers and thinkers. The dialogue between thinking and poetry, he tells us, is one that takes place between those "who dwell near one another on mountains most separate" (*GA* 9:312/237). Heidegger's dialogue with "the poet of poets," which itself goes through several stages,[36] thus takes place alongside a more direct line of development in his dialogue with philosophers, a line which goes through a number of significant texts from the mid-1930s, including the lecture courses *Introduction to Metaphysics* (1935) and *Schelling's Treatise on the Essence of Human Freedom* (1936), as well as the private manuscripts of *Contributions to Philosophy* (1936–38) and its sequel volumes, before reaching that pivotal confrontation gathered in the two *Nietzsche* volumes. In the remainder of this chapter I focus on *Introduction* and *Contributions*. The following chapter is devoted to Heidegger's reading of Schelling's philosophy of the will, and the *Nietzsche* volumes, which have been with us from the beginning of this study, are again the focus of much of chapter 6.

Violence and *Wissen-Wollen* in *Introduction to Metaphysics*

In the 1935 lecture course later published as *Introduction to Metaphysics,* composed in the aftermath of his frustrated political engagement and after his first extensive meditations on Hölderlin's poetic word, Heidegger once again takes up the question of being in dialogue with the beginnings of the Western philosophical tradition. This text is significant for its thematic exposition of the question of being and its original, if controversial, interpretations of Greek thought. In the present context, I shall keep my reflections focused on the problem of the will. This concern is, however, hardly a peripheral one; for it is in this text, more than anywhere else, that Heidegger defines the relation between man and being in "willful" terms. The language of violence and power (*Gewalt*), of man "doing battle with" and "bringing to a stand" the "overpowering onslaught" of being, pervades the work. Although the arena is no longer the war-bound politics of Hitler's regime, military metaphors and the language of power tactics are transposed onto the "more essential" realm of the question of being. Heidegger's text enacts a thoughtful battle with the powers of being for the sake of Germany, the West, and then the earth as a whole (see *EM* 32). And what is won in this battle is a retrieval of an idea of the essence of human being from the Greeks, an idea which sees man as essentially engaged in a "struggle" (*polemos* or *Kampf*) for unconcealment, that is, in a "continuous conflict [*ständiger Widerstreit*]" (146) with and for being.

The initial turn in Heidegger's thought has here already been made in the sense that the meaning of being is not approached by way of an analysis of individual Dasein, nor does even the collective Dasein of the university or the state form the focus of the investigation; rather, "the question of human being [*Menschsein*] is now determined in its direction and scope solely through the question about *being*" (156). Understanding is not grounded in Dasein's resolutely choosing its possibility-for-being, and beings are not oriented to Dasein as the ultimate for-the-sake-of-which; but rather, "apprehension happens for-the-sake-of [*umwillen*] being. . . . Being rules [*waltet*], but because it rules and insofar as it rules and appears, apprehension *also* necessarily occurs *along with* appearance" (106). Man, in belonging to being, participates in this appearing by way of apprehension. That man belongs to and participates in being remains a constant theme of the later Heidegger's thought. Yet what is crucial here is to attend to the manner in which this participation is characterized.

"Apprehension" (*Vernehmung*) is the translation Heidegger gives in *Introduction* for the Greek word *noein*. Of the latter he writes: "When troops take up a position to receive the enemy, then they will [*wollen*] to meet the enemy that is coming toward them, and meet him in such a way that they at least bring him to a halt, a stand. *Noein* involves this receptive bringing-to-a-stand of that which appears" (105). As reflected in this deployment of military metaphor, the relation between man and being is thought of in terms of power and violence, that is, as "the *polemos* of *physis* and the violent essence of human being."[37] Being (*physis*) is thought as the rising up of the "overpowering" (*Überwältigende*), while for man, "the use of power/violence [*Gewaltbrauchen*] is the basic trait not only of his action but of his Dasein" (115).

> Man is the violence-doer [*Gewalt-tätige*], not aside from and along with other attributes but solely in the sense that from the ground up and in his violence-doing he uses violence [*Gewalt*] against the overpowering [*Überwältigende*]. (Ibid.)

To be sure, Heidegger's use of the expression "doing violence" is meant to indicate something which "in principle reaches beyond the usual meaning" of "brutality and arbitrariness [*Willkür*]." Yet, it cannot be denied that a certain will-fullness is implied. In fact, it is not only implied, since Heidegger explicitly and affirmatively employs the language of "will" in this text. Man's role is said to be that of questioning being, questioning as a "*willing*-to-know" (*Wissen*-wollen), where "the willing as well as the knowing is of *a very particular kind* [ureigener Art]" (17). Knowledge in its "authentic sense" is what the Greeks originally meant by *techne;* the latter is understood as follows:

> *Techne* characterizes the *deinon*, the violence-doing, in its decisive basic trait; for to do violence [*Gewalt-tätigkeit*] is to use power/violence [*Gewalt-brauchen*] against the overpowering [*Überwältigende*]: the knowing struggle to set being, which was formerly closed off, into what appears as beings. (122)

Knowing can only take place by way of a questioning of being that involves a willful use of power/violence against its overpowering onslaught. One does not here piously wander down a *Holzweg* into an open-region of *Gelassenheit;* a clearing must be hacked open by a counterforce to the chaotic onslaught of *physis;* questioning is the woodcutter's battle ax of thought. Derrida is correct in pointing out that, at least during this period of his development, the "questioning" at the center of Heidegger's thought is a matter of willing: "To question is to will to know" (16).[38] This *Wissen-wollen* sets the tone (or the fundamental attunement) for Heidegger's thought in *Introduction to Metaphysics.*

The following year (1936) Heidegger went to Rome to assure his fellow Europeans, in a lecture entitled "Europa und die deutsche Philosophie," that the *Wissen-wollen* of German philosophy is alive and well and ready for the dual task of "protecting the European peoples from the Asiatic" and "overcoming Europe's own uprooting and fragmentation" ("EdP" 31). In conclusion to this lecture he reminds us that "true knowing is genuine will and vice versa. . . . *Wissenwollen* is the fight for truth" (41).

After his turn from the will, however, his earlier embrace of *Wissen-wollen* necessarily becomes the subject of Heidegger's explicit self-(re)interpretation and (implicit) self-critique. In a parenthetical addition to the 1953 publication of *Introduction to Metaphysics,* Heidegger attempts to defuse the willful connotations (or rather *denotations*) of the term *Wissen-wollen* by claiming that implicit therein is the idea that "all willing should be grounded in letting-be" (*EM* 16). While the original text may claim that "willing" here must be understood as of "a very particular kind," there is little in this text of 1935 to lead us to understand the violence of its willing as grounded in a non-willing letting-be. On the contrary, there is much, as we have seen, to confirm our suspicions (if suspicions that the language of "will" has "willful overtones" need confirming in the first place) that the text uses the language of "will" to mean what it says.

We must, to be sure, take care not to close ourselves off to the mutations of language in texts where Heidegger is attempting to twist through and beyond traditional dichotomies and patterns of thought in the struggle to say something different (i.e., not simply something opposite within the same domain). Indeed, a fundamental difficulty in the attempt to think a sense of "non-willing" together with Heidegger is that the accustomed terms of our tradition always seem to connote either a sense of willing or of not-willing, such that "all such names at once misinterpret [non-willing] as pertaining to the [domain of the] will" (*G* 58/80). And yet, on the other hand, we must not be overeager to find in every text from every period of Heidegger's thought only various attempts to express non-willing—i.e., as what "he must have really been trying to say." We must often resist even Heidegger's own self-(re)interpretations for the sake of forthrightly following his wandering path, a path which turns through an embrace of the will. We must learn from the points where he stumbles, and even backtracks on this path, as well as from the new clearings toward which his thought gestures.

Heidegger himself does not always shy from radically criticizing former key terms of his thought; *Wissen-wollen* is among them. In 1954 he writes:

> *Wissenwollen* and greed for explanations never bring us to a thoughtful questioning. *Wissenwollen* is always [sic!] the concealed arrogance of a self-consciousness [*Selbstbewusstseins*] that banks on a self-invented ratio and its rationality. *Willing*-to-know [*Wissen*wollen] does not *will* to abide in hope before that which is worthy of thought. (*GA* 12:95/13)

And in 1945 Heidegger writes that, although thinking understood in the traditional way is representing as a kind of willing, where "to think is to will, and to will is to think," what he is after is the authentic "essence of thinking" which is "something other than willing" (*G* 29–30/58–59). It is no longer a question of salvaging and rethinking the comportment of *Wissen-wollen*, but of admitting: "Would not then all willing-to-know be shaken from the ground up?" (*GA* 77:163). In these passages, Heidegger explicitly distances himself from the terms of his earlier thought, rather than attempting to salvage them by way of awkward or forced reinterpretation. Heidegger finally abandons the will by situating it at the core of the epoch from which he is attempting to twist free, the epoch of the culmination of metaphysics in nihilism and technological manipulation.

Before he explicitly attempts to think "something other than willing," however, he spends most of the remaining years of the 1930s searching for a proper sense of willing. In *Introduction to Metaphysics,* this proper sense is spoken of as *Wissen-wollen.* This text from 1935 remains for the most part a philosophy of will, even with the qualification that this willing is of "a very particular kind." Being rules in its overpowering onslaught; man asserts his own violent power in an attempt to bring this onslaught to a stand, as an army receives enemy troops.

> *Legein and noein,* gathering and apprehending, are a need and act of violence *against* the overpowering, but at the same time always and only *for* it. Thus the violence-doers must time and again shrink back in fear from this use of violence, and yet they cannot retreat. (*EM* 135)

Even in such ambivalent, even hesitant, formulations of the give and take, the onslaught and counter-violence between man and being, even when man is said to "shrink back and yet will to master [*Zurückschrecken und doch*

Bewältigenwollen]" (ibid.), this relation is hardly yet thought outside the domain of violence and will.

Before Heidegger comes to see the will as epochally problematical, essentially unsalvageable, in the years following *Introduction to Metaphysics* he continues the attempt to think a higher sense of will as man's proper comportment to being. This proper will, however, is increasingly thought—not as a violent response to violence, a power-asserting response to the overpowering—but as a holding back, a reticence or reservedness (*Verhaltenheit*) that corresponds to being's own extreme refusal to reveal itself in our destitute time. This is the meaning given to "the most proper will" in *Contributions to Philosophy,* written in the years 1936–38. It is to this text that I shall turn for an interpretation of Heidegger's final attempt to think a positive sense of will in the 1930s.

Prior to considering this pivotal text, however, let us note an interesting passage which signals a significant turning in this direction from "The Origin of the Work of Art," the earliest version of which was written the same year as *Introduction to Metaphysics,* but which went through "several revisions" before appearing in final form in 1960. In this essay Heidegger elucidates how a work of art can open up a world, holding together the "strife of earth and world" by a "thrust to the surface" and a "thrust down." But, now writes Heidegger, "this multiple thrusting is nothing violent" (*GA* 5:54/191); and moreover, for man to "submit to this displacement" which the work of art engenders means

> to restrain [*ansichhalten*] all usual doing and prizing, knowing and looking, in order to stay within the truth that is happening in the work. Only the reservedness of this tarrying [*Die Verhaltenheit dieses Verweilens*] lets what is created be the work that it is. This letting the work be a work we call the preserving of the work. (Ibid.)

Following this discussion of the "reservedness" which lets the work be, Heidegger then takes up once again the idea of *Wissen-wollen,* twisting the notion further from "willing" and closer to the "letting-be" of his 1953 (re)-interpretation.

> Knowing that remains a willing, and willing that remains a knowing, is the existing human's ecstatic engagement [*Sicheinlassen*] in the uncon-cealedness of being. . . . Neither in the creation mentioned before nor in the willing mentioned now do we think of the performance or act of a subject striving toward himself as his self-set goal. . . . Willing is the sober resolute openness [*Ent-schlossenheit*] of that existential self-transcendence which exposes itself to the openness of beings as it is set into the work. (55/192)

This (revised) essay thus explicitly takes up the terminology of will, attempting to think a proper sense of will (which involves restraint and letting-be) in distinction from a self-assertive sense of will as the "act of a subject striving toward himself as his self-set goal." This reflects Heidegger's approach to the problem of the will in *Contributions to Philosophy:* to think a positive sense of will (as reservedness) as the proper essence of man in distinction from a negative sense of will (as egoistic self-assertion). Let us now examine how a distinction between these two senses of will is implied in *Contributions.*

The *Beiträge's* Contributions to the Problem(atization) of the Will

In many ways Heidegger's 1936–38 *Beiträge zur Philosophie (Vom Ereignis),* translated as *Contributions to Philosophy (From Enowning),* records a major pathmark of the "transformative turn" under way in Heidegger's thought since *Being and Time.* Daniela Vallega-Neu writes in this regard: "Whereas in *Being and Time* Heidegger exposes the question of being in a way that leads *toward* the origin (the temporal occurrence of being, which in *Contributions* he will reconsider as the truth of being), in *Contributions* Heidegger attempts to think *from* the origin (the truth of being as enowning [*Ereignis*])." She adds that this "shift in directionality of thought," which has been called the *Kehre* of Heidegger's thought, is understood by Heidegger himself "as originating in a more original turning, namely, the turning that occurs in the event of the truth of be-ing [beyng] (*Wahrheit des Seyns*) as 'enowning' (*Ereignis*)."[39] While the notion begins to appear already in *Introduction to Metaphysics* (see *EM* 29), it is also in *Contributions* that a being-historical turning to "the other beginning" (*der andere Anfang*) is first explicitly thematized and developed.

With regard to the themes of a turning to an other beginning and the fugue-like turning structure of *Ereignis* itself, themes that underlie all of Heidegger's later thought, this massive set of orchestrated notes has justifiably been referred to as "Heidegger's second major work," or at least a draft form thereof.[40] On the other hand, the fact that *Contributions* was withheld from publication is perhaps a sign, not just of the unreadiness of the public in those transitional times, but also of the still-transitional status of (at least one key element of) Heidegger's thought at this time. *Contributions* is, as Vallega-Neu notes, "more a site of struggle than a systematic book."[41] This not only reflects Heidegger's belief that "the time of 'systems' is over" (*GA* 65:5); it is also, I maintain, due to the fact that Heidegger is here still struggling to find and articulate the right fundamental attunement for the transition into an other beginning. With regard to the problem of the will, it shall be demonstrated in this section that *Contributions* is indeed the struggling site of a twisting transition. As such, however, it provides us with invaluable pathmarks on the way to Heidegger's mature critique of the will and his attempt to think a turning to a way of being radically other than willing.

"In philosophy," Heidegger writes near the beginning of *Contributions*, "propositions never get firmed up into a proof" (*GA* 65:13). Proofs always come too late, and presuppose that "the one who understands . . . remains unchanged as he enacts the interconnection of representations for the sake of proof. . . . By contrast, in the first step of philosophical knowing, a transformation of the human who understands [*eine Verwandlung des verstehenden Menschen*] takes place" (13–14). Hence, what Heidegger's own thought attempts to prepare for (rather than "prove") is "a shifting into Da-sein itself" (*Verrückung in das Da-sein selbst*). Dasein is thus no longer simply a fundamental ontological name for what humans always already are, but is rather a possibility of what we may become; Da-sein is the "ground of a definite, i.e., future humanness" (300).[42] (The term "man" [*der Mensch*] now reappears to indicate those who must make the transition into Da-sein.) It should not surprise us that the possibility of this shift into Da-sein is first discussed with regard to the "fundamental attunement" (*Grundstimmung*)[43] of this other, more originary way of being.

After claiming that what is at stake in the meditations of *Contributions* is a "shifting into Da-sein itself," Heidegger then proceeds to offer the name, or rather three names, of the "fundamental attunement of thinking in the other beginning": *das Erschrecken* (startled dismay), *die Verhaltenheit* (reservedness), and *die Scheu* (awe). Although we are initially told that "there is no word for the onefold of these attunements," a lack that is said to "confirm its richness and strangeness" (22), later Heidegger adds: "unless it be with the name *Verhaltenheit*" (395).[44] The question for us is: what is the relation of this fundamental attunement to the problem of the will and/or to the possibility of non-willing? Although at first impression the notion of "reservedness" would seem to imply the passivity of a not-willing, more of a "reluctance" now than a "will to mastery," Heidegger also calls this reservedness an "ownmost" or a "most proper will" (*eigenster Wille*). What is at stake, then, is not a simple turnabout to quietism.

In *Contributions* Heidegger no longer avoids the term "will," as in *Being and Time*, nor does he simply embrace it, as he did in his political speeches of 1933–34. The term is used rather frequently in a positive sense, and in certain passages he gives us some indications for how to decisively distinguish the notion of a "most proper will" from the improper notion, let us call it "subjective will." Heidegger in fact explicitly claims here that it is necessary to adhere to the familiar sense of words, such as "decision" and presumably "will," in order to carry out the transformation at stake. He explains this process as one where, "within certain limits," one "must go a certain stretch of the way *with* ordinary opinion [i.e., the familiar sense of words], in order then at the right moment to exact an overturning of thinking, but only under the power of the same word" (*GA* 65:83–84).

This "overturning of thinking" (*Umschlag des Denkens*) is not just a matter of language and thought, or rather it demands us to rethink the capacity of "language" and "thought" themselves, such that an overturning in them would imply nothing less than "*a transformation of man himself*" (84). While this transformation is more one that man would have to undergo than one that he would bring about, in some fashion a human comportment is needed for this transformation. But if there is a "will" involved in the transition to the grounding of the other beginning, it must be then qualified as a "true will" or a "most proper will" in order to distinguish it from the self-assertive willing that characterizes the subjectivity of man in the modern epoch of nihilism.

Heidegger speaks of this most proper will in the context of the *Grundstimmung,* the fundamental attunement, in which thinking into the other beginning must take place. He characterizes this *Grundstimmung,* as we have mentioned, with three words: *das Erschrecken* (startled dismay), *die Verhaltenheit* (reservedness) and *die Scheu* (awe). Reservedness, he says, "is the *middle* . . . of startled dismay and awe. These simply make more explicit what belongs *originally* to reservedness. It determines the style of inceptual [*anfänglichen*] thinking in the other beginning [*im anderen Anfang*]" (15). As this inceptual fundamental attunement, Heidegger calls reservedness the "most proper will":

> [This] startled dismay is no mere retreat, nor is it a helpless surrender of the "will." Rather, precisely because in it the self-concealing of beyng reveals itself, and because the preservation of beings themselves and the relation to them is willed, the most proper or ownmost "will" [*eigenster "Wille"*] of this startled dismay joins together with this startled dismay from within—and this is what we have here named *reservedness* [Verhaltenheit]. (15)

It is therefore with this notion of "reservedness" that we can approach what Heidegger thinks in *Contributions* as "the most proper will." Reservedness is not a simple holding back, since it also involves the greatest venturing (*wagen*). This is the difficulty we must think. Reservedness is a comportment of holding back as the most proper will. It is essentially related to *Erschrecken,* a startled dismay which itself, however, is no helpless giving up of the will, but is the wherein of the self-opening (*sich auftut*) of the self-concealing of beyng. We are reminded of the yawning of the

Abgrund revealed in the mood of *Angst* in *Being and Time*. And yet the *Abgrund* is no longer thought of primarily as the deathliness of individualized Dasein, but is now the beyng-historical self-concealing of beyng itself. Startled dismay arises in the face of the refusal (*Verweigerung*) of beyng to come to presence. Dasein is not merely confronted with the nothingness of its individual deathliness, but with the epochal abandonment by beyng (*Seynsverlassenheit*). Beyng has abandoned us to beings; and beings, alienated from beyng, deteriorate into material for machination (*Machenschaft*), while humans, wrapped up in their subjective concern for adventure and "lived-experience" (*Erlebnis*), sink into willful and willed manipulators of this machine world.

The abyss thought here is thus not simply that of *je meiniges* Dasein, as it was in *Being and Time,* but is that of our epoch in the history of being, an epoch characterized by our own forgetfulness of beyng in relation to the refusal of beyng to come to presence. Thus, while for the Greeks the *Grundstimmung* "is the astonishment [*das Er-staunen*] that beings are," for us it must rather be a "startled dismay in the abandonment of being" (46). Our epoch is one of the utmost distress; we have forgotten the question of being in our abandonment by being. Reservedness (*Verhaltenheit*), as the creative correspondence to being's refusal, names the proper comportment (*Haltung*) to beyng in this epoch of *Seynsverlassenheit*.

By the time of *Contributions,* the Nothing to which authentic humans open themselves up is thought of as the self-concealing withdrawal of beyng, which in this extreme epoch (*epoche:* holding back, self-withdrawal) of the history of being is that of an abandonment of beyng. The message of *Contributions* is a dark one: "Our hour is the epoch of going-under" (397). We are at the end of the epochs of metaphysics, and there is as yet nowhere else to go. In our distressful times beyng speaks to us only in refusal. Yet the silence of this refusal is still a way in which it speaks to us; and we still must respond to this refusal properly. What is the proper response to a denial?

> But if beyng essences as denial [*Verweigerung*], and if this denial itself
> should come forth into *its* clearing and be preserved as denial, then
> the preparedness for the denial can consist only in *renunciation*
> [Verzicht]. (22)

Here we have yet another term added to the fundamental attunement of reservedness. *Verzicht* (renunciation) too must be understood in an affirmative sense; it is not a "mere will not to have [*Nichthabenwollen*]," but rather "the highest form of possession" (ibid.). Heidegger claims that "renunciation" must not be understood here merely negatively, for example "as weakness and avoidance, as suspension of the will," and stresses rather that it involves a "holding fast," and even its own kind of "struggle" (62). This renunciation is far from a "gloomy 'resignation,' which no longer wills" (397). As an essential note in the fugue of the fundamental attunement of reservedness, it must be thought in terms of the "most proper will." It is part of the fundamental attunement that contains "the heart of courage as the attuned-knowing will of *Ereignis*" (396).

And yet, this "most proper will" of reservedness and renunciation does imply a negation; something is renounced, something is held back. In response to the refusal of beyng, we must renounce—but renounce what? A mere affirmation of willing would fall back into the "noisy optimism" which "does not yet truly will, because it closes itself off from willing to go beyond itself" (397). The will to go beyond oneself must first of all involve a renunciation of the will to simple self-affirmation. It is such simple self-assertion of will that Heidegger sees as underlying the modern machination (*Machenschaft*) of the world, wherein the world is reduced to masses of material for production, and as underlying the clamor about "lived-experience" (*Erlebnis*), where the subject's will and representation become the ground and the measure of beings. These two phenomena are interpreted in *Contributions* as the foremost signs of our state of nihilism, our state of blind self-assertion in the void left by beyng's refusal to come to presence (see sections 61–69).

In answer to the question of what is to be renounced, and with a bit of interpretive hindsight, it is thus possible to say: *The most proper will involves a renunciation of subjective willing.* That is to say, the most proper will involves what Heidegger later (in 1944–45) speaks of as "willingly to renounce willing" (*G* 30/59). And yet the key difference between the reservedness/renunciation of *Contributions* and the *Nicht-Wollen* of "Towards an Explication of *Gelassenheit*"—the difference that marks the former as a still-transitional text with regard to Heidegger's turn from the will—lies in the manner in which the other side of this negation is articulated. The *Nicht-Wollen* of the latter text is said to also intimate "what remains outside of *any kind of* will" (ibid., emphasis added); in other words, by that time Heidegger no longer thinks that this particularly problematical word "will" carries the capacity to be "overturned" in such a way as to say something essentially different. Yet in the former text Heidegger still attempts to affirmatively think a proper sense of will. *Contributions*, with its notion of an *eigenster Wille*, still attempts to deal with the problem of the will by salvaging a will uninfected by subjective willing.

In this transitional text, the most proper will is not that of an individual subject, nor that of a state, nor even primarily that of a *Volk*, but is rather that which participates in the grander movement of the history of being itself. The most proper will is certainly not that of the apologists of subjective egoism, nor is it that of the peddlers of a philosophy of the *Volk* as a goal to be willed as an end in itself. The most proper will is that of philosophy in the highest sense, understood as "a willing to go back [*Zurückwollen*] to the beginning of history and thus a willing to go beyond oneself [*Übersichhinauswollen*]" (*GA* 65:36). In apparently stark contrast to (the common understanding of) the comportment of reservedness and reservation, *Contributions* also speaks in part in a qualified language of voluntarism. We are told, for example, that the possibility of the other beginning "opens out only in the attempt [*Versuch*]. The attempt must be thoroughly governed by a fore-grasping will [*vorgreifenden Willen*]. As a putting-itself-beyond-itself, the will *stands* in a being-beyond-itself" (475). The philosopher's and poet's "will to found and build" (98) by "grasping the knowing will [*aus dem Begreifen des wissenden Willens*]" (96), or as "the attuned-knowing will to *Ereignis*" (58), is the other side of the fundamental attunement of renunciation and reservedness.[45]

In response to beyng's refusal to come to presence, its refusal to open a world for us, we too must refuse; we must refuse to close ourselves off from beyng's refusal by fleeing into a groundless world of willful subjectivity, a world of subject-centered lived-experience and technological manipulation. The most proper will involves the refusal of such willing. Reservedness is, in this sense, a will to not will. But it is also that which first "struggles and endures [*erkämpft und er-leidet*]" (62) in a "creative holding out in the abyss" (36); it is the struggle to be responsive to the essencing of beyng in a time of *Seynsverlassenheit*. Whereas in *Being and Time* willing-to-have-a-conscience occurs as a readiness to repeat the interruptive *moment* (*Augenblick*) of anxiety, the more fundamental attunement of reservedness, as "the ground of care" (35), bespeaks rather a holding out into a creative *enduring* of our abysmal *epoch*. Only in this enduring comportment of reservedness is the *Augenblick* for responding to the call of beyng opened up (see 31).[46] Does this "struggle to be responsive" to the address of beyng intimate a dynamic comportment beyond the duality of activity and passivity within the domain of the will?

Heidegger's radical experiments with language and thought in *Contributions* resist being understood in the terms and grammar of traditional metaphysics. And yet, *Contributions* continues to attempt to express the proper manner of being human chiefly either with affirmative expressions for a "proper will," or with negative expressions of renunciation and reservedness. What each of these aspects of *Contributions'* fundamental attunement aim to leave behind is more or less clear: subjective willing (while the negative terms denounce subjective *willing*, the positive terms denounce *subjective* willing). Yet seen from the perspective of the subsequent development of Heidegger's thought-path, both of these aspects perhaps still draw too much on what they attempt to twist free from: the domain of (subjective) will. Their relation to the will is still ambiguously transitional. To be sure, this transitional character does not *only* mark a limited stage of development along Heidegger's *Denkweg;* for these expressions in their ambiguity are meant to speak from out of, as well as to, our essentially transitional historical position, which is ambiguously situated at the end of the first beginning and (perhaps) on the verge of an other beginning. Nevertheless, it remains the case that in this text Heidegger has not yet disclosed the central role of the will in the history of metaphysics; nor has he thought the turning to the other beginning in terms of twisting free of the domain of the will as such. *Contributions* still vacillates between leaving the will behind and uncovering its most proper sense.

After around 1940, Heidegger thinks the will in a decidedly more critical fashion than in *Contributions;* he no longer holds out the possibility of determining a "proper will," insofar as the language of will is found to be inextricably bound up with the history of metaphysics and its culmination in technological nihilism. The most decisive site of his turn from the will can be found in his sustained confrontation with Nietzsche's philosophy of the will to power. It is significant to note, in this regard, that in the sequel volumes to *Contributions, Besinnung* (1938–39) and *Die Geschichte des Seyns* (1938–40), Heidegger begins to develop a radical critique of the notion of "power" (*Macht*).

While *Introduction to Metaphysics* attempted to retrieve an original sense of being from the Greeks as an overpowering onslaught of *physis,* and while *Contributions* still spoke of the "disempowering" (*Entmachtung*) of *physis* since the first beginning (*GA* 65:126), in *Besinnung* Heidegger radically questions the propriety of thinking being in terms of power. In reference to his earlier comment, Heidegger writes that "speaking of disempowering is here ambiguous"; it implies not simply that *physis* remains to be recovered in its original *Machtcharakter,* but more profoundly that "in the first beginning of its essencing, beyng neither gave itself away in its proper truth nor properly grounded the essence of truth" (*GA* 66:194). In its proper truth, in its essential ground, "beyng is . . . never power and thus also never impotent [*Ohnmacht*]." Beyng should in truth be called *das Macht-lose,* not in the sense of lacking power, but as power-free in the sense of "remaining released [*losgelöst*] from [being determined according to] power" (192–93).

Thus Heidegger now writes: "Beyng—the *power-free* [Machtlose], *beyond power and un-power* [jenseits von Macht und Unmacht], or better, outside of power and un-power, essentially unrelated to these" (187–88).

In *Die Geschichte des Seyns,* Heidegger sharpens his critique of power yet further, and begins to connect it more clearly with the will. When the being of beings appears only in the distorted sense of the will to power, and when beings are then let loose into the dominion of machination, this is a sign of the utmost abandonment of being in its most proper essencing, namely, as that which remains outside the very domain of power. "The essence of power [*Macht*] as machination [*Machenschaft*] negates the possibility of the truth of beings" (*GA* 69:71).

In this critique of power the later Heidegger's critique of the modern epochs of will—from idealism's will of spirit or love, to Nietzsche's will to power, and finally to the technological will to will—is beginning to take shape, even if he is not quite ready to name the will as the core ingredient in this constellation. In the context of a critique of the reduction of beings to objects of representation, Heidegger does however write: "Behind objectiveness [*Gegenständlichkeit*] is long concealed, until German idealism and more precisely until *Schelling,* being as will [*das Sein als Wille*]— and the 'will' as a mental-spiritual [*seelisch-geistiger*] cover-name for power" (*GA* 69:62). Elsewhere in notes from 1938–39, Heidegger claims that the "will," that is to say "will as self-willing" (*Wille als Sichwollen*), is the "simplest name" for the modern metaphysical determination of the beingness of beings, a name that is first pronounced by Schelling before it is uncovered in its essence in Nietzsche's "metaphysics of the will to power" (*GA* 67:157ff.).

In the waning years of the transitional decade of the 1930s, then, Heidegger does not simply turn his back on the will and leave it behind. The term and topic of "will" do not simply vanish from the pages of his texts. The will continues to play a central role in his thought—only now he begins to turn around to critically rethink it as the heart of the nihilistic culmination of the entire history of the West.

A Radically Ambivalent Onto-Theodicy of Primal Willing: On Heidegger's Interpretations of Schelling

> Hence it is entirely correct to say dialectically that good and evil
> are the same thing, only seen from different aspects; or evil in
> itself, i.e., viewed in the root of its identity, is the good; just as, on
> the other hand, the good, viewed in its division or non-identity,
> is evil. . . . [In] this system there is only one principle for every-
> thing; it is one and the same essence [*Wesen*] . . . that rules with
> the will of love in the good and with the will of wrath in evil. . . .
> Evil, however, is not an essence [*Wesen*] but a dissonant excess
> [*Unwesen*] which has reality only in opposition, but not in itself.
> And for this very reason absolute identity, the spirit of love, is
> prior to evil, because evil can appear only in opposition to it.
> —F. W. J. Schelling[1]

In his 1809 "Philosophical Investigations into the Essence of Human Freedom and Related Matters," Schelling famously states:

> In the final and highest instance there is no being other than willing.
> Willing is primal being [*Wollen ist Urseyn*]. ("FS" 350/231)

This first explicit assertion of a metaphysics of will comes to occupy a
special place in Heidegger's history of being. Heidegger's confrontation
(*Aus-einander-setzung*) with Schelling's treatise on freedom, a text that he
refers to as "the acme of German idealism," also occupies a special place
in the development of Heidegger's thought. If Heidegger's turn from the
will can be most clearly witnessed in the increasingly critical interpre-

tation of the will to power over the course of the two *Nietzsche* volumes (1936–46), his 1936 engagement with the ambivalent root of the will in Schelling's treatise on freedom, I shall suggest in this chapter, helped clear a pivotal space for this turn.

If the question of Schelling's influence has remained a relatively neglected topic in Heidegger scholarship,[2] this is perhaps in part due to the fact that Schelling is usually referred to in Heidegger's later texts merely as a precursor to Nietzsche in the course of the modern history of the metaphysics of will. It is noteworthy, however, that *Schelling's Treatise on the Essence of Human Freedom* was one of the last of Heidegger's texts to be published (1971) during his lifetime and with his assistance. This text consists of a lecture course from 1936 and an appendix containing important selections from lecture and seminar notes from 1941–43.[3] In the 1936 course, as Jean-Luc Nancy points out, Heidegger's own discourse on the question of being provides a kind of "incessant counterpoint to Schelling's, without making the matter explicit on its own, and without the latter's discourse being given a clear interpretation by that of the former (as was the case with Kant and Leibniz)."[4] Heidegger's commentary and Schelling's text are in large part enigmatically interlaced up to the last minutes of the course, where Heidegger explicitly calls for a radical leap from Schelling's ambivalent apex of the German idealist metaphysics of the Absolute into a thinking of the finitude of being. In the course from 1941, on the other hand, Heidegger will look back at Schelling from a marked distance; Schelling's philosophy of the will is now clearly delimited as a metaphysics of "unbounded subjectivity."

Between 1936 and 1941 Heidegger wrote *Contributions to Philosophy* (and its sequel volumes) and the lectures and essays that make up most of the two *Nietzsche* volumes. In short, during these years the "history of metaphysics" is outlined, and the decisive turn from the will takes place. In chapter 6 I shall explicate Heidegger's mature critique of the will as it takes shape in the wake of this turn. The close examination of Schelling's treatise on freedom and Heidegger's reading of it given in the present chapter is necessary, not only because the impact of Schelling's difficult philosophy of (post-)idealism on the development of Heidegger's thought remains relatively little understood, but because this impact concerns precisely the question of the will. Without attempting to situate the treatise on freedom within the career of Schelling's own *Denkweg*, I begin by giving an explication of this key text in reference to Heidegger's meticulous 1936 reading.[5] I then attempt to suggest what Heidegger learned from Schelling in 1936 with regard to the problem of the will, before moving on to examine his critique of Schelling's metaphysics of subjectivity and will in the course notes from 1941–43. The 1936 course presents an important pathmark on the way to Heidegger's turn from the will; the 1941–43 course notes introduce us to his post-turn critique of the metaphysics of will.

The Will's Originary Doubling: The Principles of Ground and Existence

The will plays a central and positive role in German idealism as the essence of freedom, that is, as the autonomous faculty of giving the law to oneself. As we have seen, Heidegger problematically adopted this philosophy of the will in his interpretive appropriation of Kant's practical philosophy in 1930. In his treatise on freedom, Schelling too begins with the Kantian notion of freedom as the autonomy of self-legislation. Yet for Schelling, "idealism supplies only the most general concept of freedom, and a merely formal one." The "real and living concept of freedom," Schelling claims, is "the capability for good and for evil" ("FS" 352/233; *SA* 117/97). Schelling's decisive contribution to the idealist tradition is to have reintroduced the radical *ambivalence* of human freedom, an ambivalence, he seeks to demonstrate, that is rooted in an originary ambivalence of willing as primal being itself. It is this profoundly ambivalent character of the will that, we shall see, Heidegger encountered and grappled with in his 1936 reading of Schelling.

According to Schelling's metaphysics, willing is the unitary character of primal being; but this oneness *realizes* itself only by way of an originary bifurcation into "ground" and "existence," that is, into the "will of the ground" or "self-will" (*Eigenwille*) on the one hand, and the "will of understanding" or "universal will" on the other. The former is the irrational "realistic" principle of "darkness" or "gravity"; the latter is the rational "idealistic" principle of "light." The two principles, however, are essentially intertwined. Without the ground there is no reality; without existence there is no consciousness; and history, according to Schelling, is the very movement of reality becoming conscious—in theological terms, of God's self-revelation through time.

Schelling's concern is with the *essence* of human freedom, that is, with its fundamental place—its possibility and necessity—in this process of the self-realization of God as the Absolute. Human freedom and will must be understood on the basis of the freedom and will of the Absolute. This requires nothing less than reconciling human freedom with pantheism. Schelling admits as undeniable that "a fatalistic sense can be combined with pantheism"; for example, attributing "absolute causality to one being leaves nothing but unconditional passivity for all others." And yet, that pantheism does not necessarily lead to fatalism is confirmed, he says, by the fact that "so many people are driven to the pantheistic view precisely by the liveliest sense of freedom" ("FS" 339/222). The task Schelling sets himself is that of demonstrating how the concept of pantheism, when correctly understood, is not incompatible with human freedom; pantheism does not necessarily lead to fatalism. On the contrary, human freedom "demands immanence in God, pantheism" (SA 103/85). "Since freedom in contradiction to omnipotence is inconceivable," writes Schelling, the only way to reconcile human freedom with God's absolute freedom is "to save man with his freedom in the divine being itself," by saying that "man is not outside God, but in God, and that his activity itself belongs to the life of God" ("FS" 339/222; SA 84/70). But what does it mean to say that human freedom is "in" the absolute freedom of God; and how would this immanence make possible rather than cancel out human freedom?

For Schelling, philosophical knowledge is only possible in terms of "the whole of a scientific world view" ("FS" 336/219). To understand a part is to see it in relation to the whole. The concept of "freedom" too, "if it is to have any reality at all . . . must be one of the dominant central points of the system." And yet, as Schelling notes here at the outset of his treatise, according to an influential tradition of thought, "the idea of freedom is said to be entirely inconsistent with the idea of system." A complete system of knowledge, it would seem, cannot help but end in denying human freedom. Schelling attempts to answer two types of questions that appear as barriers to the reconciliation of human freedom with the metaphysical "system" of the Absolute: (1) Does a system of the Absolute preclude genuine human freedom; must not every such system lead to pantheistic fatalism? (2) If human freedom is the freedom for good and for evil, then evil is a positive possibility. But how can the positivity of evil be reconciled with the goodness of the Absolute? One could respond to the first dilemma by claiming that humans are not in fact free; but that would contradict the undeniable "feeling of freedom [that] is ingrained in every individual" ("FS" 336/219). One could likewise respond to the second dilemma by denying the goodness of the Absolute; but, as Schelling later puts it, the "demand for wisdom" entails a demand for a world "that has been posited wisely, providentially, freely."[6]

In order to solve these dilemmas, in order to think a "system of freedom" that allows for both the ultimate goodness of the Absolute and genuine human freedom for good and evil, Schelling introduces his crucial "distinction" (die Unterscheidung) between the "ground" of a being and its "existence." Everything depends on making the distinction "between a being [Wesen] insofar as it exists, and a being insofar as it is merely the ground of existence" ("FS" 357/236–37). Heidegger explains this distinction as follows:

> "Ground" means for Schelling foundation [*Grund-lage*], substratum [*Unterlage*], "basis," thus not "ground" in the sense of "ratio." . . . "Ground" is for Schelling precisely the non-rational. . . . Schelling uses the word existence in a sense which is closer to the literal etymological sense than the usual long prevalent meaning of "existing" as objective presence. Ex-sistence, *what emerges from itself* and in *emerging reveals itself.* (*SA* 129/107)

This fundamental distinction allows Schelling to differentiate between the ground of God and his existence, and to claim that only the latter is the self-reflectively realized "God himself." Schelling writes: "The ground of his existence, which God has within himself, is not God viewed absolutely, that is insofar as he exists; for it is only the ground of his existence, it is *nature*—in God, a being which, though inseparable from him, still is distinguished from him" ("FS" 358/237). Hence, things have "their ground in that which is in God, but *is not God himself*, i.e., in that which is the ground of his existence" (359/238). Man too is fundamentally dependent on God, and yet "dependence does not annul autonomy or even freedom" (346/227).

The identity-in-distinction of ground and existence, or what Heidegger terms the *Seynsfuge* (the "jointure" or "fugue" of being), would be what enables Schelling to think human freedom, and hence the possibility of evil, without denying God's absoluteness or his goodness. The possibility of evil can in this way be "grounded in" God (i.e., there is no need to posit a dualistic ground of evil *outside of* God), but God does not *himself* "cause" evil (*SA* 137/114). If Schelling is able to solve the dilemma of reconciling the Absolute with human freedom and evil, this is done by thinking God as a "*becoming* God," an "existing god" who is "*in himself* historical" (131/109). God goes out of his ground and exists by becoming "aware of himself" (*bei sich selbst*). God is a "life," and "life" entails contradiction and becoming. God's goodness is manifest only by way of "letting the ground operate," but in such a manner as to subordinate the self-will of the ground to his existence as the will of love.

The two principles—the will of the ground and the will of understanding or existence—are from the beginning intertwined. The "primal longing" (*die ursprüngliche Sehnsucht*) of the ground in God, the "longing which the eternal One feels to give birth to himself," is "a will within which there is no understanding." It is therefore "not an independent and complete will, since understanding is in truth [*eigentlich*] the will in willing"

("FS" 359/238). The primordial will of the ground as longing essentially calls forth its opposite, the will of the understanding, in order to truly become itself. Heidegger elaborates on this originary doubling as follows:

> In longing [*Sehnsucht*] lies a double and even *oppositional* movement: the striving away from itself in expansion, and yet precisely back to itself. . . . In that the general nature of the will lies in desiring, longing is a will in which what is striving wills itself in the indeterminate, that is, wills to find itself in itself and wills to present itself in the expanded breadth of itself. But since in this will willing is precisely *not* yet aware of itself and is not its own [*noch* nicht *bei sich selbst und sich zu eigen*], is not yet properly [*eigentlich*] itself, the will remains an improper [*uneigentlicher*] will. The will in willing is the understanding, the understanding knowledge of the unifying unity of what wills and what is willed. (*SA* 150–51/125)

Willing is this movement of ecstatic-incorporation, of expanding itself out in order to come back to itself, in order to re-present itself and thereby to come into its own. Heidegger explicitly develops here the connection between will and representation: "The craving [*Sucht*] of self-presentation is the will to bring oneself before oneself, to re-present *oneself* [*des* sich *Vorstellens*]" (151/125). Moreover, he acknowledges that this craving, this *Sucht* which characterizes the primordial longing (*Sehnsucht*) of the will to self-presentation, "means originally and still today means the disease that strives for self-expansion." Yet Heidegger's concern in this 1936 text is still predominantly with explication, and not yet with critique of the interconnection of will and representation in the metaphysics of idealism. As in the case with Nietzsche, to the extent that Heidegger's later critique of Schelling's philosophy of the will is compelling, this is due to his having first gone through a careful and largely sympathetic reading of Schelling's text. Before we turn to the critique of Schelling's philosophy of the will worked out in 1941, however, let us continue to follow Schelling's text and Heidegger's 1936 reading.

The primordial will springs forth in the darkness of the ground, but it becomes itself only in reflecting back on itself in understanding. In other words, God becomes himself by existing. And even if at times "Schelling's presentation gives the appearance that God is first only *as ground*" (*SA* 147/122) which only subsequently exists, in truth there is no precedence in time or in essence between the two principles. "In the circle out of which all things become," writes Schelling, "it is not a contradiction that what engenders one thing is itself in turn engendered by it. Here there is no first and last, because all things mutually presuppose one another" ("FS" 358/237). The two principles are co-originary and essentially in-

tertwined from the beginning. Hence, on the one hand, the primal longing is already "a will of the understanding, namely, the longing and desire
thereof; not a conscious but a prescient will [*ein ahndender Wille*], whose
prescience is understanding" ("FS" 359/238; *SA* 146–47/121–22). On the
other hand, the will of the understanding is essentially dependent on its
other, the irreducible principle of reality, the will of the ground.

It is the latter insistence that sets Schelling's (post-)idealism apart
from, for example, the idealism of Hegel's dialectic of Spirit which ultimately claims that "the real is [sublated into] the rational." For Schelling,
there is an "incomprehensible basis of reality in things, the irreducible
remainder [*der nie aufgehende Rest*], that which with the greatest exertion
cannot be resolved in the understanding." It is, on the one hand, "out of
that which lacks understanding [*Verstandlosen*]" that "understanding in
the true sense is born"; yet, on the other hand, the never fully sublatable
"unruly [*Regellose*] lies ever in the depths as though it might break out
again" to disrupt the order and form of the understanding ("FS" 359–
60/238–39).

Evil as Inversion of the Principles:
The Willful Rebellion of the Inverted God

The originary duality of the will cannot be canceled out. The ambivalence
between the two intertwined principles is essentially irresolvable. In God,
however, the two principles, the will of the ground and the will of understanding, develop together into a harmonious bond (*Band*). God becomes
himself as the harmonious dialectical identity of the two principles. Initially there is "an inward, imaginative response" which corresponds to the
primal longing to become a self, and God, who "beholds himself in his
own image," becomes "the God begotten *in* God himself" ("FS" 361/239).
Yet it is only through the creation of nature, which strives to reach ever
higher stages of a dialectical identity between ground and existence, that
God fully reveals—and thus becomes—himself. This progressive heightening of dialectical unification does not, however, entail a cancellation of
the distinction (*Unterscheidung*), that is, of the separation (*Scheidung*) between the principles. In fact, the opposite is the case. "The deepening of
the ground is the expansion of existence. Both together are the intensification of separation as the heightening of unity" (*SA* 167/139). The dialectical unity becomes stronger by becoming more diverse: "The deeper
that which unifies comes out of the ground, and the further the unification strives into the light, the *Band* becomes all the more relaxed, and the

manifold of what is bound together becomes all the more rich. . . . Ground and existence separate further and further, but in such a way that they are ever in unison in the form of an ever higher being" (164/136–37). In man, therefore, as the highest created being, "there is the whole power of the dark principle, and in him, too, the whole force of light. In man are the deepest abyss and the highest heaven, or both centers" ("FS" 363/241).

At each stage of nature prior to the appearance of man the ground is subordinated to existence; in other words, the self-will of the particular is necessarily subordinated to the universal will of the whole. Hence, the self-will of each individual animal is necessarily subordinated to the will of the species, which contributes to the harmony of the whole of nature (*SA* 168/140). Yet God, in order to ultimately realize himself, needs an "other" who stands in true opposition. Man *must* be free for God to be revealed, for "God can reveal himself only in what is like him, in free beings that act by themselves" ("FS" 347/228). Even if "only the Eternal is in itself [*an sich*], resting in itself," even if "it alone is will and freedom," human freedom is nevertheless possible, indeed necessary, as a "derivative absoluteness," that is, as a power derived from God but absolutely free to choose its essential formation.[7]

Heidegger explains this dialectic as follows:

> God is properly [*eigentlich*] himself as the Existent, that is, as he who emerges from himself and reveals himself. . . . Now every being, however, can only be revealed in its opposite (cf. Schelling's treatise, p. 373). There must be an other for him which is not God as he is himself and which yet includes the possibility of revealing himself in it. Thus, there must be something which, although it originates from the innermost center of the God and is spirit in its own way, yet still remains separated from him in everything and is something individual. This being, indeed, is man. Man must be in order for the God to be revealed. . . . But then this means: the conditions of the possibility of the revelation of the existing God are at one and the same time the conditions of the possibility of the faculty for good and evil, that is, of that freedom in which and as which man essentially is [*west*]. (*SA* 143/119)

There must be both an essential similarity and an essential difference for God to reveal himself through man as his counter-image (*Gegenbild*). Man's peculiar freedom marks both this sameness and this difference. God's freedom is at once his necessity. In God the two principles are unified in a hierarchical relation where the will of the ground is subordinated to the will of existence. This subordination is maintained, as we have noted, in the pre-human stages of nature. But because the self-will of ani-

mals is not yet capable of opposing the divine will, God is not yet fully revealed in them; both their difference from and sameness to God is limited. Human freedom, however, is absolute in that it stands, in a decisive
sense, above both principles. This absoluteness is different from that of
God, however, in that human freedom does not necessarily choose to
properly subordinate the principle of darkness to the principle of light.
This difference, which explains the possibility of evil, also opens the space
for God's revelation. Schelling writes: "If the identity of both principles
were just as indissoluble in man's spirit as in God, then there would be no
difference, i.e., God as spirit would not be revealed. The unity which is in-
divisible in God must therefore be divisible in man—and this is the possibility of good and evil" ("FS" 364/242; *SA* 169/141).

The capacity for evil is based on the separability, and hence the *reversibility*, of the principles of ground and existence in man. Evil consists
in "the positive perversion [*Verkehrtheit*] or inversion [*Umkehrung*] of the
principles" ("FS" 366/244). In Heidegger's words: "*Evil is the revolt that
consists in the reversal* [Verkehrung] *of the ground of the essential will into the
inverse* [Umkehrung] *of God's*" (*SA* 127/106). In God's existence, the will
of the ground is necessarily subordinated to the will of the understanding.
God's ground is contained within his existence. Man, on the other hand,
derives his being from the ground in God, and in him the principles are of
equal power (see "FS" 374/250). If he chooses to subordinate the ground
to understanding, he chooses good over evil; if he chooses to reverse this
proper ordering, he chooses evil over good. Heidegger explicates Schelling's idea of evil as an inversion of the harmonious ordering of the principles as follows:

> In what does the malice of evil consist? According to the given new deter-
> mination of freedom, freedom is the faculty of good and evil. Accord-
> ingly, evil proclaims itself as a position of will of its own, indeed as a way
> of being free in the sense of being a self in terms of its own essential law.
> By elevating itself above the universal will, the particular self-will [*der
> Eigenwille*] wants precisely to itself be the universal will. Through this ele-
> vation a peculiar manner of unification takes place, and thus a peculiar
> manner of being spirit. But this unification is a reversal of the original
> will, and that means a reversal of the unity of the divine world in which
> the universal will stands in harmony [*Einklang*] with the will of the
> ground. In this reversal of the wills the becoming of an inverted god [*das
> Werden eines umgekehrten Gottes*], of the counter-spirit [*des Gegengeistes*],
> takes place, and thus the upheaval against the primal being, the revolt
> of the adversary element against the essence of being, the inversion of
> the jointure of being into the disjointure [*die Umkehrung der Seynsfuge ins*

Ungefüge], in which the ground elevates itself to existence and puts itself
in the place of existence. (*SA* 172/143)

In rebelliously elevating the will of the ground over the will of understanding, self-will over universal will, the human spirit becomes an "inverted god"; and this inverted unification of the twin forces of primal willing perversely places man's own ego at the center of the world. Displaced
from its proper center in the will (love) of God's existence, the harmonious fugue of the jointure of being is distorted into the dissonance of dis-
jointure. This (dis)unity of evil is as real as it is false.

Schelling uses the analogy of "disease" to explain the parasitic
reality of evil.[8] As Heidegger explains, the negativity of evil and disease is
not merely that of privation, a mere relative lack of goodness, but rather
that of "negation placing itself in dominance." The expression *Wo fehlt es?*
(What's wrong?), when used to inquire about a sickness, really asks after
"something which has, so to speak, gotten loose from the harmony of being healthy and, being on the loose, wants to take over the whole being
and dominate it." Here "there is not just something lacking [*etwas Fehlendes*],
but something false [*etwas Falsches*]"—"false" not just in the sense of in-
correct, but "in the genuine sense of falsification, distortion, and inversion" (172–73/143).

Man's finite freedom, his "derivative absoluteness," thus entails the
separability of the principles, or more specifically, their reversibility. "Man
is placed on that pinnacle where he has the source of self-impulsion towards good and evil equally within him; the bond of the principles within
him is not a necessary but a free one" ("FS" 374/250). Man stands on this
precarious pinnacle, hovering above both principles of the will, and must
decide to orient his being towards good or towards evil. His freedom is, it
would seem, "freer" than God's—yet both Schelling and Heidegger regard the freedom that is united with necessity as higher than the freedom
of choice, which stands precariously close to pure arbitrariness wherein
"the essence of freedom dissolves into empty chance." "True freedom in
the sense of the most primordial self-determination," writes Heidegger,
"is found only where a choice is no longer possible and no longer necessary" (*SA* 185–86/154). Yet man in his finitude must first find his way to a
genuine decision that unites freedom and necessity; for Schelling this
means that human finite freedom is indeterminately strung between the
possibilities of good and evil. The absolute freedom of God, on the other
hand, is at once united with the necessity of his self-determination. Heidegger writes: "To be able to choose means to have to be finite. Such a determination is incompatible with the Absolute. On the contrary, the per-
fection of the Absolute consists in only being able to will one thing, and

this one thing is the necessity of its own essence. And this essence is love" (192/159–60).

The divine will of love is, according to Schelling, the force that unites the will of the ground and the will of understanding in their proper ordering. The divine spirit's "mystery of love" is that it holds together independent yet intertwined opposites. The "mystery of love," Schelling writes, is "that it combines what could be by itself and yet is not and cannot be without the other" ("FS" 408/278). In Heidegger's explication: "As the will of love, spirit is the will to what is set in opposition. This will wills the will of the ground and wills this will of the ground as the counter-will to the will of the understanding. As love, spirit wills the opposing unity [*die gegenwillige Einheit*] of these two wills" (*SA* 154–45/128). The will of love "lets the ground operate" in independence; it allows the insurgence of the will of the ground in order that, by ultimately subordinating this rebellious will of darkness to the order of light, it may manifest its own omnipotence (see "FS" 375/251). God lets man freely become the inverse god, so that the dissonance of evil may in the end serve as a foil for the sake of the revelation of the superior harmony of divine love. Man, standing on the pinnacle between the two forces of good and evil, can choose to become an instrument of the true center of God's love, or he can rebel and, inverting the order of ground and existence, attempt to particularize the universal, to (dis)orient the world from the false center of his own self-will.

The Pivotal Role of Schelling in Heidegger's Turn from the Will

Let us pause here in our reading of Heidegger's 1936 reading of Schelling to ask: what did Heidegger learn from Schelling's account of the radical ambivalence of the will? As we have seen, a certain "unsaid ambivalence" with regard to the will in the early Heidegger's thought gave way to an embrace of the will after *Being and Time,* philosophically in his 1930 interpretation of Kant's practical philosophy and then politically in his Rectoral Address and speeches in 1933–34. If the resoluteness of authenticity becomes a matter of concrete willing, which "actually wills willing and nothing else besides" (*GA* 31:285), then inauthenticity would appear to be a matter of failing to will rather than a failure of will, a lack of willful resolve rather than an errant will. Inauthenticity would be a matter of heteronomy, of passively deferring to the will of *das Man,* as opposed to actively taking up the autonomous task of "giving oneself the law." Yet with

Schelling, a positive possibility of "willing evil" is brought to the fore. Evil is not merely the passivity of a failure to autonomously will; it is a highly spiritual possibility of free willing. Schelling is quoted as writing that "the highest corruption is precisely the most intelligent," for "error and malice are both spiritual and come from the spirit." And Heidegger adds here the comment: "Error is not a lack of spirit, but twisted spirit [*verkehrter Geist*]" (*SA* 144/120).

Schelling's relentless exposure of the precarious ambivalence of human freedom calls into question Heidegger's all too unambivalent embrace of the philosophy of spirit and will in the early 1930s. Through his 1936 reading of Schelling, we may surmise, Heidegger gained an insight into the highly spiritual possibility of evil, the rebellious self-will that posits itself as the center of the world, and that represents beings from this egocentric perspective. It is this false center of self-will that introduces a "false tone" of dissonance into the harmony (*Einstimmigkeit*) of the world, distorting this harmony into a disharmony (*Unstimmigkeit*), throwing the *Seinsfuge* out of joint into an *Ungefüge* (172–73/143–44). This insight into the disruptive power of self-will marks a crucial step on the way to his later radical critique of the metaphysical notion of the will as such.

The turn from the will has been made by 1941, when Heidegger returns to Schelling's treatise for a second, much more critical examination. In 1936, however, Heidegger's response to the ambivalence of the will is—following Schelling in his own manner—to attempt to distinguish between a proper and an improper will, rather than to see the metaphysical concept and the fundamental attunement of the will as irredeemably problematical. He still seeks to affirm a notion of *Wissen-wollen,* his own version of a finitely concretized will of understanding (see *SA* 190/158). The voluntarism of 1930 is still echoed here in passages where Heidegger claims that "the determination of one's own essence, that is, the most primordial free element [*Freie*] in freedom, is that self-overreaching as self-grasping of oneself which originates in the original essence of the being of man" (186/155). And yet this comprehension of the essence of freedom as a knowing decision that "wills primordially" is now clearly situated within the historical occurrence of being, namely, as a resolute openness (*Entschlossenheit*) that stands "within the openness of the truth of history, the enduring standing-within [*Inständigkeit*] which carries out what it must carry out" (187/155). The authentic will is here thought to respond to the "must" of the historical occurrence of the truth of being. This will to respond to historical destiny, like the willing-to-have-a-conscience of *Being and Time,* is neither simply autonomous nor simply heteronomous, but rather simultaneously pushes up against both of these polar limits of the domain of the will. Rather than fall back into the pendulum swing between voluntarism and fatalism, Heidegger is regaining his balance and is poised once again to begin to work *through* this ambivalence, twisting free toward a way of thinking beyond the domain of the will as such.

It is noteworthy that when Heidegger returns in the final moments of the 1936 course to the issue of the "incomprehensibility of freedom," the language of "will" is curiously absent. Heidegger writes that, "however far Schelling travels on a new path into the essence of human freedom," Kant's basic insight into the incomprehensibility of "the fact of freedom" is not undermined, but only confirmed. The only thing we can comprehend (grasp), Heidegger says, is freedom's incomprehensibility (ungraspability). The question is how to indicate, point towards, the contours of this ungraspable event. Now Heidegger writes that

> freedom's incomprehensibility [*Unbegreiflichkeit*] consists in the fact that it resists com-prehension [*Be-greifen*] because being-free transposes us into the occurrence of being [*in den Vollzug des Seyns versetzt*], not in the mere representation of it. Yet the occurrence is not a blind unfolding of a process, but is a knowing standing-within [*wissendes Innestehen*] beings as a whole, which are to be endured [*auszustehen*]. This knowledge of freedom is certain of its highest necessity because it alone makes possible that position of receptive taking up [*Aufnahmestellung*] in which man stands, and is able as a historical being to encounter a destiny, to take it upon himself and to carry it beyond himself. (196/162)

Human freedom is here that enigmatic capability by which we enter into cor-respondence within the occurrence of being. However, even if no longer thought in terms of the violence and counter-violence of the 1935 *Introduction to Metaphysics,* the fundamental attunement of this correspondence has not quite yet become that of reservedness (*Verhaltenheit*), as it does in *Contributions to Philosophy,* written in the immediately following years (1936–38). By 1943 Heidegger has radically distanced his own notion of freedom as the "restrained comportment of letting-be [*die Verhaltenheit des Sein-lassens*]" (*GA* 9:190/146) from the metaphysics of will and subjectivity.

Heidegger's Schelling: A Metaphysics of Willful Subjectivity and an Onto-Theodicy of Evil

In the seminar notes on Schelling from 1941–43, Heidegger critically distances himself from the concept of "freedom" as a metaphysical name for "capability by oneself [*Aussichselbstvermögens*] (spontaneity, cause)," a concept which moved into the center of modern metaphysics as that which "unifies the determinations of cause and selfhood (of the ground as what underlies and of the toward-itself, for-itself), that is, of *subjectivity*" (*SA* 232/192). Insofar as "freedom" is restricted to this modern metaphysical determination, it is said to have "forfeited its role *originally in the history of beyng* [*Seynsgeschichtlich-anfänglich*]" (ibid.).

From this decidedly critical vantage point, Heidegger reconsiders Schelling's "system of freedom" as "another name for the system of *subjectivity*" (234/193). Schelling's system of freedom, as a system of subjectivity which declares will to be the essence of the being of all beings, is now understood not only to be the acme of German idealism, but also to express nothing less than "the essential core of all of Western metaphysics *in general*" (*GA* 49:2; *SA* 201/165).

Heidegger then returns to Schelling's quintessentially modern answer to the founding Aristotelian question of metaphysics: *Ti to on?* (What is being?)

> In the final and highest instance there is no being other than willing. Willing is primal being, and to it alone all predicates thereof apply: groundlessness, eternality, independence of time, self-affirmation. All philosophy strives only to find this highest expression. ("FS" 350/231)

Heidegger now examines in greater detail each of these four metaphysical predicates of willing as primal being (*GA* 49:84ff.; *SA* 207ff./170ff.). "Groundlessness" is said to express the fact that precisely "because being is groundlike, ground-giving, it cannot itself be in need of a further ground. The groundlike is groundless, what grounds, what presences as basis . . . is without something to which it could go back as something outside it." The ground-less is thus precisely, if paradoxically, a characteristic of the ground-like, i.e., of the *subiectum*. "Eternity" or "eternality" (*Ewigkeit*) indicates that "being means constancy in a unique presencing." "Independence of time" goes further to indicate that the constancy of being implies "untouched by succession, presencing not affected by the change of disappearing and arriving." These three predicates—groundlessness, eternity, and independence of time—together are said to clarify the metaphysical determination of being as *hypokeimenon*. The final predicate, "self-affirmation," on the other hand, points to the distinctively "modern interpretation of being," which implies: "A being is in that it presents itself to itself in its essence, and in this presentation represents, and representing, strives for itself."

Hence, in modern metaphysics "the will is *subiectum*" in the double sense of subjectivity, namely: "(1) as *hypokeimenon*, but willfully, striving (*ex ou*), 'basis,' and (2) as egoity, consciousness, spirit (*eis ho*), 'Word,' *logos*" (*GA* 49:90; *SA* 211/173). It is in this sense, Heidegger writes, that we can understand how "being as will" determines the root of Schelling's fundamental distinction between the will of the ground and the will of understanding. "The will is ground because as striving (longing) it goes back to itself and contracts itself, thus is a basis for [existence]"; and, on the other hand, the will is understanding "because it moves toward reality, unity (*universum*), presence, the presence of what the ground is, self-hood" (ibid.). In other words, Schelling's predicates for willing as primal being express the combination of *hypokeimenon* and striving for self-representation, a combination which expresses the modern determination of the *subiectum*, the ground of beings, as subjectivity. Schelling's "willing," as the most fundamental predicate of being, thus combines both a striving for oneself and a representing of the totality of the world. It is a dark longing for itself which is only brought to light and into its proper truth as universal understanding. The modern metaphysics of will thus implies a system of understanding; for, as Schelling writes, "the understanding is in truth the will in willing" ("FS" 359/238; *SA* 209/172). The primal longing for self-affirmative self-representation of the will fulfills itself in an ecstatic-incorporation of the world into the universal will of understanding.

The ego into which the world is systematically incorporated is, to be sure, not the ego of an individual human being, but the Ego of the Absolute, of God. For Schelling, the will of the ground "in God" is thus properly subordinated to the will of his existence, to the will of divine love. "True will, true being, is love." "Will truly means: to come to oneself, to take oneself together, to will oneself, to-be-a-self, spirit, *love*" (*GA* 49:91; *SA* 211/174). This will of love, in order to "come to itself" and "to reveal itself," requires the division of itself, the *Unterscheidung*. In other words, insofar as God's love is a will, it needs a ground for the self-affirmative representation of its existence; it needs to overcome opposition in order to become itself. "*Every will is oppositional-will* [Wider-wille] *in the sense of a counter-will* [Gegen-willens]" (*GA* 49:100; *SA* 217/179), and God's will of love is no exception (indeed, it is the rule). According to Schelling, the will of love requires the "relative independence" of the will of the ground, for "the ground must operate so that love may be." There "must be a particular will . . . turned away from love, so that when love nevertheless breaks through it as light through darkness, love may appear in its omnipotence [*Allmacht*]." Love requires "something resistant [*ein Widerstrebendes*] in which it can realize itself" ("FS" 375–76/251).

Heidegger interprets this philosophy of the Absolute's will of love as the acme of modern metaphysics:

In being as willing the *subiectum*-character of beings was developed in every respect. If beingness is *subiectum* in all metaphysics (Greek and modern), and if primal being is willing, then willing must be the true *subiectum*, in the unconditional manner of willing-oneself. (Hence: denying oneself, contracting and bringing oneself to oneself.) . . . Strife and opposition are willed and produced by being itself. . . . Love—as letting the ground operate (375), in opposition to which it can be itself and must be itself in order that a unifying one and unity and it itself might be. (*GA* 49:90–91; *SA* 211/173–74)

God's self-revelation through an other requires not only human freedom to reverse the principles as the *possibility* of evil; nothing less than the *actuality* of evil is needed so that God's love may realize and reveal its superior power. As Heidegger remarked in his 1936 course: "Only by letting the ground operate does love have that in which and on which it reveals its omnipotence—in something in opposition." This means that, even while the actual decision for evil is left to human freedom, the "attraction of the ground," as the "inclination to evil," "'comes' from the Absolute" (*SA* 182/151). Whereas the reversibility of the principles in human freedom explains the possibility of evil, its actuality can only be explained on the basis of this general force of evil, this "general cause" or "solicitation to evil" ("FS" 374/250). While man is free to choose either good or evil, God can only reveal himself when evil is actually chosen and then overcome by the greater power of love.

The mere possibility of evil, explained by human freedom to reverse the principles, does not yet explain its actuality, and Schelling tells us that the problem of the actuality of evil is in truth "the greatest object of question" ("FS" 373/249). Thus Heidegger concludes that Schelling's so-called "treatise on freedom" "really deals with the essence of evil, and only because it does this does it deal with human freedom." The fact that Schelling determines freedom as fundamentally the faculty for good *and* evil (not "or"), Heidegger remarks, indicates that he does not mean the freedom of choice, but "freedom as the metaphysical jointure and bond in the discord itself" (*SA* 215–16/177). The question of human finite freedom is thus thought on the basis of the question of the absolute freedom of God; and God's absolute freedom is one with the absolute necessity to actualize his love through the conquest of evil. As Heidegger writes near the end of the 1936 course: "The will of love stands above the will of the ground and this predominance, this eternal decidedness, the love for itself as the essence of being in general, this decidedness is the innermost core of absolute freedom" (193/160). Schelling's bold attempt to think a "system of freedom" as a "metaphysics of evil" in the end falls back into a "systemadicy" of the Absolute. Evil is required and justified for the sake of (*umwillen*) the revelation of the omnipotence of the divine will of love.[9]

The 1936 course ends with Heidegger's claim that Schelling failed to think a system of the Absolute as a "system of freedom" that would unite the opposition of the will of the ground and that of understanding. Schelling's claim near the end of his treatise that, although in the divine understanding there is a system, "God himself, however, is not a system but a life" ("FS" 399/270), throws into question his entire attempt to think the system of the Absolute as an intertwined opposition of ground and understanding—for now the system would be confined merely within one of the principles. This difficulty proves to be an "impasse," according to Heidegger, and Schelling's failure to think the jointure of ground and existence is said to have led him to "fall back into the rigidified tradition of Western thought without creatively transforming it" (*SA* 194/161). Heidegger interprets Schelling's doctrine of "absolute indifference"—the *Ungrund* from out of which the two principles are said to spontaneously arise—as merely a failed final attempt to salvage the unity of the system of the Absolute. "Here too," Heidegger writes, "Schelling does not see the necessity of an essential step. If being in truth cannot be predicated of the Absolute, that means that the essence of all of being is finite and only what exists finitely has the privilege and the pain of standing in being as such and experiencing what is true as beings" (195/161–62). Heidegger's step beyond Schelling entails an abandonment of the system of the infinite Absolute for a thinking of the always finitely occurring event of being. Letting go of the predicates of being as willing (groundless *subiectum*, independence of time, eternality, and the self-affirmation of subjectivity), Heidegger's path of thought ultimately leads to an attempt to think the *Seynsfuge* as the non-willing event of appropriation.

In his seminar notes from 1941–43, Heidegger critically interrelates the metaphysical concepts of the Absolute, the system, knowledge as certainty, the will, and unconditional subjectivity. He now understands his *Auseinandersetzung* with Schelling as that of "the thinking of the history of being with metaphysics in the form of unconditional subjectivity" (230/190). He also explicitly seeks to mark the essential distance of his now-central notion of *Ereignis* from the dialectical Absolute of idealism.

> Because the Absolute is thought as unconditional subjectivity (that is, as subject-objectivity), as the identity of identity and non-identity, and as subjectivity essentially as will-full reason and thus as movement, it looks as if the Absolute and its motion would coincide with what the thinking of

the history of being thinks as *Ereignis*. But *Ereignis* is neither the same as the Absolute nor is it even its contrary, for instance, finitude as opposed to infinity. (231/191)

Ereignis as the event of appropriation is above all not to be confused with the ecstatic-incorporation of the Absolute as unconditional subjectivity. Neither is it simply its dialectical opposite, disjointed "finitude" as opposed to and determined over against systematic infinitude. Indeed, Heidegger later speaks of the gathering of the fourfold "from the *in*-finite relation [*aus dem* un-*endlichen Verhältnis*]" (*EHD* 170/194), and of *Ereignis* as that which gives both being and time (*ZSD* 20/19). In these later texts, and in others such as *Identity and Difference,* Heidegger continues to stress the radical difference underlying whatever superficial similarities his thought shares with idealism. If the post-metaphysical thinking of *Ereignis* remains easily misunderstood today in terms of idealism as the crowning achievement of metaphysics, this is because in the Absolute as the infinitude of unconditional subjectivity "the abandonment of being is most of all hidden and cannot appear" (*SA* 231/191). What remains most difficult to recognize, and to think, according to Heidegger, is that beyng as *Ereignis* is neither a finite nor an infinite being, but rather the always-finite event of appropriation in which human finitude is needed/used for the historical granting-in-withdrawal of the truth of being.

Unresolved Schelling Questions

In conclusion to this reading of Heidegger's readings of Schelling, I wish to raise two sets of issues that require further investigation. The first of these issues, which I can only begin to address here, concerns the question of whether Schelling's notion of the "will of love" can, in the end, be wholly reduced to a penultimate expression of the modern metaphysics of unconditional subjectivity. According to Heidegger's later formulations of the history of metaphysics, Schelling's will of love is but a still-concealed form of Nietzsche's will to power (*GA* 9:360/273). In the lecture notes from 1941, Heidegger claims that after Schelling had revealed the essential core of modern metaphysics in the doctrine of *Wollen ist Urseyn*, where this "primal willing" is predicated as a self-affirmation or a "willing oneself," there "still remains only what Nietzsche then brings: the inversion [*die Umkehrung*]" (*GA* 49:89; *SA* 210/173). Nietzsche would, as it were, reverse the hierarchical relation between the irrational self-will of the ground and the rational universal will of understanding. Yet in this "mere inversion," would the metaphysics of the will in fact remain "essentially" the same?[10]

In the 1941 notes Heidegger also writes that in "willing as willing oneself there are two basic possibilities of essential development," namely Schelling's "unconditional subjectivity as love" and Nietzsche's "unconditional subjectivity as 'power.'" While Nietzsche's doctrine is said to be a *"willing* oneself" (*Sich*wollen) as a "going-out-beyond-oneself, as overpowering and command," Schelling's doctrine is said to be a "willing *oneself*" (Sich*wollen*) which paradoxically implies "no longer to will anything of one's own." Schelling's will of love, as a "released inwardness" (*gelassene Innigkeit*), entails "letting the ground operate," and is characterized as: "to will nothing, not anything of one's own and not anything of love, not oneself either" (*GA* 49:101–2; *SA* 224–25/185). Heidegger also writes that, whereas *Sein* signifies for the later Schelling the "own-ness" (*Eigenheit*) of "the being which has not yet emerged from itself," "love," on the other hand, "is *das Nichts der Eigenheit*, it doesn't seek what is its own, and therefore also cannot be of its own accord" (*GA* 49:93; *SA* 212/174).[11]

On the one hand, Schelling undoubtedly often thinks the Absolute in terms of the subjectivity of a personal God. The Absolute is a "personal, in the genuine sense, like us, living being."[12] Yet would the "subjectivity" of the Absolute be "essentially the same" as the human willfulness of ecstatic-incorporation? In the treatise on freedom, Schelling depicts the will of the ground as "the unruly" force that can break out from the depths at any moment to upset the order of reason, while love is the "binding" force that holds together intertwined opposites ("FS" 359/238, 408/278). In subsequent texts, however, Schelling emphasizes that the dark self-will is originally a "contractive" force that withdraws back into itself, whereas love is the expansive force that flows outward beyond itself.[13] We can perhaps relate the former to the centripetal impulse of incorporation, and the latter to the centrifugal impulse of *ekstasis*. Insofar as each of these impulses would imply the other, a kind of ecstatic-incorporation would characterize both the self-will of egoism and the divine will of love. Yet there is a radical difference of emphasis, depending on which impulse is given priority. According to Schelling, when the two impulses are harmonized in their proper hierarchical balance, with the will of the ground subordinated to the will of existence, love is manifest. When this relation is inverted, the dissonant self-will of egoism arises. Even God, according to Schelling, must "overcome divine egoism through divine love." Indeed, the "subordination of divine egoism under divine love is the beginning of creation."[14]

Even if, therefore, it were appropriate to speak of Schelling's Absolute in terms of "unconditional subjectivity," does one not at least need to mark a significant, and perhaps radical, or even essential, difference between the human subjectivity of willful egoism and the divine subjectivity of the will of love? Even if the "only" difference between "self-will" and "the will of love" were that between ecstatic-*incorporation* and *ecstatic*-incorporation, this apparently "mere alteration of emphasis" would signify for Schelling, in fact, the essential disparity between the harmony of a proper hierarchical relation and the disharmony of a rebellious inversion—that is to say, nothing less than the difference between good and evil.

A further complication is added by the fact that Schelling is prone to gesture beneath and beyond "willing as primal being" at precisely those moments when he attempts to characterize both the aboriginal beginnings and the ultimate ends of primal willing. In Schelling's *The Ages of the World*, God is said to be the pure freedom of the will at rest, and such freedom, as "the will, insofar as it does not will anything actual," is said to be "the affirmative concept of absolute eternity." Human beings too, along with everything else, are said to strive to return to this position of "willing nothing," either indirectly and naively through "abandoning themselves to all of their desires, since this person too only desires the state in which they have nothing more to will," or directly by "withdrawing from all coveted things."[15] Moreover, while the will essentially strives to cancel itself out in a post-willing "will at rest," primordial willing is said to spring forth out of an aboriginal indifference (both ontological and psychological "indifference"). This "absolute indifference" is what the treatise on freedom calls "that which was there before the ground and before existing beings (as separated)" ("FS" 406/276), in other words, what love was before it became love.

In between aboriginal absolute indifference and the realization of supreme love, however, is "the longing felt by the eternal One to give birth to itself" ("FS" 359/238). How does this will for self-revelation arise from the *Ungrund* of indifference? In the treatise on freedom, Schelling leaves us only with enigmatic suggestions. On the one hand, he says that "out of indifference, duality immediately breaks forth" (407/277). Is the *Ungrund* of absolute indifference then nothing but a logical and ontological presupposition for the absolute spontaneity (freedom) of originary willing?[16] On the other hand, Schelling also speaks of the *Ungrund* as in some sense already operating with an intentionality, namely, that of dividing itself "in order that life and love may be, and personal existence" (408/278). In later texts (notably the several drafts of *The Ages of the World*), Schelling continues to struggle with this enigma of why something (primal being as willing) arose from nothing (the *Ungrund* as absolute indifference). In any case, it remains unclear whether Schelling was ever able to radically put the ontological domain of the will in question, even when he not only boldly exposes the darker side of the will, but also traces willing as archaic being back to an an-archic indifference, and postulates the final telos of will in an eternity of pure willing which wills nothing.

Schelling's legacy with regard to the metaphysics of the will is thus itself ambivalent. We might summarize this ambivalence as that between two ways of interpreting the notion of "letting the ground operate" (*das Wirkenlassen des Grundes*). Does God's love let the ground operate for the sake of the most far-reaching revelation of his unconditional subjectivity—a self-revelation of absolute mastery that would require so much as the submission of "free slaves"? Or does this love intimate a letting-be that lets go of the will to closure of the system of the Absolute, of the very will to unconditional subjectivity itself? Does God's love ultimately incorporate the world into, or ecstatically release the world from, his (perhaps originally abnegated) transcendental subjectivity? Heidegger's critical incorporation of Schelling's treatise as the "acme of idealism" into his being-historical account of the history of metaphysics settles on the former view. Yet reading between the lines of Heidegger's critique, we may nevertheless surmise that Schelling's intimations (enigmatic as they may have remained) of an originary letting-operate, and of a freedom of "willing nothing" as the proper end of—or as the recovery from—all willing, were among the influential provocations behind Heidegger's own attempt to think a non-willing freedom of *Seinlassen* and *Gelassenheit*.[17]

The second set of issues, which I simply wish to raise here in anticipation of later discussions, concerns the question of how the legacy of Schelling's provocative rearticulations of the problem of evil and the enigma of human freedom are taken up in Heidegger's own thought. According to Heidegger, Schelling failed to work out a "system of freedom" as a "metaphysics of evil." The fact of human freedom and the positive reality of evil shatter idealism and split open the system (see *SA* 59/48, 110/91, 118/98, 121/100). It is Schelling that brought us to this impasse; and yet he himself, despite everything, is said to have adhered to the idealistic interpretation of being (see 128/106–7). According to Heidegger's interpretation, Schelling's "treatise on freedom" is founded on a "metaphysics of evil" (125ff./104ff.). "For short we call Schelling's treatise the 'treatise on freedom,' and rightly so. But it really deals with the essence of evil, and only because it does this does it deal with human freedom" (215–16/177). Moreover, for the sake of a "metaphysics of evil" Schelling must attempt to justify evil on the basis of the "systemadicy" of the Absolute. The discord (*Un-fug*) of evil would serve the role of necessary resistance for the self-revelation of the *Seynsfuge* as the system of the Absolute (216/178). But the question remains: when Heidegger attempts to think the finitude or the historicity of the occurrence of being, when he thinks the *Seynsfuge* as the event of appropriation/expropriation (*Ereignis/Enteignis*) rather than as the ecstatically incorporative system of the Absolute, what happens to the enigma of freedom and the positivity of evil?

How are the questions of freedom and evil taken up in Heidegger's being-historical thinking? The short answer is that the problem of evil is rethought as the problem of the will itself. In a dialogue written in 1945, Heidegger explicitly suggests: "Perhaps it is in general the will itself that is evil" (*GA* 77:208). In chapter 6 we shall examine how Heidegger understands the history of metaphysics to culminate in the technological *Ge-stell*, which reduces beings to the manipulations of willful subjectivity. The technological will to will ultimately threatens to strip humans of their freedom, reducing them to another cog in the wheel of machination. The proper response to this situation is not to reassert "free will" as a faculty of the subject, a power of self-determination possessed by the self-proclaimed masters of the earth. Human freedom must be rethought, according to Heidegger, from within the clearing of being as *das Freie*. Human freedom is an ecstatic engagement in this clearing, this *Da* of *Sein* that lets beings be (see *GA* 9:188/144). Human freedom is most properly an engaged *Gelassenheit* that cor-responds to the *Seinlassen* of being.

In chapter 7 we shall begin to discuss the difficult problem of the transition from the metaphysics of will to this non-willing freedom of *Gelassenheit*. Later we shall need to ask whether this transition could ever be complete, whether there could ever be an other beginning once and for all free of the will. This question shall require us, in the end, to return to the question of whether Heidegger's thinking of being has sufficiently thought, or problematically "accounted for," the recalcitrant facticity of evil, as well as to the question of what space remains in his *seins-geschichtliches Denken* for the enigma of human freedom.

5

Releasement to and from God's Will: Excursus on Meister Eckhart After Heidegger

Gott ist ohne Willen
Wir beten: es gescheh, mein Herr und Gott, dein Wille;
Und sieh, er hat nicht Will, er ist ein ewge Stille.

Der tote Wille herrscht
Dafern mein Will ist tot, so muss Gott, was ich will;
Ich schreib ihm selber vor das Muster und das Ziel.

Die geheimste Gelassenheit
Gelassenheit fäht Gott; Gott aber selbst zu lassen,
Ist ein Gelassenheit, die wenig Menschen fassen.
—Angelus Silesius[1]

Heidegger, Mysticism, and the God of Will

According to Heidegger, Nietzsche's purported "overcoming of metaphysics" succeeded merely in "overturning" metaphysical oppositions, leaving these categories as such essentially unaltered. In a parenthetical remark in an essay on Nietzsche from 1939, Heidegger also rejects "mysticism" as a "mere counter-image [*Gegenbild*] of metaphysics" (*N2* 28/182). "Still trapped in utter servitude to a metaphysics one thinks one has long since suppressed, one seeks an escape in some otherworldly realm beyond the sensuous." Mysticism would repeat metaphysical oppositions either directly or by simply "reversing" them, fleeing, for example, from the hyperrational into the irrational. Any such countermovement necessarily remains, "as does everything 'anti,' held fast in the essence of that over against which it moves" (*GA* 5:217/61).

RELEASEMENT TO AND FROM GOD'S WILL

A decade and a half later, however, Heidegger draws on the mystic Angelus Silesius's poem "Ohne warum," found in the same pages of *The Cherubinic Wanderer* as the epigraphs to this chapter, for intimations of a way beyond the metaphysical "principle of reason" (see *SG* 68ff.). Together with the idea of *Gelassenheit* (*gelāzenheit*) as ultimately a "letting go of God for the sake of God," Silesius's poetic thought of "living without why" can be traced back to Meister Eckhart. Heidegger, of course, is aware of this connection, and he is now, in 1955–56, even willing to acknowledge that "the most extreme sharpness and depth of thought belong to genuine and great mysticism. . . . Meister Eckhart gives proof of this" (71).

Might the "depth of thought" found in Eckhart's "genuine and great mysticism" point toward an alternative, "uniquely religious and non-Heideggerian way out of onto-theo-logic, a religious overcoming of metaphysics," as John Caputo has suggested?[2] Does philosophy need to thoughtfully recollect the profound dimension of experience that it has for too long dismissed as "irrational mysticism," if it is to recover from its own metaphysical amnesia? Does the mystical path, for its part, need to undergo "thoughtful repetition" in order to free itself decisively from remnants of onto-theological bondage?

Yet just as Heidegger takes care to maintain the distinction between "thought" and "poetry" precisely when meditating on their essential nearness, he is also concerned to avoid the "ring of a mystical assertion" (*SG* 183) in a thought which risks entering into dialogue with "genuine and great mysticism." When he draws on Silesius's "Ohne warum," Heidegger writes: "But one might immediately respond that this source is indeed mystical and poetic. The one as well as the other belong equally little in thinking." And yet, he adds: "Certainly not *in* thinking, but perhaps before thinking" (*SG* 69). Perhaps then for Heidegger, the word of the genuine mystic Eckhart, like the word of the great poet Hölderlin, belongs to thinking as what lies "before" it, both preceding and ahead of it. But unlike the case with poetry, about which he wrote many volumes, Heidegger never did fully clarify the relation of his later thought to Eckhart's mystical word, or indeed, for that matter, to Christianity in general.

Heidegger's profound and recurring interest in Eckhart dates back to his theological studies and is reflected, for example, in his plans in 1918–19 for a course on "The Philosophical Foundations of Medieval Mysticism" (*GA* 60:315ff.).[3] Indeed, the appreciation Heidegger shows for Eckhart late in life may signal another sense in which Heidegger's turn involved in part a return to a critical repetition of his theological origins— the background without which, Heidegger confesses, he would never have come to his path of thinking (*GA* 12:91/10).[4] Of course, even when these origins come to meet him once again from the future, Heidegger never simply returned to "theology," which remained for him a "positive science" that deals with "the highest being" and with the "certainty of faith" rather than with the piety of a responsive thinking of being.[5]

Heidegger consistently criticizes the onto-theology that posits God as "the first cause" and "the highest being"; but to what extent did he also abandon the "original experience" of Christian faith? In this regard we should recall the passage from the 1943 essay "The Word of Nietzsche: 'God Is Dead,'" where Heidegger writes that "a confrontation with Christendom is absolutely not in any way an attack against what is Christian, any more than a critique of theology is necessarily a critique of faith" (GA 5:219–20/63–64). After the turn in his Denkweg, the dimension of the divine becomes increasingly pronounced in his thinking, even if he continues to disavow theism (monotheism or polytheism) along with atheism (see GA 65:411).

In his later thought Heidegger attempted, above all through his readings of Hölderlin's poetry, to anticipate the arrival of the coming god(s) (their number is said to be undecided [see GA 65:437]). His rejection of the God of onto-theology, while giving the appearance of atheism, in fact means something quite the opposite (see N1 471/207–8), or rather something radically different, namely, the renewed search for a "divine god" before whom one can dance and fall to one's knees in awe (ID 140–41/72). And yet, the divinities (die Göttlichen) in Heidegger's later thought of the appropriating event of the fourfold no longer occupy the same central place as the God of monotheism. Is a decentered god still a God?

In any case, what is abundantly clear, and what is most pertinent to our present inquiry, is that the omnipotent Creator "God of Will" finds no place in Heidegger's topology of being. Inasmuch as God is revealed in Christianity—in the "original experience" of faith as in the theology of Christendom—as a being of omnipotent will, then it remains bound to a history of metaphysics as onto-theology. The temporal event of being, which grants-in-withdrawal the clearing wherein beings are let be, is covered over by the theology which posits an eternal being that rules over finite beings and incorporates them into (or condemns them for not freely choosing to return to) its domain.

If the history of metaphysics is a story of the rise of the will, then it is not surprising that the omnipotence of the Will of God becomes a prominent theological theme at the end of the Christian epoch of the Middle Ages. Michael Allen Gillespie, in his study on the pre-Nietzschean roots of the nihilism of willful self-assertion, argues that the increasingly bold assertion of human subjectivity and will in modern philosophers, from Descartes to Fichte and finally to Nietzsche, must be understood as a reaction against the late medieval absolutization of the Will of God. The philosophical assertion of human will, in other words, "can be understood only as a response to and secularization of the earlier notion of an omnipotent divine will." According to Gillespie, the radical nominalism of William of Ockham marks an apex in the theological history of the assertion of the absolute Will of God. For Ockham, God's power can admit of no limits, including those of his own prior creation of any immutable "universals," which would be independently accessible to human reason. Moreover, for Ockham "God's omnipotence also means that he does not create the world for man and is not influenced by anything that man does. . . . Indeed, while [Ockham] does not deny that God is a God of love, he does assert that God's love for man is only a passage back to his love of himself, that ultimately God's love is only self-love."[6] God's creation of humans and his shepherding them back into his domain would be moments in the ecstatic-incorporation of his omnipotent willing.

Does Heidegger's philosophical history of being adequately address this question of the role of medieval Christian theology in the rise of the metaphysics—and ultimately the nihilism—of the will? Gillespie asserts that Heidegger's genealogy of the rise of modern willful subjectivity was myopic in its exclusive focus on the philosophical tradition. While Gillespie agrees that the proper response to nihilism involves taking "a step back from willing," he claims that Heidegger's own attempt to do so only succeeded in reverting from an assertion of human will back into a deference to an omnipotent "will of Being."

> Heidegger either does not recognize or does not admit the connection of the two notions of will [i.e., the philosophical and the theological]. He certainly has a vested interest in distinguishing them from one another, because his own notion of Being, which he holds up as a solution to the problem of nihilism that is the product of the modern philosophy of will, draws heavily on the earlier notion of an omnipotent divine will. Being in his thought is an omnipotent power beyond nature and reason, akin to the *deus absconditus* of nominalism.[7]

Once again we find a reductive interpretation of Heidegger's later thought, one that imputes a turnabout to a purported "will of Being" to his critique of willful subjectivity. While Gillespie supplements Heidegger's critique of the will by shedding light on the late medieval theological and modern anti-theological background for the nihilism of human willful self-assertion, he fails to follow Heidegger's attempt to intimate a "step back from willing" that leads not simply "back" to a deferred-willing, but rather forward towards a *Gelassenheit* of non-willing.

In later chapters I shall discuss in more detail the ways in which Heidegger attempts to think the relation of man and being beyond the domain of the will (i.e., not simply as a reversal *within* it), but here let it suffice to point out a passage where Heidegger explicitly denies that his notion of *Gelassenheit* can be understood as a matter of deferred-willing. Near the beginning of "Toward an Explication of *Gelassenheit:* From a Conversation on a Country Path about Thinking," a text originally composed in 1944–45, Heidegger writes:

> [The] essence of *Gelassenheit* is still hidden for us. . . . And this above all in that *Gelassenheit* can still be thought of within the domain of will, as happens in the case with old masters of thought, such as Meister Eckhart. . . . From whom there is still much to learn. . . . To be sure; but what we have named *Gelassenheit* obviously does not mean a casting off of sinful selfishness and letting self-will go in favor of divine will. (*G* 33–34/61–62)

In chapter 7 we shall look at this key text in greater detail, paying close attention to its dialogical attempt to find a path of *Gelassenheit* that leads beyond the domain of the will. The question I want to raise in this chapter is whether Heidegger's dismissal of Eckhart—which ironically prefigures the manner in which his own thought gets hastily rejected by critics like Gillespie—does justice to the Rhineland mystic's notion of *Gelassenheit.*

In general I have had to limit myself in this study mainly to a consideration of the role that Heidegger's confrontations with thinkers play in the development of his own thought. There are several reasons, however, why an exception is called for in the case of Eckhart. One is that Heidegger critically appropriates the key notion of *Gelassenheit* in part explicitly from Eckhart. Another is that, unlike his critical appropriation of ideas from the philosophical tradition (e.g., his critical dialogue with Nietzsche on the will to power), Heidegger takes over the thought of *Gelassenheit* without explicitly working out in detail a critique of the limits of the idea in Eckhart's thought. The passing remark that Eckhart's *Gelassenheit* remains within the domain of the will is insufficient, not only as an interpretation of Eckhart's thought, but also as an explanation of the nearness and distance of that thought to Heidegger's own.

Eckhart and the Will: Detachment, Deference, Union, and Breakthrough

In the supplements appended to the original version of the conversation on *Gelassenheit* (*GA* 77:158), Heidegger quotes, apparently as grounds for his passing critique, the following lines from Eckhart's *Talks of Instruction:*

> Where I will nothing for myself, there wills instead my God.[8]

> For whoever has released his own will and himself has released the whole world, as truly as if it were his free property, as if he possessed it with full power of authority. Everything that you expressly do not desire, that you have forsaken and released unto God. "Blessed are the poor in spirit," our Lord has said; and this means: those who are poor in will.[9]

It is significant that Heidegger refers to this earliest vernacular work of the Dominican preacher, for it remains, relatively speaking, conservative in its emphasis on the need to let self-will go in favor of God's Will. Insofar as he restricts his critique to this early text, Heidegger might seem justified in his interpretation of Eckhart's *Gelassenheit* as a matter of deferred-willing. Friedrich-Wilhelm von Herrmann, supplementing Heidegger's critique with a number of other passages from the *Talks of Instruction,* can thus conclude: "*Gelassenheit* in Meister Eckhart is that true comportment of man to God, where man has let go of [*abgelassen*] egoistic self-will in his world-relatedness, and has released himself over to [*überlassen*] the divine Will."[10] Eckhart's *Gelassenheit* would, first of all, be a matter of detachment (*Abgeschiedenheit*) as a letting go of (*Ablassen*) self-will. This "releasement from" self-will would prepare one for a "releasement to" God's Will.

Throughout his later sermons Eckhart does, to be sure, continue to speak of being "given back to oneself" only by way of "setting one's will wholly in God's Will."[11] This abandonment of self-love is the road not only to blessedness but also to justice. "The just have no will at all; what God wills is all the same to them, however great the distress may be" ("Q" 183). And yet, particularly in his later sermons, Eckhart thinks releasement and detachment more radically still, not merely as the precondition of human deference to, or even union with, the divine Will, but as of the very nature of the divine itself. In his most radical moments Eckhart intimates a breakthrough to a Godhead (*gotheit*) beyond or before the persona of the God of Will.

Before pursuing this radical trajectory of Eckhart's thought, however, let us press the Heideggerian suspicion to its limits. Heidegger's explicit critique refers only to Eckhart's *deference* to the Will of God; yet he would presumably also be suspicious of Eckhart's more (not to say most) radical thought of a *union* with the Will of God. This more radical thought—that of thoroughly emptying oneself of self-will to the point where one does not just defer to, but rather becomes one with, the divine Will—can, in fact, already be found in the *Talks of Instruction*.

> The will is complete and just when it is no longer bound in any way to the ego [*ohne jede Ich-bindung*], and when it has forsaken itself, and has been formed and shaped into God's Will [*in den Willen Gottes hineinge-bildet und geformt ist*]. ("Q" 66)

Gelassenheit does mean for Eckhart, *initially*, giving up self-will in favor of an absolute obedience to God's Will. But obedience is still very much an imperfect *Gelassenheit;* for as long as there is a duality between master and servant, there remains a self-will that resists the one Will of God. According to the uncompromising logic of Eckhart's thought, there can be only one will; "for, where there are two, there is defection. Why? Because insofar as the one is *not* the other, this 'not,' which creates distinction, is nothing other than bitterness; there one finds no peace. . . . Two cannot subsist with one another; for one (of the two) *must* lose its being" ("Q" 389). Perfect *Gelassenheit* can thus only be approached by way of a complete "annihilation of self" ("Q" 95). This utter dispossession is necessary in order to receive the gifts of God. Our will must become God's Will, or better yet, says Eckhart, God's Will must become ours ("Q" 336). Because "God wants to give us himself and all things as our own free property, so he wants to deprive us, utterly and completely, of all possessions" ("Q" 96). The good man is "so much of one will [*einwillig*] with God, that he wills what God wills and in the way that God wills it" ("Q" 110).

It is thus not in any way a question of a balance of wills; Eckhart demands that we give up ego and self-will utterly and completely, so that we become one with the Self and Will of God. Norbert Winkler interprets this to mean that there is no "unity *between* two subjects, but rather the transformation of the one into the other."[12] This union demands a releasement *from* self-will, as a "pure cessation of will and desire," and a releasement *into* "God's good and dearest Will" ("Q" 91). Ultimately, this detachment would "willingly forgo even God's sweetness," insofar as true joy comes not from receiving God's favors but from uniting with his Will. The *Talks of Instruction* therefore ends with the statement: "One who has all his Will and his Wish has all his Joy; and no one has this whose will is not wholly one with the Will of God. May God grant us this union" ("Q" 100).

Although this union must be prepared for by actively negating self-will, and by passively opening oneself to the grace of God, the *unio mystica* itself would, strictly speaking, no longer be a matter of deferred-willing. In abandoning all resistance, the self that has achieved the union would spontaneously act out the one and only Will. Presumably, however, those who remain on the path of releasement from self-will would still need to practice detachment and deference. Of course one may, in the wake of Nietzsche, deny from the start the very possibility of releasement from self-will, and seek then to expose the covert-willing that would be found inevitably operating under the preacher's rhetoric of giving oneself wholly over to another will. But this is not the only critical question that needs to be raised. For even if we grant the possibility of a complete deference to and thereby union with the "one I" and the "one Will" of God, has the problem of the will been solved, or has it perhaps been magnified to cosmic proportions? Is the breakthrough into a mystical union with the Godhead, for Eckhart, a matter of a passage from a finite subjectivity "into a form of transcendent subjectivity," as has been suggested by some interpreters?[13] Does God represent here a meta-Subject who wills to "ecstatically incorporate" the world into his domain? Here too the will (or the Will) would be the *letzte Faktum* to which we come down, to which we "return."

This suspicion would appear to be reinforced when we examine the Christian Neoplatonic structure of Eckhart's thought. Although Eckhart does indeed claim: "Ego, the word 'I,' belongs to no one save God alone in his oneness" ("Q" 302), his God is, in fact, not simply that of a meta-Subject of immediate self-presence. Eckhart's dialectical thinking reintroduces, in its own manner, a Neoplatonic process of emanation and return that radically transforms the Scholastic onto-theology of God as an immediately self-present substance. Winkler interprets Eckhart's theological innovation as a "turn from substance ontology to a philosophy of spirit [*Geistphilosophie*]," which introduces a dialogical structure *within* the "self-grounding monologue [*Selbstbegründungsmonolog*]" of God. In other words, God is rethought as a "self-referential subject" who grounds himself reflexively through his creation of the world. "Such a God is no longer conceived of as a fixed causal substance, but rather as a God who, in relating to itself, first becomes what he is meant to be. God's self-knowledge is conceived as a self- and world-creating act."[14] It is not difficult, then, to see how Eckhart's development of Christian Neoplatonism in turn prepared the way for German idealism, and in particular for Hegel's notion of *Geist* as a transformation of substance into subject in the movement of a "self-returning circle that presupposes its beginning and reaches it only in the end."[15] We shall see how, from the perspective of Heidegger's critique of the metaphysics of will, Hegel's history of Spirit, as a return from self-alienation back into its realized subjectivity, presents a classic example of a metaphysical saga of ecstatic-incorporation. Would the same critique apply to Eckhart's theology?

Care must be taken here, however, to understand Eckhart in his own terms and not to hastily assimilate his dialectic forward into that of Hegel. Bernard McGinn summarizes the terms and structure of Eckhart's theology as "a dynamic system whose basic law is the flowing out (*exitus, effluxus, ūzvliezen*) of all things from God and the corresponding flowing back or return of all to this ineffable source (*reditus, refluxus, durchbrechen, īngānc*)." This "pattern of emanation and return" moves in two directions, each taking place in two broad stages. The "flowing out" is, first, "the inner emanation of the Trinitarian Persons" (*bullitio*) and, second, "the creation of all things" (*ebullitio*). The "flowing back" takes place first of all as the "birth of the Word [Christ] in the soul" and, second, as the "breakthrough" or "penetration of the soul into the divine ground that is the God beyond God." The "God beyond God" is the Godhead (*gōtheit*) as the "divine depth, abyss, or ground [*grunt*]," "the hidden source from which all things proceed and to which they return."[16]

The crucial matter is how to understand the relation between this abyssal Godhead and the will. It is also necessary to understand the role of the will both in the flowing out from and in the return back to the Godhead. Although references to "will" permeate his writings, it is perhaps best to see this language as one that Eckhart (deconstructively) inherits from the Scholastic tradition.[17] In opposition to the Fransciscan emphasis on the faculty of the will, as a Dominican Eckhart tends to favor the intellect as the higher faculty of the soul. But in the end he is more interested in "breaking through" all faculties of the soul to a more profound experience of the divine *grunt,* an abyssal ground that is itself beyond the personas of the Trinity and beyond such personal qualities or faculties, including the divine Will.[18] This breakthrough not only releases one from the "created" self of the faculties, but also lets go of the personal "God" for the sake of a *unio mystica* with the Godhead.

The breakthrough (*durchbruch*) opens up onto the most radical element of Eckhart's mystical thought, both in the order of knowing (or "unknowing") and in the order of being (or "nothing"). While the "flowing out" gives birth to separation (namely, the distinction and separation of creator and created), the "flowing back," as a return to oneness with the ground, overcomes all distance. Thus Eckhart, in a key passage from one of his boldest and most revealing sermons, writes:

> A great authority [a "Meister"; Eckhart is likely referring here to himself] said that his breaking-through is nobler than his flowing out; and that is true. When I flowed out from God, all things said: "God is." And

> this cannot make me blessed, for with this I acknowledge myself as a creature. But in the breaking-through, where *I stand free of my own will and of God's Will* and of all his works *and of God himself,* there I am above all created things, and I am neither "God" nor creature, but am what I was and what I shall remain, now and eternally . . . for in this breaking-through I receive that God and I are one. ("Q" 308–9, emphases added)

In perfect detachment, in true poverty of spirit where one "wants nothing, and knows nothing, and has nothing," there is no more distance from "God" and therefore "He" is no more.

The radical movement back to the abyssal *grunt* can be interpreted as taking place in three intertwined and overlapping moments: "detaching" or "cutting off" (*abescheiden*); "birthing" (*gebern*); and finally "breaking-through" (*durchbrechen*).[19] On the one hand, these can be thought of as increasingly radical stages of the return. Certainly Eckhart's most transgressive statements relate to the idea of breaking through "into the silent desert where distinction never gazed." It is perhaps not wholly misleading to provisionally separate and, in a developmental sense, think of the moment of detachment as the negation of will (not-willing), the moment of birth as the passive reception of God's Will (deferred-willing), and the breakthrough as a transgression of the domain of the will as such.

In his illuminating analyses of the complex relation between the "the birth of the Son" and the "breakthrough" motifs in Eckhart's thought, Ueda Shizuteru demonstrates how the extremes of passivity/activity are pushed to the breaking point of releasement from the very domain of this dichotomy. In general, Ueda understands Eckhart to be concerned with "a process of intensification that moves from the birth motif to the breakthrough motif."[20] The lesser intense birth of the Son in the soul takes place by way of an utter passivity, where the soul empties itself to receive the grace of God. Here the "absolute activity of God-as-giver" is coupled with "the corresponding absolute passivity of the soul-as-recipient."[21] Yet as we move toward the more intense moment of breakthrough, in "comparison to the absolute passivity of the soul in the birth of the Son, the activity of the soul here is most striking. The soul seeks to penetrate the ground of God."[22] At this moment, Eckhart writes: "delving deeper and ever seeking, she [the soul] does not rest content but quests on to find out what it is that God is in his Godhead" ("Q" 206); this "spark in the soul . . . wants nothing but God, naked, just as he is. . . . [It] wants to get into . . . its simple ground, into the silent desert into which no distinction ever gazed, of Father, Son, or Holy Ghost" ("Q" 316). Despite this apparent reversal from the passivity to the activity of the soul with regard to God, Ueda writes that we should not understand the birth and the breakthrough as two isolated events, but rather as "a *double event occurring along the same line of intensification.*"[23] He explains this continuity, where "absolute passivity experiences its transformation into absolute activity precisely because of the absolute passivity," as follows:[24]

> Perhaps the only way we can understand what Eckhart means here is to
> regard this "power in the soul" as the power of the only-begotten Son
> whom the soul has received in absolute passivity. There is nothing other
> than the absolute activity which the soul has received in absolute passivity. In the absolute passivity of its freedom, the soul receives the begetting Father's absolute activity that is now established in the soul. Eckhart
> repeatedly uses the analogy of firewood to illustrate this transition from
> passivity into activity: . . ."the fire gives birth to itself in the wood and
> gives it its own nature and also its own being, so that all is one fire, of like
> property, neither more nor less" ["Q" 117]. . . . The birth of the fire . . .
> means that the wood burns by virtue of the passive reception of the fire,
> so that "all is *one fire*" (emphasis added), in which the relationship of
> passivity-activity is suspended.[25]

In short, the *path* to the *unio mystica* thus requires (1) an initial active effort of detachment (a will not to will), (2) a passive receptivity to God's grace, and (3) a receptive-activity that breaks through to a union with the ground of the Godhead. But ultimately the union is so complete as to remove the distance required for a relation of either activity or passivity; and the "pure activity" that springs forth from this *ursprüngliche* abyssal *grunt* of indistinction would lie beyond the horizon of activity/passivity between subjects determined by the domain of the will.

The Ambivalence of Eckhart's *Gelassenheit*

The three moments—detachment, birthing, and breakthrough—are so interconnected that each one, when followed through to the end, seems to necessarily imply the others. Yet the theme of birthing, as the middle transitional term, is peculiar in that it appears both on the way back and on the way out. The birth takes place not only as an "utter passivity" of deferral, preceding the breakthrough beyond all duality, but also as the "welling up into himself" of the Godhead. The will too reappears.

> As you go completely out of yourself for the sake of God, so goes God
> completely out of himself for your sake. When both go out, what remains

is a simple One. In this One the Father gives birth to his Son in the most inward source. There blooms forth the Holy Spirit, and in God springs forth a will that belongs to the soul. As long as it stands untouched by all created things and from all createdness, this will is free. ("Q" 181)

Would this free will that the soul receives, this will that "springs forth in God"—in God who, for his part, has returned from standing outside himself in unity with the detached soul in the One—be of a radically and incomparably other nature than the egocentric or Egocentric will of ecstatic-incorporation?

To be sure, we bear in mind here that "in medieval texts 'will' and 'love' are indeed used time and again synonymously."[26] Yet the question remains: how far can "God's Will/Love" as *amor benevolentiae* be definitively distinguished from all sublated and sublimated forms of *amor concupiscentiae*? More precisely: can God's Will/Love be thought essentially otherwise than as a cosmic rendition of the will of ecstatic-incorporation? The question here is whether the Will/Love reborn in the *effluxus* of the simple One (the *exitus* out of the indistinct desert) is essentially other than idealism's will of Spirit that goes out of itself (*sich entäußert*), that releases beings into their own, only insofar as it needs this self-separation (this *Unterscheidung*) in order to finally return to itself in the fullness of its majesty. In this case, writes Heidegger: "Will truly means: to come to oneself, to take oneself together, to will oneself, to-be-a-self, spirit, *love*" (*GA* 49:91; see also 134–35). God's love of his creation would ultimately be a Self-love.

Insofar as God is thought as the One who goes out of and returns to himself, all beings, as his creatures, would appear as essentially subjected to his Will. On the other hand, however, insofar as God (as the Godhead, as *Nichts*) is "himself" perfect detachment, would his *ekstasis* (his flowing out) be that of a free giving that willfully expects no return? Or perhaps the "return" of God into the hidden Godhead could even be thought, after Heidegger, not as a willful incorporation of things, but as a withdrawal (*Entzug*) of his presence for the sake of letting things presence on, and into, their own. Would the profoundest meaning of "God" then be: "letting beings be"?

In the end we are perhaps left with an intractable ambivalence in Eckhart's preaching, an ambivalence between, on the one hand, radically breaking through and letting go of God the Father (the personal being of Will), and, on the other hand, letting him and his Will reappear ever again from out of the abyssal *grunt*. For one who takes Heidegger's critique of the metaphysics of will seriously, it is a troubling ambivalence that cannot simply be explained away by exclusive or strategically timed reference to the most intense moments of releasement in Eckhart's mystical thought.[27] One cannot help but remain suspicious that, to the extent that the "rebirth of will" would leave the categories of onto-theological Christianity immanently intact, breathing new life into them from beyond without essentially altering their internal structure and character, we fall back ever again into a localized teaching of deferred-willing. One danger of this traditional domain of religiosity—as we know too well from ongoing history—is that the call to a deference to (my) God's Will all too easily merges with a technique of covert-willing directed against those who did not happen to be born into the church, who have a different name for "God," who have a different vision and/or number of his/her personas, who prefer an atheistic spirituality, or who find all "spiritual interventions" an imposition on a direct engagement with others and with the things themselves. The detached-and-engaged mystic all too easily returns from the desert to slip back on the same old robe of the preacher (the "ascetic priest"?), who in turn all too easily dons the mantle of the missionary (if not the armor of the crusader) sent out to incorporate others (back) into the fold of the (my) Father's Will.

There is nevertheless, as we have seen, a genuinely radical thrust to Eckhart's thought that leaves both "God" and his Will behind. Eckhart intimates a passage through utter passivity that gives way to a birth of "pure activity" without a subject or an object, that is, to the spontaneous generosity of living "without why." We find this transition under way in the following lines: "Let God act as he will, and let humans stand empty/free [*ledic*]. . . . All that ever came out of God is set into pure activity [*lūter würken*]" ("Q" 306).[28] The pivotal word *ledic* (*ledig*) in this passage may be thought to refer only in retrospect to a "freedom from creatures," and only in passing even to a "passive emptiness" ready to receive God's Will. Indeed, Eckhart goes on here to say that the "highest poverty" is found in "one who does not *will* to fulfill God's Will, but who lives so that he may be free both of his own will *and* of God's Will, as when he was not (yet)." One then "stands empty of my own will and of the Will of God" ("Q" 306, 308). Having broken through both self-will and the Will of God, one stands, not just empty, but "empty and free" (*ledic und vrī*).

Ueda points out that this phrase, *ledic und vrī*, is a *Grundwort* of Eckhart's thought which reappears throughout his sermons, particular at those points where he breaks through traditional theological categories.[29] "For Eckhart," Ueda writes,

> ultimate detachment means being free from God. It means a life without God (*āne got*), wherein God himself is present as a nothingness in himself. . . . In the freedom of detachment, radical freedom from God was

able to be re-integrated with freedom *for* God. This allowed Eckhart to say: "Man's highest and dearest leave-taking is if he takes leave of God for God" ["Q" 214].[30]

More radically still, Ueda points out, "Eckhart's realization of the truest and most individual freedom" is expressed in the statement: "The just man serves neither God nor creature, for he is free" ("Q" 300). The basic term "free" thus carries in Eckhart a double meaning: "To be free means to be empty, as in the receptivity of the birth paradigm; at the same time it means to be free of God, as in the purity of the breakthrough paradigm."[31] In completely emptying itself, the self returns to the unnameable wellsprings of the pure activity of a just and blessed existence.

Here, then, is Eckhart at his most radical, where absolute passivity paradoxically releases one into an originary freedom for "pure activity." This freedom of living without why, beyond the dictates of God's Will as well as the desires of self-will, manifests itself in a "pure [egoless and non-willing] activity" that would lie beyond the horizon of activity and passivity, having radically stepped back out of Heidegger's "domain of the will."

With the idea of a *unio mystica* that completes itself in a return to "pure activity" in the midst of everyday life, Eckhart breaks with tradition by breaking through it. One of the hierarchies he upsets is that of the traditional mystical preeminence of the *vita contemplativa* over the *vita activa*. This break is particularly evident in his revolutionary interpretation of the story of Mary and Martha ("Q" 280ff.; compare Luke 10:38–42), where he reverses the traditional assessment to claim that Martha's activity, "busy about many things," is in fact a profounder expression of union with God than the passivity of Mary, who remains seated at Jesus's feet. "Eckhart not only abandoned the notion of tension-filled oscillation between action and contemplation but daringly asserted that a new kind of action performed out of a 'well-exercised ground' was superior to contemplation, at least as ordinarily conceived."[32] If at this point one is asked why he or she lives a life of good works, the answer can no longer refer to any outside reason or ground, not "for the sake of God" nor "for the sake of the moral law" and certainly not "for the sake of salvation." Eckhart writes: "If anyone were to ask a truthful man who works out of his own ground: 'Why are you performing your works?' and if he were to give a straight answer, he would say nothing else than: 'I work, therefore I work.'"[33] When one lives from out of the abyssal *grunt* of indistinction, one no longer seeks an external reason for one's works, for now "life lives out of its own ground and springs from its own source."[34] One who has emptied himself of both self-will and the Will of God, and who lives directly from out of the originary nothingness at the abyssal ground of his/God's being, would be released into a life of "pure activity" that exceeds and precedes the duality of passivity/activity. For this life of ecstatic engagement, having let go of the subjective inside, there can no longer be, nor is there any need for, an external objective answer to the question "why."[35] The life of blessedness and justice is at bottom, like Silesius's rose, without why.

Releasement: From Creatures and/or Toward Things

> Man should accustom himself to seeking and striving for nothing of his own, but rather to finding and laying hold of God in all things. . . . [One] must have a well-exercised detachment . . . ; then can one receive great things from God, and God in [all] things. ("Q" 89–90)

> The expanse of all growing things, which abide about the country path, bestows world. Its language is the unspoken in which Eckhart, the old master of reading and living, said God is first God. (D 39)

> Meister Eckhart uses the word *thing* (*dinc*) for God as well as for the soul. . . . *Thing* is here the cautious and abstemious [*enthaltsame*] name for something that is at all. . . . However, neither the general, long outworn meaning of the name "Ding," nor the Old High German meaning of the word "thing," are of the least help to us in our pressing need to experience and give adequate thought to the essential source of what we are now saying about the *Wesen* of the jug. . . . The jug is a thing neither in the sense of the Roman *res,* nor in the sense of the medieval *ens,* let alone in the modern sense of a represented object. The jug is a thing insofar as it things. (VA 169–70/176–77)

Eckhart's mystical thought, in its most radical moments, leaves both negation and deferral of will behind, pointing toward a life of "pure activity" beyond or before the duality of activity and passivity, and beyond or before either an anthropocentric demand for, or a theocentric answer to, the question "why." When Heidegger draws on Angelus Silesius's poem "Ohne warum" in *The Principle of Reason,* he writes that everything depends on hearing what is unsaid in the fragment, namely, that "man, in the most concealed grounds of his essence, first truly is when he is like the rose—

without why" (*SG* 73). Heidegger, however, cuts off his reflection on this crucial matter with the words: "we cannot pursue this thought any further here." Of course, in an important sense this matter is such that it *cannot* be pursued any further, that is, if such pursuing were to imply a seeking of reasons. But Heidegger does not mean to simply leave us with a "mystical silence," for his transformation of thinking at the end of metaphysics is precisely an attempt to think beyond the either/or of "metaphysical rationality" and so-called "mystical irrationality." Had such a transformation already been intimated in the "depth of thought" found in Eckhart's "genuine and great mysticism"? Does Heidegger's post-metaphysical thought converge with Eckhart's post-theological sermons at the moment in both where logos reaches its apex and vanishing point in the indication of a radical praxis of living "without why"?

And yet, even after we have problematized Heidegger's claim that Eckhart's *Gelassenheit* remains within the domain of the will, decisive differences do in fact remain between the two thinkers. To begin with, we need to address a second criticism implicit in Heidegger's text. In the supplements to the original version of the conversation on *Gelassenheit*, we find yet another quote from Eckhart's *Talks of Instruction:* "As far as you yourself go out of all things, just this far, not one step less or more, does God go in with all that is his" (*GA* 77:158).[36] This quotation from Eckhart, along with the two that we previously looked at, is found under the following heading in Heidegger's notes: *Vom Lassen der Dinge.* Does Eckhart's thought of *Gelassenheit* remain a detachment *from* things, whereas Heidegger, on the other hand, attempts to think a *Gelassenheit zu den Dingen* (*G* 25/55), a releasement *toward* things?

According to Emil Kettering, it is Heidegger's this-worldliness that sets "*Gelassenheit* in Heidegger's sense entirely in opposition to that of mysticism." "The way to *Gelassenheit* is for the mystics," Kettering contends, "a process of closing one's eyes to the world and an absorption in one's self," together with a corresponding "withdrawal from the world of action." On the other hand, he goes on, "Heidegger's *Gelassenheit* transforms our thinking and our acting" in such a manner that it is, "instead of a negation of earthly life, the extreme form of the affirmation of existence [*Bejahung des Daseins*]."[37] This censure of mysticism clearly does not account for Eckhart's affirmation of the *vita activa*, however much it may indeed be an appropriate criticism of the escapism and hypocritical "Self-absorption" into which "otherworldly mysticisms" all too often fall.[38]

Ueda's interpretation of Eckhart and Zen in this regard is instructive. According to Ueda, a genuine *unio mystica* paradoxically, yet necessarily, empties itself of all traces of a "mystical union" (which all too easily sublates an initial ecstatic dissolution of the ego into an expanded "Ego"), and gives way to a genuine *ekstasis* of open engagement in the world. In other words, Ueda writes, "genuine mysticism," as a dynamic movement *through* union to *ekstasis,* completes itself only in becoming "non-mysticism" (*hi-shinpishugi; der Nicht-Mystik*).[39] Ueda stresses the significance of a "dynamic Nothingness" over a "static One"; for whereas the latter implies a tendency to otherworldliness, the former leads us directly back into a profounder engagement in the extraordinary ordinariness of the everyday. He writes:

> In its existential reality, detachment displays a process that moves through a radically realized detachment back to the original, ineffable, pure ground of being and from there back into the *vita activa,* back into the reality of the world and life. There is a double return going on here, back to the original ground and back to reality in one process of realization. We may call this process a lived unity of negation and affirmation, or a union of nothingness and the here-and-now of the present.[40]

"Detachment from all created things" is, to be sure, an essential moment of Eckhart's path, one that makes for an interesting comparison with the moment of anxiety for Heidegger, in which one "lets beings as a whole slip away" in turning away from the "running around amidst beings" (*Umtrieben an das Seiende*) that characterizes the everyday life of *das Man* (*GA* 9:116/92).[41] For both Eckhart and Heidegger, however, this detachment can be understood to clear the way for a more genuine engagement with things. We have already seen how Eckhart's *unio mystica* ultimately gives way to an engaged living without why. "Such is Eckhart's this-worldliness," writes Reiner Schürmann, "which is opposed to the other-worldliness of the Neoplatonists."[42]

But do there remain certain persistent otherworldly residues in Eckhart's thought? In the *Talks of Instruction,* Eckhart writes that it is not things as such, but rather the way in which one comports oneself to things, namely, the comportment of "self-will," that is the problem. "You yourself are what hinders you in things, for you comport yourself in a crooked manner [*verkehrt*] to things" ("Q" 55). The problem is our willful comportment to creatures. What then, according to Eckhart, is the proper way to approach things? One who has a "well-exercised detachment," we are told, is able to "to receive great things from God, and God in [all] things" ("Q" 89–90). One must learn "to see God in all things" in order to one day be able "to see all things in God." But would seeing things "in God" let them be what they are; would it let them show themselves from themselves, or would it reduce them once again to "creatures" of God's design? Eckhart urges us to "find God in all things," for all the gifts God gives us are meant only to prepare us for "the *one* gift that is himself." "In every gift and work we ought to learn to look toward God, and we should not allow ourselves to be satisfied or be detained by any thing" ("Q" 89). Here perhaps returns the suspicion that Eckhart's *Geistphilosophie* ecstatically incorporates all things into the one Will of God the Father.

Yet once again we must also take into account the radicality of Eckhart's (a)theology of the abyssal Godhead, the "simple ground" or "quiet desert" "into which distinction never gazed, not the Father, nor the Son, nor the Holy Spirit." With the names "spark" or "little castle" in the soul, or the "guardian" or "light of the spirit," Eckhart names this nameless "power in the soul that is alone free." In the end, it is "free of all names and bare of all forms, entirely empty and free [*ledic und vrî, ledig und frei*], as God in himself is empty and free" when he himself is detached from all "his names and his personal properties" ("Q" 163–64). Hence Eckhart at times refers to God (or, more precisely speaking, to the Godhead—this terminological distinction is not always strictly maintained by Eckhart) as itself "nothingness" (*niht*). In his sermon on the biblical phrase: "Paul rose from the ground and with open eyes saw nothing" (Acts 9:8), Eckhart gives four interpretations of this "seeing nothing." This can mean that (1) "he saw nothing, and this nothingness was God"; (2) "he saw nothing but God"; (3) "in all things, he saw nothing but God"; and (4) "he saw all things as nothingness" ("Q" 328). The fourth meaning of nothingness, as "privation," is the most frequently employed in Eckhart's writings; insofar as God is the one and only being, all creatures are nothing in their separation from God. One must learn, therefore, to detach oneself from creatures *insofar as* they are falsely seen as independent of their ground in God. Schürmann points out that this does not mean that the creature is to be fled from because it is "inherently bad," for, strictly speaking, it is inherently nothing; "it does not exist by itself."[43]

But what does it mean to refer to God or the Godhead itself as nothingness? We have seen that the soul in its union with the Godhead finds itself "empty and free." The soul finds its freedom in an emptiness, a nameless origin that lets it be. Holger Helting interprets Eckhart in this direction, and specifically in reference (and in response) to Heidegger's thought. Helting seeks to demonstrate that Eckhart's notion of "the Will of God" cannot be understood as a "self-acting striving," but points rather toward an originary "letting." He then attempts to understand the idea of "'*Nichts*' as God/Godhead" in Eckhart's thought in the sense of a "freedom-granting letting-be" (*freigebende Seinlassen*). By way of this interpretation, Helting finds in Eckhart a profound commonality with Heidegger's thought of being as that which withdraws in order to let beings into their own being, their freedom.[44] "God" would, accordingly, signify a "nothingness," not (only) in the sense of exceeding all determination in the fullness of his exuberance, but (also) in the sense of "withdrawing" from all positive determination in order to let beings be. The Godhead would withdraw from sight as the open clearing in which things are allowed to show themselves from themselves.

The Step Back: Into Active (Wandering) Union with the Godhead of Nothingness, or Into Thoughtful Cor-respondence with the Address of Being

Yet how far can Heidegger's thought of *lethe* be understood as a "hidden Godhead"? Heidegger speaks only sparingly of "god" or "the gods." Indeed, he writes that one "who has experienced theology in his own roots [*gewachsener Herkunft*], both the theology of the Christian faith and that of philosophy, would today rather remain silent about God [when he is speaking] in the realm of thinking" (*ID* 121/54–55). In the "Letter on Humanism" Heidegger tells us that in order to raise the question of "god" and "divinity" (*Gottheit*) we must first step back to the question of "the truth of being." He thus rejects the "existentialist" label of "atheism"; but he goes on to say that his thought has also "in no way decided in favor of theism. It can be theistic as little as it can be atheistic" (*GA* 9:351–52/267). This indecisiveness is in no way, we are told, a matter of "indifference" to the question of god. Can Heidegger's reticence to speak directly of god be understood as a quiet attempt to harbor (*bergen*) "him" in his essential concealment (*Verborgenheit*), in order to "spare" (*schonen*) "him" from the modern hubristic challenging-forth of all mysteries into the bright lights of calculative reason? Heidegger does, after all, write with regard to Hölderlin: "By using the word 'the gods' sparingly [*spart*], and hesitating to say the name, the poet has brought to light the proper element of the gods" (*EHD* 20/39). In dialogue with Hölderlin's poetic word, Heidegger does, in fact, venture to speak of the "gods who have fled" and the "god who has not yet arrived." This "absence of the god," moreover, is not to be understood simply as a deficiency (28/46); for the "god comes to presence only by concealing himself" (169–70/194).

But the coming god, for Heidegger, is not the almighty and eternal God who creates and oversees the destiny of humans; "for the god too still stands under destiny [*unter dem Geschick*]" (*EHD* 169/194). The appearance of the gods, who are allotted their place as one of the quadrants of the fourfold, is dependent on the appropriating event of *Ereignis*. The gods, in order to be themselves, need to appear; and "they need the word of the poet for their appearance" (191/218). The "center" of the fourfold, Heidegger explicitly says, "is neither earth nor sky, neither god nor man" (163/188). It is this "center," as the gathering point of the "truth of being," that must first be thought if we are to once again become capable of addressing the questions of the holy, of divinity (*Gottheit*), and of the god(s). As von Herrmann puts it, "Truth, as the open of being, is not itself the god, but is rather the *Wesensraum* for the appearing or self-withdrawal of the holy, of the godly and of the god."[45] Heidegger clearly marks the distinction in *Contributions to Philosophy:* "The last god [*der letzte Gott*] is not *Ereignis* itself; rather it needs *Ereignis* as that to which the founder of the t/here [*der Dagründer*] belongs" (*GA* 65:409).

Helting, however, while not unaware of these distinctions, nevertheless attempts to find a central place for the Godhead in Heidegger's thought. He interprets Heidegger's *Gott* to be "the *appearing* of the concealed *as* the concealed" within *Ereignis* understood as "the (fourfold) clearing of the *concealed.*" The word *Gottheit*, then, could be reserved to indicate "the concealed" (*das Verborgene*) in its remaining concealed.[46] But does the expression "Godhead," as a "name" for what essentially withdraws, perhaps already "reveal" too much; does it not already give an overly determinate name to the nameless? To what extent does the expression "Godhead" inevitably tend to evoke for us the Christian "God" of revelation?[47] To the extent that this name does remain so overdetermined, the "God" in the (expression) "Godhead" would evoke the personal Father (the God of Will/Love who creates and rules over the world), not only as he who must be let go of *on the way back,* but also as he who first appears *on the way out.* Eckhart's breakthrough to the Godhead both lets go of *and* lets be (re)born the monotheistic God of Will/Love. (The wholly detached person, who lives a life of "pure activity" that is groundlessly "without why," would be released from any external idea of "the Will of God."[48] And yet, apparently, as a preacher he would still teach deference to God's Will for the sake of those who remain full of self-will and in need of a grounding reason in response to the "why.") This place reserved for the transcendent Almighty in Eckhart's thought, however preliminary or secondary it is to the breakthrough beyond God and his Will, nevertheless marks a certain decisive limit to the dialogue with Heidegger's thought.

Even if Heidegger is attentively waiting for the arrival of the future gods or for the arrival in passing of "the last god," "it" or "they" have not yet arrived and cannot yet be named, least of all, he tells us, with the name of the Christian God, whose time is past.[49] "The arrival of the presencing gods in no way signifies the return of the old gods" (*EHD* 185/212). In short: On the one hand, Heidegger does suggest that "the God-less thinking" which must abandon the God of onto-theology is "perhaps closer to the divine god" (*ID* 141/72). On the other hand, however, the "last god" anticipated in *Contributions* is said to be "totally other over against gods who have been, especially over against the Christian God" (*GA* 65:403).

But the remains of a "theological conservatism" (i.e., the preservation of a role for deference to the Will of God, before and after the radical breakthrough) in Eckhart's thought are not the only point of controversy. Heidegger would also cautiously maintain a distance from the radicality with which Eckhart speaks of the "return" (*reditus*) as a breakthrough to an *indistinct* union with the Godhead. Heidegger's "step back" (*Schritt zurück*) into a more originary relation to being is not simply a removal of distance, but also "gains distance from that which is about to arrive" (*ZSD* 32/30). This peculiar gaining of distance that is at the same time a removal of distance, we are told, is a matter of entering into a "correspondence to that which appears in the step back" (ibid.).

Jürgen Wagner's criticism of Heidegger's *Gelassenheit* from the perspective of Eckhart's *unio mystica* is relevant here, not so much as a satisfactory interpretation of Heidegger, but in that it does point toward a decisive difference between the thinker and the mystic. Wagner claims that Heidegger's *Gelassenheit* remains a matter of passivity, insofar as a distinction is maintained between the *Gegnet* (the "open-region") as "that which admits or lets in" (*der Einlassende*) and man as "that which is admitted or let in" (*der Eingelassene*) to the relation.[50] "One who has fully released himself into engagement," however, "knows nothing more of who admits and who is admitted." With Eckhart, on the other hand, the distinction between "that which lets" (*der Lassende*) and "that which is let" (*der Gelassene*) is said to ultimately disappear; even "letting" itself cancels itself out in its completion, and in favor of the self-showing of the thing that is let be. In the complete stillness of this consummated letting, it is no longer possible to make a distinction between "active" and "passive." Here, writes Wagner, "Eckhart surpasses Heidegger," and not the other way around.[51]

Heidegger's notion of *Gelassenheit* is clearly intended to exceed a mere passivity, and to intimate a relation of "letting-be" beyond the distinction of activity and passivity, that is, beyond the domain of the will (*G* 33/61). Nevertheless, Heidegger does indeed wish to maintain a certain distinction between *Sein* and *Dasein*, or between the region and the humans who dwell therein; and this may indeed mark a decisive difference from Eckhart's breakthrough to an indistinct oneness. In a certain sense it is, in fact, Heidegger that appears to remain more "conservative," even if not more "orthodox," in his respect for "transcendence." Strictly speaking, the later Heidegger drops the language of "transcendence" (*Transzendenz*), which he says is inevitably tied to "meta-physics" as a going beyond beings to being in such a way that, departing from beings, being remains thought in terms of beings (see *GA* 65:217–18). After the turn, Heidegger no longer attempts to think the meaning of being from out of Dasein's "transcendence to world," but rather to think the truth of being itself. In order to think being itself, the "reflection on the transcendence [*Überstieg*] of being over beings" must be taken as "one of those questions that stabs itself in the heart, not so that thinking may thereby die, but so that it may live in a transformed manner" (*GA* 9:417/315–16). This transformed thinking is, however, not a simple retreat to immanence, much less a "rescendence" to a technological humanism (398/301). It is rather an attempt to think the so-called "transcendence" of being *otherwise;* for any simple reversal of transcendent difference into immanent identity would precisely be another "mere counter-image of metaphysics." It is necessary to radically rethink both the sameness and the difference between being and man.

For Heidegger, "sameness" (*Selbigkeit*) comes to mean, not the abolishing of difference, but rather a "belonging-togetherness [*Zusammengehörigkeit*]" (*ID* 90/28). Moreover, he adds, it is necessary to think this "belonging-together" not in terms of "the unity of the together," but rather by way of "experiencing this together in terms of belonging" (92/29).[52] The space needed for the thinking of being, like that required for poetic naming, is a nearness that preserves an essential difference. In Heidegger's thought, "the essence of nearness appears to lie in bringing near that which is near, in that it holds it at a distance" (*EHD* 24/42).

Hence we can understand why Heidegger's conversation on *Gelassenheit,* in its original version, bore the title "*Anchibasie.*" The conversation begins by remarking that this old Greek word seemed appropriate as a name for that which the dialogue partners were looking for, namely, a kind of "knowing" that is not a willing (*GA* 77:3ff.). In the end of the conversation it is suggested that this old word, which may be translated literally as "going near" (*Nahegehen*), could be thought more precisely as a "going-into-nearness" (*In-die-Nähe-gehen*), or, literally, if still only approximately, as a "letting-oneself-into-(an engagement with)-nearness [*In-die-Nähe-hinein-sich-einlassen*]" (*G* 70/89; *GA* 77:155).

For Heidegger, then, twisting free of the will does not lead to the *unio mystica* of an indistinct identity with the Godhead, but rather to a "nearness" that preserves an essential distance. *Gelassenheit,* for Heidegger, releases one into, and itself characterizes, an a-propriating relation of cor-respondence with being. Being, for its part, is neither identical with man nor does it command man to obey its Will; nor does it "willfully appropriate" (*aneignen*) man in the sense of incorporating him into its sub-jectivity. Rather, Heidegger says, "the most profound meaning of being is letting. Letting-be beings" (*GA* 15:363). Being releases (human) beings into their own. We shall later discuss in greater detail Heidegger's at-tempts to think and to articulate this relation of *Gelassenheit* and *Seinlassen* beyond the domain of the will.

In conclusion to the present excursus on Meister Eckhart, let us re-turn to the question: to what extent is it possible to read Eckhart as hav-ing intimated a parallel, or perhaps rather an alternative, path beyond the domain of the will? On the one hand, the breakthrough to a radical union with the Godhead releases one from God's Will as well as from self-will into a life of "pure activity" without why. Does not this most radical mo-ment of a non-mystical engagement in everyday life also leave behind what Heidegger calls the "domain of the will"? To be sure, Eckhart, the preacher, does not simply announce a breakthrough to the Godhead that abandons traditional distinctions and leaves them behind. God and his Will reappear throughout Eckhart's sermons, and Heidegger would re-main suspicious of the repeated rebirth of the problem of deferred-willing.

Yet could the repeated movement between deference to and re-leasement from God's Will perhaps be understood—not just as a circle that keeps returning one to where one started, running in circles within, or rather in and out of the domain of the will—but *also* as a spiraling path of twisting free? And, moreover, would this twisting free simply lead beyond all cor-respondence to a once and for all indistinct union; or would it not be more appropriate to speak of what Schürmann calls a "wandering identity" with the Godhead in the abyssal depths of the self? According to Schürmann's discerning interpretation, "Eckhart's thought [of *Gelassenheit*] fluctuates between the demands of a law: voluntary dis-appropriation and impoverishment; and the description of a state: the original liberty which man has never lost at the basis of his being. The con-cept of releasement includes these two aspects."[53] Finite humans could never be once and for all freed from the demand to abandon their self-will, that is, from the paradoxical task of willing not to will. But neither would they be wholly confined to the domain of the will; for by way of ever again stepping back to their abyssal roots, they can rediscover an origi-nary freedom beyond or before all self-assertion and deference; they can re-tap an always-already-and-not-yet wellspring of non-willing.

To the extent that Eckhart has intimated a wandering path which commutes to this radical source of non-willing, his mystical thought could not be wholly confined within an epochal stage in the rise of the metaphysics of will.[54] But this inability to restrict Eckhart's *Gelassenheit* to the domain of the will suggests, then, the possibility of a non-historical excess to the history of metaphysics, an excess which both critically calls into question the seamless rule of its epochs and affirmatively suggests the possibility of participating in a transition to an other beginning beyond the closure of metaphysics in the technological will to will.

6

The Mature Critique of the Will

Vielleicht ist überhaupt der Wille selbst das Böse. (*GA* 77:208)

It is first the will that arranges itself everywhere in technology, that devours the earth in the exhaustion and consumption and alteration of the artificial. (*VA* 94/88–89)

As we have seen, Heidegger's path through the 1920s and 1930s can be read as a struggle to find and define the problem of the will. Despite the many foreshadowings that can be found in (or read back into) these texts, the will is first decisively and explicitly problematized beginning in the waning years of the 1930s. We have seen that *Contributions to Philosophy* still attempts to think in terms of a "most proper will," albeit one of "reservedness" rather than self-assertion, without yet seeing the very concept of "will" as inextricably embedded in the metaphysical tradition from which it seeks to twist free. Nevertheless, in *Contributions* and its sequel volumes many of the key elements of Heidegger's mature thought begin to take definite shape, including (1) the notion of the "history of being"; (2) the critique of technology or "machination"; and (3) the possibility of a turning to "the other beginning" beyond the end of metaphysics. In the latter two parts of this chapter I focus on the first two elements as they relate to Heidegger's mature (i.e., post-1939–40) critique of the will. The third element, the question of a turning to an other beginning, will be introduced in the final part of this chapter, in preparation for more detailed discussion in chapter 7 and later chapters.

   In the first section of this chapter, I discuss the decisive turn from the will which takes place during the course of Heidegger's prolonged confrontation (*Auseinandersetzung*) with Nietzsche's philosophy of the will to power. In the second section, I then show how Heidegger situates the will to power as the penultimate stage in the history of metaphysics. This history is narrated as one of an increasing withdrawal of being and an accompanying escalating prominence of the will. Metaphysically the history of the West completes itself in the will to power, which in turn finally reveals itself as the technological will to will. In the third part of this chapter I examine Heidegger's critique of the epoch of technology, wherein ultimately humans themselves are threatened with being reduced to "human resources" for the cybernetic drive of the will to will.

In the extreme distress of our abandonment into willful manipulation of beings and domination of the earth, however, Heidegger claims that there lies concealed the possibility of a change within human nature corresponding to a turning in the history of being to an other beginning. In the desolateness of this extreme epoch of will lies the possibility for a turning to a way of being other than willing, a turning to non-willing. Yet only by first plumbing the depths of our distressful times can the question of such a turning be raised; it is necessary to first of all meditate on the essence of technology, nihilism, and the will.

In this chapter more than elsewhere I shall let Heidegger's texts speak for themselves, often with an emphasis on explication and clarification rather than on critical interpretation. Heidegger never wrote the magnum opus of his later period, and thus it is necessary to orchestrate and explicate passages here from the many lectures and essays—starting with, but not limited to, those decisive texts gathered in the 1,100 pages of the two *Nietzsche* volumes—which together present a complexly interwoven critique of the will that lies at the heart of his later thought. The work of condensation and exposition in this chapter will lay the ground for the more interpretive and critical work to be carried out in later chapters.

The Critique of Nietzsche's Will to Power

The *Nietzsche* Volumes as the Site of a Crisis and a Turn

Nietzsche hat mich kaputtgemacht.[1]

Heidegger's *Auseinandersetzung* with Nietzsche was also a confrontation with his own embrace of the will. Confronting Nietzsche's radical affirmation of the will to power forced Heidegger into a crisis: to will or not to will? But is that the only way to form the question? Might there not be a third, a radically other way—to be? Heidegger's path of recovery from this dilemma in fact led neither to a Schopenhauerian resignation nor to a Nietzschean voluntarism, but rather set him explicitly on a path to non-willing.

The lectures and essays that make up Heidegger's two *Nietzsche* volumes were written between 1936 and 1946.[2] Upon the publication of these volumes in 1961 Heidegger wrote: "Considered as a whole, the publication aims to provide a view of the path of thought I followed from 1930 to the 'Letter on Humanism' (1947)" (*N1* 10/xl). In other words, the *Nietzsche* volumes are a document of the developmental turn(s) in Heidegger's thought. They both gather the thought of the early 1930s and inaugurate the later thought as found in such essays as the "Letter on Humanism." Indeed, despite the crucial steps made in earlier works, it can be said that the second decisive turn in Heidegger's thinking, the turn away from a philosophy which still all too often draws its categories and attunements from the domain of the will, takes place in the *Nietzsche* volumes.

As simplified as Hannah Arendt's comment may be, there is indeed an important sense in which in the first volume Heidegger still largely "goes along with" Nietzsche, while the second is written in an "unmistakable polemical tone."[3] In the first lecture course Heidegger gives a strikingly affirmative account of the will, or at least of that "genuine willing which surges forward in resoluteness [*Entschlossenheit*], that 'yes,' [which] instigates the seizure of our entire being, of the very essence within us" (*N1* 57/47). He thus goes so far as to equate the sense of will he finds in Nietzsche with his own notion of resoluteness: "Will is, in our terms, *Entschlossenheit*, in which he who wills stations himself abroad among beings in order to keep them firmly within his field of action" (59/48). Heidegger's turn from the will is not merely a matter of a change in terminology; it signals a fundamental change in thought inasmuch as it is precisely this characteristic of man "stationing himself abroad among beings *in order to* keep them within *his* field of action" that becomes the target of Heidegger's critique of the will as a matter of what I am calling "ecstatic-incorporation."

While in the first lecture course Heidegger largely follows Nietzsche in seeing the will as responsible for "instigating the very essence within us," and although his phenomenological description of the will remains remarkably consistent, by the time of the fourth lecture course Heidegger's *appraisal* of the will has undergone a drastic alteration, if not indeed a conversion. Moreover, the fundamental reach of the will is radically called into question. Now Heidegger writes: "For Nietzsche, will to power is the ultimate *factum* to which we come. What seems certain to Nietzsche is questionable to us" (*N2* 114/73).[4] Heidegger does in fact acknowledge the will to power as the essence of *modern* man, and indeed as the manner in which the being of beings is revealed (in extreme concealment) in this epoch. And yet he goes on to ask: "But the will to power itself—where does it originate . . . ?" (ibid.). If the will to power is in fact determined by a particular sending of being, namely as an extreme epoch of the self-withdrawal of being in its most proper essencing, then in this abandonment of beings to the will to power is concealed the possibility of a re-turn (*Einkehr*) into a more originary mode of being.

This does not imply a simple rejection of Nietzsche's thought, but rather an attempt to go beneath and beyond Nietzsche by going through him. It is by revealing the pervasiveness of the will to power in the modern epoch that the need for a turning to an other way of being can be awakened. In this sense, Heidegger will continue to "go along with Nietzsche": "the modern metaphysics of subjectity is consummated in Nietzsche's doctrine of the will to power as the 'essence' of everything real" (*GA* 5:239/83). And yet, according to Heidegger, what Nietzsche's thought claims to reveal as the unchanging essence of beings *as such*—i.e., the will to power as "the world viewed from the inside," as "the ultimate ground and character of all change" and as "the innermost essence of being"[5]—must in truth be historically situated in a particular epoch of the history of being. The will to power is the *letzte Faktum* only within what Heidegger delimits as the penultimate *epoche* of the truth of being in the metaphysics of modernity; it is preceded by the will of dialectical reason and followed by the technological will to will.

A Critical Phenomenology of the Will to Power

In chapter 1 we considered in some detail how Heidegger draws on and criticizes Nietzsche's will to power in his account of the essence of will as "the will to will," as "power-preservation/power-enhancement," or as what I am calling "ecstatic-incorporation." Here I shall summarize and supplement that earlier analysis.

Willing is always a willing out beyond oneself, and therefore must be distinguished both from a mere striving and from an egoism thought in the static sense of a solipsistic ego cut off from the world. The subject of will exists out beyond himself and is thus a particular manner of being-in-the-world. This manner is summed up by Heidegger as follows. "To will . . . is to-will-to-be-master [*Herrsein-wollen*]" (*N2* 265/194); in other words, the manner in which the one who wills exists is that of a "being-master-out-beyond-oneself [*Über-sich-hinaus-Herrsein*]" (*N1* 76/63). In willing, the subject exceeds himself only to incorporate this excess back into his subjectivity. The *ekstasis* of willing is thus always brought back into the economy of the ego; the self-overcoming of willing is always in the name of an expansion of the self, an increase in its territory, its power. Willing is essentially this reaching beyond oneself in "commanding" (*Befehlen*).

This is the manner in which Heidegger understands Nietzsche's key notion of "the will to power." For Nietzsche, he claims, the terms "will" and "power" say "the same"; but this does not make the phrase "will to power" simply redundant. On the one hand, Heidegger claims already in the first lecture course that power is "nothing else than the essence of will. Hence will to power is will to will, which is to say, willing is a self-willing" (*N1* 46/37). The will to power is ultimately the "will to will," for, as Heidegger puts it nearly a decade later: "What the will wills it has already. For the will wills its will. Its will is what it has willed. The will wills itself" (*GA* 5:234/77–78). There is thus a repetitious self-sameness to the will to power, despite its essentially ecstatic character; the will reaches out to the world only to reduce this world to more of its same.

Heidegger is careful not to reduce the phrase "will to power" to a static redundancy. "Nonetheless," he writes, "will is not simply power, and power is not simply will. Instead we can say the following: The essence of power is *will to* power, and the essence of willing is will *to power*" (*N2* 265/195). The will *to* power has a dynamic character of insatiable growth. "In will, as willing to be more, as will to power, enhancement and heightening are essentially implied" (*N1* 72/60). The will to power essentially involves the will to an increase in power. But, on the other hand, in order to will this increase, the will must first will to preserve its established domain of power. The reverse is also the case, as even "a mere pause in power-enhancement . . . is already the beginning of the decline of power" (*GA* 5:235/78); preservation of power demands a ceaseless increase in power. "Power can only empower itself to an overpowering by commanding *both* enhancement *and* preservation" (*N2* 268/197). In short, the will to power involves both moments of increase and securing, securing and increase, moments which mutually enable one other. Nevertheless, in the end, what is increased is in a fundamental sense the "same" as what is preserved; the will to power, for all its dynamism, moves in an expanding yet essentially closed circle of the "will to will."

Thus, the "will *to* will" must be thought dynamically, even if, in a more profound sense, it dynamically repeats more of the same. The will is ultimately the insatiable, ever-expanding, yet always essentially the same "will to will." "In this way [the will] continually comes as the selfsame back upon itself as the same" (*GA* 5:237/81). Despite its ecstatic character, the will is after all, it would seem, a kind of "encapsulation of the ego," not, to be sure, in the timid sense of shutting out the world, but in the aggressive sense of expanding the territory of the ego to include the world in its field of power. Ultimately: "Willing wills the one who wills, as such a one; and willing posits the willed as such" (*N1* 51/40). The will, in willing itself, reaches out to the world as something it "posits" (*setzt*) as a means for its movement of power-enhancement and hence power-preservation, power-preservation and hence power-enhancement.

The above is a condensed account of Heidegger's critical phenomenology of Nietzsche's will to power. As we shall see, this interpretation of the will to power not only serves as a basis for Heidegger's critique of Nietzsche, but, because he sees the latter's thought as the culmination of Western metaphysics and as ushering in the current epoch of technology, it also serves as a foil for Heidegger's later thought as a whole. The "positing" (*Setzen*) or "positioning" (*Stellen*) character of the will, which represents (*vor-stellt*) its objects as means to its own securing and enhancing of power, is at the heart of what Heidegger problematizes as the *Ge-stell* of technology. Hence, Heidegger explicitly makes the following connection between the power-preservation moment of the will to power and the technological reduction of the world to "standing-reserve" (*Bestand*).

> The preservation of the level of power belonging to the will reached at any given time consists in the will's surrounding itself with an encircling sphere of that which it can reliably grasp at, each time, as something behind itself, in order on the basis of it to contend for its own security. That encircling sphere bounds off the standing-reserve [*Bestand*] of what presences . . . [as what] is immediately at the disposal of the will. (*GA* 5:239/83–84)

Moreover, Heidegger claims that "the unconditional rule of calculating reason [in the epoch of technology] belongs to the will to power" (*VA* 77/75). He thus directly connects Nietzsche's will to power as the will to will with the "way of revealing beings" he calls "the essence of technology." We shall return to the crucial relation between the will and technology in the third part of this chapter. Unlike the critique of technology, which is one of the later Heidegger's own central concerns, the claims that Nietzsche's thought is the culmination of metaphysics, and the ultimate form of nihilism, attack Nietzsche's own self-understanding. Before leaving Nietzsche, then, let us briefly consider these charges insofar as they relate to the problem of the will.

Heidegger's Nietzsche: The Nihilistic Last Metaphysician

> I mistrust all systematizers and I avoid them. The will to a system is a lack of integrity. . . . Those were steps for me, and I have climbed up over them: to that end I had to pass over them. Yet they thought that I wanted to retire on them.
> —Nietzsche[6]

I am still stuck in the "abyss" of Nietzsche. (*Z* 320)

Heidegger's critical interpretation of Nietzsche is as controversial as it is influential.[7] Most important in the context of the present study, however, is the key role it plays in the development of Heidegger's own thought. My discussion of Heidegger's critique shall concentrate on four topics: (1) Nietzsche's thought as the ultimate entanglement in nihilism; (2) Nietzsche as the last metaphysician; (3) Nietzsche's own spirit of revenge; and (4) the role of "Heidegger's Nietzsche."

1. While Nietzsche claims to have revealed the essence of nihilism and the way toward a self-overcoming of nihilism, Heidegger claims that in fact Nietzsche's thought is itself the ultimate entanglement in nihilism.

Nietzsche understands nihilism as "the devaluation of the highest values," and proposes a radical "revaluation" as a means of "overcoming nihilism." Heidegger takes issue both with Nietzsche's "value thinking" and with the very idea of willing to "overcome" nihilism. Thinking in terms of "values" involves an orientation to and from the subject and his will. "Value is 'essentially the viewpoint' of the power-reckoning seeing of will to power. . . . Will to power manifests itself as the subjectivity that is characterized by value thinking" (*N2* 269–72/198–200). The "essence of nihilism," according to Heidegger, "is the history in which there is nothing to being itself" (*N2* 338/201). Nihilism is precisely the history of an increasing centralization of the subject (and his willful positing of values) who forgets that "beings are thanks to being," that is, thanks to a granting which first opens a clearing for beings to appear. Value thinking forgets being. Thus it is not by chance that Nietzsche, the thinker of will to power and the revaluation of all values, claims that "being" is nothing but a "wisp and a vapor." According to Nietzsche, what is needed is not a reopening of the question of being, but a will to power strong enough to posit its own "new values." "Value is thought as a condition of the will" (*VA* 73/72).

For Heidegger, this attempt to overcome nihilism by way of a willful revaluation is akin to an attempt to put out a fire with kerosene.

> It is precisely in the positing of new values from the will to power, by which and through which Nietzsche believes he will overcome nihilism, that nihilism proper first proclaims that there is nothing to being itself, which has now become a value. (*N2* 340/203)

Nietzsche's thought is at one and the same time the "low point" in the abandonment/forgottenness of being, and the "high point" in the subject's self-conscious affirmation of his will. Nihilism completes itself in the explicit value positing of the will to power.

> Nietzsche's metaphysics is nihilistic insofar as it is value thinking, and insofar as the latter is grounded in will to power as the principle of all valuation. Nietzsche's metaphysics consequently becomes the fulfillment

of nihilism proper, because it is the metaphysics of the will to power.
(342/204)

Heidegger concludes: "Nietzsche's metaphysics is not an overcoming of
nihilism. It is the ultimate entanglement in nihilism" (340/203). Moreover,
Heidegger criticizes the very idea of "overcoming" nihilism. Nihilism, he
claims, "does not allow itself to be overcome, not because it is insuperable,
but because all willing-to-overcome is inappropriate to its essence" (389/
243). The will-to-overcome nihilism repeats the very problem it seeks to
surmount.

2. According to Heidegger, Nietzsche's critique of metaphysics ends
up completing metaphysics by carrying out the final possibility on its horizon. Thus, "Nietzsche's countermovement against metaphysics is, as the
mere turning upside down of metaphysics, an inextricable entanglement
in metaphysics" (*GA* 5:217/61).

We have seen how Heidegger pulls the carpet out from under Nietzsche's feet by claiming that the latter's attempt to overcome nihilism by
means of willing new values is actually the most acute expression of nihilism as the abandonment of being. In a related manner, Heidegger
claims that Nietzsche's "overturning" of Platonism or metaphysics is actually the final expression of metaphysics: Nietzsche, the self-proclaimed
anti-metaphysician, is in truth the "last metaphysician."

"Metaphysical thinking rests on the distinction between what truly
is and what, measured against this, constitutes all that is not truly in being" (*VA* 118/230). Nietzsche would agree with this definition. Indeed,
Heidegger no doubt learned much from his predecessor in the critique
of metaphysics and nihilism. Nevertheless, Heidegger sees Nietzsche's
thought as a "mere inversion" that does not twist free of the "yawning gulf
between realms" (ibid.) essential to metaphysics itself. The distinction between realms, which constitutes metaphysics,

> persists even when the Platonic hierarchy of supersensuous and sensuous
> is inverted and the sensuous realm is experienced more essentially and
> more thoroughly—in the direction Nietzsche indicates with the name
> *Dionysus*. For the superabundance for which Zarathustra's "great long-
> ing" yearns is the inexhaustible permanence of Becoming, which the
> will to power in the eternal recurrence of the same wills itself to be.
> (118–19/230)

Nietzsche's "reversals" and "revaluations" do not break out of the horizon
of metaphysics and metaphysical subjectivity as such. Nietzsche's over-
turnings are "a mere countermovement" and thus "necessarily remain, as

does everything 'anti,' held fast in the essence of that over against which it moves" (*GA* 5:217/61). Nietzsche's "overman," for example, is a mere reversal of the traditional characterization of man as the "rational animal"; "he is the *animal rationale* that is fulfilled in *brutalitas*" (*N2* 23/177). Nietzsche's emphasis on the primacy of "becoming" is in the end recuperated in the thought of the eternal return which, as the supreme act of the will to power, stamps becoming with the character of being.

In short, Nietzsche's philosophy is said to invert but not twist free of metaphysics. Indeed, as "*a metaphysics of the absolute subjectivity of will to power*" (*N2* 200/147), it is the fulfillment of metaphysics, its final stage. Heidegger ultimately reconstructs, "on Nietzsche's behalf" as it were, the following outline of "Nietzsche's metaphysics":

> "Will to power," "nihilism," "the eternal return of the same," "the overman," and "justice" are the five fundamental expressions of Nietzsche's metaphysics. . . ."Will to power" is the word for the being of beings as such, the *essentia* of beings. "Nihilism" is the name for the history of the truth of beings thus defined. "Eternal return of the same" means the way in which beings as a whole are, the *existentia* of beings. "Overman" describes the kind of humanity that is demanded by this whole. "Justice" is the essence of the truth of beings as will to power. (*N2* 259–60/189)

This critical reconstruction of "Nietzsche's metaphysics" is, to be sure, highly contentious; in the end it may tell us more about Heidegger's history of metaphysics than about Nietzsche's own attempt to shake the foundations of the metaphysical tradition. Although he often calls attention to the movement character of his own path of thought, Heidegger ironically attempts to force the dynamic polylogue of Nietzsche's writing into a kind of final anti- or overturned metaphysical system, an "inverted Platonism." Only in the final productive year of Nietzsche's life, according to Heidegger, did Nietzsche's inversion within the domain of metaphysics begin to clearly become a "twisting free" (*Herausdrehung*) of it; yet "during the time when the overturning of Platonism became for Nietzsche a twisting free of it, madness befell him" (*N1* 233/202).[8] But from the start was not Nietzsche's attempt a matter of radically questioning, rather than simply inverting, hierarchical binary oppositions; was it not his intention to become, not a Dionysian madman, but a "Dionysian philosopher," in other words—those of his *first* book—"a Socrates who practices music"?[9]

Most question-worthy in the present context is the smooth systematic linking of the will to power and the eternal recurrence. In insisting that "they must say the *selfsame* thing [dasselbe]" (*N2* 17/171), Heidegger fails to explore the *tension between* these thoughts. The devastating thought of the eternal return may not simply present, as Heidegger suggests, the supreme triumph of the will to power, so much as bring the will to power to an impasse, perhaps even to a crisis through which it could pass only by way of transformation into a radically different fundamental attunement.

3. Heidegger's *Auseinandersetzung* is most provocative where he proceeds by way of immanent critique. He criticizes Nietzsche using the latter's own terms of critique when he argues that Nietzsche's metaphysics of the will to power—as ultimately the will to affirm the eternal recurrence of the same—repeats that which it was meant to overcome: the spirit of revenge (*der Geist der Rache*).

According to Nietzsche, the will comes to an impasse in the face of that which it cannot master, the unalterable past of the "it was." This impasse was for Nietzsche a prelude to the "most difficult of thoughts," the eternal recurrence of the same. A decisive question of Nietzsche interpretation is whether the latter notion is the ultimate triumph of will, as Heidegger would have it, or whether, on the other hand, it is the occasion for breaking beyond the domain of the will to power to an *amor fati* that perhaps twists free of both active assertion of will and passive resignation.[10]

The later Heidegger's interpretation of Nietzsche is not, in fact, without any appreciation for the more radical thrust in Nietzsche's thought, in this case his attempt to free himself from the spirit of revenge.[11]

> Nietzsche's thinking focuses on deliverance from the spirit of revenge. . . . The space of this freedom from revenge is prior to all pacifism, and equally to all power politics [*Gewaltpolitik*]. It is prior to all weak do-nothingism and shirking of sacrifice, and to blind activity for its own sake. . . . That is the space toward which he who crosses over is moving—the overman—"Caesar with the *soul* of Christ." (*WhD* 33/88)

Here Heidegger affirms that Nietzsche's thought on the will moves in a direction which is neither a matter of active willing nor of passive notwilling; Nietzsche's thought moves toward a space prior to the opposition of pacifism and power politics, do-nothingism and blind activity, a space other than the domain of the will.

Nevertheless, Heidegger concludes some pages later that Nietzsche does not succeed in finally breaking free of the domain of the will, but rather proclaims its ultimate triumph.

> Deliverance from revenge is [according to Nietzsche's thought] not liberation from all will. For, since will is being, deliverance as the annulment of willing would lead to a mere nothingness. Deliverance from revenge is the will's liberation from what is revolting to it, so that the will

can at last be will. . . . The will is delivered from revulsion when it wills the constant recurrence of the same. . . . The eternal recurrence of the same is the supreme triumph of the metaphysics of the will that eternally wills its own willing. (43/104)

For Heidegger, Nietzsche's "one thought" is that being is in *essentia* will to power which in *existentia* is the eternal recurrence of the same (see *N2* 260/189). The thought of eternal recurrence would thus, far from occasioning a break beyond the will to power, be the ultimate self-expression of a triumphant will. This interpretation finds support in such passages from Nietzsche as the following: "To stamp upon becoming the character of being—that is the supreme will to power. . . . That *everything recurs* is the closest *approximation of a world of becoming to a world of being*."[12] Heidegger draws the following conclusion from his interpretation of this passage:

> Does such thinking . . . overcome the spirit of revenge? Or does there not lie concealed in this very *stamping*—which takes all becoming into the protection of eternal recurrence of the same—a form of ill will *against* sheer transiency and thereby a highly spiritualized spirit of revenge? (*VA* 117/228)

4. Heidegger does not label Nietzsche "the last metaphysician" in order to dismiss the significance of his philosophy of the will to power, but rather in order to "credit" him with having (albeit inadvertently) articulated the essence of the modern epoch of the history of metaphysics. The critique of Nietzsche is thus not carried out for the sake of dismissing him; rather, in order to think through the past and present of the history of metaphysics, Heidegger urges: "We must think him" (*N1* 657/157). Heidegger's *Nietzsche* is thus not presented merely as the record of a personal confrontation, but rather as a reflection on a crucial moment of the history of metaphysics itself.

In conclusion to this discussion of "Heidegger's Nietzsche," and in transition to a broader consideration of the role of the will in Heidegger's history of metaphysics and its most extreme epoch of technology, let us remark the following three points concerning the place of Nietzsche in Heidegger's thought. According to Heidegger: (*a*) Nietzsche succeeds in giving the most direct expression to the being of beings as it reveals itself (in extreme concealment) as will in the modern epoch. In Nietzsche's will to power the will no longer assumes the guise of reason or spirit, but appears undisguised as the will to power. (*b*) However, Nietzsche does not think being as the history of being, and therefore he does not see that being appears as will only in an epoch of the abandonment of being. In this sense Nietzsche does not see the will as the sign of an estrangement, but rather sees it "metaphysically" as the ultimate *factum* to be endured and indeed affirmed. Thus Nietzsche's thought, as the attempt to willfully overcome nihilism, is paradoxically the deepest entanglement in nihilism. (*c*) But for Heidegger this deepest entanglement is not simply to be regretted. The extreme epoch of will (nihilism, technology) is Janus-faced; in the extreme distress of the abandonment of being lies the possibility of awakening to the need of being and thereby the possibility of turning to an other beginning beyond the will. The "history of being" must therefore be understood as the horizon in which Heidegger understands Nietzsche, nihilism, the will, and the possible turning to non-willing.

The Rise of the Will in the History of Being

> The word of Nietzsche speaks of the destining of two millennia of Western history. (*GA* 5:213/58)

The problem of the will for Heidegger is historically situated. Western history involves an emergence and upsurge of the will leading to Nietzsche's will to power and thereafter to the technological will to will. According to Heidegger, then, the problem of the will must be understood in the context of the "history of being" (*Geschichte des Seins* or *Seinsgeschichte*), which occurs, from the ancient Greeks to the present, as the "history of metaphysics." We have seen that Nietzsche's will to power serves as the footing and foil for Heidegger's critique of the will. The will to power is at once the historical truth of the being of beings in the modern epoch, *and* an extreme concealment of the letting-be proper to being. Will to power over beings expresses both man's historical essence in the epoch of modernity, and his alienation from a more originary response-ability to assist in letting beings be.[13]

The History of Being as a Descensional and Eschatological Continuity-of-Discontinuity

It has often been remarked that Heidegger's history of being resembles a kind of inversion of Hegel's history of Spirit.[14] Whereas Hegel sees the movement of history as one of progress toward Spirit's self-realization, Heidegger's history of being would, on this account, tell the story of a decline of the West from the allegedly "pristine origin" of the pre-Socratic Greeks, who were presumably attuned in wonder amidst the unconcealment (*aletheia*) of being, to the epoch of technology, where humans have completely forgotten or been abandoned by being in their frenzy of willful domination of the world. The escalation of the will would correspond to an increase in historical distance from the golden age of the pre-Socratics. Were this to be the case, both the story of the decline and the directives or direction for recovery would be simple to tell. If each of the epochs of being were seamlessly connected in a single process of decline, then perhaps the history of the escalation of will could be rationally deduced or at least dialectically reconstructed. And if the story were simply one of decline from a pristine origin, then this diagnosis would call for an attempted recovery of or return to this age of innocence. And yet, although Heidegger does indeed see a certain continuous decline in the history of the West, and although he does attempt to reawaken an attunement to being by way of rereading the Greeks, his thought of the history of being is more complex than this quasi-reversal of a Hegelian history of progress would account for. The question-worthy and questionable character of Heidegger's fundamental thought of the history of being shall concern us throughout the remaining chapters of this book. In this section let me begin by laying out three points that need to be kept in mind.

1. Heidegger stresses the *discontinuity* as well as the *continuity* between epochs. When specifically addressing the question of the relation between epochs, he in fact tends to stress their radical discontinuity. The continuity, on the other hand, is usually stressed directly or indirectly either when discussing the whole of the history of metaphysics, that is, the history of the increasing withdrawal of being since the time of the Greeks, or when juxtaposing the unity of this history since the "first beginning" with that of the possibility of an "other beginning" yet to arrive. The degree of discontinuity is no doubt greatest between the first beginning and the other beginning, but there is also a certain element of continuity there (i.e., the *Zuspiel*, the "interplay" between or "pass" from the first to the other beginning), just as there is an element of discontinuity between epochs within the history of the first beginning, that is, between the epochs in the history of metaphysics.

The term "epoch," Heidegger tells us, does not refer to a span of calculable time, but rather to "the fundamental characteristic of the sending, the in each case particular holding-back of itself [*das jeweilige An-sich-halten seiner selbst*] in favor of the discernability of the gift, that is, of being with regard to the grounding of beings" (*ZSD* 9/9).[15] He draws on the sense of the Greek *epechein* as "to keep in, hold back" or "to stay, stop, wait" in order to articulate the manner in which being holds itself back, withdraws so that beings may be. "As the promise of its truth, being keeps to itself with its own essence. . . . From the respective [*jeweiligen*] distance of the withdrawal . . . such keeping to itself determines each epoch of the history of being as the *epoche* of being itself" (*N2* 383/239). In self-withdrawal being delimits its originary abundance, and thereby lets beings be in their finite determinations of truth. The history of being is a sequence of epochal gifts of letting-be (*Seinlassen*).

Yet over the course of the history of metaphysics, being withdraws to the point of abandonment (*Verlassenheit*). Correspondingly, humans are progressively abandoned to their own self-assertion; the fundamental (dis)attunement of will escalates until, abandoned to the pure immanence of "the will to will," the will recognizes no other in its frenzied hunt for more control, more power, more will. The progressive emergence of the will in correlation to the increasing withdrawal of being thus provides a marked aspect of continuity to the history of metaphysics.

And yet, Heidegger also claims that each epoch originates in the *Augenblick* of a new sending of being. The history of being must be thought in this ambiguous (*zweideutig*) continuity/discontinuity: "The sequence of epochs in the destiny of being is not accidental, nor can it be calculated as necessary" (*ZSD* 9/9). Elsewhere he writes that, on the one hand "the epochs suddenly spring up like sprouts," and yet on the other hand they also unfold the continuity of a tradition.

> The epochs can never be derived from one another, much less be placed on the track of an ongoing process. Nevertheless, there is a legacy [*Überlieferung*] from epoch to epoch. But it does not run between the epochs like a band linking them; rather, the legacy always comes from what is concealed in the *Geschick*, just as if from one source various streamlets arise that feed a stream that is everywhere and nowhere. (*SG* 154)

Another metaphor that might be used is that of a chain, where each link (epoch) is uniquely determined and non-deducible from the others, yet also connected to them to form the continuity of a series. On the one hand, Heidegger refuses to claim any strictly logical continuity to his history of being, rejecting even the complex continuity of a dialectic: "In no way can it be seen that individual philosophies and epochs of philosophy have emerged from one another in the sense of the necessity of a dialectical process" (*WP* 62–63). On the other hand, there is a compelling cogency to the history he tells, which narrates an increasing forgottenness/withdrawal of being from the pre-Socratics to Plato and Aristotle, to the Latin world, to the moderns, and finally to the utmost abandonment of being in the epoch of technology.

Both continuity and discontinuity are thus essential to Heidegger's history of being, such that each aspect, taken alone, somehow misses the

mark. Borrowing a term from Nishida Kitarō, who also struggled to articulate a sense of time and history that does justice to both the continuity
of identity and discontinuity of change, Heidegger's history of being
demands that we think in terms of a "discontinuous-continuity" or a
"continuity-of-discontinuity."[16]

2. The second point to be made is that Heidegger explicitly rejects
the idea of any superficial attempt to "return to the Greeks." In this regard
he writes of "the obvious misinterpretation" of his notion of "the step
back" (*der Schritt zurück*), namely, "the view that the step back consists in a
historical return to the earliest thinkers of Western philosophy" (*ID* 118/
52). The direction of the step back is rather back to "the realm which until
now has been skipped over" (115/49), that is, the step back "moves out of
metaphysics into the essence of metaphysics" (117/51). Heidegger does
not suggest a mere chronological step back *within* the history of being, but
rather a thoughtful step back *to* the history of being, that is, to the essencing (*Wesen* understood verbally) of truth. Certainly this takes place only by
way of a conversation with past philosophies; yet this conversation is engaged in not for the sake of a historical (*historische*) "regress" to their age,
but rather for the sake of a creative "retrieval," a *Wiederholung* of the tradition on which and before which we presently stand. Heidegger attempts
to experience both what the Greeks thought and—even more important—what they left unthought. Nor is the step back simply an attempted
"retreat" from the troubles of the present; it is rather an attempt to understand and think through the historical (*geschichtliche*) unfolding of the
current epoch of technological nihilism.

3. This brings us to our third point, which is that Heidegger does not
simply disparage the willful oblivion of being as a human moral failure.
Nor does he blame Nietzsche for proffering the thought of the will to
power.

> That the being of beings becomes operative as will to power is not the
> result of the emergence of Nietzsche's metaphysics. Rather, Nietzsche's
> thought has to plunge into metaphysics because *being radiates its own
> essence as will to power;* that is, as the sort of thing that in the history of the
> truth of beings must be grasped through the projection as will to power.
> (*N2* 239/181, emphasis added)

As we shall discuss in detail below, the desolate epoch of the technological will to will is Janus-faced; for precisely in the extreme abandonment of being lies the possibility for a turning. Hence, our own extreme
epoch at the end of the first beginning of Western history is as full of potential as it is forsaken, an "evening land" (*Abendland*) at the same time as

a promise of the dawn of an other beginning. In this sense Heidegger's history of being is not merely "descensional," but rather *eschatological.*

Although in the following discussion I shall focus on the continuity of the history of being (as the history of the rise of will), we must keep these three points in mind: the continuity-of-discontinuity between epochs, the step back as a critical and creative *Wiederholung,* and the Janus-faced character of the epoch of technology. These three aspects of the history of being shall become particularly important later when we discuss the possibility of a turning beyond the epoch of will/technology, and the question of how man can and should participate in this turning, that is, how he is to cor-respond to the sending of being.

The Ambiguous Relation of the Greeks to the Will

Heidegger turns to the Greeks both in tracing the origins of the will *and* in attempting to think non-willing(ly). There is an important difference, to be sure, between the pre-metaphysical early thinkers, the so-called pre-Socratics, and the first metaphysical philosophers, Plato and Aristotle. When he traces the origin of the modern metaphysics of will back to the Greeks, it is usually in reference to the latter pair. With regard to the pre-Socratics, on the other hand, he defends them against such charges as that of anthropomorphism,[17] and looks to them for resources for thinking more original notions of truth (*aletheia*), justice (*dike*), artistic creation (*poeisis*), and knowing (*noein*). But even when he considers the pre-Socratics as pre-metaphysical, he claims that they did not explicitly *think* either their experience of *aletheia* or the attunement of non-willing; these tasks are claimed to be his and our own.

The case of Plato and Aristotle is somewhat more straightforward, but still far from unambiguous. In general, Heidegger thinks of their philosophies as the "inceptual end of the great beginning [*anfängliche Ende des großen Anfangs*]" (*EM* 137). He clearly traces the origin of the metaphysical notion of truth as correspondence to Plato (see *GA* 9:203ff./ 155ff.), and thus also the distant premonitions of Cartesian subjectivity, knowing as representation, and by implication, then, the first signs of the (dis)attunement of will. It is, however, in Aristotle that Heidegger finds the origin of the concept of the will. In the first lecture course on Nietzsche, Heidegger explicitly traces the roots of the modern notion of will back to the Greeks, and specifically to Aristotle, as follows:

> Willing is a kind of desiring and striving. The Greeks call it *orexis.* . . .
> But will, as striving, is not blind compulsion. What is desired and striven
> for is represented as such along with the compulsion. . . . What does

Aristotle teach concerning the will? The tenth chapter of Book 3 [of
De anima] deals with *orexis*, desiring. Here Aristotle says (433a 15ff.):
". . . for what is desired in the desiring moves, and the intellect, representation, moves only because it represents to itself what is desired in the
desiring." . . . Aristotle's conception of the will becomes definitive for all
Western thought. (*NI* 66–68/54–56)

In another striking passage, Heidegger traces Nietzsche's concept of the
will to power back to the central Aristotelian notions of *dynamis, energeia,*
and *entelecheia.*

No matter how decisively the interpretation of being as will to power
remains Nietzsche's own, and no matter how little Nietzsche explicitly
knew in what historical context the very concept of power as a determination of being stood, it is certain that with this interpretation of the
being of beings Nietzsche advances into the innermost yet broadest
circle of Western thought. . . . Nietzsche often identifies power with
force, without defining the latter more closely. Force, the capacity to be
gathered in itself and prepared to work effects, to be in a position to do
something, is what the Greeks (above all, Aristotle) denote as *dynamis.*
But power is every bit as much a being empowered, in the sense of the
process of dominance, the being-at-work of force, in Greek, *energeia.*
Power is will as willing out beyond itself, precisely in that way to come
to itself, to find and assert itself in the circumscribed simplicity of its
essence, in Greek, *entelecheia.* For Nietzsche power means all this at once:
dynamis, energeia, entelecheia. . . . Although Nietzsche does not appreciate
the concealed and vital connection between his concept of power, as a
concept of being, and Aristotle's doctrine, . . . we may say that the Aristotelian doctrine has more to do with Nietzsche's doctrine of will to
power than with any doctrine of categories and modalities in academic
philosophy. (*NI* 76–78/63–65)

What is even more striking is the next sentence which connects, indirectly, the will to power with the pre-Socratics: "But Aristotle's doctrine
itself devolves from a tradition that determines its direction; it is a first-
coming-to-an-end [*Zum-ersten-Ende-kommen*] of the first beginnings of
Western philosophy in Anaximander, Heraclitus, and Parmenides." To be
sure, we should take note of the fact that these passages are found in the
first lecture course on Nietzsche, where Heidegger still largely "goes along
with" Nietzsche's idea of the will to power. He thus makes these connections at this point not so much in critique, but rather to show that Nietzsche's thought is the rightful heir of the essential tradition of the history

of being. Nevertheless, these passages are important not only in that they suggest how the will might be traced explicitly back to Aristotle's thought, but also in that they suggest that the pre-Socratics might also be read as Janus-faced with regard to the will. Early Greek thought is not only *pre*-metaphysical and *pre*-will; it is perhaps also pre-*metaphysical* and pre-*will*.

Indeed, even in the third lecture course on Nietzsche, Heidegger explicitly traces the will to power back to a potential inherent in the Greek notion of *physis*.

> With this utterance, "Life is will to power," Western metaphysics com-pletes itself; at its beginning stands the obscure statement, "being as a whole is *physis*." Nietzsche's utterance, "being as a whole is will to power," states concerning being as a whole that which was predetermined as a possibility in the beginning of Western thinking and became unavoidable because of an inevitable decline from this beginning. (*N1* 492/18–19)

We should, however, add a word here about the other face of Aris-totle; for Heidegger looks to Aristotle not only for the beginning of the history of (the) metaphysics (of will), but also for the methodical expres-sion of traces of the pre-metaphysical Greek world. In many ways for Hei-degger, "Aristotle is more truly Greek in his thinking than Plato" (*N2* 409/9), and in essays such as "Metaphysics as History of Being" Heideg-ger stresses the discontinuity between Aristotle's Greek thought and its metaphysical translation into Latin. Nevertheless, here too there is conti-nuity as well as discontinuity, and Heidegger seeks to indicate both. "The pro-gression of metaphysics from its essential beginning leaves this be-ginning behind, *and yet* takes a fundamental constitution of Platonic-Aristotelian thinking along" (*N2* 410/10, emphasis added).

Concerning the essential continuity, for instance, Heidegger clearly traces the origin of metaphysics, with its temporal restriction of being to "constant presence," back to Plato and Aristotle; and to this extent the fun-damental (dis)attunement of will, at least in germ, can also be found there. Pöggeler compellingly makes this connection between the thought of being as constant presence and the will to power in the following manner:

> When pushed to extremes, the thought that being is constant presence requires the thought of will to power. If being is thought of as constantly presencing and thus as always present, it then comes to be at the disposal of the thinking corresponding to it. Indeed, being is perhaps thought of only as constant presence because thinking as representing something permanent has always been the guide for the projection of being, even if

it is concealed at first. Being is thought of as constant presence *in order that* it be at thinking's disposal. If man stands into willing-to-dispose-of, then the being of beings becomes—in modern thinking—the representedness of objects. The will must ultimately reveal itself as the essential element in representing taken as the placing-before-oneself and placing-toward-oneself. Nietzsche draws only the final consequence out of the metaphysical, recently transformed approach when he thinks of being . . . as will to power.[18]

We find Heidegger himself explicitly making this same connection, from the opposite direction, when he reads Nietzsche's remark, "To *stamp* becoming with the character of being—that is the supreme *will to power*," as meaning that the "will to power in its most profound essence is nothing other than the permanentizing of becoming into presence" (*N1* 656/156).

The Changing Essence of Truth, the Will to Salvation, and the Rise of Subjectivity

Not only is the metaphysical conception of being as permanent presence associated with the problem of the will; so too is the change of truth from the pre-metaphysical notion of *aletheia* (unconcealment) to *homoeisis* (correspondence), to *adequatio* (correctness), and finally to "certainty" (*Gewissheit*), intimately connected with the rise of the will. With this change in the essence of truth, knowing becomes a matter of representation (*Vorstellung*) where a world of objects is set over against a subject. In the change of the essence of truth from unconcealedness to the correct correspondence between an assertion and a state of affairs, a shift in the *locus* of truth takes place. "As unconcealedness truth is still a basic feature of beings themselves. But as correctness of the 'gaze,' it becomes a characteristic of human comportment toward beings" (*GA* 9:231/177). Once truth is determined as "certainty," the shift of the orientation of truth toward the subject is complete. Truth is no longer an event within which humans find themselves, but increasingly rather a matter of the correctness of their representations. Subject/object dualism is established as the epistemological framework. This dualism at once severs the subject from an originary non-dual being-in-the-world (an *ekstatisches Innestehen*), and posits the now-alienated world as matter to be conquered—in theoretical re-presentation (*Vor-stellen*) and in practical production (*Her-stellen*)—and brought back under the domain of the subject's power.

Heidegger speaks of these transformations in the history of being as the conversion of knowing to representing and truth to certainty, the subjectification of the self and the objectification of the world, and the rise of the will to technological mastery. Together these characterize the essential direction which the history of being as the history of metaphysics has taken. Let us read a particularly illuminating passage where he ties these themes together:

> In the occurrence of the default [*Ausbleibens*] of being itself, man is thrown into the letting loose of beings [*Loslassung des Seienden*] by the self-withdrawing truth of being. Representing being [*das Sein*] in the sense of beings [*des Seienden*] as such, man lapses into beings, with the result that by submitting to beings he sets himself up as the being [*als den Seienden*] who in the midst of beings representationally and productively seizes upon them as the objective. In the midst of beings, man freely posits his own essence as certainty for and against beings. He seeks to accomplish this surety in beings through a complete ordering of all beings, in the sense of a systematic securing of stockpiles, by means of which his establishment in the stability of certainty is to be completed. . . . The objectification of all beings as such, on the basis of man's insurrection on behalf of the exclusive self-willing of his will, is the essence of that process in the history of being by which man sets forth his essence in subjectivity. (*N2* 378/233–34)

In the history of metaphysics, the "subject" develops from the Greek *hypokeimenon*, as that which underlies beings as their ground, through the Latin "translation" as *subiectum*, and finally to modern metaphysics, where the "subject" is exclusively identified with the human ego as the subject of empirical knowing or transcendental metaphysics. Heidegger at times uses the neologism *Subiectität* or *Subjectität* (subjectity) to express the unity of the metaphysical determinations of being as *subiectum*, while reserving the usual term *Subjektivität* (subjectivity) for the specifically modern metaphysical identification of being as *subiectum* with "egoness, above all the selfhood of Spirit" (*N2* 451/46–47). With the advent of modernity, the human subject of will and representation, or at least man's transcendental ego, becomes the ground for all beings. The rise of the subject is at one and the same time the rise of the will; and both reach their peak in the metaphysics of modernity.[19]

> In the subjectity of the subject, will comes to appearance as the essence of subjectity. Modern metaphysics, as the metaphysics of subjectity, thinks the being of beings in the sense of will. (*GA* 5:243–44/88)

The relation between will and representation is of particular importance to understanding the modern predicament of technology, and later we shall consider this connection in greater detail. Here let us focus on the transformation of truth to certainty. "Truth . . . in metaphysics changed [from the unconcealedness of beings] to a distinctive trait of the intellect . . . [and] comes to its ultimate essence which is called *certainty*" (*N2* 422/20). As man moves to the center of the world as its ground, knowledge and truth increasingly become a matter of making the world secure for his disposal. Truth becomes "certainty as self-guaranteeing (willing-oneself)" (*VA* 81/78).

This process reaches its extreme form in the epoch of technology; but on the way Christianity, in particular the movement of the Reformation, marks an important stage. Even religion, Heidegger claims, is reduced to the form of "the subject-object relation, which is sustained by subjectivity" (*N2* 378/234). The focus of religion becomes the subject and his salvation. Thus "transcendence" itself gets reduced to a subjective concern.

> Through the insurrection into subjectivity even theological transcendence and thus the supreme being of beings [*das Seiendste des Seienden*] . . . shifts into a kind of objectivity, specifically, the objectivity of the subjectivity of moral-practical faith. It makes no difference in the essence of this fundamental metaphysical position concerning the human essence whether man takes that transcendence seriously as "providence" for his religious subjectivity or takes it merely as a pretext for the willing of his self-seeking subjectivity. (379/234)

In other words, regardless of whether the striving of religious subjectivity is a genuine concern for salvation or simply the pretext for covert-willing, the religious sphere is reduced to the domain of the subject and his will. Truth is reduced to a matter of subjective certainty, the certainty of the subject's own salvation.

Heidegger explains this development specifically with regard to Luther and the Reformation's individualization of religion. It is Luther who raises the question of whether and how a person can be certain of eternal salvation. "Luther asks how man could be a 'true' Christian, i.e., a just man, a man fit for what is just, a justified man" (*GA* 54:75/51). In this way the question of truth (*veritas*) becomes a matter of justice (*iustitia*) and justification (*iustificatio*). This concern for justification, "as the question of certainty of salvation, becomes the center of evangelical theology" (ibid.). Noting that for medieval theology justice (*iustitia*) meant the correctness of reason and will, Heidegger connects this concern for the certainty of one's personal salvation directly with the rise of subjectivity and the will to will. "Put briefly: the *rectitudo appetitus rationalis*, the rightness of will, the striving after rightness is the basic form of the will to will" (ibid.).[20]

In short, the will to salvation reduced religion to a matter of the subject's concern with his own security and/or the preservation and enhancement of his power. In this manner, "the transformation of reality to the self-certainty of the *ego cogito* is determined directly by Christianity" (*N2* 472/67).[21] This transformation to the self-certain thinking subject who represents the world as object is completed, however, only in Descartes's *cogito ergo sum*.

Descartes's metaphysics completes the transformations of truth to certainty, knowing to representation, and the world to an object for the representing subject.

> [The] objectifying of whatever is, is accomplished in a representational setting-before [*Vor-stellen*] that aims at bringing each particular entity before it in such a way that man who calculates can be sure, and that means certain, of that entity. . . . What it is to be is for the first time defined as the objectiveness of representing, and truth is first defined as the certainty of representing, in the metaphysics of Descartes. (*GA* 5:87/127)

Indeed, Heidegger goes on to say that "the whole of metaphysics, including Nietzsche, maintains itself within the interpretation of what it is to be and of truth that was prepared by Descartes" (ibid.). Descartes's philosophy is thus a decisive milestone on the road that leads to the metaphysics of the subject of representation and will to certainty, and then eventually to Nietzsche's explicit doctrine of the will to power. And yet, one may want to ask, did not Nietzsche posit the primacy of will rather *in critique* of Descartes's emphasis on the cogito?[22] Heidegger writes in this regard:

> Nietzsche refers the *ego cogito* back to an *ego volo* and interprets the *velle* as willing in the sense of will to power, which he thinks as the basic character of beings. *But what if the positing of this basic character became possible only on the basis of Descartes' fundamental metaphysical position?* (*N2* 181–82/129)

Heidegger answers this question in the affirmative, claiming that "behind Nietzsche's exceedingly sharp rejection of the Cartesian cogito stands an *even more rigorous commitment* to the subjectivity posited by Descartes" (174/123). Behind Nietzsche's opposition to Descartes lies a fundamental agreement that "being means 'representedness,' a being established in thinking, and that truth means 'certitude'" (181/129).

Heidegger's intention here is not only to connect Nietzsche back with Descartes, but also to connect Descartes forward with Nietzsche. Despite

Descartes's emphasis on the thinking subject, insofar as he thinks "thinking" as a matter of representing objects for a subject, his metaphysics marks a decisive point in the rise of the will as ecstatic-incorporation. Heidegger notes that, after all, "Nietzsche himself explained Descartes's principle on the basis of the will to truth, and will to truth as a kind of will to power. Consequently, Descartes's metaphysics is indeed a metaphysics of will to power, albeit an unwitting one" (237/179).

Nevertheless, Descartes's thought does not yet inaugurate the explicit metaphysics of the will. This is a step that Heidegger's history of being accords to Leibniz.

The Modern Metaphysics of Will: From Leibniz's *Appetitus* to Nietzsche's *Wille zur Macht*

> *Wenn das Sein "Wille" ist* . . . Durch die volle Entfaltung dieses Wenn-Satzes lässt sich das Wesen der neuzeitlichen Metaphysik darstellen. (*GA* 67:159)

For Heidegger, it was German idealism that directly prepared for Nietzsche's understanding of all that is as the will to power, namely, by forcefully and explicitly equating both being and thinking (as re-presentation) with willing. And yet the beginning of the modern completion of metaphysics in the identification of the beingness of beings with the will can be traced, Heidegger claims, at least as far back as Descartes. "[We] can see that, from the metaphysics of Schelling and Hegel, back beyond Kant and Leibniz to Descartes, the entity as such is at bottom experienced as *will*" (*N2* 342/205). "Of course," he adds, "that does not mean that the subjective experience of human will is transposed onto beings as a whole. Rather, it indicates the very reverse, that man first comes to know himself as a willing subject in an essential sense on the basis of a still unelucidated experience of beings as such in the sense of a willing" (343/205). Human willing, we are told in another text, "remains rather only the willed counterpart of will as the being of beings" (*GA* 5:279/102).

As we have noted, however, while Descartes prepares for the metaphysics of will by positing the subject of representation, he does not yet make the aspect of volition explicitly central. This vital step is first made by Leibniz, then decisively carried out by the German idealists, and finally completed by Nietzsche. Let us look at Heidegger's interpretation of the role of each of these in the rise of the metaphysics of will.

Leibniz was "the first to think clearly . . . the volitional essence of whatever is" (*GA* 5:245/90). As Michael Zimmerman elaborates, for "Leibniz, all 'actuality' was contained as representations or experiences within each individual monad. And monads, these spiritual points of experience, were self-willing agents which actualized and made present all the entities in their experience." Thus it could be said that by "introducing an Aristotelian dynamism into Descartes's static metaphysics of the subject, Leibniz opened the way for Nietzsche's doctrine that the Will to Power constitutes the being of all entities."[23] By understanding beings as monads, and these as the union of perception (*perceptio*) and volition (*appetitus*), Leibniz inaugurated the tradition of thinking the being of beings as essentially the unity of representation and will. When Heidegger says that the traditional way of understanding thinking is as a kind of willing (see *G* 29/58), this "belonging together of thinking and willing" or "representing and striving" is first explicitly articulated by Leibniz (see *GA* 77:53).

> Leibniz . . . defined the being of beings in terms of the monad as the unity of *perceptio* and *appetitus*, representing and striving, that is, will. What Leibniz is thinking comes to language in Kant and Fichte as "the rational will"; Hegel and Schelling, each in his own way, reflect on this *Vernunftwille*. Schopenhauer is referring to the selfsame thing when he gives his major work the title "The World (not man) as Will and Representation." Nietzsche is thinking the selfsame thing when he acknowledges the primal being of beings as will to power. (*VA* 110/222–23)[24]

Although the metaphysics of will is anticipated by Descartes and unveiled by Leibniz, it gets thoroughly established by German idealism. The link between *perceptio* and *appetitus*, between knowing as representing and volition, is worked out further by the idealists as that between "reason" and "will."

Kant, as the (unintentional) forefather of German idealism, plays an important yet ambivalent role in the rise of the metaphysics of will. "Kant's metaphysics resists this essential thrust of being [toward absolute subjectivity]—while at the same time laying the ground for its fulfillment" (*N2* 298/222). He resists it insofar as he emphasizes the finitude of man, and leaves the "thing-in-itself" outside the reach of the subject's representation. And yet he prepares the ground for the link between absolute knowledge and absolute will in at least two related ways. One is by linking will and reason in the ethical will as that which acts according to concepts (see 468–69/64) and as absolute self-legislation (see 298–99/222). Secondly, even though Kant rejects the idea of a human "intelligible intuition," he ambiguously places the ethical will beyond the realm of phenomena. Insofar as Kant critically delimits metaphysics, his thought forestalls the rise of the metaphysics of will and representation. And yet the "finite metaphysics" that he secures by way of his critique—both his "transcendental idealism" with its transcendental unity of apperception, and his "meta-physics of morals" with its "good will" as "absolute self-legislation"—lay the foundation for the metaphysical idealism of the absolute subject of will and reason. Nevertheless, the decisive step beyond Leibniz toward a full-blown metaphysics of the will is carried out first by Kant's heirs: Fichte, Schelling, and Hegel.

Although Heidegger does not usually emphasize Fichte's role in his summary sketches of the rise of the metaphysics of will, in Fichte's volun-taristic idealism the connection between thinking as representing and willing is clearly made.[25] Moreover, the progression of Fichte's *Wissenschaftslehre*—where the impossibility of theoretical knowledge to re-store the world to the Ego (the transcendental I [*Ich*] that originally "posited" the world as Not-I [*Nicht-Ich*]) leads to the practical imperative of "infinite striving" to shape the world according to the will of the human subject—gives a prime example of how idealism prepares the metaphysi-cal justification for a willful technological mastery of the world.[26]

In Schelling, as we have seen in chapter 4, and as Heidegger con-tinues to point out in his later writings (see *WhD* 35/90–91), the identifi-cation of the being of beings with will finds its explicit formulation: "In the final and highest instance there is no other being than willing. Willing is primal being [*Wollen ist Urseyn*]."[27] According to Heidegger, Schelling's distinction (*Unterscheidung*) between the will of the ground and the will of understanding "signifies an opposition (strife) which structures and rules all *Wesen* (beings in their beingness), all of this always based on subjectiv-ity" (*N2* 478/72). Yet despite providing the most explicit formulation of the identification of being with will, according to Heidegger it is not Schelling who most concretely worked out the idealistic equation of being and thought with the will; this is credited to Hegel.

Hegel, in "completing" Kant, takes the "absolute self-legislation" of the autonomous rational will to the metaphysical extreme.[28] Heidegger sketches the path from Kant to Hegel as follows:

> Self-legislation . . . characterizes the "will," insofar as it is determined on the horizon of pure reason. Reason, as striving reason, is at the same time will. The absolute subjectivity of reason is willful self-knowledge. This means that reason is absolute Spirit. (*N2* 299/222)

For Hegel, absolute Spirit as absolute Reason is also absolute Will in the sense that "will" is the force by which reason realizes itself through "expe-rience" (*Erfahrung*), the latter understood as the process by which Spirit, having alienated itself into "natural consciousness," progressively comes to realize itself. "Experience is the dialogue between natural consciousness and absolute knowledge" (*GA* 5:202/146). Experience is the process by which consciousness "successively absolves itself from dependence on objects by gradually realizing its own role in the constitution of these objects."[29] The will is the force of the movement of experience in which Spirit returns to know itself, achieving this self-knowledge in *parousia*, shining forth within human subjectivity. The will is the "power that prevails within experience" (*GA* 5:193/133) as the returning of Spirit to itself.

In this process of self-re-presentational experience, Spirit undergoes a process of "self-othering" (*Sichanderswerden*) for the sake of a "self-*restoring* sameness or the reflection in otherness back into itself [*die sich wiederherstellende Gleichheit oder die Reflexion im Anderssein in sich selbst*]."[30] In his idealistic remolding of the Socratic theory of knowledge as anamnesis into an ontodicy of Spirit, Hegel thinks the essence of knowledge, in stark contrast to a letting something other show itself from itself, as a "*pure self-recognition in absolute otherness*."[31] Elsewhere Hegel writes: "Every act of Spirit is thus only a grasping of itself, and it is the aim of all genuine knowledge that Spirit recognize itself in everything that exists in heaven and on the earth. Something wholly other is simply not given for Spirit."[32]

Hegel thus tells a grand narrative which recounts the experience of the realization of Spirit's self-will; Spirit reaches out to—or indeed posits from out of itself—the other than itself only to cunningly bring this other back into its original sameness. Spirit needs this reincorporation of the other even at the risk of alienating itself from itself, sacrificing its initial solitary immediacy for the sake of the incorporative transformation of all otherness into a mediated and thus self-consciously self-identical totality. Hegel's *Phenomenology of Spirit* is, in short, a metaphysical saga of ecstatic-incorporation, a meta-narrative tale of conquest which Spirit can only tell as a monologue, there being no other remaining to listen. In "absolute knowing," all *ekstasis* has been reincorporated: "The circle has closed itself [*Der Ring hat sich geschlossen*]" (*GA* 5:205/149).

According to Heidegger, for Hegel "phenomenology" means "the manner in which absolute subjectivity as absolute self-appearing representation (thinking) *is* itself the being of beings" (*N2* 299/223).

> The will wills itself in the *parousia* of the Absolute that is with us. "Phenomenology" itself is being, according to whose mode the Absolute is with us in and for itself. This being wills, willing being its nature. (*GA* 5:203–4/148)

The metaphysics of will, as the metaphysics of subjectivity and representation, approaches completion here. And yet the final step is not yet made. "Although [for Hegel] reason is will, here it is reason as representation (idea) that nonetheless decides the beingness of beings" (ibid.). In Hegel's will of knowing, just as in Schelling's will of love, the "will to power is still concealed" (*GA* 9:360/273). The final step to the preeminence of will over representation is executed only in Nietzsche's thought. Thus, although the "completion of metaphysics begins with Hegel's metaphysics of absolute knowledge as the Spirit of will . . . [the] will has not yet appeared as the will to will. . . . Hence metaphysics is not yet completed with the absolute metaphysics of the Spirit" (*VA* 72/71). Only with Nietzsche's will to power is the metaphysical road paved for the technological will to will.

With Nietzsche's thought, namely in its "nihilistic inversion of the preeminence of representation to the preeminence of will as the will to power, the will first achieves absolute dominion in the essence of subjectivity" (*N2* 300–301/224). Although representation already decisively orients the object of knowledge to the subject, making it available to his will,

> representation is still always conditioned by what presents itself to our representing. Yet the absoluteness of the will alone empowers what may be mustered as such. The essence of absolute subjectivity first reaches its fulfillment in such inverted empowering of the will. . . . Will to power is therefore both absolute and—because inverted—consummate subjectivity. (301/224–25)

While in Hegel the will is still a means to the end of absolute knowledge as the total self-representation of Spirit to itself, in Nietzsche knowledge is strictly reduced to the status of a means to the power-preservation and power-enhancement of the will. Here, although the relation of will to representation remains, the latter is now decisively oriented to and from the former. The will to power is the sole ultimate fact of existence.

Nevertheless, Nietzsche's "metaphysics of the will to power" is not yet the purest possible expression of the will to will; rather, "Nietzsche's metaphysics makes apparent the second to last stage of the will's development of the beingness of beings as the will to will" (*VA* 77/75). The last stage failed to make its appearance with Nietzsche because his thought can still be "misread" as pitting "life" (i.e., will) against thought, when in actuality it is the unification of will and representational (calculative) thinking. As we have seen, both power-preservation ("truth," "thought") and power-enhancement ("will") are bound together in the will to power. According to Heidegger, the will to power ultimately must be understood as the endless repetition of the self-willing of the will; that is to say, the two pillars of "Nietzsche's metaphysics" must be understood together as *the eternal recurrence of the will to power*, the endless repetition of the will to will.

And yet, although the "being of the will to power can only be understood in terms of the will to will," the "will to will, however, can only be experienced when metaphysics has entered its transition" (*VA* 78/76). Nietzsche's thought was itself too immersed in the will to experience it fully in its pure essence as the will to will; for this experience requires a measure of "interpretive distance." This ultimate understanding is, therefore, left to Heidegger and ourselves who would stand at "the end of [the] philosophy [of the will]," and at the brink of a possibility of thinking from a region outside of the domain of willing. The radical step back that prepares for an other beginning, however, is in turn made possible only by way of thoughtfully reflecting on the consummation of the history of metaphysics in the *Gestell* of the technological will to will.

Technology and the Unbounded Reign of the Will

> The basic form of appearance in which the will to will arranges and calculates itself in the unhistorical element of the world of completed metaphysics can be stringently called "technology."
> (*VA* 76/74)

Heidegger rejects the popular idea that "technology" (*Technik*) is merely a set of "means," or the totality of tools that can be either properly used or abused. "The essence of technology," he says, "is nothing technological" in this sense. What then does Heidegger mean by "the essence of technology"? Technology, as he defines it, is not merely a set of instruments made possible by science and subsequently abused by willful humans, but rather, prior to all this, *technology is a way of revealing* (see *VA* 16/318). Technology names a highly restrictive way in which beings are revealed, *and concealed;* for in this particular manner of revealing/concealing, beings are allowed to show themselves only as material for willful manipulation.

Heidegger draws the connection between technology and the will to power as follows:

> The uprising of man into subjectivity transforms beings into objects. But that which is objective [*Das Gegenständliche*] is that which is brought to a stand through representing. The elimination of that which *is* in itself [*Die Beseitigung des an sich Seienden*], the killing of God, is accomplished in the making secure of the standing-reserve [*Bestandsicherung*] by means of which man secures for himself material, bodily, psychic, and spiritual resources, and this for the sake of his own security, which wills dominion

over beings as potential objectivities in order to correspond to the being
of beings, that is, to the will to power. (*GA* 5:262/107)

We also read in this passage that the willful essence of man is determined
by the will as the being of beings as a whole in the modern epoch. It is in
the course of the history of being, and specifically in the epochs of modern metaphysics, that the being of beings comes to appear as will. Only
then, "correspondingly, human willing too can be in the mode of self-
assertion" where everything "turns irresistibly into material for self-
assertive production" (289/111). Thus, for Heidegger, it is not that our
willful nature has led us to treat the world technologically, but rather that
we became the self-assertive masters of objects through the being-
historical (*seinsgeschichtliche*) unfolding of the essence of technology. In
other words, the unbounded will of man is in fact bound up with a process
that "emerges from the hidden essence of technology" (ibid.).

Ge-stell: The Gathering of a Willful Setting

To understand Heidegger's critique of the will, then, it is essential to finally see it in the context of his critique of technology. Before considering
technology as such, however, let us elaborate here on a point that we have
come across time and again: the interconnectedness of representation
(*Vorstellung*) and will. This connection is crucial to understanding technology as a way of revealing beings that reduces them to standing-reserve
(*Bestand*) for willful manipulation. Contrary to a popular notion that there
is a tension or even an antithesis between knowing and willing, where the
former is thought to require abstinence from the latter (as in the case of
the "disinterested objectivity" of theory as opposed to the purposeful activity of praxis), Heidegger claims that the Western tradition has in fact
reduced knowing to a matter of willing. Knowing has become a matter of
subjective representation wherein the world is reduced to the sum total
of objects for the representing subject. Representation, or as Heidegger
sometimes hyphenates the German term, *Vor-stellung*, is a matter of "setting before," placing an object (*Gegenstand*) in the position of standing
over against (*gegen*) the subject, and ultimately at the disposal of his will.

As we have seen, Heidegger attempts to show how this linking of representation and will is explicitly made by modern philosophers beginning
with Leibniz. Thus Heidegger claims that "thinking, understood in the
traditional way, as representing is a kind of willing" (*G* 29/58). Let us draw
out this connection more explicitly, showing how in its extreme form willful representation leads to what Heidegger calls technology. "Representation inspects everything encountering it from *out* of itself and with ref-

erence *to* itself, inspects it with regard to whether and how it relates to what representation . . . requires for its own certainty" (*N2* 295/219). The subject of representation places himself in the center of beings, or even under them as their ground. Representing is not an open receptiveness to the self-showing of beings, nor is it an "engaged letting" things show themselves from themselves; it is a constitutive knowing (Kant) that commands the very terms in which beings can appear. "Representing is making stand-over-against, an oppositional-objectifying [*Ver-gegen-ständlichung*] that goes forward and masters" (*GA* 5:108/150). In the present "age of the world-picture," where all that is gets reduced to a structured image (*Gebild*) seen from the standpoint of man as subject, representation becomes a matter of "the conquest of the world as picture" (94/134). Representation is therefore not just *subsequently* linked with the will, but rather "is *in itself,* not extrinsically, a striving" (*N2* 298/221) in the sense of willing as ecstatic-incorporation.

Technology is the extreme form of this unity of representation and will. It is the way beings are allowed to show themselves only as "usable," as ready to serve man's willful projects, or perhaps in the deficient modes of "resistant to" or "not yet ready for" such servitude. Heidegger thus characterizes technology's way of revealing as follows: "The revealing that rules in modern technology is a challenging-forth [*Herausfordern*], which puts to nature the unreasonable demand that it supply energy which can be extracted and stored as such" (*VA* 18/320). Nature is reduced to a resource from which energy is unlocked, transformed, stored up, distributed, and switched about, ever at the beck and call of human will.

This way of revealing, Heidegger says, "has the character of a positioning [*Stellens*]" (20/321). The German verb *stellen* means to set or set up, to place or put into position, to arrange, or to make stand. As we shall see, Heidegger understands the basic sense of this root word as a matter of self-assertive will, and refers to various terms derived from *Stellen* in order to illustrate the fundamentally willful character of technology in its various aspects or moments. Let us read the following key passage while paying attention to the *Stellen* words in the German original.

> It is through human re-presenting [*Vor-stellen*] that nature is brought before man. Man places before himself [*stellt . . . vor sich*] the world as the whole of everything objective, and he places himself before the world. Man props up the world toward himself, and delivers nature over to himself [*Der Mensch stellt die Welt auf sich zu und die Natur zu sich her*]. We must think of this producing, this setting-forth [*Her-stellen*], in its broad and multifarious essence. Where nature is not satisfactory to man's representation, he (re)orders [*bestellt*] it. Man produces [*stellt . . .*

her] new things when they are lacking to him. Man transposes [*stellt . . . um*] things when they are in his way. Man adjusts things for himself, or even contorts [*verstellt*] them, when they [would otherwise] distract him from his purpose. Man exhibits [*stellt . . . aus*] things when he boosts them for sale and use. Man stands out when he displays [*herausstellt*] his own achievements and plays up his own occupation. By multifarious producing (or setting-forth) [*Herstellen*], the world is brought [to stand and into position [*in den Stand gebracht*]. The Open becomes an object [*Gegenstand*], and is thus twisted around toward human being. Over against the world as the object, man exhibits himself [*stellt sich . . . heraus*] and sets himself up [*stellt sich auf*] as the one who purposely prevails through all this producing (or setting-forth). (*GA* 5:287–88/110)

Heidegger then goes on in the following paragraph to explicitly connect these multifarious moments of *Stellen* with willing:

To bring something before oneself, pro-pose it—in such a manner that what has been pro-posed, having first been represented, determines all the modes of production in every respect—is a basic characteristic of the comportment which we know as willing. (288/110)

The moments of *Stellen*—representing (*Vorstellen*), producing (*Herstellen*), ordering (*Bestellen*), exposing (*Ausstellen*), distorting (*Verstellen*), etc.—reveal a comportment of self-assertive willing, and collectively they define the essence of modern technological revealing/concealing.

Heidegger thus understands the essence of technology in terms of the various interconnected moments of a willful *Stellen*.[33] Gathering these forms of *Stellen* together, Heidegger names the essence of technology with the word: *Ge-stell* (usually translated as "enframing," though, as Theodore Kisiel suggests, perhaps best translated as "com-position"). The German word *Gestell* normally refers to a "stand," "rack," or "frame" (for bottles or books, for example), but in hyphenating the word Heidegger draws attention to the prefix *Ge-*, meaning a "gathering together" (as in the word for "mountain range," *Gebirge*). The term *Ge-stell* thus indicates the gathering of the various moments of *Stellen*, a gathering which results in the total enframing or "com-posing" of the world for technological manipulation.

Bestand: The Reduction of Beings to Resources for Willful Manipulation

Heidegger characterizes modern technology as a representing that "goes forward and masters," and that reveals beings only as they show themselves to this willful "positioning that challenges-forth [*herausfordernde*

Stellen]" (*VA* 20/322). Technological revealing reduces beings to objects of manipulation and consumption; it discloses the forces of nature only as energy resources to be unlocked, stored, distributed, and used up. The current of a river is revealed as a resource for hydroelectric power, a track of land is a resource of coal or a quantity of acres for the mechanized food industry. Everything, in the end, gets reduced to a matter of quantities of power: 100 kilowatts of hydroelectric power, steam power, atomic power, all calculated as resources to be stored for distribution and used at will. Everywhere the technological will determines the way things are allowed to reveal themselves.

Heidegger considers two objections that might be raised against his critique of the pervasiveness and uniqueness of the modern technological worldview. First of all one might ask: is not a river also a landscape or a place of recreation, a place where we go to get away from the (willful) hustle and bustle of daily life, and thus a place not wholly reduced to a power supply? Heidegger responds: "Perhaps. But how? In no other way than as an object on call [*bestellbares Objekt*] for inspection by a tour group ordered [*bestellt*] there by the vacation industry" (*VA* 19–20/297). Even "nature" is enframed, like a garden terrace in an industrial complex, as part of the technological world-picture centered on human willing.

The second objection Heidegger considers concerns the uniqueness of the modern problem of technology. He claims that the challenging-forth (*Herausfordern*) of modern technology is essentially different from the bringing-forth (*Her-vor-bringen*) in the sense of *poeisis* that still resounds in the Greek notion of *techne*. While the latter bespeaks a more original creative relation to nature (*physis*), the former reduces nature to an object for subjective willing. "But does not this [technological reduction] hold true for the old windmill as well?" Heidegger asks rhetorically. His answer is: "No. Its sails do indeed turn in the wind; they are left entirely to the winds blowing. But the windmill does not unlock energy from the air currents in order to store it" (18/320). Similarly, in contrast to the modern "mechanized food industry," the farmer formerly cultivated his fields in the sense of taking care and maintaining. "The work of the peasant does not challenge the soil of the field" (ibid.); it does not "arrange [*stellt*] nature" as does the modern mechanized food industry. This distinction is crucial both for clarifying what his critique does *not* call for, namely a universal renunciation of all human doing and making, as well as intimating what it does call for, namely a way of doing and making other than that of the willful challenging-forth of technology.

Heidegger thus asks what kind of unconcealment is peculiar to the technological revealing of "positioning that challenges-forth." The answer he gives is that beings are allowed to reveal themselves only as "standing-reserve" (*Bestand*) to be used and used up as raw material for the willful projects of humanity. Heidegger defines this second key term of his critique of technology as follows:

> Everywhere everything is ordered to stand by, to be immediately on hand, indeed to stand there just so that it may be on call for a further ordering [*Überall ist es bestellt, auf der Stelle zur Stelle zu stehen, und zwar zu stehen, um selbst bestellbar zu sein für ein weiteres Bestellen*]. Whatever is ordered about in this way has its own standing [*Stand*]. We call it the standing-reserve [*Bestand*]. (20/322)

We have said that the subject of willful representation reduces things to "objects" (*Gegenstände*). But here the reduction goes a step further; for whatever "stands by in the sense of standing-reserve no longer stands over against us as object [*steht uns nicht mehr als Gegenstand gegenüber*]" (ibid.). "In the *Bestand* even the *Gegenstand* is no longer admitted [*zugelassen*], much less the thing as thing" (*GA* 79:46). Indeed, in a consummate technological world even the oppositional dualism of objects standing over against a subject would be supplanted by a homogeneous cybernetic system wherein humans and things alike are reduced to cogs in the wheel of an aimless and insatiable technological will to will.

Cybernetics: Humans Too Are Willed About by the Will to Will

When the metaphysics of willful subjectivity gives way to the extreme epoch of technology, humans themselves are threatened with reduction to standing-reserve (see *VA* 30/332). Whereas in the rise of the modern metaphysics of will things are progressively reduced to objects of human will and representation, in the extreme epoch of technology even this egocentric dualism threatens to give way to a uniform ordering about of both non-human and human beings as standing-reserve. Heidegger speaks of this extreme form of modern technology as "cybernetics."

> In the cybernetically represented world, the difference between automatic machines and living things disappears. It becomes neutralized by the undifferentiated process of information. The cybernetic world project, "the victory of method over science," makes possible a completely uniform and in this sense universal calculability, in other words the controllability of the lifeless and the living world. In this uniformity of the cybernetic world, man too gets installed [*eingewiesen*]. (*D* 142)

Zimmerman points out that in cybernetics, technology no longer centers on the striving for power of the self-interested subject, as it perhaps did with the capitalist class during the Industrial Revolution; for now "the technological disclosure of entities mobilizes everything—including people—into the project of increasing the power of the technological system itself."[34] Despite his self-image as lord of the earth, man is becoming, along with material things, merely one more nodal point in the system of the technological machine, one more cog in the wheel of the cybernetic will to will.[35] "The current talk about human resources, about the supply of patients for a clinic," Heidegger remarks, "gives evidence of this" (*VA* 21/323).

The domain of the will to will is not under human control; modern technology is "no mere human doing" (22/324). Technology is not a mere set of tools to be used, abused, or mastered, but is rather a destiny of revealing. Technology is not, in other words, simply an insurrection on the part of autonomous man, but is an extreme epoch of the history of being; technology is the way being reveals/conceals itself in utmost abandonment. Hence, the essence of technology as *Ge-stell* refers not only to human enframing the world as standing-reserve; for ultimately humans too are challenged-forth and enframed by the cybernetic processes of technology. The *Ge-stell* thus shows itself to mean "the gathering together of the positioning which positions man, that is, challenges him forth, to reveal the actual, in the mode of ordering, as standing-reserve" (24/325).

Only "to the extent that man for his part is already challenged to exploit the energies of nature can this revealing which orders happen" (21/323). Man never was "in control" of technology; and insofar as we still think in terms of losing or gaining control, we do not yet even see into the essence of technology as a destining of revealing/concealing. The forces which "drag along, press and impose man under the form of some technological contrivance or another" have "long since moved beyond his will and have outgrown his capacity for decision"; but this is because in the first place "man has not made them" (*G* 19/51). "Self-assertive man" was all along, "whether or not he knows and wills it as an individual, . . . the functionary of technology" (*GA* 5:271/116). The will, by which man asserts himself over all that is, reducing the world to objects and ultimately to standing-reserve for his projects of mastery, does not originate in man himself. Heidegger goes so far as to say at one point: "The opinion arises that the human will is the origin of the will to will, whereas man is willed by the will to will without experiencing the essence of this will" (*VA* 85/81–82). Human will is willed by the will to will. Man is a mere functionary of technology.

The question arises: Has Heidegger stripped man of all capacity for change, of the responsibility to participate in the turning to an other way of being? Can we do nothing but defer to the sending of being, in hopes that this will bring a turning beyond the cybernetic will to will? Has Heidegger here backed us into a pessimistic corner where man can do nothing but passively sit and wait? And yet, Heidegger not only rejects the very terms of optimism and pessimism (see *SP* 97/105), but also attempts to think a way of human being that is *other than* those possibilities of activity/passivity (e.g., either willful assertion or will-less waiting) available within the domain of the will.

In anticipation of more detailed discussion in later chapters, at this point let me indicate the place Heidegger preserves in his discourse on technology for a human "taking part" or "corresponding" to the revealing/concealing of being; in other words, the place he attempts to open for a "third option" beyond the domain of either assertion or deferral of human will. He writes:

> Yet precisely because man is challenged more originally than are the energies of nature, i.e., into the process of ordering, *he is never transformed into mere standing-reserve.* Since man drives technology forward, he *takes part* in ordering as a way of revealing. (*VA* 22/323, emphases added)

Human beings are never exhaustively reduced to human resources. We remain, to an extent, free in our "response-ability" to being; we "take part" in its revealing/concealing. Man cor-responds to being, even when in the deficient mode of willful forgetting. In fact, any turning in the history of being "needs and uses" man. "Man is needed and used [*gebraucht*] for the recovery from the essential occurrence of technology," but only insofar as man's essence "corresponds to that recovery" (*GA* 79:70/39).

Hence, although the greatest danger is that man may become a mere "defenseless and helpless victim delivered over to the unstoppable superior power of technology" (*G* 21/52–53), this is not an inevitable destiny. Heidegger speaks of the possibility of "bringing the measure of meditative thinking decisively into play against mere calculative thinking" (21/53). There is, then, a third possibility beyond either actively willing or being swept along involuntarily by the technological will to will. This third possibility would be one of twisting free of such dichotomies within the domain of the will by way of cor-responsive meditative thinking. In later chapters we shall explore in greater detail this possibility; here let us consider Heidegger's suggestion, not only that there remains a glimmer of hope for a turning beyond the technological will to will, but that it is precisely in the midst of this desolate age of technology that there lies the possibility for catching sight of a more originary way of being.

The Janus Face of Technology and the Possibility of a Turning

Wo aber Gefahr ist, wächst
Das Rettende auch.
—Friedrich Hölderlin[36]

> The abandonment of being contains the undecided matter of
> whether, in this abandonment as an extreme of the concealment
> of being, the unconcealment of this concealment, and thus the
> more original beginning [*der anfänglichere Anfang*], is already
> coming to light. (*N2* 471/67; see also *GA* 65:91)

Despite his disavowal of pessimism, Heidegger may be thought to have
painted a rather gloomy picture of the current epoch of the technological
will to will. And yet, the extreme epoch of technology is Janus-faced. It is
both a time of utter distress—a time where the greatest distress paradoxically disguises itself in Hollywood happy endings and shopping mall pa-
rades as a lack of distress, where the self-consumed and self-consuming
will to will apparently needs no other, even if this "needlessness is [in fact]
the most profound need" (*GA* 65:107)—and, on the other hand, a time
where, in the midst of the danger of technological abandon, we may be
able to hear a "first hint," an "echo" or a "ringing-forth" (*Anklang*) of a
more originary correspondence to being. It is in the depths of our abandonment to the will to will that the possibility of a turning beyond the will
is intimated.

Heidegger warns against any simplistic or impatient solution to the
problem of nihilism/technology/will; he rejects both the Romantic idea
of a "renaissance of antiquity" (*VA* 43/158) and the Nietzschean idea of
"overcoming nihilism." Instead, he calls for us to take "the step back . . .
to *encounter* being in its self-withdrawal" (*N2* 370–71/227). We must first
experience the essence of nihilism/technology/will. In doing so, Heidegger claims, we not only find that the technological will to will is the extreme
danger, but we also "look into the danger and see the growth of that-
which-saves" (*VA* 37/338).

> [It] is precisely in this extreme danger that the innermost indestructible
> belongingness of man within granting may come to light, provided that
> we, for our part, begin to pay heed to the essence of technology. . . .
> Thus the coming to presence of technology [*das Wesende der Technik*]
> harbors in itself what we least suspect, the possible upsurgence of that-
> which-saves. (36/337)

In other words, the "essence of technology is in a lofty sense ambiguous [*zweideutig*]" (37/338). On the one hand, insofar as "enframing challenges-forth into the frenziedness of ordering that blocks [*verstellt*] every view" into the event of being (and that means also into technology as itself an "*Ereignis* of unconcealment"), technology is the extreme concealment of a more originary relation to being and to beings. On the other hand, in the extreme abandonment of being that gives rise to enframing, humans can experience that they "may be the ones who are needed and used [*der Gebrauchte*] for the safekeeping of the essence of truth. Thus the rising of that-which-saves appears" (37/338). The task is to open the possibility of the latter experience by way of reflectively bringing to awareness the former. Precisely by way of reflecting on the essence of technology as the history of metaphysics culminating in the enframing of the will to will, man reattunes himself to his originary correspondence with being. Hence, the danger is, when seen as the danger, at once the growth of that-which-saves. "That-which-saves is not secondary to the danger. The self-same danger is, when it is *as* the danger, that-which-saves" (*GA* 79:72/42). Reflecting on the danger, we correspond to the turning as the growth of that-which-saves. By critically reflecting on the will, we attune ourselves to the possibility of non-willing.

One may still want to object that Heidegger is not clear on how this turning would take place. And yet if the clarity of giving reasons or grounds is what one seeks, this unclarity is inevitable, given the radical discontinuity between the epoch of technology and the other beginning.[37] Heidegger speaks of this discontinuity, as the suddenness and lack of mediation in the turning, as a "leap" (*Sprung*) from metaphysics into the other beginning. "When the turning comes to pass in the danger, this can happen only without mediation. . . . The turning of the danger comes to pass suddenly" (*GA* 79:73/44).

Hence there are, on the one hand, elements of continuity between the end of metaphysics and the turning to an other beginning (i.e., that-which-saves grows where the danger is, and man must vigilantly prepare for the turning by critically reflecting on the essence of the technological will to will); on the other hand, there is an element of radical discontinuity between the two (i.e., the turn happens suddenly as an unmediated leap). Here too, even when the element of discontinuity is conspicuous, the movement of Heidegger's history of being takes place in the manner of a "continuity-of-discontinuity."

But precisely how are humans to open themselves to the danger and the growth of that-which-saves? When Heidegger speaks of the "sudden flash [*der Blitz*] of the truth of being into truthless being" as the "insight into that which is [*Einblick in das was ist*]" (*GA* 79:75/47), how is man to prepare to receive or take part in this sudden insight? Heidegger writes:

> Only when human being [*das Menschenwesen*], in the appropriating event of the insight [*im Ereignis des Einblickes*] and as that which is beheld therein, *renounces human self-will* [*dem menschlichen Eigensinn entsagt*] and projects himself away from himself toward that insight, does he correspond [*ent-spricht*] in his essence to the claim [*Anspruch*] of that insight. (76/47, emphasis added)

Man must renounce his egocentric self-will in order to correspond to the appropriating event of being which clears a place and time (a *Zeit-Raum*) for an insight into that which is.

But how is man to renounce his self-will? Insofar as the essence of man in the modern epoch would be *exhaustively* determined as will, then it would seem that a fundamental change in attunement could only happen absolutely suddenly and without preparation. And yet, Heidegger here as elsewhere speaks of the necessity of "renouncing" the will; the non-willing comportments of "*Gelassenheit* towards things and openness for the mystery," he says, "do not simply befall us accidentally [*Sie sind nichts Zu-fälliges*]," but rather require a "relentless and courageous thinking [*einem unablässigen herzhaften Denken*]" (*G* 25/56). Heidegger's thought thus calls for a "twisting free" of the will. Even if the "freeing" is sudden, the twisting as preparation for the leap involves, with all its tensions, a relentless and courageous "renouncing of the will." It is in this sense necessary to speak of two aspects of *Gelassenheit;* this word not only intimates a way of being *beyond willing*, but also first of all implies *renouncing willing*. We shall return to this issue in chapter 7.

In conclusion to our present discussion of Heidegger's critique of technology, we need to address the question of what Heidegger has in mind when he speaks of freeing ourselves from technology. Does he call for a Romantic return to a world of handicraft before the Industrial Revolution? One can, to be sure, often hear in his texts a tone of nostalgia for pre-technological times: his fascination with the "hand" and handicraft, his idealized image of the life of the farmer who tills the land, his reasons for "remaining in the provinces" (see *D* 9–13). And his occasional unilateral disparagement of technological achievements in such areas as agriculture, transportation, and media (though he apparently made an exception for televised soccer games!) strikes even the most sympathetic reader today as revealing only one side of a complexly multifaceted issue.

And yet we should bear in mind that the central point of Heidegger's critique is not aimed at technological devices themselves, but at the way of revealing/concealing which they embody. "What is dangerous is not technology. Technology is not demonic. . . . The essence of technology, as a destining of revealing, is the danger" (*VA* 31–32/333). To condemn technology as the devil's work, and to attempt to overcome technology by throwing away all its devices, would be to misunderstand the essence of the problem (see *ID* 105/40). Indeed, the will to overcome technology by throwing away its devices would repeat the very problem it attempts to address: the will to mastery that characterizes human being in the epoch of technology. The essence of technology is not a tool, and does not lend itself to mastery. Thus Heidegger writes:

> It would be foolish to attack technology blindly. It would be shortsighted to want to condemn [*verdammen zu wollen*] it as the work of the devil. We depend on technical devices; they even challenge us to ever greater advances. But suddenly and unaware we find ourselves so firmly shackled to these devices that we fall into bondage to them. (*G* 22/53–54)

What, then, does Heidegger suggest we are to do in the face of the very real danger of technology and the impossibility of overcoming this danger by simply throwing away its devices? He continues:

> Still we can do otherwise. We can use technical devices, and yet with proper use also keep ourselves free of them, so that we may let go of them at any time . . . let them alone as something which does not affect our most inner and proper [essence]. . . . We let technical devices enter our daily life, and at the same time leave them outside. . . . I would call this comportment toward technology, which expresses "yes" at the same time as "no," by an old word: releasement toward things [*die Gelassenheit zu den Dingen*]. (22–23/54)

Gelassenheit is not only a releasement from willful technological manipulation; it is also a releasement into a more attentive engagement in letting things be.

Twisting Free of the Domain of the Will: On the Way to an Other Beginning of Non-Willing

The transition out of willing into *Gelassenheit* is what seems to me to be the genuine difficulty. (*GA* 77:109; *G* 33/61)

No age lets itself be done away with by a negating decree [*durch den Machtspruch der Verneinung*]. (*GA* 5:97/138)

It belongs to the essence of such transitions that, within certain limits, they must continue to speak the language of that which they help overcome. (*GA* 9:303/231)

Taking Our Bearings: Toward a Thinking of Non-Willing

Having retraced the ambivalent and often stormy course of the problem of the will in Heidegger's early and middle periods, and having mapped out the parameters of Heidegger's mature critique of the will, let us once again take our bearings on the ship of Heidegger's *Denkweg*.

According to Nietzsche, as we have seen through the lens of Heidegger's *Nietzsche*, the will to power is the ultimate fact to which we come down. This world is at bottom nothing but the will to power in its many, often self-deceptive, forms. The human or over-human task would then be to live in honest affirmation of the world as will to power, which would require weaning ourselves from all deceptive dreams of an other than willing, dreams which can only lead to degenerate forms of not-willing or deferred-willing or to convoluted forms of covert-willing. Heidegger, however, reads Nietzsche as the last metaphysician, as the thinker who has brought the more than two millennia-old history of metaphysics to completion in its last possibility, the inversion of Platonism. According to Nietzsche, there is nothing to "being" because this concept itself is nothing but an immanently posited value, a previously more or less effective fabrication for the preservation and enhancement of the life of becoming as the will to power. But Nietzsche's overturning of metaphysics is itself still an inverted metaphysics, contends Heidegger. Despite overturning many traditional metaphysical oppositions, Nietzsche remains within the domain of the terms he inverts. Nietzsche completes the history of metaphysics both by reversing its hierarchies, and thus giving expression to its final possibilities (will over reason, body over mind, the sensuous over the supersensuous, etc.), and by giving consummate expression to the descensional progression of the history of metaphysics toward a delimitation of the being of beings as the will to power.

Heidegger's *Auseinandersetzung* with Nietzsche thus becomes the focus of his confrontation with the entire history of metaphysics, and the pivotal point for his turn away from the will toward a thinking of *Gelassenheit*, that is, for his turn toward an other beginning of thinking nonwilling(ly). Nevertheless, Heidegger does not simply discredit Nietzsche's delimitation of being as the will to power; on the contrary, he affirms the truth of Nietzsche's thought, but with one crucial qualification: being is determined as (i.e., reveals/conceals itself as) the will to power only at a culminating stage of the epochal history of metaphysics. As Pöggeler puts this point: "If Nietzsche thinks of will to power as the ultimate fact, Heidegger asks . . . whether the totality of beings is basically always will to power or whether it shows itself only at a specific time, at the end of the modern age, in the light of the will to power."[1] In other words, Heidegger asks: is it not the case "that the experience of beings in light of will to power as the being of beings belongs in an entirely specific and limited history, that being has the character of historicality?"[2] By locating Nietzsche's thought at a particular juncture within the history of being, Heidegger can *both acknowledge and criticize* the pervasive reality of the will to power. He can also then preserve the possibility for an other, more originary determination of being.

While Nietzsche thought that he had brought metaphysics to an end by exposing its underside as the will to power, Heidegger, by revealing the continuity of Nietzsche's thought with the history of metaphysics, claims that the doctrine of the will to power in fact completes the descensional history of metaphysics by bringing forward its final (inverted) possibility. If there could be no twisting free of the ultimate fact of the domain of the will to power, then any twisting could only lead to a twisted (convoluted) form of the will to power. For Heidegger, however, the end to which Nietzsche brought Western thought and history is not final; rather, "this end *is* the need of the other beginning" (*N1* 657/157). Our own extreme epoch of technology, prepared for by Nietzsche's metaphysics of the will to power, is at one and the same time the extreme abandonment of being and the promise of an other beginning. In the distress of living under compulsion of the will to will lies the possibility of awakening to the need for a more originary cor-respondence with being, the need for a re-tu(r)ning to the fundamental attunement of non-willing.

What would this way of being other-than-willing be like? Heidegger offers a number of formulations which intimate a sense of non-willing. Foremost among them is the notion of *Gelassenheit*. This word speaks of a certain releasement from the will, and a releasement into a comportment, no longer of a willful commanding, but rather of a "letting-be." What is the nature of this "letting"? Letting would presumably be in some sense distinct from willing; but it must not be understood as a simple negation of will, at least not if we are to understand *Gelassenheit* as *non*-willing. Whereas *not*-willing, as it has been defined here, remains within the domain of the will as the simple negation or mere deficiency of willing, *Nicht-Wollen* in the sense of *non*-willing indicates a way of being radically other than both the active and the passive modes within the domain of the will.

Approaching *Gelassenheit* in terms of a "higher" form of will, one that would suspend and supersede the subjective will of self-assertion, also has its limits. As we saw in chapter 3, *Contributions to Philosophy* speaks of "re-servedness" (*Verhaltenheit*) as the comportment of a "most proper will" (*eigenster Wille*). Significantly, however, after the first *Nietzsche* volume, that is, after around 1939, Heidegger no longer prefers to use the language of a "higher" or "most proper will."[3] In the rare cases when he does employ such terms, it is in the context of rejecting the idea that non-willing is a matter of passivity or not-willing, and he is quick to qualify or even reject their ultimate suitability. For example, in "Toward an Explication of *Gelassenheit*" we read: "This reserved steadfastness, in which the essence of *Gelassenheit* rests, could perhaps be said to correspond to the highest will-ing, *and yet it may not*" (*G* 59/81, emphasis added).

The language of "will" is no longer seen by the later Heidegger as sal-vageable; a good or proper will cannot finally be separated out from the will of self-assertion and thirst for power. The (domain of the) will as such must be abandoned. But how? The transition out of (the) metaphysics (of will) cannot simply take place by means of a higher form of will; accord-ing to Heidegger this was, in a sense, Rilke's error. It was also Heidegger's own error in the 1930s. After his prolonged confrontation with Nietzsche, Heidegger no longer holds that the "recovery" from will can take place by means of a higher will to overcome; a higher will is neither the goal nor fi-nally even the means. Yet how, then, are we to think the transition?

The later Heidegger abandons the quest for a proper will; the domain of the will as such, in all its dimensions, is the problem. But precisely because of the radicality and reach of his critique of the domain of the will, the enigmatic character of any transition to a region of non-willing is intensified. Saturated as we are with will, bound as we are to the domain of the will, how could we make the transition to non-willing? Perhaps it is ultimately only by way of a "leap" (*Sprung*) that one could move from the domain of the will into the region of non-willing, even if a painstaking "twisting free" is needed to prepare for this leap. Perhaps this leap is made only by way of a "step back," not simply as a return to the historically prior (e.g., to pre-modern farmers or to pre-metaphysical Greeks), but as a radical step back *through* the "*non*-historical." We shall find, however, that thinking the role of the *non*-historical (as what I shall call the *in*-historical) in Heidegger's being-historical thought is as demanding as it is demanded in order to think the possibility of a transition to an other beginning of non-willing.

More Willing Than the Will to Power: The Limits of Rilke's Venture

In the 1946 essay on Rainer Maria Rilke, "What Are Poets For?" Heidegger interprets his poetry to be suggesting that the transition out of the technological will to will can be made by means of becoming "more willing" (*williger*). Rilke's poetry, as Heidegger reads it in this essay, is instructive both in its contributions to the critique of the will, and in its failure to ultimately break free of the domain of (and the metaphysics of) the will.[4]

Heidegger's essay centers on an extended interpretation of the following unpublished poem by Rilke:

> As Nature gives the other creatures over
> to the Venture [*Wagnis*] of their dim delight
> and in soil and branchwork grants none special cover,
> so too our being's primal ground settles our plight;
> we are no dearer to it; it ventures us [*es wagt uns*].
> Except that we, more eager than plant or beast,
> go *with* this Venture, will it [*es wollen*], sometimes
> more daring [*wagender*] (and not in the least from selfishness)
> than Life itself is, by a breath
> more daring . . . There, outside all caring [*Schutz*],
> this creates for us a safety—just there where the gravity

of the pure forces [*reinen Kräfte*] operates; in the end,
it is our unshieldedness [*Schutzlossein*] on which we depend,
and that, when we saw it threatened, we turned it so into the Open
in order that, somewhere in the widest orbit,
where the law touches us, we may affirm it. (*GA* 5:277/99)

According to Heidegger, "Rilke's poem thinks of man as the being who is ventured into a willing, the being who, without as yet experiencing it, is willed in the will to will" (293/115). Rilke's language of Life, Venture, Nature (conceived as a force permeating all beings), etc., reveals that he experiences the being of beings in terms of "will."[5]

For Heidegger, modern man is self-willing, self-assertive; he is "resolved to take unconditional command" (295/117). But as such man is only responding to the extreme epoch of "a world that is only admitted as will" (ibid.). "Self-assertive man . . . is the functionary of technology" (293–94/116). In chapter 6 we discussed this ambivalence between interconnected extremes within the domain of the will in the epoch of technology. In our unrestrained will to dominate the earth, we too become reduced to cogs in the wheel of an increasingly cybernetic technological will to will. Our dilemma is compounded by the fact that, as everything is running smoothly in "total organization," "technology itself prevents any experience of its essence" (295/117). Without experiencing the essence of technology as the will to will, without experiencing this abyss on which the sand castles of technological total organization are constructed, we cannot hope for the dawn of another way of being. The answer Heidegger finds in Rilke is that to "see this danger and point it out, there must be mortals who reach sooner into the abyss" (ibid.). Here again Heidegger quotes Hölderlin's lines: "But where danger is, grows/Also that-which-saves." On this point Heidegger is at one with Rilke. In order to recover from the problem of self-will, we must first peer into the abyss. However, to the question of how this transition out of self-willing takes place, to the question of what it means to reach beyond self-will into the abyss, we must begin to draw a line of critical distinction between Heidegger and (Heidegger's interpretation of) Rilke. The distinction is crucial because it concerns the very nature of that which would be other than self-will.

According to Rilke, the mortals who would reach sooner into the abyss "would be the most daring, the most ventured. They would be still more daring even than the self-assertive human being [*Menschenwesen*] which is already more daring than plant or beast" (296/118). Rilke writes that such mortals "go *with* this Venture, will it." In his interpretation of this line, Heidegger offers us the key to understanding his assessment of the path Rilke offers for transcending self-will.

But if man is the ventured being who goes with the Venture by willing it, then those humans who are at times more venturesome must also will more strongly [*müssen . . . auch noch wollender sein*]. Can there, however, be a heightening of this willing beyond unconditional purposeful self-assertion? No. Those who are at times more venturesome, then, can will more strongly only if their willing is different in essence. Thus, willing and willing would not be the same right off. Those who will more strongly by the essence of willing, remain more in accord with the will as the being of beings. They correspond sooner to being that shows itself as will. They will more strongly in that they are more willing [*Sie sind wollender, insofern sie williger sind*]. (296–97/119)

Crucial here is the connection made between *wollender* ("more willing" in the sense of willing more strongly) and *williger* ("more willing" in the sense of being willing to do something, in this case more willing to be in accord with being that shows itself as will). To be "more willing" is thus not simply an increase in the will of self-assertion: "The more venturesome ones do not venture themselves out of selfishness, for their own personal sake. They seek neither to gain an advantage nor to indulge their self-interest" (297/119). Their willing is "without care" (*ohne Sorge*), when caring "has the character of purposeful self-assertion by the ways and means of unconditional production" (298/120). Rather, their willing is "of a different essence"; the *Wollen* of those who are *williger* is a higher or more proper will.

Having passed through and beyond his own attempts to determine a "most proper will," that of *Wissen-wollen* and/or that of *Verhaltenheit*, Heidegger now critically asks whether Rilke's notion of a proper will, namely a will that is *williger*, successfully calls into question the domain of the will as such. Does it not remain rather a kind of deferred-willing, a deference to the Will of Nature? Does it not leave in place the modern delimitation of being as (the domain of the) will?

On the one hand, Heidegger is partially sympathetic to Rilke's conception of the more venturesome ones as those who are *williger*. For instance, he speaks of the *Schaffen* (creating) in Rilke's poem in nearly the same manner that he himself attempts to think a non-willing notion of poetic retrieval (*Schöpfen*). It is worthwhile to read this passage here, not only because it shows the appreciative side of Heidegger's 1946 reading of Rilke, but also because it gives us a taste of Heidegger's own attempts to think the work of art, or "building" in general, otherwise than as an artificial manufacturing, that is to say, otherwise than as an active imposing of form on a passive material according to the will of the artist (see *GA* 5:63–64/200; *VA* 154/160; *WhD* 50/15).

> The daring that is more venturesome, willing more strongly [*wollender*] than any self-assertion, because it is willing [*willig*], "creates" [*schafft*] a secureness for us in the Open. To create means to fetch from the source [*Schaffen bedeutet: schöpfen*]. And to fetch from the source [*Aus der Quelle schöpfen*] means to take up what springs forth and bring what has so been received. The more venturesome daring of the willing exercise of the will [*willigen Wollens*] manufactures nothing. It receives, and gives what it has received. It brings, by unfolding in its fullness what it has received. The more venturesome daring accomplishes, but it does not produce. Only a daring that becomes more daring by being willing [*willig*] can in receiving bring into fullness. (*GA* 5:298/120)

Heidegger's greatest sympathies with Rilke's poetry concern the receptive creativity of language. If for Heidegger language in general is the "house of being" (see *GA* 9:313/239), poetry is the temple in the center of this domicile "precinct" (*Bezirk, templum*), where the determinations of this clearing are first marked off (*bezirkt, temnein, tempus*) by the word (*GA* 5:310/132). Heidegger thus understands the question of *what* the more venturesome ones venture (a point not made explicit in Rilke's poem itself) in the following manner: "Thinking our way from the temple [*Tempel*] of being, we have an intimation of what they dare who are sometimes more daring than the being of beings. They dare the precinct of being. They dare language" (ibid.). In the daring of his poetry, even if it does not in the end manage to break out of the metaphysics of will, Rilke is acknowledged to be a "poet for destitute times."

But let us now turn our focus to the limits of Heidegger's appreciation for Rilke's idea of the more venturesome ones as those who are *williger*.

At several points in his essay, Heidegger remarks on what he holds to be the metaphysical limits of Rilke's poetry. Rilke's poetry, Heidegger claims, "remains in the shadow of a tempered Nietzschean metaphysics" (*GA* 5:286/108; see also *GA* 54:235). How does it remain in this shadow, and how does it "temper" it? Both points are important. Rilke remains in the shadow of Nietzsche's metaphysics in that he too understands the being of beings as will.

> The being of beings is the Venture. The Venture resides in the will which, since Leibniz, announces itself more clearly as the being of beings that is revealed in metaphysics. . . . Rilke, in representing Nature as the Venture, thinks it metaphysically in terms of the essence of the will. (*GA* 5:279/102)

Rilke's poetry remains in an essential sense within the metaphysics of will. Thus man, even in his most proper mode of being more venturesome, *williger*, remains thought in terms of the metaphysical notion of a representing consciousness.

> For Rilke's poetry, the being of beings is metaphysically defined as worldly presence [*weltische Präsenz*]; this presence remains referred to representation in consciousness, whether that consciousness has the character of the immanence of calculating representation, or that of the inward conversion to the Open which is accessible through the heart. (311/132)

Rilke's "logic of the heart" remains a "logic," and as such remains within metaphysics; for "only within metaphysics does logic exist" (311/133). Thus, even though Rilke's logic of the heart is the reversal (*Umkehrung*) of the "logic of reason" as "the organization of the dominion of purposeful self-assertion in the objective," this remains a reversal *within* metaphysics, and does not break out of its domain as such. For Rilke, as for Nietzsche, the determination of the being of beings as will is not thought historically, as an epochal withholding of a more originary essence of being, but is thought ahistorically as the nature of being as such. Correspondingly, "human being" for Rilke, both the being of self-assertive man and the being of the more venturesome one who is *williger*, is thought of as a "subject." Indeed, it is only "within the sphere of subjectivity as the sphere of inner and invisible presence," and only by "a conversion of consciousness," "an inner recalling of the immanence of the objects of representation into presence within the heart's space" (307–8/129), that Rilke sees the possibility of overcoming willful self-assertion.

What, then, of the notion of overcoming the will by being "more willing" in the sense of *williger*? Granted, this notion is a "tempering" of the Nietzschean affirmation of will to power. Even if Rilke's "angel" is the metaphysical equivalent of Nietzsche's "overman" (312/134), his notion of being *williger* is more decisively pitted against the will of self-assertion. But in the end even this notion of a higher will of willingness remains within the domain of the will.

To be sure: "The more venturesome ones will more strongly in that they will in a different way from the purposeful self-assertion of the objectifying of the world. Their willing wills nothing of this kind. If willing remains mere self-assertion, they will nothing" (318/140). And yet, even these more willing ones do not challenge the understanding of being as will as such. They are more willing, *williger*, in that they correspond sooner to the will which, as the Venture itself, draws all pure forces to itself as the pure whole draft of the Open. The willing of the more venturesome ones is the willingness [*Willige*] of those who say more sayingly, those who are resolutely open [*ent-schlossen*], no longer closed off in the parting against the will as which being wills beings. (319/141)

The more venturesome ones reach into the abyss, but they do not bring us across it. They might open themselves to the essence of technology as the will to will; they might reveal, by complying with, the modern being of beings as will. Yet they would not fetch from the source, or even decisively intimate, a more originary way of being.

We turn now to Heidegger's own attempt to think a path to *Gelassenheit*, a notion of non-willing which ultimately abandons the attempt to re-habilitate the will or discover its proper essence, and intimates rather a way of being *other than* willing. We shall see, however, that in the very radicality of its difference from the will, the question of the transition becomes enigmatic in the extreme.

A Conversation on the Way to *Gelassenheit*

In 1959 Heidegger published two texts in a small volume entitled *Gelassenheit:* a memorial address for the composer Conradin Kreutzer (1780–1849) given in 1955, also entitled "Gelassenheit"; and a "conversation" (*Gespräch*) between three characters, a Scientist (*Forscher*), a Scholar (*Gelehrter*), and a Teacher (*Lehrer*), entitled "Toward an Explication of *Gelassenheit:* From a Conversation on a Country Path about Thinking." The latter text (*G* 29–71) was excerpted and reworked from a much longer unpublished conversation (*GA* 77:3–157) written fifteen years earlier in 1944–45. In other words, the conversation—Heidegger's most explicit and sustained meditation on *Gelassenheit* as *Nicht-Wollen*—was originally composed precisely at the end of his prolonged *Auseinandersetzung* with Nietzsche's philosophy of the will to power. The portion published in 1959 is a slightly revised version of most of the last third of the earlier unpublished version (see *GA* 77:105–23, 138–57), which has now appeared in full in volume 77 of the *Gesamtausgabe*.

Conversation as Corresponsive Wayfaring

The sections of the conversation on *Gelassenheit* that Heidegger prepared for publication in 1959 present in a sense the finale of the (unending) conversation; but it is nevertheless important to pay attention to the unpublished sections, which include the entire first two-thirds of the conversation, for several reasons. The problem of repeating the will precisely in the attempt to overcome it, for example, receives more attention in the earlier sections. Also, the relation between the interlocutors is clearer in the longer version. While by the end of the conversation the three characters frequently appear to be speaking in tandem and finishing one another's thoughts, this is less the case in the beginning. In particular, the distance between the Scientist and the Teacher—who is called the Sage (*der Weise*)[6] in the earlier version—is more evident in the first parts of the conversation; *der Weise* is clearly pointing (*weisen*) the way from further down the path, while the Scientist often finds it rather difficult to follow these indications, as this demands thinking beyond the horizonal limits of traditional and modern concepts. To be sure, the frank obstinacy and at times impatient eagerness for clarity of the Scientist, which contrasts with and complements the radical yet guarded indications of the Teacher/ Sage, play an important role in the dialogical movement of the text. Together with the mediating role of the hermeneutically learned Scholar, it is the interplay between these characters that keeps the conversation on its way.

The dialogical (or trialogical) form of a conversation is appropriate to the task of faring a path towards a clearing, towards an explication or an "emplacing" [*Erörterung*], of *Gelassenheit*. The conversation is not a debate, nor does it move forward by collectively positing and defending a thesis in the will to win an argument. "It is doubtful," remarks the Sage at one point, "whether a conversation is still a conversation if it wills something" (*GA* 77:56). Indeed, the propriety of "questioning" itself falls into question. In a striking (self-)critical reference to "a book from our time" that sought to raise anew the fundamental question of the Greeks and of Western metaphysics (i.e., the question *ti to on*, "What is being? [*Was ist das Seiende?*]") as the question of "the truth of being [*die Wahrheit des Seins*]," the Sage suggests that "the way to the essential answer is not at all that of questioning." "It seems to me," the Sage adds, that "he who asks about being and devotes everything to working out the question of being [*Seinsfrage*], does not truly know to where he is under way" (24)!

A decade after having affirmed that "to question is to will to know" (*EM* 16), and several years prior to enigmatically stating that "questioning is the piety of thinking" (*VA* 40/341),[7] the conversation clearly suggests that "proper thinking does not at all consist in questioning," but rather in a kind of "answering" (*Antworten*). This "originary answering is not," however, "the answering of a question." "It is the answer [*Antwort*] as the counter-word [*Gegenwort*] to the word [*Wort*]. The word must first be listened to" (*GA* 77:25). To be sure, questioning too is a kind of listening, but for the most part it is said to be "a kind of willing-to-hear [*eine Art des Hörenwollens*]. " What is called for, then, is not a willful questioning which brings to a stand and schematizes the meaning of being, but rather a kind of thinking which listens and re-sponds (*ant-wortet*) to the promise (*Zuspruch*) and claim (*Anspruch*) of being. What is needed is not the positing of a horizon by way of a questioning as a will-to-know, but an engaged re-leasement which cor-responds to the regioning of the open-region. As Heidegger later writes in "From a Conversation on Language: Between a Japanese and an Inquirer," what is needed is not an objectifying speaking *about* language, but rather "reaching a corresponsive saying [*entsprechendes Sagen*] of language"; and, he adds, "only conversation could be such a corresponsive saying" (*GA* 12:143/52).

The literary form of a conversation, then, rather than a systematic treatise or a lecture that "only speaks in propositional statements" (see *ZSD* 25/24), is appropriate to this listening-corresponsive thinking. The three companions listen and respond to one another as they attempt to listen and respond to the regioning of the region of *Gelassenheit,* into the proximity or intimate-distance[8] of which their circuitous country path is slowly but surely wandering. Perhaps now we can begin to better understand the unusual title and subtitle of the original version of the conversation. As was noted above at the end of chapter 5, the title is "*Anchibasie,*" an old Greek word which the conversation ends by translating as a "letting-oneself-into-(an engagement with)-nearness [*In-die-Nähe-hinein-sich-einlassen*)]" (*G* 70/89; *GA* 77:155). The subtitle is "A Triune Conversation [*Gespräch selbstdritt*] on a Country Path Between a Scientist, a Scholar, and a Sage." As we shall see, it is the three-way conversation between these characters that clears a path toward a thinking of non-willing.

Releasement: From Assertion, Denial, and Deference

The term *Gelassenheit* is taken over from the Christian mystical tradition, in particular from Meister Eckhart's *gelāzenheit*. But, as we have seen, Heidegger is swift in marking the distance of his notion from (what he takes to be) that of Eckhart. Heidegger's critical interpretation of Eckhart in this regard is reflected in the quotation from the *Talks of Instruction* appended to the original version of the conversation: "Where I will nothing for myself, there wills instead my God" (*GA* 77:158). In contradistinction to (what is taken to be) Eckhart's notion of *gelāzenheit* as a matter of deferred-willing, the Scholar claims: "What we have called *Gelassenheit* obviously does not mean . . . letting self-will go in favor of divine will" (*G* 34/62).

As for the relation of *Gelassenheit* to the will, the participants agree near the beginning of the shorter (1959) version of the conversation that

> *Gelassenheit* lies . . . outside the distinction between activity and passivity . . . because *Gelassenheit* does *not* belong to the domain of the will. (*G* 33/61)

Gelassenheit would be distinct from the various modes of comportment within the domain of the will; with respect to the will it could only be called *non*-willing in the radical sense of *other than* willing. Indeed, one of the central themes of the conversation is how to understand *Gelassenheit* as *Nicht-Wollen*.

Heidegger is well aware that there are several ways of (mis)understanding *Nicht-Wollen* such that it would remain firmly within the domain of the will itself. Through his careful reading of Nietzsche, he learned well that the "will to destruction is will nonetheless. And, because willing is to-will-oneself, even the will to nothingness still permits willing—that *the will itself* be" (*N2* 65/31). In the original (1944–45) version of the conversation on *Gelassenheit*, several ways are listed in which the phrase *Nicht-Wollen* might be (mis)understood so as to remain within the domain of the will: it could be understood as a "self-refusal" (*Sich-Weigern*), as a "self-opposition" (*Sich-Widersetzen*), or as a "forbidding" (*Verbieten*). In each of these, it is remarked, there remains a kind of willing, namely "a will that something does not take place." They are not therefore radical negations of the will (*GA* 77:77). Next is considered the case when someone says: "I will no more." But here too—whether this is meant as "I no longer have any desire or strength to live," or "I abhor willing," or "I renounce willing"—there still lives a kind of will.

> All *Nicht-Wollen* of this kind remains throughout a transformation of willing. . . . Even though the transformation consists of a *denial* of willing, this transformation is nonetheless never a denial of the *will*, but is rather each time an affirmation of it. . . . All transformations of willing in the form of its various kinds of denial take place within the will. (78)

Heidegger makes a distinction here between *das Wollen* (willing) and *der Wille* (the will); the latter would be the root or domain of the former, such that a denial of *willing* is still based on and does not disrupt *the will*. Even if an ascetic willing not to will is a necessary first step, that is to say, even if the will must, up to a certain point, be employed in its own overcoming, in the end this transition must also "leave behind all [willful] overcoming" and somehow draw on that at which it aims: *Gelassenheit* as *non*-willing.

The Open-Region of Being Beyond the Horizon of Subjectivity

The shorter version of the conversation begins by claiming that "thinking, understood in the traditional way, as re-presenting, is a kind of willing. . . . To think is to will and to will is to think" (*G* 29–30/58–59).[9] Traditional thinking, which here means foremost that of Western modernity, involves the positing of a horizon wherein things are represented as objects for subjective consciousness. A "horizon," as a circle of vision (*Gesichtskreis*), circles the outward view (*Aussicht*) of a thing. Representational-horizonal thinking thus "steps over the appearance of the object . . . just as transcendence passes beyond the perception of objects" (36/63). Things are encountered only within the horizon posited by and centered on the subject. We encounter the tree only through what we have represented in advance as tree-like (*das Baumhafte*). We see only what we will to be seen. The subject of transcendental-horizonal representation forgets that the tree has a "backside" which both supports and withdraws from the "frontside" that is revealed as tree-like. This "backside" of the tree silently withdraws into oblivion, into forgotten concealment from the technological vision that wills the tree into boundless unconcealment as lumber-reserves.

Such subject-centered transcendental-horizonal thinking (from which even Heidegger's own early phenomenological Dasein-analysis did not yet decisively free itself) is to be left behind in the attempt to think that which lets things be, that which lets things show themselves from themselves, or that which "lets the horizon be what it is" (37/64) in the first place.[10]

> *Teacher:* What is characteristic of a horizon [*Das Horizonthafte*], then, is but the side turned toward us of an openness which surrounds us . . .
> *Scientist:* . . . But what is this openness as such, if we disregard that it can also appear as the horizon of our representing?
> *Teacher:* It strikes me as something like a region [*Gegend*], an enchanted region where everything belonging there returns to that in which it rests. (37–38/64–65)

This surrounding region, as "the region of all regions" (*die Gegend aller Gegenden*), is subsequently named in the conversation according to the old form (still spoken in some southern German dialects) of the German word for "region," *Gegnet*. This term is translated by Anderson and Freund as "that-which-regions," in order to "reflect a movement attributed by Heidegger to *die Gegnet* and further emphasized by his use of the verb *gegnen* (to region)." However, "that-which-regions" is best used as a translation for *das Gegnende* (39/65), and while we should indeed bear in mind its dynamism, I shall render *die Gegnet* rather as "the open-region," following the characterization of it as *die freie Weite*, "the free or open expanse" (39/66).

If the region (*Gegend*) were merely taken "literally" in the sense of "what comes to meet us [*was uns entgegenkommt*]," and understood as "that which comes to meet us [*das uns Entgegenkommende*]," then we would misunderstand its nature as an open-expanse that surrounds us. "In this way, indeed, we would characterize the region, just as we had previously done with the horizon, through its relation to us—whereas we are searching for what the openness that surrounds us is in itself" (39/65–66). It is for this reason that the old form *die Gegnet* is used rather than the usual *die Gegend*. The open-region is not first of all an environment centered on human projects, but rather "an abiding expanse which, gathering all, opens itself, . . . letting each thing emerge in its own resting" (40/66).

Although the Scientist takes this non-anthropocentrism of the open-region to mean that "the coming to meet us is not at all a basic characteristic of the region" (39/66), the conversation later makes clear that the open-region does "appropriate man's essence for its proper regioning" (62/83). Indeed, "without the human essence [*Menschenwesen*] the open-region cannot essence [*wesen*], as it does." Hence, the conversation attempts to think otherwise than in terms of either anthropocentrism or anti-anthropocentrism.[11] Man's essence is needed and used (*gebraucht*) for the regioning of the open-region as the coming to pass of the truth of being. If the open-region is thought as the "hidden essence of truth," we are told, then it could be said that "the human essence is appropriated over to truth, because truth needs and uses [*braucht*] man. . . . Man is he who is needed and used for the essential coming to pass [*das Wesen*] of truth" (62–64/83–85).

The "open-region" is thus the topological name given to being in the conversation. This new word characterizes Heidegger's later thinking of the "truth of being" as the "topology of beyng" (see *GA* 15:335), a development already anticipated in the notion of the "clearing" (*Lichtung*) as an open space in a forest to which woodpaths may lead. This topological thinking is reflected in the very title of the conversation as an *Erörterung*— literally an "emplacing"—of *Gelassenheit*.[12] Elsewhere Heidegger writes that *Erörterung* is to be understood first as "to point toward the place [*in den Ort weisen*]," and then as "to attend to the place [*den Ort beachten*]" (*GA* 12:33/159). We may thus understand the title, "Zur Erörterung der Gelassenheit," in the sense of pointing towards and attending to the topology of being in the other beginning of non-willing.[13]

The *Seinsfrage* then becomes a question of thinking the proper relation of man to, or the proper comportment of man within, the open-region. *Gelassenheit* is the manner of man's most proper engagement in (*Sicheinlassen auf*) the regioning of the open-region as that which lets things be by letting them come to rest in their own. Human *Gelassenheit* would cor-respond to the *Seinlassen* of the open-region, and take part in letting beings be.

How are we to understand this human participation in this letting-be? How are humans to dwell in the open-region and assist in letting things be? In contrast to transcendental-horizonal thinking, as the willful positing of a horizon that lets things show themselves only according to human designs, the conversation suggests that releasement into the open-region takes place by way of "waiting."[14] "Relating to the open-region is a matter of waiting. And waiting means: to release oneself into an engagement with the openness of the open-region" (*G* 48/72). This "waiting" must not be understood in the sense of a subservience to any would-be Will of the open-region of being.[15] For the onto-theological notion of a transcendent Will is as foreign to Heidegger's region of *Gelassenheit* as is the transcendental willing of a horizon. The open-region of being is not a domain or "regency" of a divine Will, and the "regioning" of the open-region is not an activity to which man is to merely passively subject himself. If *Gelassenheit* indicated nothing other than this, it would remain squarely within the domain of the will as a sacrificial deferral of willing.

Gelassenheit, once again, is said to lie "beyond the distinction between activity and passivity" because it "does not belong to the domain of the will" (33/61). We must attempt to think beyond the domain of this dichotomy between willful activity and will-less passivity if we are to think *Gelassenheit* as a non-willing. And yet, thinking beyond this domain is easier demanded than carried out.

Slowing Down Our Pace on the Enigmatic Path to *Gelassenheit*

Immediately following the claim that *Gelassenheit* does not belong to the domain of the will, the conversation continues:

> *Scientist:* The transition out of willing into *Gelassenheit* is what seems to me to be the difficulty.
> *Teacher:* And all the more, since the essence of *Gelassenheit* is still hidden.
> (*G* 33/61)

The conversation remains under way to this still-hidden essence of *Gelassenheit*. Only in "meditating [*Nachsinnen*] by slowing down our pace [*Schritt*]" (31/60), in not jumping ahead to a region not yet thoughtfully cleared, can we stay on track in the transition out of the domain of the will; for patient preparation is required for undergoing the radical *Schritt zurück* into the fundamental attunement of *Gelassenheit*.

Already in texts from the decade prior to the conversation, Heidegger writes of the paradoxical circularity involved in a shift in fundamental attunement. In 1936 he writes:

> This transformation is intrinsically, and not just as a consequence, a
> retuning [*Umstimmung*] into an originary fundamental attunement
> [*Grundstimmung*]. But attunements in the essential sense do not come
> about by one's talking about them, but only in action, here in the action
> of thinking. Action, too, cannot make the attunement, but only summon
> [*rufen*] it. The old difficulty which man can never overcome returns, that
> only in the completion can we attain that which must already be gained
> for this carrying out. (*SA* 126/105)

Here we are presented with one of the fundamental difficulties in thinking the transition to non-willing, namely, the problem of by what capacity one is to make the transition. On what basis can fundamental changes occur? In this case, the difficulty is that of thinking how non-willing could be achieved *either with or without* the paradoxical endeavor of "willing non-willing." The retu(r)ning to a more originary fundamental attunement, which by the early 1940s Heidegger comes to understand in terms of the transition from will to non-willing or *Gelassenheit*, cannot simply be willed, either actively by oneself or passively in deference to an other being (see *GA* 45:170). In the 1944–45 conversation on *Gelassenheit*, Heidegger patiently attempts to dialogically think through this enigmatic transition.

In order to understand the difficulty of the "transition from willing to *Gelassenheit*" at issue in the conversation, we need to bear in mind the character of the participants. Not surprisingly, it is the Scientist who has the most difficulty moving beyond the domain of the will, and he often plays the role of stubbornly dragging his feet; though at other times he is the one most eager to run ahead to stake claim on a region beyond willing. These two extremes are not unrelated, no more than are the extreme points in a pendulum swing between pessimistic skepticism and optimistic self-assuredness. Although it is through the Scientist's remarks that we get many of the clearest formulations of the difficulties as well as the "goals" of the inquiry, in their very clarity they sometimes threaten to oversimplify and lose the matter to be thought. The following is a case in point.

After the Teacher remarks: "When we engage in letting ourselves into releasement towards the open-region, we will non-willing [*Wenn wir uns auf die Gelassenheit zur Gegnet einlassen, wollen wir das Nicht-Wollen*]"—a formulation pregnant with possibilities and necessities for thought, the Scientist draws the noteworthy yet perhaps overly eager conclusion:

> Releasement [*Gelassenheit*] is indeed the release of oneself [*das Sich-loslassen*] from transcendental representation and so a relinquishing of the willing of a horizon. Such relinquishing [*Absehen*] no longer stems from a willing, except that the occasion for releasing oneself to belonging to the open-region would require a trace of willing [*bedürfe einer Spur des Wollens*]. This trace, however, vanishes while releasing oneself and is completely extinguished in releasement. (*G* 57/79–80)

This is one of the most far-reaching statements of the conversation, in that it anticipates, beyond the transition where a trace of willing is still required, a complete extinguishment of willing. This line is often cited as representative of Heidegger's post-turn stance of non-willing, which is then too often critically misinterpreted as a simple abnegation of the will that leads to a standpoint of passivism or quietism. But to think merely of an "extinguished will" would still be to think within the domain of the will. In his next statement, the Scientist himself worries about such a nihilistic misinterpretation:

> Someone who heard us say this could easily get the impression that releasement floats in the realm of unreality and so in nothingness, and, lacking all power of action, is a will-less letting in of everything and, basically, the denial of the will to live! (58/80)

The simple extinguishment of willing would achieve merely a passive willlessness; but what is wanted (*gewollt wird*) is *non*-willing. The Scholar, in response, suggests that perhaps "something like power of action [*Tatkraft*] and resoluteness also reign in releasement" (ibid.). Yet these expressions are, in turn, all too easily misunderstood in terms of willing.

Perhaps from the perspective of not-willing, non-willing could only appear as willing, while from that of willing, it could only appear as not-willing. Hence the apparent oscillation between characterizing *Gelassenheit* with terms that resound of willing and those that suggest not-willing; this particular "restless to and fro" (51/75) appears inevitable as long as we think only from within the domain of the will. Within this domain, we are only able to think in terms of either assertion, denial, or deference of willing. Moreover, as we shall see, the presumed conundrum of an either/or yes or no (see *GA* 77:124) answer to the question of whether we are always already dwelling in the open-region of *Gelassenheit,* or whether we are inescapably caught in the domain of will, exaggerates the difficulty of the transition into an impossibility.

A Transitional "Willing Non-Willing"

Let us, then, return to the more patiently nuanced (and filled with transitional tension) statement offered up for thought by the Teacher: "When we engage in letting ourselves into releasement towards the open-region, we will non-willing " (*G* 57/79). A discussion of the problematical yet key phrase, *Ich will das Nicht-Wollen,* had in fact already been a reoccurring highlight of earlier sections of the original longer version of the conversation, and looking back at these passages can help clarify the complex issue at stake. The phrase is that of the Sage (the name for the Teacher in the earlier version), but is first elicited by a question from the Scholar, who asks: "What then do you truly [*eigentlich*] will [*will*]?"[16] The Sage responds: "In our reflections on thinking, what I truly will is non-willing" (*GA* 77:51). The Scientist immediately responds to this "strange answer" as follows:

> Can one then will non-willing? Yet such a willing would only increase willing. Such willing thus always acts decisively against what it wills, namely, non-willing. (Ibid.)

The Sage at this point, far from denying this paradoxical tension, agrees by adding that this "willing against" entangles itself in willing in such a way as to lose that which is willed, non-willing. The Scientist believes the argument won, and claims several pages later that the notion of willing non-willing is after all a contradiction (59).

And yet, the Sage maintains that despite the difficulties it raises, the only answer he could give to the question of "What do you will?" was *Ich will das Nicht-Wollen* (66). This defense of his answer does not mean, moreover, merely that the original question was faulty; on the contrary, that question brings the ambivalent "on the way" character of the conversation—and presumably of our transitional times in general—clearly into view. The point is both to see the limits of the domain within which the question is framed, and at the same time to recognize those limits as still for the most part our own. Hence the Sage does not simply refuse to answer the question, but rather offers the frankly ambivalent phrase, "I will non-willing."

In fact, the ambiguity does not first appear in this phrase, but is already contained within the very term *Nicht-Wollen.* This term is ambiguous, has a double sense (*zweideutig*), insofar as, on the one hand, it means "a transformation of willing," and, on the other hand, says "that it is not a willing" (82). And the intention of the Sage with his carefully worded and repeated phrase, *Ich will das Nicht-Wollen,* was then nothing other than to disclose and "lead ourselves to this ambiguity [*auf die Zweideutigkeit hinzuführen*]" (80).

While cautiously keeping one eye trained on the ambiguity of our situation, the direction of the path of the conversation is unmistakably toward the possibility of thinking non-willing(ly), which entails not only "clarifying the essence of this non-willing" but also "letting ourselves into an engagement with this non-willing itself" (67). But is it possible, in the end, to let ourselves into an engagement with *Gelassenheit* by way of willing non-willing? The Teacher's final offering on the matter of willing reads:

> A patient noble-mindedness [*langmütige Edelmut*] would be a pure rest-ing-in-itself of that willing, which, renouncing willing, has released itself into an engagement with that which is not a will [*jenes Wollen, das, absagend dem Wollen, auf das sich eingelassen hat, was nicht ein Wille ist*]. (*G* 64/85)

A willing that renounces willing would ultimately twist free into a released engagement with that which lies beyond the domain of the will. The phrase *Nicht-Wollen,* however, insofar as it involves in part the transitional willing non-willing, retains the double meaning rephrased earlier by the Scholar (in response to the Teacher's statement *Ich will das Nicht-Wollen*) as follows:

> *Nicht-Wollen* means, accordingly: [1] willing to renounce willing [*willentlich dem Wollen absagen*]. And the term means, further: [2] what re-mains strictly outside any kind of will [*was schlechthin ausserhalb jeder Art von Willen bleibt*]. (*G* 30/59)

In thinking through the problem of the will and towards the possibility of non-willing, it is necessary to keep these two moments in mind. The first moment involves a kind of ascetic self-abnegation of willing; the second, attainable only through the discipline of the first, but also only by way of twisting free of its asceticism (*its* will), would be a way of being, not merely opposed to, but *other than* willing. Non-willing, in the most radical sense of other than willing, could only be reached by way of undergoing an ar-duous twisting through a paradoxical willing non-willing. *Nicht-Wollen* is for us today, if not always, inherently ambiguous. It is both an ascetic wean-ing from, and a way of being other than, willing.[17]

Moreover, the decisive transition from the fundamental (dis)attunement of will (back) to the fundamental attunement of *Gelassenheit,* that is, the releasement into a more originary non-willing relation with the open-region, does not take place simply by way of the human capacity to will non-willing. It is necessary to think this transition in terms of the "essential history" or the "history of the essence" (*die Wesensgeschichte*) of man; and insofar as "the *Wesen* of man does *not* experience its characterization from man" himself, but rather from "the open-region and its regioning," it is necessary to think this decisive transition in terms of "the history of the open-region [*die Geschichte der Gegnet*]" itself (55–56/78).

Seinsgeschictliche Ent-scheidung:
On Heidegger's "Decisionism"

> "Decision" can and should at first be meant as a human "act" . . . until it suddenly means the essential occurrence of beyng [*Wesen des Seyns*]. (*GA* 65:84)

The transition from (the epoch of) will to (the other beginning of) non-willing is not only a patient plodding down a country path; it is also ultimately a radical, indeed *decisive* leap into an other way of being. Let us now focus our attention on the peculiar "decisionism" involved in Heidegger's thinking of the history of being.

As we have seen, Heidegger criticizes Nietzsche's "will to overcome nihilism" as being "the ultimate entanglement in nihilism." The "will to overcome" repeats the nihilism that it purports to surmount. Nevertheless, as D. F. Krell asks, does not "Heidegger's [own] decisionism at times seem a massive voluntarism?" And yet, as Krell also cautions,[18] we must carefully explicate the sense and development of the notion of "decision" in Heidegger's thought; for if there remains a kind of decisionism in the context of his later thought of the "eschatology of being" (*GA* 5:327/18), it is hardly that of the existential voluntarism of an individual Dasein.

Whatever the ambiguities in the relation of his early notion of decision to the human will may have been, in Heidegger's later thought historical decisions occur as the sending (*Geschick*) of being itself. "The decision is never first made and executed by a human. Rather, *its* direction and perdurance decide *about* man" (*N1* 476/5). This does not mean, however, that the decision for the "rule of being [*Herrschaft des Seins*]" (ibid.) can be understood as a kind of transcendent Will of being to which humans should simply passively submit. Rather, "being needs/uses [*braucht*] man."

In the following chapter we shall return to this enigmatic yet crucially significant notion of *Brauchen,* together with the idea that being and man are "the same" in the sense of "belonging together by way of mutual appropriation" (see *ID* 90ff./28ff.). Suffice it to note here that such notions would radically distinguish Heidegger's thought of the relation between man and being from that of human obedience to a transcendent Will.

Nevertheless, Heidegger's later thought does claim that it is not first of all man, but rather being, or beyng as the event of appropriation (*Ereignis*), that decides the course of history. In texts from the late 1930s, notably in *Contributions to Philosophy,* Heidegger clearly displaces the locus of decision from individual Dasein to the history of being. Whereas *Being and Time* tended to speak of decision as a *jemeinige* affair, claiming that "only the particular Dasein decides its existence" (*SZ* 12), *Contributions* tells us that we need to move away from any "'existentiell' [self-?] misunderstanding of decision" (*GA* 65:88) to a more originary meditation on "the being-historical essence of decision" (87). To understand the latter phrase we need to rethink the "essential occurrence of decision" (*das Wesen der Entscheidung*) in such a way that decision is seen in the context of the history of being.

"Decision," Heidegger writes in *Contributions,* "comes about in stillness, not as resolve [*Beschluss*] but as resolute openness [*Entschlossenheit*]" (101). In this *Ent-schlossenheit,* he tells us in a later lecture course, "man is in a literal sense 'de-cided' [*ent-schieden*] with regard to the being of beings; that is, 'decision' means to be without a scission from [*nicht abgeschieden von*] being" (*GA* 54:111). This "without scission," or "not cut off from," however, would not imply a simple identity, but a belonging together in mutual appropriation. As the difficult language of *Contributions* puts it: "What is called here de-cision [*Ent-scheidung*] moves into the innermost essential-midpoint of beyng itself and [therefore] says: the very moving apart [*Auseinandertreten*] which divides [*scheidet*] and in dividing first comes into the play of [mutual] a-propriating [*Er-eignung*]" (*GA* 65:88). *Ent-scheidung* as de-scission thus brings together man and being into the dynamic identity of a play of mutual appropriation. As with the interrelated meanings of the "turning" (i.e., as the turning within *Ereignis* and as the turning to an other beginning of the history of being), this sense of de-scission between man and being is related to the being-historical sense of decision as that which divides one epoch from another. (In the latter case the "Ent-" would function as an intensifier rather than as a removal of the scission.) The "highest decision" in the latter sense is that which decides between the end of the history of metaphysics and the dawn of the other beginning. Whether this highest historical decision takes place or not depends on whether the de-scission between man and being occurs.

In this context Reiner Schürmann's interpretation of the later Heidegger's notion of decision is thought-provoking, in that, after stressing the non-humanistic character of being-historical decisions, he briefly raises the question of human participation in terms of "the problem of the will." Schürmann interprets Heidegger's thought to imply an "economically disjunctive decision" which is "necessarily nonhuman." He draws attention to the etymological connection, alluded to above, between *Entscheidung* and the verb *scheiden*, meaning to "separate," to point out that what is involved in the being-historical decision is the separation between two historical epochs: between, on the one hand, the first beginning as the history of metaphysics, and, on the other hand, the other beginning which is to come.[19] The history of metaphysics has culminated in an epoch of unbounded subjective will. Heidegger's thought attempts to look beyond this epoch in order to prepare for a turning to a more originary comportment to being. The decision at stake, then, cannot be a matter of subjective resolve, but must rather be a scission in the unfolding history of being itself. Schürmann writes: "A decision is, then, first of all, a matter of collective destiny. It is the disjunction between two economic eras."[20] It should also be thought of, he adds, as "aletheiological," as it "opens the space where human decisions can occur at all."

But how is man to participate in the being-historical decisive turning from an "economy" of will to one of non-willing? In this regard let us examine, in sympathetic critique, Schürmann's interpretation of that key phrase from the conversation on *Gelassenheit: Ich will das Nicht-Wollen.* Schürmann claims that, although "individual and collective decisions, our voluntary acts, are always inscribed within the horizon of economic decisions," we can choose either to attune our acts to these transitions or not: "Voluntary acts comply with economical transitions or they 'hold fast to the assertion of their stay.'" In other words: "Voluntary decisions either abandon themselves to the epoch-making disjunctive decisions or they harden themselves against those decisions."[21] This general understanding of the proper role of human action is applied in an interpretation of our present need to will non-willing:

> The will can follow the economic flow or not follow it, observe its own context or decontextualize itself. If, as has been shown, the last epochal principle, whose efficacy culminates in technology, is the subject reduplicating itself as will to will—for our age being is willing—then the will, too, is primarily contextual and only secondarily behavioral. What does it mean, in our age of closure, to follow the economic modifications? It can only mean to follow the context-setting will in its epochal decline, to

dismiss it as the last metaphysical stamp, as the being of entities, as the mark of our age. It means to "renounce willing voluntarily."[22]

Thus Schürmann interprets the phrase *Ich will das Nicht-Wollen* to mean: "To renounce willing voluntarily." And yet, if we take seriously Schürmann's own idea that economic decisions precede any voluntary acts, is not the very meaning of a "voluntary decision" itself absolutely determined by this being-historical epochal decision? Can the first "will" in the phrase "to will non-willing" unambiguously maintain the sense of a "voluntary act," when what is being decided is precisely the very nature and validity of such terms as "action" and, particularly, "volition"? Where would the impetus to voluntary renunciation of volition come from? Why would this "voluntary renunciation of willing" not simply be another example of where, as Heidegger writes, a "renunciation of will" in fact "remains throughout a transformation of willing," or where a "denial of will" is in fact "an affirmation of it" (*GA* 77:78)? In his all too brief treatment of the problem of the will, Schürmann does not sufficiently address these questions, and his notion of voluntarily following the context-setting will in its epochal decline remains a suggestive yet in the end enigmatic solution.

This is not to wholly disagree with Schürmann's interpretation, or to simply assert that the will to non-willing does not mean "to renounce willing voluntarily." However, only within the epoch of will could one simply affirm the role of the "volitional act" in making (or "following") decisions. To point out the role the "volitional act" plays is but to expose one horn of the dilemma regarding the possibility of moving beyond the will. The necessity of our recourse to "willing non-willing" is as problematical as it is undeniable. The catch-22 appears to be that, in participating in the decision between will and non-willing, we both cannot and cannot but resort to the powers of a "volitional decision."[23]

The Teacher in the conversation on *Gelassenheit* sighs at one point: "If only I had already the right *Gelassenheit*, then I would soon be relieved of that task of weaning" (G 32/60). But "the right *Gelassenheit*" is precisely that non-willing which could be reached only by "weaning ourselves from the will" (ibid.). *Gelassenheit* is both the end and the required means for twisting free of the will; this is the aporia of the transition to non-willing. But is there a "right way to enter this circle"? Is there in fact a sense in which we *do* already have—at least a trace or prenotion of—the right *Gelassenheit*? Is *Gelassenheit* or non-willing perhaps *both* that *historical* possibility toward which we are groping *and* an originary *non-historical* essence of man?

The Non-Historical as In-Historical:
Beyond the Sterile Opposition of Relativism
and Absolutism

Is it legitimate to speak of the "non-historical" in the context of Heidegger's thought of radical historicity? In order to introduce this controversial topic in such a way as to show both its necessity and its complexity, some preliminary discussion is called for.

To begin with, it is crucial to distinguish what I am calling the "non-historical" from a simple privation or opposition to the historical (i.e., from the a-historical or un-historical). The non-historical must be seen as inseparably interwoven with the historical, rather than as independently set over against it. In fact, it is only when we fall into historicism (in the sense of historical relativism) that any suggestion of the non-historical can only be heard as a failure to think historicity. Heidegger's *radical* thinking of history, on the other hand, demands that we also think its relation to the non-historical. However, the non-historical—and this is the peculiar difficulty that Heidegger's post-metaphysical thought entails—"is" only in and through its historical determinations. I suggest, therefore, that we understand the non-historical as the "*in-historical*," with the essential ambiguity of the "in-" signifying both difference and location. The non-historical as in-historical exceeds the determinations of the historical without existing anywhere else; there is no metaphysical realm of predetermined essences. Being presences only in and as its determinate sendings, without, however, being exhausted in or reducible to a specific historical determination or set of determinations. Being as the in-historical presences in withdrawal.

At one point Heidegger tells us that experiencing the essence of history remains most difficult, and is best approached by way of what is unessential to it, i.e., its *Unwesen* (*GA* 53:179). History (*die Geschichte*) must neither be thought "historiographically" (*historisch*) nor a-historically. Heidegger is less concerned with what he calls "the history-less" realm (*das Geschichtlose*) of "nature."[24] He is most concerned to warn against what he sees as the modern fall of humankind into "the un-historical" (*das Ungeschichtliche*). The un-historical (the simple negation of the historical, or rather, of the historical already reduced to the historiographical) is "the breaking off with history" in the abandonment of "the law of history" (*das Gesetz der Geschichte*). On the other hand, it is the inability to radically think "historicity" (*Geschichtlichkeit*) that has led us into the sterile opposition between "historicism" and the "absolutism" of a-historical science or unhistorical thinking. Historicism, in its one-sided negation of transcendence, reduces history to a one-dimensional temporal succession of worldviews. What Heidegger struggles to think as the "law of history" gets covered over here just as decisively as in the case of the metaphysics of transcendent eternal essences.

Indeed, Heidegger's path of thought can be read as a struggle to recover from this sterile opposition between historicism and absolutism. Pöggeler has pointed out that, under the influence of Husserl and neo-Kantianism, the young Heidegger had initially sought to show that "the validity of signification (*Sinngeltung*) was something untouched by time" as opposed to "the historical process of meaning-formation (*Sinngestaltung*)." Subsequently, in *Being and Time* and other early works, Heidegger rebelled against this strict division, but perhaps in such a way, suggests Pöggeler, as to overemphasize the historical dimension. "In his late work he rejects historicity and history as guiding principles" in favor of the idea of *Ereignis* as that which grants the *Zeitspielraum* in which the *Geschick* of being can be thought. In Heidegger's mature thought, concludes Pöggeler, "it is necessary that one critically distinguish between that which builds itself historically and that which, also seen from a historical perspective, is still more than, and different from, a historical becoming."[25]

In a detailed and illuminating study that traces the theme of historicity through the development of Heidegger's thought, Hans Ruin argues that, despite the apparent disfavor of the term "historicity" in his later texts, Heidegger had in fact always sought to think this idea beyond the opposition between the relative and the absolute; indeed, "from the beginning his affirmation of the historicity of life and of philosophy itself is seen as a remedy against historicism."[26] Ruin shows how Heidegger attempts to maintain philosophy's mission as a pursuit of origins, as *Ursprungsphilosophie*, "in explicit recognition of the foundering of this very project as previously understood."[27] For Ruin this means that the "origin" does not disappear altogether for a thought of radical historicity, yet its meaning is fundamentally transformed; the origin becomes essentially "enigmatic." "Through the thought of historicity Heidegger seeks to designate the situatedness of knowing and of existence while not admitting their relativity. It is an attempt . . . to think a constitutive finitude, the point from which the generality can be grasped in its manifestation, without taking it for granted as a given framework."[28] Ruin traces this "paradoxical logic that rules over the thought of historicity" from the notion of the *Augenblick* in Heidegger's earlier writing to the notion of *Ereignis* (noting the etymological roots of this term in *Eräugnis* and *eräugnen*) in his later thought. The *Augenblick*, he writes, is the name for "the event of understanding and meaning-enactment . . . through which the manifestation of the eternal may be grasped as such."[29] But the "eternal" here can no longer be thought as an a-historical realm of already constituted meaning, for it "is," it "comes to pass," only in its enactment in the *Augenblick* as "the moment of vision."

While remaining inherently "enigmatic"—insofar as it essentially withdraws as it grants, conceals its indeterminate abundance as it reveals a particular determination of the being of beings—Heidegger's attempt to think this non-historical origin becomes more acute. In *The Principle of Reason*, while warning against the "handy representation of history as the temporal actualization of what is supratemporal," Heidegger attempts to think "the unique concealed in the enigmatic constancy which at times erupts and is assembled into the suddenness of what is genuinely *Geschick*-like."

> The sudden is the abrupt that only apparently contradicts that which is constant, which means, that which endures. What is endured is what lasts. But what already lasts and until now was concealed is first vouchsafed and becomes visible in what is abrupt. We must calmly confess that we never reach the vicinity of the historicity that is to be thought with a view to the *Geschick* of being so long as we remain ensnared in the web of representations which, all in all, blindly take refuge in the distinction between the absolute and the relative. (*SG* 160)

The thoughtful place from which this opposition between absolute and relative can be understood in its limitation, Heidegger goes on to say, is that which brings into view "the sense in which being and ground [*Grund*] name that which 'is' the same. For this 'same' is simultaneously what is constant and what at times lights up in the suddenness of a *Geschick* of being" (161). The "same" here is, then, neither simply historical nor a-historical; it intimates what must be thought of as "non-historical." More precisely, it is that which, in the *Augenblick* of *Eräugnis*, both presences and withdraws, opening up the dimension in which humans ambivalently dwell in (excess of) the historical; it is the non-historical as in-historical.

The Non-Historical Essence of Man as (the Possibility of the Transition to) Non-Willing

Let us now set this thought of the non-historical in the context of the question of the transition from will to non-willing. We can begin by restating the aporia of this transition so as to show how it hinges on the question of the historical character of the essence of man. How is man to participate in the transition from the epoch that determines his nature as will to a time when he would be released into non-willing? How can we leave behind that by which we are still determined? We have stressed the radical difference between the (domain of the) will and non-willing; but it is the very radicality of this difference which makes the transition so enigmatic. For if the historical essence of man is to undergo a basic change, on what basis does this change occur? Insofar as in the epoch of will man's essence, his "fundamental attunement," would be *wholly* determined by the will, then a transition to non-willing could come about only as an unmediated conversion to a wholly other mode of being. And yet, is it not the case that in some sense, as Haar claims, in "addition to some new element, every transformation requires something that persists"?[30] Is there an excess to modern man's determination as willful subjectivity, a more originary fundamental attunement which endures even under the cover of the darkest night of the technological will to will? Is it on the basis of glimmers of this buried yet more originary fundamental attunement that we can participate in the transition beyond the will? Is non-willing to be understood, then, not *only* as a possibility on the hither side of the turning from the epoch of will, but *also* as man's concealed and forgotten but nevertheless somehow enduring originary essence?

Haar claims at one point that "Heidegger maintains that man is entirely and exclusively historical,"[31] and he seeks to retrieve a sense of the non-historical *after* Heidegger as follows:

> For Heidegger, the essence of man is intrinsically determined by epochality. For him there is no nonhistorical or transhistorical human essence. And yet just as the essence of being persists through its History, must there not necessarily be a human essence that does not change? The simplicity of the mortal, inhabiting the earth with others, exposed to the heavens, belongs neither to the dawn nor to the dusk; it is of all time, ageless; it is at once archaic and of an extreme, immemorial youth. Must we not ultimately counter a Hegelian and Heideggerian excess by rehabilitating the nonhistorical?[32]

Haar is thus interested in uncovering a non-historical dimension of man through and beyond Heidegger's thought, particularly with regard to the ways in which "nature" (or "the Earth")[33] and the body[34] always exceed their "worldly" (i.e., historical) determinations, even while this excess is only ever accessible in and through worldly historical disclosures. But Haar claims that he must do so "sometimes against the letter of the Heideggerian text . . . [because for] Heidegger, man is intrinsically historical, intrinsically limited, defined and determined by the epochs of the History of Being."[35] And yet, does Heidegger in fact completely give human being over to its epochal being-historical determinations; is the essence of man, according to Heidegger's thought, without excess of its historical delimitations? Is the essence of man in the modern epoch *wholly and seamlessly* confined in its definition as will? Haar himself suggests that Heidegger's notion of man as a mortal dwelling in the fourfold intimates a non-historical dimension.[36]

Before we look at some of the many intimations of a non-historical essence of man in Heidegger's texts, let us first be clear on the extent to which he does indeed stress the historicity of the essence of man. In *Introduction to Metaphysics,* where he is beginning to develop the notion of the history of being, he claims that the question which asks after the determination of the essence of man, and the decision regarding this question, are historical; indeed, "this question is the very essence of history." This is so because the "question of what man is must always be posed in an essential connection with the question of how it stands with being" (*EM* 107). And as the central insight of *Being and Time*—that the horizon of the meaning of being is time—develops into the idea that "the history of being is being itself" (*N2* 489/82), the question of "how it stands with being" is to be understood as a being-historical question. Hence, Heidegger writes in 1955–56, the "history [*Geschichte*] of thinking is the bestowing [*Beschickung*] of the essence of man by the sending [*Geschick*] of being" (*SG* 147). Man's essence is thus determined historically by the sending of being.

And yet, do we not already find the suggestion here of a non-historical aspect of the essence of man, namely, that he is called on in all ages to thoughtfully cor-respond to the sending of being, precisely in order to receive the epochal gifts of his *jeweilige* historical essence? This other side of Heidegger's thought of the essence of man, this other dimension to that essence, is from the beginning part of his conception of the history of being. A few pages after the passage quoted above from *Introduction to Metaphysics,* Heidegger writes that, in this questioning of the determination of the essence of man, "man is first brought back to the being that he himself is and must be. . . . Only as questioning-historical does man come to himself; only as such is he a self" (*EM* 110). The human essence is not only historical in the sense of being determined historically; man is also historical in that he is in all times called on to essentially participate in this historical determining. That is to say, *man's non-historical essence is in part characterized by a cor-responsive participation in the being-historical determination of the historical essence of beings, including, first of all, that of his own being.* Man is, in short, non-historically historical.

We can begin to elaborate and test out the idea of a non-historical essence of man in Heidegger's thought by looking at his notion of "that-which-saves" (*das Rettende*). What happens when we are "saved" from the historical determination of our essence as will? "To save," writes Heidegger in "The Question Concerning Technology," "is to fetch something home into its essence" (*VA* 32/333). That-which-saves thus "lets man see and re-turn to [*einkehren*] the highest dignity of his essence," namely that of "keeping watch over" the clearing of being (36/337). The reason that the extreme danger of enframing can also be the site of the growth of that-which-saves is that "it is precisely in this extreme danger that the inner-most indestructible [*innigste, unzerstörbare*] belongingness of man within granting may come to light" (ibid.). The danger is that the particular his-torical determination of the essence of man as will in the epoch of en-framing "threatens to sweep man away into ordering as the ostensibly sole way of revealing, and so thrust man into the danger of the surrender of his free essence [*die Gefahr der Preisgabe seines freien Wesens*]" (ibid.). It is precisely this intimation of an "innermost," "indestructible" and "free es-sence" of man, which exceeds the modern historical delimitation of his essence as will, that would enable a human participation in the transition to an other beginning of non-willing.

Let us look at some further passages where Heidegger speaks of this non-historical essence. In the essay "Building Dwelling Thinking," he writes that "the manner in which we humans *are* on the earth, is . . . dwelling [*das Wohnen*]. To be human means to be on the earth as a mor-tal; it means to dwell" (*VA* 141/147). Notice that he does not say "the way we once were" or "the way we could one day be," much less "the way we now are," but rather simply the way humans, regardless of time or place, are. For Heidegger, "dwelling" names "the basic character of human exis-tence [*den Grundzug des menschlichen Daseins*]" (183/215); it is a non-historical characteristic of being human. We dwell together with one an-other as mortals among things, on the earth, under the sky, and before the divinities, and this is the case even in the deprived form of a forgetfulness of this fourfold dwelling in our willful technological manipulation of en-tities. Even though there may never have been nor ever will be pure unadulterated dwelling, even though mortals must always anew find ways to dwell, we are always already in some manner dwelling; for dwelling is a non- or in-historical characteristic of being human.[37] Heidegger also claims that it is, perhaps above all else, man's subversion of the relation of dominance between himself and language "that drives his essence into alienation [*in das Unheimische treibt*]" (140/146). It is man's non-historical essence to speak in response to the saying of language; and so the mod-ern illusion that man is the master of language is not simply one histori-cal way of being among others; this hubris is (also) an uncanny alienation from our originary fundamental a-tunement to language.

The hint of an answer to the dilemma of how man can participate in the transition out of the domain of the will is that man is in fact never *ex-haustively* determined by the epoch of will; *there is a non-historical human essence of non-willing which exceeds his epochal delimitation as willful subjectiv-ity.* Were modern man to be wholly and seamlessly confined to his histor-ical essence of willful subjectivity, the "will" to non-willing would forever reduplicate the problem it aims to "overcome." Moreover, passively sub-mitting to the sending of being, as if it were a fate willed from above, would simply shift the locus of agency within rather than displace the do-main of the will as such. Yet because man is never completely severed from an a-tunement to the originary non-historical dimension of non-willing, he is already to some extent able to "take part" in the fate of technology (see *VA* 22/324, 36/337); he is always already to some extent able to "cor-respond to being" (*WP* 72ff.) or to "play along with" the sending of being (*SG* 188) in a manner that exceeds both the active and passive modes of the domain of the will.

    If this interpretation of the fundamental attunement of non-willing as the non-historical essence of man needs yet further support, let us look at a passage where Heidegger says that it is the will which alienates man from and even threatens to extinguish "his essence."

> What has long since been threatening man with death, and indeed with the death of his essence, is the unconditional character of sheer willing in the sense of purposeful self-assertion in everything. (*GA* 5:294/116)

The essence of man, Heidegger claims here, "resides in the relation of being to man. Thus man, by his self-willing, becomes in an essential sense endangered" (293/115). Man is threatened with "the death of his es-sence," in other words, with an irrecoverable estrangement from his non-historical essence of non-willing cor-respondence to being.

    In the essay "The Turning," Heidegger writes that man is needed and used (*gebraucht*) for the "recovery [*Verwindung*] from the essential oc-currence of technology," in that "in his essence" he "corresponds" to the turning of being. Yet in order to properly cor-respond within the turning of being, "modern man must first and above all find his way back into the full breadth of the space proper to his essence" (*GA* 79:70/39). It is by re-trieving his non-historical essence that man can participate in the turning to an other beginning. In the following passage Heidegger elaborates on this "great essence of man [*das große Wesen des Menschen*]" (70/40), and claims that its retrieval is necessary for the transition out of the techno-logical will to will.

> That essential space of human essence [*Wesensraum des Menschenwesens*] receives its conjoining dimension [*seine ihn fügende Dimension*] solely from out of that relation [*Verhältnis*] in which the safekeeping of being

itself is given to belong [*vereignet*] to the essence of man as the one who is needed and used [*gebrauchten*] by being. Unless man first establishes in himself beforehand the space proper to his essence and there takes up his dwelling, he will not be capable of anything essential within the destining now holding sway. (70/39–40)

In this text Heidegger goes on to speak of the "sudden flash" or "insight into what is" as that which suddenly breaks through the "truthless being" of technology and brings man back into his essence. Man, for his part, corresponds to this insight only when he "renounces human self-will and projects himself toward that insight" (76/47).

Renouncing self-will, we recall, is said to be the entrance into *Gelassenheit*. About the latter Heidegger writes: "Authentic *Gelassenheit* consists in this: that man *in his essence* belongs to the open-region, that is, he is released to it [*ihr gelassen ist*]. . . . Not occasionally, but—how shall we say it—*prior to everything* [im vorhinein]" (*G* 61/82–83, emphases added). *Gelassenheit*, as the most proper relation to the open-region, is man's innermost essence, his non-historical essence that he is called on, ever again, to help bring into history. On the one hand, the conversation tells us, insofar as "we are not and never could be outside of the open-region" (48/72), we could never be irrevocably and totally severed from *Gelassenheit*, or expelled from dwelling in the region of non-willing. "And yet again we are still not in the open-region, insofar as we have not yet released ourselves into an engagement in the open-region as such" (49/73). Hence the ambiguity in the Teacher's answer to the question of whether we were ever outside the open-region: "That we were, and yet we were not" (48/72).

In our innermost core we are beings of *Gelassenheit;* and yet perhaps we are always already to some extent alienated from this non-historical essence. In the conversation we are told that, although "the subject-object relation," which in the end reduces things to objects of willful manipulation, is "only a historical variation of the relation of man to the thing," nevertheless things "have become objects even before they attained their essence as things" (55/78). Moreover, the "same is true of the corresponding historical change of the essence of man to egoity [*geschichtlichen Wandel des Menschenwesens zur Ichheit*] . . . which likewise emerged before the essence of man could return to itself [*ehe das Wesen des Menschen zu sich selbst zurückkehren durfte*]" (ibid.).

We are charged with the task, perhaps a never-ending one, of awakening to that originary essence of human being which we always already are—even under the epochally oblivious covering of willful subjectivity—and yet have never once simply been.

8

Intimations of Being
in the Region of Non-Willing

> *Scholar:* Do you mean that everything depends on whether we
> engage in [*uns einlassen*] explaining the essence of non-willing,
> or do you mean that it depends on whether we engage in non-
> willing itself?
> *Sage:* I mean in a certain manner both. (*GA* 77:67)

Anticipatory Thinking: *Winke, Ahnungen,* and *Vermutungen*

In the opening pages of *Contributions to Philosophy* Heidegger writes that
"the time of 'systems' is over," and yet "the time of building the essential
formation of beings from the truth of beyng has not yet arrived" (*GA*
65:5). In the meantime, that is, during the "crossing over to the other beginning," philosophy must confine itself to the patient task of thinking
forward in anticipation of this other way of being. During our transitional time, "the other beginning of thinking always remains only an intimation [*das Geahnte*], though already decisive" (4). Thinking toward
the other beginning in an epoch of *Seynsverlassenheit* requires reattuning
our ear to the distant ringing-forth (*Anklang*) of beyng. The language of
"inklings" (*Ahnungen*) and "hints" (*Winke*) pervades the later Heidegger's writing as he attempts to think that which is not (yet) wholly think-
able; on the hither side of questioning and problematizing the will, anticipatory thinking attempts to listen and cor-respond to intimations of
non-willing.

Yet this reserved language is not merely intended to be a sign of our
transitional times, as if the other beginning would establish a new era of
logical certainty. Rather, the task of thinking for Heidegger becomes inherently a matter of responding to hints and cultivating intimations. In

Was heisst Denken? (*What Is Called Thinking?* or *What Calls for Thinking?*) Heidegger writes:

> Because we have for a long time become accustomed to understanding all knowing and ability in terms of the thinking of logic, we measure "inkling" [*Ahnung*] by this same measure. . . . [But] the authentic sense of having an inkling is the way in which what is essential comes to us and is given to attention [*in die Acht gibt*], so that we may keep it therein. This having an inkling is not a preliminary step on the stairway to knowledge. It is the great hall wherein all that can be known is kept concealed and harbored [*verhehlt, d.h. verbirgt*]. (*WhD* 172–73/207)

"In fact," writes Heidegger elsewhere, "we ought to ask ourselves here in a general way whether proofs of thought . . . are what is essential—or whether what is essential are hints of being [*Winke des Seins*]" (*N2* 383/238).

In a letter to a student who had asked "whence the thinking of being receives its directive," Heidegger responded as follows. On the one hand, this thinking can provide no credentials "that would permit a convenient check in each case whether what I say agrees with 'reality'"; but on the other hand, "it is just as little a matter of arbitrariness [*Willkür*]." The question for a thinking that is "on the way"—a way (*Weg*) that is always at risk of "going astray" (*Irrweg zu werden*)—is rather that of whether it is "rooted in the essential destiny of being." "Everything here is the way of a corresponding which examines as it listens [*Weg des prüfend hörenden Entsprechens*]" (*VA* 176–79/183–86). This path of a "corresponding which examines as it listens" would involve neither an assertion nor a deference of will. For "thinking," unlike "science," does not proceed by way of positing hypotheses and setting out to prove these by way of calculations of certainty; nor does it, like "theology," have an infallible Word and Will of revelation to which it can defer in faith. Rather, Heidegger suggests that we must carefully and with fore-sight (*vor-sichtig*) risk suppositions (*Vermutungen*) of thinking beyond the closure of the horizon of onto-theology.

In the previous chapter we considered the difficulties involved in (thinking) the transition from will to non-willing. How would the historical essence of man be transformed from the technological will to mastery to a way of being other than willing? If it were to be either simply by means of a will to self-determination, or simply by means of a passive submission to a higher decree, then the problem of the domain of the will would be reproduced precisely in the attempt to step beyond it. The task is to think the transition out of the domain of the will in such a manner so as not to simply switch positions within it. But would not this thinking of the transition already require a prior intimation of non-willing? "Must we not already be bound by a different measure [*Mass*] before we are capable of measuring [*Messen*] anything in that manner?" (*GA* 12:17/197). In order to think non-willing, we must already to that extent be able to think non-willingly. The problem could be expressed in terms of a kind of "hermeneutical circle": in order to think the possibility of moving beyond the domain of the will, we must already be attuned to that which lies outside. In some respects analogous to the "pre-ontological understanding of being" (*SZ* 15) that was thought to enable his early hermeneutical phenomenology, does the later Heidegger suggest a pre-turning intimation of the other beginning of non-willing?[1]

Heidegger's later texts are indeed replete with intimations of non-willing. He cultivates a thinking of, for example: a non-technological usage of things which "preserves" or "spares" (*schont*) rather than either manipulates or neglects them; an engaged knowing that is neither a blank staring nor a *Wissen-wollen;* an artistic building as a responsive "fetching from the source" (*Schöpfen*) rather than as a willful making (*Schaffen*); and an attentive listening that lets language speak by "answering" (*Ant-worten*) its word. A detailed consideration of each of these significant aspects of the later Heidegger's thought would require another study. Here, in staying focused on the key relation between man and being, I shall consider Heidegger's attempts to think this relation otherwise than in terms of the domain of the will.

In earlier chapters we have had occasion to touch upon many of the ways in which the later Heidegger tries to intimate a non-willing relation between man and being. In this chapter I shall gather, focus, and elaborate further on these attempts to think this relation beyond the domain of the will, letting Heidegger's texts say what they can with regard to this central yet most difficult of matters. By commenting on some of the most crucial, if also most demanding, passages from his later texts, I shall here continue to follow the pathway he has disclosed, and where possible attempt to further clarify the *Lichtung* to which it leads. Once this attentive (*hörende*) explication and interpretation has been carried out, we may reopen the more critical (*prüfende*) eye in our next chapter. Only then shall we be ready to turn our attention to the residual shadows in the clearing.

Opening Other Vistas: Attempting to Speak Otherwise

Beyond Humanism and Anti-Humanism: Man as the Shepherd of Being

In chapter 6 we considered Heidegger's critical account of the course of the entire history of metaphysics as culminating in the modern metaphysics of willful subjectivity and ultimately in the technological *Wille zum Willen*. In a compelling manner Heidegger reveals the complicity of many fundamental aspects of the Western tradition and the modern "world-civilization" in this metaphysics of will. He maintains, for example, that "the logic of reason" is the "organization of the dominion of purposeful self-assertion" (*GA* 5:311/133); that "values" rob things of their essential worth insofar as "what is valued is admitted only as an object for human estimation" (*GA* 9:349/265); and that "humanism" is not only "either grounded in a metaphysics or is itself made to be the ground of one" (321/245), but is in fact the pinnacle of metaphysics which places man (ultimately his will) at the center of all things. Hence, for example, "existentialism" can be a "humanism" precisely because it is a subject-centered voluntarism.

And yet, although Heidegger radically criticizes logic, values, and humanism, he is quick to point out that this criticism should not be taken to imply an affirmation of their "opposites." His critique of logic and the rational is not meant to excuse a "flight into the irrational," but rather attempts to "face a demand which is outside of the either/or of the rational or the irrational" (*GA* 9:388/294). The "liberation of language from grammar" (a liberation which is "reserved for thought and poetic creation"), he writes, does not condemn us to the lawless realm of the boundlessly illogical, but rather brings us "into a more essential framework" (314/240). And to "think against values," he says, "does not mean to beat the drum for the valueless and nullity of beings. It means rather to bring the clearing of the truth of being before thinking, as against subjectivizing beings into mere objects" (349/265). And finally, the critique of humanism "in no way advocates the inhuman" (345–46/263); indeed, far from negating the importance and uniqueness of man, Heidegger thinks "the essence of man" to be "essential for the truth of being," "insofar as being appropriates man as ek-sisting for guardianship [*Wächterschaft*] over the truth of being into this truth itself" (345/263). Although Heidegger questions whether we should keep the word "humanism" for this "curious kind of 'humanism'" which "contradicts all previous humanism" (ibid.), his thought in no way advances an anti-humanism.

In short, as with the critique of logic and values, Heidegger's "opposition to 'humanism' in no way implies a defense of the inhuman, but rather *opens other vistas*" (348/265, emphasis added). Heidegger's thought thus ultimately attempts to "open other vistas" beyond the metaphysical horizon of both logic/values/humanism *and* their opposites. That is to say, in showing how both these traditionally affirmed positions and their polar opposites are bound to the problematical domain of the will, Heidegger attempts to think toward a vista beyond the horizon of this domain, i.e., toward a region of non-willing.

How does Heidegger's *non-*humanism think the proper role of man? Set against the relief of the technological worldview, one could say that man is essentially "less than" the lord of the earth, and yet "more than" a passive link in a chain driven by the cybernetic will to will. More properly speaking, man is essentially *other than* these apparent opposites. What, then, is man most properly or "authentically"? In the "Letter on Humanism" Heidegger rethinks the notion of "authenticity" (*Eigentlichkeit*) as follows: "[The] terms 'authenticity' and 'inauthenticity' . . . imply . . . an 'ekstatic' relation of the essence of man to the truth of being" (*GA* 9:332–33/253). How would man authentically take part in this ekstatic relation?

> The advent of beings lies in the destiny of being. But for man it is a question of finding what is fitting in his essence which *corresponds* to such a destiny; for in accord with this destiny man as ek-sisting has to *guard* the truth of being. Man is the *shepherd* of being. (330/252, emphases added)

Thus Heidegger understands human "existence" no more in the sense of an existential voluntarism than in the sense of the subjectivity of the *ego cogito.* If man's essential way of being is indeed an ek-sisting, this is not to be understood in the sense of a transcendence (an *Übersteigen* or overstepping of beings) that willfully posits a horizon of meaning, but rather as a standing out that stands within—an "ecstatic standing within" (*ekstatisches Innestehen*) (325/248)—the truth of the clearing of being. Ek-sistence is an "ecstatic dwelling in the nearness of being. It is the guardianship, that is, the care for being" (343/261).

The non-willing in-historical essence of man involves "guarding," "shepherding," "watching over," or "caring" for the clearing of being; only in this manner would man most properly take part in that event which grants or lets beings be. Renouncing his lordship over beings, man opens himself to the free space, the clearing, of being; in guarding the clearing of being, man takes part in letting beings be. In his role of guarding or shepherding, man neither actively creates, nor merely passively suffers, but rather "participates" in the opening up and preserving of a world by "corresponding" to being. In each of these expressions for the essential role of man, "guarding," "shepherding," "watching over," "taking part," etc., what is at stake is hearing a "task" or "commission" that is no longer definable in terms of the opposition of passivity/activity in the domain of the will.

A Non-Passive Waiting

Heidegger wrote that since "Western languages are languages of metaphysical thinking, each in its own way," it "must remain an open question whether . . . these languages offer other possibilities of utterance" (*ID* 142/73). The "house of being" modern man inhabits is constructed within the domain of the metaphysics of will. Yet it is not possible to simply vacate the premises overnight and take up lodging elsewhere. To enter into genuine dialogue with non-Western languages or to learn to speak in new ways requires going *through* the hallways and clearing the portals of our current domicile. Hence, if we are to open a window onto another vista, indeed if we are to build a pathway for transporting and rebuilding our house in a region beyond the domain of the metaphysics of will, we must begin by learning to use the furnishings available in this house otherwise. Heidegger therefore does not just completely abandon the language of metaphysics, but frequently attempts rather to deconstructively let its words speak differently. Most often he does this starting with everyday words, which harbor latent possibilities for speaking beyond their hardened metaphysical determinations. Let us consider here one of the most counterintuitive examples, namely that of a non-passive understanding of "waiting."

Heidegger clearly denies that the job of the philosopher is to go out and actively change the world or that any "willful action" on the part of humans could bring about a revolution that would free us from the crisis of technology. "I know of no paths to the immediate transformation of the present situation of the world, assuming that such a thing is humanly possible at all" (*SP* 104/110). "We are," the Teacher claims in the conversation on *Gelassenheit*, "to do nothing but wait" (*G* 35/62). But this "waiting" does not simply stand in opposition to "doing"; it is not merely a matter of passive inactivity. To begin with, let us note how Heidegger distinguishes his notion of waiting (*Warten*) from that of "awaiting" (*Erwarten*). The latter is determined within the subjective horizon of "representing and the represented"; it involves the projecting of an object which is then expected to appear. Awaiting is thus thoroughly entwined in both the active and the passive sides of the domain of the will. Heidegger's waiting, on the other hand, would be neither a willful projection of an object nor a will-less submission to a being. In genuine waiting, "we leave open what we are waiting for . . . [because] waiting releases itself into openness" (42/68). Yet if we cannot say what waiting "awaits," what does it "wait upon," or rather, what does it wait "in relation to"? The answer Heidegger suggests is that waiting waits upon the open-region, which cannot be spoken of in terms of will (see 58/80), but is rather that open place or placing that lets beings be.

Waiting is ultimately identified, as is "thinking," with releasement to the open-region (see 50/74); "thinking changes in *Gelassenheit* from . . . a representing to waiting upon the open-region" (ibid.). Waiting, properly undertaken, is already *Gelassenheit*. It is not only the attentive anticipation of the other beginning, but is already, as the responsive attunement to the open-region, the released non-willing comportment proper to man. Thus, in the end, it is not only the case that we can "do nothing but wait for the essence of man" (57/79). Properly undertaken, such a waiting is nothing other than that "*Gelassenheit* through which we belong to the open-region" while the latter "still conceals its own essence" (ibid.); and indeed, since a self-concealing would remain an essential aspect of the event of being as a granting-in-withdrawal (as *Ereignis/Enteignis*), waiting in "openness for the mystery" would always remain an essential aspect of man's proper comportment to being.

As a transitional term, on the other hand, "waiting" can perhaps provisionally be understood as a radical passivity that interrupts active willing, and thus as a counterpart to "willing non-willing." These two together—a proper willing that "actively" renounces the will, and a radical "passivity" that opens itself to the arrival of non-willing—are perhaps complementary moments of a twisting free of the very dichotomy of activity/passivity as determined within the domain of the will. Yet ultimately, the "waiting" of which Heidegger speaks is no longer merely a transitional term; it intimates a radical break from the domain of the will as such. Waiting now names a non-passive/non-active receptive-responsiveness to the regioning of the open-region; human waiting properly corresponds to being, whose arrival in turn always waits upon human correspondence (see *GA* 9:363/ 275). Human waiting corresponds to the waiting of being itself.

Heidegger speaks of this proper corresponsive waiting, for example, in terms of a "reserved steadfast releasement [*verhalten ausdauernde Gelassenheit*]" that receives "the regioning of the open-region" (*G* 59/81). He also speaks of this engaged waiting in terms of *Inständigkeit* (indwelling). Along with *Innestehen*, this word reflects Heidegger's turn from understanding the "ek-sistence" of Dasein in any "transcendental" sense (i.e., as overstepping beings to posit a horizon) to that of a standing-out-within the clearing which "receives intact . . . the coming forth of truth's essence" (60/82). Standing within the *Da* of *Sein* requires a steadfast (*ausdauernde*) holding-out in the perdurance or "carrying-out" (*Austrag*) of the happening of truth. *Austrag* is another term that gives us a sense for this comportment beyond both passivity and activity. Joan Stambaugh provides the following helpful explication of the term:

> *Austrag* [means] literally carrying out, holding out. In a consultation Heidegger . . . stated that its basic meaning is to bear, to hold out, but without any connotation of suffering or exertion [i.e., neither passive not-willing nor active willing]. The *Austrag* is the carrying out of the "relation" of [being] and beings, endured with an intensity that never lets up.[2]

This notion of "waiting," thought as "*Inständigkeit* in *Gelassenheit* to the open-region," is so far from a mere passivity that it is referred to as "the genuine essence of the spontaneity of thinking" (*G* 60/82). Waiting is spontaneity. In thinking these apparent opposites together Heidegger attempts to twist free of the very domain which sets them in simple opposition. In a parallel manner, Heidegger suggests that in fact "movement comes from rest [*Ruhe*] and remains let into rest" (45/70), for "rest is the seat and the reign of all movement" (41/67). The way (*Weg*) of movement (*Bewegung*) is pervaded by rest; and waiting, as the *Gelassenheit* corresponding to this rest in the heart of the regioning of the open-region, is the true spontaneity of thinking. As inherently enigmatic as these intimations may remain (for the participants in the "Conversation on a Country Path" as well as for us), what is clear is that to follow the direction in which Heidegger's path of thought is leading, we must rethink words like "rest" and "waiting" otherwise than as deficient states of activity.

It is this radically other sense of "waiting" towards which Heidegger is pointing when he claims that "we are to do nothing but wait." In the conversation on *Gelassenheit* he attempts to develop, as we have seen, this non-willing sense of "waiting." In the interview with the magazine *Der Spiegel*, however, after denying that the philosopher can provide a path to the immediate transformation of the world, he also rejects the idea that we should simply (i.e., passively) wait.

> It is not simply a matter of waiting until something occurs to man within the next 300 years, but of thinking ahead (without prophetic proclamations) into the time which is to come, of thinking from the standpoint of the fundamental traits of the present age, which have scarcely been thought through. Thinking is not inactivity but is itself the action which stands in dialogue with the world mission [*Weltgeschick*]. (*SP* 104/110)

This more originary sense of the "action" of thinking must, however, be thought beyond the metaphysical opposition between theory and praxis; for thinking in terms of this horizon "blocks the way to an insight into what I understand by thinking" (104/110–11). We must therefore attempt to understand Heidegger's "thinking of being" as a matter of non-willing correspondence that radically precedes and calls into question the binary terms in which we are accustomed to understanding theory/praxis, activity/passivity, and waiting/taking action.

The Essence of Man: Thinking as Corresponding

Man's non-historical or in-historical essence, we have seen, is to corre-spond to the being-historical sending of the historical essence of beings, including first of all the historical essence of man. The question is how we are to properly think man's participation in this historical sending. Let us first note how Heidegger's thought resists the misunderstanding that the sending of the history of being takes place as a fate that compels as a will handed down from above. Man, to be sure, cannot himself "effect" the turn from the technological *Gestell* to a time beyond the epochs of meta-physics; yet neither can this turn happen without his preparation by way of stepping back to his more originary essence of thinking as non-willing corresponding. "Man is indeed needed and used [*gebraucht*] for the re-covery [*Verwindung*] from the essential occurrence of technology. But man is needed and used here in his essence that *corresponds* to that recovery" (*GA* 79:70/39, emphasis added).

The destining or sending (*Geschick*) of the history of being is obvi-ously other than a history shaped by human will; but neither is it a fate (a higher Will) which compels from above. To be sure, the "history of think-ing is the bestowing [*Beschickung*] of the essence of man by the *Geschick* of being" (*SG* 147). Yet this "bestowing" is not a willing; it is rather a *Brauchen* which not only "uses" man but "needs" him to take the leap whereby "thinking enters into the breadth of that play upon which our human essence is staked" (186). In other words, the in-historical essence of man is to corresponsively participate in the play of the *Geschick* of being wherein his own historical essence is determined. In the present situation, man must find his way back into his non-historical fundamental attunement of non-willing so that he may take part in (by way of preparing an abode for) the turning of being into a more originary revealing as the region of non-willing, a turning which would let man historically build, dwell and think according to his most originary essence as non-willing.

The *Geschick* of being is thus not a fate willed from above, but "remains the history of the essence of Western humanity insofar as historical humanity is engaged in constructively inhabiting [*bauende Bewohnen*] the clearing of being" (*SG* 157). Man is called on to participate by "constructively inhabiting" the event of the clearing of being wherein his own historical essence is in turn determined. The *Seingsgeschick* is not a master-Subject that wills the fate of its human slaves; it is an eventuation that is rather like an innocent "child that plays" (188). The human task is to properly engage in this play; the question is "whether and how we, hearing the movements of this play, play along and accommodate ourselves to the play" (188). Within the non-willing play of being, we are called on to participate in our own manner of non-willing thinking as cor-responding.

For Heidegger, then, the essence of man is thinking, the nature of which is a cor-responding to the address of being. "Man *is* essentially this relationship of corresponding to being, and he is only this" (*ID* 94/31). Although this corresponding to being "always remains our abode," that is, although it is the non-historical essence of humans to cor-respond to being, "only at times does it become a developed comportment specifically taken up by us" (*WP* 74/75). "Cor-responding to being" is thus what I have called the "in-historical" essence of man; more specifically now, it names both the non-historical essence of man and the anticipated historical awakening to this essence in the turning to the other beginning beyond the closure of the history of metaphysics—a history which both depends on and yet conceals this originary cor-respondence.

Here our concern is how to understand this in-historical human correspondence, not only in terms of the transition to the other beginning, but also as itself properly a matter of non-willing. If cor-responding (*Ent-sprechen*) to the address (*Zu-spruch*) of being constitutes the fundamental trait of our essence (see *WP* 72/73), we can provisionally isolate three moments of this corresponding: (1) renunciation (*Verzicht*), detachment (*Abgeschiedenheit*), or holding-back (*Zurück-halten*); (2) belonging (*Gehören*) or obedient (*gehorsam*) listening (*Hören*); and (3) answering or responding (*Ant-worten*). In short, the three moments are (1) restraint, (2) receptivity, and (3) response.

Thinking demands renunciation (*Verzicht*) of self-will, a detachment from beings (*Abschied vom Seienden*), and even sacrifice (*Opfer*) as a matter of "the human essence expending [*Verschwendung*] itself"; and yet this sacrifice is said to be made "in a manner removed from all compulsion [*Zwang*], because it arises from the abyss of freedom" (*GA* 9:310/236). This renunciation or sacrifice leads to the second moment: thinking is "obedient [*gehorsam*] to the voice of being" (311/237). Man, in his reception (*Empfangen*) of the address of being (see *SG* 144), belongs to being, is claimed by being (*GA* 9:358/272). "A belonging to being prevails within man, a belonging which listens to being because it is appropriated to being" (*ID* 94/31). This obedient listening gives way to the third moment: "the sole matter of thinking," in response, is to "bring to language ever and again this advent of being" (*GA* 9:363/275). Everything depends on "reaching a corresponsive saying [*entsprechendes Sagen*] of language" (*GA* 12:143/52). The address of being is not a monologue, but as "conversation" essentially calls for "a corresponsive saying."

Thinking is "determined" by being (*GA* 9:309/236). And yet, this "determining" (*Bestimmen*) is not the ordering of a will, but rather "the silent voice of being [*lautlose Stimme des Seins*]" (310/236)—a voice which elicits or evokes (*be-stimmt*) an "attunement" (*Gestimmtheit*) and ultimately an answer by way of an "echo" (*Widerhall*) from humans. "This echo is the human response to the word of the silent voice of being" (ibid.). "What appeals [*zuspricht*] to us as the voice [*Stimme*] of being evokes [*be-stimmt*] our correspondence" (*WP* 76/77). Thinking is in this sense an "attuned correspondence [*gestimmte Entsprechen*]" to being (78/79). Man speaks in correspondence with language as the house of being. Humans are ultimately response-able (*Verantwortlich*) not just to listen but to answer (*Antworten*) or respond (*Ent-sprechen*) to the address (*Zu-spruch*) and claim (*An-spruch*) of being. In short, the first moment of "renunciation" (*Entsagen*) ultimately gives way to the third moment of a "counter-saying" (*Ent-sagen*) within the speaking of the language of being.

Named retrospectively in terms of the will, the three moments might appear under the guise of (1) not-willing, (2) deferred-willing, and (3) proper-willing. There is moreover the possibility of interpreting these as indicating three moments of a transition, forming a kind of succession of (1) willing not to will, (2) waiting in radical passivity for the arrival of another beginning, and finally twisting free of even these vestiges of the domain of the will into (3) a non-willing cor-responsive participation in the appropriating event of beyng. Yet taken as intertwined moments within the region opened up in the other beginning, each of these moments would have to be rethought in its own way as other than willing.[3] In any case, in order to fully understand human cor-respondence as non-willing, it needs to be clearly shown that the first two moments of restraint and receptivity would not imply a deference to the "will" of being. To do this we need to show, yet more thoroughly, that the "activity" proper to being is essentially other than willing.

Being's Needful-Usage of Man:
The Regioning of Non-Willing

For Heidegger, the question of being and the question of man are inseparable. In asking the question of being Heidegger always found it "necessary to meditate upon the essence of man" (*GA* 9:372/282). Conversely, rethinking the essence of man corresponds to rethinking the essence (or the essencing, the *Wesung*) of being. Hence, to think the essence of man decisively beyond the domain of the will, it is necessary to think being itself (beyng) as otherwise than willing. Not only man's comportment to being, but being's relation to man must be rethought as non-willing. Heidegger struggles to find a non-metaphysical way of radically rethinking this mutual relation. We have seen that man's proper relation (*Verhältnis*) to being is a comportment (*Verhaltung*) of reserved (*verhaltene*) yet engaged cor-respondence; we shall now elaborate on being's proper relation (*Bezug*) to man as that of a needful-usage (*Brauch*) for safeguarding (*Bewahren*) its truth (*Wahrheit*).

The relation between man and being is neither that of the clash of two wills to power, nor is it that of the incorporation of man into the one Will of being as meta-Subject. In *Identity and Difference* Heidegger writes that, just as man is appropriated to being, in its own way being is appropriated to man. Being needs man: "For it is man, open toward being, who alone lets being arrive as presence [*lässt dieses als An-wesen ankommen*]. Being's coming to presence needs/uses [*braucht*] the openness of a clearing, and by this need remains appropriated over to the essence of man [*bleibt . . . durch dieses Brauchen dem Menschenwesen übereignet*]" (*ID* 95/31). In this manner, "man and being are appropriated over to one another [*Mensch und Sein sind einander übereignet*]. They belong to one another" (ibid.).

In "On the Question of Being," another important later text on the relation between man and being, we find the following key passage:

> We always say *too little* of "being itself" when, in saying "being," we omit its essential presencing *unto* the human *essence* [*das An-wesen* zum *Menschenwesen*] and thereby fail to see that this [human] essence itself co-constitutes [*mitausmacht*] "being." We also say *too little* of man when, in

saying "being" (not human-being [*das Menschsein*]) we posit man as
independent and then first bring what we have thus posited into a relation to "being." Yet we also say *too much* when we mean being as the all-
encompassing, and in doing so represent man only as one particular
being among others (such as plant and animal), and place them in relation to one another. For there already lies within the human essence the
relation [*Beziehung*] to that which—through a relation [*Bezug*], a relating in the sense of needful-usage [*Brauchen*]—is determined as "being"
and so through this relation is removed from its supposed "in- and for-
itself." (*GA* 9:407/308)

Being is neither a pantheistic "all-encompassing" nor an idealistic substance become subject "in-and-for-itself"; its essential relation to man is
not that of a substance to an accident, nor that of a Subject which posits
and reincorporates human subjectivity into its dialectical domain. As we
see in these passages, Heidegger attempts to think the relation of being
to man *otherwise* with the word *Brauchen,* which he thinks in the double
sense of a "needful-usage."

The idea that man is the site (*die Stätte*) or the "there" (*Da*) which
"being requires [*ernötigt*] in order to disclose itself" (*EM* 156) is a central
element of Heidegger's thought from early on, and even the use of the
word *Brauchen* to denote this peculiar need can be found at least as early
as the mid-1930s.[4] While this word is already used in a developed sense in
Contributions (see *GA* 65:317–18) and also, for example, in an important
section of the second *Nietzsche* volume (see *N2* 390ff./244ff.),[5] Heidegger's most explicit and sustained meditation on the term *Brauchen* is
found in the 1946 "Anaximander Fragment." There he uses this word to
translate the Greek *chreon,* which is usually rendered as "necessity." We fall
into error, Heidegger warns, if we exclusively adhere to the derived meaning of "what is coercive" (*Zwingende*) or what "must be" (*GA* 5:365–66/51–
52). The word *chreon* is etymologically connected to the word *chrao,* which
means: "I get involved with something, I reach for it, extend my hand to
it," and also "to place in someone's hands or hand over, thus to deliver, to
let something belong to someone" (ibid.).

Heidegger "dares" a translation at this point, one which does not result from "a preoccupation with etymologies and dictionary meanings,"
but rather "stems from a prior *trans*lation [Über*setzung*] of thinking" (*GA*
5:369/54) which thinks from the experience of being's oblivion, and from
the ringing-forth (*Anklang*) in that oblivion of a more originary relation
between man and being. He translates *to chreon* as der Brauch (in the English translation, "usage"). Heidegger is first of all concerned to distance
this word from any modern connotations of "utilizing." Rather, we should

"keep to the root meaning: *brauchen* is to brook [*bruchen*], in Latin *frui,* in German *fruchten, Frucht*" (367/53), which we may "translate freely" as "to enjoy" (*genießen*), not in the modern sense of "to consume or gobble up," but in its original meaning of "to be pleased with something and so to have it in use" (ibid.). Thus *Brauchen* is intended to mean: "to let something present come to presence as such; . . . to hand something over to its own essence and to keep it in hand, preserving it as something present" (ibid.). Elsewhere Heidegger distinguishes *Brauchen* both from a "utilizing" (*Benützen*) that uses up or exploits (*Ab- und Ausnutzen*) and from a leaving alone that neglects. "On the contrary: proper use brings what is used to its essential nature and holds it there. . . . *Brauchen* is: to let something into its essence and to safeguard it there" (*WhD* 114/187).

In another context Heidegger calls this kind of non-willing engagement with things a "sparing" (*Schonen*), which is said to be nothing less than "*the fundamental character of dwelling* [Der Grundzug des Wohnens]" as a mortal (*VA* 143/149). This proper using (*das eigentliche Brauchen*) that spares and preserves is said to "designate a human activity" that is nearest to us all. Yet Heidegger also claims that "proper using is rarely manifest," and even that "in general it is not the affair of mortals." Rather, "mortals are best illuminated by the radiance of [proper] use [*vom Schein des Brauchens beschienen*]" (*WhD* 115/187). Ultimately, then, Heidegger reserves the word *Brauchen* for the peculiar "activity" of being itself. It is not predicated as

> a form of human behavior; nor is it said in relation to any being [*Seiendes*] whatsoever, even the highest being [*das höchste Seiende*]. . . . [But] rather, *Brauch* now designates the manner in which being itself essences as the relation to what is present, approaching [*an-geht*] and becoming involved with [*be-handelt*] what is present as present. (GA 5:367–68/53)

Being needs man, but is not subject to human will; man is used by being, although this "using" is not a willful utilizing, but rather a handing man over to and preserving him in his essence—namely that of corresponding to being by giving expression to and watching over the clearing of its truth. *Brauchen* is ultimately not to be understood as a transitive verb; it is not the predicate of a subject that uses man as an object. Rather, we must recollect the middle voice and think in terms of *Es brauchet* (provisionally translated: "It is useful"). Commenting on the same Greek word as it appears in a fragment of Parmenides, in *What Is Called Thinking?* Heidegger writes: "*Chre* [*Es brauchet*], then, would be a sentence without a subject" (*WhD* 115/188). "As a translation of *chre,* the phrase 'Es brauchet' belongs rather in the company of 'Es gibt'" (116/189). The phrase *Es gibt* expresses the originary occurrence of being, its manner of presencing, of giving (itself) by way of letting beings presence. *Brauchen,* then, would be akin to this originary giving in that it would not be a transitive act, but a middle-voiced event.

Heidegger goes on to ask whether these "apparent opposites," *Es brauchet* and *Es gibt,* do not in fact say the same thing.

> "Es gibt" apparently names the exact opposite to "Es brauchet"; for that which "needs/uses" [*brauchet*] requires and wants rather to "have" and precisely for that reason cannot therefore "give." Yet one who advances such opinions has already again forgotten what is contained in the highest sense of *Brauchen:* letting into [*einlassen*] essence and preserving therein. Would this not be a giving? . . . Could it be that the "Es Brauchet"—once thought through sufficiently—would determine more closely what the "Es gibt" says? (*WhD* 116/189)[6]

Heidegger's notion of *Brauchen* is thus, far from any willful utilizing of man for being's ends, the non-willing middle-voiced event wherein man is given over to his own proper essence of non-willing cor-respondence.

Heidegger ultimately goes beyond, or radically steps back before, the name "being" (*Sein*) for this most originary event of needing/using/giving, and speaks rather of the "It" which gives as *Ereignis. Ereignis* is said to be "richer than any possible metaphysical definition of being" (*GA* 12:248–49/129). And yet, the dynamic relation between the correspondence of man and the *Brauchen* of being (now *Ereignis*) is carried over: "*Ereignis* appropriates [*ereignet*] man to its own needful-usage [*Brauch*]" (249/130). As the "within itself oscillating realm" which holds man and being together in holding them apart, *Ereignis* "needs" man's corresponsive thinking. Indeed, Heidegger's very thought of *Ereignis* attempts to answer to this need: "To think of *Ereignis* as *Er-eignis* means to build onto the structure of this realm oscillating within itself [*am Bau dieses in sich schwingenden Bereiches bauen*]" (*ID* 102/37–38).[7] Man receives the "tools" (*Bauzeug*) for this building from language, as "the most delicate and thus the most susceptible oscillation holding everything within the hovering structure of *Ereignis*" (102/38). In thinking, man both draws on and gives back to language as the house of being. It is this non-willing relational interplay that is named *Ereignis,* as the event of mutual appropriation between man and being. Topologically thought, the *Ereignen* of *Es gibt/Es brauchet* is the regioning of the open-region of non-willing, within which man cor-responds by way of his most proper fundamental attunement of *Gelassenheit.*

The Intimacy of *Ereignis* and *Gelassenheit*

The Event of Mutual Appropriation

In the remainder of this chapter, let us consider this key word of Heidegger's later thought, *Ereignis,* and its relation to *Gelassenheit* in some detail. In *Contributions to Philosophy* (which is subtitled *Vom Ereignis*) Heidegger began to doubt whether the term "being" (*Sein*) could be thought non-metaphysically—i.e., no longer as the beingness of beings, as the highest being, or as the first cause—and there he frequently used the alternative spelling "beyng" (*Seyn*) to indicate the non-metaphysical temporalizing/spatializing event of presencing/absencing which remains unthought in metaphysics (see *GA* 65:436). In *Contributions* Heidegger also introduces the term *Ereignis* as the most proper name for this originary event of beyng.

In his published works, a more gradual displacement of *Sein* by *Ereignis* as the central term of Heidegger's thought continues, becoming most explicit in texts such as the 1962 "Time and Being." In the "Summary of a Seminar" appended to this text we are told that, on the one hand, "the term 'being itself' already names *Ereignis*"; and yet, on the other hand, "it is precisely a matter of seeing that being, by coming to view as *Ereignis,* disappears as being" (*ZSD* 46/43).

In the 1955 text "On the Question of Being," Heidegger goes so far as to cross out "being," writing it as B̶e̶i̶n̶g̶, a gesture which is made initially "to prevent the almost ineradicable habit of representing 'being' as something standing somewhere on its own that then on occasion first comes to encounter man" (*GA* 9:411/310). Yet he goes on to say that "the sign of this crossing-through [*Durchkreuzung*] cannot, however, be the merely negative sign of a striking-through [*Durchstreichung*]. It points, rather, toward the four regions of the fourfold and their being gathered together in the point/place [*Ort*] of this crossing through" (411/310–11). In other words, the sign B̶e̶i̶n̶g̶ is not simply an abandonment of the term "being," but a more radical determination of it. The crossing-through of B̶e̶i̶n̶g̶ indicates—with its four corners—the interrelation, the identity-in-difference, of the elements of the fourfold (earth and sky, divinities and mortals), and stresses that "being" is nothing but the simple oneness of this event of the fourfold. B̶e̶i̶n̶g̶ crossed through indicates *Ereignis*.

In another context, *Ereignis* is also thought as "the same" in the sense of the "belonging-together" of man and being (*ID* 90ff./28ff.). "Being" here does not so much disappear as become decentered, such that *Ereignis* names the essential relation of dynamic interplay between man and being.

We may translate *Ereignis* as "the event of (mutual) appropriation." Depending on the context, what is thought as "mutually appropriated" are time and being, man and being, or the fourfold of earth and sky, divinities and mortals. When "world" is used to refer to the mutually appropriating event of the fourfold, the "worlding of the world" is the middle-voiced *Ereignung* of *Ereignis*. In common usage the German word *Ereignis* means "event," and *sich ereignen* means "to happen" or "to occur." Yet Heidegger draws special attention to its connection with the term *eigen* (one's own, what is proper to one). Hence *Er-eignen,* as a "dedication" (*Zueignen*) or "a delivering over into what is their own [*Übereignen . . . in ihr Eigenes*]" (*ZSD* 20/19), would be an event that brings (releases) matters into their own, into what is proper to them. *Ereignis* is neither a metaphysical ground nor a transcendental Subject; and *Er-eignen* does not appropriate (*Aneignen*) things in the sense of willfully incorporating them into a place they don't belong. It does not greedily dis-own things from, but rather generously en-owns them into their proper, their "appropriate" manner of being; it does not willfully displace things from, but rather non-willingly en-places them into, their proper (appropriate) locale.

As the event of mutual appropriation, *Ereignis* lets beings be the beings they are in their interrelation or "mirror-play" with one another. Furthermore, Heidegger is aware of the etymological connection of *Ereignis* with *Auge* (eye), and at times uses the archaic spelling of *er-eignen* as *er-aügnen* to express its character of "bringing into view" (see *GA* 12:249/ 129). *Ereignis* is thus most fully understood as the originary event wherein things are allowed to show themselves from themselves in the mirror-play of their mutual appropriation in the time-play-space of the fourfold.

Ereignis as the middle-voiced worlding of the world is a gathering onefold (*Einfalt*) in which the elements of the world are held both together in their unity and apart in their differences. While warning that we are still not able to thoughtfully experience the worlding of the world in itself (see *GA* 79:47), that we are still on the way to the thoughtful "experience" of "awakening to *Ereignis*" (*ZSD* 57/53), many of Heidegger's later texts are devoted to various attempts to indicate or at least intimate this originary event. For example, he speaks of this onefold gathering of the world as the "appropriative mirroring" (*ereigende Spiegeln*) of the fourfold, and depicts this mutual expropriative-appropriation (*enteignende Vereignen*) as follows.

> Earth and sky, divinities and mortals—being at one with another of their own accord—belong together by way of the simple one-fold of the single fourfold [*aus der Einfalt des einigen Gevierts*]. Each of the four mirrors in its own way the essential occurrence [*das Wesen*] of the others. . . . The appropriative mirroring sets free each of the four into its own, but it

binds these free ones into the one-fold of their essential [extending] toward one another [*die Einfalt ihres wesenhaften Zueinander*]. (*VA* 172/179)

Man as the mortal is called on first of all to attend to being, as the appropriating event of the fourfold, by shepherding and sheltering its clearing of truth in poetry and in thought. Moreover, mortals are called on to let things be by sparing and preserving, rather than either manipulating or neglecting them. And mortals are called on to prepare an abode for the divinities, even when this means marking the silent presence of their absence, their flight and their refusal. In each of these interrelated endeavors, man as the mortal assumes his proper place in the fourfold event of appropriation by building, dwelling, and thinking non-willingly.

Ereignis as Originary *Lassen*

Insofar as non-willing is man's proper manner of being-in-the-worlding-of-the-world, *Gelassenheit*'s relation to *Ereignis* can be understood as man's essential way of being within the essencing of beyng. Yet the relation between these terms can be thought more intimately still. *Gelassenheit* is a fundamental attunement (*Grundstimmung*) which essentially occurs in accordance (*Übereinstimmung*) with the fugue of beyng as *Ereignis*.

Von Herrmann points out the structural parallel between the notion of *Ereignis* in *Contributions to Philosophy*—as the "turning middle" between being's "appropriating throw" (*ereignender Zuwurf*) and man's "appropriated projection" (*ereigneter Entwurf*)—and Heidegger's later thought of *Gelassenheit*. According to von Herrmann, in "Toward an Explication of *Gelassenheit*," *ereignender Zuwurf* is rethought as the "admittance" (*Zulassen*) or "letting-in" (*Einlassen*) of man into the open-region, while the corresponding *ereigneter Entwurf* is rethought as man's "admitted engagement" (*eingelassene Sicheinlassen*) therein.[8] I would stress that this change of language, from that of projection (*Werfen*) to that of letting or releasing (*Lassen*), signals more than a mere swapping of terminology; it reflects an attempt to think the relation of being and man more radically outside the domain of the will. *Ereignis* as the essencing of beyng is finally expressed, not as an overpowering or even as a throwing, but rather as a "giving" or a "letting."

In "Time and Being," Heidegger speaks of *Ereignis* as the "It" (*Es*) which "gives" (*gibt*) both time and being in their belonging together (*ZSD* 20/19). In the *Four Seminars* Heidegger tells us that the "giving" in the *Es gibt* of *Ereignis* is to be understood in the sense of a "letting" (*Lassen*). "*Letting* is then the pure *giving*, which itself refers back to the It that gives, which is understood as *Ereignis*" (*GA* 15:365/60). This letting is now said to be "the most profound meaning of being" (363/59).

When the later Heidegger attempts "to think being itself," that is, to think "being without regard to its being grounded in terms of beings [*das Sein ohne die Rücksicht auf eine Begründung des Seins aus dem Seienden*]" (*ZSD* 2/2), he does so by way of thinking being as "letting-presence" (*Anwesenlassen*). This "presencing" (*Anwesen*) is no longer to be thought metaphysically in terms of "constant presence" (*beständige Anwesenheit*), but rather as a presencing/absencing, where the past and the future are also ubiquitous aspects of presencing, namely as manners of denial and withholding. *Ereignis* is thought as the opening of a fourth dimension of "time-space" for the interplay of three-dimensional time, wherein the presencing/absencing of temporal beings may take place (see 14–16/14–15). Whereas metaphysics thought this letting-presence exclusively in relation to the beings that presence (*das Anwesende*), in post-metaphysical thought the direction of the *letting* is to be emphasized. In other words, rather than attend to the ontological difference as the relation between being as letting-*presence* and the beings that presence, Heidegger attempts to think more radically in the direction of being as *letting*-presence.

> Being, by which all beings as such are characterized, being says presencing [*Sein besagt Anwesen*]. Thought with regard to what-is-present [*das Anwesende*], presencing shows itself as letting-presence [*Anwesenlassen*]. But now we must try to think this letting-presence explicitly insofar as presencing is admitted [*zugelassen*]. Letting shows what is proper to it in bringing into unconcealment. To let presence means: to unconceal, to bring into the open. In unconcealing prevails a giving, the giving that gives presencing, that is, being, in *letting*-presence [*Anwesen*-lassen]. (*ZSD* 5/5)

In the "Summary of a Seminar" this key passage is supplemented with the following clarification of the two ways or directions in which letting-presence can be thought.[9]

> 1. Letting-presence: Letting-*presence:* what-is-present [*Anwesenlassen: Anwesenlassen: das Anwesende*]
> 2. Letting-presence: *Letting*-presence (i.e., [thought] in the direction of *Ereignis*) [*Anwesenlassen: Anwesenlassen (d.h. auf das Ereignis zu)*] (40/37)

The text then goes on to clarify the crucial difference between these two orientations of thought as follows:

> 1. In the first case, presence as letting-presence [*Anwesenlassen*] is related to beings, to what-is-present. What is meant is then the difference

underlying all metaphysics between being and beings and the relation of the two. Taking the original sense of the word as our point of departure, letting thereby means: to let go [*ab-lassen*], let go away [*weglassen*], put away, let depart, that is, to set free *into the open*. What-is-present, as that which has been "released" by letting-presence, is only thus admitted as something present for itself into the openness of co-present beings. [Yet] whence and how "the open" is given remains unsaid and worthy of question here.

2. But when letting-presence is properly [*eigens*] thought, then what is affected by *this* letting is no longer what-is-present, but presencing itself. Accordingly, in what follows the word is also written as: Letting-presence [*Anwesen-Lassen*]. Letting then means: to allow [*zulassen*], give, extend, send, to *let*-belong. In and through this letting, presencing is allowed into that wherein it belongs. (Ibid.)

The first sense of letting-presence recognizes the ontological difference between being and beings, and yet thinking is here already oriented in the direction of beings, and thus in the direction of metaphysics which, in grounding the thought of being in beings, forgets the letting-be that first opens a clearing for a determination of the being of beings. What Heidegger attempts to do in the second orientation is to think being itself as letting-presence more radically, that is, away from beings (what-is-present) in the direction of the *letting* that first opens the clearing of presencing. He wishes to indicate that: "*Only because there is* [es gibt] *a letting of presencing, is the letting-presence of what-is-present possible*" (40/37).

As the *Four Seminars* elaborates, this emphasis on the *letting* opens up the thought of *Ereignis* as the "pure *giving*" of the *Es gibt*. "Presencing is no longer emphasized, but rather the *letting* itself." This letting, moreover, must not be understood either ontically or ontologically, but as the noncausal giving of the *Es gibt* of the event of appropriation. In this regard it is pointed out that three different meanings of "letting-be" (*Sein-lassen*) can be emphasized with (1) attention to beings that are let presence; (2) attention to the presencing itself (i.e., in the manner metaphysics takes over the ontological difference); and (3) attention turned neither toward beings nor toward the presencing, but rather "where the stress is now decisively placed upon the *letting* itself, that which *allows* [lässt] the presencing" (*GA* 15:365/59–60).

The pure *giving* of the *Es gibt* of *Ereignis* is thus thought as an originary *letting*-be that opens up a world wherein things are, in turn, allowed to presence. Human *Gelassenheit* too must be thought in correspondence to this originary giving/letting. Through the thought of the fundamental atunement of man as *Gelassenheit* we are taken back to an originary *Lassen* to which human *Gelassenheit* itself corresponds. Human *Gelassenheit* is a-propriated by the *Lassen* of *Ereignis*. In short, the essence of being is letting-be (*Seinlassen*); correspondingly, the essence of man is *Gelassenheit*.

Schürmann writes in this regard: "Thus we have seen releasement turn into its contrary: appropriation. This turning, however, does not result from man's taking possession of anything; it is only the return into being's original way to be. Releasement and appropriation are now names for one and the same event." He goes on to say that "these names no longer refer to any attitude of man, or to anything human. They interpret the phrases 'It gives being' and 'there is being.' Only secondarily do they imply a claim made upon man's thought."[10] Heidegger does indeed claim that human *Gelassenheit* originates in the regioning of the open-region: "Authentic *Gelassenheit* must rest in [*beruhen*] the open-region, and must have received from it the movement toward it" (*G* 49/73). But we must take care not to misunderstand the sense in which human *Gelassenheit* is "secondary" to the *Lassen* of *Ereignis* as the regioning of the open-region. Lest we understand man to be the mere "passive" recipient of the "activity" of *Ereignis*, we must bear in mind that for Heidegger human correspondence is a co-originary element of the event of presencing. Presencing (*An-wesen*) essentially involves (*geht an*) humans. "Presencing means: the abiding that always approaches man, reaches him, is extended to him" (*ZSD* 13/12).

For Heidegger the essential occurrence of beyng needs the essence of man to prepare an abode for receiving the gift of presencing. It is perhaps not surprising that Heidegger refers to Meister Eckhart—whose radical experience and thinking of *Abgeschiedenheit* and *Gelassenheit* led him to risk heresy in speaking of the divine need of man[11]—in the context of saying that man must first "establish himself in the space proper to his essence [*Wesensraum*]" in order to be capable of anything essential (*Wesenhaftes*) in the destiny of being. He writes:

> In pondering this let us pay heed to a word of Meister Eckhart, as we think it in keeping with what is most fundamental to it. It reads: "Those who are not of a great essence, whatever work they perform, nothing comes of it."[12] . . . The great essence of man consists in that he belongs [*zugehört*] to the essencing of being, and is needed/used [*gebraucht*] thereby to keep safe [*wahren*] the essencing of being in its truth [*Wahrheit*]. (*GA* 79:70/40)

The turning from the epoch of the technological will to will, Heidegger writes elsewhere, demands that "man engage [*sich einlässt*] more and sooner and ever more originally in the essence of what is unconcealed and in its unconcealment, in order that he might experience as his essence the needed belongingness [*die gebrauchte Zugehörigkeit*] to revealing" (*VA* 29–30/331). The essencing of being needs/uses the "great essence" of man, which in turn essentially corresponds to the letting-presence of being. Insofar as It is *Ereignis* which gives the truth of being, this means: the fundamental human attunement of *Gelassenheit* cor-responds to, is a-tuned to, the *Lassen* of the granting-in-withdrawal of *Ereignis* as the originary event of letting-be.

The Granting-in-Withdrawal of *Ereignis/Gelassenheit*

Let me end this chapter with a question in reference to a central, indeed the central trait (*Zug*) of *Ereignis* which has thus far remained somewhat in reserve here, namely, withdrawal (*Entzug*) or self-withdrawal (*das Sich-entziehen*). That "withdrawal [*Entzug*] must belong to what is peculiar [*zum Eigentümlichen*] to *Ereignis*" (*ZSD* 23/22) means that *Ereignis*, the It which gives as the event of appropriation, "expropriates" itself. "Expropriation [*Enteignis*] belongs to *Ereignis* as such" (23/23). This is the most peculiar property of *Ereignis*, that it "withdraws what is most fully its own from boundless unconcealment" (23/22). "By this expropriation, *Ereignis* does not give itself up, but rather preserves what is its own [*bewahrt sein Eigentum*]" (23/23). Expropriation thus indicates a concealing (*Verbergen*), which is also a sheltering (*Bergen*) of what is most proper, most intimate to the It that grants the clearing which in turn lets beings be. This means that in the sending of an epochal determination of being and time, a sending which opens a time-play-space of unconcealment for beings, "that-which-sends keeps itself back [*das Schickende selbst an sich hält*] and, thus, withdraws from unconcealment" (23/22).

This self-withdrawal, moreover, does not only characterize the "epochs" of metaphysics, that is, the space-times characterized by the oblivious absence or abandonment of beyng; on the contrary, "awakening to *Ereignis*" (see 44/41) would involve precisely an opening to the *lethe* in *aletheia*, to the inevitable and proper element of concealment in the coming to pass of truth as unconcealment. In other words, "awakening to *Ereignis*" would not imply a boundless enlightenment of being's mysteries, but rather an "openness for the mystery" (*G* 25/56) of its withdrawal as the expropriation proper to the event of appropriation.

The first part of my question is this. In the end, Heidegger tells us, all that can be said of *Ereignis* itself is *Ereignis ereignet* (*ZSD* 24/24). When Heidegger goes on, then, to reveal (often in dialogue with Hölderlin's poetic word) *Ereignis* in greater detail as the worlding of the fourfold, does this determination conceal other possibilities of configuring this originary appropriating/expropriating event of granting-in-withdrawal? The second part of my question is then: In correspondence to the letting of *Ereignis/Enteignis,* would not *Gelassenheit* too always only reveal itself in withdrawal? In accord with what is most peculiar to *Ereignis,* would *Gelassenheit* also "withdraw what is most fully its own from boundless unconcealment"? Would this mean that what is most peculiar to *Gelassenheit* could never once and for all be fully presented, definitively named? Would not all definitive names (determinate significations) for these originary non- or in-historicals of *Ereignis* and *Gelassenheit* be provisional? With the *via negativa* peculiar to the expression "non-willing," do we preserve the reserved distance necessary for an intimation of what would be other than the will to boundless unconcealment of what is most proper to (our) being?

Residues of Will in Heidegger's Thought

[The] scene of the gift also obligates us to a kind of filial lack of piety . . . as regards the thinking to which we have the greatest debt.
   —Jacques Derrida[1]

From where might one "criticize" Heidegger? From what '"point of view"? This much, however, is true: recognition of the importance of his thought . . . in no way excludes infinite mistrust.
   —Philippe Lacoue-Labarthe[2]

Confrontation [*Auseinandersetzung*] is genuine criticism. It is the highest and only way to a true estimation of a thinker. . . . To what purpose? In order that through the confrontation we ourselves may become free for the highest exertion of thinking.
(*N1* 13/4–5)

On Critically Reading Heidegger

In dealing with the early and middle periods of Heidegger's writings in chapters 2 and 3, I combined a sympathetic reading with a critical one, seeking not only to show that the problem of the will and the possibility of non-willing was often an underlying ("unthought") problematic, but also to expose the points where Heidegger failed to problematize and/or embraced the will—most devastatingly in the texts which prepared for and contributed to his political involvement with National Socialism. I have sought to show how the turn in Heidegger's thought ultimately entailed a decisive turn away from the will, a turn so decisive that he subsequently considered the metaphysics of the will to lie at the core of the modern epochal descent into nihilism. This turn was, at least implicitly, a self-critical one, insofar as the ambiguous role of the will in *Being and Time* gave way in the first half of the 1930s to a philosophical and then political voluntarism. Even after the orientation of his thought began to turn to being-historical thinking, the relation between being and man continued for a time to be thought within the domain of the will. Only after the late 1930s did Heidegger begin to clearly and thoroughly problematize this domain as such. In critically retracing this course of the early and middle periods of his *Denkweg*, I was able to draw on the later Heidegger's thought for resources to criticize his earlier moments of ambiguity and embrace.

In subsequent chapters I have attempted to explicate and interpret the critique of the will, the problem of the transition out of the domain of the will, and intimations of non-willing in the later mature period of Heidegger's thought. My approach in these chapters has been largely sympathetic, aimed at learning what we can from Heidegger on the problem of the will and the possibility of non-willing by "magnifying what is great" in his work. I have attempted to first "encounter" his thought rather than from the start "going counter" to it. In approaching Heidegger's texts in this manner I have, in fact, followed his own advice for reading.

> One thing is necessary for a dialogue [*Zwiesprache*] with the thinkers: clarity about the manner in which we encounter [*begegnen*] them. Basically there are only two possibilities: either to go to an encounter with them [*das Entgegengehen*], or to go counter to them [*das Dagegenangehen*]. If we want to go to the encounter with a thinker's thought, we must magnify still further what is great in him. Then we will enter into what is unthought in his thought. If we want only to go counter to a thinker's thought, this will [*Wollen*] must have minimized beforehand what is great in him. We then shift his thought into the obvious matters of our know-it-all presumption. It makes no difference if we assert in passing that Kant was nonetheless a very significant thinker. Such praises from below are always an insult. (*WhD* 72/77)

There is no shortage of books and articles these days that begin by stating something like "Although Heidegger's many philosophical achievements cannot be denied" and then go on to attempt to reduce his thought to nothing more than, for example, a potential, then enthusiastic, and finally unreformed philosophical Nazism. In the wake of "the Heidegger Controversy," however, equally problematical are those readings that stop at mere faithful exegesis, and therefore fail to encounter his thought in its full radicality and question-worthiness. As D. F. Krell writes: "For even more disturbing than the avidity of the Heidegger bashers is the business-as-usual attitude of the Heidegger acolytes."[3] What is called for is a careful and critical reading that involves (or at least prepares for) both an appropriation and an *Auseinandersetzung* with Heidegger's thought.

In attempting to carefully read Heidegger's text, therefore, I do not mean to sacrifice the ability and responsibility for criticism, but rather to go *through* a genuine encounter with his thought. Has this attentive reading allowed me to "enter into what is unthought in his thought"? I have suggested that the issue of the will can be read as the unthought in *Being and Time*, and have traced how this issue rises to the level of explicit critique in his later writings. Perhaps we have even come to understand the problem of the will "in Heidegger's thought-path" better than he understood it himself.

At this point we are called on—largely from out of the movement of (our reading of) Heidegger's thought-path itself—to go a step further and critically examine the "residues of will" that still remain embedded in the later period of his thought. We are called on to examine those places in his texts or in the framework of his texts where we must, as far as possible, follow "a Heidegger who thinks against Heidegger";[4] in Heidegger's own terms, we must continue to submit his thought to an "immanent critique" (*ZSD* 61/55). There are, to be sure, certain limits to a purely immanent approach, even when what one gets "inside" of is an ongoing way and not a closed system.[5] Nevertheless, a criticism of Heidegger "from without" always risks simply failing to read him, and thus failing to see what falls into question through his thought regarding one's own presumably external standpoint. What is called for, then, is a double reading of Heidegger, one which attentively follows his way and yet also at certain moments—neither rushed nor passed over—diverts (from) his path of thinking in response to demands both inside and outside his text.

This approach parallels that of Derrida when he writes of how, despite his debt to Heidegger, or rather because of it:

> I attempt to locate in Heidegger's text—which, no more than any other, is not homogeneous, continuous, everywhere equal to the greatest force and to all the consequences of its questions—the signs of a belonging to metaphysics, or to what he calls onto-theology. Moreover, Heidegger recognizes that economically and strategically he had to borrow the syntaxic and lexical resources of the language of metaphysics, as one always must do at the very moment that one deconstructs this language. Therefore we must work to locate these metaphysical holds, and to reorganize unceasingly the form and sites of our questioning.[6]

We have seen how the problem of metaphysics is intimately tied to the problem of the will, and thus what Derrida says here could be repeated in terms of this problematic. The question in this context is whether and where Heidegger remains caught in or slips back into the domain of the will—and moreover whether and where he does so precisely, if paradoxically, in those thoughts which would account for the critique of the metaphysics of will and the turning to non-willing.

I shall focus on three sites where it remains questionable whether the later Heidegger's thought freed itself from the domain of the will.[7] These three sites correspond to the following three critical questions: (1) Is man, after all, called on to defer his will to being? (2) Does "the history of being" repeat the metaphysical will to unity and system? (3) Does the eschatological idea of the other beginning reflect a will to finality?

We are by this point familiar with many ways in which Heidegger's thought resists such critical suspicions; the later Heidegger repeatedly wipes away the residues of will as often as they appear to reappear in his thought. As shown particularly in the previous chapter, Heidegger's later thought radically attempts to twist free of the domain of the will toward ways of thinking man, being, and their relation in terms of non-willing. In this chapter, however, I shall double back and ask whether and to what extent there is nevertheless reason for doubts to persist. Having previously attempted to "magnify what is great" in his vigilant and innovative attempts to think non-willing(ly), in this chapter I mean to counterbalance that sympathetic reading by highlighting points that remain troubling. These chapters must be read together; for while at times in the present chapter, in response to Heidegger's one-sided critics, I shall again show how his thought resists being reductively interpreted and criticized wholly in terms of the domain of the will, my focus shall now be on acknowledging and amplifying certain relevant criticisms that have been made, and developing further critical questions of my own concerning the residues of will in Heidegger's later thought. In the end, it is not a question of either defending or attacking Heidegger's thought, but rather of pursuing the *Sache selbst* by way of magnifying the ambiguities and ambivalences at play or in strife within the path opened up through his thinking.

A Mere Turnaround from Voluntarism to Fatalism?

A Deference of Will to Being?

According to a popular critique of Heidegger's relation to the will, the voluntarism of the early Heidegger gives way to a sheer passivity in his later thought. We have seen this view expressed by Karl Löwith, who charges Heidegger's thought with merely flipping "between willfulness and sacrificing one's will."[8] This is also the gist of Jürgen Habermas's critique when he writes:

> The language of *Being and Time* had suggested the decisionism of empty resoluteness; the later philosophy suggests the submissiveness of an equally empty readiness for subjugation. . . . Dasein is no longer considered the author of world-projects . . . ; instead, the productivity of the creation of meaning that is disclosive of world passes over to Being itself. Dasein bows to the authority of an unmanipulable meaning of Being and rids itself of any will to self-affirmation that is suspect of subjectivity.[9]

Habermas then simply (or simplistically) concludes that the *Kehre* in Heidegger's thought is nothing more than a "mere inversion of the thought patterns of the philosophy of the subject."[10] One could agree with Habermas that in an important sense "there is only a rhetorical difference between voluntaristic 'institution' and fatalistic 'dispensation,'"[11] and yet still object to a reduction of the turn in Heidegger's thought to nothing more than a flip-flopping between these two extremes within the domain of the will.

Following in the footsteps of Löwith and Habermas, Richard Wolin has written one of the most aggressive critiques of Heidegger's thought and its relation to his politics. After paying his respects to the "originality, rigor, and profundity" of Heidegger's thought in the introduction to his book (indeed, elsewhere Wolin refers to Heidegger as "probably the century's greatest philosopher"),[12] Wolin later summarizes the turn from the early Heidegger to the later as follows: "If the early Heidegger attempted to rally Dasein to 'decisiveness' (*Entschlossenheit*), the thought of the later Heidegger appears at times to be a summary justification of human passivity and inaction (*Gelassenheit*)."[13] In the later Heidegger's thought man would purportedly be absolutely submitted to passive impotence, while "Being," in its "other-worldly supremacy," "assumes the character of an omnipotent primal force."[14] Thus, Wolin concludes, so "extreme is the philosopher's reconceptualization between Being and Dasein that one could plausibly interpret the *Kehre* as a 'Reversal' rather than a 'Turn' in Heidegger's thinking."[15]

Although Wolin curiously qualifies many of his indictments with such hesitant markers as "one could plausibly interpret" or "appears at times," he fails to pursue or even to suggest alternative readings of Heidegger's thought.[16] Specifically, Wolin completely passes over both Heidegger's explicit critique of the domain of the will as such, and his attempts to think a region of non-willing beyond the very opposition of willful decisiveness and passive submission to a fate willed from above. Wolin's polemical reading fails to encounter, or even to consider, this crucial dimension of Heidegger's thought-path, despite its direct relevance to the topics he addresses. However, this is not to say that some of his (usually overstated) criticisms do not touch on certain genuinely problematical issues. Ironically perhaps, by wholly passing over the problematization of the will and the intimations of non-willing *within* Heidegger's texts, Wolin (together with Löwith and Habermas before him) highlights for us certain risks or dangers involved in the radicality of Heidegger's thought-path. These misapprehensions of Heidegger's turn toward a twisting free of the domain of the will indirectly suggest an insufficiency in articulation, or at least a tenuous subtlety, in his intimations of thinking non-willing(ly).

Let us then return to critically address the question of whether or to what degree Heidegger's intimations of a non-willing belonging to being and its sendings can dispel lingering doubts that his later thought unilaterally consigns man to a role of "passivity" with regard to the "activity" of being. In a more nuanced but no less severe critique than Habermas and Wolin, Michel Haar also worries that Heidegger's "*Kehre,* the turn, often enough begins to look like an *Umkehrung,* a turnaround."[17] "Is there not an excessive and fantastic omnipotence of being as well as an excessive depotentializing and desubstantialization of man, which would resemble an inversion of the excess of substance that metaphysics has conferred on him?"[18] In this manner, Haar asks: does Heidegger's critique of the technological will to dominate, along with his "turnaround" from his own early "existential quasi-voluntarism," in the end only show that man is "condemned to oscillate perpetually between the illusion of his power and the tragic knowledge of his impotence?"[19] Or, on the other hand, as I have suggested in response to such suspicions, is there not a third possibility intimated in Heidegger's texts, namely that of a non-willing relation between man and being which exceeds the very domain of power and impotence?

In the previous chapter we considered at some length Heidegger's thought of a human "cor-respondence" to the "needful-usage" of being, a thought which intimates a relation outside the domain of the will, and which resists the criticism that man is reduced to "impotence" and being elevated to "omnipotence." Indeed, the very opposition which sets man and being over against one another in these terms is inappropriate to Heidegger's thought of the "sameness" of their mutual appropriation and belonging together. The "task of thinking" remains a crucial and not merely "passive" role that man is called on to play. Being, for its part, must not be reified into an omnipotent Subject-being, as Heidegger stresses by finally crossing this key word through and speaking rather of *Ereignis* as the event of mutual appropriation within which man takes part. Haar argues that "*Ereignis* in Heidegger's last writings," as the attempt to think the mutual belonging together of man and being, in the end "disposes over man to the same extent and with the same total sovereignty as does being."[20] And yet, as we have seen, neither being's needful-usage of human correspondence, nor *Ereignis* as the event of this mutual co-appropriation, can be understood as the disposing of a total sovereignty over man.

Yet it must be admitted that Heidegger's "rhetorical reversals," especially when taken out of context, often seem to suggest such a turnabout from humanistic voluntarism to being-historical fatalism. Let us gather together here several of the most "suspect" passages which appear to simply reverse the "relation of dominance" between man and being.

> The opinion arises that the human will is the origin of the will to will, whereas man is willed by the will to will without even experiencing the essence of this willing. (*VA* 85/81–82)

> Man acts as though he were the shaper and master of language, while in fact language remains the master [*die Herrin*] of man. When this relation of dominance [*Herrschaftsverhältnis*] gets inverted, man hits upon strange maneuvers. (*VA* 184/214)

> The being of beings—something which man never masters [*meistert*], but which he can at best serve [*dienen*]. (*WhD* 142/235)

Can it be denied that in such turns of phrases Heidegger's thought-path (*Denkweg*) leaves behind tracks (*Wegmarken*) of a simple reversal, a depossessing man of his faculties or "powers" and an apparent transference of these to being? In radically criticizing the will of man, why use formulations that suggest a *deferral* of will, power, and dominance to being, when the task is to twist free of the domain of the will as such?

Heidegger might respond that such "apparent reversals" are initially necessary in order to turn us on our way of twisting free towards nonwilling, and that the critics' persistence in reductively misinterpreting his expressions for the peculiar "activity" of being in terms of will betrays their own failure to follow the movement of his thought-path. Nevertheless, it is our responsibility as critical readers not only to follow the intimations of his thought as best we can, but also to continue the task of immanent critique by weeding out the residues of will in Heidegger's own formulations: in this case, any residual sites of a "turnabout" on his path of "twisting free." Yet pointing out the necessity for continuing to vigilantly problematize such residues should not be conflated with excusing the one-sided distortions and dismissals of Heidegger's thought-path altogether. Before leaving this critical and controversial topic, then, let me respond a bit further to some of the debate it has aroused.

Passing over Heidegger's manifold critique of the very domain of the will, and ignoring Heidegger's relentless attempt to distinguish being from the onto-theological notion of a transcendent Subject-being possessed of will, Wolin concludes: Heidegger's later philosophy is, in short, a "philosophy of heteronomy," where "in his desperate effort to extirpate the last vestiges of a 'philosophy of subjectivity' from his thinking, Heidegger has 'succeeded' only by endowing Being with the characteristics of an all-powerful metasubject."[21] Heidegger's thought would purportedly then be "a secularized replay of medieval ontology," where man would be called on to sacrifice himself to the Will of God or now "Being."[22] Here again Wolin is echoing and amplifying Löwith's critique, which also misinterprets Heidegger's being metaphysically as "a supersensible 'hidden world' which sends us our destinings."[23] Habermas also provides a "reliable source" for this misleadingly reductive reading when he writes: "The propositionally contentless speech about Being has, nevertheless, the illocutionary sense of demanding resignation to fate."[24]

For such critics *Gelassenheit* would not be a tentative name for nonwilling, but would merely signal an onto-theological replay of human deference to a higher Will. One commentator, who prefers the "balance" struck in Heidegger's middle period between the power of Dasein and that of being, bemoans Heidegger's later language of *Gelassenheit* as supposedly simply reducing the role of man to that of total passivity. "In *Gelassenheit*, the active life of 'responding' to Being which [Laszlo] Versényi attributes to the 'middle' Heidegger (1930 to the early '50s) is destroyed. *Gelassenheit* . . . refers to a state of total self-denial and self-repression."[25] When critics insist on interpreting it merely *within* the domain of the will, *Gelassenheit* inevitably gets misunderstood as a simple negation and deference of willing or as an abnegation of all human activity as such.

But this reading entirely passes over the *non*-willing indicated by *Gelassenheit*. As Reiner Schürmann writes, there is another way of understanding the relation between the sending of being and the *Gelassenheit* of man: "Such a mittance, *geschick*, is not a matter of the will and asceticism. One has to be very released, *gelassen*, to respond properly to what destiny sends."[26] *Gelassenheit* would not be a simple denial of will, but rather an engaged releasement where man would properly "take part" (*VA* 22/324) in the sending of being which "starts man upon the way" (28/329) of revealing, but which also calls on him to "play along" (*SG* 188).

In the later Heidegger man is not after all simply stripped of all his powers, but rather, as Werner Marx points out, all of the seemingly "passive" characterizations "should not blind us to the fact that man is allotted the role of cocreating creatively in the occurrence of being. Man is thought by Heidegger as a necessary and creative *coplayer* in the play of the world." "The creative modes of human response already designated by Heidegger in forethinking, namely, poetizing, thinking, building, and dwelling, are no longer violent, but they are nonetheless, each in its own way, the expression of an enormous power of man."[27] In the conclusion to his book, however, Marx claims that "a thinking that carries on should concern itself with determining the distribution of the power and impotence [*Verteilung von 'Macht und Ohnmacht'*] between being and the essence of man more definitely."[28] There does indeed exist a need to continue to think the relation between man and being after Heidegger; yet to continue to characterize this relation in terms of a "distribution of power and impotence" misses the thrust of Heidegger's attempt to twist free of the very language of power and will. Heidegger's *Gelassenheit* neither returns us to a "medieval" submission to a transcendent Will nor does it betray, as Versényi would have it, a more acceptable "balance of power" in the middle Heidegger. As we have seen, the violent onslaught of being and the counter-violence of man in the mid-1930s gives way to a more radical problematization of the domain of the will, and not to a one-sided negation of human willing; and it is in this context that *Gelassenheit* can be understood as intimating an other than will, a non-willing.

We have also seen that man is not simply to resign himself to fate, but is called on to cor-respond to the sending of being. Thus I also cannot concur with the following accusation of fatalism that Karsten Harries makes: "Heidegger's insistence on the total domination of technology" precludes "every attempt to build from the ruins of our culture a house in which we can dwell, every attempt to criticize the modern world in order to alter it."[29] At one point Heidegger responds directly to such a concern over fatalism in the following manner: "Does this mean that man, for better or worse, is helplessly delivered over to technology? No, it means the direct opposite; and not only that, but essentially it means something more than the opposite, because it means something different" (*GA* 79:68/37). As Heidegger puts this point in a letter to a Japanese scholar: "The either/or of master and servant does not apply to the region of the determining matter at hand."[30]

Heidegger is attempting to twist free of this either/or of will and its mere negation, of master and servant, of willing one's own fate and being willed by a higher Fate. He is aware that his language of "sending" or "destining" will be misunderstood from the standpoint of will as a mere negation of the efficacy of human freedom. But he counters this suspicion by claiming that "this destining is never a fate that compels. For man becomes truly free only insofar as he belongs to the realm of destining and so becomes one who listens [*ein Hörender*], though not one who simply obeys [ein Höriger]" (*VA* 28/306, emphasis added). By properly listening, man finds his genuine freedom and his proper "activity." "For thinking is proper activity, if acting [*Handeln*] means: to lend a hand to the essencing of beyng [*dem Wesen des Seyns an die Hand gehen*], in order to prepare an abode for beyng and its essencing to bring themselves to language" (*GA* 79:71/40). Thus does Heidegger attempt to think beyond the very opposition of willful humanism and passive fatalism.

Nevertheless, it must be acknowledged that this attempt to think the relation of being and man beyond the domain of the will can be hampered by passages (such as those quoted above) where Heidegger appears to simply reverse the "relation of dominance." Perhaps, as I have suggested, such "rhetorical reversals" are provisionally useful to counteract and break us out of the prejudice of willful humanism; but they frequently remain more thorough in negating human willing than in deconstructing the "power" of being. That is to say, Heidegger's later thought, while attempting to radically twist free of the very domain of both human willful assertion and fatalistic quietism, is often more thorough in its critique of the former. Hence, even though the radical trajectory of the way opened up by his thought demands that a *deference* of human will be submitted to the same relentless problematization as the *assertion* thereof, thicker *residues* of a deferential fatalism than of humanistic voluntarism can be said to remain in some of his attempts to intimate a non-willing relation between man and being.

The Puzzling Role of the God(s)

The roles that "god" or "gods" or "divinities"—their number is said to remain undecided (see *GA* 65:437)—play in Heidegger's thought is complex and develops through the years.[31] This complexity, together with a modern philosophical bias toward atheism, has perhaps led many Heidegger scholars to downplay or neglect this aspect of his thought. Yet, granted that the notions of "the last god" and "the coming gods" are *inherently* enigmatic and indeterminate, a relative neglect on the part of scholars to interpretively clarify the role of the god(s) in Heidegger's thought may have inadvertently helped make it all too easy for his impatient and one-sided critics to reductively interpret his turn as a simple return to a deference to divine authority. Perhaps in response to this neglect on the part of Heidegger scholars, Günter Figal has gone so far as to provocatively suggest: "If one wanted to erase the theology of Heidegger's later thought, one would deprive it of its center."[32] At the very least it is undeniable that one would deprive his thought of one of the six joinings of its fugue or one of the quadrants of its fourfold. In any case, the role of the god(s) in Heidegger's thought is one of its most puzzling yet constitutive elements.

I have already given some consideration to the *Gottesfrage* in Heidegger's thought in chapter 5, and in the present context I shall restrict myself to emphasizing a couple of salient points, and raising a few further questions. Heidegger's notion of god(s) is clearly to be radically distinguished from "onto-theological" conceptions, which reduce god to the highest being or first cause, and remain oblivious to the *Seinsfrage*. The god of onto-theology is said to be a god to whom one can neither pray nor sacrifice. The god-question must be rethought from out of the thinking of being. Only from out of a thinking that leaves onto-theology behind by reawakening the wonder of the question of being can a more genuine openness to the god-question be cultivated. In 1956–57 Heidegger writes:

> Man can neither pray nor sacrifice to this god [of philosophy]. Before the *causa sui*, man can neither fall to his knees in awe nor can he play music and dance before this god. . . . The god-less thinking which must abandon the god of philosophy, the god as *causa sui*, is thus perhaps closer to the divine god. Here this means only: god-less thinking is more open to Him [*freier für ihn*] than onto-theo-logic would like to admit. (*ID* 140–41/72)

Far from promoting an "existential atheism," in such passages Heidegger calls for a recovery of a more originary experience of the divine. In this regard we should take note of the closing pages of "The Word of Nietzsche: 'God Is Dead'" (*GA* 5:259–67/105–12), where Heidegger interprets Nietzsche's proclamation to apply to the theologians' "God as the highest value," and draws attention to the madman's initial cries: "I seek God! I seek God!" "And the ear of our thinking," Heidegger asks, "does it not still hear the cry?" (267/112).

And yet, the god that Heidegger seeks would no longer have the same absolute status that "He" is accorded in the monotheistic traditions. The "last god" in *Contributions to Philosophy* cannot be understood, we are told, in terms of a "theism," be it "mono-theism," "pan-theism," or "a-theism" (*GA* 65:411). It is not a god that "grounds," but "is" only in "passing."[33] Heidegger's god(s) is no more the almighty Creator of heaven and earth than it (they) is an eternal being of self-presence. In a revealing passage from *Besinnung*, Heidegger writes:

> The gods do not create man; neither does man invent the gods. The truth of beyng decides "over" both, not by ruling over them, but rather appropriating between them such that they themselves first come into an en-counter. (*GA* 66:235)

Man's most originary relationship is, therefore, not to the god(s) but to beyng (*Ereignis*). It is only within the clearing of the truth of being that the god(s) can appear. The god(s) too depends on the granting of the clearing of being, just as do, each in their own ways, man and things. This is certainly a radical break from traditional Judeo-Christian notions of God, and its consequences are profound. In their own way the gods too "need" (*bedürfen*) *Ereignis*, and insofar as man is "needed" (*gebraucht*) by *Ereignis*, god at least indirectly depends on man. "God waits on the grounding of the truth of beyng and thus on the leap of man into Da-sein" (*GA* 65:417).

The structure of a double relation, where man is related to being and then again to *Ereignis* as the mutual appropriation of this relation itself, is first developed in *Contributions* not only in terms of man, being, and *Ereignis*, but also in terms of man, god, and beyng (as *Ereignis*). "Beyng as *Ereignis*" is the "turning middle" (*kehrige Mitte*) between god and man (see *GA* 65:413, 477), and we must prepare for the "colliding together [*Zusammenstoßes*] of god and man in the middle of beyng" (416). Thus, even while Heidegger thinks man's relation to beyng or *Ereignis* as more originary than the relation between man and a god, the latter internal relation is carried over and rethought within the former more encompassing relation. Man relates to the god(s) within "the relation of all relations," that is, within beyng as *Ereignis*.

This relativization of the man/god relation certainly profoundly alters the very sense of the relation, as well as the conception of what is related. On the other hand, Heidegger's god apparently retains enough characteristics of the traditional conceptions of the divine to go by the same name (*Gott*), and many of the same questions regarding the problem of the will with respect to these traditional conceptions need to be raised once again with regard to his thought of the man/god relation.

Von Herrmann's elaboration of Heidegger's critique of Eckhart's notion of *Gelassenheit*—namely, as purportedly remaining within the domain of the will, i.e., as a deference to the will of God—concludes as follows: for Heidegger, "the *Gelassenheit* of the experience of god takes place *within* the *Gelassenheit* that belongs to *Ereignis*."[34] But the question here is whether the *Gelassenheit* with respect to god remains one of a deference of will; how is the very character of releasement with respect to god altered by situating it within the *Gelassenheit* with respect to the appropriating event of beyng? According to *Contributions*, even if man "surpasses" (*übertrifft*) god,

god still "overpowers" (*übermächtigt*) man (*GA* 65:415); and man is still thought to "stand *at the disposal of the gods* [*den* Göttern zur Verfügung]" (18). Are we then called on not just to dance before but to "sacrifice" (our wills?) to this god?

Moreover, the infamously cryptic phrase from the 1966 *Der Spiegel* interview tells us: "Only a god can save us" (*SP* 99–100/107). One perhaps cannot help but suspect that Heidegger's later thought relegates man to a role of passivity with respect to god, when he leaves us with a statement such as this.[35] To be sure, both in *Contributions* and in the *Der Spiegel* interview, Heidegger rejects the idea of a merely passive "waiting" for a god to save us; we are called on to "prepare a sort of readiness, through thinking and poetizing" (*SP* 100/107; compare *GA* 65:417). But nevertheless, insofar as it is a god that saves, and man who merely prepares to be saved, one cannot help but suspect that Heidegger's critique of the domain of the will is here again more thorough in its repudiation of human willful assertion than it is in its disavowal of the simple sacrifice/deferral of willing. While any reading which would *only* see the later Heidegger as an advocate of quietism fails to take into account his manifold attempts to intimate a way of and toward *non*-willing—attempts that characterize what is genuinely radical, innovative, and most interesting in his thought—we must also conclude that some troubling residues of not-willing or deferred-willing remain in such places in his texts as we have considered here.

The History of Being and the Will to Unity

> What is it—the oneness of a name, the assembled unity of Western metaphysics? Is it anything more or less than the desire . . . for a proper name, for a single, unique name and a thinkable genealogy?
> —Jacques Derrida[36]

One-Track Thinking and the Will to Univocity

In the previous section we looked at certain residues of not-willing or deferred-willing in Heidegger's later thought of the relation between man and being. In this section, on the other hand, we shall examine residues of willing or covert-willing in Heidegger's thought of the history of being. Deference to the determinations of being, on the one hand, together with a certain "will" to comprehend these determinations in the unity of a "history of being," on the other, would certainly not be an unimaginable combination. Nietzsche's critique of the ascetic ideal in the "priest" sought to expose the covert-willing motivating the very spokesperson for the denial of will. One must remain suspicious of prophets who claim to represent the Will of God; why did God choose them, their nation, their mother tongue, their person to voice his Will? In (apparently) negating or deferring his own will, the (false) prophet covertly preserves and enhances his domination over others.

Does Heidegger's thought conceal an analogous strategy of covert-willing in a call for a deference to the destiny of being—a sending which happens to speak through German philosophers and poets, and which ultimately becomes revealed in Heidegger's own *seinsgeschichtliches Denken*? The line of essential history that Heidegger draws ends up being one in which all roads lead to and through Heidegger himself. The Latinization of philosophy was a downfall of the greatness of Greek philosophy, and this greatness is only retrieved in modern times with the rise of German philosophy. The German language retains an intimate connection with the Greek, and thus even French philosophers, for example, must speak German when they really begin to "think" (see *SP* 107–8/113). Heidegger himself apparently happened to be born into this privy position in the center of being's destining, and the only other "prophets" Heidegger is willing to share center stage with are selected German poets (especially Hölderlin) who, in dialogue with the thinker, are alone said to be capable of responding today to the address of being. One cannot help but suspect that a certain will to power is at work here in the very thought that would give being-historical context to Heidegger's critique of the will.[37]

The question of the willfulness of Heidegger's structuring thought of the history of being is far from a simple one, and among other things it calls for a reflection on the troubling similarities with Hegel's history of Spirit. We must, however, also note certain crucial differences in this regard. But before we qualify this critique, let us first develop and sharpen it.

The problem can be addressed in terms of the will's drive to unity, its drive to bring all others and their otherness under the rubric of its sameness; the will is the will to univocity.[38] Heidegger himself, in his critique of the technological will, warns against what he calls "one-track thinking."

> This one-track thinking [*das eingleisige Denken*], which is becoming ever more widespread in various shapes, is one of those unsuspected and inconspicuous forms of domination . . . of the essence of technology—an essence which wills and therefore needs unconditional univocity [*unbedingte Eindeutigkeit*]. (*WhD* 56/26)

Our present question is whether Heidegger's thought itself is not infected by this will of one-track thinking. Indeed, is there not ironically a trace of it here in this very passage, where he defines one-track thinking as one of the many forms of a *single* "essence of technology"? The "will to univocity" is delimited, fixed in place for critique by the very univocity of the essence of technology, an essence which defines a certain epochal climax in the course of the single Western history of being—a history which is, paradoxically, thought largely in terms of a consistent one-way rise of the will (to univocity). The doublings of will appear to infect even the structure of Heidegger's own critique of the will.

I shall propose here that a problematical will to unity in Heidegger's account of the history of being can be found at three levels: (1) each great thinker thinks only one thought; (2) each epoch is determined by one name for being; (3) the history of being is one movement from the Greeks through the Germans. Let us examine each of these problematical assertions of unity in turn.

Every Thinker Thinks Only One Thought

"Every thinker thinks only one thought" (*WhD* 20/50). Even when an apparently complex thinker's thought is "many-chambered," these are "chambers that adjoin, join, and fuse with one another [*ineinander verfügen*]" (21/51). It is noteworthy, and ironic, that Heidegger makes these statements with regard to Nietzsche, who is often considered the guerrilla enemy of the system, the thinker of polyvocity, of the aphorism as opposed to the treatise.[39] In another text Heidegger repeats this insistence on the singleness of each essential thinker's one thought:

> Nietzsche belongs among the essential thinkers. With the term "thinker" we name those exceptional humans who are destined to think one single thought, a thought that is always "about" *beings as a whole*. Each thinker thinks only one *single* thought. (*N1* 475/4)

The systematization of Nietzsche's thought (above all the smooth linking of the will to power and the eternal recurrence) is crucial for the cogency of Heidegger's history of being. This is because for him Nietzsche is to play the role of "the last metaphysician" who gathers all of the history of metaphysics into its final possibility by "overturning" it. All "the themes of Western thought, though all of them transmuted, are fatefully gathered together in Nietzsche's thinking" (*WhD* 21/51).

And yet later in this same text Heidegger himself writes that "all true thought remains ambiguous (or 'multiguous' [*mehrdeutig*])," and that we must always think "in the element of [a thought's] multiple meanings [*Mehrdeutigkeit*]" (68/71). By his own accounts, must not every univocal interpretation of a thinker conceal as much as it reveals? Does not Heidegger forget this revealing/concealing motif of his thinking when he strives to give a single account of each thinker, placing them in a single epochal notch in a single history of being?

"To think," Heidegger writes, "is to confine oneself to a single thought that one day stands still like a star in the world's sky" (*GA* 13:76/4). This will to the unity of "one thinker—one thought" is at work in Heidegger's self-(re)interpretations and later (unmarked) revisions of his own texts. In retracing the development of Heidegger's problematization of the will, we have repeatedly encountered the difficulties these self-(re)interpretations present. Heidegger persistently attempts to read his later fully developed critique of the will back into, for example, *Being and Time*, a text which is, as we have seen, deeply ambiguous with regard to the will. Despite Heidegger's own attempts to unify his long path(s) of thought, this path is as polyvocal as is that of any great thinker. In the present case, it is necessary to argue against the strict unity of his thought for the sake of following and carrying forward an important strain of that thought, namely, the vigilant problematization of the will and the intimations of non-willing afforded thereby.

One Thought Grounds an Epoch

According to Heidegger, the "one thought" of the great philosophers does not merely unify their own writings; it also determines the unity of an epoch in the history of being. In *Introduction to Metaphysics*, Heidegger writes: "Philosophizing always remains a kind of knowing that not only does not allow itself to be made timely [*zeitgemäß*], but, on the contrary, imposes its measure on the times [*die Zeit unter sein Maß stellt*]" (*EM* 6). In later texts, we are told that each sending of being determines every word of a language (see *GA* 79:63), and that the one thought of each great metaphysician grounds an epoch in the history of being.

> Metaphysics grounds [*begründet*] an age, in that through a specific interpretation of beings and through a specific comprehension of truth it gives to that age the ground upon which it is essentially formed. This ground holds complete dominion [*durchherrscht*] over all the phenomena that distinguish the age. (*GA* 5:75/115)

The history of metaphysics, as we have seen, is for Heidegger the history of the rise of the will. And yet it does not wait for the explicit epoch of the will to exhibit a kind of will to unity, namely, the will to provide a basis which "holds complete dominion over all the phenomena" of an age. These unifying thoughts underlying each age, however, are clearly witnessed only in retrospect at the end of the history of metaphysics; only at this end is metaphysics gathered so that it can be discerned by one (i.e., Heidegger) who, much like Hegel's owl of Minerva, can view the whole of this history of the *Seinsgeschick*.

Each age is founded on a "decision" in the history of being, a decision the thinker does not "make" but rather "participates in." Ultimately, Heidegger says, among thinkers "those are essential whose sole thought thinks in the direction of a single, supreme decision," namely, that which decides "between the predominance of beings and the rule of being" (*N1* 476/5). In this passage we find Heidegger at his most reductive (reducing all thinkers not only to one thought, but to their participation in the single direction of the history of being), apparently at his most "deferential" (speaking of "the rule of being"), and at his most eschatological (speaking of the supreme decision where the entire past will be gathered at the departure of an other beginning). We shall return later to the eschatological question; but for now let us focus on the problem of the unity of an age being grounded in a single thought.

Among the various problems that plague any attempt to unify the various heterogeneous phenomena or events of "an age," let us focus our attention on two problems in Heidegger's notion that an epoch is grounded in a single thought. The first concerns the matter of it being a "thought" that grounds an age. Although at times, most notably in texts from the 1930s, Heidegger also speaks of "the work of art" and "the act that founds a state" as being fundamental events that open up a world, for the most part Heidegger emphasizes the thought of the thinker or the word of the poet as being responsible for founding an epoch. As he puts it in the late 1930s, philosophy has a "hidden sovereignty" (*verborgene Herrschaft*) in that it is "*the immediately useless, but nevertheless sovereign, knowledge of the essence of things*" (*GA* 45:3). Why this "sovereignty" of philosophy; why must the relation between thought and other aspects of life be wholly unidirectional? Moreover, is there not an excessive elitism in the idea that it is only "the few and the rare" (*GA* 65:11) who can participate in this founding? Did Heidegger succumb to the philosopher's willful image of self-importance, to what Yeats called the "conspiracy" of all contemplative men "to overrate their state of life"?[40] Despite certain crucial differences (to which we shall return), there is a sense in which "for Heidegger, like Hegel before him, the history of philosophy becomes the philosophy of history."[41] For Heidegger, "*philosophia* . . . determines the innermost basic feature of our Western-European history" (*WP* 28–30).

Also relevant here is the debate regarding Heidegger's subordination of the interpersonal ethical relation to the thinking of being. For Heidegger, the "thinking which thinks the truth of being . . . is in itself originary ethics" (*GA* 9:356/271). Only from out of this thinking "can there come from being itself the assignment of those directives that must become law and rule for humans" (360–61/274). Or as he says elsewhere: "To stand under the claim of presence is the greatest claim of humans; it is 'ethics'" (*Z*273). Thus, man's relation to the presencing of being by way of essential thinking ethically precedes even the face-to-face relation with other persons. This, as is well known, is Levinas's point of critique. Levinas seeks to show that the "deposition of sovereignty by the *ego*" does not first of all take place in the realm of ontology (or with regard to the question of being), but rather in the primal dimension of ethics as "the social relation with the Other, the dis-inter-ested relation."[42] Despite the radicality of Heidegger's breaking through the traditional confines of ontology to a more originary thinking of being, his thought is said to continue the reduction of the an-archic relation to the other person to the "sovereignty of philosophy."

The second problematical aspect of the will to unify each epoch under a single thought of being is its rejection of all other events as inconsequential. In Heidegger's history of being there is a tendency to see "actual historical situations . . . as merely the *consequences* of this hidden history; as consequences they have no control over their ground" (*N1* 538/56). This problem concerns what has been called his "leveling gaze" which reduces, for example, the many complex factors of the modern age to the single problem of the "essence of technology," the *Ge-stell*. Heidegger's sustained attempt to think modern phenomena (e.g., industrialization, the tourist industry, and scientific objectification) from the single critical angle of the essence of technology marks at once the illuminating strength of his thought and, when carried to certain extremes, its limits.

In what sense can we, for example, say that even such a momentous event as World War II decided nothing "essential"? Heidegger asserts that this "world war has decided nothing—if we here use 'decision' in so high and wide a sense that it concerns solely man's essential fate on this earth" (*WhD* 65/66; see also *GA* 77:241, 244). On the one hand, this statement no doubt contains a certain important criticism of those who would, reassured in their black-and-white thinking by the outcome of the war, uncritically affirm their own values of technological thinking. Relentless retrospective critical analysis of the ghastly evils perpetrated by the defeated Nazis has perhaps often inadvertently allowed us to conveniently divert attention from certain pervasive problems within our own victorious societies and ways of thinking. Nevertheless, does not Heidegger exhibit a shockingly insensitive aspect of his essentialism when he claims that the war, in which the fascist state that "exterminated" six million Jews was defeated, "decided nothing essential"? Would nothing essential have been decided were Germany to have won the war, or—an even more troubling thought—did Heidegger still believe that the "inner truth and greatness" of the Nazi movement could have contributed (at least more than the liberal democratic countries could) to a more essential decision?

In one of his extremely rare references to the Holocaust, Heidegger did indeed condemn it—not, however, as a radically evil event incomparable in scope, intent, and monstrosity, but rather as one *exemplary* phenomenon which, among other examples, displays the essence of technology! He writes:

> Agriculture is now a motorized food industry, the same thing in its essence as the production of corpses in the gas chambers and the extermination camps, the same thing as blockades and the reduction of countries to famine, the same thing as the manufacture of hydrogen bombs. (*GA* 79:27)

This sentence is, as Lacoue-Labarthe writes, "scandalously inadequate."[43] While it may succeed in disclosing the unrecognized threat of technological reduction that underlies many of our mundane practices, it does so at the expense of leveling the atrocity of the Holocaust to one more exemplary case of the technological reduction of beings (human or vegetable) to standing-reserve. What is really needed, it suggests, is not the defeat of the particular regime that "happened to be" perpetrating this particular technological machination, but rather essential thinking which alone could free us from "the epoch of technology."

In this reduction, Heidegger's thought of the gathering of each epoch under a single thought of being reveals its most troubling face. In this case we cannot just simply ascribe Heidegger's "reduction to essence" to an instance of the perhaps perennial philosophical quest to reduce a bewildering manifold to a manageable unity. For one must concede to his less sympathetic critics that a certain "strategy of denial" may be at work here. A genuine problem is touched on in Wolin's remark that were the real culprit to be the epoch of technology sent by being, then there would "be no question of 'personal' or 'national' culpability for Germany's unspeakable crimes against the other European peoples, insofar as larger, impersonal, metaphysical forces are to blame."[44]

In this regard, Heidegger's increasing emphasis on "the abandonment of being" (*Seinsverlassenheit*) in contrast to the earlier emphasis on "the forgetfulness of being" (*Seinsvergessenheit*) is noteworthy.[45] For while, as we have seen, at his best Heidegger intimates a non-willing relation wherein man is not simply abandoned to "an impersonal metaphysical force" but is determined in a relation of belonging-together by way of correspondence to being, at times Heidegger falls back on a rhetoric which suggests a more one-sided negation of human will. If the technological will to will is not man's doing, if human willing is not responsible for itself because "man is willed by the will to will," then is man no longer responsible for the horrors committed in this epoch of the most extreme abandonment by being?[46] If this were the case, then the will to determine the unity of an epochal sending of being would disturbingly fold together with the deferral of human responsibility to higher forces.

The Unity of the History of Being

We turn our attention now to the third aspect of the problem of the will to unity in Heidegger's thought, namely, that of positing the unity of the history of being as a whole. The suspicion is that Heidegger's history of being repeats, in its own manner, a metaphysical will to system, a kind of Hegelian assertion that, standing at the end of (the) history (of philosophy), one has in view the history of the West as a whole. Krell raises this question in the following manner:

> Could it be that Heidegger's complaint that metaphysics is characterized by oblivion of Being, along with his project of inserting past thinkers into niches of the history of this oblivion, is nothing more than a case of "German scholarship," that is to say, a peculiarly convoluted expression of will to power? Is it not indeed a most virulent effusion of will to power or will-to-will to assert that one has in the course of one lifetime grasped the "essence" of two millennia of thought?[47]

To begin with, we might note a passage from a late text where Heidegger responds directly to such a suspicion. Heidegger poses the question to himself: "Is there not an arrogance in these assertions which wills to put itself above the greatness of the thinkers of philosophy?" (*ZSD* 66/60). Although he assures us that this suspicion "can easily be quelled," there remains reason for doubt. On the one hand, Heidegger rather convincingly makes the hermeneutical point that "every attempt to gain insight into the supposed task of thinking finds itself moved to review the whole history of philosophy"; moreover, he goes on to say, it must "think the history of that which grants a possible history to philosophy." In doing so, an attempt such as his own does not reach higher than all previous philosophy, but "only" tries to step back to experience the essential questions of this tradition. Such a thinking is of a "preparatory, not a founding [*stift-ende*] character"; it merely tries to awaken "a readiness in man for a possibility whose contours remain obscure, whose coming remains uncertain" (ibid.). It can neither predict the future nor can it directly affect the present industrial age, and it "necessarily falls short of the greatness of the philosophers."

But at the same time, Heidegger's attitude to "the greatness of the philosophers" is ambivalent; their "greatness" also depends on a forgetfulness; their "progress" (*Fortschritt*) is also their failure to undertake the essential *Schritt zurück*. And despite Heidegger's confession of not knowing the future or the ultimate answer to the human predicament, he does claim to know *the* question, *the* essence of the predicament, and the essential moments of "the whole history of philosophy" which has led to this predicament. In this sense, Heidegger does claim to have "grasped the 'essence' of two millennia of thought." At the peak of his arrogance, Heidegger claims in 1935 that the question of being is to be connected to "the fate of Europe, where the fate of the earth is being decided, which for Europe itself our [German] historical Dasein proves to be the center" (*EM* 32; see also *GA* 54:250). And who is to be the axis point of this center if not the philosophical Führer of the Führer, the thinker of being, namely, Heidegger himself? Despite all of his later developments and turnings, did Heidegger ever fully submit this egocentrism to question?

Gadamer, who was far more partial to Hegel than was Heidegger, nevertheless agreed that "Hegel's dialectic is a monologue" and not a genuine dialogue with the tradition.[48] Yet Gadamer also complained that in the end Heidegger's history of being was itself monological: "When all is said and done, we are forced to admit that Heidegger's thoughtful dealings with the history of philosophy are burdened with the violence of a thinker who was veritably driven by his own questions and a desire to rediscover himself everywhere."[49]

We shall return later to the differences between Heidegger's history of being and Hegel's history of Spirit. Here let us first pursue further the suspicion of a certain strategy of covert-willing, where egoism is paradoxically overcome in the name of its expansion. We have already seen that Heidegger, in what can be considered moments of indirect self-critique, claims that through "the insertion of the I into the we" "subjectivity only gains in power" (*GA* 5:111/152), and that the "concepts of 'people' and 'Volk' are founded on the essence of subjectivity and egoity" (*GA* 54:204). He thus criticizes the idea that egoism or individual subjective willfulness can be overcome by way of the creation of an authentic *Volk* as metasubject. His turn beyond the residues of subjectivity that remained, not only in his earlier Dasein-analysis, but more problematically in his *Volk* politics and philosophy of the 1930s, was made by way of attending to the larger context of the history of being, a history which determines the modern epoch as one of willful subjectivity, be it of an individual or of a group. But now we need to carry this immanent critique forward to question the very notion of the history of being itself. Does Heidegger's history of being (which like a *Volk* would gather by way of exclusion) not only give context to his critique of subjective will (egoism and/or ethnocentrism), but at the same time, despite itself, posit an even larger "We," an even more powerful inclusive/exclusive subject of "the West"? In order to address this question, let us pursue as far as possible the suspicion of what might be called a "logic of the expansion of the subject."

In *Being and Time*, Dasein, as being-in-the-world, is always already thrown into ek-sisting beyond the confines and the control of the individual ego. This thought deals a significant blow to the metaphysical subject of will and representation. Moreover, this primordial unity of being-in-the-world can never form a closed "totality" insofar as it is exposed to its finitude precisely in its most authentic moment of existence, that is, in its resolute repetition of running-ahead-towards-death. The self is neither cut off from the world nor can it ever succeed in incorporating the world. The genius of Heidegger's thought here is that it evades both a Kantianism which threatens to fall into a "transcendental alienation" *and* an idealism which recovers the thing-in-itself at the price of swelling towards a "transcendental solipsism."

And yet, as we have seen, running-ahead-towards-death not only shatters as it unifies, it also unifies as it shatters. Dasein not only disrupts the walls of the individual subject; it also, in a certain sense, threatens to expand them. Herein lies the intractable ambiguity of the will in the philosophy of *Being and Time*. We need not repeat here the account of this ambiguity given in chapter 2. However, recalling the willful aspect of this text—a certain "will to self-possession" wherein Dasein runs ahead to its death in order to authentically "choose" its ownmost potentiality-for-being—let us note a potential danger involved in what could be (mis)-taken, not as a shattering, but as an *expansion* of the subject to Dasein as being-in-the-world. For one's ownmost possibilities are now said to structure, to give meaning, not only to one's own life but to the world itself as a totality of significations. The danger of this incorporation of the world back into Dasein is the flip side of Dasein's ecstatic standing out into the world. In other words, the extension of the self from the self-enclosed subject into the unity of being-in-the-world is in dangerous proximity to being (mis)taken up as a voluntaristic philosophy of "ecstatic-incorporation."

Now, the question at hand is: what happens to this problem in Heidegger's turn to the notion of a *Volk* in the early 1930s (a turn already fore-shadowed in the later sections of *Being and Time*), and then to the "more inclusive" notion of the Western history of being? The suspicion is this: Does Heidegger's thought, precisely in those moments where it would criticize (the residues of) a certain limited ego or will (the subject, individual Dasein, the *Volk*), threaten to simply envelop this limited ego or will in a more inclusive one? Does Heidegger, despite himself, repeat the will to totality again after each of his vigilant attempts to criticize it? To the extent that this were to be the case, in each of these moments a lesser will would be negated in the name of a higher Will, a smaller ego would be required to submit to a larger Ego; hence the suspicion of deferred-willing, or, assuming these higher wills to be either fictions or disingenuous self-serving realities, of covert-willing.

There is, in fact, a certain troubling continuity between the notion of the *Volk* or the nation in Heidegger's political writings of the early 1930s and the notion of the history of being in his mature texts. Note, for example, the element of similarity of the following two passages, the first from a notification Heidegger distributed as rector to the faculty of Freiburg University on December 20, 1933, the second from the third Nietzsche lecture course from 1939:

> It is unclear how much of our transitional work will survive. What *is* clear, however, is that no work or achievement, however successful, can ever become an occasion for thrusting individual accomplishment and zeal into the limelight. What is also clear is that only the unbending will to tackle the tasks that lie ahead can give meaning and substance to our present endeavors. The individual, whatever his place, counts for nothing. The destiny of our nation within the state counts for everything.[50]

> The struggle [for the word of being in the history of the West] is in play beyond war and peace, outside of success and defeat, is never touched by clamor and acclaim, and remains unconcerned about the destiny of individuals. (*N1* 492–93/19)

The individual would be called on to sacrifice his or her will to the nation or to the history of being; in either case a higher purpose takes precedence, and Heidegger appears as its spokesperson in a position to demand this submission. This continuity leads one to suspect that the willful philosophy of the nation and its destiny is not radically negated, but rather remains sublated, appropriated into its proper place within the more lofty notion of the history of being. Does the Greco-German history of being function as a kind of sublated Ego-narrative whereby Heidegger, in a mas-

terful act of ecstatic-incorporation, covertly asserts a will to unity and mastery over the entire history and destiny of the West?

Of course, one might respond to this critique by pointing out that,
even if there do exist heavy traces of this "residual element" in his thought,
the *movement* of Heidegger's thought is not primarily that of the sublation
or the expansion of the will, but rather the attempt to twist free of its domain. The "history of being" is not simply a narrative expansion of the will
of ecstatic-incorporation, but is (also) an attempt to think the problem of
the will in its genealogical continuity and discontinuity. But we need to
point out here—in the movement through an immanent critique—how
aspects of this very idea which provides a framework for thinking the
problem of the will threaten to repeat the problem itself. For example,
just as the subject of will secures its own identity by means of alienating
and subordinating alterity, so would Heidegger's history of being gather
the essential by means of exclusion. It tends to exclude both non-Western
traditions and non-Greco-German Western traditions from the realm of
essential being-historical thought.

The Exclusion of the Non-Greco-German

With regard to the question of the exclusion of non-Western traditions
from Heidegger's being-historical thinking, there is the well-known statement in the *Spiegel* interview that "a reversal can be prepared only in the
same place in the world where the modern technological world origi-
nated, and . . . cannot happen because of any adoption of Zen Buddhism
or any other Eastern experiences of the world" (*SP* 107/113). Despite the
fact that the problem of technology has become a worldwide predicament, apparently only Western thought can contribute anything essential
to solving this crisis. And yet, at the same time, in his "From a Conversation on Language: Between a Japanese and an Inquirer" (which is, in any
case, more significant as a text of Heidegger's appropriation of, rather
than a literal account of, any of his dialogues with Tezuka Tomio and
other Japanese thinkers over the years),[51] Heidegger asks "whether it is
necessary and rightful for East Asians to chase after European conceptual
systems" (*GA* 12:83/3); they are encouraged rather "to call back to mind
the venerable origins of [their] own thinking, instead of chasing ever
more greedily after the latest news in European philosophy" (124/37).[52]

Putting the comments from these two texts together, then, it would
appear that East Asian thinkers are left in a double bind: they should turn
their attention away from "the latest news in European philosophy" and
back to their own venerable origins of thinking; and yet they should also
recognize that these Eastern traditions can, nevertheless, offer nothing

essential to the task of solving the worldwide problem of technological nihilism. Only the West can, as it were, repair what it has broken; and it must do so alone, on and according to its own. Does this mean that contemporary Japanese thinkers, who live in a society thoroughly influenced by the voluntary and compulsory "adoption" of Western ways—i.e., by what Heidegger calls the "Europeanization of man and of the earth" that "devours the wellsprings of everything essential" (*GA* 12:99/16)—should spend their time meditating on an anachronistic tradition which can do nothing to help change the world!

To be sure, many of the elements of Heidegger's statements—his stress on the importance of carefully deconstructing/retrieving the Western tradition, his skepticism toward any superficial importation of a "quick fix" from "the mystical East," and his encouragement to Asians not to forget their own traditions in the mad rush to keep up with the West—have an important point to make. Yet the severity of this *double exclusion*—of Asian thinkers from Western thought, and of Asian thought from contributing to a solution to the problem of technology—an exclusion which would once again conveniently leave Heidegger in a position of authority for essential thinking of the past and future of the world-situation, betrays a questionable willfulness. Moreover, Heidegger himself showed sustained interest in East Asian thinking, and was arguably influenced (perhaps significantly so) in particular by his contact with Zen Buddhist and Daoist thought.[53] Why then the need to exclude these resources for thinking through the problems of the world-situation? Is there at work behind this exclusion a certain will to reject the importance of that which one is not oneself capable of linguistically and thoughtfully mastering?[54]

On the other hand, it must not be overlooked that it is Heidegger himself who has often—cautiously and ambivalently, and yet with radical implications—hinted in a more pluralistic direction. In a less often noted statement a few pages prior to his rejection of the idea of countering the technological worldview by simply adopting an Eastern experience of the world, Heidegger confesses: "And [yet] who of us can say whether or not one day in Russia and China the ancient traditions of a 'thought' will awaken which will help make possible for man a free relationship to the technical world" (*SP* 106/111). In a foreword written for a Japanese translation of one of his texts, Heidegger explicitly affirmed that the *Auseinandersetzung* of Western and Eastern thinking "can contribute [*mithelfen*] to the endeavor to save the essence of man from the threat of an extreme technical calculation and manipulation of human Dasein."[55] Not only does Heidegger radically criticize "the Europeanization of man and of the earth" (*GA* 12:99/16), but he also claims on occasion to be preparing ultimately for what he calls "planetary thinking" (*GA* 9:424/321). Indeed, Heidegger has written that the "dialogue with the Greek thinkers and their language" is to be understood as the "precondition for the inevitable dialogue with the East Asian world" (*VA* 43/158), and that the recollection of the Greek beginning "can no longer remain in its Western isolation. It is opening itself to the few other great beginnings that belong with their own to the same of the beginning of the in-finite relationship, in which the earth is contained" (*EHD* 177/201).

Heidegger's preference to patiently prepare for, rather than rashly embark on this "planetary thinking"—even though this patient approach is a luxury not afforded to non-Westerners whose lives are already profoundly affected by global Westernization—should be taken as a warning to "comparative philosophers" today to proceed more cautiously in the endeavor to open up a genuinely dialogical encounter between Western and non-Western traditions.[56] The renowned specialist of Indian and comparative philosophy, Wilhelm Halbfass, concluded his review of "India in the History of European Self-Understanding" with a consideration of Heidegger's thought, affirming that it "opens more radical perspectives on the situation of the modern world and the possibility of 'dialogues' with the East than that of Gadamer or Husserl."[57] Pöggeler addresses both sides of Heidegger's ambivalent contributions to planetary dialogue when he writes: "More than any other European philosopher, Heidegger made a conversation between the West and the Far East possible; yet he takes up the themes of the great traditions only to subordinate them entirely to his dominant concerns—to the necessities that drove his thought."[58]

Then there is the massive problem of Heidegger's persistent depreciation of the Judeo-Christian traditions in his Greco-German history of being, traditions in which he was nevertheless rooted and by which he remained influenced. In a number of contexts in this study I have had occasion to remark on Heidegger's complex and highly ambivalent relation to the Judeo-Christian tradition(s), and his peculiar exclusion of these from the realm of essential thought has received much insightful attention from critics.[59] In a somewhat simplified version of a common critique, while the young Heidegger attempted to formally indicate the factical life of "primal Christianity" by freeing it from the alien shackles of the Greek metaphysical conceptuality of Scholasticism (see *GA* 60), the later Heidegger attempts rather to recover the originary Greco-German tradition of philosophy from its epochal detour through (or fallenness into) hardened Christian/Latin onto-theological concepts. In the present context, suffice it to note the tension in the fact that, in Heidegger's exclusion from essential history of all but a single line of thinkers, from the pre-Socratic Greeks to the German poets and philosophers and finally to himself, a certain will to unity (i.e., inclusion/exclusion) ironically helps provide the being-historical framework within which the metaphysics of will is criticized.

Any will to the purity and unity of the history of being from the early Greek thinkers to the German philosophers and poets, however, is already disrupted from within by certain elements of Heidegger's thought that were undeniably influenced by the Judeo-Christian origins of his thought-path,[60] as well as by other elements that were arguably influenced to a significant degree by his contact with East Asian thought.[61] Each of these non-Greco-German sources of influence on his thought throws a kink in the chain of the history of being which skips it off the "one track" running from Anaximander to Heidegger.

One may be tempted to follow Werner Marx in rejecting the "particular 'historical' binding" character of Heidegger's thought while retaining "many of [his] important and very productive and penetrating thoughts."[62] In our context this would mean attempting to retain his critique of the will and his intimations of a *Gelassenheit* beyond the will, while rejecting the exclusive structure of the history of being. One might wish to argue that there are "limited references to the history of being" in the dialogue on *Gelassenheit,* in order to distance this notion of non-willing from the problematical residues of an anthropo-ethnocentric Hegelianism.[63]

And yet matters are not this simple. Heidegger's central thoughts, *Gelassenheit* included (see *G* 55ff./78ff.), depend for their meaning and force in large measure on the account of being itself as essentially historical, and on the claim that the entire history of Western metaphysics culminates in the epoch of the technological will to will. We cannot simply shave off the being-historical account within which Heidegger develops his critique of the will. The history of being has often been considered Heidegger's "decisive innovation,"[64] and some would go so far as to say that the "whole force of Heidegger's thought lies in his account of the history of philosophy."[65] At any rate, it is not possible to *simply* extract individual elements of Heidegger's thought from their situatedness within the context of his *seinsgeschichtliches Denken.*

Beyond the Will to System?

Without attempting to address all of the question-worthy issues that have been raised, let us nevertheless look back once more at Heidegger's notion of the history of being in search of its resistances to the suspicion that it remains a convoluted repetition of the metaphysical will to system. If there remains a kind of systematic structure to *Being and Time,* a transcendental structure in tension with its own central thoughts of radical historicity and mortal finitude, Heidegger's later thought explicitly claims to abandon the systematic philosophical endeavor. This is not accidental, for beginning in the 1930s Heidegger launches a critical attack on precisely the quintessentially modern "will to system." In his lecture course on Schelling Heidegger writes: "The knowing conquest of being as jointure, system and the will to system . . . is the innermost law of existence of this whole age [of modernity]" (*SA* 39/32). And yet why does Heidegger's own structuring thought of the history of being—a history in which the will to system is itself historically delimited—appear at times to repeat this systematic will to unity?

The question is whether or not Heidegger reduplicates certain prejudices of "philosophy" (as metaphysics) at the very moment he would radically criticize this tradition for its will to subordinate beings to a higher being or to ground factical history in an underlying metaphysical process. Heidegger resists this charge, for example, when he claims that by "referring to the *Geschick* of being we are not shoving behind the history of thinking something like a deeper layer that would allow one—as with the flick of a switch—to casually continue speaking of 'the history of being' instead of 'philosophy'" (*SG* 130). Yet does not Heidegger himself posit the continuity of a "deeper layer" of "essential history," where "the fate of the West hangs on the translation of the word *eon*" (*GA* 5:345/33), or what he calls at one point a "hidden history" (*verborgene Geschichte*) of which "actual historical situations and conditions are seen as merely consequences" (*NI* 538/56)? In what way, then, is Heidegger's notion of essential history radically different from, and not simply a quasi-inversion of, Hegel's history of Spirit?

As we have seen, Heidegger claims that there is not only a certain continuity between the various epochs of the history of being (as "the history of the oblivion of being escalating itself" [*ZSD* 56/52]), but also a radical discontinuity. The decisions which lie between epochs can neither be calculated nor predicted. The shift from one epoch to another would then seem to take place by way of a radical break, as it were, "from the outside." And yet neither are the sendings of being from "the outside" in the sense of a transcendent realm that would, as it were, "will history from above." Being itself is "finite" or "historical" in the sense that it "is" only as the temporal events of revealing/concealing. The history of being is, on the one hand, the continuity of an increasing withdrawal of being (and the corresponding rise of the will), and yet, on the other hand, being is nothing but this (dis)continuous movement of revealing/concealing, granting-in-withdrawal.

Precisely herein lies the difficulty of Heidegger's thought of being as the history or sending of being. How are we to think this peculiar "continuity-of-discontinuity"? The tension between the two sides must be resolved, it would seem, and yet to do so by reducing either side to the other would repeat one or another traditional problem of the will. If one were to emphasize only the idea of continuity, one would fall into a kind of Hegelian teleology of absolute knowledge. This would make Heidegger's recollection of the history of metaphysics into a sublated metaphysics; it would, as Haar puts it, prolong "the Hegelian project of totalization which is that of Metaphysics as a whole: the will to appropriate, to possess, [would be] applied here to Western History."[66] And yet, as the seminar on "Time and Being" notes, there is an essential difference, in that "for Hegel the identity of being and thinking is really an equivalence. Thus for Hegel there is no question of being" (*ZSD* 53/49). Unlike Hegel's absolute knowing, where being as such would be fully incorporated into reason, Heidegger always reserves a difference between being and thinking; the identity of the two is a "belonging-together" in their essential difference (*Unterschied*) and not a sheer equivalence. "Being always conceals itself from thought, and perhaps this [i.e., its essential withdrawal, *Entzug*] characterizes its essential trait (*Zug*)."[67]

And yet, on the other hand, precisely here where Heidegger is most resistant to "Hegelian hubris," i.e., to the will to incorporate being without reserve into thinking, his thought threatens to fall back into a kind of deference to a transcendent will. It is for this reason that the later Heidegger's thought elicits the following type of response from his less patient readers: "Being itself was elevated to the rank of absolute subject of history and man condemned to total subjection to Being and its fateful sendings [*Schickungen*]."[68] I shall not repeat here the reasons why Heidegger's being cannot be understood as an "absolute subject," and the many ways in which man, in his cor-respondence with being, is not "condemned to total subjection."

The point I wish to make here is that if either a strict continuity or a sheer discontinuity between the epochs of the history of being is emphasized at the expense of the other, one leans back toward this or that pole within the domain of the will. In only stressing the continuity, one leans toward a metaphysical will to system, and a sublation of the factical historicity of being into thought; in only stressing the discontinuity, one leans toward a passive deference to a fate sent from above. Regardless of one's final judgment as to the success of Heidegger's attempt to twist free of this dilemma, the *task* of thinking along Heidegger's way involves avoiding being drawn back into these pitfalls of assertion or deference of will.

Eschatology and the Will to Finality

The Eschatology of Being and the Goal of Non-Willing

> Hence the originary mindfulness of thinking necessarily be-
> comes genuine thinking, which means a thinking that sets *goals*.
> What gets set is not just any goal, and not *the* goal in general, but
> the one and only and thus the singular goal of our history. This
> goal is the *seeking* itself, the seeking of beyng [*das Suchen des
> Seyns*]. It takes place and is itself the deepest find when man be-
> comes the preserver of the truth of beyng, becomes the guardian
> and caretaker of that stillness, and is decided [*entschieden*] in
> that. (*GA* 65:17)

In *Contributions to Philosophy* there is still a quest for a proper will, here
spoken of as a "seeking" that sets a single supreme historical goal, a goal
for which the preservation of the *Volk* is only a condition (see *GA* 65:60,
99, 139), the goal of the other beginning whereby "man enters a wholly
other domain of history" (227). To be sure, this proper will of a goal-
setting seeking is not the willfulness of an egocentric subject, and the goal
aimed at is itself a seeking qua caretaking. The goal sought (willed) here
is a realization of man's proper essence as "seeker, preserver, guardian,
and caretaker" of the truth of being; for "this is what *care* means as the fundamental trait of Dasein" (17).

But for all this, does not this eschatological setting/seeking/willing
of the supreme goal of an other beginning for the entire West, led by the
few and the rare of the German *Volk*, bear certain residues of willful subjectivity even as it seeks to provide the structure for "overcoming" the
epoch of subjectivity? Even after Heidegger no longer speaks of a "will to
a goal," an eschatological structure remains in his thought, and with it certain problematical residues of a *will to finality*.

Haar points out that it is in Heidegger's idea of "the eschatology of
being" that he is at once in the closest proximity and at the same time at
the greatest distance from Hegel. The proximity lies in part in the idea
that at the end of the history of metaphysics, after the gathering of its final possibility, the thinker can for the first time get into view the whole of
this history. Heidegger himself acknowledges the similarity with Hegel
when he introduces his idea of the "eschatology of being"—even while he
situates Hegel's thought itself at a particular stage within the history of
metaphysics.

> We think of the eschatology of being in a way corresponding to the way
> the phenomenology of Spirit is to be thought, i.e., from within the his-

tory of being. The phenomenology of Spirit itself constitutes a phase in the eschatology of being, when being gathers itself in the ultimacy of its essence, hitherto determined through metaphysics, as the absolute subjectity [*Subjektität*] of the unconditioned will to will. . . . If we think within the eschatology of being, then we must someday anticipate the former dawn in the dawn to come; today we must learn to ponder this former dawn through what is imminent. (*GA* 5:327/18)

What is imminent is a turning in the history of being beyond the will, a turning which is made possible by a gathering of the history of being "in the ultimacy of its destiny." "The gathering in this departure, as the gathering (*logos*) at the outermost point (*eschaton*) of its essence hitherto, is the eschatology of being" (ibid.).

On the one hand, Heidegger's thinking, not unlike (an inverted version of) Hegel's, claims to gather the essence of all that has gone before, the "essential past" (*Gewesenes*) that prevails throughout (*durchwaltet*) the tradition even though it has never yet been properly thought as the inceptual (*Anfangende*) (*ID* 114–15/48–49). He appears to repeat the gesture of a metaphysical will to a retrospective anamnesis of absolute knowing, even while this Hegelian thought would itself be inscribed within the history of metaphysics as a landmark of the modern epoch of willful subjectivity. On the other hand, Heidegger's openness to the not-yet-thought both within the tradition and beyond it—i.e., to the "provisionality" (*Vorläufigkeit*) of his own thought, and indeed to "the finitude of thinking and of what is to be thought" (*ZSD* 38/35) in general—radically distinguishes his thinking from the totalizing metaphysical will of Hegel's system of absolute knowing.

The anticipation of an other beginning also clearly distinguishes Heidegger's history of being from a (merely inverted) Hegelianism. As Robert Bernasconi notes, "Heidegger's presentation of metaphysics in its unity is always at the same time complicated by his reference to 'another beginning.'"[69] Haar writes that, despite prolonging the Hegelian project in his retrospective appropriation of the whole of Western history, "Heidegger completely abandons the Hegelian model when he says that the History of Being has ended and that it is necessary 'to leave metaphysics to itself.'"[70] And yet, precisely in this eschatological reference to another beginning, a radically other beginning which would not be (merely) a sublation (*Aufhebung*) of the tradition but (also) a decisive leap out of it, precisely here where Heidegger's thought resists the Hegelian will to incorporate (by canceling, lifting up, and preserving) the tradition into the totality of the system of absolute knowing, does not Heidegger's thought exhibit another kind of will, a will to a clean break, and in this sense a "will to finality"?

This suspected will to finality would be the residue of the voluntaristic/fatalistic aspects of Heidegger's decisionism in the 1930s. Even when Heidegger deemphasizes or even denies the willful or subjective element of decision, when he stresses that the "decision" is not ultimately a human deed but rather the event of a scission between the epochs of the history of being, even then there lurks the problem of a will to definitive solutions, a will to once and for all be done with the vigilant task of critically disclosing turnabouts and reinscriptions within the domain of the will. The suspect will to finality is here the will to sweep away the domain of the will once and for all; it is an unproblematized *will* to non-willing.

The question is this: Does the thought of an other beginning, a time-space beyond the metaphysics of the will to power and the technological will to will, imply a time-space where non-willing would be fully revealed ("boundlessly unconcealed"), its possibility finally actualized? Yet would not such a projection of a final overcoming (*Überwindung*) of the problem of the will itself involve a certain will to final results? *Or* does the later Heidegger's preference for the expression *Verwindung*, following his critique of Nietzsche's "will to overcome nihilism" (see *N2* 389/243), imply rather the need to both "recover from" *and* "cope with" the problem of the will?

My own suspicion and supposition, stated somewhat bluntly in advance of later discussions, is this: just as there never was an epoch completely severed from the non-historical (or "in-historical") possibility of non-willing, on the other hand there could never be a utopian time and place completely free of traces of the problem of willing. The problem of willing would then not be exhaustively contained within the epochs of metaphysics—for there would be a certain non-eradicable, non-historical (even if always only historically occurring) problem of willing, which I shall later call the problem of "ur-willing." (In the following chapter I attempt to indicate some sources for thinking this problem of ur-willing in Heidegger's text.) The possibility of non-willing, as the non-historical essence (*Wesen*) of man, would thus be no more once and for all completely actualizable than would it be fully eradicable, for it would always be in strife with this non-historical "dissonant excess" (*Unwesen*) of "ur-willing."[71]

The Problem of Thinking the Other Beginning: A Double Strategy?

We have gotten slightly ahead of ourselves, anticipating the issue of "ur-willing" that shall concern us in the following chapter. In the present context we are attending to the critical suspicion that there remains in Heidegger's thought a residue of a will to finality. That residue would involve a will to determine the will wholly historically, and to project the other beginning as a total overcoming of the problem of the will as such in a historical actualization of non-willing. Let us return, then, to the problematical idea of "the eschatology of being."

The eschatological thought of the end of metaphysics and the turning to an other beginning pervades Heidegger's later writings. On the one hand, this involves the idea of a final "gathering": "The end of philosophy is the place, that place in which the whole of philosophy's history is gathered in its most extreme possibility. End as completion means this gathering" (*ZSD* 63/57). We have already discussed this problematical will to unify the entire history of the West as the history of metaphysics; here let us attend to the other side of the notion of an eschatology of being, namely, the idea of an other beginning.

Although the language of an *anderer Anfang* can be found as early as *Introduction to Metaphysics* (see *EM* 29), it is in *Contributions to Philosophy* that this notion is fully developed into a structuring element of Heidegger's thought. There Heidegger characterizes his thought as a "preparatory thinking" which, by participating in the interplay or "pass" (*Zuspiel*) between the first beginning and the impending other beginning, prepares for a leap (*Sprung*) into the truth of beyng. In this leap, man would finally be transformed into Da-sein, the "there of being" as the grounding (*Gründung*) of the truth of beyng. Although much of the language and many of the thoughts of *Contributions* are subsequently modified, the eschatological idea of the other beginning remains very much a structuring element throughout the later periods of Heidegger's thought. For example, in the important text from 1951–52, *What Is Called Thinking?* we find the following statement:

> [There] is announced here a still unspoken gathering of the whole of Western destining, the gathering from which alone the Occident [*Abendland,* the "land of evening"] can go forth to encounter the coming decisions—to become, perhaps in a wholly other mode [*in eine ganz andere Weise*], a land of dawn, an Orient [*das Land eines Morgens*]. (*WhD* 67/69–70)

In this anticipation of the dawn of a morning-land "wholly other" than the final gathering of the metaphysical evening-land, we find the eschatological motif well intact in the later period of Heidegger's thought. This eschatological idea of an other beginning provides his thought with its direction and critical vantage point. The history of metaphysics as a history of the rise of the will is problematized both in order to intimate, as well as by way of intimating, a time beyond this history, a time perhaps wholly other than the epochal history of the will.

Recall the statement of the Scientist in the conversation on *Gelassenheit* who, frustrated with the doublings of the problem of the will in every attempt to negate it, ventures the bold claim that any "trace of will" "vanishes while releasing oneself and is completely extinguished in *Gelassenheit*" (*G* 57/80). Is there after all a persona of Heidegger's thought reflected in this projection of a traceless releasement from the will? After twisting free of the will by way of the complex *Wollen das Nicht-Wollen,* there would, according to this eschatological reading, come the dawn of a time of non-willing, a time no longer in need of any reference to the problem of the will. Even the expression "non-willing," and perhaps *Gelassenheit* too (as releasement *from*), would then become anachronistic, as there would be no more (domain of the) will from which to twist free and be released.

It is precisely this projection of a time no longer plagued by the problem of the will, a ~~non-willing~~ dwelling in the fourfold, which is at once one of the most enticing elements of Heidegger's thought, and one of the most question-worthy. Bernasconi writes that the idea of the *andere Anfang* "indicates what is most inviting, most challenging, and yet most disturbing in Heidegger's thought."[72] In the present context it is disturbing because Heidegger comes dangerously close to cutting short the toil of a relentless critique of the will by flirting with a kind of utopian will to decisive results. This element in his thought runs against, however, his own critique of Nietzsche's will to a revaluation of all values. As Krell notes in his insightful discussion of the problem of "results,"[73] Heidegger argues that the "very will to a new valuation, the compulsion to rescue beings as a whole and establish positive results for their history, is a metaphysical—hence nihilistic—will." Krell goes on to ask the critical question: "However, does Heidegger's thought too hope to establish results in and for the history of philosophy, precisely in its constant appeals to primordial beginnings and irrevocable ends. . . . Is its yearning for results yet another instance of metaphysical nostalgia?"[74] Is the eschatological vision of an other beginning yet another metaphysical will to final results? The question is not a simple one, not least because it is Heidegger himself who criticizes the idea of "results," which, he writes, "are given only where there is reckoning and calculation" (*N2* 85/48), that is, where there is the technological will.[75] Once again Heidegger appears to be his own best critic.

We find what often seems to be a kind of deliberate ambivalence, between the radical suggestion of a possible way of being wholly otherwise than willing, and an awareness that our own being and thinking—including the very terms in which we frame our intimations of non-willing—are (still) largely determined by the domain of the will.[76]

In general Heidegger's thought moves within a tension with regard to the relation of the first beginning and the other beginning; the latter is both a thoughtful repetition of and a radical break with the former. As *Contributions* puts it: "Reverence for the first beginning . . . must go together with the ruthless [*Rücksichtslosigkeit*, literally a lack-of-looking-back-ness] turning away [*Abkehr*] from this beginning to an other questioning and saying" (*GA* 65:6). Although the aspect of radical break is usually emphasized with regard to the degenerate end of the tradition inaugurated by the first beginning and not the greatness of its inception, the other beginning is also not to be understood as a simple return to the not-yet-degenerated start (*Beginn*) of the first beginning (*Anfang*). Consider this tension in the following passage from a letter Heidegger wrote to Gadamer: "This experiencing of *aletheia* is the step back to the 'oldest of the old,' the turning to the 'other beginning,' i.e., the one and the same single beginning of Western European thought, but this beginning thought in another manner."[77] He emphasizes both the sameness and the difference between the other beginning and the first beginning; they think the same (i.e., the "oldest of the old," the *Ursprung*), but differently.

Against the tendency of some interpreters to overemphasize the radical break involved in this thought, Bernasconi emphasizes the continuity involved.

> Far from being an attempt to accomplish a complete break, a total emancipation from the tradition, the "overcoming of metaphysics" takes place as an insight into metaphysics, a reappropriation of it. . . . "[Another] beginning" is not a new beginning, but a beginning which remembers the first beginning of the Greeks and at the same time illuminates it.[78]

In the notion of "another," he points out, "the reference to what went before is maintained in its discontinuity with it." Bernasconi's counter-emphasis is an important corrective to a tendency to attend only to the "scandalous" aspect of Heidegger's alleged "destruction" and dismissal of the entire Western tradition without attending to the "retrieval" of original (if often unthought) experiences through the *Destruktion*. As Heidegger stressed early on: "*Liberation from the tradition is an ever new appropriation of its newly recognized strengths*" (*GA* 29/30:511/352).

And yet, even after this corrective has been acknowledged, we must not fail to attend to the aspect of radical discontinuity in the thought of the other beginning.[79] There is a radical otherness of the other beginning, an otherness most explicitly witnessed in the rupture between the end of the history inaugurated by the first beginning, the extreme epoch of the metaphysics of will, and the intimated turning of being to the dawn of a "perhaps wholly other" time-play-space. In *Contributions* Heidegger suggests that in the other beginning "man enters a wholly other domain of history" (*GA* 65:227); this would entail "a complete transformation of man into Da-sein" in "another time-space" which is opened up by a "more originary essencing [*ursprünglichere Wesung*] of beyng itself" (475).

There is both innovative retrieval and radical break. This complex intertwining between retrieval of and break with the first beginning is concisely expressed in the following passage from the closing pages of *Contributions:*

> In the end the other beginning stands in a necessary and intimate but hidden relation to the first beginning, a relation which at the same time includes the complete separatedness [*völlige Abgeschiedenheit*] of both in accord with their origin-character [*Ursprungscharakter*]. (*GA* 65:504)

This inherent ambivalence in Heidegger's thought of the other beginning would presumably call for an interweaving of the two "strategies"[80] that Derrida proposes at the end of his essay "The Ends of Man."[81] The first strategy is as follows:

> a. To attempt an exit and a deconstruction without changing terrain, by repeating what is implicit in the founding concepts and the original problematic, by using against the edifice the instruments or stones available in the house, that is, equally, in language.

In our context this first strategy would involve the complex dynamic of willing non-willing. The strength of this "internal critique" is that it problematizes from within; the will becomes a problem to itself, and thus leaves no ground for retreat. The shortcoming is that it is always in danger of simply repeating the will, of sublating or sublimating it into a more or less convoluted form of the same problem. As Derrida writes, here "one risks ceaselessly confirming, consolidating, relifting (*relever*), at an always more certain depth, that which one allegedly deconstructs." Hence the need to combine this with a second strategy, namely:

> b. To decide to change terrain, in a discontinuous and irruptive fashion, by brutally placing oneself outside, and by affirming an absolute break and difference.

Although Derrida claims here that "the style of the first deconstruction is mostly that of the Heideggerian questions, and the other is mostly the one which dominates France today," we have found something like the latter very much at work in Heidegger's thought of the other beginning as a new dawn of a wholly different mode or domain of history. Thus we find *both* "strategies" at work in Heidegger. The region of non-willing, as the radical other to the domain of the will, could ultimately be entered into only by way of a radical break with the tradition of metaphysics that completes itself in the technological will. We would have to finally "leave all willing to itself," including the will to non-willing, in order to dwell within this radically other time-play-space. And yet, as Derrida notes, the danger of this second strategy of thinking is that "the simple practice of language ceaselessly reinstates the new terrain on the oldest ground," "thereby inhabiting more naively and more strictly than ever the inside one declares one has deserted." Every attempt to definitively and positively name non-willing, we have worried, threatens to simply repeat, in a disguised or hypocritical manner, a position within the domain of the will.

Despite its moments of excess and residues of will, Heidegger's thought of the other beginning leaves us held between these two "strategies," or rather "demands" for thinking. We are called on to maintain the tension between an immanent critique of the domain of the will and a cultivation of intimations of a radically other region of non-willing.

In the closing paragraphs of the 1962 lecture "Time and Being," Heidegger utters the well-known lines: "Our task is to cease [*abzulassen*] all overcoming and leave [*überlassen*] metaphysics to itself" (*ZSD* 25/24). Presumably this would also be the case with the will. We must ultimately cease all *willing* not to will in order to and by way of entering into non-willing as a radically other way of being. But we are not yet, if indeed we ever could be, at this ultimate point of departure. After the above lines, Heidegger adds the following remarks which should not be overlooked: "If overcoming remains necessary, it concerns that thinking which explicitly enters *Ereignis* in order to say It in terms of It about It. . . . Our task is to relentlessly and unceasingly [*unablässig*] overcome the obstacles that tend to render such saying inadequate" (ibid.). Analogously, with regard to the problem of the will, the task would be to *relentlessly and unceasingly* recover from (ur-)willing in order to let non-willing be.

10

The Persistence of Ur-Willing, the Dissonant Excess of Evil, and the Enigma of Human Freedom

> Philosophy is always completed when its end becomes and remains what its beginning is, the question. (*SA* 118/98)

> If you want to honor a philosopher, you must catch him where he has not yet gone forth to the consequences, in his fundamental thought; (in the thought) from out of which he proceeds.
> —F. W. J. Schelling[1]

> For every great thinker always *thinks* one leap more originally than he directly *speaks*. Our interpretation must therefore try to say what is unsaid by him. (*NI* 158/134)

Heidegger's *Denkweg*, which began by stepping back to the most fundamental questions of philosophy, moves forward as a thinking that keeps itself open to question(ing). As readers of Heidegger, we too are called into question(ing). His being-historical thinking demonstrates that a step back through the history of philosophy is a prerequisite for venturing a genuine step forward in thought; and correlatively, an attentive reading of a past thinker always already entails transgressing his text toward a present and future possibility for thinking.

My own "faithful transgressions" of Heidegger's text began with the interpretive decision (a decision made in the chiasmic exchange between reading and writing) to thematically focus on the problem of the will and the possibility of non-willing. After having followed this problematic through the course of Heidegger's *Denkweg*, and after having critically examined—largely by way of "immanent critique"—the residues of will that remain still in its later phases, we have been brought to the question of how to understand the "other beginning" with regard to the problem of the will. In this departing chapter, I shall attempt to interpretively elucidate some of the more radical implications of Heidegger's thought with respect to this question, a question that in fact necessitates readdressing two of the most difficult issues for philosophical thinking: the problem of evil and the enigma of human freedom. It will be necessary to situate my interpretations now more than ever at the ambiguous limits of reading Heidegger after Heidegger. While here too I shall attempt to keep any interpretive transgressions of the letter of Heidegger's text more or less faithful to the direction of its most radical indications, I shall leave the question open as to whether and to what extent I have in places managed to give Heidegger cause to "bow to the necessity of later being understood differently than he thought he understood himself" (*GA* 9:ix/xiii).

The Problem of the Possibility of Non-Willing

> Yanyang asked Zhaozhou: How about when one arrives carrying not a single thing [i.e., having let go of all attachments]? Zhaozhou responded: Cast that down [i.e., let go of your attachment to the idea of having let go of all attachments]!
> —*Congronglu* (*Shōyōroku*)[2]

> In the very will to protect oneself against "x" one is more exposed to the danger of reproducing "x" than when one tries to think contamination.
> —Jacques Derrida[3]

In the beginning of this study I noted that the reach of "the problem" in the phrase, "the problem of the will and the possibility of non-willing," should be understood to extend not only to "the will" but also to "the possibility of non-willing." Hence, during the course of this inquiry we have been concerned not only with "the problem of the will" but also with "the problem of the possibility of non-willing." The problem of the possibility of non-willing is not only the dilemma of how to make the transition to non-willing, but also the question of whether there could ever be non-willing, whether this possibility could ever be actualized, or in what sense non-willing is even a "possibility."

We need to keep a certain Nietzschean doubt in mind, namely, his suspicion that any attempt to wholly negate the will or to posit an other than willing can succeed only in concealing and sublating the will into covert guise. Nietzsche's "ascetic priest," for instance, only appears to negate his will, while in fact it is sublimated into the convoluted and hypocritical form of a self-serving mouthpiece for the (projected) higher Will of God. According to Nietzsche, any apparent twisting free of the will actually results only in a twisted form of willing, or what I have referred to as a covert-willing. As for the possibility of twisting free of the will into a non-willing, Nietzsche claims that the very idea that "the will would become *Nicht-Wollen*" is but an illusory "fable song of madness."[4]

Nevertheless Heidegger, while fully aware of Nietzsche's critique of covert-willing and skepticism with regard to the possibility of non-willing, does not acquiesce to the assertion that the will is the *letzte Faktum* to which we come down; for Heidegger, the predominance of the will is not a universal metaphysical truth, but is situated in a *Seinsgeschichte* as the epochal culmination of the history of metaphysics. The will is not the ahistorical essence of man, but rather his historical essence in the modern epoch. Heidegger even suggests in places, as we have seen, that the will is the historical essence of humans who are most alienated from their proper non-historical essence of non-willing. Hence, Nietzsche's rejection of the possibility of an other-than-willing would tell us as much about his own epochal limitation as it does about the genuine difficulty of escaping the domain of the will. One could then say that Heidegger's thought is aimed at thinking *through* Nietzsche's admonitions in a twisting free of the domain of the will toward a genuine non-willing, which would no longer simply repeat the will in a (self-)deceptive guise.

And yet, here at the end of this study we return to the question of whether and in what sense the other beginning of non-willing would lie once and for all beyond the problem of the will. We have found that Heidegger's thought of the other beginning is in fact stretched between two strategies or demands of thinking: (1) a plodding deconstruction of the tradition from within and (2) an anticipation of an abrupt break from without. In terms of the problem of the will, these two correspond to (*a*) a relentless critique of the (domain of the) will and (*b*) an attempt to intimate a wholly other way of being as non-willing. Would the ambivalence of this double strategy be left behind in the inauguration of the other beginning? Would a realization of non-willing leave behind the need to vigilantly problematize the will?

In fact, we find a tension in Heidegger's thought regarding the possibility of a postepochal time of non-willing. On the one hand, the other beginning would be wholly other than the history of the metaphysics of will; and insofar as the will would be an essentially historical determination, this would appear to be a time beyond the will as such. On its own, however, this view is self-contradictorily plagued by a certain "will to finality." On the other hand, I shall demonstrate below, Heidegger's thought in places may be understood to suggest that there is a certain non-historical problem of "willing," one that is not wholly contained within the epochal limits of the history of metaphysics. On this second view, then, the other beginning would not be a complete eradication of the problem of willing, but rather a vigilant opening to it, a watchful recognition of the finitude of our selves caught between this problem of willing and the possibility of non-willing. These two views of the other beginning do not simply overlap with the two strategies or demands of thinking (deconstructing from within/radical break from without), but rather the former view would involve a leap from the first strategy to the second, while the latter would involve perpetually maintaining the tension between the two strategies. In this chapter I shall develop the latter, less absolute but more radical interpretation of the other beginning in Heidegger's thought.

Before elaborating on this second view, however, let us remind ourselves of the first, namely the idea that the other beginning would be a clean break from the epoch of will to a time of unadulterated non-willing. This vision is suggested by Heidegger's more apocalyptic depictions of the end of the nihilistic history of the metaphysical will. For example:

> Before being can occur [*sich . . . ereignen*] in its inceptual truth [*anfänglichen Wahrheit*], being as the will must be broken, the world must be forced to collapse and the earth must be driven to desolation, and man to mere labor. Only after this going-under [*Untergang*] does the abrupt while of the beginning [*die jähe Weile des Anfangs*] take place [*ereignet sich*] for a long span of time. (*VA* 69/68)

Complementing the apocalyptic vision of a final overcoming of the will is the anticipatory projection of "the dawn of an altogether different age [*der Frühe eines ganz anderen Weltalters*]" (*GA* 5:326/17). This would be the dawn of a "wholly other mode [*eine ganz andere Weise*]" (*WhD* 67/70) of being where "not even a trace" (see *G* 57/79–80) of the will remains, not even the will to negate the will or the will to non-willing. The other beginning would then presumably be a time of pure *Gelassenheit* wholly unrelated to the will, a "non-willing" where even this transitional name, which still bears a trace of a relation to the will (as a radical negation of its domain), would become anachronistic, if not indeed unintelligible.

As enticing as these visions may appear to be, however, a somber suspicion of all apocalyptic final solutions, and of all utopian dreams of dwelling in communities once and for all wholly beyond the conflict of wills, gives us critical pause. Could there ever be a time where a relentless problematization of the will (including all its partial negations and sublimations within the domain of the will) would simply no longer be needed? Could we ever enter into a time of non-willing such that the problem of the will as such would dissolve and disappear? Or rather, would the other beginning be a time where non-willing, or at least decisive or incisive moments thereof, would be made possible precisely through a vigilant openness to a certain never-finally-eradicable problem of "willing"? Would the other beginning thus be a time, not of the complete eradication of the problem of willing, but one where the problem would no longer be concealed, where *das Nicht-Wollen* would, in all its complexity and sheaf of meanings, be allowed to vigilantly clear ever again possibilities, intimations of non-willing?

Heidegger's thought provides several significant resources for thinking the other beginning as an opening to the strife between willing and non-willing. To begin with, when Heidegger states that the other beginning entails an occurrence of the "inceptual truth" of being, strictly according to his understanding of truth this would *not* be an overcoming of all concealment, but rather a step back from what we might call "double concealment," that is, from forgetting the ineradicable play of revealing/concealing that characterizes the essencing of truth as *a-letheia*. The history of metaphysics is the history of the concealment of the originary essencing of truth as revealing/concealing; metaphysics involves a double concealment, a forgetting of the concealment which belongs essentially (i.e., not simply in one epoch or another) to the revealing of being.

According to *Contributions to Philosophy*, where Heidegger was developing his thought of the eschatological history of being, he states that although the essence of being (or beyng) would in some sense be "grounded" (*gegründet*) in the other beginning, this would not mean that it would once and for all be wholly manifest and made "sayable." "That the essence of beyng is never conclusively sayable does not imply a shortcoming; on the contrary: the inconclusive knowing holds fast to the *abyss* [Abgrund] and thereby to the essence of beyng" (*GA* 65:460). The essence of beyng is itself abyssal, that is, it always conceals as it reveals, withdraws as it grants.

We find this thought poignantly developed in Heidegger's 1962 lecture "Time and Being," and it becomes the topic of much of the discussion recorded in the "Summary of a Seminar" appended to the publication of the lecture. In "Time and Being," in place of the "other beginning" Heidegger speaks of entering into the event of appropriation, of "awakening into *Ereignis.*" It is necessary to note a certain doubling of the sense of *Ereignis* in its relation to history, a doubling I have attempted to characterize with the notion of the non-historical as the "in-historical" (where the "in-" signifies at once difference and location). On the one hand, *Ereignis* is thought as the non-historical "It" which gives time or sends the various epochs of being (see *ZSD* 20/19, 44/41); on the other hand, it is thought specifically as the historical event in which the epochal history of metaphysics would come to an end in the "awakening into *Ereignis* [*Das Entwachen in das Ereignis*]" (53/49).

On the one hand: "That-which-sends [*das Schickende*] as *Ereignis*, is itself non-historical [*ungeschichtlich*], or more precisely without destiny [*geschicklos*]" (44/41). The term *Ereignis* indicates the non-historical appropriating event (or eventuation) that gives rise to the epochs of history, and perhaps to a time other than the epochal history of metaphysics. On the other hand, Heidegger clearly in places thinks "the awakening into *Ereignis*" as an otherwise "historical" possibility at the end of metaphysics (i.e., at the end of history as the history of the *epochs* of being), an event where being and man would each come back more originally into their own. As metaphysics is "the history of the concealment of that which gives being [i.e., *Ereignis*]," the "entry of thinking into *Ereignis* is thus equivalent to the end of this withdrawal's history. The oblivion of being 'lifts' itself 'up' [*hebt sich auf*] in the awakening into *Ereignis*" (*ZSD* 44/41).

The awakening into *Ereignis* is thus for Heidegger the historical possibility of awakening to the It which gives history itself. *Ereignis*, as that which properly holds man and being together in holding them apart, as the mirror-play of the fourfold, is both historical and non-historical, at once the yonder side of the extreme epoch of the technological will to will, *and* that which gives both epochal and postepochal history as such. *Ereignis* is thought both as the essence of historical occurrence and as the moment of awakening, the moment of coming into its ownness, of that essence: *dann ist, für einen Augenblick, Er-eignis Ereignis* (*GA* 65:508).

Ereignis, as the event of proper mutual appropriation of man and being, or of the elements of the fourfold, is what we might call the possible event of non-willing—an event which can only come into its own once we undergo the transition out of the epoch of the technological will to will. As Michel Haar writes: "Outside the reign of this History [of metaphysics] which is both forgetful and totalizing it [*Ereignis*] opens up *a nonhistorical dimension* where man learns anew to let things simply be, to open up to the play that connects earth and sky, mortals and gods."[5] In other words, the awakening into *Ereignis* would open up a non-historical dimension where man could realize more originally his non-historical essence as non-willing. Nevertheless, this opening up occurs as an event *in* history, and even as an inaugural event *of* history, namely, as the inception of the other beginning.

The sense of *Ereignis* as the opening of a time beyond the closure of the history of metaphysics presents us with Heidegger's last word on the idea of the other beginning. Let us therefore pay special attention to the way this event is conceived. To be sure, entering into *Ereignis* would mark the end of the history of metaphysics as the oblivion of being; but this does not mean that the negativity of concealment as such would end. Rather, inasmuch as withdrawal or "expropriation [*Enteignis*] belongs to *Ereignis* as such" (*ZSD* 23/23), "the withdrawal which characterized metaphysics in the form of the oblivion of being now shows itself as the dimension of concealment itself. *But now concealment does not conceal itself*" (44/41, emphasis added). This last point is crucial: in awakening to *Ereignis* concealment is not eradicated but rather *no longer conceals itself.* On the one hand, this marks the radical difference of this time from the epochs of metaphysics, and, on the other hand, it dismisses the (metaphysical) utopian misconception of a postepochal time beyond all negativity and concealment. Thus, whereas for (a predominant interpretation of) Hegel absolute knowing would be the overcoming of human finitude,[6] for "Heidegger, in contrast, it is precisely finitude that comes into view—not only human finitude, but the finitude of *Ereignis* itself" (53/49). The other beginning would not be an "overcoming of," but rather an "awakening to" concealment and finitude.

And it is here that I shall insert my interpretive suggestion: Is there not a problem of "willing" that is an ineradicable aspect of man's ineradicable finitude? Would not a problem of "willing"—even if not that of its specific historical determinations/exacerbations in the epochs of metaphysics—remain even in the other beginning? Just as we discovered essential ambiguities in the cases of *Ereignis* and non-willing, must we not also think a dual sense of "willing"? That is to say, must we not think "willing" both in the sense of a historically determined fundamental (dis)attunement (i.e., "the will" as the historical essence of man in the modern epoch), *and* in the sense of a non-historical *Unwesen* that inevitably haunts non-willing as the non-historical *Wesen* of man? If so, then the other beginning would not be a total extinction of the problem of willing in the total actualization of the possibility of non-willing, but rather: man in the other beginning would remain vigilantly open to a certain never finally eradicable problem of "willing," and precisely and only through this vigilant openness would be attuned to the always granting-in-withdrawal possibility of non-willing. While guarding the clearing of being precisely through an engaged letting-be of its play of presencing/absencing, by letting go of the will to once and for all ground non-willing in a permanent presence, man would assist in allowing moments of non-willing to grant-in-withdrawal. Intimations of non-willing would be enabled by way of ceaselessly (*unablässig*) attending to a certain non-historical problem of "willing."

Non-willing would, then, always be accompanied by a counter-essence (*Gegenwesen*), or, more precisely formulated, by a certain originary dissonant excess (*Unwesen*)[7] that could neither be wholly eradicated from the would-be pure tonality of a univocal origin, nor dialectically sublated into the redemptive harmony of an absolute identity. This originary dissonant excess to the fundamental a-tunement of non-willing would be the origin of "the will" of metaphysics, but not yet or no longer this will itself. Insofar as "the will" specifically refers to the fundamental (dis)attunement of modern subjectivity, let us then call this originary dissonant excess, this ineradicable pre-metaphysical root and post-metaphysical seed of willing: *ur-willing*.

The Persistence of Ur-Willing

In the epoch of subjectivity, the will ultimately appears to be the essence of existence. On the other hand, at the end of this epoch of willful subjectivity, when the willfulness of subjective existence is revealed to be the fundamental (dis)attunement of ecstatic-incorporation, a more originary attunement is intimated, a more radical ek-sistence that breaks through the domain of willful subjectivity and opens to that which withdraws from the grasp of incorporation. In an open attunement to the presencing-in-withdrawal of being, mortal humans would non-willingly participate in letting beings be.

Letting beings be entails, then, a double comportment, as conveyed in Heidegger's statement: "Releasement toward things and openness for the mystery belong together" (*G* 24/54). An openness to the withdrawal of being into concealment (i.e., into the hiddenness of the mystery) enables a released engagement with (*Sicheinlassen auf*) things, where "we no longer view things merely technologically" (23/54).

Yet these two comportments are not only mutually supportive; in a certain sense, they also occur in essential tension with one another. An engagement with present beings is enabled through an openness for the granting-in-withdrawal of being, and yet this engagement is essentially always already under way toward forgetting this originary event of presencing/absencing. An intimate involvement with beings requires, and yet tends to obfuscate, an originary response-ability to ek-statically participate in the event of being which lets beings be in the first place.

In "The Essence of Truth" essay Heidegger articulates the essential ambivalence of this double comportment in his discussion of how *ek-sistence* necessarily entails the countermovement of *in-sistence*.

> Dasein not only ek-sists but at the same time *in-sists*, i.e., holds fast to what is offered by beings. . . . *As ek-sistent, Dasein is insistent.* . . . Man errs. Man does not merely stray into errancy. He is always astray in errancy, because as ek-sistent he in-sists and so already stands in errancy. (*GA* 9:196/150)

The freedom of ek-sistence—which exceeds the present determinations of beings and stands out into the clearing event of their determination—is always complemented and countered by an in-sistence which holds fast to beings, turning its back on the opening which allows them to presence in the first place. Man forgets even that "he insists only by being already ek-sistent" (ibid.). The relation between these intertwined movements is not merely conflictual, for ek-sistence itself already essentially entails a "turning away from the mystery"; the revealing of ek-sistence already essentially involves a tendency toward concealment, because it always reveals beings in a particular way (193/132). Man not only in-sists because he ek-sists, but also ek-sists by already turning toward in-sisting. Human freedom, Heidegger writes, must then be "conceived on the basis of the in-sistent ek-sistence of Dasein" (198/151).

Freedom as "letting beings be" is not a permanent state into which one enters, but can occur only "from time to time" by way of a "glimpse into the mystery out of errancy," that is, by stepping back from one's dealings with beings to expose oneself to the question of being. Being is revealed only in withdrawal, however, and thus "resolute openness to the mystery [*Ent-schlossenheit zum Geheimnis*] is as such always underway into errancy" (ibid.). Letting beings be requires *both* that we turn to and away from the mystery of being. For precisely "because letting be always lets beings be in a particular comportment . . . it conceals beings as a whole. Letting-be is intrinsically at the same time a concealing" (195/148).

Ek-sistence and in-sistence are intertwined no less than are revealing and concealing, truth and errancy. Humans in the other beginning would not overcome the ambivalent play of this intertwined duality, but would openly acknowledge and attentively participate in it. The problem of the modern epoch is not concealment as such, but rather the fact that "concealing as a fundamental occurrence has sunk into forgottenness" (195/149); the problem is not "errancy" as the counter-essence of truth, but rather that the ineradicability of this counter-essence is no longer recognized.[8] Not the failure to achieve, but the very *will* to absolute truth as "unbounded unconcealment" is the problem. "The Essence of Truth" suggests, then, that the task is not to eradicate in-sistence, but rather, by recognizing it as the counter-essence of freedom, to learn to live within "this perpetual turning to and fro" (197/151) that is the condition of our finite existence. In the very recognition of the ineradicable counter-essence of truth, the human task is to cultivate "the possibility that, by experiencing errancy itself and by not mistaking the mystery of Da-sein, one *not* let oneself be led astray [*sich* nicht *beirren lassen*]" (ibid.).

Errancy (*die Irre*) is the necessary counter-essence of truth. But what is this apparently unnecessary "letting oneself be led astray"? Everything now depends on clarifying this distinction. While "The Essence of Truth" does not elaborate in detail on this crucial point, it does contain a decisive passage that addresses the issue. After introducing the notion of concealing as that which preserves the mystery as the proper non-essence of truth, Heidegger suggests that the apparent strangeness of this idea is due to the fact that "concealing as a fundamental occurrence has sunken into forgottenness" (195/149). Man is then left to his own resources, establishing standards and goals according to his latest needs and aims. Yet in seeing himself as an autonomous positor of values and setter of standards, "man goes wrong as regards the essential genuineness of his standards." Here both an essential connection with, and a decisive distinction from in-sistence is introduced:

> Man is all the more mistaken [*vermisst sich*] the more exclusively he takes himself, as subject, to be the standard [*Maß*] for all beings. The inordinate forgetfulness [*vermessene Vergessenheit*] of humanity persists [*beharrt*] in securing itself by means of what is readily available and always accessible. This persistence [*Beharren*] has its unwitting support in that *comportment* by which Dasein not only ek-sists but at the same time in-sists. (196/149–50)

In-sistent involvement with beings and concealment of the mystery are integral moments of the occurrence of truth as the freedom of letting beings be; even errancy is a necessary counter-essence of involvement in the truth of beings. Only by ek-sisting, stepping out of our everyday involvement with beings, do we cor-respond to being so as to open up a free space (a *Da* of *Sein*) that lets beings show themselves in a particular manner. Yet correlatively, only by in-sisting, by stepping into an involvement with beings, can we engage ourselves in concretely letting them be. However, just as there is an *inordinate and excessive* (*vermessene*) forgetfulness of the mystery, persistence (*Beharren*) would be an *inordinate and excessive in-sistence,* an insistence which no longer properly ek-sists, or which ek-sists ultimately only in the malformation of an ecstatic-incorporation, a willful *Aneignung* of beings into the world-order posited by subjectivity.

Could the tendency toward this *inordinate and excessive* forgetfulness and insistence ever be finally overcome? Would the other beginning establish a time where man would release himself (or be-released) into the "turning to and fro" between ecstatic openness to the mystery and insistent involvement with beings, a time when man—precisely by way of opening himself to the "ontological" inevitability of errancy, and thereby remaining aware of the dangers of excessive in-sistence—would never again let himself be led astray into persistence, and into willful subjectivity? Or, because of the "unwitting support" of in-sistence, would there not always remain a force of temptation to persistence, a danger of falling back into willful subjectivity? The other beginning would, in that case, not only entail an attunement to the harmonious play of ek-sistence/insistence, but also a vigilant recognition of the impulse to persistence, an impulse which, when left unchecked, would pull one back towards willful subjectivity. It is this persistent impulse, this impulse to persistence, that I am referring to as "ur-willing."

There is another text where Heidegger speaks of an inordinate persistence. In "The Anaximander Fragment," where Heidegger is seeking to "anticipate the former dawn in the dawn to come" (*GA* 5:327/18), where he is attempting at once to think back before metaphysics and forward beyond metaphysics, Heidegger considers a kind of extra-metaphysical will-to-persistence as an inherent tendency in the presencing of beings. Beings come to presence, Heidegger reads Anaximander to be saying, between the twofold absence of the not-yet and the no-longer. "In this 'between' whatever lingers awhile is joined. . . . Presencing comes about in such a jointure [*Fuge*]" (355/41). Heidegger translates Anaximander's *dike* (usually rendered as "justice") as the "ordering and enjoining order [*der fugend-fügende Fug*]" (357/43).

What is important to us here is that Heidegger reads Anaximander to be stating that this "order" is let be always only by the "surmounting of disorder," *adikia*. "The fragment speaks from the essential experience that *adikia* is the fundamental trait of *eonta*" (355/42). What is the origin of this fundamental "disorder"? It is here that we may take Heidegger to be suggesting a kind of pre-metaphysical (and perhaps non-metaphysical) root of ur-willing. He writes:

> What has arrived [to linger between the twofold absence] may even
> insist [*bestehen*] upon its while solely to remain more present, in the

sense of perduring [*Beständigen*]. That which lingers persists [*beharrt*] in its presencing. In this way it extricates itself from its transitory while. It strikes the willful pose of persistence [*Es spreizt sich in den Eigensinn des Beharrens auf*], no longer concerning itself with whatever else is present. It stiffens—as if this were the only way to linger—and aims solely for continuance and subsistence. (Ibid.)

Does this "rebellious whiling" (*Aufständische der Weile*), through which "whatever lingers awhile insists upon sheer continuance" (356/43), relate to a non-historical problem of ur-willing that would not simply go away with the end of the metaphysical epochs of will? While not (yet) "the will"—i.e., the subject's will to ground and ecstatically incorporate all other beings into the (dis)order of its worldview—would not this inordinate impulse to its own *Beständigkeit des Fort-bestehens* begin to pave the road to the rise of willful subjectivity? The persistence of this lack of concern for other beings, and exclusive concern with one's own perduring presence, would make way for the will to conquest and the reduction of other beings to means for the power-preservation and power-enhancement of one's own subjectivity.

Hannah Arendt comments on "The Anaximander Fragment" as follows: "The Will as destroyer appears here, too, though not by name; it is the 'craving to persist,' 'to hang on,' the inordinate appetite men have 'to cling to themselves.'" Yet she goes on to characterize this as "Heidegger's denunciation of the instinct of self-preservation (common to all living things) as a willful rebellion against the 'order' of Creation as such."[9] Arendt problematically equates willfulness (*Eigensinn*) with the "natural inclination of beings to self-preservation," thus reading the Heidegger of this essay as proffering a kind of Schopenhauerian pessimistic metaphysics of the Will. But there is no reason to think that the so-called instinct for self-preservation, when carried out to the "ordinate" or unexcessive "natural" degree, would not be part of a being's allotted stay or "whiling" on the earth. It is perhaps when we exceed this allotted naturalness—for example in wars of conquest rather than of self-defense, or in a technological consumption of resources (*Bestand*) rather than a using which spares (*schont*) things—that we give rise to the excessive disorder of injustice. Elsewhere Heidegger writes:

> The unnoticeable law of the earth preserves the earth in the sufficiency of the emerging and perishing of all things in the allotted sphere of the possible which everything follows, and yet nothing knows. The birch tree never oversteps its possibility. The colony of bees dwells in its possibility. It is first the will which arranges itself everywhere in technology that

> devours the earth in the exhaustion and consumption and change of
> what is artificial. Technology forces the earth beyond the developed
> sphere of its possibility. . . . It is one thing just to [willfully] use the earth,
> another to receive the blessing of the earth and to become at home in
> the law of this reception in order to shepherd the mystery of being and
> watch over the inviolability of the possible. (*VA* 94/88–89)

Heidegger is thus not proffering a pessimistic renunciation of the "will-to-live," but rather suggesting a comportment (*Verhalten*) of a certain re-servedness (*Verhaltenheit*) which would reattune humans to the unnotice-able law of the jointure of things, to our place of participation in the fugue of being.

What Heidegger's reading of Anaximander does suggest, however, is that it is not *first* of all the full-blown technological will to will that dis-rupts the *Seynsfuge*. The jointure of being is always already disturbed by the *adikia* of a tendency to willful persistence. Subjective willing could be understood as exacerbating this originary willful impulse, such that the subjective ego seeks to be itself the giver of laws and the ground of possi-bilities; and the technological will to will would carry this to the extreme of no longer recognizing any *Gegen-ständlichkeit* or any law outside that of the immanent repetition of its cybernetic system of production and con-sumption. Yet there would be a continuity as well as a discontinuity be-tween, on the one hand, these metaphysical/technological forms of "will," and, on the other hand, "ur-willing" as the impulse to an inordinate and excessive persistence that always already threatens to disrupt the fugue of being. Would not the other beginning, then, be inaugurated only by way of a vigilant awareness of this ineradicable persistence of ur-willing, rather than by the presumption to have overcome all willful dissonance in a har-monious fugue of unbounded consonance?

There does seem to be a problematical aspect of anthropomorphism in Heidegger's reading of Anaximander's fragment, perhaps due to the fact that, while the fragment is concerned with *ta onta* in general, the beings with which Heidegger is predominantly concerned, here as elsewhere, are *hoi anthropoi*. But would not *human* ur-willing remain essentially different than any willful persistence that could be ascribed to animals, not to men-tion inanimate things? Heidegger most often, to be sure, insists on an abyssal distinction between humans and animals, an insistence that in other contexts (such as the question of our embodied and sentient kinship with [other] animals) appears problematic. Yet would it not be vital to mark a decisive distinction between humans and non-human animals precisely here, where it is a question of a capacity for inordinate willfulness? Are not humans radically distinguished from other animals nowhere more clearly than with respect to our disruptive ability to rebel against the natural order of things? As Heidegger himself acknowledges in his interpretation of Schelling, the possibility for evil is an essential trait of humans, one that sets us apart from animals. An "animal can never be 'evil,'" writes Heidegger, and thus "the dubious advantage is reserved for man of sinking beneath the animal" (*SA* 173–74/144; see also *GA* 29/30:286/194).

As Heidegger's reading of Schelling shows, it is this fact of human freedom for evil that shatters the *system* of idealism. Yet does Heidegger's own thinking of the *fugue* of being fully take into account this all too human problem of evil? Is the extreme dissonant excess of evil "accounted for" in a thought of the fugue of being? For Heidegger, we shall see, the problem of evil radically opens up the question of whether there is an originary strife, not just in human being, but in the very heart of being itself. We shall need to ask, therefore, whether Heidegger, in ascribing the origin of evil to a negativity in being itself, implicitly *justifies* evil as an ontologically necessitated errancy. We shall also need to ask whether this apparent displacement of evil from human freedom to an originary dissonant excess of being would relieve humans of the responsibility to, ever again, set themselves on the path to/of non-willing.

The Originary Dissonant Excess of Evil

> Each Da-sein is standing in the potentiality to comport itself in an evil manner. As an essential characteristic, each Da-sein always already has the potentiality-to-be-evil [*Böse-sein-können*] in relationship to what it encounters, whether or not it is always and expressly enacted. (*Z* 208–9)

> The question of the possibility and actuality of evil brings about a transformation of the question of being. (*SA* 117/97)

> *Das Unwesen* des Seyns—*das Böse*—*der Wille*. (*GA* 77:241)

The first epigraph here is from Heidegger's conversations with the psychiatrist Menard Boss in 1963, conversations in which the later Heidegger is willing to speak in the more familiar terms of the Dasein analysis of his early period, rather than in terms of his later thought of the history of being and its possible other beginning. Boss writes elsewhere: "Malice toward fellow men is a potentiality inherent in every human *Da-sein*. It is, then, yet another of the Existentials."[10] Regardless of the limitations of the language of "Existentials" for the later Heidegger's being-historical thinking, what is clearly suggested by Heidegger himself is that a "potentiality-to-be-evil" is in some sense an essential characteristic (*Wesenszug*) of human being. The question of being, then, must come to terms with this undeniable and ineradicable human potentiality-to-be-evil.

The second epigraph to this section is found in Heidegger's 1936 interpretation of Schelling's "Freiheitsschrift" as a "metaphysics of evil as the foundation of a system of freedom" (see *SA* 125ff./104ff.). Schelling attempts to explain man's freedom systematically as the decidedness for good *and* evil, that is, as "the unity of the will to essence [*Wesen*] and deformation of essence [*Unwesen*] aroused in him" (188/156). As we have seen, Heidegger interprets Schelling's attempt to incorporate freedom and evil into the *Seynsfuge* as the very "acme of [German] idealism." Yet the "acme of idealism" means not only its highest achievement, but also its limit and the point from which one can and must leap into another way of thinking. According to Heidegger, Schelling got "stranded with his philosophy in spite of everything" (117/97), and in the end fell back into "the rigidified tradition of Western thought without creatively transforming it" (194/161). Schelling ultimately failed to think the question of evil outside the onto-theological tradition of "theodicy" and its philosophical reiteration in the "systemadicy" of idealism.

Schelling was acutely aware of the philosophical temptation to "the escape of conceiving evil as nothing positive in order to save the system" (121/100), and indeed he himself "shows first of all how the system is split open by the reality of evil" (118/98). In a crucial passage near the end of the "Freiheitsschrift," Schelling's answer is to subordinate the system to the "life" of God: "In the divine understanding there is a system; however, God himself is not a system, but a life."[11] Here, comments Heidegger, "system is attributed only to one factor of the jointure of being, to existence. At the same time, a higher unity is posited and designated as 'life'" (194/161). This higher unity of the life of God would still serve the function of reconciling the opposites of "ground" (as the basis of assertion of self-will and thus evil) and "existence" (as the understanding or the will to universality). But this entails that, even when he places the "system" of understanding within the greater unifying force of "life," Schelling at best retreats from systemadicy back to theodicy. Evil must be not only possible but actual in order for "ground" and "existence" to be reconciled in the self-revelation of God as Absolute. This reconciliation would be made possible by positing from the start a predominance, an "eternal decidedness,"

of the "the will of love" over the "will of the ground," of God's "love for itself as the essence of being in general [*die Liebe zu sich selbst als Wesen des
Seyns überhaupt*]" over the dissonant excess (*Unwesen*) of evil. Evil must be
endured for the sake of realizing love as the telos of the theodicy of God's
life; "evil is metaphysically necessary" (193/160).

According to Heidegger, Schelling did not see "the necessity of an
essential step" into a thinking of the finitude of being itself. Heidegger's
fugue of being would no longer be either a theodicy or a systematic ontodicy of the Absolute; it would not guarantee a final reconciliation of
good and evil, but rather root them in an ineradicable strife in the finitude of being itself, a finitude which calls on man to assume the privilege
and pain of standing in the *Da* of *Sein* (see 195/161–62). Despite the radicality of his metaphysics of evil, Schelling did not ultimately take this step
which would inextricably inscribe non-sublatable negativity and finitude
into the abyssal heart of being itself.

Evil has long been associated with negativity. It has often been recognized that the "question of evil and thus the question of freedom
somehow have to do essentially with the question of the being of the non-
existent [*dem Seyn des Nichtseienden*]." For Heidegger, this means that "the
question of the nature of being is at the same time the question of the nature of the not and of nothingness" (122/101). But in the tradition of
onto-theology evil has been associated with negativity merely in the sense
of *privatio boni*. If the essence of being as God or the Absolute is goodness
or the Good, then evil must be understood as privation, as lack of being.
The *Unwesen* of evil is thus—in the final onto-theological analysis, or in the
final atonement chapter of the saga of onto-theodicy—revealed to be that
of an excess that can be resolved by returning to the wholeness of an essential goodness. For Heidegger, on the other hand, who inscribes negativity inextricably in the essential occurrence of being itself: "Nothing is
not nugatory, but rather is something tremendous, the most tremendous
element in the essence of being [*das Ungeheuereste im Wesen des Seyns*]"
(ibid.). This negativity, it turns out, is inherently ambivalent; it is potentially either the letting-be of a harmonious granting-in-withdrawal, or the
fury of an unleashing-in-abandonment. The *Unwesen* of evil, in any case, is
no longer that of either an inessential or dialectically necessary alienation
from an original plenum; it is an originary dissonant excess of the essencing of being itself. The ambivalent occurrence of being in its essential finitude entails the ineradicable possibility of evil.

The third epigraph to this section is a provocative yet enigmatic phrase
found in the supplementary notes to the third and last "Conversation on
a Country Path." This dialogue, entitled "Evening Conversation in a Pris-

oner of War Camp in Russia between a Younger and an Older Man" (*GA* 77:203–45), is significantly dated May 8, 1945, in other words, precisely at the end of the war of unprecedented devastation and systematically perpetrated evil, and when Heidegger's own sons were missing on the Russian front. This date is also exactly one month and one day after the date given to the original version of the conversation on *Gelassenheit* (April 7, 1945). Did Heidegger feel the need to supplement his thoughts on the difficult path to a releasement from the will with a reflection on an originary dissonant excess that inevitably returns to haunt the peace of *Gelassenheit*? Outside his interpretations of Schelling, this text is, in any case, one of the rare places where Heidegger explicitly reflects on the problem of evil.

The younger man begins the "Evening Conversation" by relating an experience of being suddenly overcome that morning by "something salutary [*etwas Heilsames*]" (205). The dialogue later turns to a consideration of pure waiting as a "letting come" of that-which-heals (*das Heilende*). Yet it first takes up for consideration the "devastation" (*Verwüstung*) that has been consuming the earth for centuries and that has culminated in the destruction of the war (211). The older man suggests that "this devastation of the earth and the accompanying negation of the human essence [*Vernichtung des Menschenwesens*] is somehow itself *das Böse*" (207). The younger man responds that "evil" here must not be thought of simply as "moral badness" or "blameworthiness" but rather as "malice" (*das Bösartige*). He then ventures the thought: "Perhaps it is in general the will itself that is evil" (208).

The older man shrinks back from this identification of the will with evil: "I shy from even presuming to suggest something so daring." The younger man responds that he only said "perhaps," and that the thought was in fact not his own, even though he had not been able to let go of it ever since it was proposed to him. Again it is stressed that the devastation is neither a result of moral badness, nor can it be countered by "moral indignation." Indeed, it is even suggested that morality may itself be a "monstrous offspring" (*Ausgeburt*) of evil, and Nietzsche's genealogy of morality is alluded to in this regard. Yet here we find Heidegger, once again, drawing on Nietzsche's account of nihilism while at the same time criticizing his "solution" of an affirmation of will to power—a solution which is said to be itself the deepest entrenchment in nihilism.

The younger man sharply criticizes Nietzsche's assertion that the will to power is "beyond good and evil."

> Yet given that the will itself would be what is evil, then the domain of pure will to power is least of all a "beyond good and evil"—if there otherwise can at all be a beyond evil. (210)

And if the will itself is what is evil, then we may surmise that there could just as little be a "beyond will." The younger man goes on a few pages later to suggest that "malice . . . might well remain a fundamental characteristic of being itself [*ein Grundzug des Seins selbst*]" (215). The older man again shrinks back: "But don't you also think that this idea, that being is in the ground of its essence malicious [*bösartig*], would be an altogether unreasonable demand on human thought?" The younger man responds that this thought is indeed difficult, particularly when one must abstain from considering it as "pessimistic" or in some other way "evaluating" it. Yet the demand that thinking be easy, he reminds his conversation partner, is itself rooted in the spirit of devastation.

What we find suggested in this dialogue is nothing less than the thought that the will itself is evil, and that "evil dwells in the essence of being" (215). The latter thought is not unique to this posthumously published text; we find it expressed in the following crucial, if also rather cryptic, lines from the "Letter on Humanism."

> Thinking conducts historical eksistence . . . into the realm of the upsurgence of healing [*des Heilens*]. . . . With healing, evil appears all the more in the clearing of being. The essence of evil does not consist in the mere badness of human action, but rather in the malice of rage. Both of these, however, healing and the raging, can essentially occur in being only insofar as being is itself what is in strife [*das Sein selber das Strittige ist*]. (*GA* 9:359/272)

The strife between healing and the raging of evil would occur within the very essencing of being itself. Negation, Heidegger writes in this context, does not arise first of all from the "willful assertion of the positing power of subjectivity," but rather "in being is concealed the essential provenance [*Wesensherkunft*] of nihilation" (ibid.).

Does the possibility of evil dwell even in the most proper essence of being as *Seinlassen*, in the granting of the *es gibt*? Apparently so, given that: "To healing being first grants ascent into grace; to raging its compulsion to disaster [*Unheil*]" (360/273). One is reminded here of Schelling's statement: "[In] this system there is only one principle for everything; it is one and the same essence [*Wesen*] . . . that rules with the will of love in the good and with the will of wrath in evil."[12] As with the final triumph of the will of love in Schelling, for Heidegger too, would the ascent into grace ultimately win out, insofar as "the world's darkening never reaches the light of being" (*GA* 13:76/4)? Would the world's darkening be justified in that it would, at the end of a *seinsgeschichtliche* ontodicy, allow the light of being to shine forth in all its radiance in a new beginning, a new dawn after the *Untergang* of the sun in the *Abendland*?

Does Heidegger's thought seek to justify the *Unwesen* of evil in the name of a higher essencing of the fugue of being? Is there reason to be suspicious of what Jean-Luc Nancy calls a "secret, imperceptible ontodicy" and even "despite everything, a secret egoity" of being? Nancy writes:

> [Is] it possible to say that the thinking of being, at least as Heidegger was able to announce it, has escaped the profound logic and tonality of the idealism of freedom, according to which freedom "for good and for evil" is first established and can only be established through evil, and must therefore, whether it wants to or not, in one way or another justify evil, which means dialecticize it, as is the case when "discord" is at best what makes "unity appear"?[13]

It is not my intention (no more than it is Nancy's) to find an unequivocal answer to this question; for Heidegger's thought itself may very well be ambivalent in this regard.[14] Is being a fugue into which all dissonance is in the end necessarily harmonized? Or does evil haunt the gift of being as its non-sublatable dissonant excess? If the former idea pulls Heidegger's thought back towards the systemadicy of idealism, the latter suggestion draws him forward into the uncharted region of thinking the essential negativity and finitude of being itself. Let us pursue here the latter course of interpretation.

Heidegger's claim that negativity originates in being itself certainly recalls one of the most radical theses of German idealism. Indeed, Heidegger makes explicit reference to idealism in this context. Yet he also goes on to mark a critical distance between his thought of the "strife in being itself" and idealism's dialectical positing and sublation (*Aufhebung*) of negativity.

> Nihilation unfolds essentially [*west*] in being itself. . . . Therefore the "not" appears in the absolute idealism of Hegel and Schelling as the negativity of negation in the essence of being. But there being is thought in the sense of absolute actuality as the unconditioned will that wills itself and does so as the will of knowledge and love. In this willing being as will to power is still concealed. (*GA* 9:360/273)

In the dialectical thinking of idealism, "nihilation comes to the fore . . . but at the same time is veiled in its essence" (ibid.). For idealism, the dissonant excess of evil would in the end be *aufgehoben* (back) into the higher unity of absolute subjectivity. The will of reason or love, in its systematic ontodicy or divine theodicy of ecstatic-incorporation, would serve to retrieve the negativity of evil back into the greater positivity of goodness.[15] Nietzsche reveals the essence of will as will to power, and thus unleashes nihilation from its containment within the dialectical circle of systematic or theocentric onto-theodicy. Here Nietzsche takes a step further toward revealing the essence of negativity as a non-sublatable dissonant excess, and yet in his mere "overturning" of idealism he understands negativity now only in the sense of an ontic struggle between a shifting plurality of egocentric centers of will to power. Heidegger would be the first to think negativity in terms of a non-sublatable strife between the *Wesen* and the *Unwesen*, the healing and the raging, occurring within being itself.

The originary "letting" of being would itself be radically ambivalent—it can offer a healing grace and it can unleash a malicious fury; and, unlike Schelling's God of love, there is no eternal decidedness between the two. If being is a child at play, this innocent game is capable of turning into both a joyous dance and a temper tantrum of rage. There is no ontodicy that guarantees that evil will be justified and returned to the greater egoity of being. If *Seinlassen* is the most profound meaning of being, this can occur not only as (1) the *es gibt* of *Ereignis* which lets the fourfold into the harmony of a mutual appropriation/expropriation, a harmony in which man belongs and to which he cor-responds by way of *Gelassenheit;* but can occur also as (2) the "unleashing" (*Loslassen*) of the *Ge-stell* as the "photographic negative of *Ereignis*" (*GA* 15:366).[16] The essence of technology is the extreme self-concealing negativity of an epochal sending-in-withdrawal of being—an *excessive Seinlassen*, a *Seinsverlassenheit* which abandons or unleashes (*loslässt*) beings into the pure "positivity" of "unbounded unconcealment," into standing-reserve for the machinations of the will to will.

Yet while there is no "eternal decidedness" to this strife in being, while there is no fated guarantee that the dissonance of machination in the epoch of the will to will shall give way to the harmony of *Seinlassen* and *Gelassenheit,* there is nevertheless a decisive sense in which *Ereignis* as the mirror-play of the fourfold is indeed more in accord with the negativity proper to being than is the technological nihilism of the *Gestell.* There is a decisive sense in which the originary essence (*Wesen*) of being is the generosity of a withdrawal that lets beings be, whereas the rage of evil is a dissonant excess (*Unwesen*) which feeds on the concealment of concealment, on the oblivion of the mystery.

Heidegger's radical thinking of negativity involves therefore—in opposition to all positivisms which deny the reality of negativity, and all nihilisms which mistake negativity as annihilation—an attempt to recollect a negativity *proper* to the event of being. Positivism and nihilism are two sides to the same coin of forgetting the negativity proper to the withdrawal of being. In *Contributions to Philosophy* Heidegger writes that metaphysics, in mistaking the nothing as "something negative," cannot think self-withdrawal and refusal as the "highest giving" that lets beings be. The nothing is either denied, attributed to the affirming/negating powers of subjectivity, or posited as a "goal" by the heroic conquerors of "pessimistic nihilism" (see *GA* 65:246–47, 266). In this epoch of obliviousness to the negativity of self-withdrawal that is of the very essence of beyng, "should we be surprised," Heidegger asks rhetorically, "if the 'nothing' is misconstrued as what is simply nugatory [*Nichtige*]?" (246).

The recovery from nihilism as an extreme abandonment of being could then, paradoxically, only come about by way of thinking the essential "noth-ing [*das Nichtende*] in beyng itself" (266). As Heidegger makes clear in "On the Question of Being," "the nothing" does not vanish by way of an overcoming of nihilism; rather, we begin to recover from nihilism when "instead of the appearance of the nugatory nothing, the essence of the nothing in its former kinship with 'being' can arrive and be accommodated among us mortals" (*GA* 9:410/309–10). Being, as the noth-ing of no-thing, essentially withdraws so that things may be; its withdrawal grants the free space wherein beings are let be. Yet the greatest danger lies in the exacerbation of the withdrawal (the expropriation) proper to this event into the excess of abandonment.[17] When withdrawal is forgotten, when concealment is concealed, beings are increasingly abandoned to the illusion of pure positivity; negativity is then falsely displaced from the proper essencing of being itself to a power of the subject to represent beings, to the will to power over beings, and finally to the nihilistic will to will which reduces beings to mere standing-reserve. Letting be as the negativity proper to the essence of being is essentially in strife with the dissonant excess of withdrawal, the abandonment of beings to nihilism.

Are humans simply "left in waiting" for the strife of being to play itself out? Or must they not rather thoughtfully prepare for a leap into an intimate participation in the play of revealing/concealing that lets beings be? "Must not the 'no' (and the 'yes') have its essential form in the Da-sein that is needed/used by beyng?" (*GA* 65:178). Does not the finitude of being, rather than simply abandoning humans to an indifferent play of forces, in fact call them forward into the freedom and response-ability of Da-sein?

Before turning to this question of freedom, we need to consider a certain disturbing limit to the Heideggerian thinking of evil as the dissonant excess of the negativity proper to being. For Heidegger's thought, the epitome of evil is the nihilism of the technological will to will. It presumably did not seem to him necessary, therefore, to single out the evil of the Holocaust; and in fact he apparently referred to it only indirectly and only on one occasion as an *Unheil,* "the German word for radical evil, disaster, total loss of grace."[18] The Holocaust would not, for Heidegger's thinking of evil, be an exceptionally unthinkable horror, but would indeed be *exemplary* of nihilism as the abandonment of beings to the *Gestell.* Thus Heidegger could, with no sign of hesitation, claim that "the motorized food industry" is "the same thing in its essence as the production of corpses in the gas chambers and the extermination camps" (*GA* 79:27). What is "scandalously inadequate"[19] here is that Heidegger's thought appears unable to mark an essential difference between the reduction of vegetables to standing-reserve for the production and consumption of foodstuffs and the lining up of persons to be systematically murdered.

Yet the diabolical horror of the Nazi camps was not simply that of the ultimate disappearance of humanity into the machinations of technology. While the Holocaust is no doubt exemplary with regard to the role that the "banality" of technological evil played in its mass exterminations, this explanation does not go far enough; it does not indicate the heart of radical evil that was exposed there, as elsewhere.[20] Presumably even the systematicity of the extermination camps could not allow the murderers to completely evade the faces of those who were murdered. I would suggest that the unfathomable depths of radical evil are exposed, not globally in an epochal dissonant excess of the negativity proper to the letting-be of beings, but singularly with the annihilation of the negativity proper to an always singular human being, that is, with the willful denial of the interiority of the sentient Other which presences in withdrawal (what Levinas calls the "face" would be the trace of this withdrawal), and which forever marks the irreducibility of living beings to mechanical automata.[21]

The abysmal root of radical evil is most brutally exposed, then, not in the *faceless defacing* technology of the extermination camps, but rather in the fact that it is possible—as was repeatedly (i.e., not simply "in mass," but time and again on singular occasions) made evident in the Nazi camps—for a person to look another person in the face and, clearly sensing the withdrawal of interiority, willfully pull the trigger, or point a finger in the direction of the gas chambers. The wickedness of this *face-to-face defacement*—this wicked will to power that wills the murder of the Other *as Other,* in other words, that wills to maintain a recognition of the Other precisely in order to take diabolical pleasure in annihilating his or her otherness—radically exceeds the evil of the calculating machinations of technology.

The problem of the technological will to will does not address this diabolical abyss of evil. The technological will to will would finally incorporate all alterity into the immanent repetitions of the cybernetic machine, wherein ultimately humans themselves would be reduced to a stockpile of resources. The wicked will to power, on the other hand, would not straightaway strip the Other of their humanity, that is, of their interiority which withdraws from the grasp of ecstatic-incorporation. The thoughtless reduction of the Other to a cog in the wheel of technological machination is not yet the wicked will to power that maintains a recognition of the alterity of the Other precisely in order to take diabolical pleasure in conquering her resistance and witnessing her pain. This terrible fact of evil cannot be explained technologically.

Heidegger's history of metaphysics, which proceeds to culminate in the technological will to will as the most extreme epoch of being, passes by the abyss of this wicked will to power. After Heidegger, therefore, we must step back to think the originary dissonant excess of ur-willing as the root potential, not just of the faceless defacing technological will to will, but also of this wicked face-to-face defacing will to power. Moreover, insofar as human freedom could not be detached from a responsibility with regard to this non-technological evil will to power, a limit in Heidegger's thinking of evil would also mark a limit in his thinking of human freedom. Bearing this significant limitation in mind, let us return to the question: what space for (the enigma of) human freedom is left in his thought?

The Enigma of Human Freedom and the Question of Responsibility

What happens to the question of human freedom and responsibility in Heidegger's step beyond idealism's system of the Absolute to a thinking of the finitude of being? Rooting the origin of evil in being itself, has Heidegger relieved humans of their burden of responsibility? In displacing the power of negation from subjectivity, did Heidegger manage to leave space in his thought for a peculiarly human freedom? In displacing freedom from the "faculty of free will," has Heidegger stripped humans of their capacity and responsibility for good and evil? Did Heidegger not just fail to think the radicality of the evil perpetrated by the Nazis, did he in fact, as Nancy asks, "silently justify Auschwitz?"[22] Did he excuse his own political decision by deferring the decisions for good and evil to the *Seinsgeschick*, or by insisting on the ontological necessity of "errancy"? If great thinkers must err greatly (*GA* 13:81/9), does their greatness then justify the evil assisted by their errancy?

Thinking with Heidegger against Heidegger here requires us to clearly distinguish, as I have attempted to do, between the ontological necessity of errancy and the inordinate excess of "letting oneself be led astray." This is not a question of excusing Heidegger's political misjudgment, much less his infamous silence after the war. Indeed, as Lacoue-Labarthe writes, his silence on the Nazi terror was "all the more unpardonable in that, when he wanted to, Heidegger could say something" about the deprivation of human liberty, as he did in a statement from 1952 in reference to an exhibition in Freiburg entitled "The Prisoners of War Speak": "We are not yet in the proper space to reflect upon freedom, nor even to speak of it, so long as we *also* close our eyes to this annihilation of freedom" (*WhD* 159).[23] Was Heidegger, who infamously almost never opened his mouth (or even his eyes?) to speak of the ghastly "annihilations of freedom" perpetrated by the Nazis, able to leave a proper space for a reflection on human freedom in his thought?

Nancy writes that after 1936 Heidegger abandoned the notion of freedom to the metaphysics of subjectivity; rather than attempting a "more originary thinking of freedom," Heidegger is said to have shifted the topic to *das Freie* or the "free space."[24] According to Heidegger, however, the freedom of subjectivity was abandoned precisely for the sake of a more originary thinking of freedom as ek-sisting in the clearing of being so as to "let beings be." In "The Essence of Truth" (published in 1943), Heidegger writes: "Man does not 'possess' freedom as a property. At best, the converse holds: freedom, ek-sistent, disclosive Da-sein, possesses man" (*GA* 9:190/145). In this apparent reversal, has man been deprived and relieved of the responsibility of freedom? This apparent reversal was also made, and indeed emphasized as a *Merksatz*, at the outset of Heidegger's 1936 interpretation of Schelling. In this context he writes:

> Schelling's treatise has nothing to do with [the so-called] question of the freedom of the will, which is ultimately wrongly put and thus not a question at all. For freedom is here, not the property [*Eigenschaft*] of man, but the other way around: Man is at best the property [*Eigentum*] of freedom. Freedom is the encompassing and penetrating essence, in which man becomes man only when he is re-anchored [*zurückversetzt*] there. That means the essence of man is grounded in freedom. But freedom itself is a determination of true being in general, a determination that surpasses all human being [*Die Freiheit selbst aber ist eine alles menschliche Seyn überragende Bestimmung des eigentlichen Seyns überhaupt*]. (*SA* 11/9)

If this amounts to "burying freedom more deeply in being" (Nancy), however, it is because humans themselves essentially ek-sist in or even as the *Da* of *Sein*. And thus, just here, where Heidegger appears to have deferred all human freedom over to freedom as a determination of being which surpasses all human being, a certain decisive "human participation in freedom" is revealed. The above passage continues: "Insofar as man *is* as man, he must participate [*teilhaben*] in this determination of being, and man *is*, insofar as he brings about this participation in freedom" (ibid). Man does not "possess" freedom as a faculty, he ek-sists in participation in it.

When Heidegger denies that nihilation, errancy, the will, and evil have their origin in ontic human doing, freedom and responsibility appear to have been deferred to being. And yet, man essentially *is* in correspondence to being, just as the essencing of being needs human participation. Hence, the apparent disappropriation of human freedom in Heidegger's rhetorical reversal is aimed only at one who has succumbed to "the opinion that this 'relation' [between beyng and Da-sein] would correspond to or even be commensurate with that between subject and object. But Da-sein has overcome all subjectivity; and beyng is never an object" (*GA* 65:252).

Let us reread here, with a certain emphasis and explication, the following line from the "Letter on Humanism":

> Nihilation unfolds essentially [*west*] in being itself, and not at all in the Dasein of man—*insofar as this Dasein is thought as* [i.e., *insofar as Dasein is mistaken as*, or, to the extent that thought corresponds to the historical determination of human-being, *insofar as Dasein exists in the errant aberration of*] *the subjectivity of the ego cogito.* (*GA* 9:360/273, emphasis added)

What is implied here is that when man recollects the essence of his Dasein, he would recover from the aberration of subjectivity and assume his essential participation in the *Wesung* of being. Thinking and being are the "same" for Heidegger, not in the sense of a simple identity, but as the belonging-together of call and response (see *ID* 90/28; *GA* 9:408/309). Would not human Dasein, therefore, also be co-responsible for the nihilation that unfolds in being? Even after the turn in Heidegger's thought, human Dasein would, then, in a sense remain existentially "guilty" and at least co-responsible for "being-the-ground of a negativity" (*SZ* 283). This "guilt" is not an original sin against the Will of an almighty being, but rather a (re)call to an originary response-ability to participate in the freedom and strife of being.

The strife in being is also experienced as a strife in human-being insofar as man authentically exists as Dasein. As I have interpreted it, this strife is that between non-willing and its originary dissonant excess of ur-willing. Humans can help release themselves into an attentive engagement in the "to and fro" of ek-sistence/in-sistence, or they can persist in

errancy to the point of letting themselves be led astray into willful subjectivity, and ultimately into the diabolical depths of evil. Evil thus originates
in the nihilating of being *in which humans essentially participate, and for
which they are in part responsible.*

Heidegger's turn to being-historical thinking, to be sure, introduces
a historical gap between modern humanity and authentic Da-sein. En-
trenched in the epoch of willful subjectivity, modern man has not yet
made the leap into Da-sein. The enigma of human freedom is redoubled
in this context, and the question of whether man is "free" to help "bring
about this participation in freedom" (*SA* 11/9) becomes the question of
whether man is "free" to participate in a (re)turning into Da-sein. Are humans free to respond to the "must" that requires them, "insofar as they
would be human" (ibid.), to participate in the freedom of being? If there
is an imperative in Heidegger's "originary ethics," it is, as Nancy puts it,
this "injunction to be ek-sistent."[25] But an injunction implies freedom to
respond, and humans would indeed have to have a freedom—however finite—to turn either toward or against an engagement in the free space of
truth; humans would have to in some sense be free to decide either to
help prepare for the leap into Da-sein, or to willfully persist in the epoch
of the will to will. At the end of Heidegger's deconstructions of the faculty
of free will and the power of self-legislation of subjectivity, the enigma of
this "incomprehensible fact of human freedom" (see *SA* 195–96/162) returns, as does the non-sublatable burden of human responsibility.

Modern humans are not yet in their proper freedom; we have not yet
assumed our proper response-ability for letting beings be. And yet do we
not have a finite freedom to let ourselves respond to the call to turn
toward this response-ability? Are we not finitely free to comport ourselves
toward the freedom of *Gelassenheit,* or, conversely, to let ourselves continue to be led astray into subjectivity, to persist in willing?

Remaining on the Way to/of *Gelassenheit*

> There is a person who has been on the road for ages, yet without
> ever leaving home; there is another who has left home, yet who is
> not on the road.
> —*The Record of Linji*[26]

With the question of a finite freedom for response-ability, we have returned once again to the central problematic of being on the way to
Gelassenheit, and once again to the aporia of how to participate in twisting
free of the fundamental (dis)attunement of the will on the way (back) to

the proper fundamental attunement of non-willing. A *Grundstimmung,* Heidegger writes, "can neither be simply brought into operation by man's will nor is it the effect of a cause issuing from beings operating on man. This displacement is beyond explanation, for all explanation falls short and comes too late" (*GA* 45:170). This inexplicable site of a decision between fundamental attunements is also the aporetic space of free decision, a freedom in which humans must participate but cannot grasp as a possession of comprehension. "There is not 'a thinking' of freedom," Nancy writes, "there are only prolegomena to a freeing of thinking."[27]

As one prolegomenon to twisting free into a thoughtful engagement in the freedom of letting-be, we have on several occasions given consideration to the paradoxical trajectory of "willing non-willing," where an immanent critique of the domain of the will enables and is enabled by intimations of a non-graspable other-than-willing. Let us recall that we were led to the question of whether perhaps, in decisively twisting free of the domain of the will, in entering into the region of non-willing as such, the very phrase "non-willing" would become unnecessary, even its radical negation of the domain of the will anachronistic. Yet now we are in a position to say why the ambiguous negativity of the phrase "non-willing" would in fact remain indispensable, and irreducible in its ambiguity. We have come to acknowledge a non-historical dissonant excess of ur-willing that frustrates any attempt to found a postepochal time of unadulterated non-willing. The will to overcome willing once and for all is self-contradictory; "pure non-willing" has become for us an oxymoron. If non-willing remains a "possibility," it is not in the sense of a potential actuality, but rather as something like a "quiet power of the possible" that enables in withdrawal (see *GA* 9:316–17/242). Non-willing enables us as a possibility only insofar as we remain under way, and this remaining under way involves in part a critically attuned "resolute openness" to the problem of ur-willing.

We are thus, in a certain sense, brought back to a *Wiederholung* of the "resolve to repeat the interruption of willing" which was developed as a fourth interpretation of *Being and Time*'s ambiguous, and in this case essentially ambivalent, notion of *Entschlossenheit.* Yet it is not now simply a matter of resolutely returning to where one started, of Dasein ever again turning in circles between its willed resolutions and its open resolve to repeat the interruption of willing. Our reading of the being-historical thinking of the later Heidegger allows us to differentiate between (1) what Heidegger calls "the will" of subjectivity, a fundamental (dis)attunement that has risen up and prevailed in a particular epochal history of metaphysics, and (2) what we have (interpretively supplementing Heidegger) called "ur-willing," a non-historical dissonant excess which haunts the proper essence of non-willing. When in-sistence hardens into persistence, and persistence strays into subjective willing, ur-willing is the ego-centripetal force of gravity in this fall (back) into willing. The strife between non-willing and ur-willing originates in the finitude of being itself—a strife in which humans essentially participate and are in part responsible—and being's *Sein(ver)lassen* can either release beings into a freedom of mutual letting-be or unleash them into a diabolical battle of wills to power.

Non-willing as such could never be a *fundamental* attunement in the sense of a "foundation" upon which "word, work, and deed . . . can be grounded, and history can begin" (*GA* 45:170). The other beginning would not be the basis for inaugurating a postepochal history free forever of the problem of willing. Non-willing would indicate not a ground, but a "way." We remain under way only by keeping one ear critically attuned to the problem of ur-willing, a dissonant excess in the fugue of being which threatens, ever and again, to draw us back toward willing, and ultimately toward willfully participating in the rage of evil.

On the other hand, remaining on the way responds not just to the interruptive call of conscience, but also to the appeal of a time-play-space beyond the metaphysical institutions of the will. This preparatory thinking would not involve dreaming of a utopian state of pure non-willing, but rather would anticipate a vigilant engagement in the strife between non-willing and ur-willing. The other beginning anticipated would be a time of awakening into *Ereignis* such that concealing no longer conceals itself and falls into oblivion; a time of released engagement in the play of ek-sistence/in-sistence; a time of attentive cultivation rather than technological challenging-forth; a time when humans no longer willfully posit themselves as lords of the earth but rather find their place in the mutual appropriation/expropriation of the fourfold (or indeed the "manyfold"). A resolve to repeat the interruption of (ur-)willing must in this manner be paired with a cor-responding thoughtful development of intimations of non-willing.

"Non-willing" would not simply, then, be a transitional term, to be discarded when the promised land beyond the will is reached; it is a word that doubly attunes our being underway. On the one hand, it indicates a *radical negation* of the domain of the will and a resolve to repeatedly interrupt (ur-)willing; on the other hand, it intimates a way of being radically *other than* willing. *Gelassenheit,* as another name for non-willing, likewise retains its double sense, as both a vigilant releasement *from* (ur-)willing, and an anticipatory releasement *into* a relation of non-willing correspondence with being as *Seinlassen.* If there is ultimately a repose of *Gelassenheit* to be found, it would be that of a traveler who has found his home on the way, his sojourn in the journey.

Notes

Introduction

1. References in text and notes to Heidegger's works are given according to the abbreviations listed at the beginning of this book.

2. See *GA* 12:99/16; and Heidegger's letter to Takehiko Kojima in *Japan und Heidegger,* ed. Harmut Buchner (Sigmaringen: Thorbecke, 1989), 223. On the modern problem of technological and cultural displacement and loss of place, see Edward S. Casey, *Getting Back into Place: Toward a Renewed Understanding of the Place-World* (Bloomington: Indiana University Press, 1993); and Bret W. Davis, "The Displacement of Modernity," *Dokkyo International Review* 14 (2001): 215–35.

3. Hans-Joachim Simm, ed., *Von der Gelassenheit: Texte zum Nachdenken* (Frankfurt am Main: Insel, 1995).

4. Andreas Nießeler, *Vom Ethos der Gelassenheit: Zu Heideggers Bedeutung für die Pädagogik* (Würzburg: Königshausen and Newmann, 1995), 22.

5. *Historisches Wörterbuch der Philosophie,* ed. Joachim Ritter (Basel/Stuttgart: Schwabe, 1974), 3:219–24. See also Nießeler, *Vom Ethos der Gelassenheit,* 15–23; Simm, *Von der Gelassenheit,* 151–55; and Jürgen Wagner, *Meditationen über Gelassenheit: Der Zugang des Menschen zu seinem Wesen im Anschluss an Martin Heidegger und Meister Eckhart* (Hamburg: Kovac, 1995), 22–27.

6. *Brockhaus: Die Enzyklopädie,* 20th ed. (Leipzig/Mannheim: F.A. Brockhaus, 1997), 8:263.

7. For what is probably the first occurrence of the term, see Meister Eckehart, *Deutsche Predigten und Traktate,* ed. and trans. Josef Quint (Munich: Carl Hanser, 1963), 91.

8. On the other hand, Heidegger warns German readers not to misunderstand the *Lassen* of *Seinlassen* in the active "causal" sense of "making" (*Machen*); it must be understood rather in the more originary sense of a "giving," *Geben* (*GA* 15:363–64/59).

9. See Michael Inwood, *A Heidegger Dictionary* (Oxford: Blackwell, 1999), 117.

10. See Nießeler, *Vom Ethos der Gelassenheit,* 21. Nießeler argues for the compatibility of *Gelassenheit* with the *vita activa,* and for its pedagogical significance, though he tends to understand it primarily as a positive sense of "leisure" (*Muße*) or as a "theoretical praxis" of stepping back which opens up possibilities for engaged activity (12, 50ff., 256ff.).

11. Wolfgang Schirmacher nevertheless attempts, in a rather loose fashion, to connect Heidegger's thought of *Gelassenheit* with Epicurus (interpreted as "an as-

cetic"), Spinoza, and Schopenhauer—figures of the Western tradition largely un-appreciated by Heidegger himself—as well as with Buddhism, Christian mysti-cism, and "the fatalism of Islam" (Schirmacher, *Technik und Gelassenheit: Zeitkritik nach Heidegger* [Freiburg/Munich: Karl Alber, 1983], esp. 26–27, 85ff.).

12. See Nießeler, *Vom Ethos der Gelassenheit*, 17.

13. Friedrich-Wilhelm von Herrmann, *Wege ins Ereignis: Zu Heideggers "Beiträgen zur Philosophie"* (Frankfurt am Main: Vittorio Klostermann, 1994), 374–75.

14. Emil Kettering, *NÄHE: Das Denken Martin Heideggers* (Pfullingen: Neske, 1987), 251.

15. See Holger Helting, *Heidegger und Meister Eckehart: Vorbereitende Überlegungen zu ihrem Gottesdenken* (Berlin: Duncker and Humblot, 1997); and chapter 5 below.

Chapter 1

1. John Sallis, *Double Truth* (Albany: SUNY Press, 1995), 1.

2. See the opening lines of the *Phaedrus* (227a).

3. Otto Pöggeler, *Martin Heidegger's Path of Thinking*, trans. Daniel Magurshak and Sigmund Barber (Atlantic Highlands, N.J.: Humanities, 1987), 288.

4. Pöggeler, *Martin Heidegger's Path of Thinking*, 288.

5. Hannah Arendt makes this claim in "Willing," part 2 of her *The Life of the Mind*, one-volume edition (San Diego: Harcourt Brace, 1978). She argues that Aristotle's notion of *proairesis* is (merely) a precursor for the faculty of the will, while the Greek notion of *orexis* remains a matter of "desire" and not will in the sense of free and deliberate choice (part 2, pp. 57ff.). Heidegger, on the other hand, at least in 1936, sees the Greek notion of *orexis*, in its connection with the representation of an object desired, as the notion which determines in advance the concept of will in the entire Western tradition culminating in German ideal-ism and in Nietzsche's will to power (*N1* 66ff./54ff.). For a helpful summary of the longstanding debate over whether there was already a concept of will in Aristotle, or whether it was only with Augustine and the Christian tradition that the faculty of will appears, see Otfried Höffe, *Aristotle*, trans. Christine Salazar (Albany: SUNY Press, 2003), 143–46. For more detailed treatments of this question and others re-lating to the standard history of the concept of "will" in Western philosophy, see Tomas Pink and M. W. F. Stone, eds., *The Will and Human Action: From Antiquity to the Present Day* (London/New York: Routledge, 2004).

6. See Richard Sorabji, "The Concept of the Will from Plato to Maximus the Confessor," in *Will and Human Action*, ed. Pink and Stone.

7. For Arendt's critical interpretation of Heidegger as purportedly opting for the faculty of thinking as *Gelassenheit* over the faculty of willing, see *Life of the Mind*, part 2, pp. 172ff.

8. The following are a few indications for pursuing a strict investigation of Heidegger's uses of the term *Grundstimmung*. Whereas in *Being and Time* Heideg-ger speaks of the "fundamental disposition" (*Grundbefindlichkeit*) of anxiety, a rad-ically individualizing and presumably non-historically determined mood, in 1929 Heidegger began to think a historical and communal sense of *Grundstimmung*. In

The Fundamental Concepts of Metaphysics Heidegger speaks of the need to awaken to the *Grundstimmung* of our age, which he describes as that of "boredom" (*Langweile*). In the 1930s Heidegger finds in Hölderlin the *Grundstimmung* of a "holy mourning" for the remoteness of the gods and our distance from the homeland. In *Contributions to Philosophy*, as in *Basic Questions of Philosophy* written around the same time (1936–38), Heidegger speaks of the *Grundstimmung* of the Greek "first beginning" as that of "wonder" (*Staunen*). He claims, however, that there can be no simple return to this inceptual wonder; the *Grundstimmung* of the anticipated "other beginning" need rather be one of "startled dismay" (*Erschrecken*). In later texts, however, he speaks of the need to reawaken a sense of wonder (see *G* 71/90). For a discussion of Heidegger's concept of *Stimmung*, see Michel Haar's article "Attunement and Thinking," in *Heidegger: A Critical Reader*, ed. Hubert L. Dreyfus and Harrison Hall (Cambridge, Mass.: Blackwell, 1992); and also chapter 2 of Haar's *The Song of the Earth: Heidegger and the Grounds of the History of Being*, trans. Reginald Lilly (Bloomington: Indiana University Press, 1993). I am thus taking a certain amount of interpretive liberty in directly connecting the notion of "fundamental attunement" with the will and with non-willing or *Gelassenheit*, although this connection shall prove to be far from arbitrary.

9. Although I set the following passages into the critical perspective of Heidegger's later writings (in particular those writings which begin with the fourth lecture course he gave on Nietzsche in 1940), it is significant to note here that in the 1936 lecture course Heidegger largely "goes along with" (Arendt's expression) Nietzsche's "positive" assessment of the will, going so far as to identify the will with his own key term "resoluteness" (*Entschlossenheit*) from *Being and Time* (see *N1* 51/41 and 57–59/46–48), and with "self-assertion" (*Selbstbehauptung*), a key term of his Rectoral Address of 1933 (see 73/61).

10. One might also use the expression "ecstatic-appropriation" to characterize this double-sided character of the will. But this would lead to confusion insofar as the word "appropriation" is used to translate what for Heidegger is fundamentally other than the will, what for him would be precisely a matter of non-willing: the appropriating-event of *Ereignis*. While Heidegger's *Ereignis* would refer to an a-propriating that would bring that which is appropriated into its own most proper (i.e., appropriate) essence, that is, would let it be, willful appropriation—which would generally be translated into German as *Aneignung*—is a matter of forcefully assimilating an other into the domain of one's own rule. That being said, one might nevertheless remain suspicious, as Derrida does, of whether Heidegger's *Ereignis* is free from all traces of a willful *Aneignung*, and of whether his event of appropriation in the end leaves room for letting the otherness of the Other be. (The theme of *Versammlung* in Heidegger's thought is a reoccurring site of critical questioning in Derrida's "Geschlecht" series of essays as well as in his *Of Spirit: Heidegger and the Question*, trans. Geoffrey Bennington and Rachel Bowlby [Chicago: University of Chicago Press, 1989].) I shall attempt to explicate and interpret Heidegger's intimations of a non-willing sense of *Ereignis* in chapter 8, before addressing in chapter 9 certain residues of a "will to unity" that remain in his later thought.

11. Emmanuel Levinas, *Totality and Infinity*, trans. Alphonso Lingis (Pitts-

burgh: Duquesne University Press, 1969), 229–30. While my own reading of the problem of the will in Heidegger has no doubt been to some extent influenced by Levinas's thought, in particular by the rigor of his attempt to think—or to mark the limits of thought in the face of—the radically Other which resists and exposes the egoism of the will, I cannot here take up his complex and critical relation to Heidegger. (To begin with, see Jacques Derrida, "Violence and Metaphysics: An Essay on the Thought of Emmanuel Levinas," in *Writing and Difference*, trans. Alan Bass [Chicago: University of Chicago Press, 1978], esp. 134ff., and chapter 9 below.) In the context of Levinas's thought, one question that would need to be asked is whether his idea of "radical passivity," more passive than a passivity opposed to activity, ultimately twists free of the very horizon of this dichotomy. For some discussion in this regard, see John Llewelyn, *The Middle Voice of Ecological Conscience: A Chiasmic Reading of Responsibility in the Neighborhood of Levinas, Heidegger, and Others* (New York: St. Martin's, 1991); and Thomas Carl Wall, *Radical Passivity: Levinas, Blanchot, and Agamben* (Albany: SUNY Press, 1999).

12. Nishitani, who studied with Heidegger in 1937–39, developed his own philosophy of Zen in part by way of dialogue with Heidegger's thought. See his *The Self-Overcoming of Nihilism*, trans. Graham Parkes with Setsuko Aihara (Albany: SUNY Press, 1990), chapter 8; and *Religion and Nothingness*, trans. Jan Van Bragt (Berkeley: University of California Press, 1982), esp. chapters 5 and 6. The influence may in fact have gone both ways, as Nishitani recalls having "explained quite a lot about the standpoint of Zen to Heidegger," and he even relates how "Heidegger would himself repeat these ideas in his lectures, only without mentioning [that they came from] Zen!" (Ban Kazunori, *Kakyō kara hanarezu: Nishitani Keiji sensei tokubetsu kōgi* [*Without Departing from Home: Special Lectures of Professor Nishitani Keiji*] [Tokyo: Sōbunsha, 1998], 189, 201).

13. Nishitani Keiji, *Shūkyō to wa nanika* (*What Is Religion?*), in *Nishitani Keiji chosakushū* (Tokyo: Sōbunsha, 1987), 10:264; Nishitani, *Religion and Nothingness*, 240 (translation modified).

14. Nishitani, *Shūkyō to wa nanika*, 266; Nishitani, *Religion and Nothingness*, 242 (translation modified).

15. I have treated Nishitani's Zen Buddhist critique of the will, and his philosophy of a radical step back to the "field of emptiness (*śūnyatā*)" as an originary dimension of non-willing, in the following works: "Nishitani Keiji ni okeru 'taiho': Nihirizumu o tōshite zettai teki shigan e" ("Nishitani Keiji's 'Step Back': Through Nihilism to the Absolute Near-Side"), in *"Kongen" e no tankyū: Kindai nihon no shūkyō shisō no yamanami* (*The Search for "Grounds": The Range of Religious Thought in Modern Japan*), ed. Hosoya Masashi (Kyoto: Kōyō Shobō, 2000); "The Step Back Through Nihilism: The Radical Orientation of Nishitani Keiji's Philosophy of Zen," *Synthesis Philosophica* 37 (2004): 139–59; "Kami no shi kara ishi no daishi e: Posuto-Niiche no tetsugakusha toshite no Nishitani Keiji" ("From the Death of God to the Great Death of the Will: Nishitani Keiji as a Post-Nietzschean Philosopher"), in *Sekai no naka no nihon no tetsugaku* (*Japanese Philosophy in the World*), ed. Fujita Masakatsu and Bret W. Davis (Kyoto: Shōwadō, 2005); and "Zen After Zarathustra: The Problem of the Will in the Confrontation Between Nietzsche and Buddhism," *Journal of Nietzsche Studies* 28 (Autumn 2004): 89–138.

16. Ryosuke Ohashi, quoting Heinrich Ott (*Denken und Sein* [Zollokon, 1959], 94) as writing that the primary characteristic of metaphysics is "Dasein's will-to-ground-itself [*Sich-selbst-Begründen-wollen*]," argues that "thinking as willing is precisely that thinking that is rooted in the domain of the will as the origin of metaphysics." According to Ohashi, the dilemma of metaphysics, which thinks transcendence within the domain of the will, is that "the more thinking *wills* to ground being, the more this metaphysical manner of representation hardens, which is precisely what bars thinking from the experience of being itself." The early Heidegger's thinking too, insofar as it remains a kind of "transcendental-horizontale Gründen-Wollen," was not yet free from this dilemma (Ohashi, *Ekstase und Gelassenheit: Zu Schelling und Heidegger* [Munich: Wilhelm Fink, 1975], 103–4).

17. David Michael Levin has attempted to critically supplement Heidegger's thought by pointing out the *embodied* dimension of awakening the fundamental attunement of *Gelassenheit*. He writes: "Heidegger speaks of the importance he attaches to the philosophical task of 'awakening' our fundamental attunement to and by the presencing of beings as a whole and being as such. But he does not explicitly recognize it is by grace of our embodiment that *Dasein* is disposed in accordance with this fundamental attunement." By translating the notion of *Befindlichkeit* (misleadingly rendered as "state-of-mind") as "our bodily felt sense of being in a situation in the world," Levin attempts to embody Heidegger's deconstructive step back to a recovery of our "primordial experiences" of being (see *SZ* 21). "At the level of intentionality," writes Levin, "this *Befindlichkeit* is primordially passive—more passive than passive, as Levinas would say. It is a bodily felt responsiveness that is called forth, solicited, in an immemorial time of origin *prior* to all reflective awareness, all forms of intentionality that express the ego-logical will. It is an attunement (*Stimmung*), an enjoinment (*Fuge, Fügung*) that reflection experiences as always already in effect, the *arkhé* of an immemorial 'dispensation' (*Geschick*) ruling over our embodiment and laying down the existential coordinates of our ontological disposition as beings bodily related to, and called into question by, the presencing (unconcealment) of being" (Levin, "The Ontological Dimension of Embodiment: Heidegger's Thinking of Being," in *The Body*, ed. Donn Welton [Oxford: Blackwell, 1999], 130–32; see also Levin's *The Opening of Vision: Nihilism and the Postmodern Situation* [London/Boston: Routledge and Kegan Paul, 1988], 35–46). The *Gelassenheit* that would recover this primordial embodied *Befindlichkeit*, writes Levin elsewhere, would be other than the duality of passivity and activity: "*Gelassenheit* is not willful; but it is a style of agency: it is not passivity, but rather a mode of comportment different from that which takes place according to the tensions in the opposition between activity and passivity" (*Opening of Vision*, 247).

Levin has written a trilogy of works attempting to phenomenologically, hermeneutically, and critically recollect this embodied fundamental attunement: *The Body's Recollection of Being* (London/Boston: Routledge and Kegan Paul, 1986); *The Opening of Vision;* and *The Listening Self: Personal Growth, Social Change, and the Closure of Metaphysics* (London/Boston: Routledge and Kegan Paul, 1989). Levin discusses *Gelassenheit* at some length in *The Opening of Vision*, 233–50, and *The Listening Self*, 223–35. According to Levin, the recollective recovery of *Ge-*

lassenheit as an embodied pre-ontological understanding of being would not be a simple regression to childhood or to the pre-modern, but rather a phenomeno-logical and hermeneutical step back that critically and creatively steps forward; it would be an appropriating retrieval (*Wiederholung*) of an originary embodied at-tunement of *Zugehörigkeit* to being that develops it into an authentic hearkening (*Horchen*). He suggests that awakening this fundamental attunement of hearken-ing, which requires the disciplined practice of *Gelassenheit*, would quite literally allow us to be more attuned to the song of sonorous beings, letting their singing resound "with the resonance of the field as a whole, gathering into their ring the song of Being itself" (*Listening Self*, 48, 257).

18. On Heidegger's early notion of the "it worlds," see Theodore Kisiel, *The Genesis of Heidegger's "Being and Time"* (Berkeley: University of California Press, 1993), chapter 1; and John van Buren, *The Young Heidegger: Rumor of the Hidden King* (Bloomington: Indiana University Press, 1994), chapter 12.

19. Llewelyn, *Middle Voice of Ecological Conscience*, 210; see also Charles E. Scott, "The Middle Voice of Metaphysics," *Review of Metaphysics* 42 (1989): 743–64. Llewelyn's and Scott's projects are in part inspired by Derrida, who attempts to re-cover a sense of the middle voice by deconstructing the linguistic legacies of West-ern metaphysics. In "Différance" Derrida writes: "[That] which lets itself be des-ignated *différance* is neither simply active nor simply passive, announcing or rather recalling something like the middle voice, saying . . . an operation that cannot be conceived either as passion or as the action of a subject on an object. . . . For the middle voice, a certain intransitivity, may be what philosophy, at its outset, distrib-uted into an active and a passive voice, thereby constituting itself by means of this repression" (Derrida, *Margins of Philosophy*, trans. Alan Bass [Chicago: University of Chicago Press, 1982], 9).

Heidegger lamented that "Western languages are languages of metaphysical thinking, each in its own way. It must remain an open question whether the essence of Western languages is in itself marked permanently by onto-theo-logic, or whether these languages offer other possibilities of utterance" (*ID* 142/73). Could the middle voice of non-metaphysical thinking be more successfully thought in Chinese and Japanese? On this question, see Rolf Elberfeld, *Phänome-nologie der Zeit im Buddhismus: Methoden interkulturellen Philosophierens* (Stuttgart: Frommann-Holzboog, 2004), 85–120, esp. 99–101 and 113–17. Elberfeld proposes the provocative thesis that "the basic mood of the verb in Classical Chinese is the middle voice," a thesis that can be formulated even more precisely with respect to Classical Japanese in light of its explicit grammatical form of *jihatsukei*, which El-berfeld aptly translates as the "Form der Autogenese" (100, 113).

20. Llewelyn goes so far as to suggest that "the non-naming of *Gelassenheit* is called for by *Gelassenheit*. For *Gelassenheit* is the way in which the thinking of lan-guage and the language of thinking are released from being the domination of and by denomination and assertive pro-position into letting things be" (Llewelyn, *Middle Voice of Ecological Conscience*, 236). Heidegger might respond, however, that a *poetic* naming is called for in order to let things be. "By naming," Heidegger writes, "we call on what is presencing to arrive" (*WhD* 85/120). Heidegger devel-ops this thought elsewhere by commenting on a line from the poet Stefan George:

"Where the word breaks off no thing may be." He interprets this to mean: "Only where the word for the thing has been found is the thing a thing. Only thus *is* it. Thus we must stress: no thing *is* where the word, that is, the name is lacking. The word alone gives being to the thing" (*GA* 12:154/62). Naming as such would then not be the problem; the question would be how to let naming happen non-willing(ly). Does "non-willing" properly name *Gelassenheit* and vice versa?

21. The term "twisting free" is David Farrell Krell's translation of Heidegger's term *Herausdrehung*, and has been explicated by John Sallis to imply "not merely inversion but also displacement" (Sallis, *Echoes: After Heidegger* [Bloomington: Indiana University Press, 1990], 77). While the context of both Heidegger's use and Sallis's interpretive development of the term is that of Nietzsche's inversion and twisting free of the opposition between the sensory and the supersensory worlds, I shall use this term in the context of not merely inverting but displacing the will. The notion of "twisting free" will be particularly important in the context of attempting to think the difficult transition out of (the domain of) the will. Also relevant here is the "double gesture" involved in Derrida's deconstruction of binary oppositions. He explains this strategy as follows: "On the one hand, we must traverse a phase of *overturning*. . . . [On] the other hand—to remain in this phase is still to operate on the terrain of and from within the deconstructed system. By means of this double, and precisely stratified, dislodged and dislodging, writing, we must also mark the interval between inversion, which brings low what was high, and the irruptive emergence of a new 'concept,' a concept that can no longer be, and never could be, included in the previous regime" (Derrida, *Positions,* trans. Alan Bass [Chicago: University of Chicago Press, 1981], 41–42). Non-willing would not merely invert the priority of activity over passivity within the domain of the will, but would indicate a way of being that breaks out of this horizonal regime of activity/passivity as such.

22. Nietzsche quotes in this regard the following passage from Thomas Aquinas: "In order that the bliss of the saints may be more delightful for them . . . it is given to them to see perfectly the punishment of the damned" (Thomas Aquinas, *Summa Theologiae,* III, Supplementum, Q. 94, Art. 1, as translated by Walter Kaufmann in *Basic Writings of Nietzsche* [New York: Random House, 1968], 485). In this study I cite Nietzsche's works according to part and/or section number. I have referred to the original texts in *Sämtliche Werke, Kritische Studienausgabe in 15 Einzelbänden,* 2nd ed., ed. Giorgio Colli and Mazzino Montinari (Munich: Deutscher Taschenbuch, 1988); and *Der Wille zur Macht* (Stuttgart: Kröner, 1996). I have generally used, with occasional modifications, the translations by Walter Kaufmann in *The Portable Nietzsche* (New York: Penguin Books, 1982) and *Basic Writings of Nietzsche,* and by Walter Kaufmann and R. J. Hollingdale in *The Will to Power* (New York: Vintage Books, 1967).

23. Nietzsche, *The Antichrist,* section 26. Much of Nietzsche's *Genealogy of Morals* is devoted to a critique of what I would call covert-willing.

24. Nietzsche, *The Will to Power,* section 382.

25. Heidegger, in point of in fact, consistently downplays Schopenhauer's significance, as an influence on Nietzsche and in general as a major figure in the history of philosophy (i.e., the history of metaphysics). He stresses that it is inad-

equate to "grasp Nietzsche's notion of the will as the reversal of the Schopenhauerian" (*N1* 44/34), inasmuch as the will to power is no mere "blind striving."
In my opinion, however, the continuity between Schopenhauer's and Nietzsche's
conceptions of the will is greater than Heidegger allows for, though I will not attempt to demonstrate this here. I shall also defer to another occasion the question
of an unacknowledged influence of Schopenhauer—as the first modern to understand the will wholly negatively (as opposed to its ambivalence in Schelling)—on
Heidegger's own critical turn from the will. Of course, Nietzsche's doctrine of the
will to power is indeed no "simple reversal" of Schopenhauer's denial of the will-
to-live, and Heidegger's thought of *Gelassenheit* is even less a "simple appropriation" of Schopenhauer's philosophy of renunciation.

26. Arthur Schopenhauer, *Sämtliche Werke*, vol. 1, *Die Welt als Wille und Vorstellung
1* (Frankfurt am Main: Suhrkamp, 1986), 423; Arthur Schopenhauer, *The World as
Will and Representation*, vol. 1, trans. E. F. Payne (New York: Dover, 1969), 308.

27. Nietzsche, *The Will to Power*, section 1067; see also sections 685 and 693;
and *Beyond Good and Evil*, section 36; and *Thus Spoke Zarathustra*, part 2, section 12.
In this study I shall generally have to restrict my treatment of Nietzsche to a focus
on his philosophy of the will to power as a target of Heidegger's critique of the will,
without exploring the more subtle aspects of Nietzsche's "self-overcoming of the
will to power." For a detailed treatment of the profound ambivalences in Nietzsche's philosophy of the will to power, see my "Zen After Zarathustra: The Problem
of the Will in the Confrontation Between Nietzsche and Buddhism." Referring to
a passage where Nietzsche speaks of the "strong will power" required for "learning to see—habituating the eye to repose, patience, to letting things come to it . . .
the essence of which is precisely *not* to 'will'" (*Twilight of the Idols*, part 8, section
6), D. F. Krell has provocatively suggested that aspects of Nietzsche's thought
should even be read as "an unsung precursor of Heidegger's *Gelassenheit*" (Krell,
Intimations of Mortality, 136).

28. Schopenhauer, *Die Welt als Wille und Vorstellung*, 1:515; Schopenhauer, *The
World as Will and Representation*, 1:379.

29. Schopenhauer gives only the barest hints of a possible reaffirmation of the
world after the complete renunciation of the will-to-live. "[We] freely acknowledge that what remains after the complete abolition of the will is, *for all who are still
full of the will*, assuredly nothing. But also conversely, to those in whom the will has
turned and denied itself, this very real world of ours with all its suns and galaxies,
is—nothing" (ibid., 558/411–12, emphasis added). If we were to completely give
up the will, Schopenhauer claims, "all the signs would change," and that which we
can now only refer to negatively as a "nothing" would show itself as that which truly
exists (556/410). Nevertheless, for the most part firmly remaining in "the spirit of
that against which it is 'anti,'" Schopenhauer's philosophy of resignation scarcely
develops any genuine intimations of a non-willing way of being-in-the-world.

30. Nietzsche, *Genealogy of Morals*, Third Essay, section 13.

31. Quoted in David Loy, *Nonduality: A Study in Comparative Philosophy* (New
Haven: Yale University Press, 1988), 314.

32. Even with the formulation of Kant's categorical imperative that commands one to treat others always as ends and never merely as means, there remains

the question of where we get our idea of the proper end for an other. If it is from within our own subjectivity, from the rationality of our own "good will," does not even this respect for the other as an end in him- or herself harbor the danger of imperialistic incorporation? For a treatment which sees in Kant's notion of "respect for each person as an end in itself" a source for an "ethics of *Gelassenheit*"— despite the fact that Kant is said to have "badly misstated his case by treating each individual as an instance of the law, so that it is the law . . . which endows each individual with his worthiness for respect"—see John Caputo, *Radical Hermeneutics* (Bloomington: Indiana University Press, 1987), 265–66. On the question of whether there must be a kind of "good will" involved in any genuine attempt to understand the other, or whether it is precisely this "will to understand" that does not let the otherness of the other be, see the debate between Gadamer and Derrida's thought gathered in the volume *Dialogue and Deconstruction*, ed. Diane P. Michelfelder and Richard E. Palmer (Albany: SUNY Press, 1989); see also David Wood, *Philosophy at the Limit* (London: Unwin Hyman, 1990), chapter 7.

33. In the course of this study of the problem of the will in Heidegger's thought, some consideration is given to the "will" in certain thinkers with whom he engages. For example, on Heidegger's problematical appropriation of Kant's practical philosophy of will, see chapter 3; on his engagement with Schelling's philosophy of primal willing and the divine will of love, see chapter 4; on the problem of "God's Will" in Heidegger and Meister Eckhart, see chapter 5.

Chapter 2

1. In private letters Heidegger went so far as to say: "Sein und Zeit war eine Verunglückung" (from Heidegger's 1942 correspondence to Max Kommerell as quoted in Günter Figal, *Martin Heidegger zur Einführung*, 3rd ed. [Hamburg: Junius, 1999], 48; Figal also quotes a letter to Elisabeth Blochmann in which Heidegger speaks of "die große Unvorsichtigkeit" involved in the book). As is well known, in 1926 *Being and Time* had to be quickly assembled in truncated form (missing its third division and entire second part) in an attempt to justify promoting Heidegger to the position of *Ordinariat* at the University of Marburg. For Heidegger's recollection of the rush to publish *Being and Time*, see *ZSD* 87–88/80. Ironically, the success of the book often led to its being misunderstood as representing the magnum opus of Heidegger's philosophical doctrine, rather than as an important yet incomplete—and inherently ambiguous—early way-station on his path of thought.

2. See, for example, "Plato's Doctrine of Truth," where Heidegger argues that what "remains unsaid in Plato's thinking is a change in what determines the essence of truth," namely, from unconcealment to correctness (*GA* 9:203/155, 231/177). The unsaid that I am tracking in *Being and Time,* however, is not so much that of a unidirectional transformation as that of an ambivalent oscillation which makes possible quite different, even mutually opposing, directions of later development.

3. Van Buren, *The Young Heidegger,* 99.

4. Kisiel, *Genesis of Heidegger's "Being and Time,"* 67.

5. Ibid., 226; see 301 for an account of where Heidegger finds this "middle-voiced ambiguity of action and passion" in Aristotle.

6. Charles Scott, "The Middle Voice in *Being and Time*," in *The Collegium Phaenomenologicum: The First Ten Years*, ed. John Sallis et al. (Dordrecht: Kluwer, 1988), 161.

7. Scott, "Middle Voice in *Being and Time*," 162.

8. We find a similar attack on the idea of knowing as not-willing in the early Heidegger's critique of the Rankean conception of the role of the historian as one of "self-extinguishment" (*Selbstauslöschung*), that is, as a matter of completely "suspending one's judgments" in order to disclose the pure facts of history. Charles R. Bambach, in his study of the relation of Heidegger's thought to the tradition of historicism, shows Heidegger's debt in this regard to Nietzsche's early essay "On the Advantage and Disadvantage of History for Life" (Bambach, *Heidegger, Dilthey, and the Crisis of Historicism* [Ithaca: Cornell University Press, 1995], 215ff.). The later Heidegger, however, criticizes Nietzsche's (and by implication his own earlier) conception of knowing as will and decision, without, however, simply reinstating the ideal of self-extinguishing objectivism. The proper human correspondence with the history of being must be understood otherwise than as either active willing or passive not-willing.

9. In this sense it is true, as Richard Wolin claims, that "the relationship of the early Heidegger to the legacy of philosophical subjectivism is itself aporetic" (Wolin, *The Politics of Being: The Political Thought of Martin Heidegger* [New York: Columbia University Press, 1990], 37). Wolin, however, while claiming that "the logic of *Being and Time* oscillates indecisively pro and contra the heritage of philosophical subjectivism" (ibid.), makes only passing reference to Heidegger's critique of subjective representation and no attempt to explicate the elements of a radical problematization of willful subjectivity in the text. Rather, Wolin spends most of his effort in the attempt to show that *Being and Time* essentially consists of a philosophy of decisionism and voluntarism. And while he also finds that the text "at a pivotal juncture, wittingly lapses into a type of secularized mystical fatalism" (43)—an issue to which I shall return in the following chapter—he concludes by simply stating that "the opposition between voluntarism and fatalism in *Being and Time* is never reconciled" (62–63). Without denying problematical elements of ambiguity in this regard, I shall show that the text does not *only* flip-flop between such extremes within the domain of the will; its relation to the will is far more complex and also involves moments of a radical critique.

10. Richard Polt, in his *Heidegger: An Introduction* (Ithaca: Cornell University Press, 1999), argues that: "Despite some misleading formulations" (Polt remarks: "Sometimes he even refers to ready-to-hand entities as 'entities,' pure and simple . . . [such that it] . . . appears that the environment *is* the world" [55]), "Heidegger does not want to claim that everything we do is for the sake of a product, or that the Being of the environment, the instrumental world, is equivalent to worldhood in general" (50). "In fact," Polt continues in a footnote, "it is a recurrent theme in Heidegger's writings that traditional ontology is unwittingly and in-

appropriately based on the activity of production" (Polt cites in this regard Hei-degger's 1927 text *Basic Problems of Phenomenology*, *GA* 24:148/105). But it remains a question whether or to what degree a critique of what Michael Zimmerman has called "productionist metaphysics" was already at play in *Being and Time*. Hubert Dreyfus attempts to show that *Being and Time*'s treatment of both "nature" and things as "equipment" are in fact prototypical examples of precisely the techno-logical revealing (and concealing) of the world that is the target of the later Hei-degger's critique (Dreyfus, "Heidegger's History of the Being of Equipment," in *Heidegger: A Critical Reader*, ed. Dreyfus and Hall). Zimmerman responds to and qualifies to some extent Dreyfus's charges in his "Being and Time: Penultimate Stage of Productionist Metaphysics?" (chapter 10 of his *Heidegger's Confrontation with Modernity: Technology, Politics, Art* [Bloomington: Indiana University Press, 1990]).

11. I will return in the following chapter to consider some important points with regard to the brief but significant passages in *Being and Time* that deal with "being-with" other Daseins.

12. Polt would interject here that Heidegger "never describes our relation to tools in terms of imposing our will on things," and that the language of "freeing" and "letting something be involved" in *Being and Time* should even be read as fore-shadowing his later concept of *Gelassenheit* (Polt, *Heidegger: An Introduction*, 58). And yet, without denying an element of such foreshadowing, it is hard to deny that a long shadow of the will still distinctly looms over the idea of disclosing things as first of all tools in an environment structured by Dasein's projection of a *Worum-willen*.

13. It is interesting to note in passing here that in a 1963 discussion with Menard Boss (who sought to develop a new method of psychoanalysis out of Hei-degger's Dasein-analysis), Heidegger repeats the claim that "willing" must be un-derstood from the "structure of care." Here it is a question of countering the re-ductionism of Freudian libido theory (*Z* 217). In his conversations with Boss, Heidegger not only frequently lets himself be drawn back into the language of *Being and Time*, but he is also willing to use once again the everyday, if metaphysi-cally suspect, language of will. In a comment from 1968 he states: "Willing belongs to freedom, to being-free for a claim to which I respond. Then claim is the motive for willing. I only will when I am engaged in a motive [*Ich will nur, wenn ich mich ein-lassen auf den Beweggrund*], when I take it over, accept it" (274). These comments, however, are perhaps best seen as occasional and pedagogical rather than as inte-gral moments of his evolving thought on the problematic of the "will" per se.

14. Tsujimura Kōichi makes this claim as follows: "What kind of comportment (*Verhaltung*) underlies this kind of formation of the horizon of the future with the character of an *Umwillen*? This 'attitude' Heidegger names . . . with the term 'will,' to be taken in a particular sense. Projecting the *Umwillen* out in front or beyond oneself takes place on the field of this 'will.' . . . In the sense that this 'will' forms [Dasein's] transcendence, there should be no objection to calling it a *transcenden-tal 'will'* (Tsujimura, *Haideggā ronkō* [*Heidegger Studies*] [Tokyo: Sōbunsha, 1971], 90–91).

15. In this regard, note Hannah Arendt's claim that in the first part of Heidegger's lectures on Nietzsche (1936), "the Will takes the place ascribed to Care in the earlier work" (Arendt, *Life of the Mind,* part 2, p. 176).

16. Gadamer raises the following series of questions in this regard: "Is the concretization of the factical consummation of Dasein in the form of 'care' really capable—as it is claimed—of leaving behind the ontological anticipation [*Vorgreiflichkeit*] of transcendental subjectivity and thinking temporality as being? Care is ultimately a concern about one's self, just as consciousness is certainly selfconsciousness. . . . Meanwhile, what is the authentic temporality of care? Does it not appear as a self-temporalization?" (Hans-Georg Gadamer, *Heidegger's Ways,* trans. John W. Stanley [Albany: SUNY Press, 1994], 178). Also note in this context Heidegger's statement in "The Essence of Ground": "Selfhood is never relative to a 'you,' but rather—because it first of all makes all this possible—is neutral with respect to being an 'I' and being a 'you,' and above all with respect to such things as sexuality" (*GA* 9:157–58/122). The "neutrality" of Dasein in this text is another earmark for its suspected affinity to the idea of a transcendental subject which, in its non-individuality and genderlessness, precedes and makes possible empirical subjects. This lies in tension with the emphasis in *Being and Time* on *Jemeinigkeit* and the radical individuation involved in the experience of running ahead to one's own death. This emphasis on individuality, which wanes in the 1930s, is a marked counterthrust to the transcendental subjectivity of idealism, and echoes Kierkegaardian existentialism. Yet, regardless of how we square this *Jemeinigkeit* with Dasein's "neutrality," problems relating to the will remain. Indeed, the tendency toward a radical individuation of Dasein in *Being and Time* could itself be read as a residue of the solipsistic tendency of modern subjectivity. (See Ishikura Jun, "Zenki Haideggā no tetsugakuteki tachiba" ["The Early Heidegger's Philosophical Standpoint"], *Shūkyōtetsugaku Kenkyū* 8 [1991]: 75–77.) A critique of the "individualism" of Heidegger's early notion of authenticity, and of his relative lack of attention to the authentic dimension of *Mitsein,* has been a frequent theme in Japanese interpretations of Heidegger since Watsuji Tetsurō. (See *Watsuji Tetsurō's Rinrigaku: Ethics in Japan,* trans. Yamamoto Seisaku and Robert Carter [Albany: SUNY Press, 1996], esp. chapters 10 and 11.)

17. "All 'it was' is a fragment, a riddle, a dreadful accident—until the creative will says to it, 'But thus I willed it'" (Nietzsche, *Thus Spoke Zarathustra,* part 2, section 20). See also *WhD* 38ff./93ff., and chapter 6 below, where I consider the later Heidegger's critical treatment of this idea of overcoming "the spirit of revenge" by "willing backwards."

18. See van Buren, *The Young Heidegger,* 321, who traces this critique of deference to *das Man* back to Heidegger's pre-*Being and Time* writings.

19. See Inwood, *A Heidegger Dictionary,* 186ff.; and *Etymologisches Wörterbuch des Deutschen,* 5th ed. (Munich: Deutscher Taschenbuch, 2000; Berlin: Akademie, 1993), 288.

20. See *Etymologisches Wörterbuch des Deutschen,* 288.

21. See John Sallis's translator's footnote in *Pathmarks,* 373. Sallis, however, stresses that Heidegger here (the note is appended to the line quoted from "On the Essence of Truth" in my previous paragraph) does *not* take the prefix in this

sense, but rather as privation. Thus *entschlossen* signifies in that text, Sallis writes, "just the opposite of that kind of 'resolve' in which one makes up one's mind in such a fashion as to close off all other possibilities: it is rather a kind of keeping *un-closed*." This is certainly true of the term in this later text (published in 1943). The question for us at the moment is whether, or rather to what extent, the term already unambiguously had this meaning in *Being and Time*.

22. Sallis's conversation with Heidegger was recorded in a notebook dated June 2, 1975, and the comments cited here were related to me in personal correspondence, dated August 26, 1996.

23. Jean-Paul Sartre, *Essays in Existentialism*, ed. Wade Baskin (New York: Citadel, 1968), 35–36.

24. Michel Haar, *Heidegger and the Essence of Man*, trans. William McNeill (Albany: SUNY Press, 1993), 15. We shall return in a moment to note Haar's own (partial) qualification of this critique in his chapter entitled "The Call of Conscience, or the Limits of Dasein's Self-Appropriation of Its Possibilities."

25. Complicating matters here is the problem of dating these texts and their revisions. The edition of the text of "The Origin of the Work of Art" included in *Holzwege* and now in volume 5 of the *Gesamtausgabe* was published in 1960, and is said to be "a new, slightly revised edition of the essay by the same title that appeared in . . . 1950 . . . which itself went through several printings and some changes" (*Poetry, Language, Thought*, xxiii; compare *GA* 5:377). The comment in *Introduction to Metaphysics* was added "some time prior to" 1953, and ends with the note: "See my lecture 'On the Essence of Truth,' 1930." Yet while the "Essence of Truth" does indeed contain important discussions of freedom as "letting-be," this essay is itself very difficult to date. It was first published in 1943, and although its earliest version does date back to a lecture from 1930, the content of its 1943 published version is too rich with the expressions and thought of the later Heidegger to simply assign it this early date. Unfortunately, the changes which Heidegger made to these texts are not recorded in the *Gesamtausgabe* edition of his works, which is expressly not a "historical-critical edition," but rather a "from the last hand edition" (*Ausgabe letzter Hand*). This has made it difficult to precisely determine the development of Heidegger's thought in some cases, and certain aspects of his turn through and away from the will in the transitional decade of the 1930s are a case in point. The emphatic (and repeated) wording of the editor's justification for this *letzter Hand* method may be thought to be ironic in this case: "It remains decisive that in [the collected edition] *the will of the author . . . is realized*" (*GA* 5:381). But what if the "will" of the author in his later years included a desire to cover over the "it was" of the "willful" aspects of his earlier thought, and to do so by reinterpreting the expressions of "will" in these texts so as to make them appear—in their "essence," or at least according to their "fundamental experience"—to be already unequivocally speaking of non-willing?

26. This passage goes on to give Heidegger's own account of the turn in his thought: "The adequate execution and completion of this other thinking that abandons subjectivity is surely made more difficult by the fact that in the publication of *Being and Time* the third division of the first part, 'Time and Being,' was held back. . . . Here everything is turned around [*Hier kehrt sich das Ganze um*]."

The section in question was held back because thinking failed in the adequate saying of this turning [*Kehre*] and did not succeed with the help of the language of metaphysics. . . . This turning is not a change of standpoint from *Being and Time*, but in it the thinking that was sought first arrives at the locality of that dimension out of which *Being and Time* is experienced, that is to say, experienced from the fundamental experience of the oblivion of being" (*GA* 9:327–28/249–50). Here Heidegger, on the one hand, admits at least that the turn (wherein "everything is turned around" and the abandonment of subjectivity completed) was not adequately carried out in *Being and Time*, and suggests that the reason for this failure was that the language of the book remained tethered to the tradition of metaphysics. On the other hand, he claims that the turn is not an abandonment of the basic standpoint of *Being and Time*, but rather a more radical return to the "locality of that dimension out of which *Being and Time* is experienced." And yet, recalling that Heidegger himself, perhaps more than anyone else, has taught us the intimate bonds between language, thought, and experience, we must ask whether the ambiguity of *Being and Time* can in fact be explained (away) as simply a matter of the tension between its fundamental experience and the expression thereof, or whether it must be understood in terms of that dimension wherein (the) language and experience (of metaphysical subjectivity, that is, of will) are intertwined.

27. Haar, *Heidegger and the Essence of Man*, 55–56.

28. Ibid., xxviii.

29. Ibid., 3.

30. Ibid., 10.

31. Nietzsche, *Thus Spoke Zarathustra*, part 3, section 1.

32. Haar, *Heidegger and the Essence of Man*, 16.

33. Ohashi, *Ekstase und Gelassenheit*, 102.

34. Ibid., 96.

35. Ibid., 86.

36. Georg Wilhelm Friedrich Hegel, *Phänomenologie des Geistes*, Werke 3, 6th ed. (Frankfurt am Main: Suhrkamp, 1998), 36; G. W. F. Hegel, *Hegel's Phenomenology of Spirit*, trans. A. V. Miller (New York: Oxford University Press, 1952), 19.

37. This was quoted (and commented on in a positive manner) by Heidegger from Hegel's *Phenomenology of Spirit* in *N1* 74/61.

38. Derrida makes the distinction between the "book," as the "idea of a totality . . . of signifiers," in contrast to the more open-ended (disseminated and disseminating) notion of "text" (Jacques Derrida, *Of Grammatology*, trans. Gayatri Chakravorty Spivak [Baltimore: Johns Hopkins University Press, 1976], 18). See also Charles E. Scott, *The Language of Difference* (Atlantic Highlands, N.J.: Humanities, 1987), chapter 3, for an account of how the radical finitude exposed in its own text serves to overturn the very systematic structure of the "book" *Being and Time*.

39. Charles E. Scott, *The Question of Ethics: Nietzsche, Foucault, Heidegger* (Bloomington: Indiana University Press, 1990), 99–100.

40. Scott, *The Question of Ethics*, 109.

41. See Michael E. Zimmerman, *Eclipse of the Self: The Development of Heidegger's Concept of Authenticity*, rev. ed. (Athens: Ohio University Press, 1986), 76.

42. Haar, *Heidegger and the Essence of Man*, 24.

43. Scott, *The* Question *of Ethics,* 99–100. As we shall see in the following chapter, however, in 1933–34 Heidegger fails to maintain this resolve to repeat the interruption of communal will. Moreover, he reportedly stated in his summer 1934 "Logic" lectures that "resoluteness [*Entschlossenheit*] has its own constancy in itself, so that it is hardly necessary for me to repeat the resolution [*Entschluss*]. If I must repeat the resolution, that just proves that I am not yet resolved [*noch nicht entschlossen*]" (*GA* 38:77).

44. Kusumoto Bunyū, *Zengonyūmon* (*Introduction to Zen Terms*) (Tokyo: Daihōrinkaku, 1982), 04.

45. Quoted by Heidegger in *EHD* 165/189.

46. For an introduction to the Kyoto School, see Bret W. Davis, "The Kyoto School," in *The Stanford Encyclopedia of Philosophy* (spring 2006 edition), ed. Edward N. Zalta, http://plato.stanford.edu/archives/spr2006/entries/kyoto-school.

47. Nishitani, *Nishitani Keiji chosakushū,* 10:108; Nishitani, *Religion and Nothingness,* 96 (translation modified).

48. Ueda Shizuteru, *Basho: Nijūsekainaisonzai* (*Place: Twofold Being-in-the-World*) (Tokyo: Kōbundō, 1993), 53–54.

49. Ueda, *Basho,* 58–59.

50. Ibid., 64. Elsewhere Ueda discusses the later Heidegger's thought of *Gelassenheit* from the perspective of *Gelassenheit* in the practice and thought of Zen. See Shizuteru Ueda, "Gelassenheit im Zen-Buddhismus," in *Arbeit und Gelassenheit,* ed. Ernesto Grassi and Hugo Schmale (Munich: Wilhelm Fink, 1994).

51. Shidō Bunan, *Shidō Bunan Zenji shū* (*Collected Writings of Zen Master Shidō Bunan*), ed. Kōda Rentarō (Tokyo: Shunjūsha, 1968), 31. Nishitani in fact compares this thought to a line from Abraham a Sankta Clara that Heidegger quotes in an address from 1964 (*GA* 16:598–608): "A man who dies before he dies, does not die when he dies" (Nishitani Keiji, "Reflections on Two Addresses by Martin Heidegger," in *Heidegger and Asian Thought,* ed. Graham Parkes [Honolulu: University of Hawaii Press, 1987], 152).

52. See note 14 for this chapter.

53. See Tsujimura, *Haideggā Ronkō,* 95. Does Heidegger himself intimate this attunement deeper than anxiety when in 1929 he writes: "The anxiety of those who are daring cannot be opposed to joy or even to the comfortable enjoyment of tranquilized bustle. It stands—this side of all such opposition—in secret alliance with the cheerfulness and gentleness of creative longing" (*GA* 9:118/93)? Or would even this "longing" (*Sehnsucht*), as a searching (*Suchen*) for what one does not yet possess, still remain on the horizon of what Buddhism calls "craving" (*tanhā*)?

54. Nishitani, *Nishitani Keiji chosakushū,* 10:276; Nishitani, *Religion and Nothingness,* 251 (translation modified). Nishitani's philosophy is as an attempt to "overcome nihilism by way of passing through nihilism" (*Nishitani Keiji chosakushū,* 20:192), and he interprets nihilism in Zen terms as the Great Doubt (*daigi*) of the modern age (see ibid., 11:185). According to Nishitani's thought, then, it is only by stepping back *through* nihilism as a kind of Great Death that we can reach a more originary freedom from and other than the will.

55. See Dōgen, *Shōbōgenzō*, ed. Mizuno Yaoko (Tokyo: Iwanami, 1990), 1:28–29; Dōgen, *The Heart of Dōgen's Shōbōgenzō*, trans. Norman Waddell and Masao Abe (Albany: SUNY Press, 2002), 19–20.

56. There are, to be sure, many pitfalls on the Zen path to non-willing as well. Its radical negation of the will undoubtedly can and has been misunderstood and misused as a call for deferred-willing and as a mask for covert-willing. While a consideration of such abuses is beyond the scope of the present work, as in the case with the Heidegger controversy, it is necessary both to critically throw out the bathwater and to (thereby) thoughtfully preserve the baby. See Brian Victoria, *Zen at War* (New York: Weatherhill, 1997); Christopher Ives, *Zen Awakening and Society* (Honolulu: University of Hawaii Press, 1992); James. W. Heisig and John C. Maraldo, eds., *Rude Awakenings: Zen, the Kyoto School, and the Question of Nationalism* (Honolulu: University of Hawaii Press, 1994); and for my own contribution to the debate surrounding the wartime political writings of Nishitani, "Shūkyō kara seiji e, seiji kara shūkyō e: Nishitani Keiji no tenkai" ("From Religion to Politics and Back to Religion: Nishitani's Turn"), in *Higashiajia to tetsugaku* (*East Asia and Philosophy*), ed. Fujita Masakatsu et al. (Kyoto: Nakanishiya, 2003).

57. See my works on Zen Buddhism and Nishitani cited above in note 15 to chapter 1, in particular "Zen After Zarathustra: The Problem of the Will in the Confrontation Between Nietzsche and Buddhism"; and "Kami no shi kara ishi no daishi e: Posuto-Niiche no tetsugakusha toshite no Nishitani Keiji" ("From the Death of God to the Great Death of the Will: Nishitani Keiji as a Post-Nietzschean Philosopher").

58. Nishitani, Tsujimura, and others have provocatively used many terms from the Zen Buddhist tradition to translate Heidegger's texts, one example of which is the term *hōge* (casting down) used to translate Eckhart's as well as Heidegger's *Gelassenheit*. On the notion of *hōge* in the Zen tradition, see Kusumoto, *Zengonyūmon*, 45–47, 192–94. Ohashi compares Heidegger's *Gelassenheit* with Dōgen's *datsuraku* ("dropping off," or, as Ohashi translates it, *Fallen-lassen*) in *Ekstase und Gelassenheit*, 169–78. Tanabe Hajime interpreted Heidegger's notion of being-towards-death in connection with the Great Death of Zen. (See Tanabe Hajime, *Philosophy as Metanoetics*, trans. Takeuchi Yoshinori [Berkeley: University of California Press, 1986], 162ff.) Taking his own primary impetus from Shinran's Pure Land Buddhism of Other-power (*tariki*), rather than from a so-called Zen standpoint of "self-power" (*jiriki*), Tanabe attempts to think a "total passivity" that breaks through the very dualism of activity and passivity to a "dharmic naturalness (*jinen-hōni*) beyond the opposition of self and other." In this manner he attempts to think an "Other-power *qua* self-power" and a "passivity *qua* activity" (*Philosophy as Metanoetics*, 30, 103). In his final years, in his attempt to articulate a "philosophy of death," Tanabe returned both to a profound appreciation of Zen and to a dialogue with Heidegger's thought. (See Tanabe Hajime, *Zangedō toshite no tetsugaku—shi no tetsugaku* [*Philosophy as Metanoetics—the Philosophy of Death*], ed. Hase Shōtō [Kyoto: Tōeisha, 2000], 315–429; and Tanabe Hajime, "Todesdialektik," in *Martin Heidegger zum siebzigsten Geburtstag: Festschrift*, ed. Günther Neske [Pfullingen: Neske, 1959].)

59. The relevant literature on Heidegger and Asian thought includes Parkes,

Heidegger and Asian Thought; Reinhard May, *Heidegger's Hidden Sources: East Asian Influences on His Work,* trans. with a complementary essay by Graham Parkes (New York: Routledge, 1996); Willfred Hartig, *Die Lehre des Buddha und Heidegger: Beiträge zum Ost-West-Dialog des Denkens im 20. Jahrhundert* (Konstanz: Universität Konstanz, 1997); Fred Dallmayr, "Heidegger and Zen Buddhism: A Salute to Nishitani Keiji," in *The Other Heidegger* (Ithaca/London: Cornell University Press, 1993); Yoshiko Oshima, *Zen—anders denken? Zugleich ein Versuch über Zen und Heidegger* (Heidelberg: Lambert Schneider, 1985); Caputo, *The Mystical Element in Heidegger's Thought,* 104–17; and Kah Kyung Cho, "Der Abstieg über den Humanismus: West-Östliche Wege im Denken Heideggers," in *Europa und die Philosophie,* ed. Hans-Helmut Gander (Frankfurt am Main: Vittorio Klostermann, 1993). Peter Kreeft, in his article "Zen in Heidegger's *Gelassenheit,*" *International Philosophical Quarterly* 11, no. 4 (December 1971): 521–45, points out the "Zennish" character of Heidegger's notion of *Gelassenheit,* yet problematically "assume[s] a knowledge of Zen on the part of the reader" (522–23). While a disciplined practice of Zen is increasingly taking root amidst and beyond the popular marketing images of "Zen" that continue to circulate in the West, we have still hardly begun to hermeneutically approach, much less draw out, the radical philosophical implications of this tradition.

Chapter 3

1. Friedrich-Wilhelm von Herrmann helpfully distinguishes four interrelated senses of the *Kehre:* (1) the turn from the *Zeitlichkeit* of Dasein to the *Temporalität* of being; (2) the turn from fundamental ontology to beyng-historical thinking; (3) the *Kehre im Ereignis* of which *Contributions* speaks; and (4) the impending turning from the oblivion of being of which the 1949 lecture "Die Kehre" speaks (von Herrmann, *Wege ins Ereignis,* 67–68). David F. Krell stresses the *Kehre* in the history of being, and understands the turn in three interconnected meanings: "the impending turn in the essence of technology, the unsuccessful reversal within his own project, . . . and the turning at the outermost point of or *eschaton* in the history of Being" (Krell, *Intimations of Mortality,* 108ff.).

2. In *Contributions to Philosophy* (written 1936–38) and in some texts after this time, Heidegger often (though not always consistently) uses the old spelling *Seyn* (which I translate as "beyng") rather than *Sein* to stress that being is not thought of metaphysically in terms of beings, i.e., as the highest or most general being (see *GA* 65:436).

3. See also the end of "The Essence of Truth" essay where Heidegger refers to the key phrase "the essence of truth is the truth of essence" as "the saying of a turning within the history of beyng [*die Sage einer Kehre innerhalb der Geschichte des Seyns*]" (*GA* 9:201/154).

4. See Thomas Sheehan, "*Kehre* and *Ereignis:* A Prolegomenon to *Introduction to Metaphysics,*" in *A Companion to Heidegger's "Introduction to Metaphysics,*" ed. Richard Polt and Gregory Fried (New Haven: Yale University Press, 2001). Sheehan argues that the term *Kehre* should only be understood in the sense—devel-

oped first and foremost in *Contributions*—of *die Kehre im Ereignis*. Yet he does not elaborate on the second sense of the *Kehre* in the matter itself, namely, the being-historical turning from oblivion; he also downplays the *Wendung im Denken*, agreeing with Richardson that the change is "only one of focus." Kenneth Maly emphasizes that "the turning that happens in thinking is grounded in originary turning of enowning," but also excessively asserts that, from the perspective of the originary meaning of the *Kehre* worked out in *Contributions*, "all talk of a shift from 'Heidegger I' to 'Heidegger II' . . . is, once and for all, obsolete" (Maly, "Turnings in Essential Swaying and the Leap," in *Companion to Heidegger's Contributions to Philosophy*, ed. Charles E. Scott et al. [Bloomington: Indiana University Press, 2001], 150, 157). In his article on the *Kehre* in the recently published *Heidegger Handbuch*, Dieter Thomä, on the other hand, seeks to discredit the validity of speaking of a *Kehre* at all, including in particular the sense of a "turning middle" of mutual appropriation between man and being in *Ereignis*. While he correctly criticizes the superficial reading of the turn as a simple turnabout from activity to passivity (from "decisionism" to "submission") in the relation between man and being, Thomä suggests that the ultimate problem with this reading is that it assumes, with the later Heidegger, that there is in fact this "double structure" of mutuality between man and being (Thomä, "Stichwort: Kehre: Was wäre, wenn sie nicht gäbe?" in *Heidegger Handbuch: Leben-Werk-Wirkung*, ed. Dieter Thomä [Stuttgart: Metzler, 2003], esp. 139–40). However, while one may wish to criticize in this manner the basic structure and direction of Heidegger's thought-path, this remains a highly restrictive and contentious interpretation of it.

Emil Kettering's interpretation of the *Kehre*, which sees the double-structured relation between man and being as precisely the *Sache* of Heidegger's thought, both before and after the "turn" in his attempt to think this relation, is rather more convincing here. He writes that, while the early Heidegger already thought "*from out of* the relation between being *and* human being [aus *dem Bezug von Sein* und *Menschenwesen*]," only the later Heidegger succeeds in thinking the mutuality of this relation. After the turn, Kettering writes, Heidegger thinks neither predominantly from *Dasein* nor even predominantly from *Sein*, but rather from *Seyn* or *Ereignis* as the mutual movement of the twofold relation itself. "The early Heidegger thinks man in his relation to 'being,' that is, he thinks only one aspect [*Zug*] of the mutual twofold relation [*Bezug*] of being and human being; the later Heidegger, on the other hand, thinks 'beyng' and its truth, that is, he thinks the entire mutual *belonging*-together. . . . The '*Kehre*' is essentially a '*Kehre*' in the *belonging*-together itself, that is, it is at once a turn in the thinking of man as well as in being—namely as the return [*Einkehr*] into their mutual *belonging*-together" (Kettering, *NÄHE: Das Denken Martin Heideggers*, 328–30).

5. This sending must be understood, however, not simply as a fatalism, but rather as an address that calls mortal humans into a relation of cor-respondence to being within *Ereignis* (or "beyng"). I agree with Kettering (see the previous note) that the turn at issue here is not simply one from Dasein to being, but rather to a thinking of beyng (or *Ereignis*) as the belonging-together of, or the correspondence between, being and man.

6. For some noteworthy examples, see Karl Löwith, *Martin Heidegger and Eu-*

ropean Nihilism, ed. Richard Wolin, trans. Gary Steiner (New York: Columbia University Press, 1995), 42; Jürgen Habermas, *The Philosophical Discourse of Modernity,* trans. Fredrick G. Lawrence (Cambridge, Mass.: MIT Press, 1987), 141, 152–53; and Richard Wolin, *Politics of Being,* 147. In defending the early Heidegger from charges of decisionism and the later Heidegger from charges of quietism, Mark Basil Tanzer argues for a "virtual identity between Heidegger's early and later thought." He finds a combination of "domination and submission, independence and dependence [and] activity and passivity that forges the identity between Heidegger's pre- and post-*Kehre* positions." Heidegger's turn would thus only be a change of focus or emphasis (Tanzer, *Heidegger: Decisionism and Quietism* [Amherst, N.Y.: Humanity Books, 2002], 86–88). However, because Tanzer problematically uses in this context the 1935 *Introduction to Metaphysics* as his primary reference text for "the later Heidegger," he rebuffs charges of quietism only to claim that in Heidegger's post-turn thought humanity is still "called upon to assert its will over Being," or that "although we must strive to realize ourselves by attempting to dominate Being, we must respect the fact that Being will assert itself" (115–16). His interpretive efforts to "balance" voluntarism and passivism in Heidegger thus remain for the most part squarely within the domain of the will.

7. See J. L. Mehta, *Martin Heidegger: The Way and the Vision* (Honolulu: University of Hawaii Press, 1976), 110–13; Zimmerman, *Eclipse of the Self,* xxi, 232; and Otto Pöggeler, *The Paths of Heidegger's Life and Thought,* trans. John Bailiff (Amherst, N.Y.: Humanity Books, 1997), 6. Ohashi, who also locates the turn from the will between the two *Nietzsche* volumes, understands the *Kehre* as ultimately an *Einkehr in die Gelassenheit* (Ohashi, *Ekstase und Gelassenheit,* 119–20, 153).

8. Arendt, *Life of the Mind,* part 2, p. 173. See Krell's comments in the English translation of Heidegger's *Nietzsche,* vol. 4, p. 273; and Wolfgang Müller-Lauter's criticism of Arendt's view in his *Heidegger und Nietzsche* (Berlin: Walter de Gruyter, 2000), 29–32. Müller-Lauter agrees elsewhere that there is "an increasingly *critical* posture towards Nietzsche" in Heidegger's lectures, and he writes that "characteristic of Heidegger's *earliest reception of Nietzsche*" in the period prior to the beginning of the lectures (i.e., prior to 1936), and most notably in the Rectoral Address (see *R* 13/33), "is undoubtedly the affirmation of 'will' and 'power'—as the handing over of the future to men—resulting from the acceptance of [Nietzsche's] saying [that 'God is dead']" (Müller-Lauter, "The Spirit of Revenge and the Eternal Recurrence: On Heidegger's Later Interpretation of Nietzsche," trans. R. J. Hollingdale, in *Nietzsche: Critical Assessments,* ed. Daniel W. Conway with Peter S. Groff [London/New York: Routledge, 1998], 2:148).

9. Derrida, *Of Spirit: Heidegger and the Question,* esp. chapter 5.

10. This is not the only or even the first text wherein this process can be witnessed. Already in the Logic course in the summer of 1928, as we have noted, Heidegger claims that conceptual knowledge "is grasped in its genuine content only when in such knowledge the whole of existence is seized by the root after which philosophy searches—in and by *freedom*" (*GA* 26:22–23). This freedom is later specifically connected with the will. "World, as that to which Dasein transcends, is primarily defined by the for-the-sake-of-which. . . . But a for-the-sake-of-which, a purposiveness [*Umwillen*], is only possible where there is a will [*Willen*]. . . . To put

it briefly, Dasein's transcendence and freedom are identical!" (237–38). Heidegger struggles here to distinguish this finite yet constitutive "freedom" both from the "transcendental will" of idealism and from a mere "existentiell-ontic act of will." In 1930 Heidegger continues his struggle to "think together finitude and greatness" (*GA* 31:136), a struggle that reflects both his own greatness as a thinker of finite human existence and, as his subsequent political disaster reveals, the dangers of rooting being in finite human willing.

11. Jacob Rogozinski argues that "the Heideggerian analysis depends upon, without ever calling into question, the dominant interpretation since Hegel of Kantian autonomy as 'will which wills will,' as the power of the subject to prescribe itself its own law that frees it from all external law." Against this traditional reading, Rogozinski argues for a Levinasian interpretation of the Law as that which exceeds not only the subject, but any "restriction" to a philosophy of being. Only such a Law, together with a non-technological sense of end (as in Kant's dignity of the person), Rogozinski provocatively suggests, can keep us from falling into the purportedly indistinguishable "ohne Warum" of the technological will to will and Silesius's rose that blooms without why (Rogozinski, "Hier ist kein warum: Heidegger and Kant's Practical Philosophy," in *Heidegger and Practical Philosophy*, ed. François Raffoul and David Pettigrew [Albany: SUNY Press, 2002]). And yet the technological will to will, and the will to power of the Nazi guard as an extreme self-obsession that wills to recognize no end outside its own power-preservation and power-enhancement, are utterly different from the spontaneous self-giving of the rose that blooms without asking for any return, not even for the recognition that its beauty has been seen and appreciated. There is every difference in the world here, just as there is between the plea of the prisoner to respect his person as an end in itself (i.e., *without any external reason why*), and the Nazi guard who fails to respond to this appeal with his self-insistent *kein warum*.

12. For a helpful critical analysis of the development of Kant's interconnected notions of *Wille, Willkür,* disposition, freedom, and the problem of evil, see John R. Silber, "The Ethical Significance of Kant's *Religion,*" in Immanuel Kant, *Religion Within the Limits of Reason Alone,* trans. Theodore M. Greene and Hoyt H. Hudson (New York: Harper and Row, 1960), lxxix–cxxxiv.

13. Immanuel Kant, *Immanuel Kant: Critique of Practical Reason and Other Writings in Moral Philosophy,* trans. and ed. Lewis White Beck (Chicago: University of Chicago Press, 1949), 193.

14. Kant, *Critique of Practical Reason,* 142.

15. Ibid., 87.

16. Jean-Luc Nancy attempts to articulate and develop the differences between the affirmative notion of the will in Heidegger's 1930 text and the subjective will that is the villain of Heidegger's later thought; but Nancy does this without attempting to "analyze the evolution and implications of Heidegger's thought on the will" (Nancy, *The Experience of Freedom,* trans. Bridget McDonald [Stanford: Stanford University Press, 1993], 26ff.). My own interpretation, on the other hand, is focused precisely on the place of this 1930 text within the development of the problem of the will in Heidegger's thought-path, and I am thus more concerned with an immanent critique of Heidegger here than with pursuing the differences

between the pure willing that Heidegger affirms in 1930 and the subjective will that he later claims is the essence of all previous concepts of will.

17. Günter Figal, *Martin Heidegger: Phänomenologie der Freiheit*, 3rd ed. (Weinheim: Beltz Athenäum, 2000), 23. Figal refers to Heidegger's 1930 course on Kant on p. 131. For another illuminating discussion of Heidegger's philosophy of freedom, but again one that does not breach the issue of Heidegger's decisive turn from linking freedom with the will, see John Sallis, "Free Thinking," in *Heidegger and Practical Philosophy*, ed. Raffoul and Pettigrew. In his essay for the same volume, Frank Schalow simply passes over the aspect of discontinuity in the development of Heidegger's thought on freedom and the will, and, reading the later Heidegger back into the earlier, credits the 1930 text with having carried out the shift "from a sense of freedom as the spontaneous determination of the will to the openness of letting be" (Schalow, "Freedom, Finitude, and the Practical Self: The Other Side of Heidegger's Appropriation of Kant," in *Heidegger and Practical Philosophy*, ed. Raffoul and Pettigrew, 36). Elsewhere Schalow attempts to recuperate a positive sense of will which is not only not infected by voluntarism and technological mastery, but which is said to enable a genuine openness to otherness and nullity, as well as "concrete decision making" within the context of the destiny of being (Schalow, "The Will as the Genuine Postscript of Modern Thought: At the Crossroads of an Anomaly," *Epoché* 1 [1993]: 77–104). While the attempt to recuperate a positive sense of "will" may serve to counterbalance those interpretations which see in the later Heidegger a simple passive negation of the will, it must be said that the thesis that the will is the genuine postscript of modern thought does not give due reflection to the radicality and reach of Heidegger's critique of the will.

18. But note that as late as the first Nietzsche lecture course (1936) Heidegger still affirmatively speaks of "self-assertion" (see *N1* 73/61).

19. In an opening section, entitled "Der geistig-politische Auftrag als Entscheidung zur Grundfrage" ("The Spiritual-Political Mission as Decision for the Fundamental Question"), Heidegger contextualizes his 1933 summer course on "Die Grundfrage der Philosophie" ("The Fundamental Question of Philosophy") as follows: "The academic youth are aware of the greatness of the historical moment through which the German *Volk* is now passing through. The German *Volk* as a whole is coming to itself, and this means finding its leadership [*Führung*]. In this leadership the *Volk*, which has come to itself, creates its state [*Staat*]. Having been formed into a state, and establishing duration and constancy, the *Volk* grows into a nation [*Nation*]. The nation takes on the destiny [*Schicksal*] of its *Volk*."

Heidegger then goes on to ground the destiny of the nation, however, not in the arbitrary will of a political Führer, but rather in a "spiritual-communal mission" (*geistig-volkliche Auftrag*) that it is the philosopher's job to disclose and interpret. "*All essential leadership lives from the power of a great, and fundamentally concealed destined determination* [einer großen, im Grunde verborgenen Bestimmung]. And this, in the beginning and in the end, is the spiritual-communal mission which destiny holds out to a nation. The knowledge of this mission is to be awakened and embedded in the heart and will of the *Volk* and its individuals" (*GA* 36/37:3).

20. See Philippe Lacoue-Labarthe, *Heidegger, Art, and Politics: The Fiction of the Political*, trans. Chris Turner (Oxford: Blackwell, 1990), 108.

21. Rüdiger Safranski, *Martin Heidegger: Between Good and Evil*, trans. Ewald Osers (Cambridge, Mass.: Harvard University Press, 1998), 266, citing Martin Heidegger, *Logik*, ed. Victor Farías (Madrid: Anthropos, 1991), 26ff. See also Polt, *Heidegger: An Introduction*, 154–55.

22. Wolin, *Politics of Being*, 62.

23. J. P. Stern, *Hitler: The Führer and the People* (London: Fontana, 1979), 76, as quoted in Wolin, *Politics of Being*, 183.

24. Lacoue-Labarthe, *Heidegger, Art, and Politics*, 95–96.

25. See Lacoue-Labarthe, *Heidegger, Art, and Politics*, 34; and chapters 9 and 10 below, for further reflections on this disturbing statement.

26. See Jacques Derrida, "Heidegger's Silence," in *Martin Heidegger and National Socialism: Questions and Answers*, ed. Günther Neske and Emil Kettering, trans. Lisa Harries and Joachim Neugroschel (New York: Paragon House, 1990), 148.

27. As is well known, there are two texts that initiated the most recent debate over Heidegger's politics of 1933–34 and beyond: (1) Victor Farias's polemic, *Heidegger and Nazism*, ed. Joseph Margolis and Tom Rockmore, trans. Paul Burrell (Philadelphia: Temple University Press, 1989), a much-criticized work of poor scholarship which nevertheless succeeded in calling attention to the extent of Heidegger's political errancy; and (2) Hugo Ott's more scholarly—and for this reason perhaps more condemning—study, *Martin Heidegger: A Political Life*, trans. Allan Blunden (New York: BasicBooks, 1993). See also Rüdiger Safranski's informative "philosophical biography," *Martin Heidegger: Between Good and Evil*. As a few indications of the many varied attempts to think the facts in relation to Heidegger's thought, I list the following. For a helpful categorizing of the various responses, see Polt, *Heidegger: An Introduction*, 159ff. For a variety of perspectives, see Neske and Kettering, eds., *Martin Heidegger and National Socialism;* Richard Wolin, ed., *The Heidegger Controversy: A Critical Reader* (Cambridge, Mass.: MIT Press, 1993); Arleen Dallery and Charles E. Scott, eds., *Ethics and Danger: Essays on Heidegger and Continental Thought* (Albany: SUNY Press, 1992); Tom Rockmore and Joseph Margolis, eds., *The Heidegger Case: On Philosophy and Politics* (Philadelphia: Temple University Press, 1992); and Raffoul and Pettigrew, eds., *Heidegger and Practical Philosophy*. For an informative account of Heidegger's relation to Ernst Jünger and the "reactionary modernism" movement in Germany, see Zimmerman, *Heidegger's Confrontation with Modernity*. For a rather reductionist reading of the relation between Heidegger's philosophy and his sociopolitical context, see Pierre Bourdieu, *The Political Ontology of Martin Heidegger*, trans. Peter Collier (Stanford: Stanford University Press, 1988). For a more balanced analysis in this regard, see Hans Sluga, *Heidegger's Crisis: Philosophy and Politics in Nazi Germany* (Cambridge, Mass.: Harvard University Press, 1993). For several of the most philosophically interesting works, which attempt not simply to condemn and discard but to thoughtfully question Heidegger's thought in the aftermath of his Nazism, see Derrida, *Of Spirit: Heidegger and the Question;* Lacoue-Labarthe, *Heidegger, Art, and Politics;* and Miguel de Beistegui, *Heidegger and the Political: Dystopias* (London: Routledge, 1998). For a defense of modernity and humanism and a critique of the above two works by Derrida and Lacoue-Labarthe, see Luc Ferry and Alain Renaut, *Heidegger and Modernity*, trans. Franklin Philip (Chicago: University of Chi-

cago Press, 1990). For other all-out attempts to interpret Heidegger as a potential, expressed, and then never rehabilitated Nazi, see Wolin, *The Politics of Being;* and Tom Rockmore, *On Heidegger's Nazism and Philosophy* (Berkeley: University of California Press, 1992). For an attempt to defend Heidegger's thought in all its phases from these charges, see Julian Young, *Heidegger, Philosophy, Nazism* (Cambridge: Cambridge University Press, 1997). I have learned much from many of the aforementioned works about the relation of Heidegger's Nazism to his thought, yet none of them clearly focuses on his political embrace of the will in 1933–34 in the context of the problem of the will in the path of his thought as a whole. It is in this regard that the present study attempts to make a contribution to thinking through the affair.

28. See Lacoue-Labarthe, *Heidegger, Art, and Politics,* 97 and 103.

29. Note that Lacoue-Labarthe does not simply subscribe to an internal criticism of Heidegger (see *Heidegger, Art, and Politics,* 14), despite what his critics suggest (see Ferry and Renaut, *Heidegger and Modernity,* 51).

30. Michel Haar writes that the "impatience of 1933 was a voluntaristic excess born of an ontic interpretation of *Entschlossenheit,* or 'resoluteness'" (Haar, *Heidegger and the Essence of Man,* xxxii). Relevant in this regard is Heidegger's admonition in *Contributions* specifically against the "danger of misinterpreting *Being and Time* in this direction, i.e., 'existentiell-anthropologically'" (*GA* 65:87), a danger which he admits, however, "looms and gets stronger by many things that are unaccomplished in *Being and Time.*"

31. Löwith, *Martin Heidegger and European Nihilism,* 223.

32. It is such residues which give one cause to suspect that, as Pöggeler suggests, Heidegger never truly or at least fully "emerged from the proximity of National Socialism" (Pöggeler, *Martin Heidegger's Path of Thinking,* 272). As for the other half of this well-known statement, namely, that it was "through a [not to say *the*] definite orientation of his thinking that Heidegger fell—and not merely accidentally—into [this proximity]," I have sought to expose one such tendency, and there are no doubt others, in the ambivalent voluntarism of *Being and Time.* But just as this early text also harbors significant counter-orientations, so does Heidegger's later thought carry implications radically other than even the supposed "inner truth and greatness" of his private vision of National Socialism.

33. See Beistegui, *Heidegger and the Political,* 103. Chapter 4 of Beistegui's book provides an insightful account of Heidegger's turn to Hölderlin in 1934. See also in this regard Robert Bernasconi, *Heidegger in Question: The Art of Existing* (Atlantic Highlands, N.J.: Humanities, 1993), chapter 8; and Zimmerman, *Heidegger's Confrontation with Modernity,* chapter 8.

34. Theodore Kisiel writes: "In the early thirties, Heidegger . . . concerned himself with the uniquely German possibilities that could contribute to the overcoming of nihilism and the arrest of the 'Decline of the West,' and defines 'three powers' or strengths of the German people that first emerged in their full vigor during the period (1770–1830) of the 'German movement' of the European Enlightenment: German poetry, German philosophy, and 'the new German political will of the Prussian statesmen and soldiers' [*GA* 16:291] that cooperated in the founding of the Second Reich. Heidegger seeks to inaugurate a similar coopera-

tion or conversation between poets, thinkers, and statesmen in the first years of development of the Third Reich, which he for a time, following clues in the poetry of Hölderlin, regarded as Germany's 'world time,' the grand historical moment for the German people to demonstrate its presence on the world stage" (Kisiel, "Measuring the Greatness of the Great Men of Grand Politics: How Nietzsche's 'Dynamite' Rendered Heidegger 'Kaputt,'" in *Conference Proceedings from the Thirty-ninth Annual North American Heidegger Conference*, 88). While by 1938 Heidegger had reportedly come to see Hitler as "der Räuber und Verbrecher des Jahrhunderts [the robber and criminal of the century]" (see Silvio Vietta, *Heideggers Kritik am Nationalsozialismus und an der Technik* [Tübingen: Niemeyer, 1989], 47; cited in Kisiel, "Measuring the Greatness of the Great Men of Grand Politics," 101), his belief in the importance of the German poet hardly waned. In *Contributions to Philosophy* Heidegger goes so far as to claim that the "historical destiny of philosophy culminates in the recognition of the necessity of making Hölderlin's word be heard" (*GA* 65:422). And as late as 1963 Heidegger claims that "Hölderlin's poetry is for us a fate" (*EHD* 195/224). In 1963 this "us" is presumably no longer just Germany, and no longer even just the West, but rather the entire Europeanizing earth.

35. Beistegui, *Heidegger and the Political*, 98.

36. Ibid., 178.

37. Werner Marx, *Heidegger and the Tradition*, trans. Theodore Kisiel and Murray Greene (Evanston, Ill.: Northwestern University Press, 1971), 219.

38. Heidegger later famously writes rather that "questioning is the piety of thinking" (*VA* 40/341). A critique of the willfulness of Heidegger's questioning forms one of the "four threads of hesitation" in Derrida's *Of Spirit*. This, however, is one of the most debated sections of Derrida's text, a debate encouraged by Derrida himself in a seven-page footnote (129–36) added to the text, where in response to François Dastur he recognizes Heidegger's own displacement of the primacy of the question in the name of listening to the address (*Zuspruch*) of being or language as that to which we must respond before (willfully) posing any question. See John Sallis's "Flight of Spirit" (in *Of Derrida, Heidegger, and Spirit*, ed. David Wood [Evanston, Ill.: Northwestern University Press, 1993]) for an "unraveling" of the implications of this concession for Derrida's text. For Heidegger's later claim that listening must precede any questioning, see *GA* 12:165/72; for his claim that "proper thinking does not consist in questioning," see *GA* 77:25, and pp. 194–95 below.

39. Daniela Vallega-Neu, *Heidegger's Contributions to Philosophy: An Introduction* (Bloomington: Indiana University Press, 2003), 7.

40. Prior to the publication of *Contributions to Philosophy* in 1989, Otto Pöggeler had raised high expectations by reportedly hailing the work as "obviously Heidegger's magnum opus" (quoted in Krell, *Intimations of Mortality*, 106; see also Pöggeler, *Martin Heidegger's Path of Thinking*, 286–87). In his *The Paths of Heidegger's Life and Thought*, Pöggeler more cautiously calls *Contributions* Heidegger's "second major work" (1).

41. Vallega-Neu, *Heidegger's Contributions to Philosophy*, 4.

42. Da-sein is said to be "what *simultaneously undergirds* [unter-gründet] and

elevates [überhöht] man" (*GA* 65:301); or is said to be "the between" of man and the gods (311).

43. Heidegger's defines *Stimmung* in *Contributions* as "the spraying forth of the trembling [*Erzitterung*] of *Seyn* as *Ereignis* in Da-sein" (*GA* 65:21).

44. While the term *Verhaltenheit* first plays this central role of a most proper *Grundstimmung* in *Contributions*, this is not Heidegger's first employment of the term. We find, for example, the following remarkable passage in the 1929–30 lecture course "The Fundamental Concepts of Metaphysics": "Such a relation to something, which is thoroughly governed by this letting be [*Seinlassen*] of something as a being, we are calling *comportment* [Verhalten], in distinction from the behavior of captivation. But all comportment is only possible in a certain restraint [*Verhaltenheit*] and comporting [*Verhaltung*], and a stance [*Haltung*] is only given where a being has the character of a self or, as we also say, of a person" (*GA* 29/ 30:397–98).

Yet these remarks are set in the context of an interpretation of man (or "human Dasein") as "world-forming" (*weltbildend*), as opposed to animals which are said to be "poor in world" (*weltarm*). Heidegger writes: "Who forms the world? Man, according to our thesis. But what is man? . . . For it is not the case that man first exists and then also one day decides among other things to form a world. Rather world-formation is something that occurs, and only on this ground can a human [*ein Mensch*] exist in the first place. Man as man is world-forming . . . the *Dasein in* man is world-forming. The Dasein in man forms world: [1] it brings it forth [*es stellt sie her*]; [2] it gives an image [*Bild*] or view of the world, it sets it forth [*es sellt sie dar*]; [3] it constitutes the world [*es macht sie aus*], contains and embraces it" (413–14).

While one part of the "primordial structure" of the "fundamental occurrence" (*Grundgeschehen*) of this world-formation is characterized as a comportment of "holding oneself toward something binding," the unitary character of this fundamental occurrence of world-formation is said to be "projection." "[The] essence of man, the Dasein in him, is determined by this projective character. . . . *World prevails in and for a letting-prevail that has the character of projecting*" (526–27). "In projecting [*Entwerfend*], the Da-sein in [man] constantly *throws* [wirft] him into possibilities and thereby keeps him *subjected* [unterworfen] to what is actual" (531). While this 1929–30 text is clearly not proposing a metaphysical idealism or even a simple voluntaristic existentialism, where man would unilaterally will the creation or formation of his own world, in *Contributions* Heidegger nevertheless turns decisively away from a focus on Dasein's world-forming projection by emphasizing that "the thrower itself, Da-sein, is thrown, a-propriated [*er-eignet*] by beyng" (*GA* 65:304). Moreover, Dasein is now no longer thought to be "in man," but rather man must find his way into Da-sein (see 300). In order to find his way (back) into Da-sein, that is, in order to properly correspond to the throw of beyng, a *Grundstimmung* of holding back or *Verhaltenheit* is called for.

45. Heidegger also reemploys other terms usually associated with (subjective) willing, such as "mastery" (*Herrschaft*). In a chilling passage (given the political context in which he was writing) Heidegger affirms that "mastery over the masses who have become free (i.e., rootless and self-seeking) has to be established and

maintained with the fetters of 'organization'" (*GA* 65:61). Here is Heidegger still at his political worst, that is, in his inability to critically think the dangers of collaborating with a politics of coercion for the sake of "resisting the incessant uprooting" in modern society. Despite this condemnable compromise with the anti-democratic politics of power, however, Heidegger's intent in this passage is in fact to turn our attention to what he calls the need of "another mastery [*einer anderen Herrschaft*] . . . one which is sheltered and reserved, for a long time isolating and still. Here preparation is to be made for those who are to come, those who create new sites within being itself" (62). This creation, where "beings are transformed according to beyng," requires a mastery of a sort other than that which deals in power (*Macht*) or force (*Gewalt*). A few years later Heidegger writes of the transformation of mastery (*GA* 69:21) into "the mildness of the highest mastery," a mastery that requires no power and struggle, but is rather a "force-free ruling [*Gewaltlose Walten*]" (*GA* 69:8; see also *GA* 66:16–17). This other mastery, he says in *Contributions,* "is the necessity of the free to be free. . . . Its greatness consists in its not needing power and thus needing no force and still remaining more effective than power or force" (*GA* 65:282).

46. For an analysis of the notion of *Augenblick* in *Contributions* and in Heidegger's earlier works, see William McNeill, "The Time of *Contributions to Philosophy,*" in *Companion to Heidegger's Contributions to Philosophy,* ed. Scott et al.

Chapter 4

1. F. W. J. Schelling, "Philosophische Untersuchungen über das Wesen der menschlichen Freiheit und die damit zusammenhängenden Gegenstände," in *F. W. J. v. Schellings sämmtliche Werke,* vol. 7, ed. K. F. A. Schelling (Stuttgart: J. G. Cotta, 1860), 400, 409; F. W. J. Schelling, "Philosophical Investigations into the Essence of Human Freedom and Related Matters," trans. Priscilla Hayden-Roy, in *Philosophy of German Idealism,* ed. Ernst Behler (New York: Continuum, 1987), 270–71, 278–79. In my quotations from Schelling's treatise on freedom in this chapter, I have also consulted James Gutmann's translation: *Philosophical Inquiries into the Nature of Human Freedom* (La Salle, Ill.: Open Court, 1936), which indicates the German pagination in the margins; yet I have generally followed Hayden-Roy's more accurate version. Schelling's "Freiheitsschrift" (as it is called) shall hereafter be cited as "FS" followed by the page number from the German text and then the page number in Hayden-Roy's translation.

2. For some exceptions, see Parvis Emad, "Heidegger on Schelling's Concept of Freedom," *Man and World* 8 (1975): 157–74; Michael G. Vater, "Heidegger and Schelling: The Finitude of Being," *Idealistic Studies* (1975): 20–58; Joan Stambaugh, *Thoughts on Heidegger* (Lanham, Md.: University Press of America, 1991), 77–89; Fred R. Dallmayr, *Polis and Praxis* (Cambridge, Mass.: MIT Press, 1984), chapter 4; and Christian Iber, "Interpretationen zum Deutschen Idealismus: Vernunftkritik im Namen des Seins," in *Heidegger Handbuch,* ed. Thomä, esp. 194–98. Ryosuke Ohashi's book *Ekstase und Gelassenheit: Zu Schelling und Heidegger,* while not specifically focused on Heidegger's interpretation of Schelling, is particularly

noteworthy in this context insofar as it interprets Schelling's thought as a precursor to Heidegger's attempt to twist free of the metaphysics of the will (see note 17 for this chapter).

3. The 1936 course has now been published as volume 42 of the *Gesamtausgabe*, while the complete set of notes from 1941–43 has been published separately as volume 49. Throughout the 1936 text, Heidegger follows Schelling's older spelling of *Sein* as *Seyn*, without marking (as he sometimes does in subsequent texts such as *Contributions to Philosophy*) a semantic distinction between the two. To avoid confusion, where this distinction is not specifically at issue, I have rendered *Seyn* as "being" rather than as "beyng."

4. Nancy, *Experience of Freedom*, 36.

5. On the place of the "Freiheitsschrift" in Schelling's path of thought, see Dale E. Snow, *Schelling and the End of Idealism* (Albany: SUNY Press, 1996); Andrew Bowie, *Schelling and Modern European Philosophy: An Introduction* (London: Routledge, 1993); and Alan White, *Schelling: An Introduction to the System of Freedom* (New Haven: Yale University Press, 1983).

6. Quoted from Schelling's *Der Philosophie der Offenbarung zweiter Teil* in White, *Schelling: An Introduction to the System of Freedom*, 151.

7. Schelling therefore claims, more than a century before Sartre, that "the essence of man is essentially *his own deed*" ("FS" 385/259).

8. As Dale Snow points out, this analogy works best with diseases that take on a parasitic life of their own, such as cancer, in contrast to illnesses of deficiency such as anemia (Snow, *Schelling and the End of Idealism*, 166).

9. Werner Marx supports this conclusion when he interprets Schelling's treatise on freedom to have developed, not primarily a new concept of *human* freedom, "but rather of the freedom of the Absolute." "Human freedom," Marx reads Schelling to be saying, "is finite above all because it serves God. . . . God's love can only reign if goodness has constituted itself by overcoming evil, and this means that man *must* decide on evil in order to assist the triumph of goodness and, along with it, the complete reign of divine love. This means that finite freedom has its end, its boundary, in the *telos* of the process as a whole, in the 'ultimate intention' of divine creation" (Marx, *The Philosophy of F. W. J. Schelling: History, System, and Freedom*, trans. Thomas Nenon [Bloomington: Indiana University Press, 1984], 63, 79).

10. Andrew Bowie suggests the following response to Heidegger's critique: "Heidegger claims the way subjectivity is understood by Schelling makes subjectivity into the precursor of Nietzsche's 'will to power,' the will to overcome the Other in the name of the Same. Schelling's argument can surely be read, though, as a warning against the potential domination of subjectivity, which as 'evil' tries to obliterate its relationship to the ground upon which it is dependent. . . . In this way Schelling's 'evil' could, in Heidegger's terms, actually be equated with metaphysics itself" (Bowie, *Schelling and Modern European Philosophy*, 93).

11. Heidegger makes a parenthetical reference here to *Die Weltalter, Schellings sämmtliche Werke*, 8:210. See F. W. J. Schelling, *The Ages of the World*, trans. Jason M. Wirth (Albany: SUNY Press, 2000), 5–6.

12. Schelling, *Schellings sämmtliche Werke*, 7:432. Note, however, that in the *Weltalter* Schelling says that the "Supreme Being is . . . in itself the antithesis of per-

sonality and therefore ... [an] equally eternal force of selfhood, of egoity [*Egoität*], is required so that that being which is Love might exist as its own and might be for itself. . . . Therefore, two principles are already in what is necessary of God: the outpouring, outstretching, self-giving being, and an equivalently eternal force of selfhood, of retreat into itself, of Being in itself" (Schelling, *Ages of the World*, 6).

13. Franz Josef Wetz goes too far, however, when he describes this change as an "exact reversal" (Wetz, *Friedrich W. J. Schelling zur Einführung* [Hamburg: Junius, 1996], 151, 155); for the excessive eruption of the will of the ground disrupts the harmony of the whole by drawing the whole into the false center of it self-contracting ego, while the "binding" character of love cannot be simply equated with the force of contraction, insofar as love is said to hold opposites together by letting them be in their difference.

14. Schelling, *Schellings sämmtliche Werke*, 7:439.

15. Schelling, *Ages of the World*, 24–25.

16. See Marx, *Philosophy of F. W. J. Schelling*, 67–68.

17. Ohashi's *Ekstase und Gelassenheit* is an illuminating attempt to read Schelling as a precursor to Heidegger's later philosophy of *Gelassenheit*. He interprets the entire development of Schelling's thought-path as a "way towards ecstasy" (*Weg zur Ekstase*). The specific term *Ekstase* (defined in general as a "becoming one with the infinite by way of a being-outside-oneself of the finite subject") does not appear in Schelling's text until the year after the treatise on freedom, in the 1810 dialogue "Clara." There Schelling writes of an ability to enter into the most inner center of life that is "never granted to those who will," for "*Gelassenheit* and quieting of the will [*Ruhe des Willens*] are its first condition" (Schelling, *Schellings sämmtliche Werke*, 9:105; see Ohashi, *Ekstase und Gelassenheit*, 49). According to Ohashi, the *Ekstase* mentioned by name here first plays a major role in Schelling's thought in the 1821 "Erlanger Vorlesung." There Schelling speaks of the need to become "ecstatic" in the sense of letting all willing and knowing go: "he must will nothing, know nothing, feel completely bare and poor [*bloss und arm*], give everything up, in order to gain everything" (*Schellings sämmtliche Werke*, 9:218; see Ohashi, *Ekstase und Gelassenheit*, 60). In the end, however, Ohashi finds that Schelling's *Ekstase* did not leave behind the domain of the metaphysics of will and subjectivity. Even the "Erlanger Vorlesung," where *Ekstase* as a *Willensverlassenheit* plays a prominent role, remains an ambivalent text in this regard. Ohashi writes: "What [Schelling] attempted in 1821 was nothing other than this: to develop the domain of the will into its highest form, into the system. This project was doomed to internal conflict; for that to which ecstasy in the proper sense should lead is precisely the letting go of the will, and not its development" (157). Hence, although he reads this tension in Schelling's (post-)idealism—i.e., between the will to system and *Ekstase* as a letting go of the will—as an important precursor to Heidegger's own path of immanent critique and *Verwindung* from the metaphysics of will, Ohashi concludes that "the place [*Ort*] of Schelling's 'ecstasy' is still caught up in the domain of the will, in metaphysics, while the place of Heidegger's 'Gelassenheit' has perhaps left this domain behind" (160).

Chapter 5

1. Angelus Silesius, *Cherubinischer Wandersmann*, vol. 3 of *Sämtliche poetische Werke*, ed. Hans Ludwig Held (Munich: Carl Hanser, 1949), 18, 39, 53.

2. John Caputo, *The Mystical Element in Heidegger's Thought* (New York: Fordham University Press, 1986, reprinted with corrections 1990), xviii. Otto Pöggeler suggests at one point that "Heidegger's search for a way out of the Western metaphysical tradition and its dead ends finally depends upon Meister Eckhart" (Pöggeler, *The Paths of Heidegger's Life and Thought*, 267; see, however, Pöggeler's varied reflections on Heidegger's complex relation to Eckhart, at 292ff.).

3. On the young Heidegger's extensive engagements with Eckhart's mystical thought, see van Buren, *The Young Heidegger*, esp. chapters 6 and 14. Van Buren makes a strong case for the claim that one of the first "models" of Heidegger's thought was an "Eckhartian letting-be of the mystery of the flux of the Divine Life," i.e., a "movement of overflow from the abyss of the Godhead into the analogical differentiation of actuality," where "the soul is the co-worker or co-actualizer of this differentiation" (319, 116). Van Buren concludes that "in 1915–16 Heidegger's thought ultimately *was* philosophical mysticism" (122). While references to Eckhart recede as Heidegger subsequently, in the early 1920s, turns to the "kairology" found in Paul, Luther, and Kierkegaard, as we shall see, the later Heidegger re-turns once more into a proximity with the *Hingabe* and *Gelassenheit* of medieval mysticism. For a list of the considerable number of works by Eckhart and other mystics in Heidegger's personal library at the time of his death, see von Herrmann, *Wege ins Ereignis*, 376–77.

4. Heidegger refers in this context to a line from Hölderlin which reads: "For as you begin, so you will remain" (*GA* 12:88/7); and one of the ways in which Heidegger began his path of thought is precisely in the attempt to deconstructively and phenomenologically retrieve a more primordial understanding of the Christian experience. Without this "theological background," Heidegger says, "I should never have come upon the path of thinking. But origin always comes to meet us from the future" (91/10). On Heidegger's early relation to Christianity and theology, see Kisiel, "Theo-Logical Beginnings: Toward a Phenomenology of Christianity," in *Genesis of "Being and Time,"* 69–116; and van Buren, *The Young Heidegger*, esp. chapters 6, 8, and 14.

5. See Martin Heidegger, *The Piety of Thinking*, with translation, notes, and commentary by James G. Hart and John C. Maraldo (Bloomington: Indiana University Press, 1976). This book contains, among other texts, a translation and interpretation of Heidegger's 1927 "Phenomenologie und Theologie" (*GA* 9:45–78/39–62), and the protocol of a 1953 discussion between Heidegger and a group of theologians.

6. Gillespie, *Nihilism Before Nietzsche*, 16.

7. Ibid., xxii.

8. I have translated this line as it appears in Heidegger's text: "Wo ich für mich nichts will, da will statt meiner Gott." A footnote refers us to *Deutsche Mystiker*, vol. 3, *Meister Eckhart*, selected and translated by Joseph Bernhardt (Kemten/Munich:

Jos. Kösel'sche, 1914), *Die Reden der Unterweisung*, 77n1. Josef Quint gives a slightly different rendering of this line: "Wo ich nichts für mich will, da will Gott für mich" (Eckehart, *Deutsche Predigten und Traktate*, 54). In this chapter I will for the most part translate Eckhart in reference to Quint's modern German renditions, citing the page number in his text following the abbreviation "Q." In cases where a text is not included in Quint's collection, I will refer in a note to the original text in Meister Eckhart, *Meister Eckhart: Die deutschen und lateinischen Werke* (Stuttgart: W. Kohlhammer, 1958).

9. Heidegger's reference is to *Deutsche Mystiker*, 3:79. Compare "Q" 56. Again Quint's rendering differs somewhat, but the gist remains the same.

10. Von Herrmann, *Wege ins Ereignis*, 385.

11. Eckhart, *Meister Eckhart: Die deutschen und lateinischen Werke*, 1:244.

12. Norbert Winkler, *Meister Eckhart zur Einführung* (Hamburg: Junius, 1997), 79.

13. Bernard McGinn, *The Mystical Thought of Meister Eckhart* (New York: Crossroad, 2001), 144. Winkler also speaks of the union with God as a passage from the "empirical ego" to a "trans-empirical, ideal ego" (Winkler, *Meister Eckhart zur Einführung*, 99).

14. Winkler, *Meister Eckhart zur Einführung*, 36, 42.

15. Hegel, *Phänomenologie des Geistes*, Werke 3, p. 585.

16. Bernard McGinn, "Theological Summary," in *Meister Eckhart: The Essential Sermons, Commentaries, Treatises, and Defense*, trans. Edmund Colledge and Bernard McGinn (Mahwah, N.J.: Paulist Press, 1981), 30–31.

17. Reiner Schürmann finds that there are "floating, even contradictory, expressions" on the subject of the will throughout his sermons, and concludes that there are no traces to be found in Eckhart of "a genuine philosophy of the will" (Schürmann, *Meister Eckhart: Mystic and Philosopher* [Bloomington: Indiana University Press, 1978], 40). According to Schürmann, the "authentic core of Meister Eckhart's thinking is releasement" (191).

18. In 1918–19 Heidegger writes that, with regard to the radical union of which Eckhart speaks, which intimates a sphere of mystical experience beyond or before all opposition of subject and object, it is no longer appropriate to speak of an order among the "faculties" of will and intellect (*GA* 60:316, 318).

19. See McGinn, *Mystical Thought of Meister Eckhart*, 132ff.

20. Ueda Shizuteru, "Freedom and Language in Meister Eckhart and Zen Buddhism, Part 1," trans. Richard F. Szippl, *The Eastern Buddhist*, new series, vol. 23, no. 2 (Autumn 1990): 45. (The original German version of this article was published as "Eckhart und Zen am Problem 'Freiheit und Sprache,'" *Beihefte der Zeitschrift für Religions- und Geistesgeschichte* 31 [Cologne: E. J. Brill, 1989]: 21–92.)

21. Ueda, "Freedom and Language in Meister Eckhart and Zen Buddhism," 30.

22. Ibid., 34.

23. Ibid., 54.

24. Ibid., 52–53.

25. Ibid., 43–44.

26. Helting, *Heidegger und Meister Eckehart*, 74.

27. This ambivalence in Eckhart's thought is reflected in the vacillations of

Caputo's rebuttal to Heidegger on Eckhart's behalf. On the one hand, Caputo objects to Heidegger's claim that Eckhart remains confined within the sphere of willing: "If we understand the distinction between God and the Godhead, then the completely detached soul does not reach God as possessed of will. That belongs to 'God,' to the creator, to the first cause of metaphysics. The detached soul unites with the ground of God, with a nameless and will-less divine abyss, even as the soul in its ground is nameless and will-less" (Caputo, *Mystical Element in Heidegger's Thought*, 181). And yet in the same paragraph Caputo backtracks and now claims: "But Heidegger's remark does bring out the fact that in Eckhart the soul is released to a being of infinite goodness, of perfect love and boundless care for his creation. Whether one calls this 'God' or 'Godhead,' the 'divine will' or the divine 'abyss,' still as Meister Eckhart says, there is nothing to fear in God" (ibid.). Jürgen Wagner—while himself claiming that "one can sooner agree with Eckhart than with Heidegger, when the former speaks of the 'noble' origin of the will . . . [which] wills not power but rather the good"—sharply criticizes Caputo for adhering to the traditional "positive image of God, to which humans can trustingly dedicate [*hingeben*] themselves" (Wagner, *Meditationen über Gelassenheit*, 137; see also 173). The radicality of Eckhart's mystical thought pushes us beyond this dualistic dependence on a loving, willing Father into the freer, if also perhaps more "dangerous," desert of the abyssal *grunt*. Whether Caputo remains "not only behind Eckhart, but also behind Heidegger," as Wagner avers, Caputo clearly does want to hold on to the positive image of God as the absolutely transcendent loving Father. This religious security, for Caputo, is what positively distinguishes Eckhart's Christianity from the "dangers" of Heidegger's thought of *Ereignis* as the unfathomable play of the sending of being. Caputo argues that "one of the most essential differences" between the two thinkers is that "in Eckhart *Gelassenheit* is a surrender to a loving Father, and in Heidegger it is a release into the 'play of Being'" (Caputo, *Mystical Element in Heidegger's Thought*, 199). But does not Eckhart repeatedly speak of breaking through the persona of God the Father? Has Caputo himself failed to heed the distinction between God and the Godhead?

Caputo criticizes Heidegger for purportedly leaving us helplessly exposed to the irrational whimsical play of being. Ironically, on the other hand, Caputo also wants to preserve a sense of divine absolute transcendence and omnipotent independence in Eckhart's theology; for this purpose he rejects the mystical and philosophical tradition of interpreting Eckhart in such a manner as to challenge orthodox theism by claiming that God "needs" man. This heretical notion of the "divine need of man" was, as Caputo points out, taken up and developed by later mystics, by the German idealist and, in his own way, by Heidegger. But, unlike Heidegger's being, which can never essence without beings (*GA* 9:306), Caputo assures us that Eckhart attributes a self-subsistent independence to God. "For Eckhart, God is a transcendent creator and first cause Who is above being, i.e., creation, and Who could well subsist without the creature from which He is absolutely distinct" (Caputo, *Mystical Element in Heidegger's Thought*, 184). Eckhart certainly inherits a tradition of onto-theology that speaks this language. But was he perhaps rightly accused of heresy by the Christian orthodoxy for boldly claiming: "This humble man has as much power over God as he has over himself. . . .

God and this humble man are wholly one, and not two. . . . If this man were in hell, God would have to come down to him in hell. . . . God would be compelled of necessity, such that He *must* do this; for then this man is divine being, and divine being is this man" (Eckhart, *Meister Eckhart: Die deutschen und lateinischen Werke,* 1:246–47). Eckhart also clearly states elsewhere: "It is a sure truth and a necessary truth that God has *such* a need to seek us out—exactly as if all his divinity [*Gottheit*] depended on it, as in fact it does. God can no more dispense with us than we can dispense with him" ("Q" 386).

Schürmann, who relentlessly pursues (and prefers to emphasize) the most transgressive elements of Eckhart's thought, draws the conclusion: "If we follow Meister Eckhart's thought to the bottom, we find that there is no God without man. God is placed in dependence on man, to the point of receiving his being and his life from him" (Schürmann, *Meister Eckhart: Mystic and Philosopher,* 82). Later, in the context of a discussion of Eckhart's letting God go in the releasement into a living without why, Schürmann does not hesitate to remark: "One imagines what happens to Scholastic constructions when unexpectedly a preacher comes who unveils the nothingness of foundations; the Scholastic mind is seized with dizziness. The God whom this other way of thinking annihilates in his function of foundation is indeed the God of western Christianity" (113). Yet in the radicality of his interpretation, does Schürmann give due consideration, not just to the breakthrough, but also to the repeated return of traditional (residual?) ontotheological tropes in Eckhart's preaching?

In comparison, even where he is attentive to the more iconoclastic (i.e., heretical) moments in Eckhart's thought, Caputo seems eager to weave Eckhart back into the fold of Christian orthodoxy. According to Caputo, Eckhart's originality lay in his synthesis of the traditional Christian notion of the God of Fatherly Love with the Neoplatonic mysticism of becoming one with the One. In contrast to the "Christian, Trinitarian, personalistic" idea of the "birth of the Son in the soul," the radical idea of the "breakthrough to the Godhead" is said to express a side of Eckhart that is "Neoplatonic, Unitarian, pre-personalistic" (Caputo, *Mystical Element in Heidegger's Thought,* 132). According to Caputo, these two sides are, in fact, mutually supportive; the more basic "root" moment of the breakthrough must be seen to lead to the "fulfillment" or "flower" moment of the birth of the Son; for, he hastens to remind us, only the latter tells of "the love the Father has for us" (ibid.). Yet one is left with the lingering impression that Caputo's emphasis on the absolute transcendence of God the Father signals an onto-theological retreat from the most radical thrust of Eckhart's message. When he writes that "the work of *Gelassenheit* is to let God be God. . . . That is, God might very well be self-present, if that is what He wants. What is God? Anything He wants to be" (xx), does Caputo fall back not only into an ontology of presence but also into a theology of Will?

28. Quint renders "lūter würken" as "lauteres Wirken"; Uta Störmer-Caysa renders it as "reines Tun" and relates it to the notion of *actus purus* (Meister Eckhart, *Deutsche Predigten: Eine Auswahl: Mittelhochdeutsch/Neuhochdeutsch* [Stuttgart: Reclam, 2001], 115, 181.

29. See Ueda Shizuteru, *Ekkuharuto: Itan to seitō no aida de* (*Eckhart: Between Heresy and Orthodoxy*) (Tokyo: Kōdansha, 1998), 201, 256ff., 284ff.

30. Ueda, "Freedom and Language in Meister Eckhart and Zen Buddhism," 23.

31. Ibid., 55.

32. McGinn, *Mystical Thought of Meister Eckhart*, 158.

33. Eckhart, *Meister Eckhart: Die deutschen und lateinischen Werke*, 1:92.

34. Ibid.

35. Schürmann, quoting passages where Eckhart says that all things have their origin (*ursprunc*) in nothingness, and that the will recovers its proper freedom in its first origin, writes: "In its preoriginal origin the will sets itself loose from any principle; it is anarchic" (Schürmann, *Meister Eckhart: Mystic and Philosopher*, 120). But should one still refer to this originary freedom as a "will"?

36. The reference in Heidegger's text is to *Deutsche Mystiker*, 3:81. Compare "Q" 57. Quint's rendering again varies slightly from the text Heidegger quotes, but the gist remains the same.

37. Kettering, *NÄHE: Das Denken Martin Heideggers*, 251–52.

38. Wagner not only rejects Kettering's claim that mysticism necessarily implies world-negation and withdrawal from an active engagement with things, but argues that, in fact, it was Heidegger who did not carry through to the end the return to "das unvermittelte Begegnenlassen der Dinge" that his thought is said to have announced. A "further step back" would be required, Wagner writes, "in order to realize the simple truth of things themselves, a truth to which Zen directly leads and at which a mystic like Eckhart, [albeit] with many theological and philosophical accessories, also arrives" (Wagner, *Meditationen über Gelassenheit*, 177).

39. Ueda Shizuteru, *Hi-shinpishugi: Ekkuharuto to Zen* (*Non-Mysticism: Eckhart and Zen*), vol. 8 of *Ueda Shizuteru shū* (*Collected Works of Ueda Shizuteru*) (Tokyo: Iwanami, 2002), 37ff., 328ff.

40. Ueda, "Freedom and Language in Meister Eckhart and Zen Buddhism," 57.

41. See Caputo, *Mystical Element in Heidegger's Thought*, 18ff.

42. Schürmann, *Meister Eckhart: Mystic and Philosopher*, 47. According to Schürmann, in contrast to Plotinus, in "Eckhart there is no appeal to a privileged experience, no regret of falling back into the body after a repose in the divine, and above all no opposition between a higher world and a lower world into which the soul is resigned to redescend" (15). Winkler also points out that Eckhart, in his development of the Neoplatonic idea of emanation, "eliminates the thought of a hierarchical mediation through mediating beings and the idea that God flows out into his creation, not totally, but 'proportionally'" (Winkler, *Meister Eckhart zur Einführung*, 163). Yet Eckhart does take over the notion of "privation," and creatures are said to be "nothing" in their separation from God. Moreover, insofar as the "flowing out" does take place in two stages—the *bullitio* as the inner emanation of the Trinitarian Persons, and the *ebullitio* as the subsequent creation of all things—does not a certain repetition of the metaphysical hierarchy maintain a place (continually reborn, as it were, out of the breakthrough beyond hierarchical distinctions) in Eckhart's thought?

43. Schürmann, *Meister Eckhart: Mystic and Philosopher*, 62–63. Schürmann interprets Eckhart to be saying here that "one sole and unique principle is deployed throughout the world: the superabundance of divine being which becomes visible in the objects all around."

44. Helting's thesis is best quoted in the German: "Dadurch ergibt sich als Gemeinsamkeit bei Heidegger und Eckehart, dass beide Denker die menschliche Existenz als ein freigegebenes (bzw. zu eigen gegebenes) Zugelassensein verstehen und dieses Zulassen aus der Erfahrung denken, dass in einem zulassenden Sein-lassen ein Sich-Verbergen, Sich-Entziehen (ein 'Nichts,' das Verborgene, ein Geheimnis, die *lethe*) als Urgrund waltet" (Helting, *Heidegger und Meister Eckehart*, 13).

45. Von Herrmann, *Wege ins Ereignis*, 385.

46. Helting, *Heidegger und Meister Eckehart*, 55. One passage that might be read so as to support this interpretation can be found in "Building Dwelling Thinking." In the context of a discussion of the fourfold of earth, sky, mortals, and divinities (*die Göttlichen*), Heidegger writes: "The divinities are the beckoning messengers of the godhead [*die winkenden Boten der Gottheit*]" (*VA* 144/351). Does this *Gottheit*, which withdraws in revealing itself through its messenger divinities, still refer only to one corner of the fourfold, or does it have a more intimate relation than the other three to "the simple oneness of the four"?

47. Heidegger's 1953 discussion with theologians at the Protestant Academy at Hofgeismar brought to the fore the incompatibility between his thinking of the holy in dialogue with the poet's word and the theologian's faithful articulation of the message of revelation. Heidegger is reported as stating: "When a thinker listens to a poet like Hölderlin there is something completely different—a listening in another region of 'manifestness,' the founding of which, in contrast to the already decided revelation of the word of God, the poet himself essentially participates in. . . . With respect to the text referred to from the 'Letter on Humanism,' what is being discussed there is the God of the poet, not the revealed God" (Heidegger, *Piety of Thinking*, 64–65).

48. Schürmann writes in this regard: "It is in the name of the strictness of releasement that Meister Eckhart criticizes the pretension of the supreme being, 'God,' to the rank of the origin. The supreme being still has a 'why,' namely all other beings. We speak of God as the highest reason behind life. We speak even of his will and his intention. But intentionality and purpose have no place in releasement. To think God divinely is to render his ebullience aimless" (Schürmann, *Meister Eckhart: Mystic and Philosopher*, 111).

49. While Heidegger repeatedly rejected the "atheistic existentialism" reading of his early thought, he also generally disapproved of the apologetics of theologians who would all too easily attempt to incorporate his thought back into the fold of Christian theology. If in his personal correspondence Heidegger supported, or at least showed friendly toleration toward, the theologian Bernhard Welte's attempt to rethink the question of God through his thought, this was presumably not just out of personal reasons (their families were Messkirch acquaintances, and at Heidegger's request Welte spoke at his funeral), but rather because Welte proceeded more patiently and cautiously through an engagement with his critique of onto-theology. (See Martin Heidegger and Bernhard Welte, *Briefe und Begegnungen* [Stuttgart: Klett-Cotta, 2003].) It is interesting to note that Heidegger was clearly more ready to acknowledge to Welte an overcoming of the metaphysical conception of God in Eckhart than in Thomas Aquinas (ibid., 29–30, 84–90).

50. Wagner, *Meditationen über Gelassenheit*, 88; see also 139.

51. Ibid., 90.

52. Kettering centers his entire illuminating interpretation of Heidegger's path of thought on this mutual interplay of essential nearness and distance. He capitalizes NÄHE to refer to "being itself" (i.e., beyng) as the "mutual *belonging-together* [*das wechselweise Zusammen*gehören] of being and human being" (Kettering, *NÄHE: Das Denken Martin Heideggers*, 18).

53. Schürmann, *Meister Eckhart: Mystic and Philosopher*, xiii.

54. Although Schürmann is generally an advocate of a strong interpretation of the epochality of the history of being (i.e., the view that each epoch is strictly determined by what he calls an "economy" ruled by a particular principle or *arche*), he nevertheless suggests at one point that Eckhart's *Gelassenheit* already disrupts (at least the order of) the rule of the history of being. "In the history of ideas, each epoch has its own language, and perhaps releasement precedes its own epoch. Our experience is that it reveals the framework of established metaphysics as too narrow, for releasement is as inexhaustible as being itself" (Schürmann, *Meister Eckhart: Mystic and Philosopher*, 191–92). In this crucial passage, Schürmann could be understood as suggesting a thought that I shall later try to work out in some detail: that *Gelassenheit* (together with *Ereignis*) expresses on the one hand a non-historical excess of epochal history, and on the other hand a possible way of being in a time beyond the epochs of metaphysics. Schürmann would call the latter a time beyond the rule of principles, a time of "anarchy." To follow Schürmann in his remarkable interpretation of Heidegger's thought in *Heidegger on Being and Acting: From Principles to Anarchy* (Bloomington: Indiana University Press, 1987), it would be necessary to free the expression "anarchy" of any residual connotations of willful "arbitrariness" (*Willkür*). Schürmann clearly states that his notion of anarchy is to be understood as giving way neither to the violent "power of authority, *princeps*" nor to the substitution of such by "the 'rational' power, *principium*" (6). Schürmann does speak of the "anarchy principle" (indeed, the original French title of his book was *Le principe d'anarchie* [Paris: Éditions de Seuil, 1982]), but as an inherently ambivalent transitional term on the threshold of the closure of the metaphysics of principles and the transition to an anticipated "anarchic praxis" without principles (see 6, 163, 274, 293). Meister Eckhart's "life without why" is referred to throughout *Heidegger on Being and Acting* as a prefiguration of this anarchic "practical apriori" or "existentiell ground" for thinking (see 10, 244, 260, 280). One might ask Schürmann, however, whether the notion of "anarchy" would itself become anachronistic, insofar as it still speaks in (negative) terms of *arche;* would the very domain of the duality of principles/anarchy be left behind in the recovery from metaphysics? Or would the "an-" of anarchy need to be thought in the sense of the "non-" of non-willing?

Chapter 6

1. Heidegger reportedly made this comment to his wife, who relayed it to Otto Pöggeler (see Müller-Lauter, *Heidegger und Nietzsche*, 17). Gadamer also reported hearing from Heidegger's son that Heidegger always said this in the last months of

his life. (See Babette E. Babich, "Poetry, Eros, and Thought in Nietzsche and Hei-degger," *Conference Proceedings from the Thirty-ninth Annual North American Heidegger Conference,* 82; Babich cites as her reference *Aletheia* 9/10 [1996]: 19.)

2. On the basis of the *Nietzsche* volumes, Heidegger later wrote two important essays which reflect the outcome of his *Auseinandersetzung* with Nietzsche: "The Word of Nietzsche: 'God Is Dead'" (*GA* 5:209–67), originally presented in 1943 and then revised and published in 1950 in *Holzwege;* and "Who Is Nietzsche's Zarathustra?" (*VA* 97–122), presented in 1953 and published in 1954 in *Vorträge und Aufsätze. Was heisst Denken?* (1951–52) also contains important passages on Nietzsche.

3. See Arendt, *Life of the Mind,* part 2, p. 173. Pöggeler writes in this regard: "The one who attempts to follow Heidegger's difficult attempt at interpretation encounters the further difficulty that Heidegger himself is still 'underway.' . . . For example, in the rector's address of 1933 which contained the first decisive public reference to Nietzsche, Heidegger demands nothing more decisive than the 'will-ing,' which allows the essential, that which matters, to come to 'power.' . . . How-ever, Heidegger's examination of Nietzsche finally comes to the experience that precisely the will and its wanting to create, as it becomes dominant in modern times, hinder an experience of the truth of being. . . . His examination of Nietz-sche . . . is also a decision about Heidegger's thinking, a way upon which Heideg-ger works off definite presuppositions which determined his thinking" (Pöggeler, *Martin Heidegger's Path of Thinking,* 86).

4. See Friedrich Nietzsche, *Grossoktavausgabe,* ed. Nietzsche Archive (Leipzig, 1894–1912), 14:327.

5. Nietzsche, *Beyond Good and Evil,* section 36; *The Will to Power,* sections 685, 693, and see section 1067; see also *Thus Spoke Zarathustra,* part 2, section 12. For Nietzsche, to be sure, there is no "will" in the sense of a metaphysical substrate, but only a fluctuating plurality of wills competing for power. There is no noumenal "Will," but always only ever a multiplicity of "punctuations of will [*Willens-Puktationen*] that are constantly increasing or losing their power" (*The Will to Power,* section 715). Nevertheless, "the will to power" remains the defining impulse throughout all this transformation and multiplicity. According to Wolfgang Müller-Lauter's interpretation, when Nietzsche speaks of "*the* will to power," this refers to the "sole quality" common to what is different quantitatively (Müller-Lauter, *Nietzsche: His Philosophy of Contradictions and the Contradictions of His Philos-ophy,* trans. David J. Parent [Chicago: University of Illinois Press, 1999], 133ff.).

6. Nietzsche, *Twilight of the Idols,* part 1, sections 26, 42.

7. The major reaction to Heidegger's critical interpretation of Nietzsche as the last metaphysician has been on the part of French philosophers such as Klos-sowski, Deleuze, and Derrida. (See the excellent collection of articles in David B. Allison, ed., *The New Nietzsche* [Cambridge, Mass.: MIT Press, 1977].) In a pro-grammatic passage Derrida writes: "To save Nietzsche from a reading of the Hei-deggerian type, it seems that we must above all not attempt to restore or make explicit a less naive 'ontology,' composed of profound ontological intuitions ac-ceding to some originary truth. . . . The virulence of Nietzschean thought could not be more completely misunderstood. . . . Therefore, rather than protect Nietz-

sche from the Heideggerian reading, we should perhaps offer him up to it completely, underwriting that interpretation without reserve; in a *certain way* and up to a certain point where, the content of the Nietzschean discourse being almost lost for the question of being, its form regains its absolute strangeness, where his text invokes a different type of reading, more faithful to his type of writing" (Derrida, *Of Grammatology*, 19).

See also Jacques Derrida, "Interpreting Signatures (Nietzsche/Heidegger): Two Questions," in *Dialogue and Deconstruction*, ed. Michelfelder and Palmer; Jacques Derrida, *Spurs: Nietzsche's Styles*, trans. Barbara Harlow (Chicago: University of Chicago Press, 1978); and Ernst Behler, *Confrontations: Derrida/Heidegger/ Nietzsche*, trans. Steven Taubeneck (Stanford: Stanford University Press, 1991). For Derrida, it is in fact Heidegger's own obsession with unifying and systematizing Nietzsche's thought that marks rather his own residues of metaphysical thinking. I shall return to this issue in chapter 9.

8. See John Sallis, *Crossings: Nietzsche and the Space of Tragedy* (Chicago: University of Chicago Press, 1991), 2ff.; and Sallis, *Echoes: After Heidegger*, chapter 3.

9. See my "A Socrates Who Practices Music: The Dynamic Intertwining of *Mythos* and *Logos*, Art and Science in Nietzsche's *The Birth of Tragedy*," in *Mythos and Logos: How to Regain the Love of Wisdom*, ed. Albert Anderson et al. (Amsterdam/ New York: Rodopi, 2004).

10. *Amor fati*, a Dionysian affirmation of life just as it is, would be reached by crossing over to the opposite of the will to negation (see Nietzsche, *The Will to Power*, section 1041). Note that *amor fati* would not simply be fatalism, which would merely be another form of negating the will but remaining within its domain as a mere lack of will, as not-willing. *Amor fati* would not be a simple passive acceptance of fate, but a *love* of fate. Yet what is the nature of this "love"? What is the relation of this love to the will? Why does Nietzsche speak of loving fate, and not willing fate? Ryōgi Ōkōchi asks "whether 'amor' could still be a 'will'? . . . How are 'amor' and 'will' related to one another for [Nietzsche]? Was it possible for him to overcome the will?" Ōkōchi concludes that ultimately we are left with an ambiguity; in the final stage of his thought, "the will is to Nietzsche at the same time not will, 'amor' is will and at the same time no longer will" (Ōkōchi, "Nietzsches Amor Fati im Lichte von Karma des Buddhismus," *Nietzsche-Studien* 1 [1972]: 81–85). Also in dialogue with Buddhism, I have pursued at some length the question of the ambiguities involved in Nietzsche's "self-overcoming *of* the will to power"—I italicize the "of" in order to mark a crucial *ambivalence* between the subjective and the objective genitive in this phrase. Is it possible to speak of a movement in Nietzsche's thought that leads through a "self-overcoming *of* the will to power," a movement from the subjective to the objective genitive? (See Davis, "Zen After Zarathustra: The Problem of the Will in the Confrontation Between Nietzsche and Buddhism.") Charles Scott finds in the text of *Thus Spoke Zarathustra* "a movement in the power of the idea of will to power toward an anticipated organization that is beyond the will-to-power discourse" (Scott, *The Question of Ethics*, 29). Karl Löwith has suggested that we read Nietzsche's thought as a movement from a *Du sollst* to an *Ich will* and finally to the *Ich bin* of the "cosmic child" at play. The final transformation in Nietzsche's thought is said to be from the will to power to *amor*

fati, interpreted as a "lieben" that is "nicht mehr ein Wollen," but rather "eine nichts mehr wollende Willigkeit, in der sich das Wollen als solches aufhebt." A decade later, however, Löwith concludes that Nietzsche "undoubtedly achieved the metamorphosis from the Christian 'Thou shalt' to the modern 'I will,' but hardly the crucial transformation from the 'I will' to the 'I am' of the cosmic child" (Löwith, *Sämtliche Schriften,* vol. 6, *Nietzsche* [Stuttgart: J. B. Metzlersche, 1987], 128, 201, 426).

11. Müller-Lauter finds the final phase of Heidegger's involvement with Nietzsche, in the early 1950s, to be a renewed positive assessment of Nietzsche's foresight, namely that "Nietzsche had perceived the danger that man was making himself (technologically) at home on his superficies," and that "he had been the 'the first' to be aware both of the 'danger' and the necessity of a 'transition'" (see *WhD* 24/57, 62–63/55–56). Nevertheless, since the "placement of Nietzsche in Heidegger's conception of modern metaphysics as history of the truth of Being suffers no fundamental change," Müller-Lauter finds a tension in this final phase of Heidegger's interpretation between "that Nietzsche who was incapable of surveying and seeing beyond the world of technology which, though he could not comprehend it, he had nonetheless advanced, and the other Nietzsche who was supposed to have reflected on the devastation of the earth." As for Heidegger's immanent critique of the spirit of revenge in Nietzsche, Müller-Lauter argues that, if we attend to the movement of Nietzsche's thought, "it is beyond question that Nietzsche did not in the end fall captive to the spirit of revenge which he had opposed in *Zarathustra* as Heidegger thinks he did" (Müller-Lauter, "The Spirit of Revenge and the Eternal Recurrence," 149–50, 161).

12. Nietzsche, *The Will to Power,* section 617.

13. I shall return to this point in chapter 7 where I show that the "essence of man" in Heidegger's thought is ambiguous. On the one hand this essence is, along with being itself, thoroughly historical; in this sense the essence of modern man is the will. On the other hand, through his critique of the will Heidegger attempts to intimate a more originary essence of man, an essence to which we are called upon to reattune ourselves; this suggests a non-historical (which is not to say unhistorical or a-historical) essence of non-willing.

14. On the relation of Heidegger's history of being to Hegel's dialectic of Spirit, see Robert Bernasconi, *The Question of Language in Heidegger's History of Being* (Atlantic Highlands, N.J.: Humanities, 1985), chapter 1; Krell, *Intimations of Mortality,* chapter 7; Dennis J. Schmidt, *The Ubiquity of the Finite: Hegel, Heidegger, and the Entitlements of Philosophy* (Cambridge, Mass.: MIT Press, 1988), esp. chapter 6; and Rebecca Comay and John McCumber, eds., *Endings: Questions of Memory in Hegel and Heidegger* (Evanston, Ill.: Northwestern University Press, 1999).

15. In this late essay from 1962, "Time and Being," Heidegger attempts to radically think back behind "being" as the "letting-presence" (*Anwesenlassen*) of beings to *Ereignis* as the *Es gibt* which grants-in-withdrawal the epochs of being and time. This granting-in-withdrawal of the *Es gibt,* which was not thought even by the early Greeks, is what Heidegger calls "sending" (*Schicken*), while what-is-sent (*das Geschickte*) is the series of epochs of the history of being (*Seinsgeschichte*).

16. Nishida's term is *hirenzoku-no-renzoku.* With this notion Nishida attempts

to preserve both the absolute independence and self-determining aspect of each moment of time as well as the continuity of time and the determination of the present by the past and the future by the present. Nishida, it is relevant to note, develops this idea in critique of Hegel's "process dialectic," and attempts to develop his own "absolute dialectic" of the moment-to-moment "absolute death and rebirth" (*zettai-shi-soku-fukkatsu*) and the "self-determination of the world" (*sekai no jiko-gentei*). See Nishida's texts on the philosophy of history gathered in volume 5 of *Nishidatetsugaku senshū* (*Selected Works of Nishida's Philosophy*) (Tokyo: Iwanami, 1998); and Nishida Kitaro, *Fundamental Problems of Philosophy*, trans. David A. Dilworth (Tokyo: Sophia University Press, 1970). For two solid beginnings to the momentous task of bringing Heidegger and Nishida into dialogue, see Elmar Weinmayr, "Denken im Übergang—Kitarō Nishida und Martin Heidegger," in *Japan und Heidegger*, ed. Buchner; and Ōhashi Ryōsuke, *Nishidatetsugaku no sekai* (*The World of Nishida's Philosophy*) (Tokyo: Chikumashobō, 1995), 179–98.

17. Heidegger also argues that even Protagoras's statement that "man is the measure of all things" is not to be read in the manner of modern subjectivism (*N2* 135ff./91ff.).

18. Pöggeler, *Martin Heidegger's Path of Thinking*, 102–3.

19. In general Heidegger gives a clearer and more detailed genealogical account of the development (both continuities and discontinuities) of "subjectivity" from the Greek *hypokeimenon* than he does with regard to the distant origins of the "will" in Greek thought. Müller-Lauter argues that, other than a few indications with regard to *orexis*, Heidegger "left the nature of the will in the early history of *Subiectität* in the dark" (Müller-Lauter, *Nietzsche und Heidegger*, 243–44). As we have seen, these few indications are nevertheless suggestive. I agree, however, that given the centrality of the critique of the will to will as the culmination of the history of metaphysics that began with the Greeks, Heidegger did not sufficiently clarify the will's emergence and early development. It is often thought that the concept of the will in fact fully emerged only in connection with Christianity. The history of the will in Christianity itself is immensely complex, not only with regard to human will but also with regard to the "Will of God." Michael Allen Gillespie argues that Heidegger, in his purportedly exclusive attention to the philosophical origins of modernity and nihilism, failed to account for their theological origins. Gillespie begins his own account with the late medieval absolutization of the Will of God, particularly in the radical nominalism of Ockham. It is in revolt against this omnipotent *deus absconditus*, Gillespie argues, that thinkers from Descartes to Fichte to Nietzsche gradually carried out a "transference of power" from divine to human willing. This process of the transference of omnipotent will from God to humans, culminating in Nietzsche's overman as the maximization of will to power, is argued to be the main plot behind the story of modernity's rise and descent into nihilism (Gillespie, *Nihilism Before Nietzsche* [Chicago: University of Chicago Press, 1995]).

20. In his explication of Heidegger's critique of religious justification, Michael Zimmerman writes: "Justification, then, was a product of intellectual voluntarism, the will to salvation. Various disciplinary techniques . . . were developed to promote the actualization of the soul's will to salvation. Self-denial, however,

turned out to lead not to the allegedly desired goal of self-lessness, but instead to a heightened sense of individuality and self-assertion. Beneath the veneer of medieval piety [and] asceticism . . . there smoldered the self-affirming self which would later burst forth in Descartes's thinking and culminate in that of Nietzsche" (Zimmerman, *Heidegger's Confrontation with Modernity,* 179).

21. Is this transformation characteristic of Christianity as such or does it represent a degeneration of a more original Christian experience? Although at times Heidegger writes as if the tradition of Christianity is essentially metaphysical (could this tradition do without the theological idea of God as the "supreme being"?), at other times he aims his critique rather at "Christendom," hinting at a more original realm of religious experience in Christianity. For example, in the 1943 essay "The Word of Nietzsche: 'God Is Dead'" Heidegger writes: "Christendom . . . and the Christianity of the New Testament faith are not the same. Even a non-Christian life can affirm Christendom and use it as a means of power, just as, conversely, a Christian life does not necessarily require Christendom. Therefore, a confrontation with Christendom is absolutely not in any way an attack against what is Christian, any more than a critique of theology is necessarily a critique of faith" (*GA* 5:219–20/63–64).

In his retrospective notes from 1937–38, "Mein bisheriger Weg" ("My Way up to the Present"), Heidegger wrote the following about his relation to Christianity: "And who would want to ignore the fact that the *Auseinandersetzung* with Christianity silently accompanied me on this entire path heretofore: an *Auseinandersetzung* that was and is not [simply] one 'problem' that was taken up, but rather *at once* a preservation of the origin—of the house of my parents, of my homeland and of my youth—that is most my own, *and* a painful detachment from it" (*GA* 66:415).

On the complexity of Heidegger's *Auseinandersetzung* with Christianity, see chapters 4 and 5, and pp. 248–51.

22. In point of fact, Nietzsche does not simply assert that will is more fundamental than thought. Rather, he rejects the simple distinction between the two, and indeed the very notion of a simple "will" that could be isolated from thought. Nietzsche claims that "the will is always accompanied by a ruling thought" (see *Beyond Good and Evil,* section 19), and that, conversely, there is no thinking which is not a matter of will to power. Heidegger acknowledges this point when he connects Nietzsche's will to power with the assertion of German idealism that "knowing and willing are the same" (see *NI* 68–69/56–57).

23. Zimmerman, *Heidegger's Confrontation with Modernity,* 172.

24. For a slightly earlier version of this passage, *see* WhD 35–36/91.

25. See Günter Zöller's lucid account of the intertwinement of willing and thinking in Fichte's philosophy, in *Fichte's Transcendental Philosophy: The Original Duplicity of Intelligence and Will* (Cambridge: Cambridge University Press, 1998), esp. part 3. Zöller quotes passages where Fichte writes that "willing is nothing but a [kind] of thinking," and that "I will insofar as I think myself as willing, and I think myself as willing insofar as I will" (79).

26. See J. G. Fichte, *The Science of Knowledge with the First and Second Introductions,* ed. and trans. Peter Heath and John Lachs (Cambridge: Cambridge Univer-

sity Press, 1982), 231, 238. The editors' summary of Fichte's thought in this regard bears quoting here, as it gives a good account of the interconnection of (the theoretical drive of) representation and (the practical drive of) will in his idealism: "The self is an active, striving being. In particular it has two fundamental drives, which impose upon it two different but closely interrelated tasks. The practical drive of the self is 'to fill out infinity'; this drive urges it on to engage in the activity of self-assertion without end, to transform everything into its own image, and to subject a whole world to its autonomous laws. The theoretical drive, by contrast, is one that moves the self to reflect upon itself and to know itself in splendid unity. If the practical drive is conceived as a line of activity stretching outward from the self to infinity, the drive to reflection must be thought of as checking that activity at a certain point and making it revert back toward the self" (xvii). It is not difficult to see the connection between these interrelated drives and the power-preservation/power-enhancement of the will as ecstatic-incorporation.

27. Schelling, *Schellings sämmtliche Werke,* 7:350.

28. In his lectures on the philosophy of history, Hegel affirms that "the will is only free, insofar as it wills nothing other, external, foreign—for then it would be dependent—but only wills itself, the will," and that "it is only as thinking intelligence that the will is genuinely a will and free" (quoted in Charles Taylor, *Hegel* [Cambridge: Cambridge University Press, 1975], 369–70).

29. William J. Richardson, *Heidegger: Through Phenomenology to Thought,* 3rd ed. (The Hague: Nijhoff, 1974), 339.

30. Hegel, *Phänomenologie des Geistes,* Werke 3, p. 23; Hegel, *Hegel's Phenomenology of Spirit,* 10.

31. Hegel, *Phänomenologie des Geistes,* Werke 3, p. 29; Hegel, *Hegel's Phenomenology of Spirit,* 14.

32. Georg Wilhelm Friedrich Hegel, *Enzyklopädie der philosophischen Wissenschaften 1830 Dritter Teil,* Werke 10, 4th ed. (Frankfurt am Main: Suhrkamp, 1999), 9–10.

33. Again pointing to the ambiguity of the Greeks with respect to the history of metaphysics, which culminates in the epoch of technology, Heidegger notes that this *Stellen* can be traced back to "a certain *thesis*-character concealed within *physis*" (*GA* 79:63), even though this prototypical *Stellen* is not yet that of the *Ge-Stell* of modern technology. That is, while the Greek world is fundamentally *pre*technological, it is also pre-*technological* insofar as the "essential genealogy of *Ge-Stell* [*die Wesensgenealogie des Ge-Stells*]" (65) leads back to the Greek *physis.*

34. Zimmerman, *Heidegger's Confrontation with Modernity,* 199.

35. Julian Young makes the interesting remark that the "*Ge-stell* thus determines an, as it were, 'master morality' and a 'slave morality'" (Young, *Heidegger, Philosophy, Nazism,* 210). In other words, in the epoch of technology man is, on the one hand, the master who wills to be lord over the earth, and yet, on the other hand, is himself reduced to a slave of the cybernetic system of the will to will. The epoch of the *Ge-stell* thus fulfills both extremes of activity and passivity within the domain of the will.

36. "But where danger is, grows/Also that-which-saves." From Hölderlin's poem "Patmos," in *Hymns and Fragments by Friedrich Hölderlin,* trans. Richard

Sieburth (Princeton: Princeton University Press, 1984), 88–89. These lines are frequently cited by Heidegger (see *VA* 32/333; *GA* 79:72/42; *GA* 5:296/118).

37. As Heidegger's text *Der Satz vom Grund* attempts to show, a thinking which follows or enacts the turning out of metaphysics would move through "the principle of reason" to "the leap from ground" (both are possible renderings of the phrase *der Satz vom Grund*).

Chapter 7

1. Pöggeler, *Martin Heidegger's Path of Thinking*, 106.
2. Ibid., 112.
3. The few exceptions to this rule, as we have seen, are when he is (re)interpreting his own earlier texts (such as "The Origin of the Work of Art") which had used this language.
4. In his 1942–43 lecture course, "Parmenides," Heidegger had criticized Rilke in harsher terms, attacking in particular his alleged failure to think "the Open" as the *aletheia* of being, rather than in terms of "the unrestrained progression of beings." Moreover, in claiming in the eighth Duino Elegy that "the creature sees the Open," Rilke is said to have failed to recognize that it is the unique ability of man, who alone has the word (logos), to see into the Open of being, and that it is this capacity which forms "the insurmountable essential boundary between animal and man." Heidegger concludes that Rilke's poetry remained determined by modern metaphysics, and specifically that "from a purely metaphysical point of view . . . the domain of Rilke's basic poetic experience is not at all distinct from the basic position of Nietzsche's thinking" (*GA* 54:226, 231, 235; see 225–40). I shall limit myself in this section to a consideration of Heidegger's less polemical 1946 interpretation of Rilke, without attempting to respond with a counter-reading of Rilke. In this regard see Llewelyn, *Middle Voice of Ecological Conscience*, chapter 7; and especially Haar, *Song of the Earth*, 30–33 and chapter 8. Haar compellingly argues that: "In making his entire interpretation depend on [a purported] parallel with Nietzsche, Heidegger oversimplifies and dissimulates the fundamentals of Rilke's thought more than elucidates them." Haar later goes on to ask: is not Rilke's Open, as the "withdrawn center that holds all gathered things and unites their adverse tensions," not in fact "closer to Heidegger's being than to any particular being, notably to Schopenhauer's will?" (Haar, *Song of the Earth*, 121, 130–31).
5. William Richardson explicates this key point of Heidegger's interpretation of Rilke as follows: "Being is conceived as 'Nature.' After the fashion of Leibniz' *Natura*, Nature for Rilke is the universal force that permeates all beings. . . . The result is that beings are, not simply because they are willed but because they *are-willing*, [which means] are *as* willing, by reason of the Will that makes them be" (Richardson, *Heidegger: Through Phenomenology to Thought*, 392).
6. We are told in the conversation that *ein Weiser* is not meant here in the sense of one who knows (*ein Wissender*), but in the sense of one who is able to indicate (*weisen*) the direction wherefrom hints (of being) arrive, and who is then also able to indicate the way (*die Weise*) humans are to follow such hints (*GA* 77:84–85). Why

did Heidegger change the name of *der Weise* to *der Lehrer* (teacher) in the shorter published version of the conversation? Andrew Mitchell suggests that this change implies a closer relation to the *Gelehrte* (scholar), who often provides the "historical references" (*historische Hinweise*) that help the conversation along (see *GA* 77:97). "The tight relation between *Lehrer* and *Gelehrter* in the published version of the conversation," Mitchell suggests, "would seem to underscore the necessity of an appropriation of the historical before any possible 'overcoming' of it (which is to say again that the history of philosophy must be *verwindet* and not simply *überwindet*)" (Mitchell, "Praxis and *Gelassenheit:* The 'Practice' of the Limit," in *Heidegger and Practical Philosophy*, ed. Raffoul and Pettigrew, 333).

7. See note 38 to chapter 3 above. In the 1957–58 essay "The Essence of Language," Heidegger writes: "Every posing of every question takes place within the very grant [*Zusage*] of what is put in question." Therefore, "the authentic attitude of thinking is not a putting of questions—rather, it is a listening to the *Zusage*, the promise of what is to come into question." It is in this sense, Heidegger goes on to say, that the admittedly ambiguous statement in 1953 that "questioning is the piety of thinking" must be understood. In this regard he writes: "One of the stimulating experiences of thinking is that at times it does not sufficiently review its newly reached insights, and does not properly follow them through. Such, too, is the case with the sentence just cited that questioning is the piety of thinking" (*GA* 12:165/71–72). And yet, we find that in the *Feldweg* conversation Heidegger had in fact thought this insight through already in 1944–45!

8. See Kettering, *NÄHE: Das Denken Martin Heideggers*, 256–57.

9. Günter Zöller independently confirms this claim, specifically in reference to the modern German philosophical tradition: "Since Leibniz, the inquiry into the structure of subjectivity has . . . tended to employ a double characterization of the self as subject of cognition and subject of volition. More important, the cognitive and the conative elements of human subjectivity have typically been characterized in terms of each other, stressing both the volitional component in knowing and the cognitive component in willing" (Zöller, *Fichte's Transcendental Philosophy*, 71).

10. For a phenomenological discussion which draws on both Husserl and Heidegger to distinguish between, on the one hand, the "appearance of phenomena" within the limits of the "horizon" posited by subjective volitional consciousness, and, on the other hand, the "shining-forth of things" which breaks through this horizon from a "region beyond the will," see Tadashi Ogawa, "The Horizonal Character of Phenomena and the Shining-forth of Things," *Research in Phenomenology* 30 (2000): 146–57. Ogawa, however, is not concerned here with Heidegger's radical critique of the willful positing of a horizon, but rather with demonstrating what he calls a structural relation of compatibility, a "neutralized opposition" between the horizon (i.e., the domain of volitional capability) and its Other (i.e., the region beyond the will). In his essay "Praxis and *Gelassenheit*," Andrew Mitchell, on the other hand, by focusing on the *Auseinandersetzung* with Nietzsche, interprets the later Heidegger to be saying that while a *horizon* is posited by the praxis of the will to power in order to schematize and keep in view an established realm of possibilities, and thereby "make possible a further appropriation and stabilization of

chaos (i.e., growth)," the "practice" of *Gelassenheit* would involve remaining attentively open to a surrounding *region*, wherein the limits of any given perspective, along with the hidden essence of things, are acknowledged and let be. These limits would not be merely negative (i.e., concealing)—for as the Greeks already perceived: "a limit is not an end but a beginning"—but rather would also be what positively lets determinate things appear (i.e., show themselves from themselves). Rather than the oxymoronic endeavor to willfully posit a horizon of boundless unconcealment for the human subject, an openness to the mystery of the region (the self-withdrawal of being in letting beings be), and an engaged *Gelassenheit* towards the things that show themselves in this region, would entail what Mitchell calls a "practice of letting the limit be."

11. Note in this regard that in "Time and Being" Heidegger radically rethinks "presence," *An-wesen,* as what essentially concerns or goes up to us, *geht uns an,* and the "present," *Gegenwart,* as "what comes toward us in abiding [*uns entgegenweilen*], towards we humans" (*ZSD* 12/12). For Heidegger, man is most properly neither the lord of the earth nor simply one entity among others, but rather the bearer of an enormous receptive-response-ability for participating in the event of the truth of being.

12. I have opted to translate *Erörterung* in the title as "explication," meaning literally an "unfolding," since this is at least closer to the topological sense intended than is "discussion," which etymologically implies analyzing by way of smashing into pieces.

13. See Ohashi, *Ekstase und Gelassenheit,* 131–32.

14. Mitchell shows how this "waiting" also refers to the proper comportment to things: "To wait upon a thing's thing-essence . . . is precisely not to challenge it forth, not to decide in advance how it is to be revealed (i.e., as fully in accordance with our will and greed), and not to demand that it be purely present. Rather, to wait upon a thing's essence is to let the thing rest *in its essence,* and that means *to not be purely present.* The essence of a thing is a space of concealment, a hiding place from revelation. When things are allowed to essentially show themselves (when a thing *west*), they preserve this hiddenness and self-concealment, and only then can they be said to be whole (*Heil*). The way of being in the world that lets things be what they essentially are is dwelling. . . . In dwelling . . . things show themselves according to their own measure and not as 'purely present.' The hiddenness of their essence shines in their presencing. Dwelling brings a limit to willful human encroachment" (Mitchell, "Praxis and *Gelassenheit,*" 327–28).

15. We shall return to Heidegger's attempt to think a non-willing sense of "waiting" in chapter 8.

16. *Wollen* could be translated here in the everyday sense as "to want"; yet given the significance of this word in this context, it is best translated as "to will."

17. Analogously, Reiner Schürmann elucidates two aspects or moments in the context of Eckhart's teaching of *gelāzenheit.* As we have seen, he interprets Eckhart's thought as fluctuating "between the demands of a law: voluntary disappropriation and impoverishment; and the description of a state: the original liberty which man has never lost at the base of his being" (Schürmann, *Meister Eckhart: Mystic and Philosopher,* xiii). Concerning the movement from ascetic detachment

(*abgescheidenheit*) to a releasement beyond the will, Schürmann writes: "As existence moves ahead on this road, all ascetic imperatives vanish. Thus detachment turns progressively into releasement, *gelāzenheit,* which . . . is a broader concept. The lower intensities of releasement require an effort of the will; the higher intensities of releasement exclude every voluntary determination" (85). See also John Caputo's comments on these two aspects of *Gelassenheit* in Heidegger's thought, in *The Mystical Element in Heidegger's Thought,* 177–79.

18. Krell points out that both the continuity and the discontinuity between Heidegger's earlier and later uses of the notion of decision are key to understanding the development of his thought: "Decision is therefore a bridge between Heidegger's thinking of the ecstatic temporality of Dasein and the historical unfolding of being as such; a bridge, in other words, connecting Heidegger's project of a fundamental ontology of human existence with his later preoccupation with the truth and history of being as such" (Krell, "Introduction to the Paperback Edition," in Heidegger, *Nietzsche,* vols. 1 and 2, xv–xvii).

19. Schürmann also says that we must think *Entscheidung* in the context of the following passage from the second *Nietzsche* volume: "Thinking has not yet risen out of [*ent-standen aus*] the separation [*Scheidung*] between the metaphysical being question, which inquires into the being of beings, and that question which inquires more originally into the truth of being" (*N2* 293/217; see Schürmann, *Heidegger on Being and Acting,* 246). It is relevant to note that Schürmann cuts off the last part of Heidegger's sentence, which reads: "and thus into the essential relation of being to the essence of man." It is precisely the issue of "the essential relation of being to the essence of man" that marks the limit of thinking the decision solely in non-human "economic" terms.

20. Schürmann, *Heidegger on Being and Acting,* 246.

21. Ibid., 249–50.

22. Ibid., 248.

23. In the end we shall have to return to the question of whether Heidegger left a space free for rethinking the enigma of human freedom and responsibility for decision, that is, for what Schürmann problematically refers to in the language of will as the "volitional act." After following Heidegger's thought-path through to the end, the question remains: In what sense do humans remain "free"—undecided but capable of deciding—either to set themselves on the way to *Gelassenheit* or to persist in the domain of will? In what sense are humans responsible for undertaking the step back toward a recovery of their originary response-ability of cor-respondence to the address of being?

24. Is there, however, a temporal dimension of natural things that gets covered over when "nature" is objectified as an a-historical realm unrelated to the historicality of human existence? Might a re-attunement to a "time of the earth" ground an attempt to rethink historicity other than as either willful projection or calculated clock-time? John Sallis has opened up a space for such questions, through and beyond Heidegger's thought, in his rethinking of the relation of time and earth (stone). Sallis situates Heidegger at the end of a tradition that extends from Augustine, according to which time is "withdrawn from things" and located exclusively in the soul. "As if future and past were not etched into the things that

nature sets before our vision. . . . As if time's being amidst things were not attested by the things themselves, by their giving a measure by which time is determined. As the sun provides the measure for the time of day" (Sallis, "Uranic Time," in *Time and Nothingness,* ed. Michael Lazarin [Kyoto: Institute of Buddhist Cultural Studies, Ryukoku University, 1997], 11, 13).

Merleau-Ponty looks not to the celestial bodies but first to the human body for intimations of a "natural time" that is more originary than abstract clock-time and at least co-originary with the "personal time" of Dasein's ecstatic temporality. The ecstatic "thickness" of time, he writes, is disclosed first of all in my body, which "secretes time" and "unites present, past and future" in the cyclical repetition of its "anonymous functions." "Natural time is always there. . . . I am borne into personal existence by a time which I do not constitute, all my perceptions stand out against a background of nature" (Maurice Merleau-Ponty, *Phenomenology of Perception,* trans. Colin Smith [London: Routledge and Kegan Paul, 1962], 239, 346–47, 453). In the end, however, Merleau-Ponty declines to posit an unambiguous ontological hierarchy between the "natural time" of the body and the cultural and historical time of personal existence. "Neither [the natural] body nor existence can be regarded as the original human being, since they presuppose each other" (166; see 238, 347–48). In his "philosophy of ambiguity" Merleau-Ponty attempts rather to phenomenologically articulate this originary intertwinement of the nonhistorical temporality of pre-personal nature and the personal temporality of existential historicity.

25. Otto Pöggeler, "'Historicity' in Heidegger's Late Work," in *Thinking About Being: Aspects of Heidegger's Thought,* ed. Robert W. Shahan and J. N. Mohanty (Norman: University of Oklahoma Press, 1984), 58, 69–70, 72.

26. Hans Ruin, *Enigmatic Origins: Tracing the Theme of Historicity Through Heidegger's Works* (Stockholm: Almqvist and Wiksell, 1994), 254.

27. Ruin, *Enigmatic Origins,* 10.

28. Ibid., 177.

29. Ibid., 199.

30. Haar, *Heidegger and the Essence of Man,* 177.

31. Ibid., 176.

32. Ibid., 148.

33. See Haar's *Song of the Earth,* esp. the preface, "The Limits and Grounds of History: The Nonhistorical," and part 2, "The Limits of History." See also John Sallis, *Stone* (Bloomington: Indiana University Press, 1994). Sallis writes of a "peculiar temporality of stone: stone is ancient . . . in the sense that its antiquity is of the order of the always already. Stone comes from a past that has never been present, a past unassimilable to the order of time in which things come and go in the human world" (26). This radically pre-historical temporality of stone both grants a foundation for and yet withdraws from human historical temporality; hence it is often found to be the most appropriate material with which to memorialize precisely those events which occur at the limits of human time, as when one marks an inauguration with a foundation stone or a death with a gravestone. Elsewhere Sallis characterizes this duality of the temporality of stone—what we might call its *foundational* and its *impenetrable* aspects—in terms of "uranic time" and "lithic

time." With regard to the former Sallis refers to Plato's *Timaeus,* where it is written that the sun, moon, and the planets "came into being for the determining and guarding of the numbers of time" (*Timaeus* 38c). These heavenly bodies serve to ground the measurements of human temporality in uranic time. And yet in rare moments, Sallis writes, as "a quiet receptiveness comes over one's vision . . . one will sense that the time of the stone is other than the time it measures." This "lithic time" most intimate to the stone is one "to which movement is absolutely alien"; it is a time of "utter repose" that is decisively withdrawn from human events and history (Sallis, "Uranic Time," 13–14). This attunement of quiet receptiveness to the withdrawal of stone from the grasp of human historical temporality and comprehension would perhaps open us to our own embodied finitude and to that dimension of earthly things which exceeds the measurements of our technological calculation and control.

Michael Zimmerman, commenting on a passage where Heidegger writes of "the unnoticeable law of the earth" which "preserves the earth in the sufficiency of the emerging and perishing of all things in the allotted sphere of the possible which everything follows, and yet nothing knows" (*VA* 94/88), writes: "Note that Heidegger concluded that the intrinsic 'possibilities' of living things are *discovered, not created,* in the historical world. If living things did not somehow contain their own intrinsic limit and measure, there would be no basis for objecting to the technological disclosure of things. If for something 'to be' simply meant for it to present itself in accordance with the categories imposed by an historical epoch, then there would be nothing problematic, for example, about animals presenting themselves merely as objects in the laboratory or as commodities on the factory farm. . . . Heidegger's difficulty, however, . . . was how to speak of the intrinsic measure and limit of living things ('the hidden law of the earth') without resorting to one of the foundationalist doctrines of productionist metaphysics. . . . Unwilling to appeal either to metaphysics or to science, Heidegger concluded that the 'hidden law of the earth' is an impenetrable mystery" (Zimmerman, *Heidegger's Confrontation with Modernity,* 227).

It is this attempt to speak of that which exceeds historical determinations, and yet is not a metaphysical foundation of predetermined ahistorical essences, that I am calling the "non-historical" as "in-historical" in Heidegger's thought. And Heidegger does indeed have much to say, if not by way of penetrating proof then at least by way of thoughtful intimation, concerning this "mysterious dimension."

34. With regard to the non-historical dimension of embodiment, I have already mentioned Merleau-Ponty's indications of a natural time of the "anonymous functions of the body." Drew Leder has critically supplemented Merleau-Ponty's phenomenological "primacy of perception" with an attention to the visceral dimension of our subconscious embodiment that essentially recedes, not only from the invisibility of the ideal, but also from the "visibility" of the flesh. This dimension of the self both sustains its life and its living "blood relation" with the world, and yet essentially resists comprehension and control by the conscious subject (Leder, "Flesh and Blood: A Proposed Supplement to Merleau-Ponty," in *The Body,* ed. Welton).

David Michael Levin has written of what he calls the "transhistorical" dimension of embodiment. He argues that the problem of extreme historical relativism, a problem with which Heidegger struggled from early on, "cannot be seriously contested without bringing into the debate the matter of embodiment" (Levin, *Opening of Vision,* 36–37). Levin affirms Heidegger's view that "we human beings . . . are inherently historical; [we] can never exist outside history." However, he goes on to write, "when we reflect more deeply . . . we see that we are always endowed with, and already predisposed by, a general existential attunement. . . . [Our] bodies are already attuned by Being. . . . Because we are embodied beings, we have received a primordial understanding of Being: an understanding already encoded in, and carried by, our bodily nature" (44). For Levin, it is the body which is the primordial bearer of the "pre-ontological understanding of being" of which Heidegger writes in *Being and Time,* even though Heidegger himself failed to understand it as a "'gift of nature' always carried by the body of experience" (40, 42). Levin, careful to avoid a simple biological version of the metaphysical will to univocal origins, claims that this fundamental attunement of the body, which preserves a source of resistance to extreme historical relativism, is nevertheless not simply ahistorical. He writes: "This biological preprogramming is *not* a timeless, eternal, immutable structure; but it *is* transhistorical: a condition which, though it never appears except *in* history, is yet never totally determined by historical conditions alone. It is unknowable, therefore, except insofar as it enters into history; nevertheless, it compels us to recognize that it surpasses our historical knowledge. And we do at least know this much: that it *limits* what we know, what we can think and understand, even about ourselves, and what we can become, what we can make of ourselves. Our pre-ontological understanding of Being is, then, historically relative; and yet, . . . it is not totally determined by this relation to history. It is a 'primordial' and 'transhistorical' understanding, but always channeled through the specific historical conditions into which we are thrown" (44).

35. Haar, *Heidegger and the Essence of Man,* 174.

36. At another point Haar writes: "Did not [Heidegger] himself have tacit recourse to a *nonhistorical essence of man* when presenting man solely as the one who speaks, who gives signs, who shows, who exists on the earth and beneath the heavens alongside things nearby in the openness of a world?" (Haar, *Heidegger and the Essence of Man,* xxxiv). Or again: "For someone who elsewhere refuses to admit this nonhistorical dimension, the description given of the 'world' as the 'play of the fourfold'—Earth and Heavens, Mortals and Gods—has little sense" (178).

37. Haar points out the need to vigilantly refrain from exclusively identifying the intimations of this non-historical dimension of dwelling with any particular historical age, be it that of the ancient Greeks, the pre-modern farmers of the Black Forest, or even "the future ones" of the other beginning: "For Heidegger here [in the notion of the play of the fourfold] invokes an immemorial whole that does not concern any precise epoch. This immemorial whole can and must be inserted—though it seems quite difficult nowadays!—into an historical world . . . ; yet it can never be identified with, or coincide with any epoch or with any particular History" (Haar, *Heidegger and the Essence of Man,* 178).

Chapter 8

1. In this regard note the order of the four *Bremer Vorträge* of 1949: "The Thing," "The Enframing," "The Danger," and "The Turning." The meditations on the fourfold in "The Thing" are not presented, as one might expect, *after* the lectures on technology and the turning; rather, Heidegger *begins* with intimating the possibility of recovering a non-willing sense of dwelling in the fourfold. (On this point see Kōhei Mizoguchi, "An Interpretation of Heidegger's Bremen Lectures: Toward a Dialogue with His Later Thought," in *Heidegger and Asian Thought*, ed. Parkes, 192; see also von Herrmann, *Wege ins Ereignis*, 73, where it is remarked that "the going back to the first beginning is thus already guided by a knowledge of the other beginning.")

2. Joan Stambaugh, translator's preface to Heidegger, *Identity and Difference*, 17. Elsewhere Stambaugh comments on *Inständigkeit* and *Austrag*, and their relation to the will, as follows: "The word *Inständigkeit*, indwelling, . . . points to the same phenomenon designated by perdurance (*Austrag*). . . . It is a kind of waiting, not a passive waiting, but a very attentive, intense, one. . . . *Inständigkeit* or perdurance is a kind of intensely receptive sticking something through, sticking it out. . . . A kind of non-willing (not unwilling) *exertion* distances *Inständigkeit* from all flabby passivity. To use the more familiar word, when we endure something, we are not willing it, but we are not passive either" (Stambaugh, *Thoughts on Heidegger* [Lanham, Md.: University Press of America, 1991], 117).

3. Yet in the other beginning of non-willing, one might wonder, why would there any longer be a need for detachment or renunciation? In anticipation of later discussions, let me respond here with a question. Is there perhaps a certain non-historical problem of "willing," an inextinguishable dissonant force that would haunt the region of non-willing even in the other beginning, and that would therefore need to ever again be renounced in order to restore the harmony of a non-willing cor-respondence within the fugue of being?

4. Note, however, that in *Introduction to Metaphysics* this "need" is expressed in terms of "the opposition between the overpowering [of being] and the doing violence [of humans]." "Man is forced [*genötigt*] into being-there [*Da-sein*], thrown into the distress [*Not*] of such being, because the overpowering as such, in order to appear in its power, *needs* [braucht] the site of its disclosure" (*EM* 124).

5. In these difficult pages Heidegger stresses not only that being as such always "needs" an abode and "uses" man for its arrival in this abode, but also that being essentially occurs at once as "compelling" (*nötigend*) and as need (*Not*). Moreover, in the present epoch of abandonment of being (*Seinsverlassenheit*), "the needlessness that establishes itself as the dominion of metaphysics brings being itself to the utmost limit of its need. . . . At its outermost limit, the need of being comes to be the need of needlessness [*Not der Notlosigkeit*]" (*N2* 391/245). The fact that humans feel no "need *of* being" (in the double sense of the genitive) in this epoch is itself a sign of the utmost neediness. But it is also precisely the appearance of this sign in the midst of the gravest danger that signals the possibility of awakening an attunement to the originary need *of* being, and hence the growth of that-which-saves.

6. Note that all but the last sentence of this passage is missing from the English translation.

7. *Contributions* expresses Da-sein's role within the *Schwingen* of beyng as *Ereignis* as follows: "Da-sein does not accomplish anything, unless it be to get a hold of the counter-resonance [*Gegenschwung*] of en-ownment [*Er-eignung*], that is, to shift into this counter-resonance and thus first of all to become itself: the preserver of the thrown project, *the grounded founder of the ground*" (*GA* 65:239).

8. Von Herrmann, *Wege ins Ereignis,* 384.

9. For some reason the italics, which mark the change of emphasis from letting-*presence* to *letting*-presence that is precisely at issue in these passages, were not reproduced in the English translation.

10. Schürmann, *Meister Eckhart: Mystic and Philosopher,* 212. Schürmann also finds this "paradox of releasement as the condition for thinking and as the essence of being" in Meister Eckhart: "Releasement unveils being," and yet also "the essence of being is itself releasement." He concludes that this expresses the practical condition for thinking releasement: "one must let truth be in order to understand truth as letting-be" (192–93). Elsewhere Schürmann finds this "practical apriori" for thinking *Gelassenheit* in Heidegger as well: "In Heidegger, to understand the turn, one must oneself turn about. . . . To understand releasement, one must oneself be released. . . . Through *our* releasement and on its condition alone, we are 'let into' (*eingelassen*) that other releasement—both identical and different from ours—which is the event of presencing" (Schürmann, *Heidegger on Being and Acting,* 236).

11. See, for example, Eckehart, *Deutsche Predigten und Traktate,* 386.

12. Heidegger's reference is to Eckhart's *Reden der Unterscheidung,* ed. Ernst Diederichs (Bonn, 1925), p. 8 (no. 4). Compare Eckehart, *Deutsche Predigten und Traktate,* 57.

Chapter 9

1. Jacques Derrida, *Points . . . : Interviews 1975–1994,* ed. Elisabeth Weber, trans. Peggy Kamuf (Stanford: Stanford University Press, 1995), 130.

2. Lacoue-Labarthe, *Heidegger, Art, and Politics,* 14.

3. Krell, "Introduction to the Paperback Edition," in Heidegger, *Nietzsche,* vols. 1 and 2, xxvi.

4. I borrow the phrase from John D. Caputo, *Demythologizing Heidegger* (Bloomington: Indiana University Press, 1993), 6; yet this book of Caputo's, in contrast to his earlier studies, is clearly devoted more to the "against" than to the "with." While in response to "critics [such as Wolin and Rockmore] who doubt that reading Heidegger remains a necessity," Caputo claims to "offer a justification for reading Heidegger today" (8), *Demythologizing Heidegger* nevertheless reads for the most part as a polemical declaration of independence from Heidegger's "Greco-German myth of Being" and an announcement of a new alliance with the "jewgreek myth of Justice" found at work in French deconstruction, especially in Derrida's more recent writings. In the present context, Caputo's critical "demythologizing"

of the *Seinsgeschichte* is most relevant to my second site of questioning the residues of will in Heidegger's thought.

5. See Lacoue-Labarthe, *Heidegger, Art, and Politics,* 14.

6. Derrida, *Positions,* 10.

7. These three are by no means the only sites where one could raise the question of residues of will in Heidegger's thought. For example, one could question in this regard the residues of an anthropo-logocentric philosophy of spirit and will, which perhaps refuses to think the *embodiment* of *Gelassenheit* for fear of what he calls "our scarcely conceivable, abyssal bodily kinship with the animal" (*GA* 9:326/248; see also *GA* 29/30:261ff.; *Z* 292, 306–7). On the need to think the embodiment of *Gelassenheit,* see David Michael Levin's trilogy: *The Body's Recollection of Being; The Opening of Vision;* and *The Listening Self.* On the question of animals and animality, see Derrida, *Of Spirit,* chapter 6; David Farrell Krell, *Daimon Life: Heidegger and Life-Philosophy* (Bloomington: Indiana University Press, 1992); and Bret W. Davis, "Rethinking the Rational Animal: The Question of Anthropologocentrism in Heidegger, Bergson, and Zen," *Interdisziplinäre Phänomenologie—Interdisciplinary Phenomenology* 1 (2004): 173–87.

8. Löwith, *Martin Heidegger and European Nihilism,* 42.

9. Habermas, *Philosophical Discourse of Modernity,* 141, 152–53.

10. Ibid., 160.

11. Ibid., 318. In this passage Habermas is speaking of Castoriadis, but he directs essentially the same critique at Heidegger.

12. Wolin, preface to *The Heidegger Controversy,* vii. The context of this remark is what Wolin aptly calls "one of the foremost conundrums of modern European intellectual history," namely that "probably the century's greatest philosopher" succumbed to the delusion that "the National Socialist Revolution represented the 'saving power' (Hölderlin) of Western humanity." I agree with Wolin's balanced statement in the following paragraph: "It would of course be foolish to suggest that, as a result of Heidegger's concerted, short-lived engagement on behalf of the Nazi regime, he would somehow forfeit his status as a significant contributor to the legacy of Western thought. However, at the same time, now that we know the extent of Heidegger's partisanship for the Nazi cause in the early 1930s, we cannot help but read him differently." Yet the "different reading" Wolin offers us in *The Politics of Being* hardly maintains a balanced approach, but rather polemically suggests that Heidegger's philosophical contributions can ultimately be reduced to convoluted variations of voluntarism and fatalism.

13. Wolin, *Politics of Being,* 147.

14. Ibid.

15. Ibid., 132.

16. See Young, *Heidegger, Philosophy, Nazism,* 178.

17. Haar, *Heidegger and the Essence of Man,* xxxiii.

18. Ibid., 61; see 113.

19. Ibid., 165.

20. Ibid., 66.

21. Wolin, *Politics of Being,* 149.

22. Ibid., 152.

23. Löwith, *Martin Heidegger and European Nihilism,* 127.

24. Habermas, *Philosophical Discourse of Modernity,* 140; quoted in Wolin, *Politics of Being,* 151.

25. Caputo, *Mystical Element in Heidegger's Thought,* 39.

26. Schürmann, *Meister Eckhart: Mystic and Philosopher,* 105.

27. Werner Marx, *Heidegger und die Tradition* (Stuttgart: W. Kohlhammer, 1961), 223; Marx, *Heidegger and the Tradition,* 227.

28. Marx, *Heidegger und die Tradition,* 249; Marx, *Heidegger and the Tradition,* 253.

29. Karsten Harries, "Verwahrloste Welt," in *Kunst–Politik–Technik,* ed. C. Jamme and K. Harries (Munich: Fink, 1993), 215; quoted in Young, *Heidegger, Philosophy, Nazism,* 188. Young also critically responds to this statement.

30. Martin Heidegger and Takehiko Kojima, "Martin Heidegger–Takehiko Kojima: Ein Briefwechsel (1963–1965)," in *Japan und Heidegger,* ed. Buchner, 226.

31. In *The Question of God in Heidegger's Phenomenology* (Evanston, Ill.: Northwestern University Press, 1990), George Kovacs distinguishes several phases of "the question of God" in Heidegger. The first would be the "critical perspective" of his early period, which "unearths the background and the ontological inadequacy of the causal explanation of God" (xviii). While thinkers such as Sartre took this "demythologization" to imply an atheism, Kovacs points out that the destruction of the onto-theological God seeks instead, through the next phases of Heidegger's thought, to reawaken a more original openness to the God-question. "The rethinking of the meaning of Being, then, does not sweep away but rather reawakens the sense of wonder about God" (xix).

32. Günter Figal, "Forgetfulness of God: Concerning the Center of Heidegger's *Contributions to Philosophy,*" in *Companion to Heidegger's Contributions to Philosophy,* ed. Scott et al., 199. See also Helting, *Heidegger und Meister Eckehart;* and my discussion in chapter 5 of Helting's attempt to find a central place for the Godhead in Heidegger's thought of *Ereignis.*

33. Although the last god gathers all previous gods into the final and highest essence of the divine, it is not the highest being that "grounds" all beings. As Pöggeler writes: "The god experienced from the appropriative event as the last god is only 'passing by.' He is not to be brought to a standstill and secured as the ground which grounds everything" (Pöggeler, *Martin Heidegger's Path of Thinking,* 214).

34. Von Herrmann, *Wege ins Ereignis,* 386.

35. David Wood provocatively asks in this regard: "Is not the welcoming of a god the replication of a logic of traumatic loss, which would require an absolute solution to an absolute problem, after being forcibly detached from its reliance on more subtle distinctions?" (Wood, *Thinking After Heidegger* [Cambridge: Polity, 2002], 188).

36. Jacques Derrida, "Interpreting Signatures (Nietzsche/Heidegger): Two Questions," in *Dialogue and Deconstruction,* ed. Michelfelder and Palmer, 67.

37. One may suspect, as D. F. Krell puts it, that the "will to appropriate Western history as a whole, both 'empirical' history of civilization and the intellectual tradition, shapes Heidegger's history of Being" (*Intimations of Mortality,* 121; Krell is here paraphrasing ideas from Michel Haar's article "Structures hégéliennes

dans la pensée heideggérienne de l'histoire," *Revue de la métaphysique et de morale* 85, no. 1 [January–March 1980]: 48–59).

38. In this regard, note that Derrida has persistently criticized "the privilege Heidegger grants to what he calls *Versammlung*, gathering, which is always more powerful than dissociation" (Jacques Derrida, *Deconstruction in a Nutshell: A Conversation with Jacques Derrida*, ed. with a commentary by John D. Caputo [New York: Fordham University Press, 1997], 14). See Jacques Derrida, *Spectres of Marx: The State of Debt, the Work of Mourning, and the New International*, trans. Peggy Kamuf (New York: Routledge, 1994), 27–28; and his "Geschlecht" series of essays; see also David Wood's response to Derrida on this matter in "Heidegger after Derrida," *Research in Phenomenology* 17 (1987): 103–16.

39. Derrida writes: "But who ever has said that a person bears a single name? Certainly not Nietzsche. . . . Next to Kierkegaard, was not Nietzsche one of the few great thinkers who multiplied his names and played with signatures, identities, masks?" (Derrida, "Interpreting Signatures (Nietzsche/Heidegger): Two Questions," 67). Elsewhere I argue, however, that there is a genuine tension in Nietzsche's thought between a perspectival openness to plurality and a drive to yoke this multiplicity under the rule of a single will to power (Davis, "Zen After Zarathustra: The Problem of the Will in the Confrontation Between Nietzsche and Buddhism"; see also Müller-Lauter, *Nietzsche: His Philosophy of Contradictions*, esp. 73ff.).

40. William Butler Yeats, *The Autobiography* (New York: Macmillan-Collier Books, 1965), 43; quoted in Krell, *Intimations of Mortality*, 139.

41. Wolin, *Politics of Being*, 136. Polt writes in this regard: "Common sense surely underestimates the importance of philosophy in history—but Heidegger overestimates it" (Polt, *Heidegger: An Introduction*, 133).

42. Emmanuel Levinas, *Ethics and Infinity*, trans. Richard A. Cohen (Pittsburgh: Duquesne University Press, 1985), 52. Levinas's critique of Heidegger's thought has been the subject of much debate, beginning with Derrida's "Violence and Metaphysics: An Essay on the Thought of Emmanuel Levinas." In *Totality and Infinity*, Levinas writes: "To affirm the priority of *Being* over *existents* is to already decide the essence of philosophy; it is to subordinate the relation with *someone*, who is an existent, (the ethical relation) to a relation with the *Being of existents*, which, impersonal, permits the apprehension, the domination of existents (a relationship of knowing), subordinates justice to freedom. . . . Even though it opposes the technological passion issued forth from the forgetting of Being hidden by existents, Heideggerian ontology, which subordinates the relationship with the Other to the relation with Being in general, remains under obedience to the anonymous, and leads inevitably to another power, to imperialist domination, to tyranny" (45–46).

Yet Derrida counters: "[One] cannot legitimately speak of the 'subordination' of the existent to Being, or, for example, of the ethical relation to the ontological relation. To precomprehend or explicate the implicit relation of Being to the existent is not to submit the existent (for example, someone) to Being in a violent fashion. Being is but the *Being-of* this existent, and does not exist outside it as a foreign power, or as a hostile or neutral impersonal element. . . . Quite the contrary. Not only is the thought of Being not ethical violence, but it seems that no ethics—in Levinas's sense—can be opened without it. Thought—or at least the precomprehension of Being—*conditions* (in its own fashion, which excludes every ontic conditionality: principles, causes, premises, etc.) the *recognition* of the essence of the existent (for example someone, existent *as* other, *as* other self, etc.). It conditions the *respect* for the other *as what it is:* other. Without this acknowledgment, which is not a knowledge, or let us say without this 'letting-be' of an existent (Other) as something existing outside me in the essence of what it is (first in its alterity), no ethics would be possible" (Derrida, *Writing and Difference,* 136–38).

It is in any case true that Heidegger prefers to talk about "*Gelassenheit* towards things" rather than the no doubt more difficult relation of letting other persons be. Is this an accidental tendency or an essential aspect of his thinking? Caputo writes in this regard: "The one point I would urge in dealing with [Heidegger's *Gelassenheit*] is that he tends to be a little more interested in letting jugs and bridges be and to let it go at that, and he never quite gets around to letting *others* be, to our being-with others as mortals. . . . I do not think there is anything in what he says which excludes his doing this. He just never does. So we will do it for him and, by doing so, restore to *Gelassenheit* its ethical context" (Caputo, *Radical Hermeneutics,* 266–67).

Yet in a later work Caputo changes his mind and writes: "It is not a matter, as I once suggested, of needing to extend Heideggerian *Gelassenheit* to other people instead of restricting it to jugs and bridges. The matter for thought (*die Sache des Denkens*) and the task for thought (*die Aufgabe des Denkens*) must be more profoundly disrupted by an otherness to which they are systematically made deaf in Heideggerian discourse" (Caputo, *Demythologizing Heidegger,* 146). For the later Caputo, Heidegger's exclusion of the Judeo-Christian "myth of Justice" from his Greco-German "myth of Being" meant that his thought of *Gelassenheit* was inhibited from hearing the call of the victim.

While Caputo draws on Derrida, along with Levinas, as a primary source for rearticulating the "Hebraic or jewgreek myth of Justice," Derrida's text, "Violence and Metaphysics," responds to Levinas (and hence to Caputo's critical revision of his earlier position) on this point as follows: "'To let be' is an expression of Heidegger's which does not mean, as Levinas seems to think, to let be as an 'object of comprehension first,' and, in the case of the Other, as 'interlocutor afterward.' The 'letting-be' concerns all possible forms of the existent, and even those which, *by essence,* cannot be transformed into 'objects of comprehension.' If it belongs to the essence of the Other first and foremost to be an 'interlocutor' and to be 'interpellated,' then the 'letting-be' will let the Other be what it is, will respect it as interpellated-interlocutor. The 'letting-be' does not only, or by privilege, concern impersonal things" (Derrida, *Writing and Difference,* 138).

It should be pointed out that this counter-critique of Levinas on behalf of Heidegger is only half the story of Derrida's "double reading" of Levinas, the other half of which is sympathetic to the need to deconstructively supplement Greek ontology with a Hebraic appeal to radical alterity. It is this latter aspect that Caputo provocatively picks up and runs with. On the dialogue between Derrida and Levinas, see the chapters by Levinas, Derrida, Bernasconi, and Critchley in *Re-Reading Levinas*, ed. Robert Bernasconi and Simon Critchley (Bloomington: Indiana University Press, 1991).

43. Lacoue-Labarthe, *Heidegger, Art, and Politics*, 34.

44. Wolin, *Politics of Being*, 145.

45. In *What Is Called Thinking?* Heidegger claims that what is most thoughtworthy is that we are still not thinking. And yet "the reason why thought has failed to appear is not only, and not primarily, that man has cultivated thought too little, but because what is to be thought about [*das zu-Denkende*], what truly gives itself to be thought, has long been withdrawing" (*WhD* 55/25).

46. See Polt, *Heidegger: An Introduction*, 158.

47. Krell, *Intimations of Mortality*, 115.

48. Hans-Georg Gadamer, *Truth and Method*, 2nd rev. ed., trans. Joel Weinsheimer and Donald Marshall (New York: Crossroad, 1989), 369. It should be noted, however, that Gadamer's hermeneutics itself contains a tension in this regard. On the one hand, he goes along with Hegel to assert that understanding is a kind of appropriation of the foreign: "To recognize one's own in the alien, to become at home with it, is the basic movement of spirit, whose being consists only in returning to itself from what is other" (14). On the other hand, for Gadamer, an "absolute spirit" which has canceled out all otherness is no more possible than is absolute reason, and thus there is no end to the dialogue with new and other horizons (see 276). For an excellent critical discussion of Gadamer's attempt to negotiate between Hegel and Heidegger, see Bernasconi, *Heidegger in Question*, chapter 10, esp. 186ff.; see also my essay "Taiho to kaikō: Seiyōtetsugaku kara shisakuteki-taiwa e" ("Step Back and Encounter: From Western Philosophy Toward a Dialogue of Thought"), *Nihon tetsugakushi kenkyū* (*Studies in Japanese Philosophy*) 1 (2003): 36–66.

49. Gadamer, *Heidegger's Ways*, 165.

50. Quoted from the Freiburg University archives in Ott, *Martin Heidegger: A Political Life*, 240.

51. See May, *Heidegger's Hidden Sources*, 11ff., 59ff.

52. Ironically, the "latest news in European philosophy" for the Japanese had long been Heidegger's thought itself. Indeed, the first article ever published anywhere on Heidegger's philosophy was written by Tanabe Hajime upon his return to Japan from Freiburg in 1924 (translated into German as "Die neue Wende in der Phänomenologie—Heideggers Phenomenologie des Lebens," in *Japan und Heidegger*, ed. Buchner), and an appropriation of and/or an *Auseinandersetzung* with Heidegger's thought has been a mainstay of modern Japanese philosophy ever since. See Ryōsuke Ōhashi, "Die frühe Heidegger-Rezeption in Japan," as well as the other articles and correspondence collected in Buchner's *Japan und Heidegger;* Yasuo Yuasa, "The Encounter of Modern Japanese Philosophy with Heidegger," in *Heidegger and Asian Thought*, ed. Parkes; Graham Parkes, "Rising Sun over Black Forest: Heidegger's Japanese Connections," in May, *Heidegger's Hidden Sources;* and Mine Hideki, *Haideggā to nihon no tetsugaku* (*Heidegger and Japanese Philosophy*) (Kyoto: Minerva, 2002).

53. See May, *Heidegger's Hidden Sources,* for a rather compelling (even if May's approach is a bit "prosecutorial") account of Chinese and Japanese influences (the latter are judiciously covered in Graham Parkes's appended essay) on such key elements of Heidegger's thought as "Being, Nothing, the clearing, and on the complex relations between language, Way, and Saying" (79). See also Heinrich Wiegand Petzet, *Encounters and Dialogues with Martin Heidegger: 1929–1976,* trans. Parvis Emad and Kenneth Maly (Chicago: University of Chicago Press, 1993), 166ff.; and Hartig, *Die Lehre des Buddha und Heidegger,* esp. 14–39.

54. Gadamer suggested that "Heidegger studies would do well to pursue seriously comparisons of his work with Asian philosophies." When asked about the paucity of explicit references to Asian thought in Heidegger's texts, Gadamer suggests that one reason may be that Heidegger was hesitant to refer to a thought he could not read in the original language. (This was related from Gadamer's personal correspondence by Graham Parkes in the introduction to *Heidegger and Asian Thought,* 5–7; see Heidegger's own remarks in this regard in his letter to the 1969 conference held in Hawaii on "Heidegger and Eastern Thought," in Eliot Deutsch, ed., *Philosophy East and West* 20, no. 3 [July 1970]: 221.) Perhaps this linguistic inability was also Gadamer's own excuse for confining his hermeneutics to a dialogue *within* what he calls the "single historical horizon" of the Western tradition. (See *Truth and Method,* 304.) By comparison with Gadamer's tempered Hegelianism, Heidegger's *Destruktion* of the West (*das Abendland*) and his anticipations of an other beginning as a "a wholly other mode, a land of dawn, an Orient [*das Land eines Morgens*]" (*WhD* 67/70) may indeed offer a more radical opening to a dialogue with the East. Heidegger was in fact not always so rigid in his exclusion of the possibility of a contribution to thinking from East Asia. Note that in the 1940s he attempted a translation of the *Tao Te Ching* with a Chinese scholar (see Paul Shih-yi Hsiao, "Heidegger and Our Translation of the *Tao Te Ching,*" in *Heidegger and Asian Thought,* ed. Parkes). Why would he have attempted to translate such a text if he had thought that it could contribute nothing essential to (Western) thinking?

55. Martin Heidegger, "Zur Frage nach der Bestimmung der Sache des Denkens," in *Japan und Heidegger,* ed. Buchner, 230.

56. See Reiner Thurnher, "Der Rückgang in den Grund des Eigenen als Bedingung für ein Verstehen des Anderen im Denken Heideggers," in *Europa und die Philosophie,* ed. Gander. For my part, I have attempted to begin working through the "ambivalent openness/closure of Western philosophy," specifically in Hegel, Gadamer, and Heidegger, in preparation for a hermeneutics of cross-cultural dialogue, in my essay "Taiho to kaikō: Seiyōtetsugaku kara shisakuteki-taiwa e" ("Step Back and Encounter: From Western Philosophy Toward a Dialogue of Thought").

57. Wilhelm Halbfass, *India and Europe: An Essay in Understanding* (Albany: SUNY Press, 1988), 167.

58. Pöggeler, *Paths of Heidegger's Life and Thought,* 292.

59. See Caputo, *Demythologizing Heidegger;* and Jean-François Lyotard, *Heidegger and "the Jews,"* trans. Andreas Michel and Mark Roberts (Minneapolis: University of Minnesota Press, 1990); and Marlène Zarader, *The Unthought Debt: Heidegger and the Hebraic Heritage,* trans. Bettina Bergo (Stanford: Stanford University Press, 2006).

60. For a compelling account of Heidegger's "unthought debts" to the Jewish tradition, including aspects of his conceptions of language, thought, interpretation, and being, see Zarader, *The Unthought Debt*. Van Buren reveals how many central concepts of Heidegger's early thought, including care, understanding, mood, anxiety, death, language, falling, and conscience, were first developed in his attempts to lay out the basic characteristics of factical life found in primal Christianity (van Buren, *The Young Heidegger*, chapter 8). Not the least of the ideas Heidegger adopted and adapted from the Christian tradition, of course, is *Gelassenheit*. It is interesting to note that it is in his "Conversation" with a Japanese that the later Heidegger most clearly affirms the lasting influence of his theological origins (*GA* 12:91/10).

61. These may very well include the critique of the will and the notion of *Nicht-Wollen*, which bears striking resemblances, for example, to Daoist and Zen Buddhist conceptions of *wu-wei* (non-doing). For some connections with Zen Buddhism and the Kyoto School, see the final section of chapter 2 above.

62. Marx, *Heidegger and the Tradition*, 254.

63. See Zimmerman, *Eclipse of the Self*, xxvi.

64. See Bernasconi, *Heidegger in Question*, ix.

65. Richard Rorty, "Overcoming the Tradition: Heidegger and Dewey," in *Heidegger and Modern Philosophy*, ed. Michael Murray (New Haven: Yale University Press, 1978), 257.

66. Haar, *Song of the Earth*, 75.

67. Haar, *Heidegger and the Essence of Man*, 75.

68. Winfried Franzen, *Von der Existenzialontologie zur Seinsgeschichte* (Meisenheim am Glan: Anton Hein, 1975), 125; quoted in Wolin, *Politics of Being*, 200.

69. Bernasconi, *Heidegger in Question*, ix.

70. Haar, *Song of the Earth*, 76.

71. One might here, in contrast to the later Heidegger's eschatology of the history of being, suggest *another* critical repetition of the young Heidegger's interpretation (or "formal indication") of Christian "eschatology," i.e., of the *parousia* not as a coming future "object-historical" event but as the *Augenblick* of *kairos* that is in truth always before us (see *GA* 60:148ff.). In his explication of Heidegger's 1920–21 phenomenology of religion course, Theodore Kisiel writes: "The eschatological problem, in its deep nondogmatic sense, is the very center of Christian life. . . . Against the eschatology of the late Judaism of Paul's time, which put the primacy on a future event which is to be awaited, the temporality of Christian facticity emphasizes the moment of decision between past and future in which the Christian constantly stands, in the present 'before the God of old' . . . from which the future receives its sense" (Kisiel, *Genesis of Heidegger's "Being and Time,"* 188–89; see also van Buren, *The Young Heidegger*, 190ff.). Could this original sense of Christian eschatology be borrowed and rethought as the kairotic decision between willing and non-willing modes of existence? Yet in vigilantly preparing oneself for the recovery of the always-already-and-not-yet fundamental attunement of non-willing, would it no longer arrive as flashes of insight that would come from beyond "like a thief in the night," but rather as cultivated intimations *of* (double genitive) releasement?

72. Bernasconi, *Heidegger in Question,* xxiii. For Bernasconi, what is "inviting" about Heidegger's thought of "another beginning" is that it helps us think a break with tradition that is radical and yet not an absolute "new beginning," which would in fact "remain bound to the traditional logic of oppositions and so resituate the new within the old." What is "challenging" about the idea is "the difficulty of walking this tightrope"; and what is "disturbing" is that Heidegger thought it "as the special relation between the Greek language and the German language" (xxiv).

73. Krell, *Intimations of Mortality,* chapter 9.

74. Ibid., 138.

75. See ibid., 151.

76. In this regard David Michael Levin writes: "To the extent that we can achieve *Gelassenheit,* we can break out of our metaphysical history; correlatively, to the extent that we have not achieved it, we remain situated within this ancient history. I firmly believe that, both as individuals and as collectivities, we are capable of taking significant steps in this direction. But I am also convinced that *Gelassenheit* is an ideal we cannot completely actualize, and that, for this reason, the history of metaphysics is not something that we could ever completely overcome" (Levin, *Opening of Vision,* 249–50).

Elsewhere Levin expresses the concern that Heidegger's "vision of [a] 'new beginning' hovers anxiously between an apocalyptic discourse of mysticism . . . and a more restrained discourse of diagnosis, critique, and recollection." Yet he argues that Heidegger's *Geschick,* as opposed to a fatalistic notion of *Schicksal,* should in the end be understood to imply that "the world as we know it, the world-interpretation within which we live, is inherently, radically open—open to alterations coming both from the inside and from the outside" (David Michael Levin, *The Philosopher's Gaze: Modernity in the Shadows of Enlightenment* [Berkeley: University of California Press, 1999], 160–61).

77. Hans-Georg Gadamer, *Reason in the Age of Science,* trans. F. G. Lawrence (Cambridge, Mass.: MIT Press, 1981), 67; quoted in Bernasconi, *Heidegger in Question,* 183.

78. Bernasconi, *Heidegger in Question,* 183; see also Bernasconi, *The Question of Language,* 96n15.

79. Bernasconi too recognizes that "even though there is no clean break with metaphysics there is a rupture, a discontinuity" (Bernasconi, *Heidegger in Question,* 205).

80. Derrida's use of the language of "strategy," however, ironically strikes me as itself not wholly unrelated to a kind of willing. Whether in its first dictionary meaning of "the science or art of planning and conducting a war or a military campaign," or in its second meaning of "a carefully devised plan of action to achieve a goal," a "strategy" would seem to imply—contrary, of course, to the gist of Derrida's writing—a subject who stands outside (e.g., the text to be deconstructed) and posits goals for which the strategy is employed.

81. Derrida, *Margins of Philosophy,* 135.

Chapter 10

1. As quoted by Heidegger in *SA* 10/9.

2. *Shōyōroku*, edited with commentary by Yasutani Hakuun (Tokyo: Shun-jūsha, 1973), 321.

3. Jacques Derrida, "On Reading Heidegger," *Research in Phenomenology* 17 (1987): 172. The other side of Derrida's strategy of deconstruction (i.e., of thinking contamination) is an attempt to free up possibilities of the gift, justice, hospitality, etc. Strictly speaking, these are "impossible" insofar as they could never be purely actualized, insofar as their actualization always involves contamination. Nevertheless, in Heidegger's language, they grant-in-withdrawal. As opposed to "laws" which found a state and ground decisions, Derrida writes that "justice," "in its demand of gift without exchange," is the experience of the impossible that both underlies and undermines all laws. "Deconstruction," which "is justice," "is possible as an experience of the impossible, there where, even if it does not exist (or does not yet exist, or never does exist), *there is* justice" (Jacques Derrida, "The Force of Law: 'The Mystical Foundation of Authority,'" trans. Mary Quaintance, in *Deconstruction and the Possibility of Justice*, ed. Drucilla Cornell et al. [New York: Routledge, 1992], 15, 25). The gift, writes Derrida elsewhere, is "the first mover of the circle" in which "the gift annuls itself" (Jacques Derrida, *Given Time: I. Counterfeit Money*, trans. Peggy Kamuf [Chicago: University of Chicago Press, 1991], 30–31). The gift sets economies in motion at the same time as it is annulled as soon as there is a return, that is, as soon as an economic exchange is established. Analogously, would any historical actualization of the non-historical (im)possibility of non-willing always be contaminated by an ineradicable problem of "willing"? Would interruptive and generative intimations of non-willing, then, always only be prepared for by way of ever again deconstructing such contaminations? This is the question this chapter shall attempt to address.

4. Nietzsche, *Thus Spoke Zarathustra*, part 2, section 20. This remark is made in the context of an oblique criticism of the Buddhist idea of gaining liberation from the wheel of willful karma. (I have responded to this criticism, and taken up the question of Nietzsche's ironic affinities with Buddhism, in my "Zen After Zarathustra: The Problem of the Will in the Confrontation Between Nietzsche and Buddhism.") Elsewhere in *Thus Spoke Zarathustra*, however, Nietzsche could be interpreted as suggesting that his own ambivalent ascetic path of "the self-overcoming of the will to power" would lead beyond the will, or at least beyond the heroic will to the "unharnessed will" of the "overhero." In advising an "ascetic of the spirit," Zarathustra says: "Though I love the bull's neck on him, I also want to see the eyes of the angel. He must still unlearn even his heroic will; he shall be elevated for me, not merely sublime: the ether itself should elevate him, the will-less one [*den Willenlosen*]!" (part 2, section 13). In this sense too, rereading Nietzsche after Heidegger does not only entail locating his anti-metaphysics of the will to power, his "inversion of Platonism," at the nihilistic end of the first beginning, but also attending to Nietzsche's own intimations of a twisting free.

5. Haar, *Song of the Earth*, 89.

6. The tension between two competing ways to think the other beginning in

Heidegger may in fact resemble in some respects that between two interpretations of the end of history in Hegel. D. F. Krell writes: "The 'result' of Hegel's history may be understood in two very different ways, either as the conclusive *concept*, spirit in and for itself, which would be the attained goal and absolute end of the history of philosophy, or as the ongoing *deed* or activity of thought, 'eternally producing its opposite and eternally reconciling itself to it,' which would be absolute postponement of the end and result" (Krell, *Intimations of Mortality*, 139).

Although I have in general followed the first view of Hegel—both in order to critically question residues of a "will to finality" in Heidegger and in order to highlight the radicality of Heidegger's thought of the finitude of being—this other possible interpretation of Hegel should be noted.

7. *Unwesen* generally means "nuisance" in the sense of an "excess" or "deformation of essence" that disturbs the essential order of things. The expression *jemand treibt sein Unwesen* means "someone is up to his old tricks" in the sense of "does something bad (*etwas Böses*) so as to disturb the order." The adjective *unwesentlich*, on the other hand, means "unimportant" or "inessential." Heidegger uses the term *Unwesen* in a variety of contexts, and not just in the sense of the merely "inessential." In "The Essence of Truth," for example, Heidegger thinks the mystery as "the proper non-essence [*das eigentliche Un-wesen*] of truth." He distinguishes this "proper" sense of *Un-wesen* as "pre-essencing essence" (*vor-wesende Wesen*) both from "the sense of inferiority to essence in the sense of what is universal (*koinon, genos*), its *possibilitas* and the ground of its possibility," and from the "first and for the most part" meaning of *Unwesen* (unhyphenated) as "the deformation of that already inferior essence." In any case, Heidegger adds, "in each of these significations the non-essence remains always in its own way essential to the essence and never becomes inessential in the sense of irrelevant" (*GA* 9:194/148). Michael Inwood accordingly finds Heidegger to generally use *Un-wesen* and *Unwesen* in two senses: "1. the pre-essencing essence [*vor-wesende Wesen*] before it lapses into the non-verbal essence, the universal; [and] 2. the disfigurement of the already degenerate essence into something even worse" (Inwood, *A Heidegger Dictionary*, 54). However, in the context of ur-willing as the *Unwesen* of non-willing, and later in the context of evil as the *Unwesen* of beyng, I shall venture to translate *Unwesen* as "dissonant excess" or, in order to stress that this "excess" always already and ineradicably haunts the essence of non-willing and beyng, as "originary dissonant excess."

8. "Errancy" is said to be "the open site for and ground of *error.*" Error is not thought here in the sense of an isolated mistake, but rather as "the realm (the domain) of the history of those entanglements in which all kinds of erring get interwoven" (*GA* 9:197/150). For a most rigorous pursuit of the radical implications of Heidegger's rethinking of truth, see Sallis, *Double Truth*, esp. chapters 4, 5, and 6.

9. Arendt, *Life of the Mind*, part 2, pp. 193–94.

10. Menard Boss, *Existential Foundations of Medicine and Psychology*, trans. S. Conway and A. Cleaves (New York: J. Aronson, 1979), 242; quoted by the translators in Martin Heidegger, *Zollikon Seminars*, 164.

11. Schelling, *Schellings sämmtliche Werke*, 7:399; Schelling, "Philosophical Investigations into the Essence of Human Freedom," 270.

12. Schelling, *Schellings sämmtliche Werke,* 7:409; Schelling, "Philosophical Investigations into the Essence of Human Freedom," 278.

13. Nancy, *Experience of Freedom,* 131–32.

14. Nancy, for his part, undertakes a kind of double reading with regard to the question of "the space left free" in Heidegger's thought. See *Experience of Freedom,* chapter 4, and pp. 144–47.

15. See Jean-Luc Nancy, "Heidegger's 'Originary Ethics,'" in *Heidegger and Practical Philosophy,* ed. Raffoul and Pettigrew, 81.

16. Joan Stambaugh comments in this regard: "This letting appears to contain two fundamentally diverse possibilities in itself: it can let itself loose into beings and mere beingness (*loslassen,* and this is Framing, technology, *Gestell*) or it can release itself into its own (*lassen, entlassen*), and this is Appropriation (*Ereignis*)" (Stambaugh, *Thoughts on Heidegger,* 154).

17. In his provocative essay "Nihilism and its Discontents" (in *Heidegger and Practical Philosophy,* ed. Raffoul and Pettigrew), Thomas Sheehan interprets this difference as that between an essential sense and a historical-cultural sense of "nihilism" in Heidegger's thought: "Essential nihilism is a matter of the hiddenness intrinsic to the open, and historical-cultural nihilism is a matter of overlooking that hiddenness" (295). Yet Sheehan problematically goes on to claim that not only the former, but also the latter does not have anything to do with the technological domination of nature or the degree of human control over entities. Suggesting that we "reinscribe *lethe* where it belongs: at the heart of human being," Sheehan claims that the proper response to Heidegger's thought is in fact, contrary to Heidegger's own intentions, "the task of the endless humanization of the world," for "the mystery of *Ereignis* inhabits and empowers planetary technology" (296). Sheehan sees this embrace of technological nihilism as the only alternative to Heidegger's aberrant political attempt to overcome nihilism in the 1930s. He ignores or rejects Heidegger's own claim that the will to the technological domination of the earth is inextricably tied to an oblivion of the mystery of being's essential withdrawal, a withdrawal that can no more be humanistically incorporated into human subjectivity than it can be metaphysically ascribed to "an eternal Beyond." Was not Heidegger's attempt to think the belonging-together of an identity-in-difference between man and being precisely an attempt to move beyond the either/or of anthropocentric humanism and theocentric metaphysics?

18. Lacoue-Labarthe, *Heidegger, Art, and Politics,* 40.

19. See ibid., 34.

20. In this connection see Robert Bernasconi's critique of Hannah Arendt's thesis of the "banality of evil," a thesis that would locate the origin of evil in thoughtlessness and the antidote to evil in thought. Bernasconi agrees with Levinas that "the diabolical is endowed with intelligence" and so thought can embody as well as refute it (Bernasconi, *Heidegger in Question,* 64–73).

21. Neither Heidegger nor Levinas adequately addresses the question of the face and negativity proper to non-human sentient beings; yet our mechanized meat industry does indeed proceed as if it were breeding, raising, and exterminating nothing more than mechanical automata.

22. Nancy, *Experience of Freedom,* 132.

23. This passage is not included in the English translation of *What Is Called Thinking?* For Lacoue-Labarthe's reflection on this passage, see his *Heidegger, Art, and Politics,* 116.

24. Nancy, *Experience of Freedom,* 39–40.

25. Ibid., 82.

26. Iriya Yoshitani, ed., *Rinzairoku (The Record of Linji)* (Tokyo: Iwanami, 1989), 27.

27. Nancy, *Experience of Freedom,* 206.

Bibliography

Allison, David B., ed. *The New Nietzsche*. Cambridge, Mass.: MIT Press, 1977.

Arendt, Hannah. *The Life of the Mind*, one-volume edition. San Diego: Harcourt Brace, 1978.

Bambach, Charles R. *Heidegger, Dilthey, and the Crisis of Historicism*. Ithaca: Cornell University Press, 1995.

Ban, Kazunori. *Kakyō kara hanarezu: Nishitani Keiji sensei tokubetsu kōgi (Without Departing from Home: Special Lectures of Professor Nishitani Keiji)*. Tokyo: Sōbunsha, 1998.

Behler, Ernst. *Confrontations: Derrida/Heidegger/Nietzsche*. Translated by Steven Taubeneck. Stanford: Stanford University Press, 1991.

Beistegui, Miguel de. *Heidegger and the Political: Dystopias*. London: Routledge, 1998.

Bernasconi, Robert. *Heidegger in Question: The Art of Existing*. Atlantic Highlands, N.J.: Humanities, 1993.

——. *The Question of Language in Heidegger's History of Being*. Atlantic Highlands, N.J.: Humanities, 1985.

Bernasconi, Robert, and Simon Critchley, eds. *Re-Reading Levinas*. Bloomington: Indiana University Press, 1991.

Bourdieu, Pierre. *The Political Ontology of Martin Heidegger*. Translated by Peter Collier. Stanford: Stanford University Press, 1988.

Bowie, Andrew. *Schelling and Modern European Philosophy: An Introduction*. London: Routledge, 1993.

Brockhaus: Die Enzyklopädie. 20th ed. Leipzig/Mannheim: F.A. Brockhaus, 1997.

Buchner, Harmut, ed. *Japan und Heidegger*. Sigmaringen: Thorbecke, 1989.

Buren, John van. *The Young Heidegger: Rumor of the Hidden King*. Bloomington: Indiana University Press, 1994.

Caputo, John D. *Demythologizing Heidegger*. Bloomington: Indiana University Press, 1993.

——. *The Mystical Element in Heidegger's Thought*. New York: Fordham University Press, 1986. Reprinted with corrections, 1990.

——. *Radical Hermeneutics: Repetition, Deconstruction, and the Hermeneutic Project*. Bloomington: Indiana University Press, 1987.

Casey, Edward S. *Getting Back into Place: Toward a Renewed Understanding of the Place-World*. Bloomington: Indiana University Press, 1993.

Cho, Kah Kyung. "Der Abstieg über den Humanismus: West-Östliche Wege im Denken Heideggers." In *Europa und die Philosophie*, ed. Gander.

Comay, Rebecca, and John McCumber, eds. *Endings: Questions of Memory in Hegel and Heidegger.* Evanston, Ill.: Northwestern University Press, 1999.

Dallery, Arleen, Charles E. Scott, and Holly P. Roberts, eds. *Ethics and Danger: Essays on Heidegger and Continental Thought.* Albany: SUNY Press, 1992.

Dallmayr, Fred. *The Other Heidegger.* Ithaca/London: Cornell University Press, 1993.

———. *Polis and Praxis.* Cambridge, Mass.: MIT Press, 1984.

Davis, Bret W. "The Displacement of Modernity." *Dokkyo International Review* 14 (2001): 215–35.

———. "Kami no shi kara ishi no daishi e: Posuto-Niiche no tetsugakusha toshite no Nishitani Keiji" ("From the Death of God to the Great Death of the Will: Nishitani Keiji as a Post-Nietzschean Philosopher"). In *Sekai no naka no nihon no tetsugaku* (*Japanese Philosophy in the World*), ed. Fujita Masakatsu and Bret W. Davis. Kyoto: Shōwadō, 2005.

———. "The Kyoto School." *The Stanford Encyclopedia of Philosophy* (spring 2006 edition), ed. Edward N. Zalta. http://plato.stanford.edu/archives/spr2006/entries/kyoto-school.

———. "Nishitani Keiji ni okeru 'taiho': Nihirizumu o tōshite zettai teki shigan e" ("Nishitani Keiji's 'Step Back': Through Nihilism to the Absolute Near-Side"). In *"Kongen" e no tankyū: Kindai nihon no shūkyō shisō no yamanami* (*The Search for "Grounds": The Range of Religious Thought in Modern Japan*), ed. Hosoya Masashi. Kyoto: Kōyō Shobō, 2000.

———. "Rethinking the Rational Animal: The Question of Anthropologocentrism in Heidegger, Bergson, and Zen." *Interdisziplinäre Phänomenologie—Interdisciplinary Phenomenology* 1 (2004): 173–87.

———. "Shūkyō kara seiji e, seiji kara shūkyō e: Nishitani Keiji no tenkai" ("From Religion to Politics, and from Politics to Religion: Nishitani's Turn"). In *Higashiajia to tetsugaku* (*East Asia and Philosophy*), ed. Fujita Masakatsu et al. Kyoto: Nakanishiya, 2003.

———. "A Socrates Who Practices Music: The Dynamic Intertwining of *Mythos* and *Logos*, Art and Science in Nietzsche's *The Birth of Tragedy*." In *Mythos and Logos: How to Regain the Love of Wisdom*, ed. Albert Anderson, Steven V. Hicks, and Lech Witkowski. Amsterdam/New York: Rodopi, 2004.

———. "The Step Back Through Nihilism: The Radical Orientation of Nishitani Keiji's Philosophy of Zen." *Synthesis Philosophica* 37 (2004): 139–59.

———. "Taiho to kaikō: Seiyōtetsugaku kara shisakuteki-taiwa e" ("Step Back and Encounter: From Western Philosophy Toward a Dialogue of Thought"). *Nihon tetsugakushi kenkyū* (*Studies in Japanese Philosophy*) 1 (2003): 36–66.

———. "Zen After Zarathustra: The Problem of the Will in the Confrontation Between Nietzsche and Buddhism." *Journal of Nietzsche Studies* 28 (Autumn 2004): 89–138.

Derrida, Jacques. *Deconstruction in a Nutshell: A Conversation with Jacques Derrida.* Edited with a commentary by John D. Caputo. New York: Fordham University Press, 1997.

———. "The Force of Law: 'The Mystical Foundation of Authority.'" Translated by Mary Quaintance. In *Deconstruction and the Possibility of Justice*, ed. Drucilla Cornell et al. New York: Routledge, 1992.

————. "Geschlecht: Sexual Difference, Ontological Difference." *Research and Phenomenology* 13 (1983): 65–83.

————. "Geschlecht II: Heidegger's Hand." In *Deconstruction and Philosophy: The Texts of Jacques Derrida,* ed. John Sallis. Chicago: University of Chicago Press, 1987.

————. *Given Time: I. Counterfeit Money.* Translated by Peggy Kamuf. Chicago: University of Chicago Press, 1991.

————. "Heidegger's Ear: Philopolemology (*Geschlecht* IV)." In *Reading Heidegger: Commemorations,* ed. Sallis.

————. "Heidegger's Silence." In *Martin Heidegger and National Socialism,* ed. Neske and Kettering.

————. "Interpreting Signatures (Nietzsche/Heidegger): Two Questions." In *Dialogue and Deconstruction,* ed. Michelfelder and Palmer.

————. *Margins of Philosophy.* Translated, with additional notes, by Alan Bass. Chicago: University of Chicago Press, 1982.

————. *Of Grammatology.* Translated by Gayatri Chakravorty Spivak. Baltimore: Johns Hopkins University Press, 1976.

————. *Of Spirit: Heidegger and the Question.* Translated by Geoffrey Bennington and Rachel Bowlby. Chicago: University of Chicago Press, 1989.

————. "On Reading Heidegger." *Research in Phenomenology* 17 (1987): 171–85.

————. *Points . . . : Interviews 1975–1994.* Edited by Elisabeth Weber. Translated by Peggy Kamuf. Stanford: Stanford University Press, 1995.

————. *Positions.* Translated by Alan Bass. Chicago: University of Chicago Press, 1981.

————. *Spectres of Marx: The State of Debt, the Work of Mourning, and the New International.* Translated by Peggy Kamuf. New York: Routledge, 1994.

————. *Spurs: Nietzsche's Styles.* Translated by Barbara Harlow. Chicago: University of Chicago Press, 1978.

————. *Writing and Difference.* Translated by Alan Bass. Chicago: University of Chicago Press, 1978.

Deutsch, Eliot, ed. *Philosophy East and West* 20, no. 3 (July 1970). The issue is devoted to the theme of "Heidegger and Eastern Thought."

Dōgen. *The Heart of Dōgen's Shōbōgenzō.* Translated by Norman Waddell and Masao Abe. Albany: SUNY Press, 2002.

————. *Shōbōgenzō.* Edited by Mizuno Yaoko. Tokyo: Iwanami, 1990.

Dreyfus, Hubert L. "Heidegger's History of the Being of Equipment." In *Heidegger: A Critical Reader,* ed. Dreyfus and Hall.

Dreyfus, Hubert L., and Harrison Hall, eds. *Heidegger: A Critical Reader.* Cambridge, Mass.: Blackwell, 1992.

Eckehart, Meister. *Deutsche Predigten und Traktate.* Edited and translated by Josef Quint. Munich: Carl Hanser, 1963.

Eckhart, Meister. *Meister Eckhart Deutsche Predigten: Eine Auswahl: Mittelhochdeutsch/ Neuhochdeutsch.* Edited, translated, and with commentary by Uta Störmer-Caysa. Stuttgart: Reclam, 2001.

————. *Meister Eckhart: Die deutschen und lateinischen Werke.* Stuttgart: W. Kohlhammer, 1958.

Elberfeld, Rolf. *Phänomenologie der Zeit im Buddhismus: Methoden interkulturellen Philosophierens*. Stuttgart: Frommann-Holzboog, 2004.

Emad, Parvis. "Heidegger on Schelling's Concept of Freedom." *Man and World* 8 (1975): 157–74.

Etymologisches Wörterbuch des Deutschen. 5th ed. Munich: Deutscher Taschenbuch, 2000; Berlin: Akademie, 1993.

Farías, Victor. *Heidegger and Nazism*. Edited by Joseph Margolis and Tom Rockmore. Translated by Paul Burrell, with the advice of Dominic Di Bernardi, and by Gabriel R. Ricci. Philadelphia: Temple University Press, 1989.

Ferry, Luc, and Alain Renaut. *Heidegger and Modernity*. Translated by Franklin Philip. Chicago: University of Chicago Press, 1990.

Fichte, J. G. *The Science of Knowledge with the First and Second Introductions*. Edited and translated by Peter Heath and John Lachs. Cambridge: Cambridge University Press, 1982.

Figal, Günter. "Forgetfulness of God: Concerning the Center of Heidegger's *Contributions to Philosophy*." In *Companion to Heidegger's Contributions to Philosophy*, ed. Scott et al.

———. *Martin Heidegger: Phänomenologie der Freiheit*. 3rd ed. Weinheim: Beltz Athenäum, 2000.

———. *Martin Heidegger zur Einführung*. 3rd ed. Hamburg: Junius, 1999.

Foltz, Bruce V. *Inhabiting the Earth: Heidegger, Environmental Ethics, and the Metaphysics of Nature*. Atlantic Highlands, N.J.: Humanities, 1995.

Gadamer, Hans-Georg. *Heidegger's Ways*. Translated by John W. Stanley. Albany: SUNY Press, 1994.

———. *Truth and Method*, 2nd revised ed. Translated by Joel Weinsheimer and Donald Marshall. New York: Crossroad, 1989.

Gander, Hans-Helmut, ed. *Europa und die Philosophie*. Frankfurt am Main: Vittorio Klostermann, 1993.

Gillespie, Michael Allen. *Nihilism Before Nietzsche*. Chicago: University of Chicago Press, 1995.

Haar, Michel. "Attunement and Thinking." In *Heidegger: A Critical Reader*, ed. Dreyfus and Hall.

———. *Heidegger and the Essence of Man*. Translated by William McNeill. Albany: SUNY Press, 1993.

———. *The Song of the Earth: Heidegger and the Grounds of the History of Being*. Translated by Reginald Lilly. Bloomington: Indiana University Press, 1993.

Habermas, Jürgen. *The Philosophical Discourse of Modernity*. Translated by Fredrick G. Lawrence. Cambridge, Mass.: MIT Press, 1987.

Halbfass, Wilhelm. *India and Europe: An Essay in Understanding*. Albany: SUNY Press, 1988.

Hartig, Willfred. *Die Lehre des Buddha und Heidegger: Beiträge zum Ost-West-Dialog des Denkens im 20. Jahrhundert*. Konstanz: Universität Konstanz, 1997.

Hegel, Georg Wilhelm Friedrich. *Hegel's Phenomenology of Spirit*. Translated by A. V. Miller. New York: Oxford University Press, 1952.

———. *Werke in 20 Bänden*. Frankfurt am Main: Suhrkamp, 1970.

Heidegger, Martin. *The Piety of Thinking*. With translation, notes, and commentary by James G. Hart and John C. Maraldo. Bloomington: Indiana University Press, 1976.

———. "Zur Frage nach der Bestimmung der Sache des Denkens." In *Japan und Heidegger,* ed. Buchner.

Heidegger, Martin, and Takehiko Kojima. "Martin Heidegger—Takehiko Kojima: Ein Briefwechsel (1963–1965)." In *Japan und Heidegger,* ed. Buchner.

Heidegger, Martin, and Bernhard Welte. *Briefe und Begegnungen.* Edited by Alfred Denker and Holger Zaborowski. Stuttgart: Klett-Cotta, 2003.

Heisig, James. W., and John C. Maraldo, eds. *Rude Awakenings: Zen, the Kyoto School, and the Question of Nationalism.* Honolulu: University of Hawaii Press, 1994.

Helting, Holger. *Heidegger und Meister Eckehart: Vorbereitende Überlegungen zu ihrem Gottesdenken.* Berlin: Duncker and Humblot, 1997.

Herrmann, Friedrich-Wilhelm von. *Wege ins Ereignis: Zu Heideggers "Beiträgen zur Philosophie."* Frankfurt am Main: Vittorio Klostermann, 1994.

Historisches Wörterbuch der Philosophie. Edited by Joachim Ritter. Basel/Stuttgart: Schwabe, 1974.

Höffe, Otfried. *Aristotle.* Translated by Christine Salazar. Albany: SUNY Press, 2003.

Hölderlin, Friedrich. *Hymns and Fragments.* Translated and introduced by Richard Sieburth. Princeton: Princeton University Press, 1984.

Iber, Christian. "Interpretationen zum Deutschen Idealismus: Vernunftkritik im Namen des Seins." In *Heidegger Handbuch: Leben-Werk-Wirkung,* ed. Thomä.

Inwood, Michael. *A Heidegger Dictionary.* Oxford: Blackwell, 1999.

Iriya, Yoshitani, ed. *Rinzairoku* (*The Record of Linji*). Tokyo: Iwanami, 1989.

Ishikura, Jun. "Zenki Haideggā no tetsugakuteki tachiba" ("The Early Heidegger's Philosophical Standpoint"). *Shūkyōtetsugaku kenkyū* 8 (1991): 66–78.

Ives, Christopher. *Zen Awakening and Society.* Honolulu: University of Hawaii Press, 1992.

Kant, Immanuel. *Critique of Pure Reason.* Translated by Norman Kemp Smith. New York: St. Martin's, 1965.

———. *Immanuel Kant: Critique of Practical Reason and Other Writings in Moral Philosophy.* Translated by Lewis White Beck. Chicago: University of Chicago Press, 1949.

———. *Religion Within the Limits of Reason Alone.* Translated with an introduction and notes by Theodore M. Greene and Hoyt H. Hudson, with a new essay, "The Ethical Significance of Kant's *Religion,*" by John R. Silber. New York: Harper and Row, 1960.

———. *Werkausgabe in 12 Bänden.* Edited by Wilhelm Weischedel. Frankfurt am Main: Suhrkamp, 1956.

Kettering, Emil. *NÄHE: Das Denken Martin Heideggers.* Pfullingen: Neske, 1987.

Kisiel, Theodore. *The Genesis of Heidegger's "Being and Time."* Berkeley: University of California Press, 1993.

Kovacs, George. *The Question of God in Heidegger's Phenomenology.* Evanston, Ill.: Northwestern University Press, 1990.

Kreeft, Peter. "Zen in Heidegger's *Gelassenheit.*" *International Philosophical Quarterly* 11, no. 4 (December 1971): 521–45.

Krell, David Farrell. *Daimon Life: Heidegger and Life-Philosophy.* Bloomington: Indiana University Press, 1992.

———. *Intimations of Mortality: Time, Truth, and Finitude in Heidegger's Thinking of Being.* University Park: Pennsylvania State University Press, 1986.

Kusumoto, Bunyū. *Zengonyūmon (Introduction to Zen Terms).* Tokyo: Daihōrinkaku, 1982.

Lacoue-Labarthe, Philippe. *Heidegger, Art, and Politics: The Fiction of the Political.* Translated by Chris Turner. Oxford: Blackwell, 1990.

Leder, Drew. "Flesh and Blood: A Proposed Supplement to Merleau-Ponty." In *The Body,* ed. Donn Welton. Oxford: Blackwell, 1999.

Levin, David Michael. *The Body's Recollection of Being.* London/Boston: Routledge and Kegan Paul, 1986.

———. *The Listening Self: Personal Growth, Social Change, and the Closure of Metaphysics.* London/Boston: Routledge and Kegan Paul, 1989.

———. "The Ontological Dimension of Embodiment: Heidegger's Thinking of Being." In *The Body,* ed. Donn Welton. Oxford: Blackwell, 1999.

———. *The Opening of Vision: Nihilism and the Postmodern Situation.* London/Boston: Routledge and Kegan Paul, 1988.

———. *The Philosopher's Gaze: Modernity in the Shadows of Enlightenment.* Berkeley: University of California Press, 1999.

Levinas, Emmanuel. *Ethics and Infinity.* Translated by Richard A. Cohen. Pittsburgh: Duquesne University Press, 1985.

———. *Totality and Inifinity.* Translated by Alphonso Lingis. Pittsburgh: Duquesne University Press, 1969.

Llewelyn, John. *The Middle Voice of Ecological Conscience: A Chiasmic Reading of Responsibility in the Neighborhood of Levinas, Heidegger, and Others.* New York: St. Martin's, 1991.

Löwith, Karl. *Martin Heidegger and European Nihilism.* Edited by Richard Wolin. Translated by Gary Steiner. New York: Columbia University Press, 1995.

———. *Sämtliche Schriften,* vol. 6, *Nietzsche.* Stuttgart: J. B. Metzlersche, 1987.

Loy, David. *Nonduality: A Study in Comparative Philosophy.* New Haven: Yale University Press, 1988.

Lyotard, Jean-François. *Heidegger and "the Jews."* Translated by Andreas Michel and Mark S. Roberts. Foreword by David Carroll. Minneapolis: University of Minnesota Press, 1990.

Macann, Christopher, ed. *Critical Heidegger.* New York: Routledge, 1996.

Maly, Kenneth. "Turnings in Essential Swaying and the Leap." In *Companion to Heidegger's Contributions to Philosophy,* ed. Scott et al.

Marx, Werner. *Heidegger and the Tradition.* Translated by Theodore Kisiel and Murray Greene. Evanston, Ill.: Northwestern University Press, 1971.

———. *Heidegger und die Tradition.* Stuttgart: W. Kohlhammer, 1961.

———. *The Philosophy of F. W. J. Schelling: History, System, and Freedom.* Translated by Thomas Nenon. Bloomington: Indiana University Press, 1984.

May, Reinhard. *Heidegger's Hidden Sources: East Asian Influences on His Work.* Translated with a complementary essay by Graham Parkes. New York: Routledge, 1996.

McGinn, Bernard. *The Mystical Thought of Meister Eckhart*. New York: Crossroad, 2001.

———. "Theological Summary." In Meister Eckhart, *Meister Eckhart: The Essential Sermons, Commentaries, Treatises, and Defense*, trans. Edmund Colledge and Bernard McGinn. Mahwah, N.J.: Paulist Press, 1981.

McNeill, William. "The Time of *Contributions to Philosophy*." In *Companion to Heidegger's Contributions to Philosophy*, ed. Scott et al.

Mehta, Jarava Lal. *Martin Heidegger, the Way and the Vision*. Honolulu: University of Hawaii Press, 1976.

Merleau-Ponty, Maurice. *Phenomenology of Perception*. Translated by Colin Smith. London: Routledge and Kegan Paul, 1962.

Michelfelder, Diane P., and Richard E. Palmer, eds. *Dialogue and Deconstruction: The Gadamer-Derrida Encounter*. Albany: SUNY Press, 1989.

Mine, Hideki. *Haideggā to nihon no tetsugaku* (*Heidegger and Japanese Philosophy*). Kyoto: Minerva, 2002.

Mitchell, Andrew. "Praxis and *Gelassenheit:* The 'Practice' of the Limit." In *Heidegger and Practical Philosophy*, ed. Raffoul and Pettigrew.

Mizoguchi, Kōhei. "An Interpretation of Heidegger's Bremen Lectures: Toward a Dialogue with His Later Thought." In *Heidegger and Asian Thought*, ed. Parkes.

Müller-Lauter, Wolfgang. *Nietzsche: His Philosophy of Contradictions and the Contradictions of His Philosophy*. Translated by David J. Parent. Chicago: University of Illinois Press, 1999.

———. *Heidegger und Nietzsche*. Berlin: Walter de Gruyter, 2000.

———. "The Spirit of Revenge and the Eternal Recurrence: On Heidegger's Later Interpretation of Nietzsche." Translated by R. J. Hollingdale. In vol. 2 of *Nietzsche: Critical Assessments*, ed. Daniel W. Conway with Peter S. Groff. London/New York: Routledge, 1998.

Murray, Michael, ed. *Heidegger and Modern Philosophy*. New Haven: Yale University Press, 1978.

Nancy, Jean-Luc. *The Experience of Freedom*. Translated by Bridget McDonald. Stanford: Stanford University Press, 1993.

———. "Heidegger's 'Originary Ethics.'" In *Heidegger and Practical Philosophy*, ed. Raffoul and Pettigrew.

Neske, Günther, and Emil Kettering, eds. *Antwort: Martin Heidegger im Gespräch*. Pfullingen: Neske, 1988.

———. *Martin Heidegger and National Socialism: Questions and Answers*. Translated by Lisa Harries and Joachim Neugroschel. New York: Paragon House, 1990.

Nießeler, Andreas. *Vom Ethos der Gelassenheit: Zu Heideggers Bedeutung für die Pädagogik*. Würzburg: Königshausen and Newmann, 1995.

Nietzsche, Friedrich. *Basic Writings of Nietzsche*. Edited and translated by Walter Kaufmann. New York: Random House, 1968.

———. *Der Wille zur Macht: Versuch einer Umwertung aller Werte*. 13th ed. Selected and arranged by Peter Gast with the cooperation of Elisabeth Förster-Nietzsche, with an afterword by Walter Gebhard. Stuttgart: Kröner, 1996.

————. *Grossoktavausgabe.* Edited by Nietzsche Archive. Leipzig, 1894–1912.

————. *The Portable Nietzsche.* Edited and translated by Walter Kaufmann. New York: Penguin Books, 1982.

————. *Sämtliche Werke: Kritische Studienausgabe in 15 Einzelbänden.* 2nd ed. Edited by Giorgio Colli and Mazzino Montinari. München: Deutscher Taschenbuch, 1988.

————. *The Will to Power.* Translated by Walter Kaufmann and R. J. Hollingdale. New York: Vintage Books, 1967.

Nishida, Kitaro. *Fundamental Problems of Philosophy.* Translated by David A. Dilworth. Tokyo: Sophia University Press, 1970.

————. *Nishidatetsugaku senshū (Selected Works of Nishida's Philosophy).* Tokyo: Iwanami, 1998.

Nishitani, Keiji. *Nishitani Keiji chosakushū (Collected Works of Nishitani Keiji).* Tokyo: Sōbunsha, 1987.

————. "Reflections on Two Addresses by Martin Heidegger." In *Heidegger and Asian Thought,* ed. Parkes.

————. *Religion and Nothingness.* Translated by Jan Van Bragt. Berkeley: University of California Press, 1982.

————. *The Self-Overcoming of Nihilism.* Translated by Graham Parkes with Setsuko Aihara. Albany: SUNY Press, 1990.

Ogawa, Tadashi. "The Horizonal Character of Phenomena and the Shining-forth of Things." *Research in Phenomenology* 30 (2000): 146–57.

Ōhashi, Ryōsuke. "Die frühe Heidegger-Rezeption in Japan." In *Japan und Heidegger,* ed. Buchner.

————. *Ekstase und Gelassenheit: Zu Schelling und Heidegger.* Munich: Wilhelm Fink, 1975.

————. *Hōge, shunkan, basho: Sheringu to Haideggā (Gelassenheit, Moment, Place: Schelling and Heidegger).* Tokyo: Sōbunsha, 1980.

————. *Nishidatetsugaku no sekai (The World of Nishida's Philosophy).* Tokyo: Chikumashobō, 1995.

Ōkōchi, Ryōgi. "Nietzsches Amor Fati im Lichte von Karma des Buddhismus." *Nietzsche-Studien* 1 (1972): 36–94.

Oshima, Yoshiko. *Zen—anders denken? Zugleich ein Versuch über Zen und Heidegger.* Heidelberg: Lambert Schneider, 1985.

Ott, Hugo. *Martin Heidegger: A Political Life.* Translated by Allan Blunden. New York: BasicBooks, 1993.

Parkes, Graham. "Rising Sun over Black Forest: Heidegger's Japanese Connections." In May, *Heidegger's Hidden Sources: East Asian Influences on His Work.*

————, ed. *Heidegger and Asian Thought.* Honolulu: University of Hawaii Press, 1987.

Petzet, Heinrich Wiegand. *Encounters and Dialogues with Martin Heidegger: 1929–1976.* Translated by Parvis Emad and Kenneth Maly. Chicago: University of Chicago Press, 1993.

Pink, Tomas, and M. W. F. Stone, eds. *The Will and Human Action: From Antiquity to the Present Day.* London/New York: Routledge, 2004.

Pöggeler, Otto. *Der Denkweg Martin Heideggers*. Pfullingen: Neske, 1963.
———. "'Historicity' in Heidegger's Late Work." In *Thinking About Being: Aspects of Heidegger's Thought*, ed. Shahan and Mohanty.
———. *Martin Heidegger's Path of Thinking*. Translated by Daniel Magurshak and Sigmund Barber. Atlantic Highlands, N.J.: Humanities, 1987.
———. *The Paths of Heidegger's Life and Thought*. Translated by John Bailiff. Amherst, N.Y.: Humanity Books, 1997.
Polt, Richard. *Heidegger: An Introduction*. Ithaca: Cornell University Press, 1999.
Polt, Richard, and Gregory Fried, eds. *A Companion to Heidegger's "Introduction to Metaphysics."* New Haven: Yale University Press, 2001.
Raffoul, François, and David Pettigrew, eds. *Heidegger and Practical Philosophy*. Albany: SUNY Press, 2002.
Richardson, William J. *Heidegger: Through Phenomenology to Thought*. 3rd ed. The Hague: Nijhoff, 1974.
Riedel, Manfred. "'Feldweg-Gespräche': Deuten im Wort." In *Heidegger Handbuch: Leben-Werk-Wirkung*, ed. Thomä.
Risser, James, ed. *Heidegger Toward the Turn: Essays on the Work of the 1930s*. New York: SUNY Press, 1999.
Rockmore, Tom. *On Heidegger's Nazism and Philosophy*. Berkeley: University of California Press, 1992.
Rockmore, Tom, and Joseph Margolis, eds. *The Heidegger Case: On Philosophy and Politics*. Philadelphia: Temple University Press, 1992.
Rorty, Richard. *Consequences of Pragmatism*. Minneapolis: University of Minnesota Press, 1982.
———. "Overcoming the Tradition: Heidegger and Dewey." In *Heidegger and Modern Philosophy*, ed. Murray.
Ruin, Hans. *Enigmatic Origins: Tracing the Theme of Historicity Through Heidegger's Works*. Stockholm: Almqvist and Wiksell, 1994.
Safranski, Rüdiger. *Martin Heidegger: Between Good and Evil*. Translated by Ewald Osers. Cambridge, Mass.: Harvard University Press, 1998.
Sallis, John. *Crossings: Nietzsche and the Space of Tragedy*. Chicago: University of Chicago Press, 1991.
———. *Delimitations: Phenomenology and the End of Metaphysics*. Bloomington: Indiana University Press, 1986.
———. *Double Truth*. Albany: SUNY Press, 1995.
———. *Echoes: After Heidegger*. Bloomington: Indiana University Press, 1990.
———. "Free Thinking." In *Heidegger and Practical Philosophy*, ed. Raffoul and Pettigrew.
———. *Stone*. Bloomington: Indiana University Press, 1994.
———. "Uranic Time." In *Time and Nothingness*, ed. Michael Lazarin. Kyoto: Institute of Buddhist Cultural Studies, Ryukoku University, 1997.
———, ed. *Reading Heidegger: Commemorations*. Bloomington: Indiana University Press, 1993.
Sallis, John, Giuseppina Moneta, and Jacques Taminiaux, eds. *The Collegium Phaenomenologicum: The First Ten Years*. Dordrecht: Kluwer, 1988.

Sartre, Jean-Paul. *Essays in Existentialism.* Edited by Wade Baskin. New York: Citadel, 1968.

Schalow, Frank. "Freedom, Finitude, and the Practical Self: The Other Side of Heidegger's Appropriation of Kant." In *Heidegger and Practical Philosophy,* ed. Raffoul and Pettigrew.

———. "The Will as the Genuine Postscript of Modern Thought: At the Crossroads of an Anomaly." *Epoché* 1 (1993): 77–104.

Schelling, F. W. J. *The Ages of the World.* Translated by Jason M. Wirth. Albany: SUNY Press, 2000.

———. *Philosophical Inquiries into the Nature of Human Freedom.* Translated with a critical introduction and notes by James Gutmann. La Salle, Ill.: Open Court, 1936.

———. "Philosophical Investigations into the Essence of Human Freedom and Related Matters." Translated by Priscilla Hayden-Roy. In *Philosophy of German Idealism,* ed. Ernst Behler. New York: Continuum, 1987.

———. "Philosophische Untersuchungen über das Wesen der menschlichen Freiheit und die damit zusammenhängenden Gegenstände." In vol. 7 of *F. W. J. v. Schellings sämmtliche Werke,* ed. K. F. A. Schelling. Stuttgart: J. G. Cotta, 1860.

Schirmacher, Wolfgang. *Technik und Gelassenheit: Zeitkritik nach Heidegger.* Freiburg/ Munich: Karl Alber, 1983.

Schmidt, Dennis J. *The Ubiquity of the Finite: Hegel, Heidegger, and the Entitlements of Philosophy.* Cambridge, Mass.: MIT Press, 1988.

Schopenhauer, Arthur. *Sämtliche Werke.* Vol. 1, *Die Welt als Wille und Vorstellung 1.* Frankfurt am Main: Suhrkamp, 1986.

———. *The World as Will and Representation.* Vol. 1. Translated by E. F. J. Payne. New York: Dover, 1969.

Schürmann, Reiner. *Heidegger on Being and Acting: From Principles to Anarchy.* Translated by Christine-Marie Gros and Reiner Schürmann. Bloomington: Indiana University Press, 1987.

———. *Meister Eckhart: Mystic and Philosopher.* Bloomington: Indiana University Press, 1978.

Scott, Charles E. *The Language of Difference.* Atlantic Highlands, N.J.: Humanities, 1987.

———. "The Middle Voice in *Being and Time.*" In *The Collegium Phaenomenologicum: The First Ten Years,* ed. Sallis et al.

———. "The Middle Voice of Metaphysics." *Review of Metaphysics* 42 (1989): 743–64.

———. *The Question of Ethics: Nietzsche, Foucault, Heidegger.* Bloomington: Indiana University Press, 1990.

Scott, Charles E., Susan M. Schoenbohm, Daniela Vallega-Neu, and Alejandro Vallega, eds. *Companion to Heidegger's Contributions to Philosophy.* Bloomington: Indiana University Press, 2001.

Shahan, Robert W., and J. N. Mohanty, eds. *Thinking About Being: Aspects of Heidegger's Thought.* Norman: University of Oklahoma Press, 1984.

Sheehan, Thomas. "Kehre and Ereignis: A Prolegomenon to *Introduction to Meta-*

physics." In *A Companion to Heidegger's Introduction to Metaphysics,* ed. Polt and Fried.

———. "Nihilism and Its Discontents." In *Heidegger and Practical Philosophy,* ed. Raffoul and Pettigrew.

Shidō, Bunan. *Shidō Bunan Zenji shū (Collected Writings of Zen Master Shidō Bunan).* Edited by Kōda Rentarō. Tokyo: Shunjūsha, 1968.

Silber, John R. "The Ethical Significance of Kant's *Religion.*" In Kant, *Religion Within the Limits of Reason Alone.*

Silesius, Angelus. *Cherubinischer Wandersmann.* Vol. 3 of *Sämtliche poetische Werke,* ed. Hans Ludwig Held. Munich: Carl Hanser, 1949.

Simm, Hans-Joachim, ed. *Von der Gelassenheit: Texte zum Nachdenken.* Frankfurt am Main: Insel, 1995.

Sluga, Hans. *Heidegger's Crisis: Philosophy and Politics in Nazi Germany.* Cambridge, Mass.: Harvard University Press, 1993.

Snow, Dale E. *Schelling and the End of Idealism.* Albany: SUNY Press, 1996.

Sorabji, Richard. "The Concept of the Will from Plato to Maximus the Confessor." In *The Will and Human Action: From Antiquity to the Present Day,* ed. Pink and Stone.

Stambaugh, Joan. *Thoughts on Heidegger.* Lanham, Md.: University Press of America, 1991.

Stapleton, Timothy J. *Husserl and Heidegger: The Question of a Phenomenological Beginning.* Albany: SUNY Press, 1983.

Tanabe, Hajime. "Die neue Wende in der Phänomenologie—Heideggers Phenomenologie des Lebens." Translated by Johannes Laube. In *Japan und Heidegger,* ed. Buchner.

———. *Philosophy as Metanoetics.* Translated by Takeuchi Yoshinori. Berkeley: University of California Press, 1986.

———. "Todesdialektik." In *Martin Heidegger zum siebzigsten Geburtstag: Festschrift,* ed. Günther Neske. Pfullingen: Neske, 1959.

———. *Zangedō toshite no tetsugaku—shi no tetsugaku (Philosophy as Metanoetics—the Philosophy of Death).* Edited by Hase Shōtō. Kyoto: Tōeisha, 2000.

Tanzer, Mark Basil. *Heidegger: Decisionism and Quietism.* Amherst, N.Y.: Humanity Books, 2002.

Taylor, Charles. *Hegel.* Cambridge: Cambridge University Press, 1975.

Thomä, Dieter. "Stichwort: Kehre: Was wäre, wenn sie nicht gäbe?" In *Heidegger Handbuch: Leben-Werk-Wirkung,* ed. Thomä.

———, ed. *Heidegger Handbuch: Leben-Werk-Wirkung.* Stuttgart: Metzler, 2003.

Thurnher, Reiner. "Der Rückgang in den Grund des Eigenen als Bedingung für ein Verstehen des Anderen im Denken Heideggers." In *Europa und die Philosophie,* ed. Gander.

Tsujimura, Kōichi. *Haideggā no shisaku (Heidegger's Thought).* Tokyo: Sōbunsha, 1991.

———. *Haideggā ronkō (Heidegger Studies).* Tokyo: Sōbunsha, 1971.

Ueda, Shizuteru. *Basho: Nijūsekainaisonzai (Place: Twofold Being-in-the-World).* Tokyo: Kōbundō, 1993.

———. "Eckhart und Zen am Problem 'Freiheit und Sprache.'" *Beihefte der*

Zeitschrift für Religions- und Geistesgeschichte 31 (Cologne: E. J. Brill, 1989): 21–92.

———. *Ekkuharuto: Itan to seitō no aida de* (*Eckhart: Between Heresy and Orthodoxy*). Tokyo: Kōdansha, 1998.

———. "Freedom and Language in Meister Eckhart and Zen Buddhism, Part 1." Translated by Richard F. Szippl. *The Eastern Buddhist,* new series, vol. 23, no. 2 (Autumn 1990): 18–59.

———. "Gelassenheit im Zen-Buddhismus." In *Arbeit und Gelassenheit,* ed. Ernesto Grassi and Hugo Schmale. Munich: Wilhelm Fink, 1994.

———. *Ueda Shizuteru shū* (*Collected Works of Ueda Shizuteru*). Tokyo: Iwanami, 2002.

Vallega-Neu, Daniela. *Heidegger's Contributions to Philosophy: An Introduction.* Bloomington: Indiana University Press, 2003.

Vater, Michael G. "Heidegger and Schelling: The Finitude of Being." *Idealistic Studies* (1975): 20–58.

Victoria, Brian. *Zen at War.* New York: Weatherhill, 1997.

Wagner, Jürgen. *Meditationen über Gelassenheit: Der Zugang des Menschen zu seinem Wesen im Anschluss an Martin Heidegger und Meister Eckhart.* Hamburg: Kovac, 1995.

Wall, Thomas Carl. *Radical Passivity: Levinas, Blanchot, and Agamben.* Albany: SUNY Press, 1999.

Watsuji, Tetsurō. *Watsuji Tetsurō's Rinrigaku: Ethics in Japan.* Translated by Yamamoto Seisaku and Robert Carter. Albany: SUNY Press, 1996.

Weinmayr, Elmar. "Denken im Übergang—Kitarō Nishida und Martin Heidegger." In *Japan und Heidegger,* ed. Buchner.

Wetz, Franz Josef. *Friedrich W. J. Schelling zur Einführung.* Hamburg: Junius, 1996.

White, Alan. *Schelling: An Introduction to the System of Freedom.* New Haven: Yale University Press, 1983.

Winkler, Norbert. *Meister Eckhart zur Einführung.* Hamburg: Junius, 1997.

Wolin, Richard. *The Politics of Being: The Political Thought of Martin Heidegger.* New York: Columbia University Press, 1990.

———, ed. *The Heidegger Controversy: A Critical Reader.* Cambridge, Mass.: MIT Press, 1993.

Wood, David. "Heidegger after Derrida." *Research in Phenomenology* 17 (1987): 103–16.

———. *Philosophy at the Limit.* London: Unwin Hyman, 1990.

———. *Thinking After Heidegger.* Cambridge: Polity, 2002.

———, ed. *Of Derrida, Heidegger, and Spirit.* Evanston, Ill.: Northwestern University Press, 1993.

Yasutani, Hakuun. *Shōyōroku.* Tokyo: Shunjūsha, 1973.

Young, Julian. *Heidegger, Philosophy, Nazism.* Cambridge: Cambridge University Press, 1997.

———. "Schopenhauer, Heidegger, Art, and the Will." In *Schopenhauer, Philosophy, and the Arts,* ed. Dale Jacquette. Cambridge: Cambridge University Press, 1996.

Yuasa, Yasuo. "The Encounter of Modern Japanese Philosophy with Heidegger." In *Heidegger and Asian Thought,* ed. Parkes.

Zarader, Marlène. *The Unthought Debt: Heidegger and the Hebraic Heritage.* Translated by Bettina Bergo. Stanford: Stanford University Press, 2006.

Zimmerman, Michael E. *Eclipse of the Self: The Development of Heidegger's Concept of Authenticity,* rev. ed. Athens: Ohio University Press, 1986.

————. *Heidegger's Confrontation with Modernity: Technology, Politics, Art.* Bloomington: Indiana University Press, 1990.

Zöller, Günter. *Fichte's Transcendental Philosophy: The Original Duplicity of Intelligence and Will.* Cambridge: Cambridge University Press, 1998.

Index

Absolute, the, 101, 102–4, 109, 115–17, 120–21, 291, 298; God as, 102, 114, 116, 118, 290
Absolutism, 124–25, 208–10
Activity/passivity. *See* Passivity
Amor fati, 341–42 n. 10
Anaximander, 162, 265, 286–88
Anderson, John M., 197
Anthropomorphism, anthropocentrism, 12, 33, 136, 161, 288
Anxiety, 42, 51, 53–54, 57, 59, 306 n. 5
Appetitus, 166, 169
Apprehension, 88
Arendt, Hannah, 6, 148, 306 n. 5, 365 n. 20; quoted, 43, 64, 287, 307 n. 9, 316 n. 15
Aristotle, 27, 113, 159, 161–63, 169, 306 n. 5
"Ascetic priest," 134, 252, 277–78
Atheism, 124, 134, 140, 248; existential, 42, 249
Attunement, fundamental, 6–8, 13–14, 85, 92–94, 111–12, 200, 211; and (dis)attunement, 9–10, 14, 22, 159, 163, 283, 301; of *Gelassenheit*, 23, 204, 230, 233, 235–36; of non-willing, 8–9, 32, 187, 214, 302–3, 361 n. 71; of reservedness, 95–97
Augustine, 5, 306 n. 5, 349 n. 24
Auschwitz, 298

Bambach, Charles R., 314 n. 8
Being (*Sein*), xxviii, 118, 231; crossed out in Heidegger's text, 231, 233, 296; Derrida quoted on, 357–58 n. 42; eschatology of, 271; God's Will as, 246; history of, xxiv, 157–61, 164–65, 251–62, 265–67; open-region of, 197–99; as primal force, 243; relation between man and, *see* Man; thinking and, 234,

300, (differentiated) 267; will of, 125, 143–44. *See also* Dasein; *Seinsfuge*
Being-towards-death, 25, 48, 51–53, 56, 57, 260. *See also* Death
Being-with, 83–84
Beistegui, Miguel de, 85, 326 n. 27
Bernasconi, Robert, 269, 272, 273, 358 n. 42, 365 n. 20
Bestand (standing-reserve), 13, 173, 174, 177–78, 287
Blake, William, 21
Blochmann, Elisabeth, 313 n. 1
Boss, Menard, 289–90, 315 n. 13
Bowie, Andrew, 331 n. 10
Brauchen (needful-usage), 62, 205, 224, 228–30
Brockhaus encyclopedia, xxvi
Buddhism, 10–11, 58, 306 n. 11, 341 n. 10, 363 n. 4. *See also* Zen Buddhism

Caputo, John, 123, 335–36 n. 27, 349 n. 17, 354 n. 4, 358 n. 42
Care, 38, 83, 268; notion of, in early work, 46–47; relation of, to will, 32, 34, 315 n. 13
Castoriadis, Cornelius, 355 n. 11
Categorical imperative, 66, 67, 69, 312 n. 32
Chinese language, 310 n. 19
Christ, 135; birth of, in the soul, 130, 131
Christianity, 134, 306 n. 5, 343 n. 19; Christendom, 21–22, (differentiated) 124, 344 n. 21; "God" of, 141–42, 336 n. 27; Heidegger's relation to, xxv, 123, 140, 265, 344 n. 21, 361 n. 71; medieval, 124–25; and mysticism, xxvii, 195, 306 n. 11; Neoplatonic, 129, 336 n. 27; "primal," 264, 361 n. 60; and the Reformation,

of, 287, 293; self-grounding, xxx; subjective will, 93, 206, 302; subjective willing, 97, 329 n. 45; "unbounded," unconditional, 101, 116, 118–19, (modern
metaphysics of) 117; willful, xxiv, 38,
50, 76, 178, 268, 283, (deconstruction
of) 31, (disruption of) 39, (and *Ge-stell*)
121, (metaphysics of, vs. technology)
178, (modern) 124–25, 211, 219, (as
pitfall) 79, (releasement from) xxviii;
will inseparable from, 76
Systemadicy, 116, 290–91. *See also*
Theodicy.

Tanabe Hajime, 320 n. 58, 359 n. 52
Tanzer, Mark Basil, 323 n. 6
Tauler, Johannes, xxv
Technology, xxxi, 121, 151; cybernetics,
178–80, 189, 220, 288, 298; epoch of,
158, 159, 166, 187, (Janus-faced character of) 17, 157, 160–61, 181; Heidegger's
critique of, xxiv, 45, 80, 146, 173–84,
189, 244, 247, 256, 257; manipulation
by, xxiv, 13, 33, 80–81, 90, 97; modern
predicament of, 165, 177; nihilism of,
70, 160, 181, 295–97; and will to power,
173–74; and will to will, xxiv, 17, 145,
160, 219, 288, (and evil) 297–98, (and
man's responsibility) 258, (step toward)
72–73, 149, (turning from) 180, 236.
See also Ge-stell
Tezuka Tomio, 262
"The they" (*Das Man*), 40, 49, 54, 83; deference to, 25, 38, 39, 41, 110; egoism of,
xxv; everydayness of, 26–27
Theodicy, onto-, 112, 291, 295; and
ontodicy, 291, 295; and systemadicy,
290–91
Thinking: anticipatory, 216–18; and
being, 234, 300, (differentiated) 267;
Descartes', 168; as essence of man,
224–27; one thought, 253–58; one-
track, 252–53; planetary, 263–64; as
willing, 6, 174, 197, 199, *see also* Reason.
See also Thought-path
Third Reich, 82, 328 n. 34. *See also* Nazism
Thomä, Dieter, 322 n. 4
Thomas Aquinas, 311 n. 22, 338 n. 49
Thought-path (*Denkweg*), Heidegger's,
xxiii–xxix, 56–57, 98, 185, 240–42,

243–46, 254, 265, 276, (background
of) 123, (central element in) 228,
(turn in/reversal of) xxx, 60–65, 85–
86, 90, 92–94, 98, 124, 239–40 (*see also*
"Twisting free"); Schelling's, 101
Trinity, the. *See* Christianity
Truth, 141, 182; absolute, 284–85; of
Dasein, 40; essence of, 182, (change in)
164, 166, (nonessence of) 364 n. 7;
"inceptual," 280; metaphysical notion
of, 161
Tsujimura Kōichi, 58, 315 n. 14
Turn, turning. *See* Kehre
"Twisting free," 56, 180, 207, 226, 301–2,
311 n. 21; in Heidegger's thought, 60–
61, 78, 90–91, 93, 143–44, 146, 183, 188,
247–48, 267, (of domain of the will)
17, 64, 84, 98, 112, 186, 244–45, (time
needed for) 84; Nietzsche's, 19, 154,
278. *See also* Kehre

Ueda Shizuteru, 57, 131–32, 134–35, 137–
38
Umwillen (for the sake of), 35–37, 53, 54,
88, 116, 315 n. 14, 323 n. 10
Unity/univocity, will to, 251–53; of history
of being, 258–62
University of Marburg, Heidegger's position at, 313 n. 1
"Unsaid," the, 25
Ur-willing, 270, 275, 283–87, 288, 298,
300, 302–3

Vallega-Neu, Daniela, 92
"Value thinking," 152, 219
Van Buren, John, 27, 333 n. 3, 361 n. 60
Versényi, Laszlo, 246, 247
Violence, 21, 63, 90–91, 247; and death,
52; of interpretation, 30–31; language
of, 87–88
Volk. See German *Volk*
Voluntarism, 74, 219; existential, 38–40,
42, 67, 204; and fatalism, *see* Fatalism;
Heidegger and, 25, 43, 50, 66, 70, 111,
240, 244–46, 248, 327 n. 32, (critiques)
71, 73, (turns away from) 63, 244–45;
Nietzschean, 147; reverse of, 47; tran-
scendental, 36
Von Herrmann, Friedrich-Wilhelm,
xxviii, 127, 233, 250, 321 n. 1

About the Author

Bret W. Davis is an assistant professor of philosophy at Loyola College in Maryland.